Social Justice Leadership for a Global World

A volume in
Educational Leadership for Social Justice
Jeffrey S. Brooks, Denise E. Armstrong, Ira Bogotch, Sandra Harris,
Whitney H. Sherman, and George Theoharis, *Series Editors*

Social Justice Leadership for a Global World

edited by

Cynthia Gerstl-Pepin
University of Vermont

Judith A. Aiken
University of Vermont

INFORMATION AGE PUBLISHING, INC.
Charlotte, NC • www.infoagepub.com

Library of Congress Cataloging-in-Publication Data

Social justice leadership for a global world / edited by Cynthia
Gerstl-Pepin, Judith A. Aiken.
    p. cm. – (Educational leadership for social justice)
  Includes bibliographical references.
  ISBN 978-1-61735-924-8 (pbk.) – ISBN 978-1-61735-925-5 (hardcover) –
ISBN 978-1-61735-926-2 (ebook) 1. Educational leadership–Social aspects.
2. Critical pedagogy. 3. Education and globalization. 4. Social justice.
I. Gerstl-Pepin, Cynthia I. II. Aiken, Judith A.
  LB2805.S687 2012
  371.2–dc23

                                                    2012023948

Copyright © 2012 Information Age Publishing Inc.

Printed in the United States of America

DEDICATION

To Cynthia's sons, Reid and Ethan, and to her husband Craig,
for their love, support and inspiration

To Judith's father, Allen Sr., her mother, Dorothea, and her husband, Richard,
for teaching compassion, care, and conviction.

To social justice leaders everywhere, for their relentless efforts and dedication
in fostering more just, humane, and inclusive schools and communities.

CONTENTS

SECTION III

STRATEGIES FOR DEVELOPING SOCIAL JUSTICE LEADERS

SECTION IV

STRATEGIES FOR K–12 SOCIAL JUSTICE LEADERSHIP

SECTION V

STRATEGIES FOR HIGHER EDUCATION SOCIAL JUSTICE LEADERSHIP

SERIES EDITOR'S PREFACE

Jeffrey S. Brooks

I am pleased to serve as series editor for this book series, *Educational Leadership for Social Justice*, with Information Age Publishing. The idea for this series grew out of the work of a committed group of leadership for scholars associated with the American Educational Research Association's (AERA) Leadership for Social Justice Special Interest Group (LSJ SIG). This group existed for many years before being officially affiliated with AERA and has benefited greatly from the ongoing leadership, support, and counsel of Dr. Catherine Marshall (University of North Carolina at Chapel Hill). It is also important to acknowledge the contributions of the LSJ SIG's first Chair, Dr. Ernestine Enomoto (University of Hawaii at Manoa), whose wisdom, stewardship, and guidance helped ease a transition into AERA's more formal organizational structures. This organizational change was at times difficult to reconcile with scholars who largely identified as non-traditional thinkers and push toward innovation rather than accept the status quo. As the second Chair of the LSJ SIG, I appreciate all of Ernestine's hard work and friendship. Moreover, I also thank Dr. Gaetane Jean-Marie, the third Chair of the LSJ SIG for her visionary leadership, steadfast commitment to high standards, and collaborative scholarship and friendship.

I am particularly indebted to my colleagues on the LSJ SIG's first Publications Committee, which I chaired from 2005 through 2007: Dr. Denise Armstrong, Brock University; Dr. Ira Bogotch, Florida Atlantic University; Dr. Sandra Harris, Lamar University; Dr. Whitney Sherman, Virginia Com-

Social Justice Leadership for a Global World, pages xi–xii
Copyright © 2012 by Information Age Publishing

monwealth University; and Dr. George Theoharis, Syracuse University. This committee was a joy to work with, and I am pleased we have found many more ways to collaborate—now as my fellow Series Editors of this book series—as we seek to provide publication opportunities for scholarship in the area of leadership for social justice.

This book, *Social Justice Leadership for a Global World,* edited by Drs. Cynthia Gerstl-Pepin and Judith A. Aiken, is the seventh in the series. The book breaks new ground by connecting and extending many ideas discussed among educational leadership into various international and global perspectives. We are excited to help provide a forum for this important work in the ongoing conversation about equity and excellence in education and the role(s) that leadership can assume in our rapidly changing world.

Again, welcome to this seventh book in this Information Age Publishing series, *Educational Leadership for Social Justice.* You can learn more about the series at our web site: http://www.infoagepub.com/series/Educational-Leadership-for-Social-Justice. I invite you to contribute your own work on equity and influence to the series. We look forward to you joining the conversation.

—**Dr. Jeffrey S. Brooks**
Iowa State University

PREFACE

Social Justice Leadership
for a Global World

*While it is appropriate to link values... and the development of practice to the local
context, to do so without placing them within the global enterprise of education
diminishes the role of leaders, renders it inward-looking and unlikely to fit staff
and learners to take their place within a globalised world.*

—Lumby, 2008, p. 4

INTRODUCTION

The global economic meltdown has highlighted the interconnectedness of
nations. This book seeks to provide an overview of topics, issues, and best
practices related to defining social justice leadership given our increasingly
global world. Refugees and immigrants from around the globe now inhabit schools and institutions of higher education across the nation and U.S.
students, teachers, and leaders are traversing international boarders both
physically and virtually through international collaboration, technology,
and exchange programs. Although there have been increased efforts and
scholarship in support of diversity and multicultural awareness, these efforts
have largely focused on the U.S. (Banks, 2006; Brooks & Normore, 2010;
Gay, 1998; Hickman, 2010; Lindsay, Robins, & Terrell, 2009; Marshall & Oliva, 2006; Moodian, 2009). We acknowledge that many leadership theories
are "domestic" (Adler, 1997) in that they typically incorporate U.S. perspec-

Social Justice Leadership for a Global World, pages xiii–xxvii
Copyright © 2012 by Information Age Publishing
All rights of reproduction in any form reserved.

tives or a single-culture description of effective leadership. Therefore, the purpose of this book is to seek a deeper understanding of diverse and multicultural perspectives as they relate to a world that is becoming increasingly interconnected economically, socially, and culturally. An emerging concept of social justice leadership in global context would focus on cross-cultural interactions that require a new type of cultural intelligence and intercultural competence. In this book we pay particular attention to providing specific strategies for social justice leaders within the context of promoting effective leadership that reflects multicultural understanding of the diversity both within and outside the U.S. In other words, within the context of leadership practice, the concept of globalization offers new insights and ideas about leadership aims, processes, and competencies as a means for addressing equity concerns throughout PK–20 education (Kezar, 2009).

Within the changing global educational context, the degree to which educational leaders are prepared with the tools and skills to build and support positive multicultural communities and interpersonal relationships, as well as the ethical values and beliefs to support social justice leadership, emerge as important areas of inquiry. Thus, more knowledge is needed related to how educational leaders develop and practice culturally sensitive practices as they work directly with teachers, other education personnel, and communities in order to bring about positive change in their schools and institutions. This line of inquiry acknowledges the increasing number of students and staff in schools and higher education from other countries and recognizes the pressing need for greater understanding of other cultures. Additionally, attention is needed in the field of educational leadership to how leaders can promote social justice by encouraging the growth of teachers and staff, using multiculturally appropriate approaches to collaborate with education personnel, and connecting with students and their families. Thus, strategies and perspectives that support social justice leadership in a changing world is the major focus of this book.

Recent efforts in the leadership literature have demonstrated an increased focus on and attention to issues of equity and social justice (Brown, 2004; Dantley & Tillman, 2006; Marshall & Oliva, 2006; Scheurich & Skrla, 2003; Shepherd, Hasazi, & Aiken, 2008; Tillman, Brown, Jones, & Gonzalez, 2005). However, within the current education environment where goals for greater accountability for student achievement have taken center stage, other concerns arise. Schools and institutions of higher education are and always have been both socializing institutions and educating institutions (Henze, Katz, Norte, Sather, & Walker, 2002). As stated by Henze and her colleagues (2002), "Schooling tends to reflect the social patterns of the larger society, including its structural inequalities based on class, race, gender, and so on. Not only does it reflect these unequal relations; it also tends to reproduce them" (p. 2). Thus, the role of educational leaders to respond to these patterns is also to recognize that in multicultural and more global environments and classrooms, the influence of cultural diversity and social justice brings new perspectives to diversity and plays an important part toward the development of safe and nurturing learning spaces for all students, staff, and teachers.

Educational leadership serves as a major function of organizational transformation and is inextricably linked to teaching and the academic success of students, as well as the growth and effectiveness of organizations. However, educational leaders and supervisors are too often unaware, unknowing, and unappreciative of how diversity, culture, ethnicity, race, language, religion/faith, sexual orientation, gender expression, and/or gender affect learning (adapted, Gay, 1998, p. 1217) and their own professional practices as leaders. Coupled with this lack of understanding, leaders also require the requisite knowledge and skills to apply cultural diversity in leadership practice. Generally, the preparation and development of educational leaders has been grounded in cultural assumptions defined by North American values and beliefs (Dalton, 1998). However, in the current changing and global environment, it is important that those of us in higher education think more broadly toward leadership practices that span multiple cultures and the changing demographics of our schools, institutions, and communities. As suggested by Williams (2006), we need "more innovative forms of global leadership accountability . . . as well as the preparation of leaders who can steer humanity through intelligent responses to global information, not through outdated beliefs" (p. 229). As we begin to face a new global order, leaders are challenged by changes such as increasing cultural diversity, changing demographics, economic exigencies, complexity and technology, social changes, social media, and information dissemination, classism and values tensions, as well as expressions of spirituality, religion or faith. Although more attention has been given to the importance of rethinking educator preparation in order to develop more culturally responsive "teachers" for our nation's schools who can use research-based pedagogy that is responsive to the learning, emotional, cultural, and social needs of ethnically and linguistically diverse students, the extent to which multicultural education has been incorporated into programs that prepare educational leaders who are able to assess, evaluate, and promote the growth of culturally responsive teachers and students and organizations within a global context remains less clear.

At the same time, state and national accountability measures have focused much attention on student achievement and the elimination of the achievement gap, and on the restructuring of curriculum and instruction to ensure all students meet high standards. Such pressures have added to the importance of school leaders and supervisors and their critical role to promote student learning for all students within diverse learning communities. Such concerns require a refocusing of preparation programs for school leaders. For many, this has meant that programs need to create opportunities for leaders to learn across cultures and to acquire "learning-oriented competencies" (Dalton, 1998, p. 396) that are important within a global context. Additionally, those who prepare leaders need to "prioritize social justice issues" (Cambron-McCabe, 2006, p. 121) and pay attention to culturally responsive practices inherent in ethical, multicultural environments (Beckner, 2004; Gerstl-Pepin & Aiken, 2009; Gross & Shapiro, 2002; Hafner, 2005; Marshall & Oliva, 2005; Rodriguez & Baum, 2005; Shields, 2004; Theoharis, 2007; Tillman, Brown, Jones, & Gonzalez, 2005). A central goal of these programs should be to foster the development of leaders who are able and willing to probe and challenge existing practices, structures, and policies to "gain an understanding of how they contribute to injustices" (Cambron-McCabe, 2006, p. 121) and cross-cultural understanding within their institutions. As stated by Gerstl-Pepin (2001), we need to develop leaders who can move beyond "discussions of how the system works and what is wrong with it, to encompass discussions of how programs can give leaders the skills to be advocates for disadvantaged children, parents, teachers, and communities" (p. 20) within a global context.

There have been increased efforts to support diversity training and leadership development in support of social justice (Dantley & Tillman, 2006; Gerstl-Pepin & Aiken, 2009; Hafner, 2005; Larson & Murtadha, 2002; Marshall & Gerstl-Pepin, 2005; Marshall & Oliva, 2006; Nieto, 2004; Straub, 2009; White & Henderson, 2008; Young & Laible, 2000). Multicultural responsiveness requires the skills, knowledge and capacities to function effectively in education environments and responds to the changing demographics in our nation and educational institutions. In order for teachers and staff to adequately serve students who represent and/or live in communities of diversity, we need leaders who are culturally responsive and multiculturally literate. This requires increased knowledge and consciousness about ethnic, racial, and culturally diverse environments and how these can be transformed into multiculturally competent and socially just leadership practices (Asante, 1996; Blackmore, 2002; Campbell, 2000; Dantley & Tillman, 2006; Gross & Shapiro, 2002; Gurin, Dey, Hurtado, & Gurin, 2002; Hurtado, Milem, Clayton-Pedersen, & Allen, 1998; Lee, 2002; Smith, 1997, 2000; Walters, 1996, 2002; Zúñiga & Nagada, 2002). Thus, this book adds to the growing literature about the practices and preparation of socially just leaders for our educational institutions.

For purposes of this book, our working definition of culturally responsive leadership and socially-just practices is influenced by several writers (Banks, 2006; Gay, 1998, 2000; Marshall & Oliva, 2006; Starratt, 2003; Straub, 2009) who conceptualize these constructs as a philosophy, a values orientation, and a set of democratic tenets framed around principles of social justice, equity, trust and respect. Culturally-responsive leadership supports a view of cultural pluralism that recognizes and affirms different cultural groups (i.e., race, ethnicity, gender, gender expression, class, ability, age, sexual orientation) and a belief that all students and faculty, regardless of backgrounds, are "empowered and enabled for maximum intellectual, personal, social, and emotional development" (Gay, 1998, p. 1218). These leaders engage in practices that foster equitable institutions, promote democratic environments, advocate for socially just policies, and demonstrate courage and skill to work against educational practices that sustain inequities. Such leaders value diversity, engage in cross-cultural communication, model inclusive practices, and engage in critical reflection about one's values and beliefs about leadership and social justice. Given our changing global context, and implicit in the ideas of globalization, leaders will need to find a balance among culture, values, practices (Lumby, 2008).

SITUATING SOCIAL JUSTICE LEADERSHIP
IN A GLOBAL WORLD

The discussion among scholars and practitioners has expanded the various perspectives of what it means to be a leader for social justice and how various forms of social justice can be enacted in professional practice (Banks, 2006; Grogan, 2002; Marshall, 2004; Marshall & Oliva, 2006; Nieto, 1996; Straub, 2009; Tillman, 2002). Understanding and valuing diversity and multiculturalism represents an essential knowledge base for leaders in today's increasingly diverse schools and institutions of higher education. It is intended that a better understanding of how to foster and develop culturally responsive leaders who are more conscious about the presence and influence of cultural diversity and social justice in their institutions within a global context will add to the literature base in the field of social justice educational leadership. In this volume we examine issues, practices, and strategies that impact leadership in our changing world and present ideas that are important to a variety of audiences, including a) leaders who serve in our public schools and participants in leadership development programs; b) administrators and campus leaders who are concerned with issues of multiculturalism and social justice; and c) faculty in higher education who are concerned with the development and a cadre of aspiring leaders who serve in non-profit and educational institutions. This book will not only introduce the readers to cultural and global dimensions of social justice leadership and supervision, but will develop new understanding and skills that they can bring to their work as well. It is also intended that this work will support the development of educational leaders who can manage and facilitate the growth and improvement of their respective staff and "supervisees," who can then better achieve higher levels of multicultural competence and cultural responsiveness in practice. This edited book and related research has the potential to engage aspiring and practicing leaders and supervisors with new approaches and perspectives that reflect the contemporary challenges and global forces they face or will face in professional practice.

ORGANIZATION OF THE BOOK

This preface frames the entire book and sets the stage for Sections I through V. The first section provides some broad frameworks for conceptualizing inequity and the need for a more global understanding of social justice leadership. The second section then provides perspectives on social justice leadership from international and U.S. scholars and sets the stage for understanding how social justice leadership is no longer a domestic endeavor. The third section then provides strategies for educational leadership programs to develop globally aware social justice leaders. The fourth section then provides specific strategies K–12 leaders can utilize to promote social justice, and then finally, the fifth section provides strategies higher education leaders can use to promote social justice. The authors in this book represent a diverse group of scholars in the area of social justice leadership in both K–12 education and higher education. Some are working in international settings, some in the U.S., and some have immigrated to the U.S. but have strong cultural ties to their home countries. Next, detail on each chapter is provided, and its contribution to the conceptual framework of the book is explained.

Section I: Frameworks for Conceptualizing Inequity

This section of the book will set the stage for the various chapters by presenting an overview of how inequity has been conceptualized and provokes thinking about some of the changing roles and responsibilities of educational leaders. Each chapter reinforces the need for the development of culturally responsive social justice leaders within a changing, diverse and global context. This section will make a case for why we need to move out of a U.S. centric understanding of leadership with attention to beliefs, practices, and specific strategies for social justice leadership and supervision within a global context. In Chapter 1, the author examines the role of culture in addressing America's achievement gap, given that by 2035 most K–12 students will be minorities. In Chapter 2, lesbian, gay, bisexual and transgender (LGBT) educators' perceptions of school climate is examined by investigating these educators' perceptions of their workplace climate and the impact of school leaders on that climate. Chapter 3, "Overcoming Cultural Collision in Educational Leadership: A Global Ethical Analysis," provides an ethical framework to guide intercultural collaborations for U.S. education workers entering other countries and introduces a possible common language and a theory of practice to facilitate productive international or cross-cultural interactions.

Section II: International and Global Perspectives on Social Justice Leadership

This section will address topics and issues related to organizational culture and learning. Chapter 4 discusses the prevalence of conflict, contestation over goals, bargaining and negotiation in institutions of higher education, and cultural and belief systems that lead to unequal power relations. The author examines power conflict through the leadership roles and practices of college heads of single-sex colleges in a primarily rural region of Pakistan. In an interesting cross-cultural comparison, Chapter 5 reports on a comparative case-study of the influence of national reform policies on school leadership in American and Chinese schools. Chapter 6 discusses the leadership challenges as well as the motivations and beliefs that a Taiwanese elementary school principal faces implementing mandates around the new immigrant education in Taiwan. This study suggests that school principals need to explore their personal histories, prejudices, and stereotypes toward new immigrants, and construct their worldviews toward multicultural leadership reflectively.

In Chapter 7, issues related to teacher leadership and how teacher leaders are being met with increasingly complicated experiences compared to a decade ago, as well as finding themselves in contexts and environment that are incompatible with the experiences they gained in their preparation programs are examined through a study of teacher narratives in the U.S. and New Zealand. The authors describe the incompatibility of the different narratives from school sites and from those in teacher leadership programs, using examples from two programs, one in the United States and one in New Zealand. Chapter 8, "Lessons From Differences: The Search for Social Justice Leadership in Education," expands upon the construct of narrative learning. Three education professors—two Caribbean and one Indian—in rural New York explore and write narratives about how their leadership style in a search for social justice has been shaped by culture and identity. Section II closes with Chapter 9 "Crumbling Barriers: A Comparative Study of International Teachers' Experiences of Educational Leadership in Their Home Countries and the United States" explores the potential for educational leaders to conceive of foreign-born and educated teachers as potential change agents in their schools.

Section III: Strategies for Developing Social Justice Leaders

The chapters in this section invite readers to explore leadership learning possibilities through curriculum and pedagogical change in leadership preparation programs. In many ways the authors in this section are developing innovative teaching and learning approaches and strategies needed to engage future school leaders to rethink their beliefs, attitudes, and dispositions toward culturally responsive and socially just practices, especially within a global context. Chapters 10 through 14 taken together provide a range of ways to transform the classroom dialogue, promote deep reflection, and to rethink personal and ethical dilemmas towards transformative and socially just actions. Chapter 10 describes how the use of documentary films offers a dynamic medium for use as a component part of an engaging curriculum in the educational leadership classroom. Through the use of both domestic and international documentaries, this chapter reveals how film can contribute to a more sophisticated global vision that uniquely informs socially just and culturally responsible dispositions of leaders. Chapter 11, "Transpositions Toward Becoming Leading Subjects," describes how these authors teach a seminar sequence through which they examine issues of diversity where they "actively de-center" what they and their students know about race, class, globalization, ability, gender, and other social and cultural categories. This chapter is aimed at looking at the graduate classroom as a place of teaching and learning that fosters greater capacity for leaders and aspiring leaders to understand and negotiate successfully the tension between their commitment for positive social change and the multiplicity of political forces that work to produce and sustain the challenging effects and affects of globalization.

The leadership challenges that result from the moral and ethical dilemmas leaders face, as well as perceptions of their own failures, offer rich opportunity for leadership transformation in Chapter 12. The author discusses a newly designed leadership preparation program that is grounded in the ideas of "relational humility." In this chapter some of the leadership and policy implications of educating leaders for social justice through relational humility are explored, and the chapter highlights the ways "case-in-point teaching" used in the program reflects the development of relational humility to better meet the global realities of schools today. Chapter 13, "Transformative School Leadership: Deconstructing Self and Agency in a Globalized World," broaches a similar topic of principal development that requires a model of leadership that transcends epistemological and national boundaries to nurture learning organizations that produce students who are equipped to engage in the global economic context and engage as citizens of the world. The authors offer an approach to educational leadership preparation programs that utilizes narrative self-reflection for transformation and introduce the importance of developing a "glonacal agency heuristic" to reframe their model of school leader development to provide for a critical multiculturalist lens occurring through an authentic, inquiry-based approach. Chapter 14 reminds us that the demographic composition of the United States is changing rapidly and that diverse ethnic groups will soon comprise a larger percentage of the student body in our schools than the traditional white majority. This chapter focuses on the assurances that all students have the opportunity to succeed in school, which is a vital element in a democracy. They add to this how the impact of globalization is changing the social, technological, and economical aspects of our lives, and the pressure on teachers and leaders to ensure that all students can succeed in a globalized world is increasing. They describe changes to principal preparation programs in order to adequately prepare future school leaders for the cultural competency challenges they will face as they prepare today's students, who will inherit a society that has become progressively more interdependent globally.

Section IV: Strategies for K–12 Social Justice Leadership

The fifth section provides strategies that K–12 leaders can utilize to promote social justice in their schools and among members of their school communities. Leadership development, crossing cultural boundaries and relevant leadership strategies comprise several of the themes presented. Chapter 15 opens the section by providing a framework for engaging diverse groups of people in complex educational change processes for social justice. Through a new synthesis of theoretical ideas and practical examples that applies cultural analysis, activity theory and complex systems theory, new forms of collective consciousness and agency concerning issues of diversity and equity emerge. The authors present several cases from practice for leading change in complex systems. Chapter 16 reminds us about research findings that leadership in urban schools, particularly in high poverty communities, demands stronger connections between school and community to serve the needs of underserved children and families. The authors make a case for "whole school reform," such as the community school approach, as an "antidote to endemic problems" facing communities and present findings from their study on cross-boundary leadership and how the community school model builds capacity to educate children and transform communities. The role of school and community is further addressed in Chapter 17. This chapter casts an idealized understanding and rationale for school leaders who are part of a global community and who are culturally responsive to the school community and lead with a conscience for social justice. While the author establishes implications for social justice leadership in K–12 schools, she uncovers a more critical requisite that hones in on important conventions in leadership preparation that develops leaders who are resilient, champion the call toward equity, and whose actions create space and access for all students in the school community.

Chapter 18, "Narrative Inquiry As A Culturally Relevant Leadership Strategy for Social Justice," examines narrative inquiry as an instructional approach that offers assistance to administrators serving as educational supervisors. The authors emphasize the power of stories to bring people of diverse origins together and unite them as they work towards a common goal, with a goal of helping educators become not only competent in multicultural diversity but committed to social justice. Chapter 19 examines the ongoing effort to promote culturally responsive leadership strategies, designed to provide a successful model for multicultural education for urban students. Given the lack of reference to multicultural education in American schools, especially at-risk schools, the authors make a case that succeeding in school is yet a challenge for multicultural children; and their opportunity in obtaining a high school diploma with advanced training in order to succeed in a more globalized labor market is more critical than ever. This chapter discusses issues and the role of educational leadership in promoting student success in urban areas.

Section V: Strategies for Higher Education Social Justice Leadership

This section explores strategies for higher education social justice leadership that spans various roles of administrators seeking to change the cultures of their institutions. Themes of equity, diversity, communication and student experiences at U.S. institutions and campuses are examined. Chapter 20, "Think Justice: Pushing the Boundaries of Black College Presidential Leadership," discusses historically black colleges and universities (HBCUs) that were established shortly after the Civil War in an effort to educate the former slaves. Created separately from the already existing colleges and universities due to the immense discrimination haunting the country at the time, these institutions became responsible for educating the African American middle class as we know it today. The contemporary environment in which HBCUs exist calls for strong leadership aimed at supporting social justice. In this chapter the authors address profiles of several HBCU leaders who are leaders for social justice in varying ways. Chapter 21 expands the conversation about higher education's role is promoting social justice, as the author offers a strategy for identifying and closing gaps in educational outcomes between underrepresented and other students in an effort to meet President Obama's goal to produce eight million more graduates by 2020. This chapter discusses ways colleges made progress towards closing these gaps by using the *Equity Scorecard.*

Chapter 22, "Making A Case for Evaluation with a Diversity Lens," reveals an emerging approach that seeks to engage multiple perspectives into the evaluation process and serves as an alternative to pre-determined evaluation methods to provide for a more culturally responsive evaluation. The diversity lens, through which interpretations are made purposefully, includes multiple stakeholders including the "voice" of program recipients. In this chapter the author examines the importance of understanding the cultural context in evaluation practice when a minority or marginalized group is the target program recipient and seeks to encourage educational leaders to explore non-traditional evaluation strategies in an effort to gain a cultural understanding of programs that serve predominantly minority or marginalized populations within a domestic or global context. In Chapter 23, concerns for social justice are expanded to an understanding of international students and their unique multifaceted needs and challenges they face while attending U.S. institutions of higher education. Due to globalization and an increased need for a high quality education, the number of individuals attending higher education in foreign countries continues to grow. Therefore, the purpose of this chapter is threefold: a) identify challenges that foreign students face while attending U.S. institutions of higher education, b) identify coping strategies used to effectively navigate these challenges, and c) identify suggestions to improve the international student experience.

Section V closes with an important chapter titled, "Do You Hear What I Hear? Culture and Communication in Teacher Education." Chapter 24 provides background information on the roles of race and culture in teacher education supervision. Two cases are presented that highlight the benefit of supervisor knowledge related to cross-cultural interpersonal communication and to cultural values and learning styles. Given the changing context of schools and the changing cultural backgrounds of students and teachers, this study highlights the importance of the supervisor in working across cultural differences.

These chapters, when taken together, present different pieces of the puzzle related to understanding the multiple ways social justice leadership can be conceptualized, taught, researched, and enacted. These chapters speak to the complexity of defining and understanding social justice leadership, which is constantly shifting and changing related to organization, cultural, social, economic, and political changes in society that reveal deep connections to the rest of the world.

A FINAL REMINDER

The authors within these pages remind us of the critical need for social justice leadership that encompasses awareness of the increasing interconnectedness of the world and the need for more cross-cultural understanding. More traditional notions of leadership may not fit as well within culturally diverse environments that experience both internal and external forces that impact the intellectual, social and emotional experiences of children, students, families and those responsible for their education. Multiple and evolving conceptions of social justice leadership are needed that bring about new social relationships, enhanced programs of learning, and expanded strategies to bring about positive change in the new and constantly shifting global world.

REFERENCES

Adler, N. J. (1997). Global leadership: Women leaders. *Management International Review, Special Issue 37*(1), 171–196.

Adler, N. J. (2009). Global leadership and women leaders. *Management International Review, 36,* 135–143.

Asante, M. K. (1996). Multiculturalism and the academy. *Academe, 82*(3), 20–23.

Banks, J. A. (2006). *Cultural diversity and education foundations: Curriculum and Teaching.* Boston, MA: Pearson.

Beckner, W. (2004). *Ethics for educational leaders.* New York: Pearson.

Blackmore, J. (2002). Leadership for socially just schooling: More substance and less style in high-risk, low-trust times? *Journal of School Leadership, 12*(2), 198–222.

Brooks, J. S., & Normore, A. H. (2010). Educational leadership and globalization: Literacy for a glocal perspective. *Educational Policy, 24*(1), 52–82.

Brown, K. M. (2004). Leadership for social justice and equity: Weaving a transformative framework and pedagogy. *Educational Administration Quarterly, 40*(1), 79–110.

Campbell, A. (2000). Cultural diversity practices: What we preach in higher education. *Teaching in Higher Education, 5,* 373–384.

Cambron-McCabe, N. (2006). Preparation and development of school leaders: Implications for social justice policies. In C. Marshall & M. Oliva (Eds.), *Leadership for social justice: Making revolutions in education* (pp. 110–129). Boston, MA: Pearson.

Dalton, M. A. (1998). Developing leaders for global roles. In C. F. McCauley, R. S. Moxley, & E. Van Velsor (Eds.), *The center for creative leadership handbook of leadership development* (pp. 379–402). San Francisco, CA: Jossey-Bass.

Dantley, M., & Tillman, L. C. (2006). Social justice and moral transformational leadership. In C. Marshall & M. Oliva (Eds.), *Leadership for social justice: Making revolutions in education* (pp. 16–29). Boston, MA: Pearson.

Firth, G. R., & Pajak, E. F. (1998a). (Eds.). Handbook of research on school supervision. New York, NY: Simon & Schuster Macmillan.

Firth, G. R., & Pajak, E. F. (1998b). Supervision as a field of study. In G. R. Firth & E. F. Pajak (Eds.), *Handbook of research on school supervision* (pp. 35–38). New York, NY: Simon & Schuster Macmillan.

Gay, G. (1998). Cultural, ethnic, and gender issues. In G. R. Firth & E. F. Pajak (Eds.), *Handbook of research on school supervision* (pp. 1184–1227). New York: Macmillan Publishers.

Gay, G. (2000). *Culturally responsive teaching: Theory, research, and practice.* New York: Teachers College Press.

Gerstl-Pepin, C. (2001). *Social justice and administrative licensure in Georgia.* Paper presented at the American Educational Research Association, Seattle, Washington.

Gerstl-Pepin, C., & Aiken, J. (2009). Democratic educational leaders: Defining ethical leadership in a standardized context. *Journal of School Leadership, 19*(4), 404–444.

Grogan, M. (Ed.). (2002). Leadership for social justice. A special issue of *Journal of School Leadership, 12*(2).

Grogan, M. (2002). Introduction. Special issue on social justice. *Journal of School Leadership, 12*(2), 112–115.

Gross, S. J., & Shapiro, J. P. (2002). Toward ethically responsible leadership in a new era of high stakes accountability. In G. Perreault & F. C. Lunenburg (Eds.), *The changing world of school administration* (pp. 256–281). Lanham, MD: Scarecrow Press, Inc.

Gurin, P., Dey, E. L., Hurtado, S., & Gurin G. (2002). Diversity and higher education: Theory and influence on educational outcomes. *Harvard Educational Review, 72*(3), 330–366.

Hafner, M. M. (2005). Teaching strategies for developing leaders for social justice. In C. Marshall & M. Oliva (Eds.), *Leadership for social justice: Making revolutions in education* (pp. 167–193). Boston, MA: Pearson.

Henze, R., Katz, A., Norte, E., Sather, S. E., & Walker, E. (2002). *Leading for diversity: How school leaders promote positive interethnic relations.* San Francisco, CA: Corwin Press.

Hickman, G. R. (Ed.). (2010). *Leading organizations: Perspectives for A New Era* (2nd ed.). Los Angeles: Sage Publications.

Hurtado, S., Milem, J., Clayton-Pedersen, A. R., & Allen, W. R. (1998). Enhancing campus climates for racial/ethnic diversity: Educational policy and practice. *The Review of Higher Education, 21*(3), 279–302.

Kezar, A. (2009). *Rethinking leaders in a complex multicultural and global environment.* Sterling, VA: Stylus.

Larson, C., & Murtadha, K. (2002). Leadership for social justice. In J. Murphy (Ed.), *The educational leadership challenge: Redefining leadership for the 21st century* (pp. 134–161). Chicago, IL: University of Chicago Press.

Lee, W. Y. (2002). Culture and institutional climate: Diversity in higher education. *The Review of Higher Education, 25*(3), 359–368.

Lindsey, R. B., Robins, K., Terrell, R. D. (2009). *Cultural proficiency: A manual for school leaders.* Thousand Oaks, CA: Corwin Press.

Lumby, J. (2008, September). *International perspectives on developing educational leaders.* A paper presented at annual meeting of the Commonwealth Council for Educational Administration and Management, International Convention Centre, Durban, South Africa.

Marshall, C. (2004). Social justice challenges to educational administration: Introduction to a special issue. *Educational Administration Quarterly (EAQ), 40*(1), 3–13.

Marshall, C., & Gerstl-Pepin, C. (2005). *Reframing educational politics for social justice.* Boston, MA: Allyn & Bacon.

Marshall, C., & Oliva, M. (2005). *Leadership for social justice: Making revolutions in education.* Boston, MA: Pearson.

Moodian, M. A. (Ed.). (2009). *Contemporary leadership and intercultural competence: Exploring the cross-cultural dynamics within organizations.* Thousand Oaks, CA: Sage Publications.

Nieto, S. (1996). *Affirming diversity: The socio-political context of multicultural education.* White Plains, NY: Longman.

Nieto, S. (2004). *Affirming diversity: The sociopolitical context of multicultural education.* New York, NY: Pearson.

Rodriguez, G. M., & Baum, J. (2005). LEADing for social justice: A journey of inquiry & reflective practice. *Journal of School Leadership, 16*(2), 126–141.

Scheurich, J. J., & Skrla, L. (2003). *Leadership for equity and excellence.* Thousand Oaks, CA: Corwin Press.

Shepherd, K., Hasazi, S., & Aiken, J. (2008). Preparing school leaders to build and sustain positive connections with families and communities. In R. Papa, C. Achilles, & B. Alford (Eds.), *NCPEA Yearbook, 2008: Leadership on the front line: Changes if professional practice.* Ypsilanti, MI: NCPEA Press.

Shields C. M. (2004). Dialogic leadership for social justice: Overcoming pathologies of silence. *Educational Administration Quarterly, 40*(1), 111–134.

Smith, D. G. (1997). Institutional transformation: Findings from comprehensive campus commitments to diversity. In D. G. Smith (Ed.), *Diversity works: The emerging picture of how students benefit* (pp. 39–45). Washington, DC: Association of American Colleges and Universities.

Smith, D. G. (2000). The benefits of diversity: What research tells us. *About Campus, 5*(5), 16–23.

Starratt, R. J. (2003). *Centering educational administration.* Mahwah, NJ: Lawrence Erlbaum Associates, Publishers.

Straub, K. J. (2009). Facilitating supervisee cultural fluency for a multicultural society. *Perspectives on Administration and Supervision, 19,* 45–50.

Theoharis, G. (2007). Social justice educational leaders and resistance: Toward a theory of social justice leadership. *Educational Administration Quarterly, 43*(2), 221–258.

Tillman, L. (2002). The impact of diversity in educational administration. In G. Perreault & F. Lunenburg (Eds.), *The changing world of school administration* (pp. 144–156). Lanham, MD: Scarecrow Press.

Tillman, L. C., Brown, K., Jones, F. C., & Gonzalez, M. L. (2005). Teaching for transformative leadership for social justice. *Journal of School Leadership, 16*(2), 207–209.

Walters, E. (1996). Embracing the spirit of multiculturalism in higher education as a means of black and Hispanic student retention. *Equity & Excellence in Education, 29*(3), 43–47.

Walters, E. (2002). Institutional commitment to diversity and multiculturalism through institutional transformation: A case study of Olivet College. *Journal of College Student Retention, 3*(4), 333–350.

White, J. L., & Henderson, S. J. (2008). *Building multicultural competency: Development, training, and practice.* Lanham, MD: Jason Aronson.

Williams, C. (2006). Global leadership, education, and human survival. In W. E. Rosenbach & R. L. Taylor (Eds.), *Contemporary issues in leadership* (6th ed.) (pp. 215–236). Cambridge, MA: Perseus.

Young, M. D., & Laible, J. (2000). White racism, antiracism, and school leadership preparation. *Journal of School Leadership 10*(5), 374–415.

Zúñiga, X., & Nagada, B. A. (2002). Intergroup dialogues: An educational model for cultivating engagement across differences. *Equity & Excellence in Education, 35*(1), 7–17.

SECTION I

FRAMEWORKS FOR CONCEPTUALIZING INEQUALITY

CHAPTER 1

SOCIOCULTURAL FACTORS AFFECTING MINORITY ACHIEVEMENT

What Every School Leader Should Know

Charles Williams

INTRODUCTION

Today, in the United States, a consensus stands on the role of education in the fight for equality. However, the nation's ability to ensure that equality by accommodating the educational needs of all its students, particularly minority students, has become a matter of great concern. Policy leaders, professional educators, researchers, and legislators have become increasingly frustrated by America's lopsided educational outcomes, as a disproportionate number of minority students often find themselves left behind, which becomes even more troubling when one considers the U.S. census data showing that the majority of primary and secondary students in the United States will be ethnic and racial minorities by 2035 (Tomlinson et al., 2003). This inevitable demographic shift has caused discussions regarding minority achievement to take center stage in America's education debate.

Social Justice Leadership for a Global World, pages 3–21
Copyright © 2012 by Information Age Publishing
All rights of reproduction in any form reserved.

Moreover, global competitiveness, combined with the inconvenient truth about America's lackluster education rankings, have led many to question the true value of a U.S. high school diploma. And while some education and policy leaders have gained a sense that the current process by which we educate in the U.S. may not adequately address the needs of all students, there is no consensus on either the true nature of the problem or an effective intervention to address this challenge.

The role of teacher preparation and school leadership programs cannot be understated, given that it will require an increased emphasis on training school leaders to develop effective policies and strategies that address the needs of a diverse student population. Where we were once a world separated by racial and ethnic tribes, spread out in faraway lands, unheard of by members of other tribes, business, technology and a desire to lend support to countries and societies facing challenges such as civil wars and natural disasters, such as hurricanes and earthquakes, have drawn us together. However, the challenge is ensuring that a fair cultural exchange takes place, in the absence of racial, ethnic or cultural hegemony. In the midst of this new type of global interdependence is an opportunity to create a more egalitarian and just world.

Specifically, school leaders must create and support policies whereby education is viewed within a larger sociocultural context (Vygotsky, 1981, 1986), moving beyond a single-minded focus on content and curriculum knowledge, toward promoting the need for school leaders and professional educators to recognize that teaching and learning takes place within a broader context—including culture, home and community life.

This new approach would take into consideration what noted education scholar Pedro Noguera (2010) termed in an essay *A New Vision of School Reform*—attending to the "whole child." To that end, school leaders must support evidence-based strategies that can lead to academic success for minority students in order to reach beyond the classroom, such as in mentoring and parent support initiatives. However, central to any discussion about school success, as it relates to educating minority students, has to include a conversation regarding the biases and perceptions of what minority students can or cannot achieve—what some refer to as "soft bigotry." Interestingly, though, the ability to recognize that education in America may require a new type of pedagogical dynamism, undoubtedly encouraged in part by the U.S.'s growing minority student population, could lead to greater success rates for all students. It is important to note, as we begin our discussions regarding the achievement gap and minority students, that a degree of heterogeneity exists within minority student groups as relates to achievement. That is to say, some minority students are currently excelling in academically rigorous courses and go on to attend some of the nation's most competitive institutions of higher learning. However, the purpose of this chapter is to examine some of the plausible challenges and solutions to why minority students face disproportionate school failure rates in the United States.

DEEMPHASIZING THE *WHAT* AND FOCUSING ON THE *HOW*

America's achievement gap may be more about critically reevaluating the processes (pedagogy) by which we educate minority students, as opposed to issues related specifically to content such as math or science. Moreover, as one author put it, in the absence of a thorough and honest assessment of teaching as a practice, we risk repeating the failures of the past (McMillian, 2003). That is to say, while the need for new academic programs cannot be overlooked, what is also needed is a thorough discussion about employing a more culturally sensitive and inclusive pedagogy, ensuring that minority students are more, rather than less, likely to succeed. Such an approach could in fact take precedence over emphasizing core content areas such as math and science (STEM). Specifically, if as some suggest, minority students are less engaged, often feeling misunderstood and culturally marginalized, how does funding a new, state-of-the-art science lab address such impediments to their academic success? Such impediments are firmly rooted in the *how* rather than the *what* of education.

How we engage minority students in formal learning settings is of the utmost importance when considering the achievement gap. For example, there is research that suggests that minority students, specifically African American students, may disproportionately face harsh school disciplinary practices, such as in-school detentions, out of school suspensions, disciplinary transfers and expulsions (Bradshaw, Mitchell, O'Brennan, & Leaf, 2010), because professional educators may misinterpret cultural behaviors—body language, communication styles, and attitudes. For the purposes of this chapter, minority students will refer to African American, Latino, and Native American students, students typically identified as lagging in achievement; these students may also be identified as "native minorities" (Warikoo & Carter, 2009).

ECONOMIC, ECOLOGICAL AND CULTURAL REALITIES

Researchers such as Bronfenbrenner (1977) and Ogbu (1991), who specifically focused on African American children, argue that environmental and cultural influences must be taken into consideration when examining various outcomes for students; considering such variables as family systems, economics, and parenting can account for the differences observed in achievement between groups. Employing such an approach to explaining the differences experienced by various racial and ethnic groups as it relates to educational achievement is often referred to as taking a cultural-ecological perspective. This approach attempts to identify aspects of culture as well as environmental structures that may affect achievement (Eamon, 2005; Warikoo & Carter, 2009). For example, Ogbu (1991) posits through his cultural-ecological perspective that African American children experience observable cultural differences, which must be taken into consideration when discussing the achievement gap. Specifically, he argues that African American children experience primary cultural differences such as language, behavior and thinking, and secondary cultural differences related to their interaction with society's dominant culture.

An example of a secondary cultural difference for an African American student might be a propensity to question the motives and intentions of an adult in a position of authority, not assuming that their actions are pure and benevolent; this may not necessarily be the case for white students, thereby indicating a different world view ostensibly influenced by culture. However, it is safe to assume that many professional educators lack this understanding of the influence of cultural difference and its impact on teaching and learning. Moreover, the absence of this critical knowledge can negatively influence teachers' attempts at engaging minority students in formal learning environments. Also, a lack of familiarity and understanding regarding culture's influence on teaching and learning may range from harmful ignorance to a tacit contempt for minority students, leading to what can be termed an "engagement gap." That is to say, given that minority students do not feel valued, respected, or understood, from a cultural standpoint, they are likely to become disinterested and disengaged. Their disengagement may, in turn, lead to frustration on the part of professional educators, causing them to become less likely to either encourage or support such students. In a sense, this engagement gap speaks to a hidden danger, likely poisoning the student-teacher dyad, which is critical to academic success. However, if professional educators were aware of this factor, it may prevent its occurrence.

Poverty: The Cost of Achievement

Paik and Walberg (2007) utilize an economic stress model to assert that many of the achievement challenges faced by black children can be linked to their families' poor economic conditions, which is plausibly the case for other types of poor minority children, e.g., Latino or Native American. Eamon (2005) goes on to further posit that economic factors may have a profound impact on the disparity in educational outcomes for Latino youth, specifically. The influence of poverty on achievement is echoed by researchers such as Gerstl-Pepin (2006), who states that poverty and low achievement stand as a sort of self-perpetuating harmful narrative. Available data make the relationship between poverty and academic achievement impossible to ignore. The National Assessment for Educational Progress (NAEP) (National Center for Educational Statistics, 2009), also known as the Nation's Report Card, states that students from low economic backgrounds score lower on every content area measured (math and reading), and they also score lower on both the verbal and mathematics sections of the Standardized Achievement Test or SAT (Taylor, 2005).

Family and Community Stressors: Minority Students' Narrative

The research is pretty clear that family life—including social, emotional, and academic outcomes—can have a significant impact on the overall life trajectory of a child. Healthy and stable families contribute to better outcomes for children and youth (Boulter, 2004; DeRosier & Gilliom, 2007; Draper, Siegel, White, Solis, & Mishna, 2009). However, the families of many minority students face unique challenges, which may lead to poor academic outcomes. Specifically, many minority students come from households where the educational attainment of the primary caregiver is low— for instance, he or she lacks a high school diploma or possesses very little to no post-secondary training. Roach (2004) also adds that parents of minority children may suffer from a lack of "sophisticated parenting" or a stimulating home environment.

Fetsch, Yang, and Pettit (2008) suggest that parents from low income communities are faced with a level of stress and overall life dissatisfaction, which may make them less inclined to focus on effective parenting strategies. Moreover, due to stressful living and social conditions, largely brought on by poverty, the parents of minority children may actually engage in ineffective parenting strategies, such as harsh disciplinary practices and physical maltreatment, making it more likely that their children will suffer from emotional challenges and poor social skills, a major corollary to academic achievement (Gresham, 1986, 1988; O'Shaughnessy et al., 2002; Williams, 2006). All of these challenges are further complicated by the fact that minority students are more likely to be reared in single-parent homes; and single-parent headed households are much more likely to face economic challenges. As one could also imagine, being reared in a single-parent home places additional stressors on the family, given that a single caregiver must shoulder the multiple burdens of child rearing, which includes being the sole breadwinner. Also, poverty rates for single-headed households are more than four times higher than those for households headed by two parents (Thomas & Sawhill, 2002).

TEACHER EXPECTATIONS, SCHOOL CLIMATE AND STUDENT ENGAGEMENT

The confluence of cultural and ecological realties mentioned in the previous section create a most challenging scenario for school leaders, as they are charged with ensuring that minority students achieve; however, such corollaries to low achievement are exaggerated by the presence of what was referred to as "soft bigotry" by former U.S. education secretary Roderick Paige (McMillian, 2003). Specifically, the idea is that some professional educators hold onto a myth, reinforced by racial and ethnic bias, that poor minority children are unable to learn, or that they learn more slowly than non-minority children. One could extend this argument to reasonably assume that the presence of soft bigotry may stand as its own challenge, cultural and ecological realities and stressors notwithstanding. The Council of the Great City Schools highlighted this in its report *A Call for Change: The Social and Educational Factors Contributing to the Outcomes of Black Males in Urban Schools*. In the report the authors point out that African American students who do not face harmful economic conditions still lag behind their white counterparts (Council of the Great City Schools, 2010). Such an occurrence may support the notion that some professional educators do not feel, even in the absence of economic challenges, that minority children are capable of achieving.

Zero Tolerance: The Color of Discipline

Often times, discussions about student achievement focus on issues related to funding or curricular issues, all of which, subsequently, affect achievement for minority students. However, an area that may require much more attention is the aggregate impact of school disciplinary policies and practices, which may actually stifle minority student achievement (Townsend, 2000). Researchers suggest that this may be due to a lack of understanding regarding the culture behaviors of minority youth. This lack of cultural understanding and responsiveness can lead professional educators to misjudge the behaviors of minority students as negative or harmful. That is to say, teachers being unaware of the conditioned cultural norms and practices of minority students can lead them to consider certain cultural norms and communication styles as threatening or incommensurate with what they perceive to be appropriate student conduct (Warikoo & Carter, 2009). This lack of cultural understanding, coupled with soft bigotry, may lead some educators to seek official school sanctions or punishment at disproportionately higher rates for minority students, particularly boys, than non-minority students.

School Connectedness, Acceptance and Engagement

As Ibañez, Kuperminc, Jurkovic, & Perilla (2004) point out, feeling connected to school is correlated with school success. School connectedness essentially means that students feel respected, accepted, included, and supported. A considerable body of research has shown that when minority students do not feel that their values, cultures and beliefs are considered, they are more likely to be disengaged in the school environment, which correlates significantly with poor academic achievement (House, 2003; Nel, 1994; Warikoo & Carter, 2009). Therefore, the false assumption that minority students are not as motivated to achieve is often made, based upon cultural, racial or ethnic bias. Many, however, would argue that the problem is that such students are not motivated to achieve, given that they do not see themselves in the policies, practices, curriculum or culture of schools. This, of course, may serve as a natural disincentive for their efforts. If students feel more connected, culturally and socially to formal learning environments, it probably follows that they are more likely to be engaged and are therefore likely to achieve school success at higher rates.

The Psychology of the Minority Student: Opposition as a Necessary Defense?

Related to discussions about school engagement for minority youth and school discipline policies is the often unexplored notion discussed by Portes and Zhou (1993), which states that minority youth from economically disadvantaged neighborhoods, where residents also experience social and political marginalization, may develop a strategy to cope with such harsh realities beyond their control. They may create and adopt what can be called an adversarial subculture. This concept warrants a deeper examination. Essentially, the idea supported by researchers such as Ogbu (1991), though not universally accepted, is that minority youth develop a high degree of skepticism and open opposition towards what they consider to be mainstream culture, a culture they see as unresponsive to their specific needs; and that offers very little opportunity for them to express views, ideas and concepts indigenous to their culture. For example, there is a tendency to value written expression over oratory ability, which may be somewhat problematic given that some cultural anthropologists suggest that many minority groups come from a rich and proud tradition whereby important histories, concepts and ideas are expressed and transmitted orally (Shuldiner, 1998). Moreover, it can be argued that this unwillingness to allow for orality—the verbal expression of intellectual concepts and ideas within formal academic contexts—stands as a type of cultural hegemony, further encouraging minority students to become disengaged in formal learning environments. Therefore, in the eyes of many minority students, formal education (school) exists as a sort of extension of a larger oppressive force. So, why would they want to engage it?

CHALLENGES SPECIFIC TO POPULATIONS OF MINORITY STUDENTS

The U.S. government has identified three specific groups of students as having the greatest risk for school failure—African American, Latino and Native American students. In the following section, a brief discussion about challenges for specific groups of minority students is presented.

African-American Students

Roach (2004) reminds us that according to data compiled by the National Assessment of Educational Progress (NAEP), sometimes referred to as the "Nation's Report Card," the average African American 12th grader has a level of proficiency in basic skills that matches that of the average white eighth grader. McMillian (2003) points out that for about 30 years the gap between the highest achieving African American high-school students and their white counterparts has remained static. For math the situation appears to be even more tragic, as only 5% of African American students perform at or above proficiency in math. As was mentioned earlier, some researchers suggest that central to this unfortunate reality may be a propensity for some educators to misinterpret certain behaviors (cultural norms) of African-American students (e.g., Neal, McCray, Webb-Johnson, & Bridgest, 2003), behaviors that may be then labeled as inappropriate, thereby serving as justification for harsh school sanctions, such as suspension or expulsion (Townsend, 2000; Tyler, 2006; Tyler, Boykin, Miller, & Hurley, 2006). If students are expelled or suspended, they miss out on important instructional time, creating a situation where they are constantly struggling to play catch up, aiding in their academic failure. In this sense, a lack of cultural knowledge and racial bias on the part of professional educators may prevent African American students from fully benefiting from formal learning environments, given that they are often struggling with being misunderstood culturally or having to deflect negative stereotypes being forced upon them, leaving little opportunity for them to feel safe, connected and supported.

Latino Students

In discussing the importance of addressing low achievement among Latino youth, Ochoa and Cadiero-Kaplan (2004) state that "maintaining a free and open democracy demands that we actively pursue equity and excellence for Latino youth" (p. 27). Latino achievement becomes even more salient when demographic trends are considered. Latinos currently constitute the largest minority population in the United States, according to the U.S. census (U.S. Census Bureau, 2009). However, it is a community facing many challenges. In fact, nearly one in three Latino youth live in poverty, which is three times higher than the poverty rate for non-Hispanic whites (Eamon, 2003). Eamon and Mulder (2005) go on to mention that Latino youth face other home and community stressors, making them more likely to face school failure. Specifically, Latino youth tend to disproportionately reside in single-mother, large family homes, where the head of household may also have limited English proficiency.

According to the National Clearinghouse for English Language Acquisition & Language Instruction Educational Programs, 80% of the 4.5 million students of limited English proficiency are Spanish-language speakers; this, according to some researchers, places Latino students at a significant disadvantage compared with their peers (Roach, 2006). Also, a high rate of Latinos in the U.S. are born to teenage mothers (Eamon & Mulder, 2005). Adding to the aforementioned stressors is the challenge of acculturation, which is likely influenced by English language ability and residential status, for instance, if the parents are recent immigrants. Kalogrides (2009) suggests that Latinos who reside in poor urban environments may face discrimination and structural barriers, which may impact their level of interest and effort in formal learning environments.

Native American Students

Native American students face unique challenges to their academic achievement—challenges that are often unexplored or over looked in most discussion regarding America's achievement gap. Nel (1994) reminds us that cultural discontinuity experienced by Native American students when entering mainstream society can cause them to struggle with feelings of inadequacy, anxiety and alienation. Many Native American students often report feeling rejected, depressed and withdrawn when educated in formal learning environments that do not incorporate or acknowledge their cultural values, traditions and beliefs. Moreover, research shows that Native American adolescents "have a lower self-image than any other minority group" (Nel, 1994, p. 169). These negative affective experiences can often preclude Native American students from achieving at an optimum level (House, 2003). For example, Native American students are disproportionately underrepresented in the top 5% of those taking the American College Testing Program assessment (House, 2003). These psychological and emotional challenges significantly compromise the academic performance of Native American students (House, 2003).

ERASING THE ACHIEVEMENT GAP

In order to start a discussion about culturally relevant and inclusive practice, it must be reemphasized that the achievement gap may be a byproduct of a lack of cultural understanding and responsiveness on the part of school leaders and professional educators. Further, formal learning environments often fail to acknowledge or accommodate the cultural realities of minority students. Moreover, it is probably safe to assume that many professional educators and school leaders hold biased assumptions about the abilities of minority students. The purpose of this section is to inform educational leaders about the evidence-based strategies and interventions available to them, which may lead to the obliteration of America's so-called "achievement gap." Reemphasizing the overall theme of this chapter, strategies that affect minority achievement may require efforts that reach beyond core content and curricular knowledge.

Curricular Choices: Cultural Understanding and Inclusion

As Davis (2007) states, professional educators need to learn about other cultural and ethnic groups as part of their formal education; and this learning will influence their ability to support the success of minority students. A part of this education has to include, however, recognizing their own soft bigotry, which may lie dormant and unexpressed until confronted with a classroom full of minority students. In the U.S. we are constantly inundated with messages that minority students are intellectually inferior and less capable, which many minority students internalize, negatively affecting their motivation to achieve. However, it is the responsibility of professional educators to impress upon minority students that they in fact do have the ability to achieve, even in the face of daunting challenges. This process, however, has to start with the educator first believing in the ability of minority students.

Also, as has been mentioned, traditional education often fails to incorporate the cultures of diverse communities within the formal curriculum. Students need to learn that diverse groups have participated and continue to participate in the development of academic thought and intellectual interrogation, both within and outside the U.S. In order to put this notion into practice, it may quire a "cultural audit" of a school or district's curriculum, to ensure that from a content standpoint, learning materials reflect and highlight the value that different cultures contribute to areas such as math, science and philosophy. Such a move would allow both minority as well as non-minority students to recognize that minorities are not just poor, marginalized peoples, but rather intelligent and productive thinkers and doers. This also allows the minority student to view herself in a more positive light, which can boost self-concept; and non-minority students get an opportunity to be exposed to positive images and contributions of students who are often viewed through a lens of negative stereotypes and low expectations.

ELL/Biliteracy Programs

Ochoa and Cadiero-Kaplan (2004) suggest that English language learner (ELL) programs can offer significant support to minority students for whom English is not their native tongue. To some extent this is self-evident, given that one could rightfully assume that instruction and course materials will most likely be presented in English; therefore, even before engaging the content, minority students who are not proficient in English are at a severe disadvantage. Moreover, the inability of English language learners, who are more than likely recent immigrants, to understand and communicate in English may cause them to engage in school-avoidance behaviors, such as excessive and unexcused absences and lateness or even dropping out of school. This type of school-avoidant behavior may also be unwittingly reinforced by parents with no or limited English proficiency, which is why there is a need to make available effective, quality ELL and biliteracy programs that may include providing education and language support to the parent or caregiver.

As was previously mentioned, English proficiency remains a challenge for many Spanish speaking students, which supports the need for effective ELL programs in U.S. schools and at times can run up against politics of language and ethnicity (Ochoa & Cadiero-Kaplan, 2004). Another effective strategy to address the needs of ELL students would be to implement biliteracy programs. Biliteracy is a process by which English language learners are allowed to develop content knowledge utilizing their first language, while simultaneously continuing to develop proficiency in English (Crawford, 1999; Ochoa & Cadiero-Kaplan, 2004). By engaging in this dual process, ELL students are able to develop English proficiency, while simultaneously learning content such as math, science and social studies. In the absence of such an approach, ELL students risk falling behind, as they struggle with academic content as well as language proficiency, concomitantly. When effective ELL and biliteracy programs are put in place, ELL students can eventually be mainstreamed into classes along with their English proficient peers, without having to wrestle with issues of efficacy and self esteem—thereby aiding in their eventual academic success. Educators need to be aware of the needs of English language learners, particularly their fears and anxieties around being non-English proficient. This once again brings to the fore issues related to cultural awareness and sensitivity. To a certain extent, English language learners are a part of a sub-culture, which must be fully explored and understood if professional educators are to reach and educate them.

Cultural Connections: Pathways to Success

Allowing minority students to develop and maintain connections with their cultural heritage may also support their academic achievement (Xie & Greenman, 2005). Moreover, research demonstrates that having a solid connection with their cultural heritage and traditions may also serve as a protective factor for minority students (Xie & Greenman, 2005). In a practical sense, aside from putting in place specific programs aimed at encouraging minority students to both seek and embrace cultural connections, it also means that school leaders and professional educators should ensure that minority students do not feel as though efforts at connecting with their culture will cost them in any way. That is to say, a climate and culture needs to be fostered whereby diversity is understood, valued and respected.

BEYOND THE CLASSROOM: MENTORING AND PARENT ENGAGEMENT

Classroom strategies alone, however, may not be enough to support students. Both student mentoring and parental engagement are strategies outside of the classroom that have been effective at supporting minority student achievement.

Mentoring

Mentoring programs developed to support minority students have proven effective in a number of circumstances (Brown & Henriques, 1997; Cheng et al., 2008; Gordon, Iwamoto, Ward, Potts, & Boyd, 2009; Whiting & Mallory, 2007; Zand et al., 2009). Group mentoring may boost achievement particularly for minority youth, given that it offers the opportunity for the expression and sharing of important cultural and ethnic traditions within a supportive environment; such an intervention would also allow for the development of strong intra-cultural social ties, which can also aid in minority achievement (Portes & Rumbaut, 2001). This has been demonstrated in such programs as the Puente program for Latino youth, an intensive mentoring program in California that promotes cultural and ethnic pride, which has been shown to lead to high rates of college attendance for participants (Gandara, 2002). Moreover, an evaluation of the Juvenile Mentoring Program (JUMP), serving minority students, demonstrated that 30% of youth participants improved school attendance, 30% demonstrated academic progress, 35% improved their general behavior, and there was a 48% increase in overall positive peer interaction (Brown & Henriques, 1997).

Mentoring appears to increase students' overall positive outlook and attitude about school and learning (Converse & Lignugaris-Kraft, 2009; Whiting & Mallory, 2007). Therefore, it would behoove school leaders interested in preventing or closing the achievement gap to support mentoring programs for minority students.

Engaging Parents

As Pedro Noguera has stated—"there's a lot more parents can do" (cited in Roach, 2004, p. 23). However, many parents challenged by racial, ethnic, social, and economic barriers require support and training in doing what is necessary to support the academic success of their children. As has been discussed, parents and caregivers play a critical role in the social, emotional and intellectual development of youth, minorities notwithstanding. Parents of minority youth can face challenges often related to such things as poverty or their own lack of successful engagement with formal education environments.

One of the ways in which to address this is through parent support programs. Parent support programs are created to increase positive and effective parental involvement, which studies show can lead to increased school attendance and self-efficacy (Drolet, Paquin, & Soutyrine, 2007). Studies also suggest that parents who participate in parent support programs can acquire greater parenting skills over time and can become more supportive of their children; this, in turn, can lead to better outcomes (Colarossi & Eccles, 2000). Another component of successful parent support programs is skills development. This would include teaching parents to set limits and to utilize effective discipline. In a randomized, controlled study of a multicomponent parenting support program, which involved teaching social skills to parents, parents who participated in the program made significant gains in their ability to encourage and support their children (DeRosier & Gilliom, 2007). Parent support programs have been proven particularly successful in engaging minority parents (Chang, Park, Singh & Sung, 2009). This also provides an opportunity for schools and colleges of education to underscore for pre-service educators the notion that educating the whole child involves successful parent engagement, which includes both understanding and facilitating these types of parent support efforts. Such an effort could take place at the start of the school year, as a type of parent orientation–parent support workshops.

FINAL THOUGHTS

The aim of this chapter was not to offer an exhaustive list of challenges that serve as impediments to minority student achievement or to merely cast blame; rather the intent was to highlight and discuss some of the challenges. Additionally, this chapter reiterates the idea that any efforts created to address the achievement gap have to start with educating school leaders and professional educators of the role that culture and cultural understanding play in unequal educational outcomes. Beyond that, school leaders and professional educators must do a self-assessment as it relates to their own racial and ethnic biases to ensure that such biases are not operating at a subconscious level, unwittingly hindering efforts at encouraging minority student achievement. Such inventories could include:

- Georgetown University—Self-Assessment Checklist for Personnel Providing Behavioral Health Services and Support for Children, Youth and their Families could be slightly modified for use in educational settings.
- Harvard University—Implicit Association Test (IAT)
- Cultural Competence Self-Assessment Questionnaire (CCSAQ)
- Beliefs, Events and Values Inventory (BEVI)
- Cross-Cultural Adaptability Inventory (CCAI)
- Global Awareness Profile (GAP Test)
- Global Mindedness Scale

If teacher and leadership preparation programs fail to adequately prepare professional educators to successfully engage and educate minority students, then the onus is placed on school leaders to draft policies and practices that would allow for professional educators (in-service) to learn the skills necessary to create a classroom and school climate that encourages the high achievement of all students. However, this may require that specific types of trainings and workshops be mandatory, realizing that important concepts and ideas about culturally responsive practices may have not been taught to pre-service teachers or practicing leaders. This conversation is also important, given the fact that the world has become more globally connected and interdependent, with various individuals of various cultural, racial and ethnic backgrounds sharing living spaces. As noted in the introduction, this new global interdependence provides an opportunity to create a more egalitarian and just world.

At the center of such an effort would be the role of education and its leaders. Possessing an understanding of and having respect for cultural, racial and ethnic difference is not something that will happen by chance; rather it must be fostered, cultivated, maintained, supported and expected by all who engage in the one science and art of education, which, plausibly has the power to right many wrongs, not just in the U.S., but in many regions of the world where entire populations are marginalized due to economic, social and political inequalities. School leaders must lead an effort to ensure that education serves as the bridge to opportunity for marginalized children and youth from around the world, offering a chance for education to serve as a tool of individual empowerment and transformation. Practically speaking, education has been shown to improve quality of life—leading to better economic, health and political outcomes for all who are privileged enough to access it fully and equitably. However, this can only occur if school leaders create, implement and assess policies and practices that integrate into both school culture and curriculum a whole child approach, acknowledging that the education of diverse student populations does not start or end at the school house door. That is to say, school leaders must encourage and hold educators accountable for understanding the sociocultural contexts that affect the experiences of such students, recognizing, respecting and accommodating their multiple traditions, heritages and world views within the teaching and learning environments. In the absence of such an understanding, an almost perfect opportunity is missed to ensure that no child is relegated to a future of repeated oppressions.

REFERENCES

Boulter, L. (2004). Family-school connection and school violence prevention. *Negro Educational Review, 55*(1), 27–40.

Bradshaw, C. P., Mitchell, M. M., O'Brennan, L. M., & Leaf, P. J. (2010). Multilevel exploration of factors contributing to the overrepresnation of black students in office disciplinary referrals. *Journal of Educational Psychology. 102*(2), 508–520.

Bronfenbrenner, U. (1977). Toward an experimental ecology of human development. *American Psychologist, 32*(7), 513–530.

Brown, P. & Henriques, Z. (1997). Promises and pitfalls of mentoring as a juvenile justice strategy. *Social Justice, 24,* 212–233.

Chang, M., Park, B., Singh, K., & Sung, Y. (2009). Parental involvement, parenting behaviors, and children's cognitive development in low-income and minority families. *Journal of Research in Childhood Education, 23*(3), 309–324

Cheng, T. L., Haynie, D., Brenner, R., Wright, J. L., Chung, S., & Simms-Morton, B. (2008). Effectiveness of a mentor-implemented violence prevention intervention for assault-injured youths presenting to the emergency department: results of a randomized trial. *Pediatrics, 122*(5), 938–946.

Colarossi, L. & Eccles, J. (2000). A prospective study of adolescents' peer support: gender differences and the influence of parental relationships. *Journal of Youth and Adolescence, 29*(6), 661–678.

Converse, N. & Lignugaris-Kraft, B. (2009). Evaluation of school-based mentoring program for at-risk middle school youth. *Remedial and Special Education, 30*(1), 33–46.

Council on Great City Schools. (2010, November). *A call for change, the social and educational factors contributing to the outcomes of black males in urban schools.* Retrieved from http://www.cgcs.org/publications/achievement.aspx

Crawford, J. (1999). *Bilingual education, history, politics, theory, and practice* (4ᵗʰ ed.). Los Angeles, CA: Bilingual Educational Services.

Davis, P. E. (2007). Something every teacher and counselor needs to know about African American Children. *Multicultural Education, 15*(3), 30–34.

DeRosier, M. E. & Gilliom, M. (2007). Effectiveness of a parent training program on improving children's social behaviors. *Journal of Child and Family Studies, 16*(5), 660–670.

Draper, K., Siegel, C., White, J., Solis, C., & Mishna, F. (2009). Preschoolers, Parents, and Teachers (PPT): a preventive intervention with an at-risk population. *International Journal of Group Psychotherapy, 59*(2), 221–242.

Drolet, M., Paquin, M., & Soutyrine, M. (2007). Strengths-based approach and coping strategies used by parents whose young children exhibit violent behavior: collaboration between schools and parents. *Child and Adolescent Social Work Journal, 24*(5), 437–453.

Eamon, M. K. (2005). Social-demographic, school, neighborhood, and parenting influences on the academic achievement of Latino young adolescents. *Journal of Youth and Adolescence, 34*(2), 163–174.

Eamon, M. K., & Mulder, C. (2005). Predicting antisocial behavior among Latino young adolescents: An ecological analysis. *American Journal of Orthopsychiatry, 75,* 117–127.

Fetsch, R., Yang, R., & Pettit, M. (2008). The RETHINK parenting and anger management program: A follow-up validation study. *Family Relations, 57*(5), 543–552.

Gandara, P. (2002). Addressing educational inequities for Latino students: The politics of "forgetting." *Journal of Hispanic Education, 4,* 295–313.

Gerstl-Pepin, C. I. (2006). The paradox of poverty narratives: Educators struggling with children left behind. *Educational Policy, 20*(1), 143–162.

Gordon, D., Iwamoto, D., Ward, N., Potts, R., & Boyd, E. (2009). Mentoring urban black middle school male students: implications for academic achievement. *The Journal of Negro Education, 78,* 277–289.

Gresham, F. M. (1986). Conceptual issues in assessment of social competence in children. *School Psychology Review,* 16, 78–88.

Gresham, F. M. (1988). Social skills: Conceptual and applied aspects of assessment, training and social validation. In J. C. Witt, S. N. Elliott, & F. M. Gresham (Eds.), *Handbook of behavior therapy in education* (pp. 523–543). New York: Plenum Press.

House, J. D. (2003). A longitudinal assessment of cognitive-motivational predictors of the grade performance of American Indian/Alaska Native students. *International Journal of Instructional Media, 30,* 303–314.

Ibañez, G. E., Kuperminc, G. P., Jurkovic, G., & Perilla, J. L. (2004). Cultural attributes and adaptations linked to achievement motivation among Latino adolescents. *Journal of Youth and Adolescence, 33*(6), 559–568.

Kalogrides, D. (2009). Generational status and academic achievement among Latino high school students: Evaluating the segmented assimilation theory. *Sociological Perspectives, 52,* 159–183.

McMillian, M. (2003). Is No Child Left Behind 'wise schooling' for African American male students? *The High School Journal, 87,* 25–33.

National Center for Education Statistics. (2009). *Indicators of school crime and safety, 11th Edition.* Retrieved from http://nces.ed.gov/programs/crimeindicators/crimeindicators2009/key.asp

Neal, L. I., McCray, A. D., Webb-Johnson, G., & Bridgest, S. T. (2003). The effects of African-American movement styles on teachers' perceptions and reactions. *Journal of Special Education, 37*(1), 49–57.

Nel, J. (1994). Preventing school failure: the Native American child. *Preventing School Failure, 67*(3), 169–174.

Noguera, P. (2010, May, 27). A new vision for school reform. *The Nation.* Retrieved April 15, 2011, from http://www.thenation.com/article/new-vision-school-reform

Ochoa, A. M. & Cadiero-Kaplan, K. (2004). Towards promoting biliteracy and academic achievement: Educational programs for high school Latino English language learners. *The High School Journal, 87*(3), 27–43.

Ogbu, J. (1991). Immigrant and involuntary minorities in perspective. In M. Gibson & J. Ogbu (Eds.), *Minority status and schooling: A comparative study of immigrant and involuntary minorities* (pp. 3–33). New York: Garland.

O'Shaugnessy, T. E., Lane, K. L., Gresham, F. M., & Beebe-Frankenberger, M. E. (2002). An integrated model to address academic underachievement and problem behavior. In K. L. Lane, F. M. Gresham, & T. E. O'Shaugnessy (Eds.),

Interventions for students with or at-risk for emotional and behavioral disorders. New York N.Y: Allyn-Bacon.

Paik, S. J. & Walberg, H. J. (Eds.). (2007). *Narrowing the achievement gap: strategies for educating Latino, Black, and Asian students.* New York: Springer.

Portes, A. & Rumbaut, R. G. (Eds.). (2001). *Legacies: The story of the immigrant second generation.* Berkeley, CA: University of California Press.

Portes, A. & Zhou, M. (1993). Interminority affairs in the U.S.: Pluralism at the crossroads. *Annals of American Academy of Political and Social Science, 530,* 74–96.

Roach, R. (2004). The great divide: racial achievement gap gains recognition as national concern, but solutions continue to elude educators, scholars and policy-makers. *Black Issues in Higher Education, 21,* 22–25.

Roach, R. (2006, September, 21). Jump starting Latino achievement: The nation's largest minority group has fallen behind academically, but dedicated scholars and programs are working to close the gap. *Diverse Issues in Higher Education.* Retrieved April 15, 2011, from http://diverseeducation.com/article/6428/

Shuldiner, D. (1998). The politics of discourse: An applied folklore perspective. *Journal of Folklore Research, 35,* 189–201.

Taylor, J. A. (2005). Poverty and student achievement. *Multicultural Education, 12*(4), 53.

Thomas, A. & Sawhill, I. (2002). For richer or for poorer: Marriage as an antipoverty strategy. *Journal of Policy Analysis and Management, 21,* 587–599.

Tomlinson, C. A., Brighton, C., Hertberg, H., Callahan, M. C., Moon, T. R., Brimijoin, K., . . . Reynolds, T. (2003). Differentiating instruction in response to student readiness, interest and learning profile academically diverse classrooms: A review of the literature. *Journal for the Education of the Gifted, 27,* 119–145.

Townsend, B. L. (2000). The disproportionate discipline of African American learners: Reducing school suspensions and expulsions. *Exceptional Children, 66,* 381–391.

Tyler, K. M., Boykin, A. W., Miller, O. A., & Hurley, E. A. (2006). Cultural values in the home and school experiences of low income African American students. *Social Psychology of Education, 9,* 363–380.

Tyler, K. M., Uqdah, A. L., Dillihunt, M. L., Beatty-Hazelbaker, R., Conner, T., Gadson., . . . Stevens, R. (2008). Cultural discontinuity: Toward a quantitative investigation of a major hypothesis in education. *Educational Review, 37,* 280–297.

Vygotsky, L. S. (1981). The development of higher forms of attention in childhood. In J. V. Wertsch (Ed.), *The concept of activity in Soviet psychology* (pp. 189–240). Armonk, NY: Sharpe.

Vygotsky, L. S. (1986). The genetic roots of thought and speech. In A. Kozulin (Trans. & Ed.), *Thought and language.* Cambridge, MA: MIT Press.

Warikoo, N. & Carter, P. (2009). Cultural explanations for racial and ethnic stratification in academic achievement: A call for a new and improved theory. *Review of Educational Research, 79,* 366–394.

Williams, C. A. (2006). *The effects of social skills and media on student achievement in elementary school students.* UMI (Dissertation).

United States Census Bureau News Room. (2009). Texas gains the most in population: Last state population estimates before 2010 census counts. Retrieved

July 31, 2009, from http://www.census.gov/newsroom/releases/archives/population/cb09-199.html

Whiting, S. & Mallory, J. (2007). A longitudinal study to determine the effects of mentoring on middle school youngsters by nursing and other college students. *Journal of Child and Adolescent Psychiatric Nursing, 204*, 197–208.

Xie, Y. & Greenman, E. (2005). Segmented assimilation theory: a reformulation and empirical test. Research Report No. 05-581. Ann Arbot, MI: Population Studies Center.

Zand, D., Thomson, N., Cervantes, R., Espiritu, R., Klagholz, D., LaBlanc, L., & Taylor, A. (2009). The mentor-youth alliance: The role of mentoring relationships in promoting youth competence. *Journal of Adolescence, 32*, 1–17.

CHAPTER 2

CREATING SAFE LGBT SCHOOL ENVIRONMENTS FOR STUDENTS AND STAFF

Tiffany Wright and Nancy Smith

INTRODUCTION

Effective school leaders strive to maintain safety within their schools (Lezotte, 1997). Bucher and Manning (2005) described a safe school as "one in which the total school climate allows students, teachers, administrators, staff, and visitors to interact in a positive, non-threatening manner that reflects the educational mission of the school while fostering positive relationships and personal growth" (p. 56). Edmondson, Fetro, Drolet and Ritzel (2007) found that safety for their study respondents included protection from bodily harm, emotional turmoil, harassment, and rumors. Students need to feel safe and accepted in order to take the important risks associated with their academic and social development (Bluestein, 2000; Merrow, 2004). Discrimination against LGBT educators is damaging not only to those employees, but also to students who witness that discrimination (Eckes & McCarthy, 2008). Support for LGBT issues varies globally due to cultural differences, with developing countries more likely to be supportive. Without equipping educators to talk about LGBT parents and people, schools in the U.S. cannot be fully safe.

Social Justice Leadership for a Global World, pages 23–38
Copyright © 2012 by Information Age Publishing
All rights of reproduction in any form reserved.

LGBT people need to be seen within the curricula and as visible members of the community (Moll, 2011).

Educators also need to feel safe and accepted in order to provide the best education for their students. Leithwood and McAdie (2007) found that teachers who felt safe had higher levels of efficacy. Historically and presently, gay, lesbian, bisexual, and/or transgender students and staff have felt unsafe in many school environments due to their sexual and gender orientations (Markow & Fein, 2005).

Within the past decade, educators have increasingly included gay, lesbian, bisexual and transgender (LGBT)[1] issues in the scope of teaching and learning about diverse populations within multicultural education (Rottman, 2006). This focus has assisted many schools in creating safer climates for diverse populations, including LGBT students and staff. The Gay, Lesbian, Straight Education Network (GLSEN) has surveyed students and teachers to understand not only what experiences exist in schools for LGBT students and teachers, but also to understand what mechanisms and pedagogy support positive experiences for these populations (Markow & Fein, 2005).

Despite this minimal progress, schools continue to struggle with how to improve experiences for LGBT students. School leaders' acknowledgement and improvement of the experiences of LGBT educators is nearly nonexistent. In fact, many LGBT educators report feeling that an unstated "Don't ask; don't tell" policy is in effect in reference to discussing their sexual orientation (Smollin, 2011). Extant literature revolves around three themes: a) the history of LGBT educators (Blount, 1996, 2000; Khayatt, 1992; Kissen, 1996; Lugg, 2006); b) the climates they have faced and currently face within schools (Blount, 1996, 2000; Griffin & Ouellett, 2003; Harbeck, 1997; Khayatt, 1992; Kissen, 1996; Yared, 1997); and c) the individual experiences of LGBT educators or pre-service educators (Evans, 2002; Ferfolja, 1998; Griffin, 1992; Jackson, 2007; Jennings, 1992; Juul & Repa, 1993; Litton, 1999; McCarthy, 2003; Melillo, 2003; Resenbrink, 1996; Woods & Harbeck, 1992; Woog, 1995). The majority of these studies have employed qualitative methods and focused on a single LGBT educator or on a small group of LGBT educators. Prior to 2007, one published comprehensive quantitative study (Juul & Repa, 1993) examined factors that influenced LGBT educators' job satisfaction, although the results are dated.

Specifically, this study presented in this chapter sought to understand factors related to the school climate, defined here as LGBT educators' perceptions of safety through policies, principal support, and perceptions of homophobia[2] and the impact these perceptions have on their levels of outness,[3] which has been linked to teacher effectiveness (Juul & Repa, 1993). This research provided new knowledge for school leaders committed to creating safer and more inclusive school environments for LGBT educators and insights for those unaware of the need to improve school environments for educators.

HISTORICAL LITERATURE

Blount (1996, 2000, 2005) and Harbeck (1997) examined how LGBT educators' professional experiences have been influenced by cultural shifts in the larger society. Although men were the earliest educators, savvy money-managers began using the accepted practice of hiring single females at lower salaries. In spite of the poor salary, these single women earned enough money to live independently of men or with each other, and this profession and lifestyle attracted a number of women who by today's standards would be defined as lesbians (Blount, 1996). These female educators also advanced into educational leadership positions until the 1920s, when researchers began to study and publicize information about sexuality, which began the process of scrutinizing teachers' personal lives (Blount, 2000). This scrutiny promoted gender role polarization, homophobia, and heteronormativity (Blount, 2000; Melillo, 2003; Sumara & Davis, 1999), defined by Berlant and Warner (1998) as "institutions, structures of understanding, and practical orientations that make heterosexuality seem not only coherent—that is, organized as a sexuality—but also privileged" (p. 548). Since this time, court cases, cultural shifts, backlashes, and public perception of the morality of sexual orientation have impacted the professional experiences of LGBT educators.

CONTEMPORARY RESEARCH ON LGBT EDUCATORS

Using survey data, Juul and Repa (1993) examined the relationship between levels of job satisfaction and stress for LGBT educators and levels of outness to others within the school setting. Their subjects varied by gender, geographic location, race, ethnicity, and teaching experience. They found that LGBT educators who rated themselves as more out had higher scores on the job satisfaction survey. Teachers who rated themselves as more out to administrators scored higher on the job satisfaction survey and were more willing to be noticed for successful performance within their jobs. Finally, Juul and Repa (1993) concluded that teachers who rated themselves as more out felt more engaged in the social and interpersonal role of being an educator. This study did not, however, address factors that influenced outness or reasons for comfort levels.

Jackson's (2007) nine LGBT participants identified support (especially from administrators) within the school as a major factor that impacted their level of outness in the workplace. Based on these findings, Jackson (2007) developed a theory that defined stages of professional development for LGBT educators that were unique and separate from the stages of professional development for heterosexual teachers. These stages were: pre-teaching, closeted, and post-coming out. During the pre-teaching stage, participants considered entering the teaching profession from traditional college teaching preparation programs, careers similar to education, or careers different from education. During this phase, participants did not believe that gayness and teaching were compatible, and accepted their sexualities to different degrees (also see Khayatt, 1992). As closeted teachers, participants first experienced a super-teaching phase, proving their worth as educators while suppressing their gayness. During the latter period of the closeted teacher stage, described as the on-the-verge, participants felt guilt and dissonance, realizing that remaining closeted negatively impacted the climate for their students and themselves. During the initial period of the post-coming out stage, educators often acted, either voluntarily or involuntarily, as gay "poster children" and resources for all on gayness. During the second period of the post-coming out stage, described as the authentic teacher phase, participants felt as if they could bring their true selves to their teaching. They developed mutually respectful relationships with their students and colleagues based on honesty and trust. Woods and Harbeck's (1992) participants had similar experiences.

Jackson's (2007) participants all agreed that being out and reaching the authentic teacher phase benefited them and their students because they felt as though they were "all the things a Good Teacher is expected to be" (p. 73) while also being self-actualized and humanized. LGBT teachers who had reached the authentic teacher phase in their development were more willing and able to confront issues of homophobia within the classroom, school and curriculum. Those schools that employed these teachers better supported all LGBT individuals in schools. Conclusions from other qualitative studies (Leithwood & McAdie, 2007; McCarthy, 2003; Melillo, 2003; Rensenbrink, 1996) further supported a positive relationship between a better environment for LGBT educators and benefit to their students.

NEED FOR RESEARCH

McCarthy (2003) identified a dichotomy for LGBT educators in schools. On one hand, schools are institutions in which traditional gender roles and "gender presentation"[4] (p. 182) have been passed through generations. On the other hand, gender roles have been challenged in schools. The extant literature suggested, therefore, that LGBT educators need to be honest with their communities about their orientations to best serve their students as positive role models and feel empowered as people and educators.

Many LGBT educators, however, are still not out. Researchers have identified several reasons why they may feel wary about being out. Prior to the Employment Non-Discrimination Act (ENDA)[5] being passed in November, 2007, thirty-one states allowed workplace discrimination based on sexual orientation, and thirty-nine states allowed it based on gender identity. This means that people (including educators) were not protected from discrimination in terms of their employment by these laws or by district policies (Lugg, 2006). This legal environment contributed to complex climates for LGBT educators; they experienced dissonance because they want to protect and be role models for LGBT youth without risking their employment status (Griffin, 1992; Litton, 1999). Even if laws are in place to protect them, LGBT educators have experienced covert discrimination, such as unpleasant assignments and negative gossip (Harbeck, 1997). Jackson's (2007) research on the stages of development of LGBT educators found that all participants believed that it was not the experience of being gay or lesbian that made being an educator difficult, but being so in the context of a heteronormative society (see also Melillo, 2003). This is why many educators still perceive an unwritten "Don't ask; don't tell" policy in reference to discussing their sexuality if something other than heterosexual (Smollin, 2011).

Researchers have identified gender role polarization (Blount, 1996, 2000), homophobia, heteronormativity (Jackson, 2007; Melillo, 2003; Sumara & Davis, 1999), and Gay Straight Alliance (GSA) existence as factors that impact the workplace for LGBT educators. Factors that have been found to positively impact the workplace environment are heterosexual allies in the building as advocates (Ferfolja, 1998; Woods & Harbeck, 1992), visible LGBT heroes and figures present in the curriculum (Ferfolja, 1998), and the presence of an LGBT educators' support group (Griffin, 1992).

Ultimately, many LGBT educators fear rejection by their students as a consequence of their sexual orientations (Kissen, 1996). High levels of stress and guilt associated with balancing honesty about their gender identity and sexual orientation and distancing themselves for safety causes health risks for LGBT educators. (Ferfolja, 1998; Khayatt, 1992; Woods & Harbeck, 1992; Yared, 1997). Jennings (1992) highlighted this by quoting an interview with Pat McCart, a lesbian principal: "We (educators) are probably the most deeply closeted group in the gay community... It's not okay. You are not fit to teach children. You are fired!" (p. 55)

Research since McCart's statement shows professional experiences for some LGBT educators have improved. Qualitative researchers have reported a sense of empowerment and energy by LGBT educators from opening up and being honest about their orientations (Woog, 1995). Studies about the experiences of LGBT educators have relied on data from small groups of educators and employed qualitative methods. Not one major quantitative research study had been conducted prior to 2007 that evaluated professional experiences for LGBT educators that could be used to draw broad or generalizable conclusions.

PURPOSE OF THE STUDY

This study addressed gaps in the current literature, examining factors related to LGBT educators' perceptions of school climate, defined here as perceptions of safety through policies, principal support, and school homophobia and the impact these perceptions have on their level of outness, which has been linked to teacher effectiveness. It is based on data collected through the *2007 National Lesbian, Gay, Bisexual and Transgender (LGBT) K–12 Educators Survey* (Smith, Esposito, Wright, & Reilly, 2006).

Preliminary conclusions based solely on demographic data from this study indicated that overall, LGBT educators reported that schools were difficult places for them to work during the 2006–2007 school year (Smith, Wright, Reilly, & Esposito, 2008). Many respondents reported hearing homophobic comments regularly without intervention from colleagues or school leaders; approximately half of the respondents reported feeling unsafe in schools, and many of those reported experiencing harassment. It is troubling that so many educators find their work place climate to be hostile. Further analysis of the survey data provided new knowledge for school leaders that can help them create the best possible school climate for all teachers, therefore likely enhancing student achievement.

METHODS

In September 2005, four researchers collaboratively developed a survey, a valuable tool in measuring perceptions (Gay & Airasian, 2003). Topics were identified based on the GLSEN survey, the extant literature, suggestions from LGBT teachers, and personal experiences. Domains impacting the climate for LGBT educators were identified. Each domain consisted of several survey items. The original instrument contained the five domains of interest to the research team (see Table 2.1). Next the team composed and revised drafts of items via email correspondence that were rewritten using the formats in SurveyMonkey.com. Three local LGBT educators with varied professional experiences reviewed the survey for face validity and suggested revisions to improve clarity of items. Their responses demonstrated that the items measured climate for LGBT educators.

TABLE 2.1 Domains and Survey Item Topics Related to Each

1	Homophobia	Homophobic comments by teachers or support staff, with administrator present, among a group of teachers
2	Principal Support	Frequency of intervention when administrator hears homophobic comments; principal reaction to students' use of homophobic language; level of comfort talking to supervisor about LGBT issues
3	Policies	Domestic partner benefits; civil rights protected by state law, local ordinance, and by union contract; policy regarding homophobic and transphobic language
4	Safety	Harassment based on LGBT identity-rumors, written communication, and phone calls; employment at risk if out to faculty, students, administrators
5	Level of Outness	To principal(s), assistant principal(s), at school, number of colleagues to whom one is out (administrators, office staff, parents/guardians, students)

In 2006, the instrument was piloted. A snowball sampling of teachers with whom the researchers had personal contacts was initiated. Responses were collected from thirty teachers representing elementary, middle and high schools in five different states.

Data was collected for the national survey during spring of 2007, to represent LGBT educators' perceptions of experiences during the 2006–2007 school year. Purposive sampling through various educational organizations, liberal faith organizations, academic organizations and conferences, and national LGBT organizations and snowball sampling were used to recruit 514 participants. Participants received a web-based link to the national survey (Smith et al., 2006) and responded via computer. The participants represented teachers in all disciplines, counselors and librarians from all grades and from all 50 states and included educators in public, charter, private, parochial, and technical schools in urban, suburban, and rural settings.

Instrument Reliability and Instrument Construct Validity

Six educational professionals ranked each item's contribution towards an identified set of factors using a Likert scale to validate the final survey instrument. For the entire instrument, reliability was excellent ($\alpha = .82$). For selected domains (homophobia, $\alpha = .82$; principal support, $\alpha = .61$; policies, $\alpha = .62$; safety, $\alpha = .69$; and outness, $\alpha = .83$) reliability ranged from excellent to moderate.

The SPSS factor analysis program was used to test for construct validity of the three domains in this study: principal support, policies, and safety. Not only was construct validity established, but two of the domains each yielded two factors. For homophobia and principal support, only one factor was extracted. Policies yielded two factors: policies of human rights and policies of bullying language. For safety, two factors also were extracted: personal safety and job safety. This in itself can be considered a finding, since none of the literature or research to date had delineated types of safety. Finally, outness yielded one factor. Items were selected for the factor analyses based on their connectedness to the domains.

The SPSS ANOVA program was used to identify any significant differences in perceptions of the seven factors representing the five original domains: homophobia, principal support, policies of human rights, policies of bullying language, personal safety, job safety, and outness across demographic, school, and personal categories. The structural equation modeling software (hereafter EQS) was used to test the hypotheses that principal's support, policies of bullying language and human rights, and homophobia would predict safety; and this further tested whether safety is a mediating factor in predicting levels of outness based on the homophobia, domains of principals' support, policies of bullying language and human rights, and personal and job safety (See Figure 2.1).

RESULTS

The first hypothesis stated that LGBT educators will perceive their school climates as hostile. This hypothesis was overwhelmingly supported. The second hypothesis stated that there will be a significant difference in perceptions of homophobia based on respondents' demographic, personal, and professional characteristics, as well as school characteristics. This hypothesis was not supported.

The third hypothesis, that there will be a significant difference in perceptions of principal support based on respondents' demographic, per-

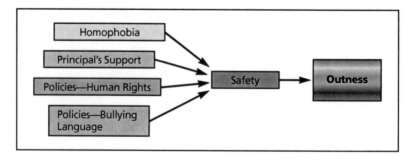

Figure 2.1 Predictive model for research hypotheses 6 and 7.

sonal, and professional characteristics, as well as school characteristics, was partially supported. Respondents ages 43 to 50 felt significantly less supported by their principal than respondents ages 18 to 25 or ages 34 to 42. There was an overall significant difference found in the years of teaching experience of respondents but no significant differences in the post hoc tests for this hypothesis.

The fourth hypothesis, that there would be a significant difference in the existence of LGBT inclusive policies based on respondents' demographic, personal, and professional characteristics, as well as school characteristics, had two parts. The part relating to bullying language was partially supported. Respondents whose schools were in the Midwest experienced more support through policies of bullying language than did those respondents whose schools were in the Southwest. The part relating to policies of human rights was not supported.

The fifth hypothesis stated there would be a significant difference in perceptions of safety based on respondents' demographic, personal, and professional characteristics, as well as school characteristics, and also had two parts. The first part related to perceptions of personal safety and was partially supported. An overall significant difference in the number of absences of respondents and reports of personal safety was found, but there were no significant differences in the post hoc tests.

The second part, that there would be a significant difference in perceptions of job safety based on respondents' demographic, personal, and professional characteristics, as well as school characteristics, was mostly supported. Respondents with 11–15 years of experience felt significantly safer in their jobs than did those with 0–5 years or 21–30 years of experience; respondents whose schools were in New England felt significantly safer in their jobs than those participants whose schools were in the South or Midwest; respondents whose schools were in the Mid-Atlantic felt significantly safer in their jobs than those participants whose schools were in the South; respondents who worked in private or independent schools felt significantly safer in their jobs than those who worked in regular public schools; respondents who worked in K–8 schools felt significantly safer in their jobs than did respondents who worked in K–5 schools and middle schools, and those respondents in K–5 schools and middle schools felt significantly safer in their job status than did those who worked in K–4 schools; respondents who worked in K–12 schools, high schools, or those schools described as "other" felt significantly safer in their jobs than those who worked in K–4 schools; and respondents who were absent zero times felt significantly safer in their jobs than those who were absent two or three times. An overall significant difference in respondents' GSA involvement was found, but post hoc tests revealed no further significance.

The sixth hypothesis, that there will be a significant difference in outness based on respondents' demographic, personal, and professional characteristics, as well as school characteristics, was partially supported. Results indicated that respondents who described themselves as GSA advisors were significantly more out than those who described their involvement in GSAs as "other."

The seventh hypothesis, that perceptions of homophobia, perceptions of principal support, the existence of policies relating to bullying language, and the existence of human rights policies will significantly predict perceptions of job and personal safety when controlling for respondents' demographic, personal, and professional characteristics, as well as school characteristics was significant for policies of human rights predicting job safety and policies of bullying language predicting personal safety ($p < .05$). However, the model did not demonstrate goodness of fit, and this research hypothesis was only partially supported.

The eighth hypothesis, that perceptions of homophobia, perceptions of principal support, the existence of policies relating to bullying language, the existence of human rights policies, and perceptions of safety will significantly predict levels of outness when controlling for respondents' demographic, personal, and professional characteristics, as well as school characteristics was significant for the following factors: 1) policies of human rights predicting job safety, which in turn predicted outness and 2) policies of bullying language predicting personal safety, which in turn predicted outness ($p < .05$). However, the model did not demonstrate goodness of fit, so this research hypothesis was also only partially supported.

LIMITATIONS OF THE STUDY

This quantitative study of a national sample of LGBT educators generated new knowledge about this population's perceptions of its workplace climate. The study's finding that LGBT educators perceive their workplace climates as homophobic confirms quantitatively what has been suggested qualitatively. The findings about differences in perceptions of principal support among LGBT educators suggest some progress in the field with younger educators reporting greater principal support than older educators, but the study also suggests that there is more work to be done. Progress has been uneven, with some regions in the nation having more progressive human rights policies than other regions. An important finding of the study is that safety is best understood in two dimensions—personal safety and job safety—a delineation not found in prior research. This study strongly suggests that to feel safe within their schools, LGBT educators need the support of administrators and policies to ensure equal rights and protection.

The study's primary limitation affecting generalizability is the design of the survey instrument that resulted in missing data. The length of the survey may have caused some participants not to complete it. There may be other reasons for non-completion of particular items within the survey, which may be worth further analysis.

CONCLUSIONS

The findings of this study lead to seven overall conclusions about the perceptions of LGBT educators surveyed. First, school climate is perceived as homophobic by LGBT educators across all ages, years of experience, races, grade level of position, area of instruction and sex. Second, the age of LGBT educators influenced perceptions of principal support. Third, few LGBT educators in the sample population perceived an inclusion of LGBT rights within their districts' policies of human rights, including domestic partnership benefits. Fourth, LGBT educators were more likely to be advisors for GSAs if they were out on the job. Fifth, impact on job safety had three parts: a) LGBT educators with 11–15 years of experience perceived a higher level of job safety than those with much less experience (0–5 years) or more experience (21–30 years); b) LGBT educators in New England and Mid-Atlantic states perceived a higher level of job safety than those in the South; and c) LGBT educators of older students perceived a higher level of job safety than those of younger students. The sixth hypothesis related to personal safety and has two parts: a) Policies of bullying language that include homophobia and high levels of perceived principal support directly influence perceptions of personal safety for LGBT educators; and b) Policies of human rights (like union contracts allowing for domestic partnership benefits) directly influence perceptions of job safety for LGBT educators.

Seventh, outness, has two parts, which are best viewed as tentative: a) Policies of bullying language that include homophobia and high levels of perceived principal support may directly influence perceptions of personal safety, which in turn may influence levels of outness for LGBT educators; and b) Policies of human rights (like union contracts allowing for domestic partnership benefits) may directly influence perceptions of job safety, which in turn may influence levels of outness for LGBT educators.

Implications for Research

There are four primary research implications from this study. These relate to a) a comparative study of the influence of domestic partner benefits on LGBT employees' perceptions of job safety; b) a study of age and years of teaching experience in relation to perceptions of principal support and job safety; c) an analysis of the open-ended items; and d) a revision of the survey instrument to yield results that can lead to more definitive results and generalizability. Gay and Airasian (2003) observed that studies relying on self-reported data often suffer from a lack of participant responses; therefore, to generate the most complete results, surveys should be brief. The 2007 National Lesbian, Gay, Bisexual and Transgender (LGBT) K–12 Educators Survey (Smith et al., 2006) has been shortened, re-named and re-released as of April 15, 2011 (Wright & Smith, 2011).

The first implication for research concerns the impact of domestic partner benefits and other human rights policies on perceptions of job safety. Few participants perceived support from LGBT inclusive policies in regards to human rights, and this factor could potentially predict job safety. Perceptions of job safety, in this study, emerged as the factor that demonstrated the most significant differences among demographic items. In order to understand the impact of domestic partnership benefits on the workplace climate for LGBT employees, more research is needed. Leithwood and McAdie (2007) indicated that positive feelings of safety lead to higher professional efficacy.

The second implication for research concerns the impact of age and years of teaching on the factors identified by this study. According to the results of this study, respondents ages 43–50 felt significantly less supported by their principals than those of two younger age groups. Also, respondents with 11–15 years of experience perceived a higher level of job safety than those with much less experience and a little more experience. Research from a generational perspective, not part of extant literature, is warranted.

Implications for Practice

Three practical implications relate to a) administrative practices that lead to perception of support for LGBT employees; b) educating school employees and the community on the differences between pedophilia and homosexuality; and c) providing domestic partnership benefits for all school employees to foster perceptions of job and personal safety.

Khayatt (1992) found that LGBT teachers experienced unsupportive treatment from school administrators. For example, participants reported that administrators would not allow LGBT teachers who were out to chaperone field trips and questioned their motives with children. Litton's (1999) participants also felt that administrators would not support them being honest about their sexual orientation. Similarly, when McCarthy's (2003) case study participant's car was vandalized, she felt that her administrators did not act in a supportive manner.

Jackson (2007) identified principal support as the most important source of support for LGBT educators and administrative practices that could lead to higher perceptions of principal support. One strategy would be providing professional development on LGBT issues and infusing these issues into the curriculum. In addition, if administrators would fight for domestic partner benefits, LGBT educators would perceive positive support from their principals. Administrators could also demonstrate support for GSAs and for policies of bullying language that include homophobia. These policies would include levels of discipline and education for those students who bully according to LGBT (or perceived LGBT) identities.

The second implication for practice is that school employees and the greater community need to be educated on differences between pedophilia and homosexuality. Participants in this study who worked with younger children perceived lower levels of job safety than did teachers of older children. Harbeck (1997) also contended that many people equated homosexuality with pedophilia and molestation. Blount (2000) and Evans (2002) noted that the general public believed that homosexuals were a threat to children.

The conflation of homosexuality and pedophilia may be one of the bases for the historical and current discrimination against LGBT educators. Harbeck (1997), Khayatt (1992), and Blount (1996, 2000) described the various forms of discrimination that LGBT educators have experienced, including the risk of losing their jobs simply because of their LGBT identities (Griffin & Oullett, 2003). In the 1970s, Anita Bryant, in Florida, and Senator John Briggs, in California, proposed and encouraged the passage of laws that limited the rights of homosexuals (Harbeck, 1997). Even during a recent election (November, 2008), voters in California and several other states passed laws (called Proposition 8 in CA) that denied LGBT people the right to marriage benefits. Much of the campaign in California depicted LGBT families' involvement in schools as a scare tactic to convince California voters to pass Proposition 8.

The third implication for practice is for school leaders to provide or advocate for domestic partnership benefits for school employees. Respondents of this study perceived a higher level of job safety when they felt supported by union contracts that provided domestic partnership benefits. These respondents also indicated a higher likelihood of outness with a higher perception of job safety. Jennings (1992), Woog (1995), and others discussed the importance of LGBT educators being out and the positive impact this had on their professional efficacy, their students, and the school climate as a whole.

It is the role of school leaders in a democracy to support all teachers, including LGBT educators, to realize their full professional potential. Although the U.S. is considered to be more supportive of LGBT issues than many developing countries, this research shows that this is an area educational leaders need to address. This time of high teacher attrition, professionally demanding environments, and federal mandates for highly qualified teachers requires it. Studies indicate that teacher satisfaction and retention are directly related to issues of safety and student achievement. The results of school leaders effectively creating safe school climates for LGBT educators will be more effective educators and higher achieving students, thus fulfilling the role of the school leader to create school climate conducive to learning.

NOTES

1. These four groups of individuals identify with each other and are frequently analyzed as one because members of these groups share many of the same experiences in regards to discrimination, negative public opinion, and targeting from conservative religious organizations. However, one must recognize that heteronormativity and hegemony have worked in different ways against each group as well.
2. Homophobia can be described as: 1) Hatred of homosexuality or homosexuals; 2) fear of gays and lesbians; or 3) a desire or attempt to discriminate against homosexuals (Religious Tolerance, 2008).
3. Levels of outness are defined within the survey instrument (Smith, Wright, Reilly, & Esposito, 2006) by four levels: out to everybody, out to most, out to only a few, or not out to anyone.
4. The external presentation or appearance of a person as it relates to the traditional stereotypes of male and female. It includes appearance, mannerisms, dress, hairstyle, speech patterns, and social interactions (EQUAL!, 2008).
5. This federal law adds sexual orientation to the list of protected populations in reference to employment discrimination. In order to have the bill passed, the sponsors had to eliminate gender identity as a protected class (Human Rights Campaign, 2008).

REFERENCES

Berlant, L. & Warner, M. (1998). Sex in public. *Critical Inquiry, 24,* 547–566.

Blount, J. M. (1996, Summer). Manly men and womanly women: Deviance, gender role polarization and the shift in women's school employment, 1900–1976. *Harvard Educational Review, 66*(2), 318–338.

Blount, J. M. (2000, Spring). Spinsters, bachelors, and other gender transgressors in school employment, 1850–1990. *Review of Educational Research, 70*(1), 83–101.

Blount, J. M. (2005). *Fit to teach: Same-sex desire, gender, and school work in the twentieth century.* Albany: State University of New York Press.

Bluestein, J. (2000, Summer). Create a caring classroom. *Instructor, 110*(2), 35–37.

Bucher, K. T. & Manning, M. E. (2005). Creating safe schools. *The Clearing House, 79*(1), 55–60.

Eckes, S. E. & McCarthy, M. M. (2008). GLBT teachers: The evolving legal protections. *American Educational Research Journal, 45*(3), 530–554.

Edmondson, L., Fetro, J. V., Drolet, J. C., & Ritzel, D. O. (2007). Perceptions of physical and psychosocial aspects of a safe school. *American Journal of Health Studies, 22*(9), 1–9.

EQUAL. (2008). *TG interest group basic transgender definitions.* Retrieved June 4, 2008 from http://www.tgender.net/taw/defn.html

Evans, K. (2002). *Negotiating the self: Identity, sexuality, and emotion in learning to teach.* New York: RoutledgeFalmer.

Ferfolja, T. (1998). Australian lesbian teachers: A reflection of homophobic harassment of high school teachers in New South Wales government schools. *Gender and Education, 10*(4), 401–415.

Gay, L. R. & Airasian, P. (2003). *Educational research: Competencies for analysis and applications.* Upper Saddle River, NJ: Pearson Education.

Griffin, P. (1992). From hiding out to coming out: Empowering gay and lesbian educators. In K. M. Harbeck (Ed.), *Coming out of the classroom closet: Gay and lesbian students, teachers and curricula* (pp. 141–166). Binghamton, NY: Haworth.

Griffin, P. & Ouellett, P. (2003). From silence to safety and beyond: Historical trends in addressing lesbian, gay, bisexual, transgender issues in k–12 schools. *Equity & Excellence in Education, 36*, 106–114.

Harbeck, K. M. (1997). *Gay and lesbian educators: Personal freedoms, public constraints.* Malden, MA: Amethyst Press and Productions.

Human Rights Campaign. (2008). Employment non-discrimination act. Retrieved May 11, 2008 from http://www.hrc.org/laws_and_elections/enda.asp

Jackson, J. (2007). *Unmasking identities: An exploration of the lives of gay and lesbian teachers.* Lanham, MD: Lexington Books.

Jennings, K. (Ed.). (1992). *One teacher in 10: Gay and lesbian educators tell their stories.* Los Angeles: Alyson Publications.

Juul, T. & Repa, T. (1993). *A survey to examine the relationship of the openness of self-identified lesbian, gay male, and bisexual public school teachers to job stress and job satisfaction.* Paper presented at the Annual Meeting of the American Educational Research Association, Atlanta, GA.

Khayatt, M. D. (1992). *Lesbian teachers: An invisible presence.* New York: State University of New York.

Kissen, R. M. (1996). *The last closet: The real lives of lesbian and gay teachers.* Portsmouth, NH: Heinemann.

Leithwood, K. & McAdie, P. (2007). Teacher working conditions that matter. *Education Canada, 47*(2), 42–45.

Lezotte, L. (1997). *Learning for all.* Okemos, MI: Effective Schools Products.

Litton, E. F. (1999). *Stories of courage and hope: Gay and lesbian catholic elementary school teachers.* Paper presented at the Annual Meeting of the American Educational Research Association, Montreal, Canada.

Lugg, C. A. (2006). Thinking about sodomy: Public schools, legal panopticons, and queers. *Educational Policy, 20*(1), 35–58.

Markow, D. & Fein, J. (2005). *From teasing to torment: School climate in America a survey of students and teachers.* New York: Harris Interactive, Inc. & Gay, Lesbian & Straight Education Network.

McCarthy, L. (2003). Wearing my identity: A transgender teacher in the classroom. *Equity & Excellence in Education, 36,* 170–183.

Melillo, S. M. (2003). *Heteronormativity and teaching: A phenomenological study of lesbian teachers.* Paper presented at the Annual AERA National Conference, Chicago, IL.

Merrow, J. (2004, Fall). Safety and excellence. *Educational Horizons, 83*(1), 19–32.

Moll, A. (2011). *Sixth graders offer college students some perspective.* Retrieved March 1, 2011, from http://www.hrcbackstory.org/2011/02/sixth-graders-offer-college-students-some-perspective

ReligiousTolerance.org. (2008). *About homophobia: What it is; its cost; what fuels it.* Retrieved May 18, 2008 from http://www.religioustolerance.org/hom_fuel1.htm

Rensenbrink, C. W. (1996, Summer). What difference does it make? The story of a lesbian teacher. *Harvard Educational Review, 66*(2), 257–270.

Rottman, C. (2006). Queering educational leadership from the inside out. *International Journal of Leadership in Education, 9*(1), 1–10.

Smith, N. J., Esposito, J., Wright, T., & Reilly, C. (2006). LGBT teachers school climate survey. Unpublished survey instrument.

Smith, N., Wright, T., Reilly, C., & Esposito, J. (2008). *A national study of LGBT educators' perceptions of their workplace climate.* (ERIC Document Reproduction Service No. ED501252). Retrieved March 13, 2010, from ERIC Education Resources Information Center database.

Smollin, M. (2011). *'Don't ask don't tell' is alive and well for gay educators.* Retrieved February 28, 2011, from http://www.takepart.com/article/2011/02/25/dont-ask-dont-tell-alive-and-well-gay-educators

Sumera, D., & Davis, B. (1999). Interrupting heteronormativity: Toward a queer curriculum theory. *Curriculum Inquiry, 29*(2), 191–209.

Woods, S. E., & Harbeck, K. M. (1992). Living in two worlds: The identity management strategies used by lesbian physical educators. In K. M. Harbeck (Ed.), *Coming out of the classroom closet: Gay and lesbian students, teachers and curricula* (pp. 141–166). Binghamton, NY: Haworth.

Woog, D. (1995). In or out: Two teachers' decisions. In D. Woog (Ed.), *School's out: The impact of gay and lesbian issues on America's schools* (pp. 109–115). Boston, MA: Alyson Publications.

Wright, T. & Smith, N. J. (2011). National survey of educators' perceptions of school climate. Unpublished survey instrument.

Yared, C. (1997). Where are the civil rights for gay and lesbian teachers? *Journal of the Section of Individual Rights & Responsibilities, 24*(3), 22–24.

CHAPTER 3

OVERCOMING CULTURAL COLLISION IN EDUCATIONAL LEADERSHIP

A Global Ethical Analysis

Lisa Bass

When you run alone, you run fast; but when you run together, you run far.
—Zambian Proverb

INTRODUCTION

In *The World is Flat,* Friedman (2005) explains the convergence of nations primarily as a result of technology, key historical events, and supply and demand in the global economy. This merging and flattening of national borders suggests that the nations of the world are becoming more similar, and that these similarities can act as a foundation on which to build partnerships and a united international community. All countries participating in cross-cultural partnerships potentially benefit from the collaborations when facilitated in such a way that each group is respected and the goals of the collaboration honor the goals of participating partners. However, given the ingrained nature of culture, it is inevitable that two cultures attempt-

Social Justice Leadership for a Global World, pages 39–55
Copyright © 2012 by Information Age Publishing

ing to merge knowledge, beliefs, morals, laws, customs, and other elements that comprise habits and habitus will face conflict as they negotiate the dimensions of culture necessary to arrive at a working basis for collaboration. As such, cultural collision is said to result when two or more cultures experience difficulty while merging their ideas in an attempt to collaborate (Grantham, 1997). Cultural differences, no matter how noble the intent, often make collaboration difficult, as each culture is organically wed to its own belief system (Buono, Bowditch & Lewis, 1985). Workers in the field of education are not exempt from such cultural dissonance.

U.S. educational policy makers and leaders are often included on teams sent out to "improve" and "inform" education practices abroad. Additionally, education scholars also create their own opportunities to collaborate with other nations as they write grants and seek opportunities to work on projects abroad. The motives behind these missions are most often pure and well intended. In fact, they usually reflect an ethic of care (discussed below); however, the approach sometimes taken by U.S. education workers does not always match the intent. This is a reflection of the privileged nature of Americans, who are primed to believe that they always have something to offer to the benefit of "less fortunate" countries.

Americans are known for going into international spaces with a "silver bullets" and a savior mentality. U.S. representatives sometimes enter relationships with representatives from foreign countries before thoroughly investigating and analyzing the host culture in order to understand how culture shapes policies and practices and how best to honor the host country with ideas for reform and/or collaboration. Further, some U.S. representatives fail to consider the strengths of their hosts before imposing North American values, practices, and policies. So despite the intent to be helpful, American educational experts can potentially insult representatives of host countries without recognizing their passive insensitivity. Lack of consideration while conducting foreign affairs and collaborations, coupled with the ethnocentrism embodied by many American diplomats, is what lead to the conceptualization and development of the term "ugly American"[1] (Lederer, 1958). The purpose of this chapter is to provide an ethical framework for educational leaders and policy makers for negotiating cross cultural collaborative relationships while working abroad.

CULTURAL COLLISION

The benefits of cross-cultural collaboration are clear. Scholars (Bullinger, Anderson, Cella, & Aronson, 1993; Henderson, 2000; Parekh, 2003; Suarez-Orozco, 2005) across disciplines acknowledge that borders between nations are becoming less and less conspicuous. Youth culture also merges nations as youth culture from country to country is beginning to express similar tastes and preferences in art, music, and media. This merging and flattening of borders suggests that the nations of the world are becoming more similar and that these similarities can act as a foundation on which to build partnerships and an international community. Globalization is the broad term used to describe this phenomenon (Lam, 2006).

Globalization, or the shrinking globe, is at the center of many discussions on educational reform. According to Suarez-Orozco (2005), globalization is about demographic and cultural transformations. However, as cultures are transformed and molded through globalization, stark differences between cultures and different parts of the world still exist. These cultural differences make this part of collaboration difficult, as each culture is organically wed to its own belief system (Buono, Bowditch & Lewis, 1985). As such, cultural collision is said to result when two or more cultures experience difficulty in merging their ideas while attempting to collaborate (Grantham, 1997).

In spite of these conflicts, researchers, policy makers, and other stakeholders in educational leadership are becoming increasingly aware of the value of international and intercultural collaboration and of observing best practices from a comparative and international perspective. As technology and the recent increase in global outreach unite the countries of the world, educational leaders recognize the need to develop common understandings and a common language. According to Lam (2006), we need to "reconsider notions of culture and identity, of agency and learning, and of societal engagement and educational of our multicultural youth population" (p. 215). Though this statement refers to multicultural youth in the United States, the same can be said for the international community.

As the globe shrinks and becomes more flat, the problems experienced among nations are becoming increasingly similar. Negotiating youth culture and adopting models to improve education are examples of issues with which many nations are currently grappling. As the issues and challenges become similar across nations, educational leaders could benefit from appreciating the cultures of other nations, yielding to the ideal that we can address common struggles together, and working to develop productive reciprocal relationships with educational leaders from other nations. Without such relationships, future generations of children will be adversely impacted because they will not be equipped to function in a diverse world. According to Suarez-Orozco (2005):

> The skills and competencies needed for identifying, analyzing, and mobilizing to solve problems from multiple perspectives will require individuals who are intellectually curious and cognitively flexible, tolerant of ambiguity, able to synthesize knowledge within and across disciplines, culturally sophisticated, and able to work in groups made up of individuals from diverse backgrounds. (p. 212)

This is the skill set and competencies necessary for leaders who will be successful in leading the next generation of worldly, boundary spanning and crossing, trailblazing, technologically savvy, youth. Educational leaders will need the ability to see beyond their current situations to a whole world of possibilities. Such insight will provide the blueprint for more effective building and district level leadership.

GLOBALIZING ETHICS TO OVERCOME CULTURAL COLLISION

According to Suarez-Orozco (2005), "globalization engenders complexity" and "is generating more intricate demographics, economies, politics, environmental choices, scientific realities, technology and media, cultural facts and artifacts, and identities" (p. 211). These factors make cross-cultural collaboration difficult. The difficulty of working with individuals from a different culture can cause conflict that hinders productivity. Cultural collision is a term used to describe uncomfortable, counterproductive friction that can occur when representatives of two or more different cultures attempt to collaborate or come together on an issue. As such, cultural collision prevents cultures from existing as equals (Grantham, 1997). This term has been used to describe the ancient interactions between Englishmen and Chinese men as they attempted to build a trading relationship in 1793 (Cranmer-Byng & Levere, 1981). In this case, cultural collision resulted when the goals of the British and the Chinese were confused and remained unmet due to cultural differences. The British, desiring to establish a trading relationship with China, sent scientific gifts that the Chinese regarded as toys. There was a fundamental difference in the way the British and the Chinese understood and responded to the scientific innovation because of the lack of communication between the two nations. The difference in their beliefs about science hindered the creation of trade agreements.

Beachum and McCray (2004) discuss the impact of cultural collision in the educative process of urban African American youth. They assert that the educative experience of African American youth is compromised because the culture of mainstream U.S. schools is so vastly different from the hip-hop and television media that these children are acculturated with. They suggest the utilization of cultural pluralism in schools to better meet the needs of all students. Vargas (2000) uses the concept of cultural collision to introduce a model for sustainable development education. Vargas notes that sustainability requires the utilization of various types of resources and knowledge: indigenous, traditional, and modern. She discusses the potentially detrimental effect of cultural collision when different cultures representing different forms of knowledge are not able to achieve common understandings.

Cultural collision in a global context is problematic if present when nation states representing different cultures attempt to work together. Cross-cultural collaboration is not possible unless all parties feel equally valued in any attempted collaborative efforts. Without parity and equality, parties will likely feel misunderstood and disrespected and rendered unable to produce the desired results. Therefore, when cultural differences emerge as we endeavor to work across international boundaries and in more interdependent ways, we may experience greater levels of cultural collision. Thus, it is imperative to overcome cultural collision before engaging in further collaborative efforts. In response to these changes, I propose a set of ethical frameworks as a basis for facilitating discussion on how to best come together as a global community to solve common problems.

Ethnocentrism: A Force Behind Cultural Collision

International super powers have long existed and have served to lead and set the pace for less powerful and developing nations in education. The United States, in particular, exports missionaries and educational experts to other nations in mass numbers, and on a regular basis, in an attempt to "improve" systems and conditions in the countries they inhabit. Educational leaders are often included when groups are formed to work in other countries. Scholars of educational leadership also create their own opportunities for international partnerships as they write grants and applications for international research and teaching, with the intention of working overseas temporarily to better conditions in a foreign country. This mission is noble and is connected to the ethic of care (discussed below); however, the approach often taken by educational leaders does not always properly analyze or take into account the culture of the host to understand how culture shapes policies and practices, nor does it always consider the strengths of the host before imposing U.S. values, practices, and policies. Though U.S. missionaries and educational experts enter countries with the intent to help, they often insult their beneficiaries without recognizing their error. This type of attitude is what has led to the development of the term "ugly American." Cranmer-Byng and Levere (1981) note the following when discussing the British and how they are perceived when they move in to help another country: "[I]s there any country on the globe that Englishmen visit where they do not display the pride of themselves and that contempt of others which conscious superiority is apt to inspire?" Although this passage was referring to Englishmen, the same is often said for Americans when they go to work in other countries. Americans are known for going into international spaces with the savior mentality.[2] This attitude sends the message that "our way is the best way" and that we are here to rescue less powerful or struggling nations by teaching them our way of operating. In the context of schooling, American educators and educational leaders often enter foreign countries to show the other how to "do school." We look at the systems of the other through the eyes of ethnocentric pride and are quick to suggest that others adopt U.S. ways of life and of doing school. In this sense, doing school refers broadly to manner in which the day-to-day business in and about schools is conducted. The business of school includes details such as the curriculum, staffing, training (teacher/parent/staff), scheduling, parent and community relations, and handling school funding and finances. Although there are clearly instances in which other nations can benefit from and welcome U.S. knowledge, we must be careful in how we approach international spaces and the manner and spirit in which we offer this knowledge. The manner in which the business of school is conducted may also be closely aligned with local culture. This alignment increases the probability of cultural collision when the cultures of the entering educational leader and the host are different.

Confronting my own Ethnocentric Biases

I was once the outsider who was sent by an agency to help a developing nation and to show them the U.S. way of operating. I spent a year in Ghana as an agent of a non-governmental organization (NGO). Before my departure, I had in mind that I was going to Ghana to teach and to make a difference. As a matter of fact, the brief training I received encouraged me to enter the country with the purpose of improving the small village where I was sent to live. My primary goal (as dictated by the funding NGO) was to open a center that would provide technological and other educational resources to educators and to teach the local educators how to use the center I created. I also taught at the teacher's training college where I was stationed. However, I was not taught about the potential benefits I would receive, nor about how much I would learn from the Ghanaians with whom I so closely lived. Nor was I taught how to enter the country as a participant observer before implementing the program I was sent to introduce.[3] As a participant observer, I would have first observed, then participated in the daily lives of my hosts before attempting to change anything. However, before taking in and attempting to learn the local culture, I found myself looking at how my hosts went about life and comparing everything to the way things were done in U.S. environments with which I was more familiar. While in the country, I often found myself saying, "At the school I worked, we..." and "we do it this way where I come from...," as though to suggest that the way people from the country I was visiting were doing things wrong. This attitude was even more evident as I recall conversations I had with other Americans at other posts throughout the country. I shamefully recall several conversations with other Americans from the program that I was involved with regarding the "backward" way things were being done in the country. I did not take into consideration the culture of the hosts until months after I arrived in the country. The longer I spent in the country, the more I understood Ghanaian culture and the reasons the Ghanaians I worked with did things the way they did. My American frame of reference did not always allow me to agree with the difference in our ways of operating and being. I experienced cultural collision as I was not yet enlightened on how to respect and interact with a different culture. This process took a period of months for me, as I had never been introduced to the ethics of engaging a host country as a visitor. However, in time and with new cultural eyes and ears, I did come to understand, love, and appreciate Ghanaian culture. Had I entered the country seeking to understand their culture, my approach to my responsibilities would have been very different. I would have demonstrated my appreciation for Ghanaian culture and drawn from the strengths of their culture and incorporated these into my suggestions for change. I also would have waited until asked to draw comparisons between U.S. and Ghanaian lifestyle and way of being and doing. Thankfully I was in the country long enough to demonstrate my appreciation for Ghanaian culture and of my experience while in the country. After several months, I realized I was gaining far more than I was able to give during my short tenure in the country. The year I spent in Ghana has forever changed the way I view the world, the way I view my responsibility as an educator and global citizen, and the way I approach intercultural collaboration and interactions. That being said, I believe I was able to successfully shed my savior mentality and to become an appreciator of my hosts before lasting damage was done between my gracious host country and me.

AVOIDING CULTURAL COLLISION

It is important for agents serving less wealthy, less developed nations to know that the savior mentality is offensive and not well received by the other and that it demonstrates a lack of appreciation or acceptance for the culture of their host. This lack of acceptance hinders relationship development and potential effectiveness in the outsider accomplishing the highest purpose of their visit to other countries (Parekh, 2003). Outsiders are much more effective when they attempt to build relationships before imposing belief systems, methods and personal and sometimes self-serving agendas from the outside (Henderson, 2000; Parekh, 2003). So although the intention to help is usually genuine, the approach often taken by more powerful nations risks being perceived as disingenuous by cultures that are encroached upon by the different values and cultural norms of the outside other. When this occurs, the nation on the receiving end of the "help" may feel obligated to show gratitude and appear to accept what the aiding agent has come to offer. However, when the agent of the country aiding the host country has returned to their home country, the host country often returns to their former ways of operating because the changes suggested by the outside experts did not take the culture of the host into consideration. As a result, both countries may miss a valuable opportunity to benefit from each other's influence (Henderson, 2000; Parekh, 2003).

Upon entering a host country, American educators, educational leaders, and policy makers should enter countries with the intent of "being schooled" rather than seeking to impart U.S. knowledge on "how to do school." Americans, as well as delegates from other countries, should build time into their pre-departure and in-country training plans to simply observe and attempt to learn the culture of their hosts. During their time of observation, they should seek to build close, positive working relationships with delegates from the host country. Not only is it important for U.S. education workers to learn the culture of their hosts, but they should also strive to learn the culture of schools and schooling, the history of education in their host country, issues that relate to gender, race, and social class, and how poverty impacts education in the host country. The delegate should strive to understand school policies and the engine that drives the origin and enforcement of such policies: whether or not there is a public school system, whether or not all children are educated in pubic schools or independent school systems, the range in quality and type of schools are available, ways in which the quality of schools is measured, the proportion of children who attend average to above average schools, teacher education, administrator education, and any other information pertinent to the project, program, or reform they will be implementing.

In an ideal situation, the agent from the outside country would enter the host country and simply observe and build a relationship with people from the country whom they intend to aid before any action is taken. Ideally, outside agents would invest time in visiting a variety of schools and other local institutions, enjoy meals and conversation with their hosts, and attempt to appreciate the country with the eyes of a participant observer rather than as an outsider within.[4] They would take time to build relationships with locals, learn the local language, and accept what they observe without passing any judgments or opinions. This type of relationship building demonstrates honor, and shows that the dignity of the people and culture visited is recognized and appreciated before imposing an alternative agenda. Before getting to this point, the individuals visiting would reflect and journal about their experiences rather than being overwhelmed with the opinions of others (either from the country they are visiting or from their own home culture). They would take the necessary time to appropriately frame their program implementation as they learned to appreciate the culture of people with whom they came to work. They would not engage in such conversations relating to changes until they had fully immersed themselves in the new culture and made sense of it for themselves. Otherwise, their perceptions might become tainted and their efforts misinterpreted.

After outside agents have come to appreciate the culture of their hosts, they may then begin to work collaboratively with others to implement new programs. Outside agents should fully consider the culture and its strengths as they unfold their agenda, whether research based or humanitarian (Parekh, 2003). When outsiders demonstrate appreciation for their hosts and other cultures, the conditions are right for the hosts to trust the outside agents and share valuable insider information. They are also more likely to receive the program or suggestions made by the outside agent and to be inquisitive about the cultures and ideas from the outside agents' countries. Thus cultural competency and international ethics should be employed to promote global citizenship and productive intercultural partnerships, and to avoid cultural collision.

CULTIVATING INTERDEPENDENCE: FACILITATING CULTURAL COHESION

As the nations of the world grow closer they will accomplish more by recognizing and fostering a spirit of interdependence. However, the spirit of interdependence is in direct contrast to the independence most nations fight for and relish. Nationalism is a powerful driver internationally as nations celebrate their freedom and desire not to be controlled by other nations. They celebrate their freedom to worship as they please, their political autonomy, and their freedom to establish the types of educational system, structures, and policies they choose.

Acknowledging interdependence means recognizing and celebrating the fact that what happens in one nation eventually impacts what happens in other nations. Interdependence recognizes that no nation is an island unto itself and that all nations are connected whether they choose to acknowledge their interconnectedness or not (Lam, 2006; Spring, 2008; Suarez-Orozco, 2005). The interconnectedness and interdependence of nations can be compared to the idea of the canary in the mine (Singham, 1998). Before scientific advances, canaries were taken into coal mines to test air quality. If the canaries fainted or died because of toxic or low quality air, this meant that miners would eventually experience the same fate if there was no intervention to improve the quality of the air. Singham (1998) applied this as a metaphor to the black/white achievement gap. He compared black students to the canaries sent to the coal mines. Singham indicated that black students are the lowest performers in the U.S. educational system, and the most likely to fail in U.S. educational systems. This lower performance, he argued, is indicative of the toxicity of the educational system, which will eventually negatively impact all students. I apply this metaphor to international interconnectedness in this chapter.

When the canary in the mine metaphor is applied to nations, any phenomenon affecting poor or weak nations will eventually reach wealthier nations, and vice versa because we are all connected. Therefore, educational leaders should become scholars of global education and continue to acknowledge global interconnectedness in decision-making processes. Educational leaders and policy makers should find ways to collaborate and to improve educational outcomes for all nations. They will benefit from not only studying successful systems, but by also studying systems that are failing to see what may also be learned from struggling systems. Further, educational leaders who understand international interdependence seek to participate in organized efforts to aid failing educational systems, not only because it is the just thing to do, but also because they are aware that what happens in failing systems will eventually impact them either directly or indirectly.

An acceptance of interdependence on the part of educational leaders requires a degree of humility and an acknowledgement that neither they nor their own educational systems are invincible. They must also acknowledge that their mode of operating is not the only or most correct way of negotiating educational leadership. When representatives of a more powerful nation enter less powerful nations with the intention of helping, those entering the outside country must be careful about not berating or disrespecting the cultures of those they came to help.

Acknowledging interconnectedness is generally positive, but it also means risking complete independence. It also means trusting outside agents from other nations and at times allowing them into closed national systems. Interconnectedness will likely mean that the closeness shared between nation states partnering together may promote the cultural collision that we seek to avoid. The contrasting desire for simultaneous cross-national interdependence while overcoming collision justifies the need for a framework that can facilitate the desired relationship (Parekh, 2003).

AN ETHICAL FRAMEWORK FOR OVERCOMING CULTURAL COLLISION

Educational administrators and policy makers have an ethical responsibility to overcome cultural collision in order to reap the full benefits of cross-cultural collaboration. I believe that we can work to overcome cultural collision by using ethical frameworks as a basis for the discussion. Through a process of global ethical analysis, we are better positioned to build collaborative and interdependent relationships across international borders. Ethical frameworks included in this discussion include the ethic of care (Goldstein, 1998, 1999; Noddings, 1984, 1988, 1992), the ethic of community (Furman, 2003, 2004), and the ethic of critique (Frick & Frick, 2010; Starratt, 1991).

The *ethic of care* suggests that everyone has a right to be cared for and that we should be moved by needs, inequities, social ills, and problems faced by the other. According to this ethic, concern must meet corrective action (Goldstein, 1998, 1999; Noddings, 1984, 1988, 1992). Those motivated by an ethic of care are moved to action to attempt to change what they view as uncaring where their actions are motivated by their feelings of concern for others (Goldstein, 1998, 1999; Noddings, 1984, 1988, 1992). For purposes of this analysis, I extend this definition to reflect an international focus. I refer to this expanded definition as a *global ethic of care.*

In the context of global citizenship and cross-cultural relationships, a *global ethic of care* suggests viewing the world as one large interconnected, interdependent community (Furman, 2003, 2004). As such, a caring citizenry acknowledges inequities on a global scale and takes action toward erasing such inequities as much as is within their own power. This acknowledgement stems from the understanding that all citizens are significant and that we can all benefit from a collaborative relationship. In short, caring global citizens recognize the importance of interdependence. Hence a global ethic of care also means taking the time to establish relationships with other citizens of the world and making a concerted effort toward understanding the cultural beliefs of others. This entails studying the cultures of other citizens that you will either work with or attempt to help, attempting to learn their language, and allowing the appropriate wait time before suggesting changes to their method of operating. The understanding attained by properly approaching the other reduces incidences of cultural collision by encouraging healthy and functional working relationships and productive international collaborations. Operating from a global ethic of care reduces the possibility of ethnocentrism and national superiority that a person from the helping nation may have otherwise exhibited. It further promotes the level of trust between nations necessary for them to act as a global community rather than as individual nations.

The *ethic of community* (Furman, 2003, 2004) is diametrically opposed to the natural inclination toward self-interest and self-preservation (Shapiro, Gross & Shapiro, 2008). According to the ethic of community, one considers the community as a whole over individual concerns. Genuinely acting out of an ethic of community can aid in overcoming fears and anxieties of the other and allow individuals to realize the benefits of membership in an international community and of being an international citizen. The ethic of community, as employed in global citizenship, recognizes that consideration of the community is linked to self-preservation because of international interconnectedness and interdependence. Therefore, the ethic of community will be referred to as the *ethic of global community* in the remainder of this analysis.

Employing the *ethic of global community* is vital in overcoming cultural collision because it encourages selflessness over acting out of more selfish interests. As related to international relationships, conflict can occur when nations prioritize their perceived needs as individual nation-states rather than recognizing and prioritizing the collective needs of all nations. An example of this might be if a seasoned educational leader entered a host country to teach a leadership framework that he or she developed. If after observing the cultural and educational context of the host country the leader can see that another framework would work better, then the leader should forego his/her plan to introduce his/her own framework and share the framework that is most appropriate to the host country—even if the leader risks losing expected financial gain. A simple example relating to culture might be that the visiting educational leader may be ready to conclude his/her work in the host country but needs to collect data for another week. If the following week is a holiday week for the hosts, the culturally conscious leader would respect the plans of his/her hosts and wait until the festivities have concluded before pressing forward with his/her research plans.

This type of selflessness is difficult, especially within the context of international, cross-cultural relationships. In such relationships, the spirit of self-preservation and competition can rouse fears and apprehensions regarding the other to the point of promoting distrust. Distrust can hinder collaboration and progress when actors focus on past history and former relationships rather than focusing on the possibilities for the future. According to the ethic of global community, people overcome the inclination to be governed by selfish interests by understanding that their own success is linked to the successes of the many others they are inevitably connected to and by recognizing that the success of other global citizens is central to their own success.

The ethic of critique provides the impetus behind proactive gestures and volunteerism taken on behalf of other nations (Shapiro, Gross, Shapiro & 2008). According to Frick and Frick (2010) "the moral focus of a critique perspective is concerned with making known and acting upon those circumstances that silence, oppress, or discriminate" (p. 120). The ethic of critique stirs nations to question the status quo (Shapiro & Stefkovich, 2001; Starratt, 1991) of nation-states or the injustices they witness on a global scale. Frick and Frick (2010) note that "the disproportionate benefit of some groups over others as a result of political, economic, and judicial hegemony are moral concerns" that must be addressed (p. 120). Or, as Starratt (1991) stated, "the theme of critique forces administrators to confront the moral issues involved when schools disproportionately benefit some groups in society and fail others" (p. 190). As such, these global injustices may take the form of national elitism, gross inequalities from nation to nation, or oppressive actions perpetrated by one country upon another. Since the actions of nations are being questioned rather than the actions of individuals, the ethic of critique will be expanded to encompass international relations and will henceforth be referred to as the *ethic of global critique.*

The *ethic of global critique* is necessary for corrective action to occur as stated above. When people witness injustices perpetrated by other nations, the ethic of global care moves them to act on the issues they have critiqued. There are many prevailing examples of U.S. and international IGO and NGO agencies reaching out to end apparent injustices. One example of this is the effort extended to liberate and educate oppressed women and girls from nations that fail to equitably educate girls. Because a critical mass of global citizens questioned the gross inequitable treatment of girls in several nations, IGO's and NGO's have made girls' education a priority (Spring, 2008). The ethic of global critique promotes social justice as global citizens committed to worldwide equity and equality implement plans of action to improve unjust global issues. Table 3.1 provides a list of questions for leaders to ask of themselves as they interact with host cultures to prevent cultural collision.

TABLE 3.1   Ethical Considerations in Decision Making

Ethic of International Critique	Ethic of International Care	Ethic of International Community
Do I allow the host's goals for his/her schools to shape my goals?	Do I find out what the host thinks is important?	Do I help the host find his/her own solutions?
Do I fully weigh the pros and cons of situations before imposing my opinion or belief system?	Do I avoid causing the host to feel vulnerable or inadequate?	Do I approach problems in a way that leads to mutual problem solving?
	Do I honor and distinguish the host's strengths and expertise? Do I use language to acknowledge this expertise?	Do I work with the host to determine how to share responsibilities (in the project)?
	Do I work with the host to build a sense of trust?	Do I use practices that involve the host in mutual decision making?
	Do I demonstrate my respect for the host?	

CONCLUSION: PROMOTING ETHICAL
INTERNATIONAL COLLABORATIONS

The formation of international partnerships and cross-cultural collaborations are popular features of almost all industries. Business, medicine, and engineering all recognize the benefit of knowledge sharing and incorporating international perspectives. The field of education has joined the ranks of the industries seeking to improve systems and processes through international collaborations. The United States plays a dual role in international collaboration. Sometimes the country is involved in humanitarian efforts—those that involve representatives who do the work of churches, IGO's, and NGO's—and sometimes the country is involved in collaborative work in which both countries enjoy marked benefits. In either case, cultural appreciation and understanding is necessary before productive international work can be done. This type of understanding can be achieved when nation states employ global ethics. The global ethics above promote the ethics of care, community, and critique. This fusion of ethics promotes mutual respect and understanding over ethnocentricity, pride, and selfishness. Countries are more likely to respond positively and interactions are more likely to result in higher levels of productivity when countries feel that they are respected or regarded in higher esteem. As such, the prescribed ethical approach to global relationships creates space for comfort and mutual trust in interactions. Finally, it is the ethical responsibility of administrators to work collaboratively with both their local and international communities so that they create an environment where their students and the students of the world can flourish.

As discussed above, cross-cultural collaboration is an inevitable part of growth and development in the field of education and educational leadership. Educational leaders will need to possess a skill set that includes cross-cultural competence if they are to be successful in leading the next generation of multi-talented and enthusiastic young people. They will be charged to lead in such a way that encourages students to be innovative and to perform at their personal best. Educational leaders will need to be technologically savvy, flexible, and understand and implement international ethical frameworks, including international ethics if they are to be effective with the next generations. Leaders who are competent in this area will be equipped to successfully lead students into becoming world changers. The international ethical framework suggested provides a starting point for educational leaders who will be collaborating with people from other cultures either inside or outside of the United States.

Leadership preparation programs are practical learning environments to teach international ethics to pre-service or practicing leaders. Such programs are charged with preparing leaders to work successfully in all types of educational environments. Programs of educational leadership can be successful at this type of training, as indicated by a six-year study within the leadership program at the University of Vermont (Gerstl-Pepin, Killeen, & Hasazi, 2006). Their study found that training (social justice and ethics) is especially effective when integrated throughout the curriculum and over time in the program. In this study, students were taught in a program that implemented an ethic of care framework in which they were purposely exposed to diversity and equity issues. The conclusion was that the introduction of such material was effective, but that integration would have made the introduction to the ethics of care and social justice even more successful. From this we learn that leadership training programs should include and integrate international ethics throughout the curriculum and that this material must be presented via multiple modalities in most, if not all, educational leadership courses. Findings from the Gerstl-Pepin, Killeen, and Hasazi (2006) study indicate that leaders exposed to this type of training will likely be more effective, caring, ethical, and democratic leaders who will have the power to raise the quality of education over time.

NOTES

1. The term "ugly American" was first coined by Eugene Burdick in 1958 and made into a book title. It has been used since then to describe the arrogant behavior of Americans while traveling abroad.
2. The term "savior mentality" or "savior complex" has been used over time to describe a person who does not believe that certain things can be done or accomplished unless they come in to act as "savior." The origin of this term is not known.
3. From Kluckhohn (1940), the participant observer in research is regarded as a member of the community in which he has entered. Participant observation is conscious and systematic, sharing in life activities and, as permitted, in the interest and affects of a group or person. The objective of participant observation is to obtain data in such a manner that the distraction of the agent being an outsider is reduced to a minimum.
4. "Outsider within" status connotes being an integral part of a community without being fully respected as a group member. Collins (1986) uses this term to describe the marginalized status of black women in society. In the context of serving as a global citizen, this could manifest as one spending significant time on projects in other nation states, yet never being fully accepted as part of the community.

REFERENCES

Beachum, F. D. & McCray, C. R. (2004). Cultural collision in urban schools. *Current Issues in Education, 7*(5), 1–8.

Bullinger, M., Anderson, R., Cella, D., & Aronson, N. (1993). Developing and evaluating cross cultural instruments from minimal requirements to optimal models. *Quality of Life Research, 2*(6), 451–459.

Buono, A. F., Bowditch, J. L., & Lewis, J. W. (1985). When cultures collide: The anatomy of a merger. *Human Relations Journal, 38*(5), 477–500.

Collins, P. H. (1986). Learning from the outsider within: The sociological significance of black feminist thought. *Social Problems, 33*(6), S14–S32.

Cranmer-Byng, J. L. & Levere, T. H. (1981). A case study in cultural collision: Scientific apparatus in the McCartney Embassy to China. *Annals of Science, 38*(1981), 503–525.

Frick, J. E. & Frick, W. C. (2010). An ethic of connectedness: Enacting moral school leadership through people and programs. *Education, Citizenship and Social Justice, 5*, 117. DOI: 10.1177/1746197910370729.

Friedman, T. L. (2005). *The world is flat: A brief history of the twenty-first century.* New York: Farrar, Straus and Giroux.

Furman, G. (2003). Moral leadership and the ethic of community. *Values and Ethics in Educational Administration, 2*(1), 1–7.

Furman, G. (2004). The ethic of community. *The Journal of Educational Administration, 42*(2), 215–235.

Gerstl-Pepin, C., Killeen, K., & Hasazi, S. (2006). Utilizing an "ethic of care" in leadership preparation: Uncovering the complexity of colorblind social justice. *The Journal of Educational Administration, 44*(3), 250–263.

Goldstein, L. (1998, April). *Taking caring seriously: The ethic of care in classroom life.* Paper presented at the meeting of the Annual Meeting of the American Educational Research Association, San Diego, CA.

Goldstein, L. (1999). The relational zone: The role of caring relationships in the co-construction of mind. *American Educational Research Journal, 36*, 647–673.

Grantham, N. (1997). Simms's frontier: A collision of cultures. In J. C. Guilds & C. Collins (Eds.), *William Gilmore Simms and the American frontier* (pp. 105–117). Athens: University of Georgia Press.

Henderson, H. (2000). Transnational corporations and global citizenship. *American Behavioral Scientist, 43*(8), 1231–1261.

Kluckhohn, F. R. (1940). The participant-observer technique in small communities. *The American Journal of Sociology, 46*, 331–343.

Lam, W. (2006). Culture and learning in the context of globalization: Research directions. *Review of Research in Education, 30*, 213–237.

Lederer, W. J. (1958). *The ugly American* (1st ed.). New York, NY: Norton Press.

Noddings, N. (1984). *Caring: A feminine approach to ethics and moral education.* Berkeley, CA: University of California Press.

Noddings, N. (1988). An ethic of caring and its implications for instructional arrangements. *American Journal of Education, 96*, 215–230.

Noddings, N. (1992). *The challenge to care in schools.* New York, NY: Teachers College Press.

Parekh, B. (2003). Cosmopolitanism and global citizenship. *Review of International Studies, 29*(1), 3–17.

Shapiro, J. P., Gross, S. J., & Shapiro, S. H. (2008). Ethical decisions in turbulent times. *School Administrator, 65*(5), 18–21.

Shapiro, J. P. & Stefkovich, J. A. (2001). *Ethical leadership and decision making in education.* Mahwah, NJ: Lawrence Erlbaum Associates.

Singham, M. (1998). The canary in the mine: The achievement gap between black and white students. *Phi Delta Kappan, 80*(1), 8–15.

Spring, J. (2008). Research on globalization and education. *Review of Educational Research, 78,* 330. DOI: 10.3102/0034654308317846, 330-353.

Starratt, R. J. (1991). Building an ethical school: A theory of practice for educational leadership. *Educational Administration Quarterly, (27)*2, 185–202.

Suarez-Orozco, M. (2005). Rethinking education in the global era. *Phi Delta Kappan, 87*(3), 209–212.

Vargas, C. M. (2000). Sustainable development education: Averting or mitigating cultural collision. *International Journal of Educational Development, 20*(5), 377–396.

SECTION II

INTERNATIONAL AND GLOBAL PERSPECTIVES
ON SOCIAL JUSTICE LEADERSHIP

CHAPTER 4

CONTESTED POWER!

College Heads in the Muslim Society of Pakistan

Saeeda Shah

INTRODUCTION

Power is contested on educational sites. The prevalence of conflict, contestation over goals, bargaining and negotiation in institutions of higher education, and cultural and belief systems create unequal power relations. These conflicts mean that "the decision making process is likely to be determined ultimately according to the relevant power of the participating individuals and groups" (Baldridge, 1971, p. 41). Pakistan is a Muslim society with feudal patriarchal structures and traditions. The Constitution of Pakistan (Khan, 1973) claims to ensure that all laws and practices are in accordance with the Islamic Sharia. Sex-segregation is perceived as a recommended feature of Islamic societies, and accordingly, in Pakistan there are generally separate institutions for males and females at all levels. Gender segregation, however, is observed more stringently in rural regions than it is in urban areas, and at post-primary-to-pre-university levels, which cover the secondary education and the college sector. This age group is perceived

Social Justice Leadership for a Global World, pages 59–76
Copyright © 2012 by Information Age Publishing
All rights of reproduction in any form reserved.

as sexually vulnerable within socio-religious discourses, which contributes to the emphasis on educating females and males separately (Shah, 2009). This chapter examines power conflict through the leadership roles and practices of college heads of single-sex colleges in a primarily rural region of Pakistan.

DISCOURSE METHODOLOGY

All of the public colleges studied in the region were single-sex, known as *zanana* (female) colleges and *mardana* (male) colleges. These colleges offered secondary to post-secondary education. The college heads, who were called principals, were academic leaders as well as administrators. There were sixty-eight colleges (thirty female and thirty-eight male[1]) in the region at the time the study was conducted. The invitation to participate in the study was sent to all sixty-five principals. However, only ten female and fourteen male principals confirmed availability during the period of my visit to Pakistan for data collection. These twenty-four principals were interviewed individually, and eleven of them participated in two mixed-sex focus group discussions following the one-to-one interviews. Each individual interview generally lasted from 60 to 90 minutes, while the focus group meetings were each approximately two hours long. Further data was collected from six senior managers (five male and one female) in the education department who were line managers for the principals and also participated in policy making at the regional level. All interviews were tape-recorded, and the interviewees were each given a code name and number for data recording, retrieval and presentation purposes. PM1, PM2 and so on were code names used for the participating male principals and PF1, PF2 for the participating female principals, while PSM was the code used for the six senior managers in the education department; as there was only one woman in this group the coding did not signal gender for the purposes of confidentiality.

The multiplicity of interacting discourses constructed in the interviews and focus groups pointed to the web of inter-relationships and power differentials active in the context. According to Foucault (1980), patterns of discourses are produced culturally and socially, and power is exercised through discourse. Social institutions like educational organizations and the practices therein are made up of diverse and often contradictory discourses (Kenvey, Wallis, Blackmore, & Jenny, 1994). The aim of the study was to search for "regimes of truth" (Foucault, 1980) as historically and culturally situated, recognizing that discourses are constituted in time and space (Best & Kellner, 1991; Foucault, 1980, 1991; Usher & Edwards, 1994). Each formation can be seen as consisting of a set of shifting and dynamic discourses, where multiply-positioned subjects discursively constitute meanings and truths:

> Truth is a thing of this world: It is produced only by the virtue of multiple forms of constraint. And it induces regular effects of power. Each society has its regime of truth, its 'general politics' of truth: that is the types of discourse which it accepts and makes function as true; the mechanisms and instances which enable one to distinguish true and false statements, the means by which each is sanctioned; the techniques and procedures according value in the acquisition of truth; the status of those who are charged with saying what counts true. (Foucault, 1980, p. 131)

In the interplay of competing truths and contesting discourses, meaning making becomes a political act. To understand situations, Knight, Smith, and Sachs (1990) advise looking into "discursive assumptions" underlying reading of "competing texts." They emphasize that "only when the 'official' authority of the text as knowledge and its source as guarantor of its truth are transcended, can the construction of really useful knowledge begin" (Knight et al., 1990, p. 34).

CONTESTED POWER

Colleges are complex organizations perceived as needing leaders possessing both legal authority (positional power) and professional competence (expert power). The research findings suggested that in colleges, positional power and expert power became virtually equal to zero power when not supplemented by socio-political influence in that particular context, where the latter frequently appeared to supplant the other two. This observation required further investigation of the socio-political "technologies of power" that deprived the *de jure* authorities of their authority and of how these "technologies" operated and interacted with formation of practices.

Rose (1996) defines technologies as "hybrid assemblages of knowledges, instruments, persons, systems of judgment, buildings and spaces, underpinned at the pragmatic level by certain presuppositions about, and objectives for, human beings" (p. 132). For example, in the context of disciplining of students, Grant (1997) examines technologies of domination wielded through discourses such as "what is a good student" to achieve specific ends. Similarly, myriad discourses surrounding *Muslimness*, family, education, and knowledge were some of the technologies deployed to create regimes of subjectification in the research context. The relative power of the principals was determined by the dominant discourses validated as appropriate by the cultural and belief systems.

There can be no similar explanations for matching facts or statistics across cultures; for example, barriers to exercise of power for women principals in a Muslim Asian segregated society might be very different from barriers to women principals in a Western context. Often, causes are diverse, contradictory, and complex, depending upon power relations and cultural systems in that society. Subjects are constituted by the operation of power, which affects their ways of perceiving things or conceiving of world (Foucault, 1980). Dreyfus and Rabinow (1982) argue that "to understand power in its materiality, its day-to-day operation, we must go to the level of micro-practices, the political technologies in which our practices are formed" (p. 185).

Foucault (1991) argues that practices are not just governed by institutions, prescribed by ideologies, or guided by pragmatic circumstances through the production of truth/s. He draws attention to pluralization of causes governing practices, and suggests to analyze "regime of practices," which have both prescriptive effects regarding what is to be done and what is acceptable at a given moment, and codifying effects regarding what is to be known. Placed in a position of authority in the formal educational structure, the participating principals emerged ineffective and helpless, with little or no agency.[2] This feeling of being powerless on the part of the principals affected their leadership roles and practices. The Islamic philosophy of education and the prestige and status associated with teaching in Islam formulated a rhetoric of *bazurgi* (greatness), *izzat* (honor) and *roub* (awe), fusing *ilm* (knowledge), *taqwa* (righteousness) and leadership in the role of *moallam* (teacher), who was expected to provide knowledge and guidance, and accordingly had the highest claims to obedience. These claims (as source of teacher power) were mainly determined by her/his claims to *taqwa* and knowledge, and the learners' submission was extended according to their perceptions of "knowledge." This re-enforcement of the rhetoric of academic excellence empowered the principals with claims to status and respect validated by the religion.

In Muslim societies, where stories abound that reinforce obeying the teacher and view the teacher as the savior (spiritual and moral), where knowledge is perceived as the legacy of prophets as guides to mankind (Quran, 12:22, 12:68, 28:24), this discourse has been a source of power for the principals. However, increasing socio-political and economic changes have shifted the focus from spiritual and intellectual to material and pragmatic, and with that the value system also underwent a change, with a relocation of priorities. Socially and ideologically, the principals desired to command respect and obedience to facilitate management; politically they needed power to function in their job positions without being paralyzed by counter-powers in a complex socio-political situation. Significantly, the demand was not for more powers. What they explicitly (through clearly worded statements) and implicitly (through stories and examples) asked for was a situation favorable to the "exercise of the powers"—powers structurally granted to the principals in the formal system—or a retrieval of their agency.

EXPLORING THE ISSUES

The perceived disempowerment of the principals, according to this research, has multifarious sources and dimensions, interacting within multiple spaces and relationships. Very broadly, these can be categorized in the following groups:

- patterns of cultural existence (kinship patterns and extended networks)
- structural loopholes
- socio-political pressures
- professional organizations
- gender

The principals in the study had associations with power, linked up with legal position/authority, academic status and professional expertise. At the same time there was a conflict around "the exercise of power," not only on the professional site but in the wider culture as well. This required political skills that Kotter (1988) defines as the ability to understand and develop power relationships or build coalitions. Significantly, in practice, power was seen as being usurped both on the cultural and the professional sites: through networks of relationships, extended families, *bradaries* (clans), and pressure groups on the one hand, and on the other by those above in the hierarchy as well as those below.

Tension and Ambiguity Around Power

According to the research participants, those above did not heed the principals, particularly in matters relating to staff appointments and transfers, financial requests, and even in matters concerning work quality, efficiency, and discipline. Those below (experienced/skilled office staff) usurped power through their skills, such as competency in handling the accounts/finances and office procedures and so on, and thereby rendered the principals less confident and less independent. In view of these constraints from seniors and restraints from juniors, authority of the position was not accompanied by the power to exercise that authority. Gordon (2002) argues that "people can be unobtrusively constrained by historically constituted codes of order or, as they are termed here, deep structures" (p. 156). These structures are a major factor in determining the exercise of power.

Peter Watkins (1989) in an interesting discussion of power relations between the super-ordinates and subordinates stresses their relational nature that "even if one recognizes that there may be large disparities in the availability of resources between the parties, the relational notion of power ensures that subordinates have some measure of autonomy while super-ordinates have some measure of dependency" (p. 26). As Giddens (1982) notes:

> Power relations in a social system can be regarded as relations of autonomy and dependence; but no matter how imbalanced they may be in terms of power, actors in subordinate positions are never wholly dependent and are very often adept at converting whatever resources they possess into some degree of control over the conditions of reproduction of system. (p. 32)

This tension and ambiguity around power-sites contradicted the Islamic construction of teacher's status and added to the de-powering of the leaders. Theoretically the principals were entitled to ideological authority, social status, and adequate structural powers to support their leadership roles and practices. The contention was that in practice all of that was rendered as mere rhetoric divested of any reality in a highly politicized context of power-play. A principal without influence became insecure and consequently ineffective, which was echoed by these participants:

PM1: I would say that only that principal can be somewhat successful who has a political back. Without that it is hard to survive. If a brother or a relative is in government then the principal would feel secure; and perhaps would perform better. If a principal has no such support, s/he is totally insecure; s/he cannot make any decision.

PF6: There are barriers in exercising your legal powers. People threaten you . . . Everybody thinks that he can get his way contrary to rules. They believe themselves as powerful . . . Just a *parchi* (a piece of paper with instructions) arrives [telling the principal what is required].

PM2: Legal authority! Yes. But no *de facto* powers. It is a political set-up. The director, the secretary, the principal, they are all powerless in spite of their legal powers. We are not really practicing democracy. A principal can make appointments up to scale seven, but during my six years of headship I could not make a single independent appointment. Instructions will arrive from high-ups and we would go through a fake procedure to adjust the recommended person.

If a principal did not bow to unreasonable demands, "false reports and complaints would be sent to the higher authorities, poisoning them against the principal. It increases the pressure. There is no probe in the matters" (PM8). A senior line manager argued:

> Unless you end this politicization, even if we make the head all-in-all s/he would be paralyzed in practice, by the ruling party's students' wing...there is political interference—it would remain a direct or indirect problem. They [in power] would find ways and means; if nothing else there would be a transfer [of the un-compromising principal]. (PSM3)

Political Interference

The principals stressed that the pressures on their decision-making were often not in the interests of the students or institutional management. Almost every principal had examples where a disciplinary action against a student or an expulsion order had to be rescinded due to political interference, which encouraged malpractice and increased problems for the principals. The interference was not limited to matters related to the students. The staff and the public also used political contacts to pressurize the principals and to get their way. Political manipulations superseded professional procedures, which affected performance and quality. According to the interviewees, the staff focus in the circumstances was no longer on work and performance but on seeking effective contacts.

Professional organizations of different categories of staff were also blamed for using pressure tactics to support their members. These were viewed by the majority of the interviewees, the principals and the senior managers, as another political agency influencing the principals' roles and practices. They were perceived as using the politicians or at times being used by them, to protect vested interests, and consequently rendered the principals helpless, as highlighted in this quote:

> Those who have contacts with government (political leaders) won't even take their classes, boasting of their relationships with the sitting MLAs or Ministers. If you write an adverse ACR, it will be used against you. They will gather under the umbrella of their professional organization and make situation difficult for you. (PM1)

The senior managers confirmed the problematic role of different professional organizations:

> Professional organizations, the so-called associations, are a serious issue. They function on local and regional levels...Their role has been pre-dom-

inantly negative. Instead of being a help in administration, they erect barriers in solving the issues—and cause problems at times. For example, they blackmail the administration—for petty gains; and bring infamy to the whole system. (PSM3)

There was a consensus that management effectiveness could be enhanced by acknowledging the principals' powers and by giving them "a free hand." Absence of a free hand converted the commanding spiritual parent into a *bechara/bechari* (helpless). In spite of religious, social, political, and professional discourses of status and authority, the principals emerged powerless, caught in a situation where decisions, options, and choices could not be exercised.

Gender Norms

Gender was another barrier to power in that traditionally feudal Muslim society and complicated the situation further for women principals. A structure, evolved from localized social and behavioral norms, was exploited to marginalize women in the name of religion and culture. Women, even when in positions of authority, were disciplined by the patriarchal norms, and became subject to a complicated multi-dimensional power-play. Social construction of women contributed to their "marginality both in their professions and in the public mind" (Curry, 2000, p. 4). On the college sites, a submission to barriers by the women and associated discomfort and uncertainties at moving across/between the boundaries (*zanana/mardana*) became indicative of role stereotyping in a particular professional context where almost all the people in main stream management and in finance-related positions (seniors and juniors) were men. The discourses of *izzat*, gender, *veiling*, labor-division, education and religion interacted to produce relationships of power and modes of ordering relationships that interacted deeply with leadership role and practice (Shah, 2009). Kezar (2000) defines "history of relationships" as a "power condition," which defines relative power in professional relationships. Women principals in this study felt restrained by cultural norms, by restraints on female mobility, and by the barriers in net-working. They were further de-powered by subordinate finance staff who all happened to be males in that research context. Prone to be easy victims to social indictment and scandal, women opted out of visibility for social survival.

Threatened by the patriarchal norms and surveillance dominating in the public, women principals appeared to feel secure and confident in the reconstruction of colleges as "family." However, the tensions between the Islamic and the patriarchal notions surfaced when "religious content" (Sharma, 1980) was replaced by patriarchal content and disseminated under "religious cover." For example Islamic injunctions regarding rights and status of a wife and mother were reconstructed as "discourse of motherhood and wifely duty to household for honorable, implying otherwise who extend the sphere of activities" (Afshar, 1987, p. 73),[3] and thus effectively confined women. They were culturally constructed as "site of familial honour" (Afshar, 1994, p. 129), and thus the "guardian," as pronounced by the Quran, became "the guarded" in practice, and subject to surveillance and manipulations. By being constructed as "the guarded," the women lost their agency and subject position.

Recurrent references to the educational sites as "family" at one level of analysis emerged as "a tool of social control centrally involved in the propagation, selective dissemination, and social appropriation of discourses" (Ball, 1990b, p. 3). It marked a significant shift from the Islamic ideology of education and social existence. These segregatory and exclusionary modes affected women's leadership roles and created issues particularly in finance management, public-relations, and net-working. They promoted male control by subjecting women to "surveillance" and "disciplining" (Foucault, 1980). In addition to that, feudal orientation of Muslim societies in general (Ahmed, 1992), and given interpretations of sexuality and family law in Islam, further strengthened patriarchal practices (Mernissi, 1991) leading to the exclusion of women from the sphere of public activities such as finance management.

Moreover, double moral standards for men and women (Afshar, 1994) and a politically constructed notion of *izzat* controlled women in public and private alike and promoted male control. It was their acceptance of the latitude culturally granted to men that became an oppressive tool in a patriarchal society, as it conversely affected female mobility and participation in the public. The separate patterns and standards of conduct/character applied to men and women were socially endorsed as propounded by Islam; and women, by not having access to places of interpretation, submitted to those with serious implications for their professional roles. Reinforced by cultural norms, this controlled their professional performance and participation. The discourses were manipulated and misappropriated to "blackmail" women into silence and invisibility, subjecting them to surveillance, as mentioned by many women participants. They were further encouraged to become invisible through given interpretations of the notions of motherhood and family (Brock, Dada, & Jatta, 2006). However, women's admitted acceptance of higher pertinence of *izzat* for females made the issue more complicated:

> Power operates visibly and invisibly through expectations and desires. It operates visibly through formal, public criteria that must be satisfied. It operates

invisibly through the way individuals think of themselves and operate. (Cherryholmes, 1988, p. 35)

This double standard also raises the issue of interpretations of religious teachings; who occupies the spaces for interpretation, how these are availed, and for what purposes. Male occupation of the places of religious interpretations and control over discourse formations led to gendered discourses of izzat, segregation, wifely duties, and motherhood, effectively confining and marginalizing the women, thus negating the Islamic teachings of gender equality, women's rights and social justice. The skewed codes of conduct constructed by male authority posed threats to women who chose or dared to move in the positions of visibility. Incriminating the moral character of a woman in a visible leadership position de-powered her, particularly if she happened to be without a socio-political umbrella. Attributes like "seditious, corrupt, or prostitution granted freely to women but not to their male 'accomplices'" (Afshar, 1987, p. 74) proved effective technology to render women invisible.

Women managers who were interviewed emphasized that they were often playing in a defensive position. They compulsively relinquished equal freedom of mobility in the work context to protect themselves socially, but it negatively impacted their professional performance, progression and effectiveness. These discourses were reinforced by patriarchal power-play aiming at restraining exercise of power through weakening women's hold over power and resources. The women principals felt under pressure because of these constructions of across gender relationships, as PF8 angrily protested that "if a woman works with male colleagues, there is a scandal...There can be relationships without corruption!"

ALTERNATE EMPOWERMENT STRATEGIES

The principals, both men and women, claimed being rendered helpless by multiple forces and elements, but they also appeared to maneuver the same or similar elements to empower themselves that have been manipulated to de-power them (Shah, 1999). An intricate interplay among dominant discourses of economic, political, religious/ideological, socio-cultural and professional/educational regimes contributed to the construction of leadership roles and practices of the principals, and towards the determination of their power and authority. The principals were located within and across multiple discourses, which constituted their subjectivities and their individual and collective positioning. Their subject positions were multiple with inherent contradictions and dissensions. They brought their socio-political subjectivity to their professional positioning—to be regarded an influential principal or powerless. The interplay was among multiple discourses including family background, contacts, and political influence. Within colleges there were relationships with the students, staff, and senior bureaucracy, besides reputation and image as a teacher and academic, which extended to the wider society. Furthermore, there were gender relationships in a predominantly sex-segregated context in a post-colonial Muslim society influencing the exercise of power.

The power relations emerged as sites of struggle for dominance and resistance. Social and political contacts with the educational bureaucracy and political regimes added another dimension to the power play. The principals emerged as participants in diverse formulations, in spite of the professed impotence of their roles as discussed earlier. Social obligations and relationships in the cultural context, political pressures and maneuverings in a particular Muslim society, and the structuring of the regional post-colonial education system all contributed towards de-powering the principals. Interestingly, the same contexts were manipulated for "empowerment" through the production of "reverse discourses" (Foucault, 1980). The managers availed certain discourses in interplay with a web of relationships to regain the structural powers they were denied. Stephen Ball (1990a) argues that:

> Managements, as localised practices, are micro-power structures and power relations that touch every aspect of organizational life and are serially related. They are special applications of power. They embody very specific mechanisms, procedures, and techniques with particular economic and political utility. (p. 165)

In this Muslim society, the traditional discourses surrounding teacher/ teaching were still powerful, particularly regarding the relationship between the teacher and what was taught. The principals referred to themselves as *ustaad* or *moaullim* (teacher), showing a re-appropriation of the discourse. In spite of a declared high work-load, many principals stated that they occasionally taught in the classes to, as they claimed, "establish contacts with the students" or probably to retain control of a powerful discourse. The positional powers as principals, denied due to social and structural barriers as discussed earlier, were re-appropriated through a religious discourse and availed to perform as effective principals.

Besides the integration of religious, social and professional discourses, a network of contacts and relationships also contributed to counter the de-powering factors. These networks were a specific feature of the regional socio-cultural scene (Shah, 1999) and comprised of familial relationships, socio-political contacts and the families of the students. An additional aspect was personal influence through the community of ex-students—their families, contacts, and jobs—the majority of whom would be anxious to be of any service to an honored teacher (an integration of social and religious discourses). Significantly, these empowerment strategies were accomplished through re-conceptualizing the college as "private space." The elements that acted as de-powering forces in a professional position in the public space were noticeably manipulated as empowerment strategies through a re-positioning of the space from the public to private. This practice invested the principals with the *de facto* authority accorded to "the head of the house" in the religious, socio-cultural and patriarchal discourses. Multiple references to the principals as the parent, teachers as siblings/family, and students as children showed the construction of a metaphorical space of "resistance" where de-powering in the public could be effectively countered. Foucault interprets power as a constantly shifting dynamic relationship between individuals, affecting each other's actions (Foucault, 1977). Discussing Foucault's notion of power, Harvey (1990) maintains that:

> Close scrutiny of the micro-politics of power relations in different localities, contexts, and social situations leads him (Foucault) to conclude that there is an intimate relation between the systems of knowledge ('discourses') which codify techniques and practices for the exercise of social control and domination within particular localised contexts. (p. 45)

Interplay of systems of knowledge and techniques of social control produces regimes of power. In that regional culture, family served as an organizational model and as a site of social control. Both women and men participants conceived colleges as family. It is interesting to analyze how it was availed across the gender divide for similar ends but by adopting different technologies. Within different societies and cultures, Muslim women have been confined to the private through inclusionary, exclusionary, and segregatory modes of control, reinforced by given discourses of "veiling" (Ahmed, 1992; Al-Hibri, 1982; Mernissi, 1991). What could not be made invisible was the status of women in the role of mother and their rights as a member of the family, "because of the Quranic rights given to women, which protect their property, give them inalienable rights of inheritance, and . . . allow them to keep their name" (Afshar, 1994, pp. 13–14).

In view of this comparative empowerment of women in the private, they might have felt stronger to re-conceive colleges as family, placing themselves in the role of mother, who is to be obeyed and honored as a passport to heaven (Ahmed, 1988). The integration of religious and social discourses invested them with a status and authority where gender discrimination could be resisted, "seeing motherhood and sexuality as source of women power" (Schrijvers, 1993, p. 155). The women participants' emphasis on re-conceptualizing colleges as family reflected at alternate strategy, which confirms Fennell's (2002) claim that women "have often expressed discomfort with structuralist perspectives of power and sought alternative theories of power" (p. 100).

In the case of women, over-emphasis on family and domestic roles might have resulted from submission to dominant discourses disseminated by renowned religious scholars such as Maududi (1979), who recognize women's physical and mental equality and acquisition of knowledge, but still strongly argue that "her sphere of activity is home" (p. 152). Or it might have stemmed from the Islamic discourse where private, conceived as *Harim*, is a place "not to keep women in but to keep the intruders out" (Helms, 1995, p. 65). However, it was effectively availed to restrict male interference in the *zanana* colleges, as claimed by a principal, "Non-students infiltrate and create a crisis [in *mardana* colleges]. This does not happen in girls colleges" (PM8).

For men, mixing and reshaping of discourses around educational institutions and family implied an unchallenged right to operate in the public. It confirmed authority of the feudal lord over the family with access to extra structural powers. It entitled them to command respect and obedience, and to make decisions and transactions on behalf of other members. Furthermore, it gave them the right to establish social and political contacts and networks, which were again manipulated for the exercise of their professional. Those principals who had powerful social and political contacts seemed to be in stronger positions to exercise their roles, as highlighted by a participating principal:

> I would say that only that principal can be somewhat successful who has a political back. Without that it is hard to survive. If a brother or a relative is in government then the principal would feel secure; and perhaps would perform better. If a principal has no such support, s/he is totally insecure; s/he cannot make any decision. (PM1)

CONCLUSION

The data highlighted that for principals in the study, power was a contested field. Power relations emerged as two way phenomenon, reflecting a complex interplay of dependence and autonomy. Giddens (1984) explains power as the capacity to achieve desired and intended outcomes. In spite of a proclaimed helplessness and perceived challenges in exercising their leadership roles, the participating principals did appear to exercise considerable power by availing cultural and belief systems to reproduce power relations that enhanced their positional power and enabled them to perform their roles. Giddens (1979) posits that:

> Power relations are relations of autonomy and dependence, but even the most autonomous agent is in some degree dependent, and the most dependent actor or party in a relationship retains some autonomy. (p. 93)

The participating men and women principals positioned their own subjectivities, submitted to the discourses, as well as reshaped them through resistance. The discursive practices involved in discourse formations pointed to the complex research context and the power-plays operative therein, which shaped the roles and practices of the principals and defined their power. The metaphorical shifting of sites and political formulations of reverse discourses contributed to empowering the de-powered principals in different ways through diverse modes of ordering.

Leadership roles of both women and men appeared to be defined by the structural as well as social, economic and political factors embedded in the context. The prioritized issue in the research context was an "infiltration free zone" to exercise the role, while the debates around leadership roles and practices in international literature tend to emphasize "techniques and skills to be effective—[and for] developing a better way of thinking about their role" (Fullan, 1992, p. 31), and often ignore the broader and different problems in developing countries (Legotlo & Westhuizen, 1996). All the participating principals complained of malpractices, corruption, and multiple pressures while women principals mentioned added challenges of male-dominated offices, segregation, and restrictions on female visibility and mobility. These factors on the one hand unveiled a complex power-play operative at cultural and societal levels and on the other hand drew attention to the issues of social justice and equality. In spite of the fact that social justice and equality are propounded by Islam and the Quran, the accepted practices in that Muslim society deprived the principals of their rights in the professional domain.

The empirical evidence highlighted that gender and given interpretations of Muslimness constrained women principals in particular. Gender emerged as a source and tool of exploitation rather than a celebration of difference as presented in the Quran. The participating women principals were constrained by specific social and structural conditions. Major challenges for women were domestic responsibilities, family obligations, social values, patterns of behavior, restrictions on mobility and participating in the public, and finance management because of the male-dominated finance offices. For male principals, main challenges were conceptualization of the *mardana* colleges as male space or public that rendered them open to *baradari* (clan) pressures, political interferences, social obligations and pressures from unions, professional organizations and other pressure groups.

The research provides evidence that roles and practices cannot be decontextualized. In the Muslim society of Pakistan, empowerment for a male or a female principal was linked to their being a member of that faith community or the *Ummah*.[4] The emphasis by all the participants on their Muslimness, and justifying the appropriateness of their roles and practices through the lens of religion points to the influence of religion and belief systems on professional roles and practices. Stepping outside the dominant religious discourse/s was not seen as good for their sense of self, and probably for their role as principal as well. Women principals accepted and emphasized their family responsibilities as Muslim women over their professional role and career progression. For male principals, self-projections as practicing Muslims supported the good Muslim image. Interestingly, this need to identify with religion was sometimes exploited, as reflected in the example mentioned by one of the participants:

> A group of lecturers made a practice of not sending leave applications when they were absent... By the end of the year, when the principal wrote in the ACR that they were not regular, or their performance was not good, or that they did not co-operate, they ganged up to propagate that the principal was an Ahmedi. They accused him of blasphemy and similar things... *molvies* (Mosque *imams*) criticized him during Friday *khutbas* (sermons); and soon the principal was running hard, and explaining hard, that he was a Muslim and believed in Quran, and that Mohammed was the last prophet. (PSM1)[5]

Religion was a dominating discourse holding validating authority, and the principals, both male and female, felt compelled to submit to it. Educational leadership emerged as a complex discursive field underpinned by the issues of religious identity and ideology. Being a male or female principal had its own associated challenges. The research offers an exploration of the roles and practices of women and men principals, and acknowledges the plurality and fragmentation of their subject positions and their efforts at adjustment in a complex context. The study attempts to make visible the challenges facing principals in a specific Muslim society and the alternate strategies deployed by them to perform their roles, affirming that "in reality, power... passes through much finer channels, and is much more ambiguous, since each individual has at his disposal a certain power, and for that very reason can also act as the vehicle for transmitting a wider power" (Foucault, 1980, p. 72).

Foucault (1977) conceptualizes power as a non-linear, shifting, and dynamic relationship between individuals. He argues that subjects are constituted by the operation of power, which affects their ways of perceiving things or conceiving of world. How participating women and men principals conceived, perceived, and exercised their roles appeared to be determined by the power relations and role perceptions in that traditionally feudal patriarchal segregated Muslim society, rather than by their professional positions, confirming that "power is not localized in state apparatuses and nothing will change in the society if the mechanisms of power that function outside, below and alongside the state apparatuses on a much more and minute level are not also changed" (Sarup, 1988, p. 86). The study affirmed that the practices and discourses that are shaped by cultural belief systems can be grave barriers to equal rights and social justice as evidenced in the case of women and men principals who felt deprived of their professional rights and powers in that particular society. It also highlighted that to change the practices for improved social justice, policy changes are not enough unless, as quoted above, "the mechanisms of power that function outside, below and alongside the state apparatuses on a much more and minute level are not also changed" (Sarup, 1988, p. 86).

NOTES

1. This was the total number of single-sex colleges for boys and girls in that region at the time the data was collected.
2. Bhabha offers an interesting interpretation of the notion of agency as the apparatus of contingency, and "ambiguity of such phenomenon" (1994, p. 187).
3. See also Afshar, 1992, p. 211; Fernea and Bezirgan, 1977, Introduction; Wolkowitz, 1987; Weiss, 1994.
4. Ummah is the overarching concept used for Muslim community with associated responsibilities and obligations as its member.
5. Ahmedis are declared non-Muslims in the Constitution of the Islamic Republic of Pakistan (1973).

REFERENCES

Afshar, H. (1987). Women, marriage and the state in Iran. In H. Afshar (Ed.), *Women, state and ideology* (pp. 70–86). London: Macmillan Press.
Afshar, H. (1992). Women and work: Ideology not adjustment at work in Iran. In H. Afshar & C. Dennis (Eds.), *Women and the adjustment policies in the third world* (pp. 205–229). Basingstoke: Macmillan Press.
Afshar, H. (1994). Muslim women in West Yorkshire. In H. Afshar & M. Maynard (Eds.), *The dynamics of race and gender: Some feminist interventions* (pp. 127–147). London: Taylor and Francis.
Ahmed, A. S. (1988). *Discovering Islam.* London: Routledge and Kogan Paul.
Ahmed, A. S. (1992). *Post-modernism and Islam: Predicament and promise.* London: Routledge.
Al-Hibri, A. (Ed.). (1982). *Women and Islam.* Oxford: Pergamon Press.
Baldridge, J. V. (1971). *Power and conflict in the university: Research in the sociology of complex organizations.* New York: Wiley.
Ball, S. J. (1990a). Management as moral technology. In S. Ball (Ed.), *Foucault and education: Disciplines and knowledge* (pp. 153–166). London: Routledge.

Ball, S. J. (1990b). *Politics and policy making in education: Explorations in policy sociology.* London: Routledge.

Best, S., & Kellner, D. (1991). *Postmodern theory: Critical interrogations.* London, Macmillan.

Bhabha, H. K. (1994). *The location of culture.* London: Routledge.

Brock, C., Dada, J., & Jatta, T. (2006). Selected perspectives on education in West Africa, with special reference to gender and religion. In R. Griffin (Ed.), *Education in the Muslim world: Different perspectives* (pp. 211–238). Oxford, UK: Symposium Books.

Cherryholmes, C. (1988). *Power and criticism: Poststructural investigations in education.* New York: Teachers College Press.

Curry, B. K. (2000). *Women in power: Pathways to leadership in education.* New York, NY: Teachers College Press.

Dreyfus, H. L. & Rabinow, P. (Eds.). (1982). *Michel Foucault: Beyond structuralism and hermeneutics.* Brighton: Harvester.

Fennell, H. A. (2002). Letting go while holding on: Women principals' lived experiences with power. *Journal of Educational Administration, 40*(2), 95–117.

Fernea, E. W. & Bezirgan, B. Q. (Eds.). (1977). *Middle Eastern Muslim women speak.* Austin, TX: University of Texas Press.

Foucault, M. (1977). *Discipline and punish: The birth of the prison.* A. Sheridan (Trans.). London: Allen Lane.

Foucault, M. (1980). *Power/knowledge: Selected interviews and other writings, 1972–1977.* Brighton: Harvester Press.

Foucault, M. (1991). "Questions of Method," and "Politics and the study of Discourse." In G. Burchell, C. Gordon, & P. Miller (Eds.), *The Foucault Effect: studies in governmentality.* London: Harvester Wheatsheaf.

Fullan, M. (1992). *What is worth fighting for in headship? Strategies for taking charge of the headship.* Buckingham: Open University Press.

Giddens, A. (1979). *Central problems in social theory: Action, structure, and contradiction in social analysis.* Berkeley, CA: University of California Press.

Giddens, A. (1982). Power, the dialectic of control and class structuration. In A. Giddens and G. MacKenzie (Eds.), *Social class and the division of labour* (pp. 29–45). Cambridge: Cambridge University Press.

Giddens, A. (1984). *The constitution of society: Outline of the theory of structuration.* Berkeley, CA: University of California Press.

Gordon, R. D. (2002). Conceptualizing leadership with respect to its historical—contextual antecedents to power. *The Leadership Quarterly, 13*(2), 151–167.

Grant, B. (1997). Disciplining Students: the construction of student subjectivities. *British Journal of Sociology of Education, 18*(1), 101–114.

Harvey, D. (1990). *The condition of postmodernity: An enquiry into the origins of cultural change.* Oxford: Blackwell.

Helms, L. M. (1995). The Haram as a Sacred Space for Muslim Women. *Muslim Education Quarterly, 12*(3), 62–72.

Kenvey, J., Wallis, S., Blackmore, J., & Jenny, L. (1994). Making "hope practical" rather than despair convincing. *British Journal of Sociology of Education, 15*(2), 187–210.

Kezar, A. (2000). Pluralistic leadership: Incorporating diverse voices. *Journal of Higher Education, 71*(6), 722–743.

Khan, S. M. I. (1973). *The Constitution of the Islamic Republic of Pakistan*. Lahore, Pakistan: Khyber Law Publishers.

Knight, J., Smith, R., & Sachs, J. (1990). Deconstructing hegemony: Multicultural policy and a populist response. In S. Ball (Ed.), *Foucault and education: Disciplines and knowledge* (pp. 122–152). London: Routledge.

Kotter, J. P. (1988). *The leadership factor*. New York: Free Press.

Legotlo, M. & Westhuizen, P. (1996). Coming on board: Problems facing new principals in developing countries. *Journal of Educational Management and Administration, 24*(4), 401–410.

Maududi, S. A. A. (1979). *Birth control: Its social, political, economic, moral and religious aspects*. K. Ahmad & M. Faruqi (Trans. & Eds.). Pakistan: Lahore, Islamic Publications.

Mernissi, F. (1991). *Women and Islam: A historical enquiry*. Oxford: Basil Blackwell.

Rose, N. (1996). Identity, genealogy, history. In S. Hall & P. du Gay (Eds.), *Questions of cultural identity* (pp. 128–150). London: Sage.

Sarup, M. (1988). *An introductory guide to post-structuralism and post-modernism*. Harvester: Wheatsheaf.

Schrijvers, J. (1993). Motherhood experienced and conceptualized. In D. Bell, P. Caplan & W. J. Karim (Eds.), *Gendered fields: Women, men and ethnography* (pp. 143–158). London: Routledge.

Shah, S. (1999). *Education Management: Braving boundaries*. Islamabad, Pakistan: National Book Foundation.

Shah, S. (2008). Women and educational leadership in a Muslim society: A study of women college heads in Pakistan. In H. Sobehart (Ed.), *Women leading education across the continents: Sharing the spirit, fanning the flame* (pp. 344–381). Lanham, MD: Rowman & Littlefield.

Shah, S. (2009). Why Single-Sex Schools? Discourses of culture/faith and achievement. *Cambridge Journal of Education, 39*(2), 191–204.

Sharma, U. (1980). *Women, work and property in North-West India*. London: Tavistock Publications.

Usher, R. & Edwards, R. (1994). *Post-modernism and education*. London: Routledge.

Watkins, P. (1989). Leadership, powers and symbols in educational administration. In J. Smyth (Ed.), *Critical discourses on teacher development* (pp. 9–37). London: Cassell.

Weiss, A. M. (1994). Challenges for a Muslim woman in a postmodern world. In A. S. Ahmed & D. Hastings (Eds.), *Islam, globalization and postmodernity* (pp. 127–140). London: Routledge.

Wolkowitz, C. (1987). Controlling women's access to political power: A case study in Andhra Pradesh, India. In H. Afshar (Ed.), *Women, state and ideology* (pp. 204–225). London: Macmillan Press.

CHAPTER 5

INSTRUCTIONAL LEADERSHIP IN AMERICAN AND CHINESE SCHOOLS

A Comparative Case Study

Anna Q. Sun

INTRODUCTION

Over time, changes in public education in the United States have become more precise and demanding, driven in particular by the intensification of federal, state, and local governments' school-based accountability mandates. The No Child Left Behind Act (NCLB) of 2001 has further energized this trend toward test-oriented accountability in its attempt to close the achievement gaps that exist among diverse student populations who attend public schools (Abernathy, 2007; Irons & Harris, 2007; Sloan, 2007). The current "Race to the Top" educational reform initiated by President Obama is also an attempt to enhance educational reforms at state and district levels, which are funded by the American Recovery and Reinvestment Act of 2009 (U.S. Department of Education, 2009).

Social Justice Leadership for a Global World, pages 77–93
Copyright © 2012 by Information Age Publishing
All rights of reproduction in any form reserved.

China, since initiating open-door policies in late 1970s, is restructuring its educational system, stressing creative thinking and hands-on skills. In 1985, the government issued the "Decision to Reform Educational Structure," which established policies to decentralize education based on the principle of "local responsibility and administration by level" (Tsang, 2001). More specific goals concerning decentralization were set forth:

- Authority should be "devolved" to local levels.
- The central government will continue to monitor the process and provide basic guidelines, but local governments will have more power and bear financial costs.
- Secondary schools will offer dual tracks, allowing students to choose higher education or vocational-technical education combined with some devolution of authority and financing.
- Devolution of authority for the nine-year compulsory system is to be gradual, based on a regional approach in the order of coastal cites, developed interior regions and cities, and less developed interior.
- The power for administration of elementary education belongs to local authorities.
- Multiple methods of financing will be implemented (Hawkins, 2000).

The 1986 Compulsory Education Act and the 1995 Education Act, which initiated a fiscal decentralization of education in China, granted local governments at village, township, and county levels the autonomy to retain a greater share of their revenue. In return, local-level governments were made responsible for generating revenue to meet their respective shares of expenditures, including education (Hawkins, 2000; Liu, 2009; Zhao, 2009). In doing so, the Chinese government has tried to systematically implement a nine-year compulsory education plan throughout the entire country to improve the country's quality of education.

Indeed, in enacting these reforms, policy-makers in both the U.S. and China seem to "have taken an unprecedented interest in public education and in charting a new mission for school reform" (Fullan, Hill, & Crévola, 2006, p. 1). Under increasingly intensified education reforms, finding ways to improve the quality of education in public schools seems to have drawn greater attention in both developed and developing countries, and both the United States and China are in the midst of working toward national educational reforms. A variety of factors, most notably policies, context, and environment, have a great impact on school improvement. School leaders in both countries have primary roles in exerting powerful influence on "restructuring" (Hargreves, 1994) and "reculturing" schools (Fullan, 2001). Given that leadership is increasingly recognized as a significant factor in the improvement of student achievement (Hallinger & Heck, 1996, 1998;

Huber, 2004; Jacobson & Bezzina, 2008; Leithwood & Riehl, 2005; Muijs & Harris, 2002), it is reasonable to look into the approaches school leaders should take to improve education quality.

Utilizing the theoretical framework of instructional leadership, this chapter reports on the findings of a comparative study based on two cases—Water Fall High School in the United States and Yellow Star High School in China (both are pseudonyms). After carefully identifying the leadership approaches adopted by the schools' respective principals, the study examined, within their particular contexts, the effectiveness of the principals' leadership at each school. It will be shown that their instructional leadership approaches were different in addressing accountability, development and deprivatization of professional practices, changing school cultures, and so on.

The next section will review the literature on educational changes in the United States and the evolution of the instructional leadership, followed by the section that will examine the two cases—Water Fall High School in the U.S. and Yellow Star High in China. The comparative perspectives of the instructional leadership approached by the two principals will be examined. At the end of the chapter are a conclusion and sections on implications and future research.

CHANGES IN INSTRUCTIONAL LEADERSHIP IN THE U.S.

In the U.S. in the past three decades, three waves of educational reforms have had great impacts on the development of school leadership. The 1983 publication by the National Commission on Excellence in Education of *A Nation at Risk: The Imperative for Educational Reform* launched these three waves of reform in public education (Giles & Foote, 2007; Hawley, 1988; Razik & Swanson, 2001).

The first wave of reform, in the early 1980s, concentrated mostly on student academic performance and teachers' instructional practices by means of standardizing curricula, regulating teacher certification, and increasing state-mandated testing (Carr & Hartnett, 1996; Metz, 1988). Echoing the initiatives of the first wave of reform, the effective schools research (Levin & Lezotte, 1990) focused on instructional leadership, which was an approach that was centered more on classroom instruction and curriculum improvement (Hallinger, 2003). Typically, the features of instructional leadership are identified as defining the school's mission, managing the instructional program, and promoting the school's learning climate (Hallinger, 2003).

Proponents believe that instructional leadership is at the core of making programmatic changes that lead to the improvement of schools (Bossert, Dwyer, Rowan, & Lee, 1982; Hallinger, 2003; Hallinger & Murphy, 1985; Hallinger & Heck, 1996). Hallinger (2003), a major advocate of this model, however, has admitted that instructional leadership focuses "too much on the principal as the center of expertise, power, and authority" (p. 330). He agrees with Barth (1990) and Lambert (1998) that "in many cases principals have less expertise than the teachers they supervise" (Hallinger, 2003, p. 335), adding that, because of its "direct involvement in teaching and learning," the instructional leadership approach "is unrealistic in a larger school, be it elementary or secondary level" (p. 334).

With its constantly changing external context, instructional leadership has evolved over time. Blasé and Blasé (1999), after a thorough review of the literature and an investigation of 809 teachers, stated that "effective approaches to instructional leadership...should integrate many specific elements...[for example] collaboration, peer coaching, inquiry, collegial study groups, reflective discussion, and action research" (p. 17). The report argued that this model is "a collaborative endeavor enacted in a supportive environment that leads to an all-school action plan" (Blasé & Blasé, 1999, p. 3). Marks and Printy (2003), in their study of 24 nationally selected restructuring schools, characterized this model as "shared instructional leadership." Marks and Printy (2003) assert that the principal is the "leader of instructional leaders, who has shared responsibilities with teachers for staff development, curriculum development, and supervision of instructional tasks" (p. 3).

The report of the Carnegie Forum on the Education and the Economy, *A Nation Prepared: Teachers for the 21st Century,* started the second wave of reform in 1986, which focused its attention to the restructuring of schools and the empowering of teachers as professional educators (Hawley, 1988; Marks & Printy, 2003). Teacher empowerment, a core element in the second reform wave, drew praise because it increased the possibilities of decentralization along with empowerment (Giles & Foote, 2007). The products of this movement were decentralization and whole-school improvement initiatives such as the "Coalition for Essential Schools," which reinforced teacher empowerment compared to conventional school-based practices (Heller & Firestone, 1995).

Critics, however, think that so-called "large-scale" school reform approaches were flawed in that they did not specifically focus on how to improve teaching and learning (Giles & Foote, 2007). The potential failure of the second-wave reform resided in its vague views of restructuring, which, Fullan (1991) points out, are changes implemented "'on the surface' by endorsing certain goals, using specific materials, and even imitating the behavior without specifically understanding the principles and rationale of the change" (p. 40).

The third wave of education reform, in the early 1990s, was what Razik and Swanson (2001) called "systemic reform," which was driven by the need for efficiency, effectiveness, accountability, and economy (Youngs, 2007).

Giles and Foote (2007) viewed the third wave as systemic change that is mainly focused on student learning, and "when taken together, the second and third waves of reform are complementary, comprehensive, and ambitious" (p. 2). According to Razik and Swanson (2001), Kentucky's educational reforms may best demonstrate so-called "systemic change, where all elements of the education system have been modified, including its governance and finance" (p. 17). More examples resulting from the second and third waves of reform movements include the decentralized Chicago school system (Dunn, James-Gross, & Trampe, 1998; Hess, 1991; Hess, 1999; Razik & Swanson, 2001), charter schools (Finn, Manno, & Bierlein, 1996; Office of Educational Research and Improvement, 1998; Razik & Swanson, 2001), the Florida voucher programs, and parental choice (Razik & Swanson, 2001).

The No Child Left Behind Act of 2001 brought to the United States greater and more demanding intensification of school-based accountability measures at federal, state, and local levels. School principals themselves can no longer shoulder those intensified mandates. School leadership simultaneously is evolving itself to a new approach called distributed leadership (Gronn, 2000, 2002; Harris, 2005; Ogawa & Bossert, 1995; Spillane, 2005, 2006). Among those who have studied this model, Spillane (2005, 2006) is in the forefront of its theoretical conceptualization.

Spillane (2005), in an empirical study of 13 elementary schools in Chicago, characterizes distributed leadership "as a product of the interactions of school leaders, followers, and their situations . . . rather than as a function of one or more leaders' actions" (p. 144). Apart from the traditional organizational theory framework, he argues that leadership tasks should be distributed among multiple leaders, and that "multiple individuals [should] take responsibility for leadership in schools." Spillane (2005) adds "[the] situation defines leadership practice in interaction with leaders and followers" (p. 144). Leadership resides in expertise, and in both formal and informal positions.

EDUCATION IN CHINA

With a population of approximately 1.3 billion, China has an education system that is vast and complex. Generally speaking, the system consists of kindergarten, primary, secondary (middle and high schools), higher and adult education. Since the promulgation of the Compulsory Education Law of the People's Republic of China in 1986, a policy requiring nine years of compulsory education has been implemented nationwide, comprising six years of primary and three years of middle school schooling (grades one through nine). At the end of the final year of compulsory education, students are required to take end-of-term examinations to get their diplomas, which is the basic qualification for moving on to high schools. Test scores are also used to determine what kind of high schools students can apply to in order to gain admission.

High school comprises three years and is not compulsory. Parents have to pay tuitions and fees. It consists of two sectors: regular secondary and vocational secondary education. Regular secondary schools are academically oriented for students who want to pursue higher education; their courses and curriculum are geared toward the highly competitive national college entrance examination. Vocational secondary schools train skilled personnel for non-professional fields of work. The duration of study in those schools runs two to four years.

The 1985 Decision to Reform Educational Structure policy issued by the Chinese government established policies that decentralized the management and financing of the educational system to local levels (Tsang, 2001). Under the new policies, principals at elementary and secondary schools could make decisions on hiring, staff allocation, student recruitments and teacher evaluation. As a result, schools enjoyed more autonomy in their day-to-day management during the 1980s and 1990s, however, curriculum and college entrance examinations are highly centralized.

As a trade-off for such greater empowerment, school principals also became responsible for their schools' finances, as reductions in funding by the central government also transferred financial responsibilities to the local governments. In return, the local governments shifted the financial burdens to the individual schools, resulting in the schools having to generate their shared funding by various means (Tsang, 2001).

In 2001, non-governmental funding generated by schools accounted for 21 percent of total school revenues (Liu, 2002), much of which came from charges levied on students and parents. But in time, because of the heavy extra taxes and fees levied on people by the local governments, the government, since early 2000s, re-centralized the funding of education, especially in rural China, reducing "the economic burden that nine years of compulsory education had imposed on poor township governments and on rural households" (Liu, 2009) in order to reduce the burden on local students' families. Both the U.S. and China have undergone significant restructuring and reform processes but within two policy and cultural contexts. The next section will outline the methodology utilized in the study.

METHODOLOGY

A case-study method was utilized (Creswell, 1998). The data were collected through multiple techniques, including participant and non-participant observations, in-depth interviews, extensive field notes, official documentation, and school/district websites. The data for Water Fall High School in the United States were collected in the fall of 2007 and included school observations, two formal interviews of the principal, and several informal interviews with the principal, two assistant principals, three administrative staff members, and five teachers. The data for Yellow Star High School in China were collected in the summer of 2008 and included participant observation (when taught at the school) and three formal interviews of the principal. It was not always possible to take complete notes, so abbreviations and code words were used during observations, which were re-written and expanded later with more details and further thoughts while everything was still fresh. Semi-structured, face-to-face interviews were used to obtain more specific and story-telling data to obtain perceptions and views from others on the school principal's leadership. The interviews were transcribed and served the purpose of supplementing the field notes. Besides field notes and interviews, the data were also gathered from a wide range of sources such as official school documents, minutes of meetings and school websites. Field notes, interview data, and documentary material was then coded into separate domains, using taxonomic and componential analysis methodology to look for recurring patterns of leaders' behavior across the two schools (Spradley, 1980).

FINDINGS

Case#1—Water Fall High School in the United States

Situated in a middle to upper middle class suburban community of 115,000 in western New York State, Water Fall High School provides a public education for a student body of approximately 1000 in grades nine through 12, with about 86 full and part time faculty and three administrators. The school's academic reputation is reflected in terms of its high state-testing results and college acceptance rates. Most students at Water Fall take New York State regents-level courses. Many have pursued accelerated courses before entering ninth grade, and go on to Advanced Placement courses when they enroll in Water Fall. Water Fall also has a good number of students who have special needs in education, whose parents have high expectations of the school and are hopeful their children will obtain a quality education while they receive support from the school. It is the oldest of three public high schools in its district. When Mr. Smith (pseudonym) became principal in 1999, Water Fall staff were concerned the school had focused on maintaining the status quo rather school improvement.

A Whole-School Action Plan

The principal of Water Fall High School holds a bachelor's degree in science and a master's degree in education. Before becoming principal in 1999, he had served as a middle-school principal for four years and a high-school assistant principal for four years. Mr. Smith thought internal and external forces drove the need for school improvement at Water Fall. Internally, the chief driving force for changes was that the previous principal ran the school with a divisive and controlling leadership style, which he carried out by grouping "his own people" to oppose those who disagreed with him. Externally, the main force for changes was the implementation of the federal No Child Left Behind Act under Title 1, which emphasizes "changes in state and local accountability, public school choice, supplemental educational services, 'highly qualified' staff, unsafe school choice, and parents' 'right to know'" (No Child Left Behind Act: Consolidated Application Update 2005-2006). To implement this, New York State mandates school districts and individual schools to design and adopt school improvement plans. The emphasis on accountability is largely measured through school outcomes on high-stakes tests and published school report cards.

Mr. Smith aimed to create an environment at Water Fall in which all stakeholders would participate in the decision-making process, particularly teachers. He realized that because his predecessor was controlling and exerted his power over faculty, he had to persuade teachers that they needed to be involved in the school's decision-making process. To achieve this, the school's faculty meetings are illustrative. Mr. Smith made use of faculty meetings to get teachers involved in formulating school policies and decisions. He used the first part of each faculty meeting for discussing issues proposed by the administration teams and encouraged his teachers to offer their ideas, opinions, and suggestions. He described his concept about involving teachers in the decision making in this way:

> Some issues are not just black and white, and you need to discuss them with your faculty. I want the faculty meeting to be for administrative purposes as well, so the faculty could step forward and identify themselves as leaders. I want them to feel that they are responsible for the school.

Building trust and instilling respect was the remedy Mr. Smith adopted to get everybody involved in a whole-school action plan. An assistant principal recalled, "I have never taken charge of the school summer program, and Mr. Smith encouraged and supported me to do it, but he held accountability as well." Mr. Smith encouraged young teachers to explore new classroom pedagogies by offering them academic support. He gave teachers who made mistakes another chance and let them know he believed in them, saying:

> If they [teachers] make a mistake, don't bury them. You don't have to repri-
> mand them severely. Give them another chance…There is nothing wrong
> with giving teachers a second chance to explore themselves. At the same time,
> you can also give people suggestions in a positive way.

Mr. Smith believed that trust was a crucial element in the empowerment process. He believed that trusting teachers would give them the confidence to make a difference in their teaching, and eventually to change students' learning outcomes. He also emphasized the need to treat teachers with dignity and respect.

Mr. Smith managed to instill high expectations in everyone—teachers, students, administrators, and parents. Most important, he thought he should first set high expectations for himself. In his pursuit of the school's primary goal—raising the levels of student academic learning—Mr. Smith recognized the importance of effective professional instruction as the core requirement for student achievement. In addition he actively maintained ongoing staff development strategies such as having teachers attend conferences and bringing consultants into the school. He also cultivated instructional expertise within his school. He believed that his teachers were educational experts, as he openly stated:

> You got very skillful faculty and staff, so what's wrong with the expertise in
> your building, you do have expertise in your building. They [teachers] don't
> mind to share, but you have to ask them if you are a good principal. It all de-
> pends on your skill and talent to make it happen.

In accord with what he said, Mr. Smith urged teachers to share their instructional methods and pedagogies in faculty meetings by means of de-privatizing their classroom practices. Case #2—Yellow Star High School in China

Yellow Star High School is one of five municipal top academic high schools in a major metropolis in China that has a population of nine million. The school has approximately 3,000 students in grades 10 through 12, 146 faculty members, and five administrators. The municipal Ministry of Education allows Yellow Star to select students from the entire city, based upon the applicants' scores on a competitive entrance exam. Unlike in the United States, most of China's cities are significantly more developed than its suburban and rural towns and villages. Parents who live in more developed cities such as Yellow Star's have more access to higher ranked high schools, are usually more educated, have high expectations for their children's education, and seek to send their children to schools with high college-entry rates. Yellow Star, therefore, attracts a large number of students who are academically capable and who want to pursue higher education.

With a long established reputation of high college-entry rates, Yellow Star's mission statement prioritizes the objective of the school as ensuring all of its students score high enough on the college to enroll in higher education institutions. All of the school's courses are geared toward the National College Entrance Examination. In 2008, 99 percent of its graduates went on to higher education, 80 percent of whom were admitted to the country's top academic higher education institutions. Student outcomes such as test scores and college entrance rates drive China's educational system. Mrs. Sue (pseudonym) and other administrators were under intense pressure to maintain Yellow Star's high academic status when she started her principalship in 1999.

Creating a Learning Environment in School

The principal of Yellow Star, Mrs. Sue, graduated from a teacher training college with a bachelor's degree in the 1970s and had been a math teacher at Yellow Star ever since. In 1994, she was promoted to assistant principal, and in 1998 she became principal upon the retirement of the former principal. At that time, Yellow Star's reputation as a top academic school was suffering because of declining student scores on the National College Entrance Exam. There was concern that the students' low performances in the exam might lead to a decline in enrollments in Yellow Star and, ultimately, affect the school's income from students.

Instructional leadership is often defined by several tasks, such as supervision of classroom instruction, staff development, and curriculum development (Smith & Andrew, 1989), which is consistent with the situation at Yellow Star High School. Mrs. Sue believed that modeling, promoting, and supporting teachers within classrooms was conducive to professional growth. Her strategy for school improvement was to focus on teachers and on supporting them in their classrooms. In her implementation of a new curriculum required by the municipal Ministry of Education, Mrs. Sun started a project called "New curriculum, innovative pedagogies," to improve teachers' professional knowledge and skills in classroom settings. Here is what she did for the project:

- Invited educational experts or model teachers (inside and outside the school) to the staff meetings to introduce and demonstrate classroom innovations,
- Established a staff training program in conjunction with two universities,
- Encouraged peer classroom observations within or across subject areas,
- Increased principal's and assistant principals' classroom observations,
- Set models of innovative classroom teaching and shared them via the requirements of peer observations, and
- Changed content-area teams as a mandate and required all teachers to be involved in half- day meeting/developing schedule.

Mrs. Sue asserted that good teachers do not just present materials to students, but also have to find effective means to teach students how to learn. For example, she encouraged Yellow Star teachers to explore cross-subject teaching pedagogy by modeling how a math teacher could teach math in English. She also supported the innovation of having geography and history teachers co-teach their subjects. Mrs. Sue also equipped all teachers with laptops to enable teachers to prepare their teaching plans effectively.

Recognizing that a rising influx of new teachers creates added pressure on the need for staff development (Hopkins, West & Beresford, 1998), she set up training programs for young teachers with less than five years' experience, and organized required partnership teams composed of new and experienced teachers. Through such efforts, she created a culture of professional growth and self-improvement. Her innovative leadership approaches worked, and the school's college admission rates have been rising consistently since 2001. Having carefully examined instructional leadership performed by the two principals, the next section will discuss the differences between the two.

DISCUSSION

The differences between the two principals' leadership approaches are significant. The principal in Water Fall High School *listened to* what teachers say by seeking their ideas, thoughts, and suggestions in the process of making policies and decisions. The principal in Yellow Star High School *talked to* teachers about a common vision of what good instruction should consist of, emphasizing unitary and score-based results. In addition to the possible culture impacts on their leadership approaches (the cultural value of individualism in the U.S. and the cultural value of collectivism in China), Gordon states that "the practice of instructional leadership has often been limited primarily to one of inspection, oversight, and judgment of classroom instruction...control supervision still dominates professional practice (as cited in Blasé & Blasé, 1999, p. 351)." In this respect, the Yellow Star principal is exercising what is known as "position-based authority" (Giles, Johnson, Brooks, & Jacobson, 2005, p. 521).

The Water Fall High principal seems to spend relatively less time on teaching and learning—a core of the school—and lacks a specific orientation toward student learning. Mr. Smith appears torn between a call for the school to be innovative toward equity and social justice on the one hand, and a need to comply with the tight accountability mandated by the state and school district on the other hand. The principal at Yellow Star High seems to focus solely on teachers' classroom teaching, while neglecting teachers' empowerment in school decision-making on school missions and instructional programs.

Spillane (2005) argues that "multiple individuals [should] take responsibility for leadership in schools," and "[the] situation defines leadership practice in interaction with leaders and followers" (p. 144).

The two schools in this study are under pressure from accountability-driven reforms. The United States' Water Fall High School has to comply with a state-mandated school improvement plan measured by students' learning outcomes in high-stakes testing; China's Yellow Star High School is under pressure to maintain high college entry rates and to improve their students' performance in the national testing—an outcome that is vital to their recruitment of sufficient numbers of top-notch students who are vital to the school's potential for generating greater revenues (a high school education is not compulsory in China).

Both principals in this study devote extensive time, effort and attention to professional development, because they recognize that teaching and learning are at the core of students' ultimate achievements. This recognition is reflected in the Hallinger's *School Leadership Development* (1999), in which he states:

> Provision of professional development should be eclectic and dependent upon the needs identified by school leaders and the capacity of organizations to meet those needs...[and] professional development of school leaders must take place in a broader context of professionalization among educators. (pp. 47–48)

Teaching is a process geared to develop cognitive skills and social awareness in students, and to help them make good use of those attributes. The objective of leadership is to facilitate and support valuable approaches to teaching and learning. Water Fall High School in the U.S. is innovative in its use of faculty meetings to create opportunities for the sharing of classroom experiences among faculty, which promotes de-privatization of professional practices within classrooms. At Yellow Star High School in China, the principal encourages peer observations and content-area teams, which foster professional learning and sharing.

CONCLUSION AND IMPLICATIONS

Fullan (2001) says: "The job of the principal, or any educational leader, has become increasingly complex and constrained" (p. 156). Most educational leaders tend to restructure and reculture their organizations effectively to move their schools forward. It is, however, worth noting that "because each school's culture is unique, being successful as a leader in one school does not automatically predict a similar experience in the leader's next appointment" (Stoll & Fink, 1995, p. 107). Issues concerning leadership dominate the recent debates in both the United States and China as global economic competition places pressure on each country to increase test scores in international comparisons. Research on the effectiveness of leadership theory and practice continues to be of interest in both countries. Based on his understanding of U.S. schools, Leithwood (2003) identifies three components for successful school leadership: 1) setting the direction; 2) developing people; and 3) redesigning the organization. In his analysis, he claims that such an approach concentrates on developing shared school visions, commitments and capacities of members in organizations, and collective actions that generate empowerment for those who participate in the change process (Leithwood, 2003)

The process of setting the direction through a shared school vision should be carefully undertaken by both schools and should involve the leadership in interaction between leaders and followers on shared intention and purpose (Burns, 1978). However, U.S. leadership theories around school reform may not be easily transferable to Chinese schools. In the U.S. there tends to be a strong belief and research that suggests that teachers, parents, students, and staff should all have a say on how to improve student learning and on what policies and programs should be implemented in schools. These stakeholders interact daily with students and are most knowledgeable as to what the best practices are for students—this type of input was not evident in the leadership approaches at either school.

In traditional bureaucratic organizations, many factors influence how school leaders exercise their knowledge and skills to provide instructional leadership at their schools. As discussed in this chapter, the intensification by states and local districts in the United States to advance school-based accountability as a means of measuring school performance may influence the kinds of approaches the school leaders take. However, the current pursuit of higher student scores on standardized tests may in time over-burden school leadership, and therefore there is a need for schools to develop a new leadership approach—distributed leadership (Gronn, 2000, 2002; Harris, 2005; Ogawa & Bossert, 1995; Spillane, 2005, 2006).

Developing people, for example, is what principals need to support by developing a collaborative environment that can facilitate distributed leadership in schools, which will give all members at the school opportunities to get involved in leadership activities and to be part of its leadership team. Hulme (2006) pointed out that "leaders create the conditions for professionals to work and learn together to create a synergy greater than the sum of individual effort" (p. 3). The principal in the U.S. school seems to utilize a distributed leadership approach. He sought to empower teachers to get involved in the decision-making process, according to U.S. literature on what constitutes best practice. The school principal in China needs to develop a distributed approach, although this may be challenging in a political system where decision making is very top down. Therefore, in the long run, all educational leaders may have to continually confront issues of the effectiveness of school leadership and take into account the cultural and political contexts in which they operate if they are improve student learning in both countries.

This study serves as a starting point to explore the complex nature of school reform challenges in both China and the U.S. Future research, however, is needed that explores how teachers, district administrators, students, and parents view the effectiveness of principals' leadership approaches. Because this study focused only on one high school principal in each country, future research is needed that studies more principals in both countries. Elementary and middle school leaders should be studied as well to see if there are different trends and perceptions of school leadership at different instructional levels. Moreover, this research suggests the need for additional research that explores how differing political and cultural contexts in individual countries may influence instructional leadership.

REFERENCES

Abernathy, S. F. (2007). *No Child Left Behind and the public schools.* Ann Arbor, MI: The University of Michigan Press.

Barth, R. (1990). *Improving schools from within.* San Francisco, CA, Jossey-Bass.

Blasé, J. & Blasé, J., (1999). Principals' instructional leadership and teacher development: Teachers' perspectives. *Educational Administration Quarterly, 35*(3), 349–378.

Bossert, S. T., Dwyer, D. C., Rowan, B., & Lee, G. V. (1982). The instructional management role of the principal. *Educational Administration Quarterly, 18*(3), 34–64.

Burns, J. M., (1978). *Leadership.* New York: Harper & Row.

Carr, W. & Hartnett, A. (1996). *Education and the struggle for democracy: The politics of educational ideas.* Bristol, PA: Open University Press.

Creswell, J. W. (1998). *Qualitative inquiry and research design: Choosing among five traditions.* Thousand Oaks, CA: Sage Publications.

Dunn, R. J., James-Gross, L., & Trampe, C. (1998). Decentralized budgeting: A study in implementation and implications. *The Journal of School Business Management, 10*(1), 22–28.

Finn, C. E., Jr., Manno, B. V., & Bierlein, L. (1996). *Charter School in action: What have we learned?* Indianapolis, IN: Educational Excellence Network, Hudson Institute.

Fullan, M. (1991). *The new meaning of educational change.* New York, NY: Teachers College Press.

Fullan, M. (2001). *The new meaning of educational change* (2nd ed.). New York, NY: Teachers College Press.

Fullan, M., Hill, P., & Crévola, C. (2006). *Breakthrough.* Thousand Oaks, CA: Corwin Press.

Giles, C. & Foote, M. (2007). Facing down four decades of standardized educational reform. Buffalo, NY: GSE Publications/SUNY Press.

Giles, C., Johnson, L., Brooks, S., & Jacobson, S. (2005). Building bridges, building community: Transformational leadership in a challenging urban context. *Journal of School Leadership, 15,* 519–545.

Gronn, P. (2000). Distributed properties: A new architecture for leadership. *Education Management and Administration, 28*(3), 317–338.

Gronn, P. (2002). Distributed Leadership. In K. Leithwood & P. Hallinger (Eds.), *Second International Handbook of Educational Leadership and Administration: Part 2* (pp. 613–696). Dordrecht, Great Britain: Kluwer Academic Publishers.

Hallinger, P. (1999). School leadership development: State of the art at the turn of the century. *Orbit, 30*(1), 46–48.

Hallinger, P. (2003). Leading educational change: Reflections on the practice of instructional and transformational leadership. *Cambridge Journal of Education, 33*(3), 329–351.

Hallinger, P. & Heck, R. (1996). Reassessing the principal's role in school effectiveness: A review of empirical work. *Educational Administration Quarterly, 32*(1), 5–44.

Hallinger, P. & Heck, R. (1998). Exploring the principal's contribution to school effectiveness: 1980–1995. *School Effectiveness and School Improvement, 92*(2), 157–191.

Hallinger, P. & Murphy, J. (1985). Assessing the instructional management behavior of principals. *Elementary School Journal, 86*(2), 217–247.

Hargreaves, A. (1994). *Changing teachers, changing times: Teachers' work and culture in the postmodern age.* New York, NY: Teachers College Press.

Harris, A. (2005). Leading or misleading? Distributed leadership and school improvement. *Curriculum Studies, 37*(3), 255–265.

Hawley, W. D. (1988). Missing pieces of the educational reform agenda: Or, why the first and second waves may miss the boat. *Educational Administration Quarterly, 24*(4), 416–437.

Hawkins, J. N. (2000). Centralization, decentralization, recentralization: Educational reform in China. *Journal of Educational Administration, 38*(5), 442–454.

Heller, M. F. & Firestone, W. A. (1995). Who's in charge here? Sources of leadership for change in eight schools. *The Elementary School Journal, 96*(1), 65–86.

Hess, G. A., Jr. (1991). *School restructuring, Chicago style.* Thousand Oaks, CA: Corwin Press.

Hess, J. K., Jr. (1999). Understanding achievement (and other) changes under Chicago school reform. *Educational Evaluation and Policy Analysis, 21*(1), 67–83.

Hopkins, D., West, M., & Beresford, J. (1998). Creating the conditions for classroom and teacher development. *Teachers and Teaching: Theory and Practice, 4*(1), 115–141.

Huber, S. G. (2004). School leadership and leadership development: Adjusting leadership theories and development programs to values and the core purpose of school. *Journal of Educational Administration, 46*(6), 669–684.

Hulme, G. (2006). Distributed leadership: An evolving view of school leadership. *Professional Association of Georgia Educations, 9*(1), 1–4.

Irons, E. J. & Harris, S. (2007). *The challenges of No Child Left Behind.* New York: Rowman & Littlefield Education.

Jacobson, S. & Bezzina, C. (2008). The effects of leadership on student academic/affective achievement. In G. Crow, J. Lumby & P. Pashiardis (Eds.), *International handbook on the preparation and development of school leaders* (pp. 80–102). Thousand Oaks, CA: Sage Publications.

Lambert, L. (1998). *Building leadership capacity in schools.* Alexandria, VA: Association for Supervision and Curriculum Development.

Leithwood, K. (2003, April). *What do we already know about successful school leadership?* Paper presented at the annual conference of the American Educational Research Association, Chicago.

Leithwood, K. A. & Riehl, C. (2005). What do we already know about educational leadership? In W. A. Firestone & C. Riehl (Eds.). *A new agenda for research in educational leadership* (pp. 12–27). New York: Teachers College Press.

Levine, D. U. & Lezotte, L. W. (1990). Unusually effective schools: A review and analysis of research and practice. Madison, WI: Center for Effective Schools Research and Development.

Liu, M. (2009). Education management and performance after rural education finance reform—evidence from Western China. *International Journal of Educational Development,* doi:10.1016/j.ijedudev.2009.04.013

Liu, X. H. (2002). China's Educational Needs. Retrieved from http://icfdn.org/aboutus/publications/China%20Education%20Needs.doc

Marks, M. & Printy, S. (2003). Principal leadership and school performance: An integration of transformational and instructional leadership. *Educational Administration Quarterly, 39*(3), 370–397.

Metz, M. H. (1988). Some missing elements in the educational reform movement. *Educational Administration Quarterly, 24*(4), 446–460.

Muijs, D. & Harris, A. (2002). Assistant and deputy heads: Key leadership issues and challenges. *Management in Education, 17*(1), 6–8.

No Child Left Behind Act (NCLB) of 2001, 20 U.S.C. Sec. 6301 (2002).

Office of Educational Research and Improvement. (1998). *A national study of charter schools, 1998.* Washington, DC: U.S. Department of Education.

Ogawa, R. T. & Bossert, S. T. (1995). Leadership as an organizational quality. *Educational Administration Quarterly, 31*(2), 224–243.

Razik, T. & Swanson, A. (2001). *Fundamental concepts of educational leadership* (2nd ed.). Upper Saddle River, NJ: Merrill Prentice Hall.

Sloan, K. (2007). *Holding schools accountable.* Lanham, MD: R&L Education.

Simth, W., & Andrews, R. (1989). *Instructional leadership: How principals make a difference.* Alexandria, VA: Association for Supervision and Curriculum Development.

Spillane, J. P. (2005). Distributed Leadership. *The Educational Forum, 69*(2), 143–150.

Spillane, J. P. (2006). *Distributed Leadership.* San Francisco: Jossey-Bass.

Spradley, J. P. (1980). *Participant observation.* Austin, TX: Holt, Rinehart and Winston.

Stoll, L. & Fink, D. (1995). *Changing out schools.* Philadelphia, PA: Open University Press.

Tsang, M. (2001). *Intergovernmental grants and the financing of compulsory education in China.* New York, NY: Teachers College Press.

U.S. Department of Education. (2009). The American Recovery and Reinvestment Act of 2009. Retrieved January 21, 2011, from http://www.ed.gov/

Youngs, H. (2007). Have the "presence" and courage to see beyond the familiar: Challenging our habitual assumptions of school leadership. Paper presented at 2007 ACEL & ASCD International Conference, Sydney, Australia.

Zhao, L. T. (2009). Between local community and central state: Financing basic education in China. *International Journal of Educational Development, 29*(4), 366–373.

CHAPTER 6

SOCIAL JUSTICE AND MULTICULTURAL LEADERSHIP IN TAIWAN

Empowering New Immigrants

Yu-Min Chien and Hsiang-I Chiu

INTRODUCTION

Multicultural education acknowledges differences between ethnicities and cultures. It seeks to promote educational equity, allowing students of different genders, socioeconomic classes, and ethnicities to receive equal education (Banks, 1993; J. A Banks & C. A. M. Banks, 2005; Bennet, 1995; Chen, 2000; Green, 1998; Sleeter, 1996; P. L. Tiedt & I. M. Tiedt, 1990). The objective of multicultural education is to emphasize diversity, differences, and social action (Liu & Chen, 2000). Specific goals include developing equal educational opportunities, creating a fair and just society, understanding and supporting diversity, fostering cultural self-identification, respecting differences, developing inter-group relations to enhance societal harmony, and empowering social action (Banks, 1994; J. A. Banks & C. A. M. Banks, 2005; Chiang, 1997; Gay, 1995; Gollnick, 1980; C. J. Lin, 1997; Sleeter &

Social Justice Leadership for a Global World, pages 95–113
Copyright © 2012 by Information Age Publishing
All rights of reproduction in any form reserved.

Grant, 1994; Tan, Liu, & Yu, 2003). Due to the growing population of students from various cultures and ethnic backgrounds (Garrett & Morgan, 2002; Walker & Dimmock, 2005) and an influx of new immigrants (Lee, 2006; H. H. Huang, 2005), schools in Taiwan have begun to pay greater attention to multicultural education (J. C, Chang, 2000; Chiu & Chien, 2007; Liu, 2005).

The term "new immigrants" refers here to women from Southeast Asian countries and mainland China. These new immigrants are in transnational marriages with Taiwanese men, who mostly work as fishermen, farmers, and blue-collar workers. New immigrants, therefore, can constitute a population characterized by "triple jeopardy" (H. Y. Chen, 2006; Silverstein, 2006), in terms of gender, ethnicity, and socioeconomic class. Since the 1990s, the population of new immigrants and their children in Taiwan has swelled to 440,000 (Ministry of the Interior, 2011). This population has grown by 50 % in the past eight years (Ministry of Education, 2011). The proportion of new immigrant births out of all births spiked from 5.1% to 13.37%, and then it has fallen to 8.7% in the past twelve years. While the proportion of new immigrant births has gone up to 4.45% (rising from 13,904 to 14, 523), the total number of new births for Taiwanese dropped by 40.84% (falling from 257,546 to 152,363). As the total number of births in Taiwan has fallen significantly (38.52%), the birth rate of the new immigrant population has increased. As a result, Taiwanese society has become more diverse and the student population more varied. Therefore, the need for the inclusion of multicultural perspectives into educational services provided for new immigrants has become an important emerging issue in Taiwan.

Central and local government agencies, such as the Ministry of Interior, Ministry of Education, Council of Labor Affairs, Department of Health, Awakening Foundation (2003) and other groups in the private sector have striven to provide services for new immigrants who face challenges in adapting to personal, familial, and social circumstances—including language barriers, difficulties adapting to Taiwanese culture, unstable arranged marriages, difficulty connecting with children and schools, lower status in their homes, being forced to work outside the home due to economics, and weak social support networks (H. H. Huang, 2005; M. Y. Huang, 2006; Lee, 2006).

These population changes and the circumstance faced by new immigrants have led to an increased interest in multicultural education in Taiwan as a way to support new immigrants. Research from the U.S., Canada, and Taiwan has shown that principals play a pivotal role in the process of educational reform (e.g., Fullan & Clark, 1994; Leithwood, Jantzi, & Stainbach, 1999; M. D. Lin, 2003; Peterson, 1989; Riehl, 2000; Sergiovanni, 1992). In the pursuit of justice in educational reform, the principals' leadership is critical to the success (e.g., Chien, 2001; Chien & Capper, 2001; Capper, Theoharis, & Keyes, 1998; Deering, 1996; Fullan & Clark, 1994;

Leithwood, Jantzi, & Steinbach, 1999; Kugelmass, 2003; Riehl, 2000; Sergiovanni, 1992). Specifically, school principals must play a proactive role in preparing to welcome students from various cultural backgrounds (Boothe, 2000; Chiu & Chien, 2007; Garrett & Morgan, 2002), cultivate an inclusive environment (Adalbjarnardottir & Runarsdottir, 2006; Chiu & Chien, 2007; Walker & Dimmock, 2005), and be considerate of both learning efficacy and fairness (Chien, 2001; Chien & Capper, 2001).

In recent years, a considerable amount of research in multicultural education related to issues of social justice has been conducted in Taiwan. This research, however, has tended to emphasize teaching-related concepts, such as instruction, curriculum and teaching materials, and instructional beliefs and implementation. Few empirical studies that have been conducted are related to the leadership of principals in multicultural education. Of these, J. S. Chen (2004) and L. Y. Chen (2000) constructed indicators on the perception of multicultural education of elementary and middle school principals, while Chiu and Chien (2007) examined the development of new immigrant volunteer training courses and their effectiveness. These studies, however, did not examine in depth the principals' leadership in implementing multicultural education, nor did they explore the implementation process. This study seeks to fill this void by learning from an exemplary principal who utilizes multicultural leadership to support new immigrants.

CONCEPTUAL FRAMEWORK

This study was employed within the framework of the leader professional awareness model, which was used to understand leaders' pedagogical visions and reflections on their roles, while promoting students' social, emotional, ethical, and civic growth (Adalbjarnardottir, 1994; Adalbjarnardottir, 2010; Adalbjarnardottir & Runarsdottir, 2006; Adalbjarnardottir & Selman, 1997; Runarsdottir & Adalbjarnardottir, 2000). This model was originally developed to explore the work that teachers considered personally and professionally meaningful (Adalbjarnardottir, 1994). Thereafter, it was also applied to leaders' professional awareness as they support effective teaching that fosters students' wellbeing and intercultural education (Adalbjarnardottir & Runarsdottir, 2006). According to Adalbjarnardottir and Runarsdottir, motivation/life history, aims, and strategies/styles are integrated into a leader's pedagogical vision. Thus, leaders' pedagogical visions are constructed and reconstructed through their personal life histories and professional experience, which form their motivation and drive their leadership. These practices can shape leaders' experience personally and professionally. Such a process is regarded as a cycle of learning. Thus, our study utilized this model to interpret an elementary school principal's pedagogical vision, and how it was interwoven with his personal experience, as well as his multicultural beliefs and implementation.

METHODOLOGY

This study employed an exemplary case study method (Stake, 1995) in order to learn from a leader who was considered highly effective in supporting inclusive new immigrant education. To that end, we chose Principal Huang at "the Center for New Immigrant Learning" at Jong Jen Elementary School.[1] Jong Jen, located in Tao-Yuan County, is a large elementary school with about 2400 students, including nearly 38% of disadvantaged groups that comprise 17% of children of the new immigrants, 13% of children from single parent and grandparents' families, 6% of aboriginal students, and 1.4% of low-income students. The school had been selected in 2004 by the Ministry of Education of Taiwan as a site to establish the Center for New Immigrant Learning in the northern region of Taiwan due to its high number of new immigrants in the county and successful services provided to new immigrants. Under the leadership of Huang and collaboration among staff, the center received the top award of excellence for four consecutive years, making the center a benchmark for other schools and institutions in Taiwan.

This study was conducted from January 2006 to January 2009. The participants of this study comprised 14 educators and volunteers, involving Huang, four school administrators, two teachers, three administrative members of the center, and four volunteers of the new immigrants. Data collection included in-depth interviews, participatory observation, document analysis, and reflective research journals. We utilized Glaser and Strauss's (1967) open coding, axial coding, and selective coding to analyze the data collected. Similarly, we used the six steps of the constant comparison method (Glaser, 1978) to further interpret the data. Finally, triangulation, feedback, and member check were used to ensure the trustworthiness of this study.

FINDINGS

Our study was aimed at gaining a better understanding of how Huang engaged as a multicultural leader for social justice. In particular, we wanted to learn how he explored his own personal histories, examined his own prejudices and beliefs, supported new immigrants, and how he viewed his role as a multicultural leader. At the outset, Huang proactively engaged the center's visions and goals. Seeking input from the administrative team and new immigrants through various meetings, he put forth the slogan "we are family" for a vision and set the goal as "respecting cultural diversity and pursuing fairness and justice" (Document, September 24, 2008). As we sought to understand Huang's transformation as a leader, three primary themes emerged: 1) developing a transformative vision for new immigrant education, 2) putting new immigrant educational leadership into practice, and 3) outcomes and challenges in leading new immigrant education. In the next sections we will provide an overview of the themes.

Developing a Transformative Vision for New Immigrant Education

Huang had not received formal training in multicultural education prior to the establishment of the center. When the center was first established, Huang traveled to Australia with Ministry of Education officials to observe new immigrant education. Upon his return, Huang's sense of mission led him to raise expectations for himself as a leader in new immigrant education for Taiwan. Huang stated:

> The formation of my ideas regarding leadership in multicultural education involved continual modification and accumulation through personal experience. The more I came to know and understand new immigrants, the more keenly I felt my own inadequacies; the more I saw the needs of new immigrants, the more I became aware of my own responsibility.

Huang's concept of multicultural leadership was deeply influenced by his direct interactions with new immigrants and observation of new immigrant education in Australia. Before the establishment of the center, Huang's perceptions toward new immigrants were characterized by negative impressions primarily derived from newspapers, magazines, and other media. His perception of new immigrants transformed in three ways; he reinterpreted his view of multicultural education from antagonism to inclusion, saw new immigrants for their cultural potential rather than economic challenges, and started to value diversity.

Huang's perceptions of new immigrant education were originally derived from the province affiliation problem. Due to the "228 Incident,"[2] Taiwanese and mainland Chinese developed an antagonistic "province affiliation complex" in Taiwan. Though with the passage of time, historical wounds healed, and Taiwanese and mainlanders learned to coexist peacefully, ethnic identity issues sometimes are manipulated by politicians nowadays. Huang reinterpreted multicultural education after the number of new immigrants increased. Huang noted,

> The influx of new immigrants was creating a multicultural society in Taiwan. . . . I think that our society was capable of accepting diversity and would

not exclude cultures that differed from ours. Even if some Taiwanese could not accept difference, people still could get to know them through the growth of the new immigrants.

When Huang encountered new immigrants at the center, he discovered that the primary reason that new immigrants are considered disadvantaged was that they had married into disadvantaged families. In reality, however, when they participated in the classes and activities of the center, Huang found they were highly engaged learners. Though most new immigrants were from Southeast Asian countries, Huang believed that, "in looking beyond per capita income, these countries actually had abundant cultural assets, including language, food, customs, and historical monuments."

Initially Huang believed that the best way to help new immigrants was to consider how to educate or train them to adapt to the lifestyle and culture of Taiwan. However, as he grew to understand the value of immigrant culture, he recognized that multicultural education should not entail assimilating new immigrants into Taiwanese culture. As one administrator of the center stated:

> We used to think that she [the new immigrant] should learn Mandarin. We, however, do not think of the idea of appreciating the beauty of his language and culture. Why don't we learn [her native language]?

Huang's leadership supported the idea that it was important to empower immigrants, enabling them to participate and learn so they would feel a sense of belonging, thereby contributing to their communities, schools, and society.

Huang believed that after new immigrants arrive in Taiwan, Taiwanese people clearly see cultural differences. Huang's vision articulated these differences as beautiful: "If only one species were planted in a habitat pool, then the habitat pool would not be so pretty." Therefore, Huang suggested that new immigrants are not necessarily disadvantaged, but they can enrich multicultural education in Taiwan.

Huang also saw the need to encourage immigrants to participate. As the director of pupil services noted, "some new immigrants were married to individuals with low levels of education or socioeconomic background." Some are generally regarded as brides engaged in a "mercenary marriage," which, together with the language barrier and hostile environment, can cause them not to participate in school and community. As Huang noted:

> They experienced a gradual freezing [because] what they were capable of had been restrained. Thus, all they had left in their lives were the tasks of raising children, cooking three meals a day, and washing clothes. Their lives are very hard and depressing.

Huang hoped to provide diverse opportunities for new immigrants to allow them to demonstrate their abilities, and resolve the helpless feeling of "gradual freezing" so they could participate in the center.

Huang's transformative vision entailed not only helping new immigrants learn to read and adapt to life in Taiwan, but also to assist them in finding greater happiness and meaning in life, so that they would feel the importance and value of existence, and pursue education with more enthusiasm. He said:

> It is the most important thing that she is happy and has a meaningful life. It comes to second to taking care of children and to helping others. Being an independent person, full of laughs in her life is the most important meaning.

Putting New Immigrant Educational Leadership into Practice

Huang was tireless in his pursuit of new immigrant education. His transformed beliefs encouraged him to take leadership toward a number of practices and strategies to support the success of new immigrants, both students and their families. Based on our analysis, seven leadership strategies emerged to support immigrant education, including establishing a comprehensive framework, offering diverse courses, encouraging volunteering, creating opportunities to outside of school, using a word-of-mouth network, developing various resources, and creating a sense of *houtoucuo*.[3] These strategies will be explained in greater detail below.

The center was supported by the county governor and guided by the Department of Education officials; in addition, school administrators and new immigrant volunteers actively participated in the center, forming a comprehensive organizational structure. At one point when the center was short-staffed, the county government allocated 330,000 U.S. dollars to the center to hire two contractual employees.

Huang emphasized that the development of classes at the center should consider the needs of new immigrants. In addition to basic literacy and lifestyle adaptation classes, the center also introduced Mandarin, Taiwanese and Hakka language courses to help new immigrants understand domestic languages and cultures; concurrently, the center also offered Vietnamese language classes for the family members of new immigrants, to facilitate communication between new Vietnamese immigrants and their Taiwanese family members. Other classes introduced by the center included parenting education and secondary skill training in accordance with the diverse capabilities and interests of new immigrants.

The new immigrant volunteer service is a distinctive aspect of the center, and is an innovation in multicultural education in Taiwan. Huang actively trained new immigrants as volunteers, seeking out at least one volunteer from each country to ensure that new immigrants from each country could be well served. Huang also provided opportunities for volunteers to be lecturers, cultural tour guides, and to aid in cultural exchange, communication, consultation, and translation work. The director of pupil service expressed that it was not difficult to recruit volunteers; it was more difficult to help volunteers feel a sense of accomplishment and consequently empower their intrinsic motivation.

Huang encouraged new immigrants to move beyond the center, in addition to providing their services at Jong Jen Elementary School and its Community Center. For example, Fang-fang (pseudonym) was selected as the female lead for a television drama "Nyonya's Taste of Life," winning the award for Best Leading Actress in 2007 in her first foray into acting.[4] In addition, the center also assisted Shuang-shuang (pseudonym) in creating an internet blog and selling Cambodian pastries to resolve her family's plight.[5] As a result, new immigrant volunteers gained confidence and recognition from their family members, reversing stereotypes and biases against new immigrants. Thus, Huang brought new immigrant volunteers with him to join his lectures or interviews, and arranged them to share their life stories, helping the public better understand the new immigrants and their cultures.

Activities offered by the center included four major areas. First, courses related to society adaptation emphasized personal growth and development, becoming the distinct features of the center. These courses included literacy, lifestyle adaptation, computer, and driving courses. Huang stated, "The first time you see one of them weeping with joy at receiving a driver's license, you feel moved and satisfied." Second, the center provided family activities, helping new immigrants interact with their family members through reading storybooks to children and going on a trip. Third, the center offered training related to technical education aimed at helping new immigrants receive various certifications, such as Chinese Chef and beautician, in order to gain employment to resolve financial difficulties. Fourth, the most common activities of the center were multicultural exchange events. The center hosted roughly 100 multicultural events every year, including lectures, heritage exchanges, dances, and singing. A word-of-mouth network of successful implementation of multicultural education was thus established.

Huang actively sought social resources to complement the funding provided by the county government. For instance, they held an event with the Center for Space and Remote Sensing at National Central University, whereby new immigrants could see their homelands through a telescope. When new immigrants saw their homelands—and even their old rooftops—they were moved to tears. One administrative staff stated:

> Like the Taiwanese language [course] we have now, he [Huang] fought for
> it...Others like our Vietnamese language course, Space Camp for parent-
> child learning of new immigrants, the Summer Camp which is just ended,
> and many others, like offering scholarship for the new immigrant' children to
> visit their native countries...He always actively seeks resources for organizing
> activities as long as new immigrants can participate in.

Through the promotion of multicultural education, the public could better understand new immigrants and their cultures and would not stereotype them.

Finally, Huang hoped that the center could provide new immigrants with
a sense of *houtoucuo*, meaning an environment that made new immigrants
feel warmth and comfort as if they were in their homes. As a result, the
center provided holistic care for new immigrants. In addition to providing
services for learning and lifestyle adaptation, Huang was also concerned
with the marriages, careers, and parenting of new immigrants. One administrative staff compared Huang's caring for new immigrants to "a small diamond glittering on the roadside." He emphasized that even the smallest
care is precious like a diamond.

Outcomes and Challenges in Leading New Immigrant Education

Under the proactive leadership of Huang, gains were made in the three
aspects of new immigrant volunteers, new immigrants in Jong Jen community, and new immigrants' education at a national level. As noted earlier,
new immigrant volunteers benefited greatly from their participation in the
center's activities. They felt a sense of belonging and were accepted by their
families. New immigrants treated each other like family members. Volunteers addressed each other as sisters, encouraging and caring for each other. Li, the head of the volunteers, suggested that "the volunteers only came
together because of the center. Because of their care and love for each
other, the volunteers became a family regardless of nationality (research
journal, September 9, 2008)." This feeling inspired Li to write the song,
"We Are Family," the first song written by a new immigrant in Taiwan.[6]

Most of the family members supported the new immigrants to be volunteers and encouraged them to participate in activities. When a small
number of family members of new immigrant volunteers became skepti-
cal,[7] center administrators would invite family members to participate in
the activities, or recorded activities for them to take home, thus soothing
the worries of family members by helping them understand the services
involved. For example, Yi served as a lecturer during Thai Culture Month.
Her husband initially thought she was joking, only to find that she was ac-

tually discussing Thai customs and culture when he visited the center. Yi's husband and son consequently felt very proud of her.

The center held a multicultural month every year, in which volunteers from each country would break ethnic barriers by learning and introducing customs from other cultures. For example, volunteers of different ethnicities all acted as guides for Vietnamese Culture Month. In addition, volunteers interacted regardless of nationality to learn about one another's food, dances, and songs. One administrator of the center said: "They [the new immigrants] broke ethnic barriers, shared and learned with each other, making the center a type of 'cultural salad.'" Though individuals of different ethnicities participated in activities together, they showed mutual respect and appreciation.

In addition to learning how to read and make lifestyle adaptations, the new immigrant volunteers also proactively participated in activities outside of their families, and gained recognition in the process of serving. Volunteers displayed abundant self-confidence when they introduced their countries and cultures to teachers, students, public, and participating agencies. Volunteers also traveled to other schools and cities to provide lectures and share their own learning experiences, in this way rebuilding their own self-confidence. Each new immigrant had different talents; they were able to showcase their abilities to the public through voluntary services, thereby increasing the affirmation and acceptance of family members and the public. New immigrants were no longer viewed as people who made trouble for the family, caused problems for the school, and became burdens of the society. Instead, they were considered in a positive light, and were viewed as a significant human resource for Taiwan.

Through mutual observation and learning, new immigrant volunteers were able to grasp the essentials of the food, song, dance, and culture of other Southeast Asian countries, allowing them to act as multicultural ambassadors. They established supportive social networks among themselves through inter-cultural exchange and mutual learning.

The establishment of the center in the Jong Jen community was also highly beneficial for parents of school-age children and new immigrants in the community. First, the center provided free consultative services, helping to relieve homesickness through technical support. Huang said:

> The Skype phone, you know. We have two. The PChome Online Inc. donated two telephones to us, offering 10 minutes free phone call services to their home towns for the new immigrants. Through taking courses and having free phone calls, they are encouraged to come to the center under the condition of their financial disadvantage. Therefore, it is another incentive for [them to come to] our center.

Second, the center became the *houtoucuo* of the new immigrants, who were able to find support and comfort at the center. When they were victimized at home and were unable to find support in their families, they sought comfort at the center. One volunteer of the new immigrant said that "Principal Huang is very kind to us and cares about us a lot." Third, the diverse range of courses offered by the center provided new immigrants with many opportunities for growth. For example, Taiwanese language courses allowed the immigrants to engage in casual conversations with their neighbors in daily life; participating in parent-child conferences improved their parenting abilities; and family outings improved family relations and home atmospheres.

The establishment of the center constituted a milestone for the development of new immigrant education in Taiwan and attracted public attention to new immigrant education. Additionally, the center proactively integrated social resources to develop new immigrant education, helping new immigrants resolve their personal and family issues; the center topped the rankings in evaluations of new immigrant education. Jong Jen Elementary School became a benchmark elementary school in the drive for new immigrant education. Personnel or agencies from other cities and counties that had established new immigrant education programs or planned to provide services to new immigrants were frequent visitors. Finally, the center established a high degree of recognition and became the focus for promoting cultural exchange in Taiwan.

Although Huang achieved significant accomplishments during his leadership of the center, he also faced several challenges. In terms of leadership, Huang was burdened with the expenditure of considerable time, the playing of multiple roles, and the opposing voices from some teachers for dividing limited resources between the school and the center. In terms of administration, Huang was forced to address the challenges of restriction on the use of funds, being understaffed, difficulties in collecting cultural artifacts from Southeast Asia, and inflexibility in expenses written off. In terms of implementation, Huang had to deal with insufficient care-givers and funding related to childcare along with the courses and programs, the role of acting as a bridge to communicate between new immigrants, difficulties in constantly maintaining the visibility of the center, and lower than expected influence on curriculum and instruction related to multicultural education at Jong Jen Elementary School.

DISCUSSION

We constructed a model of Huang's multicultural leadership based on Adalbjarnardottir and Runarsdottir's (2006) model of "leader's professional awareness." The model of multicultural leadership comprises four dimensions, including motivation, belief, practice, and outcomes that form an interactive and circular process. This study found that though Huang was not formally trained in multicultural education, he was able to perform the role of a multicultural social justice leader. This result is consistent with Arredondo and Perez's (2003) conclusion, that if a principal maintains concern and passion, and persists in becoming an advocate for multicultural education, he/she is able to successfully perform multicultural education.

Huang's earlier concepts or perceptions of multicultural education originated mostly from the media, newspapers, and magazines' negative portrayals. After his travel to Australia and interacting with new immigrants, he changed his thinking and saw their strengths and value and often reflected upon the stereotypes and biases of mainstream society. This finding echoes social contact theory in that contact across ethnic groups may facilitate the understanding, sensitivity, and accommodation of various cultures (Lopez, 2004; Mahiev & Clycq, 2007). Furthermore, Liu (2005) stated that what is urgently required for multicultural education is not the promotion of culture and self-identification of disadvantaged groups, but confronting the entrenched ideology of assumptions of cultural superiority. For instance, "inability to see" and "unwillingness to see" (Liu, 2005, p. 34) are problems that fall under this category. The inability to see is due to limitations in life experience, while the unwillingness to see is often the unwillingness to relinquish power.

Huang's emphasis that "differences are beautiful" is consistent with the views of Adalbjarnardottir and Runarsdottir (2006) and H. T. Chang (2005), in that "difference" is the theoretical basis for multicultural education, and that schools should assist students in respecting common social values and various ways of life." As Liu (2005) further explains, though multicultural education can assist individuals in perceiving the differences and oppression that are present in education, simply embracing and appreciating differences is insufficient. Multicultural education should become a force of action in rebuilding society. This view confirms Huang's efforts at eradicating the myth of new immigrants as a disadvantaged group, and his strategy of empowering new immigrants.

Huang also constantly reflected on his practice and readjusted his beliefs and strategies. These practices are consistent with J. S. Chen's (2004) recommendations that self-reflection and critical thinking are necessary during the process of promoting multicultural education. In addition, Huang established Vietnamese language courses, encouraging new immigrants and their Taiwanese family members to engage in two-way communication. This is consistent with Wen (2010), who indicated that learning one's native language not only has the potential to increase self-identification of new immigrants, but also furthers the understanding of Southeast Asian languages, cultures, and customs. Furthermore, Huang actively provided various cultural and artistic performance opportunities for new immigrants, thereby facilitating cooperation and discussion among new immigrants to innovate ways of performance. This not only increased the self-affirmation of new immigrants, but also highlighted their unique abilities. These results echo the research by Arredondo and Perez (2003) that principals must be able to observe and uncover personal strengths, provide services to meet individuals' needs, and support professional growth. Further, the support of family members was the key to effective new immigrant education, which echoes Wu's (2006) findings. Lastly, the center's courses, free consulting services, and Skype phone services provided new immigrants with opportunities for self-growth and education. This result is in accordance with the research of L. Y. Chen (2000), who indicated that school education and community are interconnected. Therefore, school and community resources should be combined to better serve new immigrants.

After establishing the Center for New Immigrant Learning, Huang began the journey of exploring the reciprocal and mutually influencing relationships among motivations, beliefs, practices, and outcomes of multicultural leadership (see Figure 6.1). The multicultural leadership model is comprised of the following five characteristics that reflect Huang's journey. First, the model is developmental; Huang does not have a static view of multicultural leadership. Not only does he actively adjust his lens in viewing

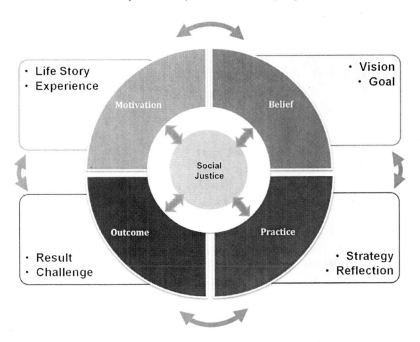

Figure 6.1 The model of a principal's multicultural leadership.

new immigrants with a positive light, he also develops new beliefs on new immigrant education, from appreciating the beauty of differences, reengaging the mindset of helplessness of those who are "gradually freezing," and assisting new immigrants to find meaning in life. Second, the model emphasizes learning and reflection. The multicultural leadership model is developed through constant learning and reflection, in the process of implementation, the passing of time, the changes accumulated from experience and the environment. Huang learns from his interactions with new immigrants, and also learns through self-reflection. As a result, Huang is leading by learning, and learning by leading. Third, the model is a dynamic process. Each dimension evolves over time through interaction with the other three dimensions. For instance, Huang's belief is not static, but evolves in a dynamic process. Through the guidance of personal vision and goals, he developed new beliefs concerning multicultural education and leadership. Fourth, the model is a circular process in two directions with mutual influence of motivation, belief, practice, and outcome in clockwise and counter-clockwise directions. Likewise, the four dimensions also mutually interacted among each other. For example, Huang's life history and experience provide the basis for his leadership strategy; simultaneously, Huang's strategy decisions also become part of his experiences, and his beliefs also influence practice. Therefore, the results and challenges faced by the principal during implementation also facilitate the adjustment of his own beliefs toward new immigration education. Fifth, social justice is the core of the model. The ultimate goal for a multicultural leader is to create an inclusive, fair, and just environment conducive to empowering new immigrants. Huang showed his sincere care for new immigrants and advocated for the best interest of them. He also devoted his time and energy to promote multicultural education at school, community, and national levels.

IMPLICATIONS

Social justice has always been an essential part of multicultural education. In the case of Huang, we learned that multicultural leadership was derived from sincere caring, inclusion, respect, passion, and persistence, in particular in support of new immigrants in Taiwan. Strategies used by multicultural leaders include leading through an inclusive vision, emphasizing future-oriented thinking, being a role model in language and behavior, empowering new immigrants to regain confidence, taking a public stance on issues related to new immigrants, learning through reflective practices, devoting time and energy to leadership, and being committed to social justice. Our study revealed that Huang has adopted these values, beliefs, and practices. We have learned that with the increasing number of new immigrants in

Taiwan, the need to prepare school leaders with multicultural competence is critical. Second, prospective school principals should have the opportunity to explore their personal histories, to examine their own prejudices or stereotypes toward new immigrants, and to construct their worldviews toward multicultural leadership reflectively. Third, school principals should engage in reciprocal learning between themselves and new immigrants. In doing so, school principals and their students will learn from each other, grow together, and become leaders of social justice.

NOTES

1. Jong Jen Elementary School was first established in 1960 to accommodate military dependents, who used to be stationed in the northern Thailand and Yunnan regions of anti-Communist National Salvation Army. Over the past ten years, the community was influx of new immigrants and then developed into a diverse ethnic community.
2. The "228 Incident" refers to an incident where, following the end of World War II, troops under the command of Chiang Kai-shek landed in Taiwan and subsequently became involved in armed conflict and bloodshed against civilians on February 28, 1947. The conflict became a political incident and led to ethnic conflict between Taiwanese and mainlanders, producing the historical tragedy known as the "228 Incident."
3. "Houtoucuo" refers to the home where a woman lives before getting married. Huang hopes to provide the new immigrants with a place where they can express their feelings freely and receive assistance and support.
4. The director was looking for a new immigrant female to play the leading role of his new television drama, "Nyonya's Taste of Life." Huang introduced several new immigrant volunteers to audition for the drama. Fang-fang was selected and her first performance won her the Golden Bell Award for Best Leading Actress in 2007.
5. Shuang-shuang's husband became comatose due to an accident, putting her family at risk. Huang and administrators of the center helped her to sell pastries through an internet blog. In addition, whenever Huang attended events or meetings with other people, he brought the pastries along as a gift to help market her pastries, and ultimately the family's financial situation improved.
6. The lyrics to the song, "We Are Family" are as follows: "Ladies of Southeast Asia, you have come to Taiwan to be wives; beauties of Southeast Asia, you have come to Taiwan to find better lives. No matter who you are, we are family! New immigrants are the center of our warm love—never forget, we are family."
7. Some husbands or mothers-in-law of new immigrants sometimes expressed their concerns of letting the new immigrants out of the house. They worried that their wives or daughters-in-law would meet friends who had bad influence on the new immigrants' thoughts and behaviors. Or even worse, they suspected the new immigrants of going out on dates, stealing money for their original families, and so on.

REFERENCES

Adalbjarnardottir, S. (1994). Understanding children and ourselves: Teachers' reflections on social development in the classroom. *Teaching and Teacher Education, 10,* 409–421. doi: 10.1016/0742-051X(94)90022-1

Adalbjarnardottir, S. (2010). Passion and purpose: Teacher professional development and student social growth. In T. Lovat, R. Toomey, & N. Clement (Eds.), *International research handbook on values education and student wellbeing* (pp. 737–764). New York: Springer.

Adalbjarnardottir, S. & Runarsdottir, E. M. (2006). A leader's experiences of intercultural education in an elementary school: Changes and challenges. *Theory into Practice, 45*(2), 177–186.

Adalbjarnardottir, S. & Selman, R. L. (1997). I feel I have received a new vision: An analysis of teachers' professional development as they work with students on interpersonal issues. *Teaching and Teacher Education, 13,* 409–428. doi: 10.1016/S0742-051X(96)00036-4

Arredondo, P. & Perez, P. (2003). Expanding multicultural competence through social justice leadership. *The Counseling Psychologist, 31,* 282–289.

Awakening Foundation. (2003). *Why are you calling me a "foreign bride?" I'm already so old, so stop calling me a "foreign bride!"* Retrieved from http://www.awakening.org.tw/chhtml/topics_dtl.asp?id=98&qtagword

Banks, J. A. (1993). Multicultural education: Characteristics and goals. In J. A. Banks & C. A. M. Banks (Eds.), *Multicultural education: issue and perspectives* (pp. 2–26). Boston, MA: Allyn & Bacon.

Banks, J. A. (1994). *An Introduction to Multicultural Education.* Boston, MA: Allyn & Bacon.

Banks, J. A. & Banks, C. A. M. (2005). *Multicultural Education: Issues and Perspective.* Hoboken, NJ: John Wiley & Sons, Inc.

Bennet, C. I. (1995). *Comprehensive multicultural education: Theory and practice.* Boston, MA: Allyn & Bacon.

Boothe, D. (2000). How to Support a multiethnic school community? *Principal Leadership, 1*(4), 81–82.

Capper, A. C., Theoharis, G. T., & Keyes, M. W. (1998, November). *The principal's role in inclusive schooling for students with disabilities, empowering and democratic schools, and restructuring schools: A comparative analysis.* Paper presented at the University Council for Educational Administration Annual Conference, St. Louis, MO.

Chang, H. T. (2005). Multicultural education and school management. *School Administration Bimonthly, 35,* 60–71.

Chang, J. C. (2000). *Multicultural education: Our lessons and others' experiences.* Taipei, Taiwan: SHTA Books.

Chen, H. Y. (2006). *New Resident Education Auxiliary Plan of Taipei County—An Initial Exploration of Issues Related to Education of New Taiwanese (23 March 2007).* Retrieved from http://share.tpc.edu.tw/neo/DocLib17/Forms/AllItems.aspx

Chen, J. S. (2004). *Perception and implementation of multicultural education by elementary school principals in Taipei City and Taipei County.* Unpublished master's thesis, National Taipei Teachers College, Taipei, Taiwan.

Chen, L. Y. (2000). *Cognition and schooling of multicultural education by elementary school principals in Hualien County.* Unpublished master's thesis, National Hualien Teachers College, Hualien, Taiwan.

Chen, M. R. (2000). *Beliefs and practices on multicultural curriculum.* Taipei, Taiwan: SHTA Books.

Chiang, H. L. (1997). *Multicultural education.* Taipei, Taiwan: SHTA Books.

Chien, Y. M. (2001, November). *Effective for whom: A study of two principals.* Paper presented at the Annual Conference of University Council for Educational Administration, Cincinnati, OH.

Chien, Y. M., & Capper, C. A. (2001, April). *Beyond inclusion.* Paper presented at the Annual Conference of American Educational Research Association, Seattle, WA.

Chiu, H. I. & Chien, Y. M. (2007, January). *An exploratory study of multicultural leadership: Building a learning community of immigrant brides.* Paper presented at Hawaii International Conference on Education, Oahu, HI.

Deering, P. D. (1996). An ethnographic study of norms of inclusion and cooperation in a multiethnic middle school. *The Urban Review, 28,* 21–39.

Department of Household Registration, Ministry of the Interior. (2011). *The statistics of native countries for newborn babies' mothers.* Retrieved from http://www.ris.gov.tw/version96/population_01_C_03.html

Department of Statistics, Ministry of Education. (2011). *The statistics of the elementary and secondary graders of foreign brides.* Retrieved from http://www.edu.tw/files/site_content/b0013/fomas.xls

Fullan, B. & Clark, P. (1994). Raising school effects while ignoring culture: Local conditions and the influence of classroom tools, rules, and pedagogy. *Review of Educational Research, 64,* 119–157.

Garrett, J. E. & Morgan, D. E. (2002). Celebrating diversity by education all students: Elementary teacher and principal collaboration. *Education, 123*(2), 268–275.

Gay, G. (1995). Curriculum theory and multicultural education. In J. A. M. Banks (Eds.), *Handbook of research on multicultural education* (pp. 25–43). New York: Macmillan.

Glaser, B. (1978). *Theoretical sensitivity: Advances in the methodology of grounded theory.* Mill Valley, CA: Sociology Press.

Glaser, B. & Strauss, A. L. (1967). *The discovery of grounded theory: Strategies for qualitative research.* Chicago, IL: Aldine.

Gollnick, D. M. (1980). Multicultural education. *Viewpoints in Teaching and Learning, 56,* 1–17.

Green, J. M. (1998). Educational multiculturalism, critical pluralism, and deep democracy. In C. Willett (Ed.), *Theorizing multiculturalism: A guide to the current debate* (pp. 422–448). Malden, MA: Blackwell Publishers, Inc.

Huang, H. H. (2005). The new immigrant families and education of their children. *New Horizon Bymonthly for Teachers in Taipei, 135,* 19-25.

Huang, M. Y. (2006). *Current state of basic education for new immigrants of elementary schools in Taoyuan County.* Unpublished Master's thesis, Taipei Municipal University of Education, Taipei, Taiwan.

Kugelmass, J. W. (2003). Inclusive leadership: Leadership for inclusion. *Full international practitioner enquiry report.* Nottingham: National College for School Leadership.

Lee, Y. (2006). An examination of moving toward learning and teaching regarding "others" and "empowerment" for new immigrant females. *Journal of Education Research, 141,* 25–36.

Leithwood, K., Jantzi, D., & Stainback, R. (1999). *Changing leadership for changing times.* Buckingham: Open University Press.

Lin, C. J. (1997). Multicultural education and educational reform. *Proceedings of The Theory and Practice of Multicultural Education Conference* (pp.24–32). Taipei, Taiwan: National Taiwan Normal University.

Lin, M. D. (2003). *Educational administration: Theory, research and implementation.* Taipei, Taiwan: McGraw-Hill.

Liu, M. H. (2005). What has multicultural education accomplished in Taiwan? *Taipei County Education, 51,* 30–36.

Liu, M. H & Chen, L. H. (2000). The theory and practice of the multicultural curriculum. *Journal of National Hualien Teachers College, 10,* 101–126.

Lopez, G. E. (2004). Interethnic contact, curriculum, and attitudes in the first year of college. *Journal of Social Issues, 60*(1), 75–94.

Mahieu, P. & Clycq, N. (2007). School leadership and equity: the case of Antwerp: A report on good practices in three primary schools. *School Leadership and Management, 27,* 35–49.

Peterson, K. (1989). *Secondary principals and instructional leadership: Complexities in a diverse role.* Madison, WI: National Center on Effective Secondary Schools.

Riehl, C. J. (2000). The principal's role in creating inclusive schools for diverse students: A review of normative, empirical, and critical literature on the practice of educational administration. *Review of Educational Research, 70,* 55–81.

Runarsdottir, E. M. & Adalbjarnardottir, S. (2000). Who wants to employ a bossy loudmouth? Teacher's pedagogical vision and strategies when promoting students' self-perception and social awareness. In A. Ross (Ed.), *Developing identity in Europe: Citizenship education and higher education* (pp. 461–467). London: CiCe.

Sergiovanni, T. J. (1992). Reflections on administrative theory and practice in schools. *Educational Administration Quarterly, 28*(3), 304–313.

Silverstein, L. B. (2006). Integrating feminism and multiculturalism: Scientific fact or science fiction. *Professional psychology: Research and Practice, 37*(1), 21–28.

Sleeter, C. E. (1996). *Multicultural education as social activism.* Albany, NY: SUNY Press.

Sleeter, C. E. & Grant, C. A. (1994). *Making choice for multicultural education: Five approach to race, class, and gender.* New York: Merrill.

Stake, R. E. (1995). *The art of case study method.* Thousand Oaks, CA: Sage Publications.

Tan, G. D., Liu, M. H., & Yu, M. H. (2003). *Multicultural Education.* Taipei, Taiwan: Jong Yu.

Tiedt, P. L. & Tiedt, I. M. (1990). *Multicultural teaching: A handbook of activities, information, and resources.* Boston, MA: Allyn & Bacon.

Walker, A. & Dimmock, C. (2005). Leading the multiethnic school: Research evidence on successful practice. *The Educational Forum, 69*, 291–304.

Wen, M. L. (2010). Reconstruction of subjectivity in ethical education in Taiwan: We can create the future. *Bimonthly Journal of Educational Resources and Research, 96*, 1–26.

Wu, C S. (2006). Beliefs and Practices of Teacher Education. *Journal of Educational Research and Development, 2*(1), 14–25.

CHAPTER 7

CONSIDERING INCOMPATIBILITY

Promoting Culturally Relevant Teaching and Learning in the United States and New Zealand

Jennifer J. Huber, Anne Hynds, Seena Skelton,
Amy M. Papacek, Taucia Gonzalez, and Lisa Lacy

INTRODUCTION

Culturally and linguistically diverse students are at heightened risk for identification in specific high-incidence categories such as intellectual disability, specific learning disability, and emotional disturbance (Donovan & Cross, 2002). Research demonstrates that there are far lower placement rates of culturally and linguistically diverse students in gifted programs; and overall achievement gaps persist between students of color and their white peers (Ford, 1998; Artiles, Harry, Reschly, & Chinn, 2002). Current research about the achievement of culturally and linguistically diverse (CLD) students,1 however, confirms that *all* students can and do achieve given the right learning conditions (Donovan & Cross, 2002; Gándara, 2000). Un-

Social Justice Leadership for a Global World, pages 115–131
Copyright © 2012 by Information Age Publishing
All rights of reproduction in any form reserved.

examined indicators of issues related to power and privilege, educators' lack of knowledge about culturally responsive instructional practices, and cultural mismatch between home and school expectations are three significant factors contributing to achievement gaps among student groups. This suggests that many schools are not addressing the educational needs of students from non-dominant backgrounds, such as those students considered as having ability differences, low socio-economic status, or culturally and linguistically diverse backgrounds as indicated by national, state and district achievement and discipline data (e.g., Apple, 1996).

Education, however, has the potential to be transformative (Freire, 1970). For this to happen, educational experiences need to be structured in ways that allow all members of the system to participate meaningfully and authentically so that all students achieve their full capacities and potential. Educators bear responsibility to promote equitable and socially just systems as they educate all students. Nonetheless, educational professionals may hold harmful narratives that are subconscious attitudes, beliefs, or dispositions (Visser, Bizer, & Krosnick, 2006) that create oppressive experiences for many students. Yet educators may be unaware of their influence; reflective awareness requires explicit mediation to uncover "beneath-the-surface" consciousness. This kind of deficit theorizing remains a persistent and damaging problem in schools across the world, with students from marginalized communities often viewed by educational professionals as lacking the necessary skills, abilities and dispositions to succeed (Shields, Bishop, & Mazawi, 2005; Gonzalez, Amanti, & Moll, 2005). Consequently, solutions to addressing achievement gaps are constructed in compensatory ways to address perceived student deficits, rather than investigating the cultural norms embedded within practice that privileges and protects dominant groups (Artiles & Kozleski, 2007). Teachers, as educational leaders in their classrooms, are in a unique position to facilitate transformative systems that free students from oppressive structures by incorporating culturally responsive teaching and learning practices; however, such transformation only happens when educators critically examine their own and others' assumptions about why certain students are less successful.

The purpose of this chapter is to examine how professional learning communities aimed at supporting Culturally Responsive Teaching and Learning[2] (CRTL) can negotiate schooling narratives that do not support CRTL. Specifically, two models are examined aimed at supporting CRTL in real-world contexts. The incompatibility of narratives in schools is used to indicate implications for measuring CRTL and to provide examples of ways to partner with schools implementing CRTL. Lessons learned about effective embedding of CRTL in schools with incompatible narratives are presented, including professional learning about identities, distributed leadership, school and cultural contexts, and classroom practices.

CONCEPTUAL FRAMEWORK

According to Gloria Ladson-Billings (1994), culturally responsive teaching, "... is an approach that empowers students intellectually, socially, emotionally, and politically by using cultural referents to impart knowledge, skills and attitudes" (p. 18). The use of cultural referents in teaching bridges and explains the mainstream culture, while valuing and recognizing the students' own cultures. Recognizing students' identities and the similarities and differences to teachers' identities in terms of their racial, ethnic, linguistic, and cultural backgrounds is important, but it is not enough to effectively teach an increasingly diverse student population. Becoming a culturally responsive teacher requires continuous learning that expands one's knowledge, skills, dispositions, and experiences in order to increase capacity to effectively teach culturally and linguistically diverse student populations (Banks, 1993). Culturally responsive teachers not only recognize, but even more importantly, respect and use students' identities to employ instructional strategies that are connected to students' lived experiences for the purpose of creating positive learning opportunities for all students (Lee, 2007). While there are many instructional strategies that can be considered culturally responsive, in this chapter we will focus on two foundational practices: a) using cultural referents and presenting multiple perspectives to honor and build on students' lived experience to bridge to new learning; and b) teaching multiple codes to help students learn to navigate various cultural contexts.

Incorporating culture in teaching and learning includes both teacher and student identities. These two identities, when brought together in meaningful ways, contribute to the building of a culturally responsive classroom. By embracing students' personal culture, the strengths each student brings to school are acknowledged, fostered, and built upon within the classroom (Cole, 1996). In doing so, student achievement is promoted and learning is enhanced. Creating and sustaining a culturally responsive learning environment begins with educators increasing their own cultural proficiency. Cultural proficiency means having thorough competence in understanding the effect culture has on teaching and learning and acting in ways that ensure educational equity and responsive instruction for all students, and specifically culturally and linguistically diverse groups of students (Rogoff, 2003). This level of proficiency is only derived from ongoing study, reflection, and focused discussion and practice. Being culturally responsive involves more than using a specific set of teaching practices; being culturally responsive means bringing culture to the foreground of educational decision-making (Artiles, 2003). Culturally responsive educators focus their discourse, attention, practice, and decisions toward the goal of increasing access, participation, engagement, and improving the learning and social outcomes of all students.

SITUATING OUR WORK

As educators with many years of experience, we can testify to the prevalence of mixed messages that proliferate many educational settings. Each of us can remember attending professional development or in-service meetings year after year that felt like a shiny new box without any connection to previous packages. However, this reality is seldom situated in research literature, and it is well documented that research often misses the practice context. Thus, we seek to connect and situate our work in real schools and situations. We use critical reflection (Freire, 1970; Freire & Macedo, 1987) to reflect on our experiences working with two programs (one in the U.S. and one in New Zealand) aimed at exploring culturally competent teaching and learning. Given that our goal is to consider the many diverse narratives experienced in schools, we engaged in critical reflection about the competing narratives lived in schools. In this section, we consider the narratives operating in each program site. The Veranda project is a collaborative, university-school partnership to implement a special education master's program in the United States, while the Te Kauhua is a collaborative action research project aimed an improving Maori student achievement in New Zealand. In the next two sections, we describe the specifics of each of the two programs.

Veranda (United States)

As Joy, Christalynn, and Sarah stood before their thesis committee unraveling their journeys of self-interrogation to understand their own identities and biases, they felt the enormity of the Veranda mission. Traditional teacher-learning programs in special education had curricula situated around technical knowledge, but the students defending before us were participants in a teacher learning program that was far from traditional; these teachers were graduating from a program that emphasized the need for identity work in efforts toward prioritizing inclusive, culturally responsive teaching and learning because "we teach who we are" (Oyler, 2011, p. 213).

Veranda is a partnership between a public university and the local school district at three of its nearby urban schools: Washington, Elliot and Muir. The three school sites for Veranda are similar yet also different. The schools are nestled into the urban landscape that is also part of this town's diverse fabric. Within the school's boundaries are children who live in working class neighborhoods, some whom call the Yaqui Indian Community home, and children who live on tree lined streets in suburban neighborhoods with a beautiful manicured park and playground equipment. Each school is comprised of students from a host of racial, cultural, linguistically diverse as well economically unique backgrounds. It is this richness in diversity that enhances the educational opportunities in which students are able to take part and grow academically. In these contexts, the Veranda teacher learning program stresses that inclusive and culturally responsive classrooms are necessary to reduce or thwart the common practice of "deficit thinking" that students confront on a routine basis, and the viewpoint that teachers regularly impose upon students who may be seen as "different" not atypical. This narrative of difference constructed as deficits is commonly communicated in schools.

The Veranda teacher learning program is therefore committed to developing culturally responsive teaching practices that provide an equitable and inclusive education for all students; every child has the right to a high-quality education in which his or her own diverse racial, language, and dis/ability are respected and valued. In conceptualizing the Veranda teacher learning program, practices associated with professional development schools and professional learning communities were considered; however in Veranda's model, a professional learning school partnership was created that deliberately placed a priority on educational equity. The idea was to create a partnership that embedded researchers, professors, instructors, and university personnel at the school sites in a partnership with already existing or developing professional learning communities (Kozleski & Waitoller, 2010).

Veranda is a graduate program in special education that immerses teacher leaders in 800 hours of teaching and/or co-teaching in one of the three professional learning schools. In addition, the teacher leader participants of Veranda take four semesters of course work at their school locations and in online or hybrid courses. The curriculum focuses on inclusive, culturally responsive practices and co-teaching with four overarching themes: identity, culture, learning and assessment. Each of the four semesters includes formative and summative performance-based assessments, which allow the students to explore what it means to work with diverse populations in urban classrooms. Additionally students develop a deep understanding of issues of identity, culture, learning, and assessment in their teaching practice.

The teacher leaders involved in the Veranda program also receive support and spaces for professional discourse and growth through their coursework. Each school site at which Veranda teacher leaders are placed has a site professor, a site coordinator, and a program coordinator that oversees the program. The university site professors spend one day per week at the

school sites coaching and providing feedback. The site coordinator is at
the school sites full time and is able to support Veranda students. In addition, researchers, a site council with members from multiple perspectives,
and principal investigators are intimately connected to the school sites and
Veranda program.

The Veranda partnership between the university and the three local
school sites has allowed us to hear and experience the schooling narratives
Veranda teachers lived and experienced. We hold steadfast to the belief
that systemic change is a complex, difficult process that requires much negotiation along the way. We are in the middle of that negotiation process.
Watching Veranda students such as Joy, Christalynn, and Sarah question the
role their biases play in the educational system represents a new trajectory
and narrative that has been laid out in three schools: a narrative of professional learning that has the potential to create systemic change toward
more equitable schools.

Te Kauhua (New Zealand)

In Aotearoa New Zealand two reports (2001, 2002) on student achievement patterns highlighted ongoing and historically prevalent underachievement by some ethnic groups, particularly indigenous Māori students. Consequently the Ministry of Education funded a new action research initiative
in volunteer schools across the country. This initiative aimed to improve
teaching practice and outcomes for Māori students through the development of culturally responsive practices.

Volunteer schools were grouped in clusters, with each cluster employing a facilitator to develop and implement a new professional development
program. In the context of Te Kauhua action research uncovered multiple
narratives. In enacting the initiative, schools undertook to: a) collect baseline data on Māori student achievement and identify students' learning
needs; b) develop and implement culturally responsive pedagogies across
the school; c) observe and record changes in Māori student outcomes; and
d) assess the impact the program had on Māori student outcomes and family-school relationships.

The evaluation of the first phase of this program, conducted in 2003, indicated positive signs of progress towards reframing the mainstream school
experience for Māori students within several schools (Tuuta, Bradnam,
Hynds, Higgins, & Broughton, 2004). However, recommendations made
in the report stated that further research was needed on partnership processes between Māori and non-Māori and the sustainability of such work.
There was a need to investigate partnership processes over time, so part of
the context of Te Kauhua was embedding researchers who were working to

answer the following question: What influences the acceptance and practice of teachers' collaborative partnership work when Māori and non-Māori teachers work together on a school reform project?

In Aotearoa New Zealand, non-Māori researchers are expected to abide by the terms of the Treaty of Waitangi[3] and engage in inquiry with Māori in an open and respectful manner. Māori centered research protocols as defined by Bishop and Glynn (1999) were used to guide the development of trusting and respectful relationships with participants (Hynds, 2007). Semi-structured, in-depth interviews were conducted with 77 participants (teachers, students, parents/caregivers, principals and in-school action research facilitators) within two schools that had volunteered to take part in the first phase of the government funded action research initiative. Over the course of 12 months, two interviews were conducted with each participating teacher (seven Māori and ten Pakeha/New Zealand European) in order to track their experiences of partnership work and their perception of change. The first interviews were conducted with teachers during the latter half of 2003 and the second towards the end of 2004. For the purposes of triangulation, interviews were later conducted in 2004 with 15 Māori students and their parents/caregivers and 15 non-Māori students and their parents/caregivers. Inductive analysis was used to ensure that codes, themes and patterns emerged from the collected evidence (Charmaz, 2000). Participants were asked to comment on emerging themes throughout the research process, in a series of "member checks." Throughout the research process, a research journal was kept to chart turning points in the researcher's thinking as she moved back and forth over time, revisiting notes and different sets of data (Hynds, 2007).

COMPETING NARRATIVES

In our efforts to promote change through leader development, our intentionality with Veranda and Te Kauhua was to engage in discourse around issues of educational equity. Specifically considering culturally responsive teaching and learning, we strive in both settings to communicate the messages illustrated above. Yet, because both Veranda and Te Kauhua are situated in authentic educational settings, we find that our narrative of equity is diluted and sometimes incompatible with the messages promoted at the school sites. These competing narratives center around the nature of reality, the nature of knowledge, and the nature of the practical school experiences in which participants engaged.

Nature of Reality

Culturally responsive teaching and learning is grounded in a sociocultural perspective about learning. In this tradition, that which is real is dynamic, changing in different contexts, interpreted differently by different people, in different cultural situations. Therefore, what is "real" is not considered an immovable, un-negotiable existence of something but instead, the private experiences and unique interpretations of individuals become their reification. That is, reality is a social and cultural construction of individuals (e.g., Vygotsky, 1978). This view of reality grounded the work in the Veranda and Te Kauhua projects and thus affected the interpretation of culturally responsive teaching and learning for participants. For example, during the first semester of the Veranda program, the theme of identity is explored in online coursework, face-to-face classes, and residency experiences at the elementary schools. Exploring the ways the teachers saw themselves and explained their conceptualization of their teacher roles was central to the work because it uncovered their theories about difference, the ways in which the teachers thought about teaching, their purposes for education, and other self-constructions that influence the schooling context (Holland & Lachicotte, 2007).

However, in the school contexts in which they worked, only the dominant culture's views of reality were legitimized. The nature of reality espoused in schools was, for the teachers, not the theoretical constructs we were teaching in our programs, but a fixed reality, based on what the people in power valued and set forth as important. A pervasive example of this was the pressure felt by school leaders related to high-stakes testing. While the aim of our narrative was to consider students' realities such as the funds of knowledge at home, their interests and hobbies, and so on, the competing narrative for school leaders was that they were accountable for high test scores on standardized, high-stakes assessments. In response to the rewards and sanctions associated in federal legislation (i.e., NCLB) with the results of high-stakes assessments, school leaders at all levels enacted the dominant narrative of emphasizing the reality reflected on assessments; this was a fixed reality incompatible with the nature of reality espoused by our program. The results of the incompatible narrative related to high-stakes assessment were complicated; for example, standardized teaching approaches that relied on scripts were dominant yet conflicted with the ways we advocated for teaching and learning that was responsive and foregrounded culture as a primary mediator of learning experiences. Diana, a teacher, explains:

> There are so many set guidelines on what we can do based on the curriculum map and based on the Harcourt that we have. I can implement, but it was hard to kinda share what I'm learning with my pod. I could share individu-

ally with my teacher next door. I could share things that I've been doing in my classes at [the university] with her, but it's kind of hard to share as a team because there's so many time limits on what we can and can't do.

Kelly, also a teacher, echoed Diana's frustrations about the reliance on curricular scripts and maps but adds the role of principal leadership:

> The district decides what we're supposed to use and then the principal decides—I mean some schools, it's a little bit more lenient, but Carmen is pretty much a stickler to the reading is just—you know, you need to be doing Harcourt materials. We don't want—like even during our small groups, she doesn't want us to pull in chapter books because it's not part of Harcourt. We have to read the Harcourt books.

Tina, a teacher, also discusses the difficulties inherent in the overdependence on standardization that she felt was occurring at her school site:

> I feel constrained that I can't do—if it's not on the lesson plan, I can't do it. If somebody walks through and it's not on the lesson plan, you're questioned, 'Well, why are you doing it?' There's no time for those creative teaching tools that you learned in college or anything like that, so no, everything has to be on the lesson plan. Every single teacher in second grade has to be teaching it the same way, so there are a lot of restraints.

Narratives about high-stakes testing and scripts are among many incompatible discourses our participants faced about the nature of reality. Below, we continue to outline incompatible narratives. Specifically, we turn to discourse about the nature of knowledge and the ways in which incompatible views of knowledge are translated to school leadership practices.

Nature of Knowledge

In the schools, the dominant narrative was that educational leaders are directly responsible for the promotion of knowledge. Participants observed this narrative translated into what Freire (1970) called the banking model of education. Made manifest, the banking model of education in the schools in which our work was situated resulted in teachers viewed as experts who were to "deposit" knowledge into the minds of their students. However, the ways in which our program advocated culturally responsive teaching and learning (described above) viewed learning as a social construction created in the context of culture. In a culturally responsive educational model, all are considered experts and participate together in the construction of knowledge (Gay, 2002; Villegas & Lucas, 2002).

An incompatible narrative in the area of content instruction was evident in language arts. School leaders experienced a narrative that reduced language arts to a form of reading that relied heavily on word calling rather than creating meaning. However, viewed from a culturally responsive perspective, literacy is a critical event framing a learner's ability to not only negotiate meaning from text, but also to use text to transform themselves and society. The ways in which literacy is conceptualized ranges from a tool to read the word and the world (Freire & Macedo, 1987) to learning skills such as decoding, fluency, and literary elements. Detrimentally, as accountability pressure increases, the scope and depth of these conceptualizations are becoming narrower and a conceptualization of literacy more closely aligned to what will be encountered on standardized tests. This narrow conceptualization has resulted in reading and writing becoming boxed into narrow confines, when in fact reading and writing do not fit in boxes. The attempted boxing of literacy was evident at the three school sites participating in the Veranda partnership. Books in the classroom were scarce and shadowed with cards and charts. Students worked through blends chart, they changed initial sounds, and they choral read word family sounds. It was like an onomatopoeia factory with *ch, ch, chs* and *th, th, ths* filling up and spilling out of student mouths.

Attempting to confine literacy into neat boxes disregards literary practices that cannot be easily measured. While word recognition, automaticity and decoding do hold a place in literacy, they alone will not equip students with the breadth and depth of literacies they will encounter and need in their lived experiences outside of school. We must look at literacy practices beyond tests that assess how many words per minute children can read and visualize the possibility of using literacy as a tool students will use to make sense of the world. Culturally responsive teaching, therefore, includes critical literacy as a tool for full democratic participation and an understanding of one's self in the world.

Even the ways participants unpacked the results of knowledge building in their schools often manifested in incompatible narratives. While features of culturally responsive teaching and learning include examining evidence of outcomes, such evidence is multidisciplinary, mutli-modal, and robustly diverse. The narratives Veranda and Te Kauhua advocated included examining data from students' families, peers, and informal learning environments as well as formal assessment. However, there was a clear emphasis in schools on formalized data; the use of data to make educational decisions relied heavily on only one kind of data: formal, standardized assessment. In discussing the impact of our work, a principal pointed to formal data to indicate growth observed in two of her teachers:

Really. I really looked at Teacher M's scores and Teacher W's scores and Teacher G's scores; all three of their scores are really good. In DIBELS, yeah, in just DIBELS so far because that's the only data we have. You'll see that we moved a lot of our intensive kids to Benchmark.

Another principal similarly characterized student learning based solely on formal data gathering:

Six hundred and some odd kids, and so we were just going through the data, and changing our data boards, and just doing all of that. This is what's most current now. So, the red down here represents the kids that we really have to look at seriously. They're in dire need. They need to be in the emergency room, more or less. The emergency room—like, if I was a doctor or something, these would need more of an emergency type of a situation. They'd need a lot more care. Of course, the ones on green—they're doing really well, but we still need to watch what they're doing. There's not as much care needed for them. Then, of course, the ones in the middle—we still have to watch them. This is what we have been doing.

Nature of the Practical School Experiences

When Te Kauhua teachers were first interviewed in 2003, many spoke about the positive changes that had resulted from their engagement in the new type of professional development program. For example, fourteen teachers (seven Māori and seven Pakeha/New Zealand European) explained that the incorporation of Māori cultural values, language and/or practices had been an important element of new partnership work. Seven of the ten New Zealand European teachers explained that they were now talking more openly with Māori staff members and seeking their support to improve aspects of their pedagogy, and twelve of fifteen Māori students told us that they had noticed that New Zealand European teachers had incorporated cultural values and practices into their teaching practices. Participants identified improvements in practice as: a) respecting and valuing Māori culture and incorporating bi-cultural dimensions within their teaching practice; b) raised expectations of teachers and increased risk-taking and experimentation in class with new pedagogies; c) teachers collectively analyzing Māori student achievement data with others and using such data to plan teaching interventions; d) a focus on peer tutoring, group work and/or cooperative learning; e) valuing and drawing on the prior knowledge and cultural capital of Māori children and young people; and f) co-construction or power-sharing strategies with students, whereby students voiced their own ideas and made decisions in the classroom.

After the first interviews with teachers the signs looked good—as if teachers' new partnership work would be furthered developed and sustained in both schools. However, analysis of subsequent sets of interviews conducted a year later indicated that competing narratives of power relationships and privilege disrupted and influenced the acceptance and practice of new collaborative partnership practices in the everyday practical school experiences.

Unexplored Privilege

Interviews were conducted with Pakeha/New Zealand European parents and caregivers a year later in 2004. As this stakeholder group spoke about their own interpretations of teachers' collaborative partnership work, it became clear that the majority of the parents and caregivers resisted the reform work being undertaken in their children's school. Twelve out of fifteen expressed concerns; they felt that their children's identities and learning opportunities were now being threatened by the increased focus on pedagogies responsive to the needs of Māori students. One principal described how a group of non-Māori parents/caregivers openly threatened to withdraw their children because of their concerns:

> We faced…really negative reactions from…non-Māori parents to the amount of te reo (Māori language) being used in school and especially spoken in classrooms. They have…seen this as detrimental to their children's learning. A few parents…said that they would pull their children from the school, particularly when we appointed our Deputy Principal, who is Māori, and there have been some families who have withdrawn their children…. (Principal, New Zealand European)

The majority of interviewed non-Māori parents/caregivers wanted to ignore cultural and ethnic differences and diversity, rather than acknowledge and value it as fundamental to learning. One participant viewed the school's reform work as threatening the collective identity of "New Zealanders," something she believed we should all hold.

> No, I don't want any information on how Māori and non-Māori teachers are working together! …like I said to my daughter…I think it's time we stopped looking at the color of people's skin and started treating everyone like New Zealanders, and…treating people equally. (New Zealand European parent/caregiver)

Other parents and caregivers believed that the new reform work was racist, while still others concluded that by addressing the needs of Māori students, teachers would ignore the needs of their own children. They also espoused the idea that teachers should ignore racial differences, claiming acknowledgement of such differences to be a type of racism:

> It's like it's racist…I don't get this race difference, like, to me everyone is even and we should be treated the same…like, to me, let's get over this race thing and try and get all our kids achieving… (New Zealand European parent/caregiver)

> …this Pakeha and Māori nonsense has got to stop. We are all New Zealanders…like we're all offered the same opportunities in life and if you want to take those, then take them, and if you don't, then you suffer the consequences. (New Zealand European parent/caregiver)

Subsequent member checks with Māori participants in both school communities indicated that new reform practices were being diluted due to growing resistance to new pedagogies and approaches. Over time interview evidence revealed that the reform programs in both schools ground to a halt. Addressing the issue of the dominant non-Māori majority and of their fears and prejudices, Bishop and Glynn (1999) have argued that contemporary educational policies and practices within Aotearoa New Zealand have developed from a framework of colonization, and as a result, "the system continues to serve the interests of a monocultural elite" (p. 12). There appeared to be a fundamental contradiction in the narratives of the Te Kauhua schools. While educators were trying to develop culturally responsive pedagogies and approaches, such practices were already evident and in place but were responsive to and privileged the needs of the dominant group (White, Paheka New Zealand European community members). Existing systems of privilege and power relationships thwarted real attempts at change and transformation for Māori students within both schools.

Another example of incompatibility involved the conceptualization of inclusive teaching and learning. The issue about inclusive education was especially apparent in the Veranda schools around language acquisition and instruction. For example, in an attempt to meet the linguistic needs of emerging bilingual students, the school district implemented a program that it believed would assist linguistically diverse students in acquiring the necessary English skills for academic success. Kevin, a teacher in one of the district's schools and a master's student in the Veranda program, struggled with a tension between doing his job in the ways the university master's program promoted as best practices (i.e., inclusive teaching and learning) while meeting the district's expectations for the cultural and linguistic instructional programming for his students. He taught thirty students in his classroom, at various stages in their English Language Development (ELD). In this classroom Kevin also had four students who were identified with learning disabilities. During the reading instructional block, Kevin's students were placed in homogeneous ability groups based on data derived from formal assessments. This notion of group memberships determined by ability as measured on formal assessments felt problematic to Kevin. For example, the students were relying on each other as their English language models yet had few advanced English proficiency models given the structure of the ability groups. Herein lay the tension between what Kevin knew to be best for his students based on his understanding of being a culturally responsive teacher and the district expectations for classroom instruction in English. He became a vocal opponent of the segregated model of ELD instruction; he wanted to be allowed to teach in a manner that is meaningful for his students, in ways that captured and respected their multiple ways of knowing. In fact, Kevin began to teach an alternative curriculum on Tuesdays, rooted in the principles of culturally responsive pedagogy, under a false guise. Although this action plan is steeped in deception, this felt to Kevin as the only way to deviate from a regimented lesson plan; he believed it was imperative to allow for his students' cultural and linguistic identities to complement his curricula in ways that valued all members as knowledge seekers and producers.

LESSONS LEARNED AND IMPLICATIONS

One of our goals in this chapter was to make manifest incompatible discourse that is often held latent. That is, rather than provide simplistic answers to complex issues facing educational leaders, we hoped to engage in a scholarly narrative dialogue that surfaced hidden or latent issues. We discovered the crux of the problem lies in understanding how leaders who are working to be change agents can help educators who are grappling with new ways of thinking to negotiate the competing forces that are alive and well in the context of schools. Given our analysis, we suggest three approaches that can aid in supporting CRTL. Educational professionals can a) actively practice their own agency by resisting problematic narratives and working for change; b) work within the incompatibility by engaging in thoughtful, strategic compromise, recognizing limitations and initiating baby steps towards change; and c) use the disequilibrium that incompatibility creates to promote growth and continuous improvement as part of professional learning. That is, leaders must reframe what they think of as incompatible and view it as part of a change process that includes discomfort, pushback, and tension as part of the nature of change.

In schools teaching and learning occur within complex systems that are constantly changing. These systems are a constellation of components including the people that populate schools and districts, the policies that guide decision-making, and the practices or everyday interactions that occur among adults and students. Moreover, these components also reflect the beliefs, values, mores and the legacies related to the meaning and purpose of education for individual students, as well as certain groups of students. Entrenched and seemingly intractable are certain narratives about how schools should be organized that are incompatible with the changing world and expectations of the twenty-first century. The fact is that all students, including culturally and linguistically diverse students, need educational experiences that are student-centered, inclusive and culturally responsive—that will teach them to be critical consumers of information, problem solvers and to be able to build relationships with people who are different from them. These experiences happen in schools where teachers understand that teaching and learning are culturally and socially mediated activities. However, it is not enough for students to experience sporadic exposure to this kind of learning environment. Culturally responsive instruction should be a part of every student's learning, everyday, in every classroom and in every school. Culturally responsive practices must be they way of doing business in schools throughout the district. Classrooms, schools and districts must be transformed into culturally responsive learning systems. While individual agency is important, system-wide transformation only occurs when there is a critical mass. To bring about the kind of change that sustains culturally responsive practices at all levels of the system and to effectively address incompatible narratives, every component of a school organization must be examined and addressed. A systems perspective examines the whole organization and the interrelationships among its component parts (Ferguson, Kozleski, & Smith, 2005). Educational professionals must work with their colleagues across disciplines to examine and recreate systems of learning that promote and sustain educational equity.

NOTES

1. Language is a powerful yet often problematic means of representing and reifying concepts and populations. Throughout this chapter, we attempted to represent populations in non-essentializing ways. However, we recognize that any label is insufficient in the ways it homogenizes a very heterogeneous population.
2. We deliberately choose to capitalize Culturally Responsive Teaching and Learning because we want to message that it is a set of specific educational actions. However, we wish to note that CRTL is not a singular approach to teaching but is instead a complex, integrated, and critical perspective, or way of being, that educators embody and act out in their classroom and school contexts.
3. This treaty was signed in 1840 and formed an agreement between the Māori and the British Crown.

REFERENCES

Apple, M. W. (1996). Power, meaning and identity: Critical sociology of education in the United States. *British Journal of Sociology of Education, 17*, 125–144.

Artiles, A. J. (2003). Special education's changing identity: Paradoxes and dilemmas in views of culture and space. *Harvard Educational Review, 73*, 164–202.

Artiles, A. J., Harry, B., Reschly, D. J., & Chinn, P. C. (2002). Over-identification of students of color in special education: A critical overview. *Multicultural Perspectives, 4*(1), 3–10.

Artiles, A. J. & Kozleski, E. (2007). Beyond convictions: Interrogating culture, history, and power in inclusive education. *Language Arts, 84*, 357–364.

Banks, J. (1993). Approaches to multicultural curriculum reform. In J. Banks & C. Banks (Eds.), *Multicultural education: Issues and perspectives* (pp. 195–214). Boston, MA: Allyn & Bacon.

Bishop, R. & Glynn, T. (1999). Culture counts. Changing power relations in education. Palmerston North, New Zealand: Dunmore Press.

Charmaz, K. (2000). Grounded theory: Objectivist and constructivist methods. In N. K. Denzin & Y. S. Lincoln (Eds.), *Handbook of qualitative research* (pp. 509–535). London: SAGE Publications.

Cole, M. (1985). The zone of proximal development: Where culture and cognitions create each other. In J. V. Wertsch (Ed.), *Culture communication, and cognition: Vygotskian perspectives* (pp. 146–161). Cambridge, MA: Cambridge University Press.

Cole, M. (1996). *Cultural psychology: A once and future discipline.* Cambridge, MA: Harvard University Press.

Cole, M. & Engeström, Y. (1993). A cultural-historical approach to distributed cognition. In G. Salomon (Ed.), *Distributed cognitions: Psychological and educational considerations,* (pp. 1–46). New York: Cambridge University Press.

Donovan, M. S. & Cross, C. T. (2002). *Minority students in special and gifted education.* Washington, DC: National Research Council.

Engeström, Y. (1987). *Learning by expanding: An activity-theoretical approach to developmental research.* Helsinki, Finland: Orienta-Konsultit Oy.

Ferguson, D. L., Kozleski, E. B., & Smith, A. (2005). Transformed, inclusive schools: A framework to guide fundamental change in urban schools. *Effective Education for Learners with Exceptionalities, 15*, 43–74.

Ford, D. Y. (1998). The underrepresentation of minority students in gifted education: Problems and promises in recruitment and retention. *Journal of Special Education, 32*(1), 4–14.

Freire, P. (1970). *Pedagogy of the oppressed.* New York: Herder and Herder.

Freire, P. & Macedo, D. (1987). *Literacy: Reading the word and the world.* Westport, CT: Bergin & Garvey.

Gándara, P. (2000). In the aftermath of the storm: English Learners in the Post-227 Era. *Bilingual Research Journal, 24*, 1–13.

Gay, G. (2002). Preparing for culturally responsive teaching. *Journal of Teacher Education, 53*, 106–116. doi: 10.1177/0022487102053002003

González, N., Moll, L. C., & Amanti, C. (2005). *Funds of knowledge: Theorizing practices in households, communities, and classrooms.* Mahwah, NJ: Lawrence Erlbaum.

Holland, D. & Lachicotte, W., Jr., (2007). Vygotsky, Mead, and the new sociocultural studies of identity. In H. Daniels, M. Cole, & J. V. Wertsch (Eds.), *The Cambridge companion to Vygotsky* (pp. 101–135). Cambridge, NY: Cambridge University Press.

Hynds, A. S. (2007). *Navigating the collaborative dynamic: Teachers collaborating across difference.* Unpublished doctoral thesis, Victoria University of Wellington, New Zealand.

Kozleski, E. B. & Waitoller, F. R. (2010). Teacher learning for inclusive education: Understanding teaching as a cultural and political practice. *International Journal of Inclusive Education, 14*(7), 655–666.

Lee, C. D. (2007). *Culture, literacy, and learning: Taking bloom in the midst of the whirlwind.* New York, NY: Teachers College Press.

Oyler, C. (2011). Teacher preparation for inclusive and critical (special) education. *Teacher Education and Special Education, 34*, 201–218.

Rogoff, B. (2003). *The cultural nature of human development.* New York: Oxford University Press.

Shields, C. M., Bishop, R., & Mazawi, A. E. (2005). *Pathologising practices: The impact of deficit thinking on education.* New York, NY: Peter Lang Publishing.

Tuuta, M., Bradnam, L., Hynds, A., & Higgins, J. with Broughton, R. (2004). *Evaluation of the Te Kauhua Maori mainstream pilot project. Rangahau Matauranga Maori.* Wellington: Maori Education Research, Ministry of Education.

Villegas, A. M. & Lucas, T. (2002). *Educating culturally responsive teachers.* New York, NY: State University Press.

Visser, P. S., Bizer, G. Y., & Krosnick, J. A. (2006). Exploring the latent structure of strength-related attitude attributes. *Advances in Experimental Social Psychology, 38*(1), 1–67.

Vygotsky, L. S. (1978). *Mind and society: The development of higher psychological processes.* Cambridge, MA: Harvard University Press.

CHAPTER 8

LESSONS FROM DIFFERENCES

The Search for Social Justice Leadership in Education

Dennis Conrad, Deborah Conrad, Anjali Misra, and Michele Pinard

INTRODUCTION

In our consideration and representation of the ongoing lessons of leadership as minority, non-U.S. born faculty, we (Anjali, Deborah, and Dennis), together with our colleague Michele as critical friend, focus on three professional frames of reference. These professional frames include our teaching and learning contexts, the influence of cultural identity on our learning and teaching, and how these intersect with our roles as social justice teachers and educational leaders.

The Inclusive Context

As leaders in teacher education instructional programs, we interact with learners who are different in age, gender, race, ethnicity, socioeconomic

Social Justice Leadership for a Global World, pages 133–150
Copyright © 2012 by Information Age Publishing
133

status, religious beliefs, culture, sexual orientation, academic success, and abilities. In addition to diverse populations, we note that the numbers of students with disabilities being placed in regular education U.S. class placements have increased from 24.6% in 1984 (Raymond, 2004) to 48.2% in 2004 (Friend & Bursuck, 2009). Donovan and Cross (2002) assert that it is bio-social and poverty issues, referral and assessment procedures, and ineffective instruction that facilitate overrepresentation of these populations and create urgent challenges for educating students in inclusive settings. Losen and Orfield (2002) question whether teachers are being adequately prepared to teach diverse learners. Further complicating matters, according to 2006 Census figures, the teacher population is not in sync with the changing student demographics, with 84% of teachers being female, European-American, and non-disabled. A cultural dissonance between the lived experiences of these teachers and the students they serve often results in disaffection and resistance to culturally responsive pedagogy (McFalls & Cobb-Roberts, 2001). To minimize this phenomenon, it has been suggested that teacher preparation programs need to create opportunities that untangle interwoven relationships of language, culture, and power in schools (Cochran-Smith, 1995). Specifically, it is imperative that programs prepare teachers as "insiders" (Banks, 1998) who have both content mastery and are culturally responsive (Gallavan, 1998; Harry, Kalyanpur, & Gay, 1999). Within the frameworks outlined, we view disability, inclusive educational practices, and social justice as intertwined, wherein inclusive education becomes about social justice (Sapon-Shevin, 2007).

Cultural Identity, Learning, and Teaching

Tomlinson (2003) refers to cultural identity as a robust, evolving, resilient response of a community to other, sustaining connections among person, geographical places and cultural experiences. In rural northern New York, where the majority of our students are decidedly white and abled, ethnic and national minority populations strive to navigate in a mainstream community in which values such as tolerance dominate amidst a population where many are unaware of their privilege (McLaren, 1999). In fact, Au and Blake (2003) contend that minority teachers have different interpretations of cultural influences than majority members, while Meece (1997) asserts that majority members are less likely to have stereotypical views of minorities when they have more understanding of their own ethnic identity. According to Hamilton (2002), identity requires balancing individualism with connectedness to others.

Leadership programs (Sheets & Hollins, 1999), cultural therapy (Spindle & Spindle, 1993, 1994), and multicultural education techniques, including drama, metaphor, self-study and diverse community experiences (Allison, 2003; Banks, 2004; Hoelscher, 1998), are among identified strategies to achieve heightened cultural literacy. Educational programs and courses designed to address underlying issues of diverse populations and social justice themes can bridge communities and decrease strains between individualism and segregated communities, forging public good. Autobiography and journal writing are common student assignments within education courses. These represent two possible beams upon which teacher candidates may balance how they construct their selves (i.e., personal and cultural identities) and how they build positive diverse relationships. They also represent tools with which to determine whether, why, and how we practice what we preach as teachers (Loughran, 2004; Bullough, 1997).

Social Justice and Educational Leadership

Bell (2007) argued that "the goal of social justice is full and equal participation of all groups in a society that is mutually shaped to meet their needs" (p. 1). Gewirtz (1998) asserts that there are two dimensions to social justice—the relational, and the distributional. The relational refers to the nature of and equity within relationships, addressing power issues. Distributional dimensions refer to equity in accessing and distributing resources. We embrace Bogotch's (2002) challenge that social justice cannot be separated from educational leaders' responsibilities or practices. We endorse Theoharris' (2007) position that educational leaders engage in social justice by centering their advocacy, vision, and practice on issues of race, class, gender, disability, sexual orientation, and other marginalizing conditions. Schrag (1979) links social justice to moral action, arguing that leaders committed to social justice should exemplify informed, reflective, empathetic practice with colleagues and subordinates. Choules (2007) argues further that social justice is about advocacy and change on behalf of the less privileged. Both education and schooling are important avenues for such social justice practices.

Kraft (2007) cautions that social justice leadership involves facilitating both a commitment to socially just teaching, and the nurturance of a socially just school community, with the former being easier to realize. Among key principles associated with building school community, Carlisle, Jackson, and George (2006) list: 1) articulating concerns about inclusion and equity, 2) having high expectations, 3) building reciprocal community relationships, 4) adopting a system-wide approach, and 5) focusing on direct social justice education and interventions. Bosu, Dare, Dachi, and Fertig (2009), however, warn that striking a balance between competing stakeholders is challenging and remains a leader's primary responsibility.

Our understanding of social justice is characterized by becoming involved in exercises that alter entrenched institutional arrangements that marginalize and exclude others, instead preferring to engage in those that build cultures of respect, care, recognition, and empathy (Gewirtz, 1998; Goldfarb & Grinberg, 2002). Such activities involve engagement in reclaiming, advancing, and sustaining inherent human rights and addressing issues of equity, equality, and fairness. By engaging in self-study, we explore how the frames of social justice, cultural identity, and context provide both frames and evolving frameworks for understanding our selves and our practices as teacher-leaders.

CO-AUTOETHNOGRAPHIC STUDY

This co-autoethnographic study involved three international special educators and one American-born "critical friend," who are colleagues in a university-based teacher education program. The research explored educational leadership issues by answering four essential questions: 1) How have our cultural and professional identities evolved and how do they relate to our leadership practice? 2) How have we enacted social justice in our educational leadership? 3) What were the key challenges to our efforts at social justice? And 4) How do we sustain our ability to enact social justice in our leadership roles? (Feldman, 2003).

Primary Participants and a Critical Friend

Deborah is an Associate Professor and Coordinator of the Childhood/Early Childhood program in the Department of Curriculum and Instruction. Born in San Fernando, Trinidad and Tobago, she served as a regular and special education teacher before completing her Ph.D. in the U.S. and assuming a position at SUNY Potsdam. Both Dennis and Deborah completed graduate work at Virginia Tech. Dennis is the Chair of the Department of Special Education and an Associate Professor. Also born in San Fernando, Trinidad and Tobago, Dennis has served as a regular and special educator and principal of an alternate school. A board member of the Eastern Educational Research Association (EERA), he is also the immediate past Chair of the Caribbean and African Studies SIG of the AERA. Anjali is a Professor in the SUNY Potsdam Department of Special Education and was largely responsible for developing that thriving program. She was born in New Delhi, India, where she taught children and adolescents with special needs. She completed doctoral studies at Pennsylvania State University and serves on the editorial boards for the *Journal of Disability Policy Studies* and the *Journal of International Special Needs Education.*

Michele, who served as critical friend, is a clinical faculty member in the Department of Curriculum and Instruction and doctoral candidate at McGill University, Montreal, Canada. She is a U.S. native who has studied, traveled and taught extensively abroad. Her research interests include experiential and intercultural education around social justice issues.

As partners in a collaborative community of learners, the primary participants (Dennis, Deborah, and Anjali) wrote responses to the essential questions, then shared their perspectives with each other, as well as with their critical friend and co-researcher, (Michele). All participants have established relationships; two of the primary participants—Deborah and Dennis—as partners for 15 years, have known each other and have access to family members and archives that support or refute each other's narratives. Dennis and Anjali have been colleagues within the same department for ten years, researching and presenting together. The primary researchers have worked with Michele for over seven years. The critical friend's role was to address the verifiability of the narratives by challenging or seeking clarification to the initial and ongoing responses of the primary participants. In so doing, she added her perspective as an outsider to discussions that occurred among the special education teacher-leaders as they explored the essential questions.

During this iterative research process, the participants and the critical friend critiqued and interrogated each other's narratives, pressing to clarify factors that shaped each other's cultural identities, evolutionary roles as social justice teachers, and practices as educational leaders, especially in the shared and current context of educating pre-service teachers. Personal narratives were scrutinized using constant comparative methods (Maykut & Morehouse, 1994) to elicit themes that would respond to the construction, interpretation, and valuing of the primary participants as learners and leaders. All co-researchers listened, reflected, and learned from each other (Poirer, 1992), emphasizing the trustworthiness of the narrative (Hamilton & Pinnegar, 2000).

EMERGENT SOCIAL JUSTICE THEMES

Several themes emerged from question one: How have our cultural and professional identities evolved and how do they relate to our leadership practice? They were notions of ethnicity and race, religion or spirituality, friendships and family, and schooling and early teaching experiences. Retaining a sense of being a minority, remaining student centered and being responsive, assuming advocacy roles, and adopting a willingness to model alliance building proved to be important elements in response to question two: How have we enacted social justice in our educational leadership? In response to question three: What were the key challenges to our efforts at social justice?, we found a common thread in "resistance." Finally, several responses emerged to question four: How do we sustain our ability to enact social justice in leadership roles? They were interacting with family and friends; maintaining spirituality, collegiality, and a belief in advocacy; retaining a commitment to education; becoming change agents; and identifying and owning social justice issues.

This collaborative self-study, including the invaluable role of the critical friend, afforded a deeper understanding of our selves and contributed to our current sustenance as teacher-leaders. The process of our engaging in this project helped to reaffirm, shape, align and balance our multiple selves, including that of maintaining our roles as leaders for social justice in a predominantly "majority" culture.

Emergent Cultural and Professional Selves

Ethnicity and Race

These were identified as influencing the evolution and current state of the three leaders' identities both culturally and professionally. Dennis and Deborah emphasize their "selves" as primarily ethnically derived. They describe their sense of selves—also referred to by both as identities—as convergent; as a blending of ethnicity and race; religion and spirituality; friendships and family; and school and early teaching experiences. Both Deborah and Dennis celebrate their multiethnic ancestries. Using the analogy of tapestry, Deborah acknowledges her African and Irish roots along with other ethnicities that constitute her being Trinidadian. Dennis relates to this theme of multiple aspects of his identity to include being Trinbagonian, Caribbean, multiethnic, and black. Anjali, despite having lived in the U.S. longer than in India, also identifies her self as Indian. Her identity is shaped by her Indian roots and upbringing and, like Dennis and Deborah, has been influenced by educational, spiritual, and familial experiences. This consolidation, a merging of personality and cultural descriptors, serves as a foundation from which they differentiate themselves from others in the U.S. context.

Religion and Spirituality

These elements influenced all three educators' social justice worldviews. Anjali grew up in a nation with linguistic, cultural and genetic diversity, exceeded only by those on the continent of Africa (Library of Congress, 2004). Every major religion is represented in India, where Hindus constitute 80.5% of the population, 13.5% are Muslims, 2.3% are Christian, while Sikhs, Buddhists, Jains, Zoroastrians and Jews make up the remaining 4%. This diversity shapes Anjali's acceptance and understanding of all religious practices. The intertwining of her personal religion, Arya Samaj, in which the core message is one of spiritual goodness, not the teachings of a specific deity or adherence of ritualistic practice, has influenced her innate acceptance and sense of social justice toward others.

To varying degrees, the other participants concurred about religion and spirituality as factors shaping their identities. Deborah identifies religious experiences as being critical to her sense of self. She links religious foundations and spirituality to her upbringing:

> I grew up participating in many religious experiences. My parents modeled tolerance for all religious groups. I was able to feel comfortable in a Hindu puja or an evangelical worship session. Within my family's preferred way of worship, I also developed a sense of community, purpose and spirituality. Moral expectations were high. Education was a must.

Dennis is from a working class family with multiple religious practices. He recognizes the role religion played in his identity formation and acknowledges that his sense of equity and social justice was born in his search for, and a belief in, a higher order. He shares that his extended family members belong(ed) to different Christian denominations, with each being the "one true way." These include family who are Catholic, Shouter Baptists, Seventh Day Adventists, Pentecostals, and Anglicans.

> I had *very* special friends and colleagues, like Beulah and Cilda, who were model Christians...also the Catholic Youth and Youth for Christ organizations. These inspired me to value myself and to see all as "children of God" regardless of socioeconomics, education, or race.

Family and Friendships

Other important factors shaping the identities of all primary participants were social influences. For Deborah, her friendship experiences align with her notion of family, especially with her "sisters" (used figuratively). They constitute the consistent energy that supports a sense of purpose and community. For Dennis, friendships are "the oases in the desert." Anjali shares with Deborah and Dennis a belief in the influential impact of friendships over one's lifetime in shaping identity, particularly given the absence of extended family living in the United States. The value of friendships over time is common to all the participants.

Deborah's parents were very family-oriented, and her sense of belonging extended from both church and community definitions of "family." As the third of four siblings in their nuclear family, she also had four older step-siblings. Her father brought firm parenting and much laughter, while her mother was very service-oriented to both church and non-church members. Dennis is the eldest of seven children. While Deborah and Dennis are the first of their family to complete college, neither of their parents completed high school.

For Anjali, also first-born, her experience among four siblings was decidedly different. Both her parents had graduate degrees, and she was surrounded by family and friends who were successful and lived comfortable lives. Anjali grew up in a relatively protected environment, mindful that she uphold cultural and societal values expected of her gender and social status. At the same time, she sought and was afforded an opportunity, after initial resistance, to follow a path that led her to study in the United States. Her entrepreneurial grandfather, a progressive thinker, had established a school that followed the philosophy that no child deserved corporal punishment. This went against common practice in Indian public education. Anjali relates her social justice commitment to being influenced directly by her grandfather's humanitarian efforts and vision.

Early Schooling and Teaching Experiences

Regardless of their socioeconomic backgrounds or particular social influences, the three participants concurred that early school and teaching experiences influenced their evolution as current social justice educator leaders. Coming from working class backgrounds and having earned their high school degrees, both Deborah and Dennis participated in diverse educational communities. Understanding and navigating among racial, religious, and ethnic groups consistently nurtured their respect of and value for difference. They realized early on that education would become a means for addressing social inequity. According to Dennis, "I grew up with a clear awareness of the 'haves and the have-nots.' There was no escaping the reality that education is the way forward for the ordinary person. And I was *very* ordinary."

Although schools were the center stage for cultivating a sense of self beyond initial social and religious experiences, schooling was not pain-free. Deborah elaborates how at the age of 11, she began secondary school after years in an all girls' parochial elementary school. She felt overwhelmed as she sought to navigate the teasing, bold and rough world of boys. Deborah also recalls her visual challenge:

> After doing well for the first four years of schooling, I began to fall back in my work, especially in mathematics. When I got my first pair of glasses at age 10 and looked at the chalkboard I understood only too well what I had struggled with for over two years of my schooling.

Dennis contrasts the social contexts of his school setting with his more humble origins: "Not only was I in a prestigious Catholic boys' school but here was where I had to face my lack of 'class,' poverty, and inadequacy." Anjali too was enrolled in a private Catholic school. Her parents believed doors would open for her in society if she developed into a well-educated, English-speaking, cultured young woman; she would be sought after in a society that preferred arranged marriages. Anjali comments:

> I was always a high achiever...and internally motivated. My parents expected me to get an undergraduate degree [but] my father was puzzled that I would want to continue on to graduate school. Going to the U.S. for higher education met with resistance, but he could not stop me because I was married and not living at home. I pursued higher education because of my desire to learn [and] to spread my wings and explore beyond...family, societal traditions, and restrictions.

Ironically, none of the primary co-researchers initially planned to become teachers. Deborah waivered between becoming a nurse or dietitian, and Dennis wanted to be a writer. Both were encouraged to pursue teaching and served as assistant teachers before completing their initial professional studies at a teachers' college. They were recruited to special schools after teachers' college and teaching in regular schools. Dennis was eventually appointed an alternate school principal. Anjali had dreamt of becoming a physician, like her aunt, who did not encourage her, so she attended a teacher preparation college. After achieving a Masters in Child Development, her father felt it appropriate that she teach in the school established by her grandfather. Anjali had been deeply affected by her interactions with children with intellectual disabilities, who were provided no resources and were largely neglected. She decided to work in a school for students with disabilities, realized the need for further training, and completed related graduate and post-graduate work in the U.S. Later, she returned to India to start a small school for children with disabilities. Unfortunately, she could sustain it for no more than one year due to lack of funding.

Ethnicity and race, religion or spirituality, friendships and family, schooling and early teaching experiences were factors that shaped the teacher-leaders' evolutionary sense of selves. There was also the pervasive thread of difference that ran through narratives, exposing individualized and rich experiences with diversity issues. The primary participants discovered by exploring question one—"How have our cultural and professional identities evolved and how do they relate to our leadership practice?"—that factors such as notions of ethnicity and race, religion or spirituality, friendships and family, and, schooling and early teaching experiences had an impact on the origination and evolution of their current roles as social justice educational leaders.

Impact of Identity on Leadership

The three primary participants also wrote narratives to define how they enact social justice in their educational leadership roles. Themes that emerged include: retaining a sense of being a minority, remaining student centered and being responsive, assuming advocacy roles, and, adopting a willingness to model alliance building.

Sense of Being a Minority

All three primary participants contend that their personal and professional lives have become melded, but that their individual identities and leadership roles are reflected in a consciousness about being a minority in multiple ways. They are among the decidedly visible minority faculty on campus, yet all three attest to being comfortable with this "difference." Nevertheless, they remain alert as to how they are perceived by students and colleagues alike—particularly as being Caribbean and black, in the case of Dennis and Deborah, and to being Indian, in the case of Anjali. For the women, their minority status in leadership roles is extended by cultural difference and compounded by gender, placing upon them mixed demands. Anjali makes it a point to dispel student wariness by initiating conversation about her origins, upbringing, and journey to the United States. However, Anjali contends that:

> Some colleagues, especially staff, have had difficulty accepting a minority female as a leader who communicates in a direct, assertive style. I think I sometimes ruffle the majority expectation that a minority elevated to a leadership position must simply continue to work efficiently but not truly "lead." My vision for change with its demands for rigorous work ethic, and . . . excellence are often misinterpreted. I do not believe this would be the case if I were not seen as the other.

Anjali struggles to find an optimal blend between her cultural identity and leadership roles. She no longer wants to be the token minority who fills the vacancy on every committee, unless she can effect real change, acceptance, and acknowledgment of her voice. For Deborah, cultural stewardship has been personified differently; she acknowledges that she sees herself as an ambassadress for all black Caribbean women within her professional context.

Dennis acknowledges that while conscious of being a leader who is a minority, he refuses to be manipulated because of his identity or to use it to manipulate others. He views leadership in a professional role as temporary, asserting that leaders must not get too carried away with the apparent power the role affords. He asserts that leaders should be committed to service for the community, genuinely striving to understand the community through building relationships. He posits that one's strength comes from the confidence and trust of the followers. This does not mean those served will agree with the leader *nor* does it mean that leadership is about doing their will or pleasing them—particularly in an educational and/or transformative context. Dennis claims that it is also about the leader being informed, caring, sensitive, and confident. He shares the challenge of building bridges in competitive communities, where colleagues might value individualism beyond community.

Student Centeredness and Responsiveness

All primary participants describe their professional practices as student centered and responsive. As leader exemplars, they are committed to modeling respect and appreciation for differences and flexibility. Although not exclusive to their experiences with special education, they celebrate how working with persons with disabilities has contributed to their sense of personal and professional identity. Deborah believes that there are two common threads that connect her special education and teacher educator selves—the readiness to work with teacher candidates' individual needs and her mission of ensuring that they achieve content mastery through differentiated instruction. "I feel the concerns of the mothers in class, the single, and the newly married. I understand the sacrifice that is real for many completing college. I see myself in their shoes many times." Likewise, Dennis shares that his professional self, after 28 years in special education, cannot be unraveled from his personal identity. He values each of his students and strives to be caring and authentic.

Assuming Advocacy Roles

Anjali believes that her worldview, actions, and philosophies are exemplified by advocacy and continually influenced by her special education teaching. She shares that she wants her students to be the best they can to become effective and excellent teachers of children with disabilities and

> . . . to be strong advocates for the rights of those who may not have a voice.
> I want them to truly believe in the abilities, potential, and strengths of those
> who are disabled and in their personal responsibility and power.

Anjali has assumed national and international leadership roles throughout her special education career. She initiated development of the special education graduate program at SUNY Potsdam, opening doors to teachers and learners who had no access to such services in northern New York. Anjali coordinated and chaired teacher education and special departments for 13 years, served on search committees for hiring faculty, and took an active position on the executive committee of the faculty union—positions that also put her in advocacy roles.

Deborah considers herself as an advocate and leader for social justice. She has evolved through community roles as a Brownie leader, youth camp organizer, and lead elementary teacher. She held positions in church leadership, as head of her department in her special education position, as a former executive membership in the faculty senate and in an eight-year coordinator role in the Childhood/Early Childhood Education Programs at her current institution.

Dennis' leadership and connections to social justice also extend to professional service. These include serving as a special education teacher and as a teacher's union activist for special education. He developed a special education teacher education in Trinidad and Tobago when there was none and served as an alternate school principal (Emotional and Behavioral Difficulties) and on the executive of several national and international education associations.

Modeling Alliance Building

Beyond professional affiliations, all three educators addressed how their current leadership facilitates the sharing of their professional selves. Anjali takes every opportunity to highlight diversity issues and emphasize the responsibility teacher candidates must share in facilitating social justice for their students:

> I find my presence gives voice to students from multicultural backgrounds. As department head, I fought for the rights of students to receive a quality education and opposed the fiscally motivated agenda to fast-track certification requirements... offering courses taught by minimally qualified faculty.

She has mentored young faculty and advised them to be self-advocates and to voice their opinions. "I spent countless hours supporting three Asian faculty when they were treated unfairly by their colleagues and administrators."

Deborah and Dennis share a relational leadership style. Deborah describes herself as a "reflective listener" who maintains some distance between herself and her students, while being no less responsive to their needs. Dennis portrays himself more as a student-centric risk taker, pushing students to be self-advocates committed to collaborative practice and community building. He targets dispositional consciousness and self-directed change.

> I try to create contexts that facilitate problem solving, the sharing of feelings, and collaborative practice opportunities. In the style of Miss Frizzle [from the Magic School Bus series] our classroom is the place to make mistakes and miracles.

To accomplish creating a balance between becoming an advocate and ally, Dennis strives to understand the contexts of students' followership experiences, giving much attention to their opinions, being sensitive while also seeking win–win, practical solutions where possible.

Challenges to Social Justice Leadership

That there are inherent challenges to social justice leadership in education is evident from the self-study. Trying to build community among diverse stakeholders requires overcoming communication hurdles; facing resistance was the strongest factor that emerged in the participants' narratives when they responded to the question, "What were the key challenges to our efforts at social justice?" Leadership requires connectedness to community. Deborah and Dennis emphasize building community with colleagues and being authentic in their interactions with others. While the demands of a young family and their roles as college faculty do not allow much time for socialization beyond the campus, this sense of community is a key aspect of their cultural identity and belongingness. Deborah recalls her first year experiences at SUNY Potsdam that went beyond course preparation. Understanding the dynamics of organizations and governance in the U.S. proved quite a challenge coming from a non-U.S. setting. She also struggled to determine her "fit" and which contributions she could make to the college.

While Dennis enjoys a very good relationship with faculty and students alike, he is keenly aware of possible pitfalls, including lack of institutional knowledge and communication differences that are culturally specific. This includes his tendency to be expressive, to hug, touch, and share his perspectives candidly. He remains sensitive to how some readily join the rhetoric of quality more by obstructive gate keeping than through opening doors, albeit with conditions. He contends: "Though this is philosophical in nature, there is a need for leaders to review their philosophical biases with the changing times and needs."

Longevity may not erase these differences, as Anjali's 20 years of leadership have shown. Her efforts have resulted in a multitude of ambivalent experiences and feelings, alternating between a sense of empowerment and even professional satisfaction and cynical, confused, frustrated questions. She wonders whether the deep-rooted status quo of current leadership can ever accept change. She acknowledges having received tremendous support when she was elected chair of a large department:

> I was praised for my hard work, organization, fairness, and knowledge. That experience made me assertive, decisive, insightful, and aware of my leadership abilities. However, I realize that many of these traits are not valued by others when they seek a leader. They want a non-threatening, agreeable, and likeable individual. Is leadership from a minority female acceptable only when coupled with compliance and non-assertiveness?

Yet, she also acknowledged that her leadership was not always valued or supported and wonders if her minority status had an effect on how her leadership was viewed.

Sustaining Social Justice Leadership

In spite of forms of resistance faced by all three primary participants, interacting with family and friends; maintaining spirituality, collegiality, and a belief in advocacy; retaining a commitment to education as a means of addressing social injustice; becoming change agents; and, identifying and owning social justice issues have all become important and integrated themes for Dennis, Deborah and Anjali in their leadership roles. These themes were addressed "holistically" in response to the last question. How do we sustain our ability to enact social justice in leadership roles?

Anjali has served the campus community the longest of her co-researchers. Her experiences as a social justice educator, minority female, and special education leader have ranged from positive and self-fulfilling to negative and demoralizing. She believes that her unshakeable belief in the power and value of education, inculcated since childhood, has propelled her throughout the years. She has never lost sight of the population she serves when making decisions. Retaining commitment to this vision (as her grandfather did) has also provided strength during times of adversity. Anjali attributes her successes to supportive colleagues, friends, and family members who were sounding boards and stood by her when needs arose.

Deborah celebrates her spirituality as a key element in supporting her sense of mission. "This is what keeps me centered . . . a reminder that there are forces beyond us that we are accountable to." While acknowledging that her church going has declined, she asserts that her spiritual life has blossomed. Deborah keeps very close to her friends and family members both within and outside of the U.S. (as her telephone bills can attest!). Her friendships transcend campuses, nationalities, and distance. She cherishes openness and honesty among her "sistren." Her kitchen is the main center of operations for coordinating her affiliations, and she prides herself on her multitasking skills.

When he accepted a position at Potsdam, Dennis was mindful that he was risking marginalizing himself and his family from all his key support systems. Nevertheless, work in Potsdam requires sacrifices beyond airport, geographic location, or snow. Dennis concedes he was ignorant of the north country and its culture. Yet, he has few regrets. As a whole, the campus community welcomed and supported him and his family beyond his expectations in the past eleven years. He has stayed connected to his cultural roots, helping to keep his "mojo" or his spirit for social justice leadership. He has also maintained—and developed new—international connections in order to keep himself academically marketable. Although Potsdam is not primarily a research university, Dennis has been able to maintain an active scholarship agenda, heeding advice from a "brother" in Pennsylvania. He utilizes collaborative research practices with colleagues at different institutions, including those in the Caribbean. All energize and sustain his leadership practice.

Perspectives from a Critical Friend

Accepting the critical friend role allows one to collegially seek connections between lived experiences, narratives witnessed, social justice education and leadership roles observed; to verify or challenge perspectives; and to share in lessons learned. This type of scholarship has unique and unrealized potential on campus for students, faculty, and broader communities served. Refocusing leadership lenses on social justice issues urges educators to go beyond traditional quantitative or Eurocentric research methods.

Colleagues who welcome opportunities to pause and listen to each other, as teachers and students do in healthy dialogical relationships, will recognize, as I have, that becoming a critical friend, is a means of connecting early experiences with leadership training. I gained points of entry in "the conversation" as first generation SUNY Potsdam students do who often come from relative poverty themselves by relating to allies not as the "other" but by listening to their narratives to hear nuggets of my own. When my colleagues described their struggles, I saw how our students may also relate to how education systems as a "way up and out." For social justice educators, the unfulfilled American dream is one in which too many children are left behind—in both policy and practice. If we can engage teacher candidates and practicing teachers in conversations such as those we begun, I hope that we may build socially just communities.

Educational institutions must spawn teacher candidates that explore roles of diversity and advocacy in leadership—purposefully and often. Sharing stories of minority faculty, as we did in this research, is to respond to the challenge of creating a new generation of social justice leaders. Trusting critical friends reminds one of the everyday leadership steps, rather than strides, that colleagues make in their personal and professional lives. Their vulnerability inspires us collectively to also not forget that the struggles faced are communal and that, even more importantly, goals for students are inclusive.

CONCLUSION AND RECOMMENDATIONS

These narratives of three co-researchers, supported by the role of a critical friend, reveal the importance of recognizing cultural identity in leadership when characterized in a social justice education framework. The participants' reflective and collective understanding of their multiple selves acknowledged factors that have contributed to the complex relationships among leadership, education, and social justice in their lives. Influences on the origins and evolution of their social justice leadership included ethnicity and race; religion or spirituality; friendships and family; and schooling and early teaching experiences. Factors affecting how they enact social justice in their current educational leadership practice include acknowledging the sense of being minority, remaining student centered and responsive, assuming advocacy roles, and modeling how to build alliances. A key challenge experienced to promote social justice leadership was "resistance." Finally, sustaining their ability to enact social justice in leadership roles requires interacting with family and friends; maintaining spirituality, collegiality, and a belief in advocacy; retaining a commitment to education; becoming change agents; and identifying and owning social justice issues.

Evidence presented from the research narratives indicated that common factors influenced these three special educators' leadership development. In spite of their minority faculty status, cultural and professional identities have merged, they have become the "other," and they have continued to build alliances to assume effective leadership roles and practices. Themes reflected ongoing intersections with challenges special educators face in rural, homogenous college communities. They also underscored the need for teacher educators and educational leaders to deeply reflect on how a sense of self and community influences professional identity development, particularly when one is committed to inclusive dispositions and responsiveness to issues of educational and social inequities and needs in the community at large. If social justice leadership is to be realized, we need more understanding of the experiences of minority faculty born outside of the U.S. in terms of challenges and the potential for sustaining relationships when enacting social justice leadership.

REFERENCES

Allison, B. N. (2003). Multicultural classrooms: Implications for family and consumer sciences teachers. *Journal of Family and Consumer Sciences: From Research to Practice, 95*(2), 38–43.

Au, K. H., & Blake, K. M. (2003). Cultural identity and learning to teach in a diverse community. *Journal of Teacher Education, 54*(3), 192–205.

Banks, J. (1998). Citizenship education and diversity. *Journal of Teacher Education, 52*(1), 5–16.

Banks, J. (2004). Multicultural education: Characteristics and goals. In J. Banks & C. Banks (Eds.), *Multicultural education: Issues and perspectives* (pp. 3–30). San Francisco, CA: Jossey-Bass.

Bell, L. A. (2007). Theoretical foundations for social justice education. In M. Adams, L. Bell, & P. Griffin (Eds.), *Teaching for Diversity and Social Justice* (2nd ed.; pp. 1–14). New York, NY: Routledge.

Bogotch, I. E. (2002). Educational leadership and social justice: Practice into theory. *Journal of School Leadership 12*(2), 138–156.

Bosu, R., Dare, A., Dachi, H. A., & Fertig, M. (2009). *School leadership and social justice: Evidence from Ghana and Tanzania.* EdQual Working Paper No. 17. Retrieved from http://www.edqual.org/publications/workingpaper/edqualwp17.pdf

Bullough, R. V., Jr. (1997). Practicing theory and theorizing practice in teacher education. In J. Loughran & T. Russell (Eds.), *Teaching about teaching: Purpose, passion and pedagogy in teacher education* (pp. 13–31). London: Falmer.

Carlisle, L. R., Jackson, B. W., & George, A. (2006). Principles of social justice education: The social justice education in schools project. *Equity & Excellence in Education, 39,* 55–64.

Choules, K. (2007). The shifting sands of social justice discourse: From situating the problem with "them" to situating it with "us." *Review of Education, Pedagogy & Cultural Studies, 29,* 461–481.

Cochran-Smith, M. (1995). Colorblindness and basket making are not the answers: Confronting the dilemmas of race, culture, and language diversity in teacher education. *American Educational Research Journal, 32*(3), 493–522.

Donovan, S., & Cross, C. T. (2002). *Minority students in special and gifted education.* Washington DC: National Academies Press.

Feldman, A. (2003). Validity and quality in self-study. *Educational Researcher, 32*(3), 26–28.

Friend, M., & Bursuck, W. D. (2009). *Including children with special needs* (5th ed.). Upper Saddle River, NJ: Merrill.

Gallavan, N. P. (1998). Why aren't teachers using effective multicultural education practices? *Equity & Excellence in Education, 31*(2), 20–28.

Gewirtz, S. (1998). Conceptualizing social justice in education: Mapping the territory. *Journal of Education Policy, 13*(4), 469–484.

Goldfarb, K. P., & Grinberg, J. (2002). Leadership for social justice: Authentic participation in the case of a community center in Caracas, Venezuela. *Journal of School Leadership, 12,* 157–173.

Hamilton, L. (2002). Constructing pupil identity: Personhood and ability. *British Educational Research Journal, 28*(4), 591–602.

Hamilton, M. L., & Pinnegar, S. (2000). On the threshold of a new century: Trustworthiness, integrity, and self-study in teacher education. *Journal of Teacher Education, 51*(3), 234–240.

Harry, B., Kalyanpur, M., & Gay, M. (1999). *Building cultural reciprocity with families: Case studies in special education.* Baltimore, MD: Paul H. Brookes.

Hoelscher, S. D. (1998). *Heritage on stage: The invention of ethnic place in America's Little Switzerland.* Madison, WI: University of Wisconsin Press.

Kraft, M., (2007). Toward a school-wide model of teaching for social justice: An examination of the best practices of two small public schools. *Equity & Excellence in Education, 40,* 77–86.

Library of Congress. (2004). *Country profile—India.* Retrieved from http://lcweb2.loc.gov/frd/cs/profiles/India.pdf

Losen, D., & Orfield, G. (Eds.). (2002). *Racial inequality in special education.* Cambridge, MA: Harvard Education Press.

Loughran, J. J. (2004). Learning through self-study. In J. J. Loughran, M. L. Hamilton, V. K. LaBoskey, & T. L. Russell (Eds.), *The international handbook of self-study of teaching and teacher education practices, Volumes 1 & 2* (pp. 151–192). Dordrecht: Kluwer Academic.

Maykut, P., & Morehouse, R. (1994). *Beginning qualitative research: A philosophic and practical guide.* New York, NY: Falmer.

McFalls, E., & Cobb-Roberts, D. (2001). Reducing resistance to diversity through cognitive dissonance instruction: Implications for teacher education. *Journal of Teacher Education, 52*(2), 164–172.

McLaren, P. (1999). A pedagogy of possibility: Reflecting upon Paulo Freire's politics of education: In memory of Paulo Freire. *Educational Researcher, 28*(2), 49–54.

Meece, J. L. (1997). *Child and adolescent development for educators.* New York, NY: McGraw-Hill.

Poirier, C. F. (1992). A student teacher's voice: Reflections of power. *Journal of Education for Teaching, 18*(1), 85–92.

Sapon-Shevin, M. (2007). *Widening the circle: The power of inclusive classrooms.* Boston, MA: Beacon Press.

Schrag, F. (1979). The principal as a moral actor. In D. A. Erickson & T. L. Reller (Eds.), *The principal in metropolitan schools.* Berkeley, CA: McCutchan.

Sheets, R. H. (1999). Human development and ethnic identity. In R. H. Sheets & E. R. Hollins (Eds.), *Racial and ethnic identity in school practices: Aspects of human development* (pp. 91–101). Mahwah, NJ: Erlbaum.

Sheets, R. H., & Hollins, E. R. (Eds.). (1999). *Aspects of human development: Racial and ethnic identity in school practices.* Mahwah, NJ: Erlbaum.

Schrag, F. (1979). The principal as a moral actor. In D. A. Erickson & T. L. Reller (Eds.), *The principal in metropolitan schools* (pp. 208–232). Berkeley, CA: McCutchan.

Spindler, G., & Spindler, L. (1993). The process of culture and person: Cultural therapy and culturally diverse schools. In P. Phelan & A. L. Davidson (Eds.), *Renegotiating cultural diversity in American schools* (pp. 21–51). New York: Teachers College.

Spindler, G., & Spindler, L. (Eds.). (1994). *Pathways to cultural awareness: Cultural therapy with teachers and students.* Thousand Oaks, CA: Corwin.

Theoharris, G. T. (2007). Social justice educational leaders and resistance: Toward a theory of social justice leadership. *Educational Administration Quarterly, 43*(2), 221–258.

Tomlinson, J. (2003). Globalization and Cultural Identity. In D. Held and A. McGrew (Eds.). *The global transformations reader* (pp. 269–277). Cambridge: Polity Press.

CHAPTER 9

CRUMBLING BARRIERS

A Comparative Study of International Teachers' Experiences of Educational Leadership in Their Home Countries and the United States

R. Martin Reardon and Risha R. Berry

INTRODUCTION

This study focused on the extent to which the concept of educational leadership plays out narrowly in terms of the U.S. context, as interpreted through the experience of teachers on temporary visas from countries other than the United States (mainly Jamaica and Colombia). The participants were invited to compare their experience in the U.S. with their experience at home through the lens of a contemporary best-practice model (Fullan, 2010). The participants were English-speaking teachers with Master's degrees (mainly science and mathematics teachers) who were recruited to teach on a temporary basis in schools districts located in two U.S. Mid-Atlantic states.

Social Justice Leadership for a Global World, pages 151–170
Copyright © 2012 by Information Age Publishing
All rights of reproduction in any form reserved.

Fusarelli and Boyd (2004) typified the prevailing sociopolitical context in America as "multicultural, multifaith, with alarming inequalities and permeable borders penetrated by globalization, by immigration (often illegal), and by international terrorism" (p. 5). They acknowledged the problematic nature of their portrait, but went on to propose that cultural conflict "both internal to the United States and external between the affluent, westernized world and Islamic underdeveloped nations" (Fusarelli & Boyd, 2004, p. 5) was a force for cultural change at a deep level, with the potential to impact the institution of the common school. Fusarelli and Boyd portrayed the pressure on the institution of common schooling as emanating from a number of sources including the accommodation of diversity (for example, Gándara & Contreras, 2009), the cultural pressure of "moral federalism" (Wolfe, 2000), and questions surrounding whose values should be taught in school (for example, McDonnell, 2004) and whose historical experience was to be respected (for example, Epstein, 2000).

The ongoing debate surrounding these far-reaching issues has been complicated by the unflattering comparisons of U.S. students' academic achievement with that of their international counterparts—especially in mathematics and science. For example, the Program for International Student Assessment (PISA, 2009a, 2009b) findings have prompted a range of reactions from warnings of the potentially negative economic outcomes of continued low performance (for example, Cheung & Chan, 2008; Hanushek & Woessmann, 2010) to a need for more effective educational leadership (Schleicher, 2009).

There is strong pressure from the No Child Left Behind Act of 2001 (NCLB, 2002) for every student to reach proficiency and for a qualified teacher in every classroom while there is a shortage of U.S. teachers in critical areas. Recruiting teachers from other countries is part of a coping mechanism designed to overcome this shortage, which is not a new phenomenon. Indeed, Sedlak and Schlossman (1986) asserted that "teacher shortages have been commonplace throughout the twentieth century" (p. vii). Towards the close of the previous century, the shortage was adverted to by others in contexts that included the raising of standards for teacher certification (for example, Darling-Hammond, 1999) and teacher turnover (for example, Grissmer & Kirby, 1997; Ingersoll, 1997). Nor is the shortage of teachers limited to the U.S., as evidenced by Mansell (2000), who noted the easing of restrictions on employing non-European teachers by the British government in response to the under-recruitment of local entrants into teacher education programs.

In what could be described as a transitional sociopolitical context in the U.S., a teacher from another country who has been hired to teach in the United States (referred to subsequently as an "international teacher") is in a potentially unsettling situation by virtue of a) coming to terms with expectations of his or her role that differ from his or her experience, and b) seeking the firm ground of established practice at a time when the field of education in the U.S. is intensely scrutinizing values and struggling to engender systemic change. Consequently, while school districts seek a strong return on their investment in recruiting the international teacher, the international teacher may not be in a good position to contribute strongly. Fuller (1969) pointed out how the concerns of teachers vary depending on their level of professional comfort with their teaching environment, and cultural disorientation as one attempts to adjust to a multi-faceted environment that is itself in a state of change is destined to promote professional discomfort. There is little literature in this field. For example, Hutchison (2006) asserted that there was a "serious gap in the literature concerning international teachers' pedagogical experiences in American high schools" (p. 6). In focusing on the cross-cultural issues that challenged four science teachers from three different countries (Ghana, Britain, & Germany) when they immigrated to teach in U.S. high schools, Hutchison delineated between issues that were support-related (not directly related to the classroom) and teaching-related issues (such as organizational expectations, assessment, communication, textbooks, pedagogical approaches, and student-teacher interactions).

This study goes beyond Hutchison's (2006) work to address what is proposed as a crucial third area: educational leadership. As the Council of Chief State School Officers (CCSSO, 2008) highlighted, amidst the uncertainty surrounding public education as an institution, one element that is not in doubt is the "high profile demands placed on education leaders to raise student achievement" (p. 1). However, Heck and Hallinger (2009), among others, have pointed out that leadership has an indirect effect on student achievement. Reardon (2011) pointed out the irony of the situation whereby the principal is held directly responsible for the educational outcomes of the school even though the effect of the school leader on learning is indirect. What is regarded as effective leadership in the U.S. may be less highly regarded in the country in which the international teacher taught before being recruited. Of course, the principal is not the only leader in the school, and this study set out to compare the difference between the broadly conceived educational leadership experienced by the participants in the U.S., compared to their home countries.

In the following, we briefly highlight the inequality of educational outcomes that typify public education in the U.S. before we present an overview of a range of perspectives on what constitutes educational leadership in the U.S. Our intention is to set equality of educational outcomes as the bar for effectiveness and to position a range of approaches to educational leadership with potential impact on this bar. We will then narrow our focus to what we selected as one of the more compelling systemic approaches to educational leadership that fits the U.S. context (Fullan, 2010), and how we interpreted the major emphases of Fullan's approach in the context of survey-based research. After describing the method and results of our study, we will conclude by discussing our findings.

INEQUALITY OF EDUCATIONAL OUTCOMES

In his foreword to Fullan (2010), Senge asserted that "tragic results" (p. vii) have attended the efforts that have been made over the course of a quarter century in the U.S. to improve educational outcomes for students. Senge singled out unwelcome human and societal outcomes for indictment. For example, Senge declared that for over ten years it has been "more likely that a young African American boy growing up in an American city will go to prison than to any form of post-secondary education" (Fullan, 2010, p. ix). The fact that this unhappy fate does not befall students equally gave rise to the harsh criticisms regarding alarming inequalities in the previous century (for example, Kozol, 1991), and the more contemporary critiques of public education as an institution that is rife with racial inequality (for example, Fusarelli & Boyd, 2004).

EDUCATIONAL ACHIEVEMENT GAP

The difference between the expected outcomes of schooling for black and white children has been commented on for many years. For example, Jencks and Phillips (1998) declared that the persistence of the black-white gap on testing outcomes was a major hurdle to be overcome in the quest for racial equality. However, Magnuson and Waldfogel (2008) pointed out that the dimensions of the test-score gap are subject to change over time. The project of the contributors to Magnuson and Wadlfogel's edited text was to link the social and economic factors that predominated in the society at large with the closing or widening of the historical educational achievement gaps. Despite the historical fluctuations, however, Magnuson and Waldfogel concluded that "the persistent gap in test scores between Black and White children remains one of the greatest challenges of our time" (p. 20).

The test-score gap is not limited to the comparison between white and black students. As Gándara and Contreras (2009) pointed out, in a national sample of kindergartners, "with the exception of Native American students, Latinos were the most likely of all groups to fall into the lowest quartile of performance" (pp. 18–19). Gándara and Contreras's summary of the National Assessment of Educational Progress (NAEP) testing at fourth grade and eighth grade in reading and mathematics shows black, Native American, and Latino students interchanging percentage-proficient figures, but always below the 20 percent level (compared to between 40 and 50 percent or higher for white and Asian students on the same tests). A test-score gap of this magnitude is not acceptable regardless of the ethnicities involved, but, given the high growth rate of the Latino population, it is of great concern that unless the situation changes, Gándara and Contreras asserted, "we will have created a permanent underclass without hope of integrating into the mainstream or realizing their potential to contribute to American society" (pp. 13–14).

EDUCATIONAL LEADERSHIP APPROACHES

A widespread malaise such as the achievement gap demands a broad-spectrum response from educational leadership. In this section we offer a brief overview of some of the educational leadership approaches and responses that have been proposed to engender systemic reform.

A Moral Community

Glickman and his colleagues (for example, Glickman, Gordon, & Ross-Gordon, 2010) have for many years advocated the formation of a moral community as a way to bolster democracy and enhance the community in which schools operate. A moral community focuses on care (adults being open and receptive to students), wholeness, connectedness, inclusion, justice, peace, freedom, trust, and empowerment. According to this concept, once the school rests on the firm foundation of a moral community, then teaching and learning can flourish in fertile ground.

Developmental Supervision

The moral community is supported in the work of Glickman et al. (2010) by specific attention to details. Some of the most pertinent details involve what they termed developmental supervision. Developmental supervision invokes assistance to teachers from educational leaders that is individualized to each teacher's characteristics. Glickman et al. (2010) envisaged a continuum of individualized assistance to teachers as a way to combat "isolation, psychological dilemmas, routine, inadequate induction of beginning teachers, inequity, lack of career stages, lack of professional dialogue, lack of involvement in school decisions, lack of a shared technical culture, and conservatism" (p. 21).

Financial Resources and Equity

Grubb (2006) asserted that discussions about equality have permeated public discourse in the United States since the Revolution "introduced an egalitarian rhetoric to an unequal society" (Pole as cited in Grubb, 2006, p. 157). Various ways of providing financial resources to schools have been implemented in an attempt to ensure equality. Grubb delineated between the provision of simple resources (such as per-pupil-funding, teacher salary enhancement), compound resources (such as class-size reduction in conjunction with a supply of able teachers), complex resources (such as enlightened pedagogical approaches), and abstract resources (such as teacher stability, coherent curriculum, and distributed leadership). Distributing more money to schools, from Grubb's perspective, will increase the simple resources, but such an increase is only marginally related to improved student educational achievement. The larger effects are associated with the provision of the higher-order compound and complex resources. Grubb argued not for simply providing additional finance, but targeting finance specifically at resources likely to make an impact.

Educational Leadership Standards

There is little doubt that the standards for educational leaders developed by the Interstate School Leaders Licensure Consortium (ISLLC, CCSSO, 1996) have been "widely used as a model for state education leadership policies" (CCSSO, 2008, n.p.). The ISLLC standards have largely shaped the understanding of the components of effective instructional leadership in U.S. schools. The subsequent document, which was dubbed "ISLLC 2008" (CCSSO, 2008), maintained the "footprint" of the earlier document, but reflected "the wealth of new information and lessons learned about education leadership over the past decade" (p. 1), and was endorsed by the National Policy Board for Educational Administration.

All Systems Go

Fullan's (2010) proposal for addressing the challenges faced by public education was developed from his integral involvement with initiating educational change in Canada. While the two North American public school cultures are generically similar enough to lend credibility to Fullan's perspective south of the border, the international roots of his proposal render it particularly appropriate in the context of this study.

The pillars supporting Fullan's (2010) approach included a focus on a) whole-system reform (as opposed to isolated pockets of excellence), b) clarity of understanding relating to the resources that may bring about a change in performance, c) utilization of existing resources, d) knowledge of the current state of affairs, e) engaging individuals in building their capacity, and f) fostering the political will to change the status quo. Fullan's approach was adopted as the framework for this study, as is explained in the survey instrument section below.

METHODOLOGY

Participants

All international teachers who had been accepted into a post-Master's degree course in Leadership Studies at a large, research extensive university in a Mid-Atlantic state were invited to participate. They were contacted through the emails they used at the time of their enrollment. Thus, the online survey was distributed to 142 international teachers. Two email addresses were school district addresses, which were no longer active, and a further 15 email addresses "bounced."

An announcement email was followed by an email with the url of the survey website and the study permission details. Three reminder emails were sent over the two-week collection period, with the Internet server set to only remind those who had not already replied. We received 32 responses from 125 active email addresses, yielding a 25% response rate (although not all questions were answered by all respondents). In terms of non-response bias, two non-respondents contacted us to explain why they had not responded. One requested a Likert-scale survey, and indicated that the survey asked for too much detail. The level of detail may well have been a factor in the incomplete responses of 13 of the participants. The other non-respondent who contacted us asserted she could not respond because she was not in a leadership position. The irrelevance of her current position to the survey was explained, but she still did not respond. In summary, we received 14 responses from the 61 Jamaican international teachers, seven responses from 27 Colombians, three from six Romanians, two responses each from the six Canadians and four Ecuadorians, and one response was received from the four South Africans, and the two Kenyans. The lone Zimbabwean and Austrian also responded. We received no responses from the three Filipinos, the two Costa Ricans, the two Venezuelans, or the single international teacher from each of the United Kingdom, Bulgaria, Argentina, Belize, El Salvador, and Mexico.

Survey Instrument

As mentioned above, Fullan's (2010) proposal for reform provided the framework for this study. It is not unusual for international teachers to have the equivalent of a U.S. Master's degree, as did all participants in this study. However, even though international teachers are recruited from competent applicants, the nuances of written English can be lost on them. To prompt reflection along our intended path, we decided to provide visual referents for each survey question, and to invite participants to provide and explain visual referents in their responses. Epner and Baile (2011) adopted a similar visual approach in developing a conceptual framework to encourage medical students to reflect on their relationships with their patients.

The six-question survey opened with Fullan's (2010) emphasis on engaging individuals in building their capacity. This was associated with the image of a mirror. Participants were invited to hold a mirror to their practice in their U.S. and home contexts. The overall prompt was "Who am I as a teacher?" Second, fostering the political will to change the status quo was associated with the image of a flag. The overall prompt was "In what ways does your country hope your people will benefit from education?" The third question focused on the knowledge of the current state of affairs. The image was a map, and the key question was "What lies ahead?" The fourth question addressed the utilization of existing resources, which was associated with the image of a paper bag, and the key question "What do I bring?" The fifth question addressed clarity of understanding relating to the resources that may bring about a change in performance. Finally, the sixth question invited respondents to directly compare their experience of the impact of educational leadership on their performance as teachers.

RESULTS

In reporting the survey results of each of the six questions, we begin with a focus primarily on the responses from the Jamaican respondents—typified by the response of one participant named Amelia. We broaden the focus from Amelia to consider the nuances contributed by other Jamaican participants before moving on to the Colombian respondents. Finally, we consider other participants' views before offering a final summary of the results from our perspective. (Note that all names are fictitious. The appropriate form of the pronoun is used in agreement with the gender connoted by the fictitious name.)

Question 1: Individual Capacity

In terms of individual capacity, respondents were asked to look at themselves as teachers by holding a mirror to their practice in their home country, compared to the corresponding situation in the U.S. Amelia (from Jamaica) used terms that evoked a utopian identity at home, in stark contrast with her identity in the U.S. Amelia portrays herself as a relaxed professional in Jamaica, but is tightly constrained ("trapped," confined emotionally and by administrative requirements) and unfulfilled in the U.S. She is "stuck" in a number of aspects of her practice—a term that indicates the task involved in facilitating her growth as an instructional leader in the U.S. The "babysitter" image Amelia chose, together with her description, is evocative of a teacher at the "survival" stage of Fuller's (1969) stages of concern. The survival stage typifies a teacher whose focus is on lasting through the day—as opposed to contributing to the lasting development of the students. Amelia's "extra-firm" approach may be the outcome of her feeling timid and overwhelmed in the U.S., in comparison to the "relaxed" but intensively engaged image she associated with her teaching at home in Jamaica.

Amelia's view of herself in Jamaica is echoed by her compatriots. Bruce (also from Jamaica) described himself as an inspirer and leader—as the wind beneath the wings of others—and Elise (Jamaican) described herself as "compassionate" and "enthusiastic." In contrast, in the U.S., Bruce typifies himself as a user of technology, and Elise is "conservative, withdrawn," and, in a compelling image, is "confined in a box." Equally compelling is Cora's (Jamaican) U.S. image of herself is of a "sad, scared, fairly young female." Frank (Jamaican) joined Bruce in describing himself also as "in tune with technology" in the U.S., compared with his image of being "conscientious" in Jamaica. In a perspective that evokes the land of opportunity theme, Gail (Jamaican) paired her images. In Jamaica, she is a "pencil;" in the U.S. she is an "electric pencil sharpener." Gail described herself as working on her own initiative in both contexts, but in Jamaica her potential is latent, whereas in the U.S. she is sharpened, and "able to do anything, to the point where I am amazed."

Among the Colombian respondents, Joan's response is a close parallel to the dominant Jamaican theme. In Colombia, she is "nurturing, understanding," with an image of knowledge-provider. In the U.S., besides the provision of knowledge, she demands "full attention at all times," and suggests an image of "a teacher who engages students." There is a sense of efficiency in Joan's U.S. persona that is echoed in Ian's (Colombian) "competent" description of himself in the U.S., and his image of "qualifications and certifications." However, Helga proposed "a building being built" as her Colombian image, compared to "a happy face" in the U.S., both of which are compatible with the sense of nurturing suggested by Joan. It is interesting to note in passing that the Jamaicans were much more forthcoming than the Colombians, arguably because the Jamaicans were responding in their first language.

Among the other respondents, Michael (from Austria) was an exception to the generally favorable portrait participants painted of their teaching at home. He described himself as "de-motivated, though engaged and well-liked by students," whereas in the U.S., he is "highly motivated" and still well-liked. Perhaps "bored" might have been a more appropriate term than "de-motivated," but, regardless, Michael's self-critique contrasts to Lisa's (from Ecuador) description of herself as "proactive, hands on and concerned about children's development." Lisa stresses the need to be "aware of all the regulations and laws" in the U.S. The image Michael chose to describe his teaching in Austria was quite thought-provoking and will be highlighted in the closing discussion. Suffice it to note here that Michael's Tarot image was quite different from Lisa's Ecuadorian "butterflies." Norah (from Romania) depicted herself as a "marathon runner [with] half the time allotted for this race" at home. One gets the impression of a lot of work to do in a short period of time, which is surely a challenge, but this is surmountable, compared to the "overloaded truck, but still running" that Norah used as an analogy in the United States.

Summary. Participants' individual capacity in the U.S. was consistently reported as different from their home country. Participants reported a distance between themselves and students in the U.S. There is a sense of having more time to be personable at home, and a sense of their being challenged by different and extensive demands in the U.S. to optimize class time, and be a sharpened pencil. These teachers have not lost their individual capacity, but teaching in a different system constricts their well-developed practices, while simultaneously extending their teaching repertoire.

Question 2: Outcomes of Education

In terms of the outcomes of education, respondents were asked to reflect on what school leaders in their home country hoped to see as a result of education compared to their perceptions of what school leaders in the U.S. hoped to see. Amelia emphasized the role that education plays in Jamaica in offering the potential for liberation from "poverty and oppression" by means of engendering innovation and a deep respect for others. She typifies this by reference to an image of "most Jamaican international teachers." The emphasis changes in the U.S., with school leaders portraying education as opening opportunity, but promoting somewhat self-serving process for the school. Teaching in the U.S. is portrayed as an opportunity to demonstrate technical proficiency, thereby gaining credibility and resources. The school has an imperative to deliver a product and is judged by measurable outcomes—giving rise to Amelia's "car salesman" image. In terms of Grubb's (2006) nomenclature, Amelia portrayed teaching in the U.S. as focusing on securing the availability of simple resources.

Cora's Jamaican views resonate with Amelia's. Cora depicted a situation where each generation builds on the work of its predecessor to progress down the "avenue out of poverty"—a theme that was common to all the Jamaican responses. For example, David cast education as "important for survival," and differentiating between "a middle-class person [and] a homeless person." In comparison, Cora tersely commented that in the U.S., school leaders believe it is "their job to educate." Elise (Jamaican), after referencing the role of education in providing social mobility in Jamaica, described U.S. school leaders as "overzealous," and as urging teachers to excel because "it helps the organization to be noticed and recognized, which, in return, is good for [the leader's] standing." Gail's (Jamaica) images are evocative of the comments of Glickman et al. (2010) with respect to the moral community. Her image of the educational leadership task in Jamaica was of a "wheelbarrow containing students being pushed"—moving her nation to a thriving economy—but she described a sense of aimlessness in the U.S. by reference to "a blindfolded person."

Very similar themes emerged from the Colombian responses. Ian used an image of a "population free of social and economic problems" to describe Colombia's leaders' vision. Helga juxtaposed an image of "happy people" in Colombia to "money" in the U.S. Joan (Colombian) referred to education in the U.S. as "an option students have; not their only option," a factor that she saw as creating an imperative for teachers to make learning attractive. Ian's image of educational leaders in the U.S. as focused on "students being helped individually" may provide a counter to an otherwise pejorative frame of reference.

Two of the other respondents, Kurt (from Zimbabwe) and Lisa (from Ecuador) also identified education as the "gateway to success" and "the only way to ensure well being." In contrast, Michael's (from Austria) response varied from this theme, as he advocated a more philosophical approach and suggested that in Austria "general knowledge" was intrinsically valued. In terms of their U.S. experience, all three of these respondents emphasized education as the path to success—with Michael adding the emphasis that in the U.S. success is expected of every single student. Lisa's images are informative: In Ecuador, she likened education to a plant being grown to harvest, whereas in the U.S., education was a silver coin because success in the U.S., she asserted, is equated to one's financial well-being.

Summary. The impression is that public education in the U.S. is a well-oiled, political process while also being somewhat mindlessly pursued—or pursued for self-serving reasons—both by educational leaders and students. The path out of poverty has been traversed successfully, and educational leaders are selling a worthy product (car sales), in an arrangement that may not have a strong long-range perspective (blindfolded), and that may not be oriented towards self-fulfillment (money). The blending of the paths requires aims all aligned to make all systems go.

Question 3: Goals of Education

This question invited participants to suggest what school leaders in their home country think U.S. education is about, and what school leaders in their home country could learn from the U.S. With her image of a "goal- and objective-driven businessman," Amelia (Jamaican) returned to the product delivery motif that she created in her previous response, but this time there is a tone of appreciation for the quality of the process and the teaching tools that facilitate the process. There is a sense that emulation would be a good thing. The image of a "child in a NEW school" (capitalization in the original) appears to convey a certain longing for contemporary relevance that is also redolent of the moral community invoked by Glickman et al. (2010).

Cora disclaimed any Jamaican preoccupation with education in the U.S., but she compared an appropriate Jamaican stance on the outcomes of education to the connoisseurship of "a skillful sculptor or painter" who is exceedingly selective about what medium to use. Such an approach would see education tailored to meet "the needs of an increasingly diverse population." Gail compared the situation of Jamaican educational leaders to a "person in a small room looking out through a tiny peephole," and was attracted, in contrast, to the U.S. image of "a motivational speaker." Gail translated the motivational speaker image into the Jamaican context, and suggested that such a leader would be able to provide expertise in how to "channel funds... to make the greatest impact," and to "motivate and train... staff to make a huge difference in the lives of their students." Elise (Jamaican) was attracted by the prospect of change. Her desire was to see an approach "other than the British system... that has been engrained in our culture and our lives."

Among the Columbians, Joan and Ian both depicted educational leaders in Columbia as believers in technology. They both depicted Columbian educational leaders as trying to prevent the local context from falling behind the pace set by the U.S., but being hampered by insufficient resourcing. On a somewhat different note, Helga (Colombian) suggested an image of testing as characterizing U.S. education, but went on to suggest that Colombian educational leaders should learn from the U.S. to be more discerning regarding roles and approaches to improving education, offering as her image "a school counselor."

Summary. In reflecting on the current state of affairs, participants were aware of what their home countries could learn from the U.S. There was a sense that the U.S. emphasis on testing is not something that they value, but that a focus on goals and objectives, together with the leadership skills to inspire teachers towards the vision was desirable. With limited funds available, it is crucial that money is spent wisely on activities with maximum leverage. Resourcefulness seemed to be highly valued by the participants. They valued the expenditure of limited funds on high-leverage activities.

Question 4: Personal Talents

This question delved into the difference between the participants' home country context and the U.S. context in terms of supporting the full expression of the respondent's talents for teaching. On the one hand, the timidity and reticence that Amelia depicted in Jamaica in Question 1 is supplanted by a range of strengths in Question 4. However, on the other hand, something of Amelia's *joie de vivre* in Jamaica ("team spirit, love/grace," "innovation, endless creativity") appears to be sublimated into "determination, resilience," and "hard work." Both of Amelia's home and U.S. skill sets are consonant with the skills and dispositions of educational leaders as delineated in CCSSO (1996), but her comparison is thought-provoking, and will be returned to later in the discussion.

Gail was harshly critical of the educational leadership she experienced in Jamaica. The image she invoked was of "an innocent man in jail [who was] never evaluated fairly." She believed her leader focused on her weaknesses and ignored her strengths. By contrast, the image she called to mind in the U.S. was of "a painter reworking a masterpiece." This is as strong a commendation of her U.S. experience as it is an indictment of her Jamaican experience. Taking account of both Gail's and Amelia's experiences brings into focus the need for developmental supervision (Glickman et al., 2010). The starkly different experiential base that these two teachers brought with them to the U.S. highlights the imperative for instructional leadership to be tailored to the needs of those being led.

Aside from Amelia's and Gail's responses, the other Jamaicans mentioned a wide range of characteristics of educational leaders, including differentiation of instruction, high expectations (Bruce), organizational skills (Cora), helping students (David), and flexibility and adaptability (Frank). Different permutations of these characteristics are echoed in the U.S. context, with the addition of comparative cultural skills "especially in content areas" singled out for mention by Elise (Jamaican).

Similarly with the Columbian respondents, there is no clear basis for delineation between the home and U.S. contexts. Possibly Joan conveys more of "a surprise box" persona in the U.S., compared to her "open book" image in Columbia, but both Helga (from Colombia), and Ian (Colombian) seem to indicate little change in the utilization of their personal talents.

Summary. The participants' talents appear to be recognized and well utilized in both their home and U.S. experiences—although local conditions may mitigate the enthusiasm of the teacher. This suggests that the skills and dispositions of educational leadership are transferable across cultures and contribute to the sense of collective capacity. As alluded to above, the circumstances can impact the degree to which such skills and dispositions are expressed.

Question 5: Lasting Memories

This question invited participants to reflect on their lasting memories of teaching in their home country compared to teaching in the U.S. Amelia's images succinctly summarize her written responses. Amelia conveys the essence of "a proud mom" towards her students in her lasting memories of teaching in Jamaica, and she comes across as the intrepid explorer in the U.S.—effectively declaring that indeed the world is round to her incredulous students.

Bruce recalled "teaching in an overcrowded classroom with limited resources" in Jamaica. He described this experience as uncomfortable, but also as fun and challenging. The common feature of all of the Jamaican and two of the U.S. memories is that they are so reminiscent of a stereotype—for example, helping a bird afraid to come out of its shell to find its wings (David), and a smiling face (Frank and Gail). However, there are U.S. exceptions. Bruce, having memorialized teaching with limited resources, regretted "having the right resources but not appreciative students," which highlighted his appreciation for the under-resourced Jamaican context. Cora similarly did not have positive recollections of "very undisciplined students thriving in a school culture where they are not [held] accountable for their inappropriate behavior," and evoked an image of "tears." In comparison to these clearly negative memories, David enigmatically referred to an enduring memory of his U.S. "students, of course," and invoked an image of "a black-and-white painting," describing himself as being puzzled by the instructional environment.

The Columbian teachers' memories of teaching at home were a little less sanguine. For example, Helga remembered her concern regarding "job security," and described a fear of being left behind economically. However, both Ian and Joan described positive memories of "another family at school," and students excitedly showing what they had learned at school, respectively. In terms of the U.S., Joan remembered an innovative approach she took that resulted in "students working hard as a team." Two of the other Columbian teachers had nuanced memories of their U.S. teaching. Helga referred to an image of "taming a lion" following a description of "uncertainty," and Ian cited an image of "maintaining faith in humanity" following an expression of appreciation for "little students coming from diverse backgrounds."

Summary. Teaching in the U.S. personally challenged the respondents both emotionally and professionally, although it was not without its satisfactions. At the same time, their memories of teaching in their home country are not uniformly sanguine. One is left with an impression of education being an easier process to engender and sustain in an environment in which its value is immediate and undeniable. The apparent inadequacies of an under-resourced culture are deceptive. Resources are not inevitably linked to the holistic quality of the education.

Question 6: Teacher Evaluation

Finally, the survey invited participants to reflect directly on how teaching performance was evaluated. They were invited to compare how teachers were evaluated in their home country with how teachers' performance was evaluated in the U.S., and were asked specifically which approach was better and why it was better. From the Jamaican perspective, Amelia asserted that both systems were similar, but with the addition of a self-evaluation step in the United States.

Apart from nuances, there is little diversity of opinion among the Jamaicans. Cora appeared unimpressed by the use of an instrument in her U.S. district that administrators were "just being trained to use." Gail asserted that the "U.S. version is better," although she saw the process in both countries as "somewhat intimidating." She also reported that, in Jamaica, assessors used a range of "very broad and vague criteria," which may relate to her earlier image of an unjustly condemned prisoner. Bruce cautioned that the use of "student achievement and test scores" for evaluation in the U.S. was sometimes unreliable, and suggested the use of "alternative assessment methods." With the exception of Gail (whose critical perspective was muted in response to this direct question), the Jamaicans appeared comfortable with the teacher assessment processes in both countries. In a response hearkening back to the moral imperative discussed by Glickman et al. (2010), Frank suggested that the touchstone was for a teacher to be "teaching heart, and soul, and mind for the students."

The Colombians were less unanimous. Helga felt that the process at home was better. She put emphasis on the role of test scores in the U.S., as opposed to what seems to be a more personalized system of advice in

Colombia. Joan felt that the systems were different just in terms of the different contexts in which they played out. Ian gave a sense of a more holistic process in Colombia, but emphasized that whatever process was considered, it should focus on the whole year performance of the teacher and involve both observations and student performance.

Summary. The importance of the evaluation of teacher performance is accepted both in the U.S. and in the international teachers' home countries. The processes also seem to be quite similar, although there is a sense that the process at home is more holistically oriented, whereas in the U.S., the emphasis in heavily placed on empirical measures.

DISCUSSION AND CONCLUSION

International teachers are recruited to teach in the U.S. because they possess subject-specific expertise. The expectation is that the international teachers will bring their subject-specific expertise with them (a quite reasonable expectation), and the students they teach will acquire subject-specific expertise because they are being taught by an appropriately credentialed teacher. This latter expectation is too simplistic, but it cannot be summarily dismissed lest one finds oneself arguing in favor of out-of-field teaching.

The discomforting international comparisons of student achievement lend impetus to the U.S. initiative to ensure teachers are teaching within their areas of academic expertise. However, teaching is an inherently complex activity, and the international teachers are more than heads for hire. When international teachers come to teach in the U.S., they bring with them an extensive skill set (as Amelia highlighted in reflecting on her talents). However, in the U.S. context, some home-grown skills are superfluous (for example, creativity in terms of instructional resources), and latent potentialities come to the fore, or have to be brought into existence (as highlighted by Gail's "pencil," "electric pencil sharpener" pairing).

The international teachers who responded to this survey appear to be grappling with their identity from a leadership perspective—especially in terms of seeking a synthesis between the expectations they had woven into their practice at home, and the expectations they encountered in the U.S. In general, effective teaching at home was interpreted in terms of the value teachers added to their students' education in a holistic sense. The change is subtle, but in the U.S., while the value added by teachers is still based on individual students' improvement, "value" is more empirically defined. In both instances, the hypothesis seems to be that society will improve because the educated student will make individual choices that will accrue to the better good of society. This seems to be close to Adam Smith's theories of economic progress—which are not widely supported currently. Rather, the aggregation of individually advantageous decisions does not accrue necessarily to societal advantage because of bounded rationality. The decisions individuals make are rational within their limited or bounded view of the world, but the collective of these decisions may not contribute to the welfare of the wider context. Educated people, in the absence of the holistic emphasis which the international teachers see as their stock-in-trade in their home countries, are not more likely to make decisions for the good of society than anyone else.

INDIVIDUAL AND COLLECTIVE CAPACITY

From a leadership perspective, how do teachers work to make improvements? They see a need for collective reform, but they are unable to impact decisions at a systems level. Consequently, they work at reforming themselves as a response to their perceived need for systems reform. However, as Grubb (2009) phrased it, "many of the most effective resources are not improvements of what individuals can make working alone, but rather are *collective* resources that can be improved by teachers and leaders working collectively" (p. 208, emphasis in original). Grubb's assertion highlights the imperative for leaders to work with their international teachers to integrate and refine the talents that their new teachers bring. This, in turn, highlights the imperative for the type of leadership that Glickman et al. (2010) have proposed for many years—leadership that fosters both moral and technical proficiency in teachers.

International teachers who have developed their competence in a foreign country grapple with the contrast between what they know their expertise to be in their home countries and what they are challenged to produce in the U.S. Their talents are diluted. They are, in effect, potential change-agents precisely because they have a dual perspective. This potential goes untapped when they are treated kindly, but also a little like exhibits, or simply like heads for hire. In some cases, the international teachers appear to be place-holders, when, if their potential was tapped, they could enliven the quality of the whole system. Herein lies the challenge to the educational leadership of the U.S. schools in which the international teachers teach: to create the conditions under which their international faculty can bring into play their full range of teaching talents as well as the richness of their diverse backgrounds.

Michael, the Austrian participant, integrated images from the Tarot throughout his responses, providing an enigmatic, yet compelling extended visual analogy that serves well as a concluding motif for a study that utilized images to delve beyond the written word. Michael's images invoked the Fool and the destruction of the Tower. One interpretation of the Fool/

Tower reference (according to http://www.aeclectic.net/tarot/learn/meanings/tower.shtml) describes the Fool coming upon a Tower that he had helped to build in an earlier time when he was striving to prove his superiority to others. The Tower was a symbol of his self-aggrandizement. The Fool sees himself at this stage of his spiritual journey as similar to those to whom he previously sought to prove himself superior. He now does not inhabit the Tower, having expanded his understanding through his journey. Coming upon the Tower again, he is amazed at how clearly he sees his earlier folly, and disavows his former attempts to prove himself superior. His disavowal of the Tower results in its crumbling before his eyes. By overcoming his earlier resistance to change and his fear of death, and relying on his new respect for moderation and the exercise of power, the Fool has opted to base his life on truth.

Without belaboring the analogical references, we would suggest that the presence of international teachers in school districts provides a currently under-utilized opportunity for both subject-specific and cultural learning. International teachers have the potential to enrich the learning of both the students and the educational leaders with whom they interact. Their potential will be better realized when the cultural barriers, or maybe the Towers, crumble.

REFERENCES

Cheung, H. Y., & Chan, A. W. H. (2008). Understanding the relationship among PISA scores, economic growth and employment in different sectors: A cross-country study. *Research in Education, 80*, 93–106.

Council of Chief State School Officers (CCSSO). (1996). *Interstate School Leaders Licensure Consortium: Standards for school leaders.* Washington, DC: Author.

Council of Chief State School Officers (CCSSO). (2008). *Educational leadership policy standards: ISLLC 2008.* Retrieved from http://www.ccsso.org/Documents/2008/Educational_Leadership_Policy_Standards_2008.pdf

Darling-Hammond, L. (1999). *Solving dilemmas of teacher supply, demand, and standards: How can we ensure a competent, caring, and qualified teacher for every child?* New York, NY: National Commission on Teaching and America's Future. Retrieved from http://www.nctaf.org/documents/supply-demand-standards.pdf

Epner, D. E., & Baile, W. F. (2011). Wooden's pyramid: Building a hierarchy of skills for successful communication. *Medical Teacher, 33*, 39–43. doi: 10.3109/0142159X.2010.530316

Epstein, T. (2000). Adolescents' perspectives on racial diversity in U.S. history: Case studies from an urban classroom. *American Educational Research Journal, 37*(1), 185–214.

Fullan, M. (2010). *All systems go: The change imperative for whole system reform.* Thousand Oaks, CA: Corwin.

Fuller, F. F. (1969). Concerns of teachers: A developmental conceptualization. *American Educational Research Journal, 62*(2), 207–266.

Fusarelli, B. C., & Boyd, W. L. (2004). Introduction: One nation indivisible? An overview of the Yearbook. *Education Policy, 18*(5), 5–11. doi: 10.1177/0895904803260356

Gándara, P., & Contreras, F. (2009). *The Latino education crisis: The consequences of failed social policies.* Cambridge, MA: Harvard University Press.

Glickman, C. D., Gordon, S. P., & Ross-Gordon, J. M. (2010). *Supervision and instructional leadership: A developmental approach* (8th ed.). Boston, MA: Allyn & Bacon.

Grissmer, D., & Kirby, S. N. (1997). Teacher turnover and teacher quality. *Teachers College Record, 99*(1), 45–57.

Grubb, W. N. (2006). The elusiveness of educational equity: From revenues to resources to results. In D. K. Cohen, S. H. Furhman, & F. Mosher (Eds.), *The state of education policy research* (pp. 157–178). Mahwah, NJ: Lawrence Erlbaum Associates.

Grubb, W. N. (2009). *The money myth.* New York: Russell Sage Foundation.

Hanushek, E. A., & Woessmann, L. (2010). *The high cost of low educational performance: The long-run economic impact of improving PISA outcomes.* Organization for Economic Co-operation and Development. Retrieved from http://www.all4ed.org/files/OECDReport011910.pdf

Heck, R. H., & Hallinger, P. (2009). Assessing the contribution of distributed leadership to school improvement and growth in math achievement. *American Educational Research Journal, 46*(3), 659–689.

Hutchison, C. B. (2006). Cross-cultural issues arising for four science teachers during their international migration to teach in U.S. high schools. *School Science & Mathematics, 106*(2), 74–83.

Ingersoll, R. M. (1997). Teacher turnover and teacher quality: The recurring myth of teacher shortages. *Teachers College Record, 99*(1), 41–44.

Jencks, C., & Phillips, M. (Eds.). (1998). *The black-white test score gap.* Washington, DC: Brookings Institution Press.

Kozol, J. (1991). *Savage inequalities.* New York, NY: Crown.

Magnuson, K., & Waldfogel, J. (2008). *Steady gains and stalled progress: Inequality and the black-white test score gap.* New York, NY: Russell Sage Foundation.

Mansell, W. (2000, September 29). Teacher training misses its target. *Times Education Supplement.* Retrieved from http://www.tes.co.uk/article.aspx?storycode=338979

McDonnell, L. M. (2004). *Politics, persuasion, and educational testing.* Cambridge, MA: Harvard University Press.

No Child Left Behind Act (NCLB) of 2001, 20 U.S.C. Sec. 6301 (2002).

Program for International Student Assessment. (2009a). *Mathematics literacy performance of 15-year-olds.* Retrieved from http://nces.ed.gov/surveys/pisa/pisa-2009highlights_3.asp

Program for International Student Assessment. (2009b). *Science literacy performance of 15-year-olds.* Retrieved from http://nces.ed.gov/surveys/pisa/pisa2009highlights_4.asp

Reardon, R. M. (2011). Elementary school principals' learning-centered leadership and educational outcomes: Implications for principals' professional development. *Leadership and Policy in Schools, 10*(1), 63–83

Schleicher, A. (2009). Lessons from the world. *Educational Leadership, 67*(2), 50–55.

Sedlak, M., & Schlossman, S. (1986). *Who will teach?* Santa Monica, CA: RAND Corporation. Retrieved from http://www.rand.org/content/dam/rand/pubs/reports/2007/R3472.pdf

Wolfe, A. (2000, March 29). Uncle Sam doesn't always know best. *Wall Street Journal,* p. A22.

SECTION III

STRATEGIES FOR DEVELOPING
SOCIAL JUSTICE LEADERS

CHAPTER 10

USING DOCUMENTARY FILM TO TEACH SOCIAL JUSTICE AND GLOBAL AWARENESS IN EDUCATIONAL LEADERSHIP

Joseph A. Polizzi and Erin San Clementi

I don't know what truth is. Truth is something unattainable. We can't think we're creating truth with a camera. But what we can do, is reveal something to viewers that allows them to discover their own truth.

—Michel Brault

INTRODUCTION

The traditional classroom approach to the training and preparation of school leaders is fast changing. Classroom teaching methods and techniques have evolved, and using multiple approaches to the planning and delivery of lessons is now more than common but expected. Exclusively online versions of classes at the higher education level and "hybrid" methods of delivering instruction (classes that both meet in person as well as online, or require an online component) have become acceptable prac-

Social Justice Leadership for a Global World, pages 173–187
Copyright © 2012 by Information Age Publishing
All rights of reproduction in any form reserved.

tices. Curriculum modules that make use of diverse instructional platforms and media are the ingredients of any well designed and delivered syllabus. This includes the use of online instructional technology, virtual forums for discussion, blogs and online journals, social-media networks, and video and audio replication available through websites like YouTube and podcasts. The ease of access to relatively obscure, more academic film titles available via online Internet streaming from websites like Netflix, Discovery Education, Annenberg Learner, EduTube, The Futures Channel, SnagFilms, Top Documentary Films, and other similar sites all bring feature, non-fiction and documentary films that once may have been doomed to a narrow audience, into the forefront of mainstream culture, beyond the urban art house theater and available in the classroom.

As the method of delivery of information has changed rapidly over the latest decades, so has the message. The very technology that has greatly influenced these new modes of communication has also influenced the content of those messages because that technology has made the world smaller; for instance, we now talk about a global community. Access to immense amounts of information to satiate the curiosity across the spectrum—from the idly curious Wikipedia tourist to the deeply devoted research scholar—has raised awareness and societal familiarity with an ever-expanding range of topics. With this expansion of issues for consideration—portrayed and delivered through media around the globe—we believe there is a particular need for a critical lens that creates practicable knowledge from these stories.

In 1964, Marshall McLuhan aptly stated that "the medium is the message" (1964/1997). The difference now, almost 50 years since first written, is the scale of interconnectedness that the advent of social action media has produced. McLuhan's reminder resounds as multifaceted messages are able to cut through and reach mass quantities of people due to visually networked, minutely personal and targeted outlets.

Clearly, the age of connectivity is upon us, but this connectivity challenges traditional notions of communication and community and offers in its place globalized knowledge-making and unchartered social and organizational dynamics (Mehlenbacher 2010). The rapidly advancing challenges brought on by technological advancement diminish previous boundaries. Now, there is the particular opportunity and strong reasoning for educational leaders to harness these means for an educative end. Such diminishing boundaries and the sheer volume of images that characterize our global community further engender the need for internationally informed and culturally sensitive educational leaders who can respond to the ever-growing obligations of social justice. The necessity of researchers and university professors to become masters of a variety of visual and technological mediums becomes an act of civic responsibility as well as a much-needed tool in the arsenal for framing issues and presenting alternative or counter-cultural visions and arguments.

Through verisimilitude, or rather what Rhodes and Springer (2006) call "image technology tied to cultural codes of verisimilitude" (p. 8), documentary films can deliver a keen understanding of social justice to the educational leadership student in immediately authentic ways. In this chapter, we discuss how documentary films offer a dynamic medium for use as a component part of an engaging curriculum in the educational leadership classroom. The particular documentary film titles selected for discussion in this chapter serve two aims: a) to introduce wide-ranging social justice themes and topics that exist outside of the education discipline but still affect the classroom; and b) to more deeply and expansively inform an epistemologically local mindset. The opportunity for school leaders to travel beyond their local or regional area for professional development and their exposure to cultures outside of their own is often limited. Further, school district personnel tend to reflect local demographics, and school communities sometimes pride themselves on maintaining their administrative personnel from a local talent pool, believing that this resident staff will reflect sensitivity to community needs and values. However, this regionalism faces newfound incongruence with our shrinking world and its subsequent growing community. It is a certain type of parochialism that can result from a too-local mindset that a careful and thoughtful approach using documentary films with current and future educational leaders can address. The use of documentary films can contribute to a growing sophisticated local—and global—vision that uniquely informs a socially just and culturally responsible disposition on the part of school practitioners.

ON DOCUMENTARY FILM THEORY AND ANALYSIS

There is a large body of research that discusses the use of *feature* films as part of the curriculum of the university classroom.[1] As it is becoming commonplace to the field of educational leadership, there are a number of strands of research that look specifically at the issues inherent in the use of feature films in this field.[2] However, throughout the research literature pertaining to the use of films on the university level, there is little discussion on the use of *documentary* films in the educational leadership classroom.[3] In searching new, valuable curriculum material and mediums that can inform and transform the work of education administrators, instructors may find that documentary film is especially powerful in a number of ways. Documentary films "stimulate epistephilia (a desire to know) in its audience and convey an informing logic, a persuasive rhetoric or a moving poetics that promises information and knowledge, insight and awareness" (Nichols, 1991, p. 40).

This access to verisimilitude, when incorporated into the curriculum of the educational leadership classroom, provides an opportunity for intellectual probing different from that offered by other materials. It also requires the activation of new levels of criticism that pulls the viewer away from the familiar and comfortable consideration of characters in a story and projects them, sometimes unsettling them, into the uncertainty of actuality. Questions arise demanding new kinds of consideration and investigation, and the dissonance is rife with the kinds of challenges educational leaders must be prepared to meet.

Documentary films show real life, interpreted through an artistic lens. The simplest and clearest definition of exactly what a documentary film is comes from the famous father of documentary film John Grierson, who stated that documentary films "offer the creative treatment of actuality" (as cited in Ellis, 2000, p. 13). This verisimilitude can be dangerous if unaddressed by critical viewing, as in the case with the recent and popular education documentary film *Waiting for Superman* (Guggenheim, 2010). Careful analysis of this film reveals its character as propaganda. According to Sheryl Tuttle Ross (2002), in order for a work to be considered propaganda, it must be epistemologically suspect/defective and used with the intention to persuade the beliefs, opinions, desires and behaviors of a socially significant group of people on behalf of a political organization, institution or cause. A conscientious contemplation of propaganda is necessary to constructively understand its function and categorize its effect. Just because something has the characteristics of propaganda, as many documentary films are susceptible, does not make it invalid or not worthwhile of consideration. As documentary films and social action media are becoming more commonplace, and more often appearing as interventions in the policy-making process, critical analysis devoted to understanding the tenets of propaganda and agnotology, the study of culturally induced ignorance (Proctor, 2008), become crucial. *Waiting for Superman* benefits from an exceptional composition, which enables the film to inspire emotional and involved reactions from its audience, but a critical analysis includes questions about what was *not* chosen to be included in the film as well as questions about what was.

When incorporated into the curriculum of the educational leadership classroom, a documentary film provides an opportunity for intellectual probing unique from those offered by the traditional academic mediums. Documentary film analysis requires the activation of new levels of critical investigation that pull the student away from the familiar and comfortable consideration of a textbook case study or the analysis of research findings presented in an article. A documentary film has the power to project research findings and ideas that can be unsettling and even epistemologically defective (i.e., wrong) into the actuality of the everyday life of a school leader. This requires the viewer to look *through* what is portrayed on the screen and to further seek out additional academic sources that reveal a deeper truth. In the case of *Waiting for Superman*, this activity is an extremely powerful practice that reveals deeper cultural, statistical, and educational revelations that lurk beneath the surface of this film. Academic research into the filmmaker's claims reveals a selectively specious (yet effective) argument and issues like public school quality, poverty, unions, teacher tenure, learning outcomes, and many others that are superficially addressed with partial information. Research counterbalances a deeper understanding of the complexity of these issues.

SOCIAL JUSTICE, GLOBAL AWARENESS AND VISUAL CRITICAL LITERACY

Deepening social justice leadership in a global context is an expansive mindset and can be difficult to define in concrete terms. Yet we believe that at the heart of an equitable and socially just supervisory disposition is a continuous, amorphous, active learning domain. Rather than being an ideology, a system, or a set of policies in itself, the concept of social justice is a value framework that provides a basis for evaluating and critiquing ideologies, systems, and policies (Hendry, 2007). As social justice encompasses life-altering experiences; this implies that professors of educational leadership need to reconceptualize and expand upon the core delivery method of the field's knowledge base if social justice is to have any lasting effect on future school leaders (Shoho, Merchant, & Lugg, 2005, p. 61).

David Baker and Gerald Letendre's (2005) discussion of the global expansion of schooling realizes that a world culture of education has emerged, shaping similar values, norms and even operating procedures in schools across all kinds of contrasting nations. As evidenced by the work of the *International Successful School Principal Project* (Moos & Johansson, 2009), many scholars and practitioners around the world are in agreement as to what a good school looks like across international boundaries (Jacobson & Ylimaki, 2011). Yet awareness of diversity continues to grow through rapidly advancing communication technology and distinct questions arise: Does a world that is growing smaller through awareness necessarily become homogenized? How can education serve the needs of rapidly changing societies, exposed to ever increasing quantities and qualities of information, while still remaining sensitive to the variety of cultures that compose those societies? Further, as Shoho, Merchant and Lugg (2005) ask, What can university administrative preparation programs do, beyond asserting sensitivity by extolling the value of socially just policies and practices in schools? Using documentary films in the educational leadership curriculum offers windows into cultures and contexts seemingly wildly different and distant, yet linked to the viewer through the common bond of humanity. Because of this, particular challenges to the viewer's positionality in relation to the wider world they inhabit begin to emerge as they gaze at the screen. In the words of Cassidy (2010):

> What may be the most difficult element of vision to make conscious is the dynamics of power involved in gazing and being gazed upon. Visual cultural studies point out that to gaze at photographs [documentaries] suggests that the viewer is a spectator. In many cases, particularly in relationship to photographs of suffering, being a spectator implies more power than the object of the gaze. The person who gazes is the subject of agency, one who can act. The one who is gazed upon is captured in the frame of the photograph as the object. (p. 200)

Using documentary films to nurture a disposition that understands and engages social justice requires this understanding of power and action. The films presented below enable discussions about basic human rights, dignity, and the inter-connectedness of people across national and cultural boundaries. This may at times require focusing a critical lens on policies, practices and people that act against the best interest of schools and children. Such an examination allows for, and even requires, the consideration of events that occur in quite distant places and their possible relevance to local circumstances and contexts.

The concept of critical literacy was developed by educator and theorist Paolo Freire to instruct the illiterate and disenfranchised poor of the Brazilian countryside by teaching more than letters and the sounds associated with them (Gutek, 2005). Researcher Allison Skerrett (2010) explains Freire's focused approach as "literacy education that empowers citizens to read both the word and the world" (p. 54). This approach, first introduced by Freire's seminal work *Pedagogy of the Oppressed* (1970/2009), stems from a foremost concern for social justice and a belief that the status quo is not preeminent fact regardless of time and place, and that by learning to read, a person becomes literate *and* empowered—empowered to learn and empowered to change the world around him or her.

Critical literacy requires the reader, regardless of age, background or education, to question as he or she reads: Who wrote this story? When was it written? Why was it written? What is its intention? Who was the intended reader? How is that reader supposed to feel about this work? How is that reader different from me? How is he or she the same? How has the intended meaning changed depending on the identity of the audience? In this way, through critical questioning (and answering), the reader is guided toward a deeper probing of the myriad perspectives that can inform meaning, and from that position open to being transformed by resulting discoveries, as the self becomes as subject to questioning as the thing examined. This type of metacognition is more than an analytic approach to literacy because it necessarily requires change; it insists that learning is transformational, and that the learner is thus charged with action towards social justice.

Henry Giroux theorizes (2001) that such a critical literacy, as developed by Freire, expanded into an overarching critical pedagogy that encompasses all of education, learning, social identity and citizenship. Critical theory, Giroux (2001) explains,

> ... refers to the nature of self conscious critique and to the need to develop a discourse of social transformation and emancipation that does not cling dogmatically to its own doctrinal assumptions. In other words critical theory refers to both a 'school of thought' and a process of critique ... it exemplifies a body of work that both demonstrates and simultaneously calls for the necessity of ongoing critique, one in which the claims of any theory must be confronted with the distinction between the world it examines and portrays, and the world as it actually exists. (p. 8)

Visual critical literacy aimed at film media, specifically documentary film, has the potential to elevate the viewing experience into a transformative engagement that promotes action towards first global awareness, then—necessarily—social justice. Viewing the documentary film whose subject examines an issue of social justice, an example of conflict between ideology and actuality, or documents otherness, as in each of the films discussed below, requires an interpretation that asks critical questions in order to form meaning through the experience of viewing the film: Who are the filmmakers? What are they trying to say? What are their inherent beliefs on which their positions rest? Who is their intended audience? What is the intended effect of the film on this audience? How does what I know, and what I do not know, influence my understanding of this film? Through such a cinematic critical literacy, the audience does not have to either agree or disagree with the point of view of the filmmaker, but only seek to understand that point of view in the context of the film as well as the context of the world that enabled its production. The activity of questioning is a practice that enables the viewer to realize dignity and a radical sociality by interrogating how his or her privileges may be located on the same map as the subjects' suffering (Cassidy, 2010).

There are three questions that can guide the educational leadership classroom in investigating the roles of social justice and global awareness with regard to the relevant edification of school leaders through the tangibility of documentary films: a) Of what practical use is being globally aware toward informing disposition for defining social justice for school leaders? b) In what way can documentary films aid in this disposition and inform how we think about educational leadership for social justice in a global context? and c) Which documentary films can be used in an educational leadership classroom to develop social justice leadership in a global context? The educator that presents the documentary film in the classroom should not ask students "What have you learned?" but rather "How have you changed?"

SELECTED DOCUMENTARY FILMS

Three films are discussed below: *Baraka* (1992), *Schooling the World: the White Man's Last Burden* (2010) and *Which Way Home* (Cammisa, 2009). Each was carefully selected after consideration of many documentary films that would fit the criteria for aiding educational leaders to approach the aims of global awareness and social justice. *Baraka* was selected for its unconventional approach, powerful insight, and ability to afford interpretations of the human condition from many perspectives. *Schooling the World* is included for its particularly critical perspective of the Western approach to education and real and perceived impact in non-Western countries and the potential implications. *Which Way Home* is here for its depiction of the immigration issue in the United States and Mexico and the ethical concerns and questions that viewers will be led to consider from watching.

While not a documentary in the familiar or traditional sense, *Baraka* (1992) is a wide ranging, ambitious film endeavor that attempts to portray the complex natural, physical, cultural, industrial, and spiritual world by juxtaposing visually dramatic footage filmed in 24 different countries on six continents. As the film travels the globe, in no particular system or order, and accompanied by an instrumental score as diverse as the visuals, it refuses to reveal any context for the stunning images depicted on the screen. It is possible through research to discover the origins of the images of mountain ranges, tribal dances, sex workers, urban landscapes, migrating birds, monkeys, factory floors, various religious rituals, shantytowns and other locales. Through specialized film techniques, such as time lapse, the filmmakers are able to present so much information in such a fluid, lyrical cinematic composition. Each frame of the film is captured by cameras in real time and then played back at a much faster rate. This time lapse approach enables the vision of a flower actually sprouting, growing and blooming in a few seconds; or viewing the rhythm and pace of people, cars and commerce on a busy urban street corner throughout an entire day over just a few minutes.

The word "*baraka*" is used by many languages, predominantly in a religious or spiritual context. In Arabic, it means spiritual gifts or protection transmitted from God; it is further defined as the greater good derived from any act. In Hebrew, spelled *berachah*, it denotes a place of blessing; in French it is a term used for luck. Baraka is essentially a sacred word that connotes divine grace and the power of sanctity or virtue as an inherent spiritual power (Hawley, 1987). *Baraka* (1992) is difficult to categorize, much like one's spirituality. It does not *look* familiar to viewers in its structure or subject matter; it does not portray people who are in leadership positions, nor are there any actors in this film, or dialogue or narration or talking at all; although viewers may find conflict in a more abstract sense, there is no story arch or plot for characters. These departures from convention leave us with a film that is rife with multiple interpretations, an experience that can widen the longitudinal scope of the use of film to affect a more globally travelled and spiritual ambient experience when applied to a multi-dimensional approach in the educational leadership classroom.

While the film *Baraka*'s inherent abstraction is not so abstract that it is unrecognizable as mini-stories of life, its deliberate lack of information—as in any indication of where the vignettes take place, of what or whom they are shot, or any significance of sequence—often leads audiences in the leadership classroom to question the purpose of the film. In fact, without the benefit of explicit exegetical commentary by the filmmaker, the viewer is unaware if the footage captured is real, doctored, staged, spontaneous, unusual, controversial or routine; the composition of coherent threads is entirely in the realm of the imagination of the viewer. As such, *Baraka* is both a visually pleasurable experience as well as an intellectually laborious one. It poses a series of unfolding questions that encompass the nature of this film specifically, non-fiction film in general, and how the viewer influences both; it primes the viewer to ask, "What am I watching and how do I know?" At the same time, it allows the viewer the opportunity to depart from typical observational behaviors because they will not be as useful while watching this film, nor appropriate—it becomes an audio-visual step back and step closer all at once. The film's concept is humanity's relation to the eternal, and it was made as a guided meditation without actors, words or a story—a series of images and music takes you to the inner essence of the concept (Fricke, as cited in Nair, 2005).

Schooling the World: The White Man's Last Burden (Black, 2010) examines the formal educational system at work in the Ladakh region of India, and the ideological conflict between Western, "modern" forces of progress and industrialization and its effects on the traditional indigenous cultures and practices of the region. The film challenges the notions of a consummate modern—or Western—schooling system, and emphasizes the value of the more local and traditional forms of knowledge that have fostered sustainability and survival of the local culture over hundreds and even thousands of years. *Schooling the World* presents for consideration the overestimation of such an application of Western education systems, and their inherent cultural values, as they are exported into communities and societies in which they were not generated. In doing so, these school systems assume an international homogeny for the standardization of curriculum, and as such presume to benchmark instruction according to a universal standard that postmodern learning has shown us not to exist, as if attempting to educate all students around the world in the same exact way was even possible, let alone advantageous.

The film is composed of traditional documentary elements, juxtaposing candid footage of indigenous populations, at home and at school, with interviews with concerned parties, spanning students, parents, school administrators and a slew of scholarly education and anthropology experts. The tone cannot be mistaken: the filmmakers avidly oppose what is presented as an ideological invasion of an alien value system into disappearing cultures whose erosion is accelerated by the dangerously benevolent mentality of a contemporized "white man's burden," a position the film's subtitle foreshadows. The fervor with which the filmmakers harbor this position is subtle through the polished professionalism of the documentary product, but unmistakably present through editing and scholarly commentary, and the message is not meant to be objective as much as persuasive; the filmmakers hope to educate the viewer and in doing so persuade them to their position.

The traditional form of the media coupled with the position diametrically opposed to formal Western education systems create an interesting problem for the viewer, especially if that viewer is an educator engaged with furthering a post graduate education for his or her self in a formalized western setting. *Schooling the World* presents an ideological dilemma that cannot be easily assuaged, and the internal strife it might inspire is particularly useful in the educational leadership classroom as fertile ground for self-evaluation and potential growth. The contemplation does not, however, solely rest on the details of cultures thousands of miles away from our classroom, but also on the details of our own experiences, the students we work with and the education systems we serve—how are values therein determined, who makes those determinations, and who do those values benefit? The film is as much about critically defining "progress" abroad as at home.

Which Way Home (Camissa, 2009) is a documentary film by director Rebecca Camissa, who received a Fulbright grant to conduct her documentary research, about the journey that many Mexican children undertake each year in their attempts to immigrate to the United States in search of family, fortune and a better life. The film's emphasis is on an examination of the situation, and its prerogative of educating otherwise unknowing parties of frightening details surrounding an issue at the forefront of national debate. Perhaps it is this position, which does not include a perspective on any potential solutions, which makes it so difficult to watch, but it is so imperative to a multifaceted dialogue on the issue of immigration itself.

The film follows seven children, Fito, Yurico, Jairo, Jose, Olga and Freddy, and Juan Carlos, over the 1,700 mile journey from Central America, through the length of Mexico, to the United States border, riding atop

"The Beast," a series of corporately owned freight trains that carry goods along the course. Countless migrants, usually adults, but approximately 5% children, make the extremely dangerous journey through Mexico by jumping these trains and riding them all the way to the border, before attempting the further perilous crossing into the United States, either through the desert or across the river. The odds of success even before reaching the border are dismal. The documentary captures the unshakeable conviction of the would-be child immigrants, traveling without their parents, even in the face of death or dismemberment—a fate akin to death because of its prohibition of any chance to work, one of the main motivations for the journey in the first place, after family.

The film is expertly crafted and deeply moving; it presents a complicated problem with wide ranging humanistic ramifications, but does not suggest any particular course toward solutions, which would be necessarily guided by a specific ideological perspective or other, and its own political stakes. By focusing on the journeys of children, some as young as six, some who left their mothers secretly in the night, some without any mothers at all, the film captures the magnitude of the gut wrenching harshness of the problem and boldly challenges an audience's passive viewing posture. Issues of justice, care, cohesion and the ethical dilemmas that arise when considering the repatriation of immigrant children back into the high risk environments they sought to escape arise through the viewing of this film.

The current political climate surrounding the issue of illegal immigration through the Mexican border is turbulent and impassioned, growing more intense daily with news reports of floundering employment rates, national deficits, health care crises, and the Mexican Drug War claiming growing numbers of lives in the tens of thousands, and spilling onto American soil. While this documentary neither openly advocates nor condemns illegal immigration, it does attempt to put a penetratingly human face on the issue, and the faces best able to tear deeply into the hearts of audiences are those of children. Although using children as the vehicle for the difficult story seems like a choice rife with manipulative motivations, the filmmakers indirectly comment on their own susceptibility to that charge by including the reactions of various adults involved in the children's journeys, including government and immigration officials, police officers, parents, and other adult migrants reacting to their presence on the journey. In the end the story is much more complicated than a heart-string pulling exploitation because the filmmakers take pains to step away from a hero-villain dynamic to the story; no one, including the children, is presented as morally exalted, and the humanity of all involved parties is presented for examination.

Immigration is a powerful vector of change (Suarez-Orozoco, 2001), and it will continue to play a significant role in the lives of teachers and school administrators throughout the first half 21st Century.

> Census Bureau data shows we are on track to add 130 million more people
> to the U.S. population in just the next 40 years, primarily due to future im-
> migration. Without a change in immigration policy, the nation is projected to
> add roughly 30 million new residents each decade for the foreseeable future.
> Assuming the current ratio of population to infrastructure, adding roughly
> 30 million each decade will mean building and paying for 8,000 new schools
> every 10 years. (Camarota, 2010)

Due to the pace and reality of migrations, with or without any significant
change to our current immigration policy, school leaders must begin to
clarify and clearly articulate distinct educational missions that incorporate
the diverse needs and multidimensional talents of a growing immigrant
population. *Which Way Home* offers a vehicle for beginning this discussion.

CONCLUSION

The films selected here for use in the educational leadership classroom are
challenging and thought provoking. Our experience using documentary
films has added significant nuance to our discussions of global awareness
and social justice. We encourage educational leaders and professors to devise a teaching practice that makes use of the abundance of documentaries available, and in so doing help others come to realize the possibilities
of social justice as an educational construct in such a way that displays a)
education as a basic right; b) that social justice as an educational construct
exists beyond schooling, yet it connects children, adults and schools to society; and c) critiques and experiments within education to show discourse,
advocacy and activism (Bogotch, 2008).

Alfred Hitchcock is often quoted as saying, "In feature films the director
is God; in documentary films God is the director."[4] If this is true, image,
symbol, music, iconic representations, interviews, environments, dialogue,
creativity, all as represented in the craft of documentary filmmaking, provide a window into the complexity of human experience and the multi-
faceted and varied collective and individual experiences of truth. As such,
these films work to influence and challenge school leaders to enhance an
embodied supervisory disposition that is critical yet empathetic of others.
This in turn enables the creation of and service towards goals and objectives
that aim to improve the overall human condition.

Media of an expanding variety penetrate all levels of our lives, and growing availability and access to multitudinous information and perspective
through technology can either overwhelm us or inspire us, and equip us to
face the very challenges they document. In order to determine our relationship with this ever-evolving condition, we, especially educators, must invite
the contemplation into the fabric of our instruction. The proliferation of

documentary films, the targeted and influential nature of the stories depicted, and the seemingly infinite outlets for their screening make the medium a productive subject and essential tool for investigation; the critical consideration of this form of communication is necessary study. Our understanding of documentary film is not so much on *what* creative techniques are used, but on *how* they are used, and to what extent the film succeeds in yielding a "truthful" representation or reflection of reality. The art of documentary films acts as a penetrating visual language in service to global awareness and social justice.

NOTES

1. This research includes its role in such courses as psychology (Dorris & Ducey, 1978; Gladstein & Feldstein, 1983), sociology (Demerath, 1981; Shdaimah, 2009), business and law (Berger & Pratt, 2004; Gerde, Shepard & Goldsby, 1996), and medicine (Alexander, Pavlov, & Lenahan (2004; Self, Baldwin & Olivarez, 1993).
2. These include the portrayal and deconstruction of school leaders, principals and school superintendents within the school setting (Dalton, 1999; Smith, 1998; Thomas, 1998); the diverse interpretation of specific feature films and their relevance to educational theories, classroom and organizational practice (Billsberry & Gilbert, 2008; Bumpus, 2005; Champoux, 1999; Shouse, 2005); and the use of historical and or biographical feature films to discuss the moral and ethical decisions faced by leaders portrayed in them (English & Steffy, 1997).
3. Though Scherer and Baker (1999) created an entire course on social institutions using the documentary films of noted cinematographer Frederick Wiseman to teach organizational theory concepts, this course was not specifically designed for school leaders.
4. This quote is widely referenced to Alfred Hitchcock, but is difficult to find the primary source. An excellent source of compiled quotes on documentary film making can be found online through the University of California at Berkeley Library Media Research Center at http://www.lib.berkeley.edu/MRC/reel-life/quotes.html.

REFERENCES

Alexander, M., Pavlov, A., & Lenahan, P. (2004). *Cinemeducation: A comprehensive guide to using film in medical education.* Oxford, UK: Radcliffe.

Baker, D., & Letendre, G. (2005). *National differences, global similarities: World culture and the future of schooling.* California: Stanford University Press.

Berger, J., & Pratt, C. (1998). Teaching business communication ethics with controversial films. *Journal of Business Ethics, 17*(16), 1817–1824.

Billsberry, J., & Gilbert, L. H. (2008). Using Roald Dahl's *Charlie and the Chocolate Factory* to teach different recruitment and selection paradigms. *Journal of Management Education, 32*(2), 228.

Black, C. (2010). *Schooling the world: The white man's last burden.* [motion picture] Malibu, CA: Lost People Films.

Bogotch, I. (2008). Social justice as an educational construct. In I. Bogotch, I. Blount, F. Beachum, J. Brooks, & F. English (Eds.), *Radicalizing educational leadership: Dimensions of social justice* (pp. 79–112). Rotterdam, Taipei: Sense Publishers.

Bumpus, M. (2005). Using motion pictures to teach management: Refocusing the camera lens through the anfusion approach to diversity. *Journal of Management Education, 29*(6), 792–815.

Camarota, S. (2010). *Census: Population up 27 Million in Just 10 years.* Center for Immigration Studies. Retrieved on April 14, 2011 from http://www.cis.org/2010CensusPopulation

Cammisa, R. (Director). (2009). *Which way home.* (Documentary Film). Guatemala: Documentress Films.

Cassidy, L. (2010). Picturing suffering: The moral dilemmas in gazing at photographs of human anguish. *Horizons, 37*(21), 95–223.

Champoux, J. (1999). Film as a teaching resource. *Journal of Management Inquiry, 8*(2), 240–251.

Dalton, M. (1999). *The Hollywood curriculum: Teachers and teaching in the movies.* New York, NY: Peter Lang.

Demerath, N. J. III. (1981). Through a double-crossed eye: Sociology and the movies. *Teaching Sociology, 9*(1), 69–82.

Dorris, W., & Ducey, R. (1978). Social psychology and sex roles in films. *Teaching of Psychology, 5,* 168–169.

Ellis, J. C. (2000). *John Grierson: Life, contributions, influence.* Carbondale, IL: Southern Illinois University Press.

English, F., & Steffy, B. (1997). Using film to teach leadership in educational administration. *Educational Administration Quarterly, 33*(1), 107–115.

Freire, P. (2009). *Pedagogy of the Oppressed.* New York: Continuum. (Original work published 1970)

Gerde, V., Shepard, J., & Goldsby, M. (1996). Using film to examine the place of ethics in business. *The Journal of Legal Studies Education, 14*(2), 199–214.

Giroux, H. (2001). *Theory and resistance in education.* Westport, CT: Bergin & Garvey.

Gladstein, G. A., & Feldstein, J. C. (1983). Using film to increase counselors empathic experiences. *Counselor Education and Supervision, 23,* 125–131.

Guggenheim, D. (Director). (2010) *Waiting for Superman.* (Documentary Film). United States: Participant Media.

Gutek, G. L. (2005). *Historical and philosophical foundations of education: A biographical introduction.* Upper Saddle River, NJ: Pearson Education, Inc.

Hawley, J. S. (Ed.). (1987). *Saints and virtues.* (Comparative studies in religion and society, vol. 2). Berkley: University of California Press.

Hendry, S. J. (2007, May 25). Block vs. Hendry on social justice at Loyola University. Retrieved on April 1, 2011 from http://www.lewrockwell.com/block/block76.html.

Hurst, J. (Producer) & Black, C. (Director). (2011). *Schooling the world: The white man's last burden* [Motion picture]. United States: Lost People Films.

Jacobson, S., & Ylimaki, R. (2011). First International Successful School Principal Project (ISPP) Conference held May 2010. *UCEA Review, 52*(1), 25.

Magison, M. (Producer) & Fricke, E. (Director). (1992). *Baraka* [Documentary Film]. United States: Magison Films.

Mehlenbacher, B. (2010). *Instruction and technology: Designs for everyday learning.* Cambridge, MA: MIT Press.

McLuhan, M. (1997). *Understanding media: The extensions of man.* Cambridge, MA: MIT Press. (Original work published 1964)

Moos, L., & Johansson, O. (2009). The international successful school principalship project: Success sustained? *Journal of Educational Administration, 47*(6), 765–780.

Nair, R. (2005). Dubai as international film festival: Cinema as meditation. Retrieved on April 11, 2011 from http://diff2005reports.blogspot.com/2005/12/cinema- as-meditation-ronfricke.html.com

Nichols, B. (1991). *Representing reality: Issues and concepts in documentary.* Bloomington: Indiana University Press.

Proctor, R. N. (2008). *Agnotology: The making and unmaking of ignorance.* Palo Alto, CA:Stanford University Press.

Rhodes G., & Springer, J. (2006). *Docufictions: Essays on the intersection of documentary and fictional film making.* Michigan: McFarland & Co.

Ross, S. (2002). Understanding propaganda: The epistemic merit model and its application to art. *Journal of Aesthetic Education, 36*(1), 16–30.

Scherer, R. F., & Baker, B. (1993(9)). Exploring social institutions through the films of Frederick Wiseman. *Journal of Management Education, 23,* 143–153.

Self, D., Baldwin, D., & Olivarez, M. (1993). Teaching medical ethics to first-year students by using film discussion to develop their moral reasoning. *Academic Medicine, 68*(5), 383–385.

Shdairmah, C. (2009). The power of perspective: Teaching social policy with documentary film. *Journal of Teaching in Social Work, 29*(1), 85–100.

Shoho, A., Merchant, B., & Lugg, C. (2005). Social justice: Seeking a common language. In F. English (Ed.), *The Sage handbook of educational leadership* (pp. 47–67). Thousand Oaks, CA: Sage.

Shouse, R. (2005). Taking Lulu seriously: What we can learn from *To Sir with Love. Journal of Educational Administration, 43*(4), 357–367.

Skerrett, A. (2010). Teaching critical literacy for social justice. *Action in Teacher Education, 31*(4), 54–65.

Smith, P. (1998), Sex, lies and Hollywood's administrators: The (de)construction of school leadership in contemporary films. *Journal of Educational Administration, 37*(1), 50–66.

Suarez-Orozoco, M. (2001). Globalization, immigration and education: The research agenda. *Harvard Educational Review, 71*(3), 345–366.

Thomas, R. A. (1998). As they are portrayed: Principals in film. *International Journal of Education Management, 12*(2), 90–100.

CHAPTER 11

TRANSPOSITIONS TOWARD BECOMING LEADING SUBJECTS

Kelly Clark/Keefe and Vachel Miller

INTRODUCTION

As educational leadership faculty interested in helping shape emerging and current leaders' discursive literacy, we began reading closely the work of transcontinental philosopher and feminist Rosi Braidotti (1994a, 2006), focusing our gaze especially on her conceptualization of *transpositions*, mining it for possibilities of thinking about our pedagogical aims and means anew. We have begun to see her ideas as offering a generous and flexible cartography, helping point a way to teaching and learning that fosters an ability and desire to negotiate successfully the complex tension between the commitment to positive, emancipatory social action *and* the multiplicity of political forces that work to produce and sustain the effects and affects of globalization. This chapter is a carefully considered beginning—an entrance to Braidotti's ideas as a way of both understanding past teaching enactments and as an avenue for incitement to future engagement with transpositioning our students and ourselves. In this spirit, the work is not a "naming" of what we have done. Instead, it stands as an invitation to oth-

Social Justice Leadership for a Global World, pages 189–208
Copyright © 2012 by Information Age Publishing

ers in this volume and beyond who are thinking with and teaching across disciplinary discourses to help shape not just what *is* but also what *could be* socially just educational leadership in a global context.

As a whole, this chapter centers on the concept of *transpositions* as articulated by philosopher Rosi Braidotti (2006). Hers is a work of immense proportion, and the discussion here takes up just a fraction of her concerns with nomadic subjectivity and transpositionality. Before moving to the heart of what we, in relation to becoming-leaders with our students, believe Braidotti's work has to offer, it is necessary to briefly introduce two particular bodies of thought or theoretical orientations—*poststructuralism* and *material feminism*—each of which function as crucial, interrelated undercurrents, helping to produce Braidotti's broader conceptualization of transpositions. *Transpositions* (2006) as a text and a set of ideas, is, in several important ways, a graduated outgrowth[1] of Braidotti's (1994a, 2002, 2006) multiple and deep analyses of these two critical postmodern discourses; hence it seems prudent to foreground them, moving (perhaps all too swiftly) to consider the particular ways that each illuminate notions of the contemporary leading subject[2] within multicultural educational contexts, a project that we believe important, yet heretofore, has not been taken up in any depth.[3] Our efforts at thinking *with* Braidotti's notion of transpositions involve discussing first the basic premises for each guiding body of thought (poststructuralism, material feminism, and transpositions respectively), glimpsing what each do to notions of educational leadership and leading subjectivity. Between each, we travel with the theory through what we are calling *pedagogical interludes* which illustrate putting each theoretical orientation "to work" in our doctoral seminars—as part of course design and/or retrospectively. In this way, we both join and expand Braidotti's general notion of transpositions, grounding a complex set of concepts in a specific pedagogical context to envision what new understandings may emerge.

POSTMODERNISM, THE "LINGUISTIC TURN," AND CONSTITUTING THE LEADING SUBJECT IN POSTSTRUCTURALIST DISCOURSE

The 21st century educationally leading subject is both born into and invested in shaping the broad socio-political narrative landscape that historically has and continues to define what education is and should be. Contemporary conditions of globalization, characterized by hyper-connectivity to information networks, increasing realization of ecological interdependence, intensive promotion of market-oriented reforms across social sectors, and pervasive social inequalities and tensions among/within states and nations have produced complex and often contentious discourses that shape what it means to be and act as an educational leader (Bottery, 2004). As Mike Bottery (2004) observes:

> Leaders need, as never before, to be 'ecologically aware'—to be cognizant of those forces that impact upon not only their own practice, but upon the attitudes and values of the other educators within their organizations, the aspirations and endpoints of their students, and upon those in the wider communities they serve. (p. 25)

With the complexity of global, political, economic and ecological circumstances in clear view, our pedagogical work in these doctoral seminars has become increasingly invested in attending to *the constitution of* leading subjects. Through foregrounding postmodernist sensitivities about the role that language plays in the production of and performances by contemporary leading subjects in education, we begin to glimpse the work and worth of developing the sort of "ecological awareness" that Bottery (2004) advocates and, as discussed later, that Braidotti compels us towards.

It is a vast understatement to say that the term postmodernism carries variable and contested meanings. Indeed, *meaning* itself is a central notion that postmodernity, as a current of thought and expression, calls into question. Whether taken as a set of ideas, a historical marker, or a group of strategic and critical practices that put to work concepts such as difference (Deleuze, 1968/1994; Deleuze & Guatarri, 1980/1987), the trace, (Derrida 1967/1976), or genealogy (Foucault, 1977), postmodernism signals an expressed dynamic aimed at undoing, shaking-up, or otherwise calling into question taken-for-granted assumptions about the objective nature of knowledge and truth. In the wake of Jean-François Lyotard's (1979/1984) key essay popularizing what many were only beginning to understand as the "postmodern condition," educational philosophers, researchers, and theorists especially interested in the structural arrangements and enactments of power, as well as the master narratives that govern and shape how we have come to understand (and value) teaching, learning, and organizational life in education, have been able to gain a critical foothold, generating a proliferation of discourses that center a *social constructivist* perspective. The postmodern outlook has challenged theoretical paradigms that assert themselves as the "one best way" to do research or leadership, and has cleared ground for the profusion of critically oriented perspectives, such as postcolonial, critical race, and queer theories. Such post-oriented perspectives have decentered the normative white/male subject to give more space for the telling of the complex, particular stories of social and educational life on the edges of traditional categories.

As foreshadowed, language plays a particularly important role in postmodernist thinking and is central to social constructivist viewpoints. A species of postmodernist thought known as *poststructuralism* marks especially this turn to language and is frequently pointed to as the intellectual engine fueling the "linguistic turn;" the centering of *text* and *discourse* as the mechanism by which cultural, social, and subjective constructions (such as "education" and "student") get shaped (and are involved in the shaping). Educational theorists working from a poststructural perspective turn to discourse as the primary site for analysis, emphasizing language as being constitutive of reality and meaning being generated through the relationship of differentially defined terms (i.e., I can only know the meaning of "cat" because of a language system that systematically differentiates it from "dog". What links the word "cat" with what I see, sense or say *as* "cat" is not its intrinsic "catness," but instead the use of language that relies on the logic and learning of *difference*.) The concept *difference* is at the heart of both structuralism and poststructuralism. However, unlike the structuralist perspective that holds difference as an *embedded* mental structure, poststructuralists believe that language rules are, like the meanings they produce, radically contingent and mutable.

In addition to centering language, one of the most significant practices that educational researchers and theorists working from a poststructural perspective have brought to the social sciences of education is *deconstruction*. Deconstruction means different things to the various writers, philosophers, and researchers who would claim to employ its "logic" (MacLure, 2003). To deconstruct a discourse "is to unravel hidden assumptions, internal contradictions, and [for those adopting a psychoanalytic perspective] repressed meanings" (Gemmell & Oakley, 1992, p. 114). Authors Gary Gemmill and Judith Oakley (1992) offer what we have discovered to be one of very few writings that takes a deconstructionist approach to the discourse of leadership (see Bottery, 2004; Maxcy, 1994 for additional postmodern treatments of leadership). Through examining various popularized views and writings about "the leader" and "leadership," Gemmell and Oakley (1992) surface several underlying assumptions and hidden presuppositions "in order to reveal the hidden political and social beliefs implied in the text[s]" (p. 114). Relevant to our conversation about the educationally leading subject are thoughts by these authors about the role of reification, or the social process of converting a mental concept or construct (leader) into a reality. Through deconstructive moves, the "conversion" begins to reveal itself in particular ways: through reification the social construction of leadership is mystified and accorded an objective existence. With reification, social progress is viewed as "caused" by or "determined" by a leader, a cadre of leaders, or "leadership." It is assumed by researchers and practitioners that because there is a word ("leader" or "leadership"), there must be an independent objective reality it describes or denotes. Reification functions to trap such labeled individuals within a mode of existence that serves to meet various unconscious emotional needs of members of an organization and of a society (Gemmell & Oakley, 1992).

One of the most powerful and productive moves in deconstruction then is, as Maggie MacLure (2003) asserts, to "spot the ways in which texts are 'articulated'—that is, joined or stitched together" (p. 9), with reification being one such stitching device. As MacLure (2003) goes on to note, however, it is the setting up of *binary oppositions* that is "[o]ne of the most general and commonplace ways in which this articulation gets done" (p. 9). "Such binary oppositions," MacLure (2003) attests, "are one of the key ways in which meaning and knowledge are produced" (p. 10). Joining Jacques Derrida, MacLure (2003) notes:

> One 'side' achieves definition—comes to meaning—through its *difference* with respect to a constructed 'other' which is always lacking, lesser or derivative in some respect. According to Derrida (1998), this oppositional logic reflects a form of 'metaphysical' thinking that has been practised by Western philosophy from Plato onwards, and which he called 'logocentrism.' Some core principle or concept is established as the superior term—the first, last, deepest, universal, central, purest or most fundamental of all—in a violent 'hierarchy' of meaning. (p. 10)

So, what happens to the educationally "leading subject" under poststructuralist circumstances, where the words locate the person it intends to describe within a "particular morale universe" (MacLure, 2003, p. 9)? What are the accumulated resonances behind the words that shape what we understand to mean "leader"—where, as Bakhtin (1981) has taught us: "Each word tastes of the context and contexts in which it has lived its socially charged life" (p. 294)?

With poststructural skepticism of binary logic in mind, our attention now turns to the first of three pedagogical interludes where theories and the concepts they engender are enlivened by their use in helping leadership students encounter (and question) "common sense" but nonetheless under-examined frames of reference for categories in 21st century education. In the first interlude, poststructuralism's aims and means are "put to work" toward understanding what is involved in going behind the scenes of myriad discourses that signal and produce durable difficulties in education, such as discrimination and oppression.

PEDAGOGICAL INTERLUDE I

Putting Poststructural Theory to Work:
Discursive Literacy and the Leading Subject

As foreshadowed in this chapter's introduction, the pedagogical land-scape for this interlude and those that follow involves work done along-side students in an educational leadership doctoral program[4] and centers a pair of courses entitled *Multidisciplinary Seminar I & II: Emerging Issues in Education.* In opening this sequence of seminars, we blend customary read-ings that center the sociology of education with less conventional readings that introduce students to the premises behind and purposes for discur-sive literacy (see especially, Bettie, 2003; Gannon & Davies, 2007; MacLure, 2003; St. Pierre, 2000). We discuss the central tenets of postmodernist and poststructural thinking, namely that meaning is shaped through discourses that, over time, get repeated and repeated, until they become ubiquitous, cognitive short-cuts, imbued with "common sense." We contemplate and inevitably debate the radically poststructural summarization by Patti Lather (1991), that "whatever 'the real' is, it is discursive" (p. 25).

Our attention turns swiftly to one of the central features of poststructural thought: that speech, text, and symbolism derive much of their meaning in and through the linguistic structure of difference; that what we experience by way of being worded or viewed as a "woman," for example, surfaces from what we understand ourselves not to be (a "man"). We discuss the idea that poststructuralism is particularly keen to call this oppositional logic out, con-sidering it dangerous and the underpinnings for inequities because the two sides of the opposition are never neutral. Terms on both sides of the binary are weighted along lines of historically and politically determined value, engendering and reproducing power arrangements that, based on one's social, racial or cultural positioning, always already classify certain people and/or groups above versus below, advantaged versus disadvantaged, and so on. In a transdisciplinary fashion, we put poststructuralist theory to work on our common sense understandings of sociology's and cultural theory's regularly constructed markers of "class," "immigrant," "race," and "gen-der;" on economic discourses of "developed" and "third world;" and on psychological and bio-medical conceptualizations of "ability," "normally developing," "child well-being," and so on. We work to become increasingly adept at asking ourselves and each other: *How do terms constructed along lines of difference shape and produce what we can and cannot know about individual and collective lives, especially those lived on the edges of what we have come to recognize, to "know" as "normal"?* We also begin to contemplate our role as social agents and as leaders, where what we "know" as "typical" or "correct" (for example, discussing students as educationally under-prepared vs. academically gifted) can be conceived and acted upon as both, and where the oppositional logic and the categories it produces is resisted and slid across. Here the impression is one of dissociation, disorderly conduct, and leaderly undecidability. What does it look like when the binaries holding the logic of opposition in place start to rupture and fail? Who can imagine such a subject, such a leader?

We turn with our students to glimpsing *Leadership Zombidom* (Figure 11.1[5]) in light of some of the possible technologies of binary thought at work specifically on and by them as emerging and/or current leading subjects. We work to call out the side-by-side, powerful pairs: the oppositional logic on which leading identities are often built, made recognizable, and over time, experienced as "real" (i.e., reified). We discuss how the historically and politically imbued *valuing* of each side of any binary, as well as the pull for leaders to identify with either this or that set of ideological beliefs, is what is at issue here. As MacLure (2003) and other deconstructionists point out, binaristic categories structure power relations that bifurcate and imprint on our collective psyche. This process establishes conceptual order and gives the impression of decisions being made along lines of, in this case, the leader's perceived allegiances with, for example, promoting global competitiveness over more local community-driven needs and service provision. Discourses that circulate to produce the competing social aims surrounding schooling also function to invest the school-community's stake in one or the other side of the binary, placing the leading subjects in an always already dualistic set of relations with education.

While not directly associating leaders who attempt to slip across or disrupt binaristic notions with zombies, we do take up this *figuration* (Braidotti, 1994b) as a transpositional point of departure for exploring how, for example, marginality and discrimination functions in general and in education in particular. In Braidotti's (1994b) early feminist writings on female subjectivity, she refers to the use of figurations as "a style of thought that evokes or expresses ways out of the phallocentric vision of the subject" (p. 1). In this spirit, the zombie figure is intended as a positive lever or provocateur, stirring "a real urgency to elaborate alternative accounts, to invent new frameworks, new images, new modes of thought" (Braidotti, 1994b, p. 1). Conjuring the legendary and ceaselessly intriguing figure of the zombie derived from Haitian cultural and folkloric traditions (Cussans, 2004), the figure roams as a powerful assistant, guiding leadership students' considerations of the logic and power of binary oppositions in producing and maintaining pernicious stereotypes related to gender, race, ability and so on, as well as the fear surrounding the dissolution of these oppositions. The not-quite-dead/not-quite-alive figure that has, overtime and with Hollywood's help, become sinister and suspect, functions as a "new mode of thought" (Braidotti, 1994b, p. 1), a new way of accounting for the us versus them binary

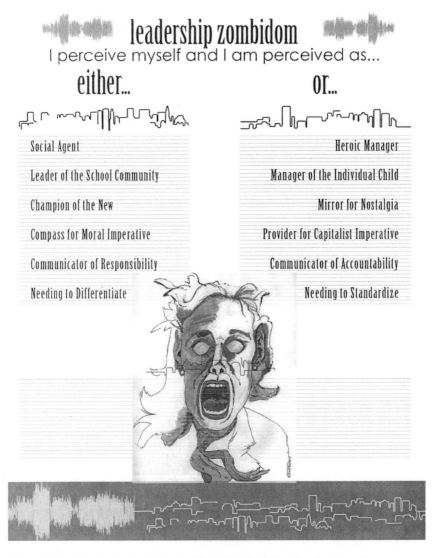

leadership zombidom

I perceive myself and I am perceived as...

either...   or...

Social Agent	Heroic Manager
Leader of the School Community	Manager of the Individual Child
Champion of the New	Mirror for Nostalgia
Compass for Moral Imperative	Provider for Capitalist Imperative
Communicator of Responsibility	Communicator of Accountability
Needing to Differentiate	Needing to Standardize

Figure 11.1 *Leadership Zombidom* by Clark/Keefe, 8.5 × 11, mixed media.

that serves to separate and in some cases judge individuals or populations unfairly. With the undecidable or indeterminate figuration of the zombie, we begin pressing open the tightly stitched meanings—the naturalness and inevitability—of identities, values and concepts such as ability versus disability or alien versus citizen. As leading subjects, we put this discursive literacy to work, approaching anew various theoretical, political, and historical discussions that debate, for example, the natural and/or socially constructed experiences of homosexuality, Christianity, teen pregnancy, race, citizenship, or other difficult differences as markers of identity.

Deconstructing binaries, rather than resting comfortably within them, can be disorienting. Reports of melancholia and frustration during this sort of deconstructive work are common. "So where do we go from here?" How can deconstruction (which often registers as *destruction*) possibly be constructive? With the realization of the proliferation of unequal power relations embedded in not only the everyday language we use but also the very means by which discourse is produced (and which produces us), we can become overwhelmed; as one student put it, "I'm speechless."

ON NOT THROWING THE LEADING AND FOLLOWING BODY OUT WITH THE LINGUISTIC BATHWATER: THE MATERIAL DIMENSION

Acutely conscious of enfolding lessons learned from postmodernism's and poststructuralism's "linguistic turn," we have in our teaching grown interested in making matter matter more while attempting understanding of how and why difference, divisions, and devaluation circulate to become what we can and cannot know as leading subjects in the 21st century. In the above noted student's speechlessness, for example, within his/our *embodied* learning instance where words would not or could not be surfaced, resides a whole host of important and we believe productive resonances that, as teachers, we want to honor.[6] With Braidotti, we want to turn towards rather than away from the body's stammer, the conceptual shudder that poststructuralism so often produces, refusing the binary of mind/body and working "bewilderment for all its worth" (St. Pierre, 1997, p. 281).

Amidst the groundswell of still-needed attention being paid to the textual, linguistic, and discursive, another paradigmatic "turn" has been brewing: the "affective turn," where it is discourse that is de-centered (not dismissed) to allow for a focus on materiality and affect.[7] Writers and researchers taking a material feminist perspective see the potential in expanding current linguistic considerations of subjectivity and the social (including education) to include a focus on physical bodies alongside socio-cultural discursively constituted bodies. As teachers who have witnessed the sensory affects of our own and our students' learning, the material of encountering the new or of the gnawing away of previous knowledge, we have become increasingly drawn to practices that draw on and retain elements from both the discursive *and* the material without privileging one over the other. In this way, we join Braidotti (2006), Clough and Halley (2007), Alaimo and Hekman (2008) and others in their efforts to not throw the discursively constituting and constituted body out with the linguistic bathwater:

> Even though many social constructionist theories grant the existence of mate-
> rial reality, that reality is often posited as a realm entirely separate from that
> of language, discourse, and culture...We need a way to talk about the mate-
> riality of the body as itself an active, sometimes recalcitrant force. (Alaimo &
> Hekman, 2008, pp. 3–4)

But what can we learn about and from the educationally leading subject's
body? And what are the dangers of doing so, especially in the context of
doctoral studies? Even if we, as teachers, students, or as leading subjects
accept that bodies are not merely conduits for conceptual understandings
and that corporeality and intercorporeality are implicated in all of our discursive arrangements, how do we work productively from our sensorial reg-
ister of pleasure and pain when in so doing, we run the risk of satisfying "all
the prerequisites of a moral panic" (Piper & Stronach, 2008, p. 3)? How
do we begin to take seriously, analyze, and construct a vision for teaching
enactments that think and work from the body?

One interesting way in which the embodied work of leaders is becoming
more popularized in professional literature is through the building upon of
Daniel Goleman's (2006) previous work on emotional intelligence. Goleman
has written recently about social intelligence, focusing on the neural-emo-
tional resonance of leaders' bodies in setting a tone in their organizations.

In the past five years, research in the emerging field of social neurosci-
ence—the study of what happens in the brain while people interact—is beginning to reveal subtle new truths about what makes a "good leader." The
salient discovery is that certain things leaders do—specifically, exhibit empathy and become attuned to others' moods—literally affect both their own
brain chemistry and that of their followers (Goleman & Boyatzis, 2008).

While honoring the inter-corporeal flow of emotion among leaders/
followers, Goleman's perspective can reinforce a universalized subjectivity,
abstracted from the matrix of socially-marked and culturally-nuanced experience of emotion. Studies that appropriate technologies that help us map
the biological onto the social and vice versa are important, yet as feminists
have been especially keen to point out, we do run the risk of producing an
over-essentialist view. Here again, we're to keep lessons from the linguistic
turn from sliding under the seduction that "hard" science and empirical
truths invite, namely the reproduction of grand narratives that perpetuate a supposed split between affect and reason. How can we as teachers,
with our affinity for alliances with and for the leading/learning subjects in
our classes, act on "semiotic flows, material flows, and social flows simultaneously" (Deleuze & Guattari, 1980/1987, pp. 22–23), helping to foster a
materially-discursive literacy for culturally responsive leadership?

PEDAGOGICAL INTERLUDE II

Putting Material Feminism to Work: Tuning-In and Turning Toward Social Sense Making

In the previous interlude we conjured our multidisciplinary seminars as sites where we worked with students to go behind the scenes of language and symbols of the self, of cultures, of scientific explanations, professional practices, socio-political structures, and so on to examine not only what they mean but how they come to mean what they do and how their recognition as something we *know* could be otherwise. Glimpsing the *Leadership Zombidom* (Figure 11.1) figuration, for example, we were able to see how oppositions establish conceptual order along lines of *either/or* distinctions, how the sides of the binary get and produce their meaning over time through discursive categorizing that favors or elevates one term over the other, and how performing, for example, as leading follower/following leader disrupts clear and stable categories. We put poststructuralist perspectives to work and became more "discursively literate" in the process (MacLure, 2003). The deeper we headed into poststructuralist territory, the more apparent the embodied and embedded conditions of our sense/abilities became. In these particular moments, with their molecularly detected stammering, we sometimes took risks and turned toward the partially *ineffable* sense of our work, capitalizing on the lack of recognition and/or the inability to say what we nonetheless felt. Alternative assignments, where speechlessness was the "rule," involved corporeal and intercorporeal *encounters* with thought, where we were forced to think different thoughts differently.

One such encounter included a graduated set of activities with inanimate and eventually animate objects. Here, to begin, a simple water bottle was presented to students as "not a water bottle," but instead as a material object that was available to the group as a possibility—a thing which, depending on their encounters with it, could come to mean something other than what they knew or recognized it to be. In their encounter, the only rule was that speech was not an option. Several tasks ensued, where students were instructed to give the object power and to take power away,[8] eventually doing so through different disciplinary discourses in order to notice what these scholarly texts do to the embodied stories they were able to tell. For example, through enacting competing economic development discourses (human resource development vs. human capacity development; see especially Levinger, 1996) that center child well-being and nutrition, the water bottle quickly became the site for being filled up, emptied out, placed horizontally and moved as if on an assembly line, being swaddled, being hidden and so on. Processing this initial step, students identified various durable symbolisms at work in their decisions about when, how, and why to interact with the water bottle. They spoke about how others' actions compelled their own, how certain positionings, especially horizontal arrangements, made them uncomfortable, and how seeing the competing discourses materialize through embodied gestures not only helped them see the physicality of theorizing but also helped them sense that even subtle shifts in their enacting power arrangements was cause for incitement—that knowledge production as well as social and intellectual life were all open to shifts, to new agencies—to materially-discursive transpositionings. Tacking back and forth between the specifics of what happened in silence and the ways in which the discourses invested their own and others comportment, the bottle became a "safe enough" site for exposing how the body becomes implicated in the ways power is understood and used.

Building on the momentum of this warm-up activity, students were then challenged to shift their attention from a single, passive object (the water bottle) to a group of "learners" (a carefully selected group of stuffed animals). Attributes, such as gender and race were ascribed, as were several difficult differences, including "reading disabled," "gay," "immigrant," "gaming addicted," and so on. The same "rule" applied in terms of working in silence. To center the challenge of agency, these "learners" were further "marked" as all making insufficient progress on key benchmarks for academic progress. Further reflecting the notion that subjectivity, as Braidotti (1994a, 2006) so forcefully promotes, is always already in motion, nomadic and never self-contained, our work with these "learners" plunged us deeply into an embodied sense of the ways in which categories, and the discourses that produce and reproduce them are divisive—how physically and conceptually "marked" bodies absorb, disperse, separate and congeal on the basis of being separate, as being "that type," "those people," and "not me." Reflecting on the potential for such "serious play" (Davies & Gannon, 2006) among doctoral-level learners and leading subjects, we recognize that the risk of bringing the body into pedagogical arrangements is one we need to keep taking.

TRANSPOSITIONS: CULTIVATING A DESIRE
FOR SUSTAINABLE ETHICS AMONG AND
FOR EDUCATIONALLY LEADING SUBJECTS

With the first two sections of this chapter's focus on poststructuralism and material feminism as pedagogical coordinates, this third section turns to transpositions. Braidotti[9] (2006) discusses the term's "double source of inspiration: from music and genetics," (p. 5) thus provoking and shaping her own use of the term:

> [Transpositions] indicates an intertextual, cross-boundary or transversal trans-
> fer, in the sense of a leap from one code, field or axis into another, not merely
> in the quantitative mode of plural multiplications, but rather in the qualitative
> sense of complex multiplicities. It is not just a matter of weaving together dif-
> ferent strands, variations on a theme (textual or musical), but rather of playing
> the positivity of difference as a specific theme of its own. (p. 5)

Thinking the term's use in music, Braidotti (2006) explains that "transposition indicates variations and shifts of scale in a discontinuous but harmoni-
ous pattern" (p. 5), noting further that in music, a transposition "is thus
created as an in-between space of zig-zagging and of crossing: non-linear
but not chaotic; nomadic, yet accountable and committed; creative but also
cognitively valid; discursive and also materially embedded—it is coherent
without falling into instrumental rationality" (p. 5).

Discussing the term's use in the case of genetics, Braidotti emphasizes
the central role that material embodiment has in transpositions within and
among living organisms. In contemporary genetics, there is a growing understanding of the mutable and interdependent processes and bonds that
align, split, or otherwise influence genetic elements. Braidotti (2006) sets
the stage in exacting terms: "Nobody and no particle of matter is independent and self-propelled, in nature as in the social" (p. 6). Leaning into
biophysicist and social scientist Donna Haraway, who as Braidotti attests
"sums it up brilliantly" (p. 6): "A gene is not a thing, much less a master molecule, or a self-contained code. Instead the term 'gene' signifies a
mode of durable action where many actors, human and non-human meet"
(Haraway, 1997, p. 142). It is this non-unitary, bio-cultural, durable action
conceptualization of subjectivity—of life—that spurs us in our teaching to
attend to the *physicality* of our *theorizing* the social, to highlight and harness
the transmission of affect (Brennan, 2004) as *effecting* what we can and cannot know as learners and leaders.

In our teaching subjectivities, we gravitate toward Braidotti because she
honors the loss that comes with nomadicism: the loss of home, of unitary
selfhood, the loss of a culturally- and economically-valued way of being that
has limited our deep understanding and enjoyment of intercorporeality, of
living in a life larger than one's own. Braidotti beckons the leading subject
from an open space beyond: "The qualitative leap through pain, across the
mournful landscapes of nostalgic yearning, is the gesture of active creation
of affirmative ways of belonging" (2006, p. 84).

Our emerging project, still (always) in draft form, is to enact a Bradiot-
tian ethical/philosophical disposition—in other words, to teach transposi-
tionally. And so we ask ourselves: What happens to the educationally leading
subject under pedagogic conditions that foreground Braidotti's transpositions? What new modes of identification with "leader," "education," "self,"
and "other" emerge under such conditions? What does it mean to lead

from a nomadic, poly-centric identity zig-zagging toward relation and in-betweenness, toward a "social horizon of hope" (Braidotti, 2010, p. 141)? And what alternative formulation of accountability and sustainability might be assembled in the process?

PEDAGOGICAL INTERLUDE III

Putting Transpositions to Work: (G)localizing the Leading Subject

Common sense tells us that the world is divided into local issues and global issues, with the local being close at hand and the global being far removed. In our seminars, we pose a set of assignments intended to compli-cate students' common sense vision of the world around them. One project invites students to create a multi-media narrative that speaks of "global-ization in my backyard" through one of several interactive digital media, including wikis and digital storytelling. Their task: to unravel the global entangled in the local. Once the unravelling starts, they glimpse how far it goes. A Christmas tree farm on a local hillside becomes a site to unpack issues of ecology and global consumerism, where seasonal workers from Mexico produce a "local" crop to compete with plastic trees from China. A paper-bead necklace from a downtown shop gets unraveled to speak of Af-rican women's material survival strategies in the context of global trade in notions of craft and justice. A plate of food gets traced back to distant soils, opening questions about the global energy resources used to sustain our lo-cal bodies. Problems with the disposal of dead computer equipment begins to reveal toxic lumps under the surface of a flattening world. In developing their "backyard" stories, doctoral students begin to see how familiar objects and their own cultural practices are imported/exported in non-innocent ways. The local/global binary springs a thousand leaks, and it becomes evident that the way we think/talk/act "at home" is already infused with globally-circulating discourses. The local becomes decentered, non-unitary, multi-textual, no longer a bounded "here" that can be separated from a distant "there"—just as we, as leading/living subjects, cannot be separated from "them," from the distant "other."

At another level, such work challenges the commonsense understanding that our doctoral program is a training ground for local practitioners, a site where the local reproduces itself to maintain its meaning and identity. In our more radical moments, we might think of our project as making stu-dents unfit for local leadership—in other words, that they won't be "local" anymore in their leading subjectivity, that they will be positively unsettled in their own locations and pose positively unsettling questions about issues of identity and justice.

UNLEARNING THE "OTHER," DOING POSITIVE DIFFERENCE, AND LIVING TO LEAD WITH AFFECTION: A MOMENTARY EXIT

Life in you does not bear your name; it is only a time-share.
—Braidotti, 2006, p. 277

How does living in a Braidottian subjectivity—a life that we cannot own, but only time-share—speak to our desire to educate globally-aware, multicultural, ethical, and materially-discursive literate leaders? Honoring the nomadic and partial nature of the subject, for Braidotti, affirms hybridity, multi-locality, and ever-becomingness as a basic condition of consciousness *with* materiality (Daniell, 2002). Braidotti (2006) explains: "Non-unitary subjectivity here means a nomadic, dispersed, fragmented vision, which is nonetheless functional, coherent and accountable, mostly because it is embedded and embodied" (p. 4). The subject is always "in transit;" thus, we are inevitably "global citizens" in any place we live—inevitably plural, inevitably situated and enfleshed, inevitably unfinished and becoming. Thus, Braidotti affords the leading subject a deeply multicultural (un)grounding. In this way, with Braidotti, we have realized that we do not achieve a multicultural identity through arriving at a particular set of values or cultural understandings, or even through embracing an assumed "otherness." Each of us is not ourselves alone; we are "the effect of irrespressible flows of encounters, interactions, affectivity and desire, which one is not in charge of" (Braidotti, 2006, p. 269). By rejecting the unitary, individualist, self-contained subject, Braidotti seeks to affirm our ethical indebtedness to others. When the life we lead is not our own, leading subjects can let go of the burden of acquiring multiculturalism, since multiple otherness has already constituted us.

As we enter into dialogue with Braidotti as pedagogues, we employ a vocabulary that the discourse of educational leadership might find too theoretical, too foreign, even downright too "undecidable." But we believe that we must risk such an unsettling to make sense of unsettled times. We take issue with those who argue that embracing a post-modern outlook is to flee down a discursive rabbit hole and hide from the hard-felt struggles of a world in crisis. Standing embodied here and now, we see clearly the multiple challenges before us: transitioning to sustainable energy, affirming human rights and achieving durable democracy, renegotiating public support for public education, and rebalancing an economically and ecologically tilting planet. As Bottery (2004) contends, the challenges that the leading subject faces in the 21st century are significant and thorny.

Doctoral courses informed by poststructural, embodied sensibilities offer no clear way forward; instead, we offer a way behind the dilemmas, a way to crack open the ascribed meanings, binary structures, and associated somatic disequilibrium that can trap us in the common sensical. We offer the unsettling conclusion that settlement of tensions is not the goal. We invite students to see difference differently, to ask different questions differently, to loosen their grip on certainty. In Braidotti's ethical vision, it is possible, even necessary, to hold both poststructural skepticism about the tight bond between words and truth, *and* an affirmative vision of a more just world.

We invite leading subjects to notice where they get stuck identifying themselves and the world in terms of definitive, unitary categories that constrain their knowing, valuing, and acting—and to push toward structures of meaning making that do not rely on unfair parings of supposedly fixed categories. What if the leading subject, ever nomadic, wanders between moments of theorizing practice and practicing theory? What if the work of doctoral study slips behind those categories into a space of unpredictable learning, unique to the becoming of each student? What if doctoral study was about increasing the leading subject's capacities for multiplicity of knowing, doing, relating? We invite leading subjects to develop a materially-discursive literacy: an ability to get behind discursive constructions with an exquisite attention to bodies as always already implicated in our meanings and their making—an affirmation of text *with* flesh.

What kind of leadership are we talking about here? Leadership, our textbooks tell us, means influencing a group to achieve a shared goal (Northouse, 2007). The leader is expected to articulate a well-defined vision, a collective destination, to motivate followers to expend energy toward reaching that place. Rather than fixing a future, Braidotti's (2006) nomadic ethics invites the leading subject to let go of knowing where a process of becoming arrives. While Braidotti (2006) places a more life-giving future as a target on the horizon, she invokes the image of a "Zen archer" who releases her arrows with eyes shut. The leading subject aims for a target she cannot see and cannot define for others. A nomadic, embodied ethic of becoming "plunges us into the unprogrammed-for and hence the unheard-of, the unthought-of.... To desire a vibrant, affirmative and empowering present is to live in intensity and thus to unfold possible futures" (Braidotti, 2006, p. 154). An intensity of living is not a determining or defining—not hardening—but becoming more porous. Giving up to become more capable of relationship. As Braidotti (2006) insists:

> Inter-relations occur on the basis of affinity, in a pragmatic mode of random attraction. It is life on the edge, but not over it. It is not deprived of violence,

but deeply compassionate. It is an ethical and political sensibility that begins with the recognition of one's limitations as the necessary counterpart of one's forces or intensive encounters with multiple others. (p. 163)

Leading subjects transpositioned in education today cannot not know that they are worded (and word their way) into a historicized and politicized consciousness about who they are or what they can or should become. In climbing behind the scenes of their own and others' linguistic shaping, they may be less likely to become "leader" without consciousness or control over how meaning resides and slides in and through their own and others bodies. In our reading of Braidottian transpositions, we glimpse the challenges as well as the possibilities of a *transpositional pedagogy* that takes us past nostalgia for a simpler era of leadership, and past anxiety about survival in a cutthroat global marketplace, toward an unmeasured, immeasurable sense of affirmation—affirmation of inter-being and inter-becoming, of the leading subject as inhabiting and expanding a free and generous space of vitality in which we can all thrive together.

NOTES

1. Braidotti (2006) would reject my use of the term "outgrowth" due to its connotation of linearity, insisting instead that transpositions is reflective of a much more complex set of "creative links and zigzagging interconnections between discursive communities" (p. 7) that have not necessarily behaved, unfolded, or developed along a humanist conceptualization of time.
2. In using the phrase "leading subject" (rather than "leader"), we join other postmodernist thinkers who revise the terms "identity" and "self" to allow for a more dynamic, non-linear, less essentialist concept of subjectivity and the subject. Braidotti, following especially French Continental philosopher, Gilles Deleuze, foregrounds a nomadic, non-unitary vision of the subject, believing that we have reached "the end of pure and steady identities" (Braidotti, 2006, p. 79) that have limited our capacity to move (and be) beyond fixed notions of who a leader is. From a Braidottian (2005) perspective, "an exclusive focus on unitary identity, especially in the liberal tradition of individualism, is of hindrance rather than assistance. Identity involves a narrowing down of the internal complexities of the subject for the sake of social conventions" (p. 266).
3. Notable exceptions that take especially a poststructuralist view of leadership or of schools with some attention to leadership behaviors include Maxcy (1994) and Piper and Stronach (2008).
4. The doctoral program is situated at a comprehensive regional university in a rural, mountainous area of North Carolina, in the southeastern United States. In the program, most students have or aspire to have full-time jobs as educational leaders in either K–12 public school systems or within the state's large

community college system. They typically conceive their degree (an Educational Doctorate or Ed. D.) as a needed credentialing for their upwardly mobile professional trajectory. A smaller percentage of students enter (or leave) the program without aspirations for administrative leadership positions and instead seek to secure college or university teaching positions.

5. This original illustration was inspired by an image appearing in Jeff Collins and Bill Mayblin's book, *Derrida for Beginners* (1996, p. 20–21).

6. While little research has been conducted on the role of silence and especially speechlessness in doctoral-level classroom dialogue, researchers Dennis Kurzon (2007) and Charles Berger (2004) offer comprehensive typologies on these related concepts, distinguishing important attributes (between, for example, silence that can signal presence but decision or refusal to respond and non-presence, which can signal preoccupation or daydreaming), causes, emotional or situational features, as well as personal and/or social consequences. While a certain level of what Thomas Bruneau (1973) refers to as "sociocultural silence," whereby groups of people in certain contexts (i.e., churches, hospitals, libraries, schools, courtrooms, etc.) are known or learned to be known as places of institutionalized silence, doctoral seminars often function explicitly or tacitly as spaces for scholarly dialogue. Silence and speechlessness is, within this presumed space of adult learners—more equitable power relations, at the very least, considered unproductive and, I would suggest, also deemed suspect.

7. See especially Clough, 2007, 2009; Coole & Frost, 2010.

8. The authors wish to acknowledge our friend and colleague, Peter "PJ" Nelsen, who first passed along this water bottle activity as something he used in one of his foundations of education courses.

9. Rosi Braidotti was born in Australia and currently resides in Utrech, The Netherlands, where she is Distinguished Professor and Founding Director of Women's Studies. As a "materialist nomadic feminist philosopher" (Braidotti, 2006, p. 30), Braidotti leans heavily into especially continental philosophers Gilles Deleuze and Felix Guattari, taking up their complex and far reaching discussions of "reterritorialization"—of what it means, or could mean, to be in the world, with all the discursive, symbolic, political and material implications that mark and are marked by our real and perceived existence.

REFERENCES

Alaimo, S., & Hekman, S. (Eds.). (2008). *Material feminisms.* Bloomington, IN: Indiana University Press.

Bakhtin, M. (1981). *The dialogic imagination.* Austin, TX: University of Texas Press.

Berger, C. R. (2004). Speechlessness: Causal attributions, emotional features and social consequences. *Journal of Language and Social Psychology, 23*(2), 147–179. doi: 10.1177/0261927X04263821

Bettie, J. (2003). Women without class: Girls, race, and identity. Berkeley: University of California Press.

Bottery, M. (2004). *The challenge of educational leadership: Values in a globalized age.* Thousand Oaks, CA: Sage.

Braidotti, R. (1994a). *Nomadic subjects: Embodiment and sexual difference in contemporary feminist theory.* New York, NY: Columbia University Press.

Braidotti, R. (1994b). Toward a new nomadism: Feminist Deleuzian tracts; or metaphysics and metabolism. In C. V. Boundas & D. Olkowski (Eds.), *Gilles Deleuze and the theater of philosophy* (pp. 159–186). New York, NY: Routledge.

Braidotti, R. (2002). *Metamorphoses: Towards a materialist theory of becoming.* Cambridge, UK: Polity Press.

Braidotti, R. (2006). *Transpositions: On nomadic ethics.* Malden, MA: Polity Press.

Braidotti, R. (2010). Powers of affirmation: Response to Lisa Baraitser, Patrick Hanafin and Clare Hemmings. *Subjectivity, 3,* 140–148.

Brennan, T. (2004). *The transmission of affect.* Ithaca, NY: Cornell University Press.

Bruneau, T. J. (1973). Communicative silences: Forms and functions. *Journal of Communication, 23,* 17–46. DOI: 10.1111/j.1460-2466.1973.tb00929.x

Clough, P. T. (2009). The new empiricism: Affect and sociological method. *European Journal of Social Theory, 12*(43), 43–61. DOI: 10:1177/1368431008099643

Clough, P. T. with Halley, J. (Eds.). (2007). *The affective turn: Theorizing the social.* Durham, NC: Duke University Press.

Collins, J., & Mayblin, B. (1996). *Derrida for beginners.* Cambridge, England: Icon Books Ltd.

Coole, D., & Frost, S. (Eds). (2010). *New materialisms: Ontology, agency, and politics.* Durham, NC: Duke University Press.

Cussans, J. (2004). Tracking the zombie diaspora: From subhuman Haiti to posthuman Tucson. In P. L. Yodder & P. M. Kreuter (Eds.), *Monsters and the monstrous: Myths and metaphors of enduring evil* (pp. 203–214). Retrieved from http://www.inter-disciplinary.net/publishing- files/idp/eBooks/Monsters%202.1 rev.pdf

Daniell, A. (2002). Figuring subjectivity for grounded transformations: A critical comparison of Rosi Braidotti's and John Cobb's figurations. In C. Keller & A. Daniell (Eds.), *Process and difference: Between cosmological and poststructuralist postmodernisms* (pp. 147–166). Albany, NY: State University of New York Press.

Davies, B., & Gannon, S. (2006). *Doing collective biography.* New York, NY: Open University Press.

Deleuze, G. (1994). *Difference and repetition.* P. Patton (Trans.). New York, NY: Columbia University Press. (Original work published 1968)

Deleuze, G., & Guattari, F. (1987). *A thousand plateaus: Capitalism and schizophrenia* (B. Massumi, Trans.). Minneapolis, MN: University of Minnesota Press. (Original work published 1980)

Derrida, J. (1976). *Of grammatology* (G. C. Spivak, Trans.). Baltimore, MD: Johns Hopkins University Press. (Original work published 1967)

Foucault, M. (1977). *Language, counter-memory, practice: Selected essays and interviews.* Ithaca, NY: Cornell University Press.

Gannon, S., & Davies, B. (2007). Postmodern, poststructural, and critical theories. In S. N. Hesse-Biber (Ed.), *Handbook of feminist research: Theory and praxis* (pp. 71–106). Thousand Oaks, CA: Sage.

Gemmill, G., & Oakley, J. (1992, February). Leadership: An alienating social myth? *Human Relations, 45*(2),113–130.

Goleman, D. (2006). *Emotional intelligence: Why it can matter more than I.Q.* New York, NY: Bantam Dell.

Goleman, D., & Boyatzis, R. (2008). Social intelligence and the biology of leadership. *Journal of the Training Management Institute, 36*(2). Retrieved from http://cte.rockhurst.edu/s/945/images/editor_documents/GOLEMAN%20%20BOYATZIS%20%20Social%20Intelligence.pdf

Haraway, D. J. (1997). *Modest_witness@second_millennium. FemaleMan©_meets_onco-mouse™: Feminism and technoscience.* New York, NY: Routledge.

Kurzon, D. (2007). Towards a typology of silence. *Journal of Pragmatics, 39,* 1673–1688. DOI: 10.1016/j.pragma.2007.07.003

Lather, P. (1991). *Getting smart: Feminist research and pedagogy with/in the postmodern.* New York, NY: Routledge.

Levinger, B. (1996). Capacity, capital and calories. Retrieved from http://www.21learn.org/site/archive/capacity-capital-and-calories/

Lyotard, J. F. (1984). *The postmodern condition: A report on knowledge* (G. Bennington & B. Massumi, Trans.). Minneapolis, MN: University of Minnesota Press. (Original work published 1979)

MacLure, M. (2003). *Discourse in educational and social research.* Philadelphia, PA: Open University Press.

Maxcy, S. J. (1994). *Postmodern school leadership: Meeting the crisis in educational administration.* Westport, CT: Praeger.

Northouse, P. G. (2007). *Leadership: Theory and practice.* Thousand Oaks, CA: Sage.

Piper, H., & Stronach, I. (2008). *Don't touch!: The story of an educational panic.* New York, NY: Routledge.

St. Pierre, E. A. (1997). An introduction to figurations–A poststructural practice of inquiry. *International Journal of Qualitative Studies in Education, 10*(3), 279–284.

St. Pierre, E. A. (2000). Poststructural feminism in education: An overview. *International Journal of Qualitative Studies in Education, 13*(5), 477–515.

CHAPTER 12

LEARNING FROM FAILURE

Relational Humility and Leadership for Global Realities[1]

Francois J. Guilleux

INTRODUCTION

In the summer of 2009, the University of Pittsburgh launched its redesigned principal preparation program. The result of two years of research and cultivating partnerships, the new program entitled Leadership Initiative For Transforming Schools (LIFTS) sought to respond to the various calls for reform found in the educational leadership literature and being required by state legislative bodies (Darling-Hammond, LaPointe, Meyerson, Orr, & Cohen, 2007; Davis, Darling-Hammond, LaPointe, & Meyerson, 2005; Jackson & Kelley, 2002; Levine, 2005; U. S. Department of Education, 2004).

The LIFTS program is defined by three themes that are introduced during the first of the four curricular blocks that make up the fifteen-month program: a) ethics as the wisdom to lead schools well in complex and uncertain times; b) inquiry as understanding the dynamics of the production of knowledge; and c) integrity to navigate the moral context of education for and with diversity. Inspired by the standards for the dispositions of edu-

Social Justice Leadership for a Global World, pages 209–226
Copyright © 2012 by Information Age Publishing
All rights of reproduction in any form reserved.

cational leaders to be lead learner, the introductory block called the *Leader as Learner* also reflects a disposition Dalmiya (2007) calls relational humility. In her challenge to re-conceptualize educational leadership for the new globalized reality of capitalism, often reflected in the academy, Dalmiya (2007) suggests that education for social justice should be supportive of the disposition of relational humility. This chapter explores how learning from one's failures through case-in-point teaching (Heifetz, Sinder, Jones, Hodge, & Rowley, 1989; Parks, 2005), the pedagogy used in the introductory leadership institute of LIFTS, is a perspective shifting experience and a powerful catalyst for encouraging a disposition of relational humility in principal preparation. In this chapter, I review Dalmya's notion of relational humility, then describe the use of case-in-point teaching, a leadership pedagogy used with aspiring principals that draws on participants' experiences of leadership failure. I will suggest that in addition to helping future school leaders to develop more complex perspectives about their leadership and organizations, case-in-point encourages the disposition of relational humility. The chapter closes with several implications and recommendations for principal preparation programs seeking to educate administrators for the complexities of schools in the 21st century within a global context.

DALMIYA'S RELATIONAL HUMILITY

In her essay, *Unraveling Leadership: Relational Humility and the Search for Ignorance* (2007), Dalmiya argues for a re-conceptualizing of leadership and educational policy-making in light of the increased need to educate for responsible citizenship and social justice in the globalized and free market model of the academy. Drawing on feminist and post-colonial criticism and the traditional Indian narrative of the *Mahabharata*, Dalmiya (2007) offers a model of leadership grounded in the virtue of relational humility. By relational humility she means the "disposition to authorize others as knowing while giving up the claim to know oneself" (p. 314). Dalmiya uses relational humility to join Noddings' (2002) ethics of care and Mohanty's (2003) notion of inter-historicity with the story of the *Mahabharata* in the hopes of deconstructing contemporary notions of leadership.

From Noddings (2002), Dalmiya (2007) draws the relational emphasis in the notions of "caring for" and the global and justice implications of "caring about." For Noddings, the purpose of education should be developing men and women with an attentiveness for not doing harm as individuals and citizens. Dalmiya highlights that for Noddings the impersonal "caring about" depends on the experience of "caring for" and being "cared for". This becomes important for Dalmiya's view of education and educational leadership. Despite Noddings' insistence of the relational nature of caring for (in opposition to caring for as a virtue), Dalmiya argues that both caring for and caring about depend on an ethical ideal like the virtue of relational humility. She suggests that the "shared control" involved in Noddings's third step of caring for is actually facilitated by the disposition of relational humility. She states, "relationally humble agents, alone, can enter into caring relationships which are ones in which they must relinquish control" (Dalmiya, 2007, p. 313).

Drawing from the work of Mohanty (2003), Dalmiya (2007) highlights the Feminist Solidarity model as a model for resistance to what she sees as the market driven "imperative for multicultural exposure" (p. 302) in the academy. Feminist Solidarity calls for an attentiveness to relations of power at work in definitions of cultural and experiential differences in the lives of women. For Dalmiya, Feminist Solidarity encourages an exploration of the social and historical processes of oppression and privilege that implicate us all. Dalmiya emphasizes that Feminist Solidarity is "a self-reflexive and comparative praxis" (2007, p. 303) with political and ethical dimensions for the academy in the exploration of what comes to be taught. Education in this model seeks to develop a de-colonization of the mind by the recognition of the "intertwined histories" of oppressed communities and the naturalization of ideologies at the center.

Despite Mohanty's (2003) critique of the emphasis on a-historical, personal relations in "caring for," Dalmiya (2007) argues that Noddings' (2002) intersubjective emphasis complements Mohanty's inter-historicity. Dalmiya (2007) writes: "Historicized subjects remain psychological subjects, even though they are not *merely* so" (p. 306; italics in original). While both theories support a search for ignorance and recognition of knowledge in the margins—two characteristics of relational humility—Dalmiya believes that a notion of subjectivity found in a traditional Indian narrative offers a common foundation for a synthesis of these different kinds of relations.

The third voice Dalmiya (2007) brings to the discourse on leadership in education for social justice is found in the traditional Indian story of *Mahabharata* (van Buitenen, 1973). The portion of this multi-volume story she focuses on is the re-education of a Brahmin named Kausika through his interactions with a housewife and a hunter from the low caste of society. While a traditional reading of the story is of learning the value of practical wisdom, Dalmiya reads the *Mahabharata* as proposing a vision of education as personal transformation through the realization of the other at the margins as the source of knowledge. Unlike other virtue models of humility and modesty involving self-knowledge (e.g., modesty as undervaluing one's worth), Damliya's (2007) definition of relational humility as "the self-ascription of ignorance along with other-ascription of important knowledge" (p. 310) does not embrace a universal human fallibility nor deny one's own knowledge. A relationally humble person does not underestimate what one knows but rather seeks to discover the incompleteness of one's knowing.

Dalmiya (2007) sees the *Mahabharata* as providing a bridge between the personal intersubjectivity of Noddings' ethics of care and the inter-historicity of Mohanty through an acknowledgement that the "psychic dispositions can be obstacles or opportunities for political transformation" (p. 312). The incomplete knowing, or the "unknown to self" quadrants in Lufts and Ingham's Joharri's window[2] (Luft & Ingham, 1955), is due in part to one's social and historical positioning.

Using Noddings (2002), Mohanty (2003), and the *Mahabharata* narrative (van Buitenen, 1973), Dalmiya (2007) re-conceptualizes agency as the purpose of education. Education for justice must address all three levels—inter-subjective, inter-historicity and the virtue of relational humility. Attending to the power relations involved in the construction of knowledge, education structured around relational humility becomes a search for ignorance intended in its exploration to expose and disrupt the forces that marginalize and silence differences. Relational humility involves the acknowledgment of the conditions that produce our own privileged voice (self-knowledge) along with the recognition that those conditions also silence others. Thus relational humility encourages a praxis (the interaction of theory and practice) of recovering voices at the margins.

RELATIONAL HUMILITY AND LEADERSHIP

What are some of the leadership and policy implications of educating leaders for social justice through relational humility? Dalmiya (2007) points out that according to Noddings (2002), in order for teachers in the classroom to engage in relations of care with students, they must have experiences of being cared for. Leaders, she argues, must reflect relational humility, with its recognition of the importance of the knowledge held by disenfranchised others, not simply as a virtue but as a political praxis engaging the voices from the periphery in ongoing conversation in order to sustain justice-informed transformation in education. I would suggest that a much closer and daily experience of being cared for can occur from the teachers' experiences of supervision by educational administrators. Dalmiya believes that cultivating relational humility among teachers begins with relationally humble school leaders whose orientation towards the importance of the knowledge others bring reinforces the holding environment for teacher leaders.

According to Dalmiya (2007), leading with relational humility involves leading through starting an *epistemic contagion*—a process by which one leads change by demonstrating the change one seeks to bring about while also being open to being led by others. This dynamic approach encourages the development of "a community of trust" where one "catches" a new way of being that leads to change (Dalmiya, 2007, p. 319). Moving beyond leading by example, leading by epistemic contagion is a relational, other-focused action. It shifts the focus away from trying to develop in the self a particular way of being that can be modeled by others to being in touch with the needs of the followers through a relationship. To lead with relational humility, Dalmiya says, is to be in community with and value others because of an appreciation for dynamics of privilege and oppression. Unlike other modes of leadership, which Dalmiya (2007) acknowledges are at times necessary, leading by epistemic contagion works because "being around people who are relationally humble in the specific sense is to be around people who see, appreciate and are willing to act on their understanding of the connections of privilege and oppression" (p. 319). This type of leadership Dalmiya suggests requires a leader to look to others for solutions and even be open to be led themselves.

Dalmiya (2007) primarily argues that her notion of relational humility as a leadership praxis rooted in the subjective, inter-subjective and historical offers a model for principal preparation. In many ways, relational humility aligns with the disposition and praxis for educational leaders to be lead learners. The modeling of learning as an approach to school leadership requires each principal to begin with a disposition that encourages one to know what one knows and what one does not know, and with a movement to the fourth quadrant of Joharri's window, recognizing that what one does not know may or may not be known by others (Luft & Ingram, 1955). This kind of epistemic leadership, Dalmiya argues, is not the same as leading by example where one demands others replicate the example. Rather it is sharing a way to see and analyze schools and students through a relationship that allows one to "catch" a vision for change.

In the rest of this chapter, I describe the use of case-in-point teaching in a leadership education course. In offering some of the results of a study on the experiences and learning of aspiring principals who participated in the course, I highlight the ways case-in-point teaching used in the Leadership Institute reflect Dalmiya's development of relational humility to better meet the global realities of schools today.

THE LIFTS LEADERSHIP INSTITUTE

The *Leader as Learner* block takes place during the first summer term of the principal certificate program. The block includes a day-long orientation, a networking event with principals, and a week-long leadership institute. The summer term also includes a class on health, mental health and school safety from the instructional leadership block and 45 hours of internship. The day-long orientation serves as an introduction to the program and its requirements, as a cohort-building initial event, and as the introduction to the leadership institute. In addition, the students are introduced and coached in Core Communication (Miller, 2007), a communication skills model encouraging self-awareness, conflict-resolution and collaborative problem-solving.

The Leadership Institute takes place six to eight weeks after the orientation and offers students an introduction to leadership theory and organizational analysis with an emphasis on human development theory. Two theoretical streams informed the design of the institute. From psychology, the program draws upon the work of Robert Kegan on adult development as meaning-making (Kegan, 1994; Kegan & Lahey, 2009). From leadership studies, we integrate the work of Ron Heifetz on adaptive leadership (Heifetz, 1994; Heifetz, Grashow, & Linsky, 2009). In addition to the unique theoretical blend, the institute uses case-in-point teaching (Heifetz, et al., 1989; Johnstone & Fern, 2004; Parks, 2005), an experiential pedagogy that opens the class as a social system for the study of leadership and groups as well as engaging the students' past experiences of leadership. Through the Institute, students are introduced to the theory and practice of adaptive leadership and organizational behavior. In addition to the work of Ron Heifetz (Parks, 2005), the case-in-point teaching used in the institute draws on a number of inspirations including the work of Linda Powell (2002) at Harvard and Teachers College and Terri Monroe at the University of San Diego.

LEADERSHIP FAILURE CASES

The case study method developed at the Harvard Business School has been imported into a number of disciplines (Martynowych, 2006). Learning from other people's mistakes through case studies has become a standard pedagogical tool in many professional graduate programs. Case-in-point teaching used in the LIFTS Institute draws on the case study method, but with a twist on the traditional method—students take as case studies their *own* leadership failures. A recent study on the learning and experiences of the participants in the LIFTS Leadership Institute shows case-in-point teaching to be a powerful leadership pedagogy that helps aspiring principals shift their perspectives on themselves, leadership and organizations (Guilleux, 2010).

In listening to the students reflect on their experiences and in reading their writings about their learning, a learning process becomes clear that is in part and perhaps unintentionally, a result of the course design. The leadership failure case plays a large role in their perspective shifting. There is an iterative process of reflection on the personal failure cases while encountering new perspectives that seems central to the resulting perspective shifts on their understanding of themselves and their organizations. Kim, an Institute participant, described the growth she experienced during the Institute this way:

> I cannot explain it physically or mentally, but I felt a shift in my thought process with this particular experience. For the first time, I was seeing beyond my own perspectives. I was seeing beyond my own lenses and opening up to those around me.

Tammy reflecting on her learning wrote,

> My perspective shifted when I started to look at my role in different levels and how one impacted the other. This shift was supported by presenting my case and being asked to honestly look at myself critically as a learner and as a leader and ask what I observed in relation to class, to lab class, and to leadership.

The first reflection on the leadership failure case occurs prior to the Institute in the preparation of the case study for presentation. This process occurs as the students are reading the theoretical frameworks of the course. Most of the students begin to integrate their understanding of concepts found in the readings. This shapes the questions they bring to their small group. While students attempt to use new language to analyze their cases, mostly the case analyses reflect a very intra or interpersonal perspective of the leadership failure and the system in which it occurred.

The second reflection on the case occurs in their consultation group. For most students this is a small group of six or seven colleagues where each will present their case for consultation. For each presentation, one person is selected to lead the group in its task. The rest of the group serves as consultants to the case. As the consultants unpack the case with the presenter, many receive interpretations about their situation they had never considered. Tara, for example, remembering her consultation group, said,

> While identifying the adaptive challenges, the small group consultation constructed certain hypotheses to apply to my case. One hypothesis that never even crossed my mind at all was based upon gender: I may have been given authority through the higher ranks, but the males may not see me, a female, as an authority based upon my gender.

These new interpretations change the presenters' perspectives of their roles and their organizations. Some students even reported being distracted and even feeling guilty when acting as consultants to others' cases because the interpretations offered in the small group stimulated their thinking about their own cases.

The third reflection is found in the work of a final assignment where the students are encouraged to integrate their learning during the Institute and the theoretical frames of the course to write a new analysis of their leadership failures. In this iteration of the cycle, the point of view encountered is the integration of theory and practice—including their reflections on the Immunity to Change exercise, a developmentally inspired reflective process that offers insight on personal barriers to change and improvement (Kegan & Lahey, 2009)—as experienced in the laboratory of the class.

This iterative process of reflection and encounter with new points of view creates for students a scaffold as their learning and perspective shifts. These shifts in perspectives are often towards more complex ways of understanding themselves, their leadership, or the schools in which they work. One way to understand the shifts that some students described in their writing is in terms of their own level of adult development as evolving into more complex meaning-making (Kegan, 1992, 1994). The characteristics of the shifts for some students involve a broadened perspective-taking that increases the complexity of how they make meaning of themselves and their world and that for which they take responsibility. Cook-Greuter (2004) characterizes this kind of shift in perspective-taking as transformative to contrast it with the traditional, informative professional development often found in schools. Several authors have argued that the development of more complex perspective-taking, or ways of knowing, is an important asset for the leaders of schools and organizations facing today's rapidly changing global and local realities (e.g., Garvey Berger, forthcoming; Helsing, Howell, Kegan, & Lahey, 2008; Kegan & Lahey, 2009).

RELATIONAL HUMILITY, GLOBALIZATION AND CASE-IN-POINT TEACHING

Ordonez (2007) notes that despite the growing universality of communication mechanisms distinctive of globalization, large international organizations to small informal work groups are becoming characterized more by diversity than homogeneity. Leaders, he notes, can no longer assume to have "the credibility of being able to state clearly defined destinations for the rest of the group" (Ordonez, 2007, p. 250). Hershock (2007) argues that in addition to making sense of increasingly complex systems, the impact of changing global realities found in education requires educational leaders to lead with a humility that recognizes and values the diversity of meaning-making and experiences found in schools and communities. Another way to think about the learning of aspiring school leaders in the LIFTS Institute is that offering a developmental framing for case-in-point teaching supports the development of relational humility in response to global realities leaders face. Beyond being a perspective-shifting experience, case-in-point embodies several characteristics that Dalmiya (2007) describes in her reconceptualization of education and leadership for a globalized world. The following section describes how case-in-point teaching supports the development of relational humility.

As demonstrated by the Brahim in the *Mahabharata*, relational humility requires that one displays a deference to others (Dalmiya, 2007). This deference to others is a combination of the recognition of self-ignorance and ascription of knowledge to others. The consultation groups offer an opportunity to practice both of these dispositions through the presentation of personal leadership failure cases. The consultation process after being modeled twice by the teaching staff early in the week of the Institute, occurs in small group meetings lasting an hour at a time and growing in frequency later in the Institute.

Due on the first day of class is a case developed as a narrative of a personal leadership failure the student experienced. One unique characteristic of the case study assignment is the unresolved nature of the failure experience. This is one of the requirements of the case. In the assignment *unresolved* is described as *continuing to have an emotional hold on you,* or *something that you have not made peace with.* The cases that the students, who have ranged in years of professional experience from three to twenty, bring to the institute—some having occurred many years prior—represent situations that continue to have a negative emotional connection for them. It seems that the reflection and meaning they have created of the situations has not relieved the tension they experienced during the events described in the case. A resolution to the failure involved in the case has eluded them. The assignment asks them to not only acknowledge this point by writing the unanswered questions they still have about the situation, but also to make this recognition of self-ignorance public through the presentation of the failure to their small group (and in some cases to the whole cohort).

The case presentation and consultation engage the presenter in a relinquishing of control around something personal and often difficult. The relationships among the presenter, the consultants, and the person who chairs the consultation group is an opportunity to practice caring for, relinquishing control and developing shared meaning. After presenting his or her case, the presenter surrenders to the questions and consultations of colleagues on the leadership failure. The opportunity to care for is something the students easily recognize and negotiate differently as the institute progresses. After a few consultations, the students come to realize that the withholding of interpretations about the case for fear of hurting the presenter can actually be a disservice to the presenter's learning. What emerges is the shared meaning between the consultants and the presenter of the case. As mentioned earlier, many students described how the consultation process broadens their perspectives on their cases, sometimes introducing meanings they had never considered. Tammy, one of the participants, said,

> I guess I would say one of the, one of the wonderful things would be that I was able to go through that failed leadership attempt. And in the beginning it was just sort of an, "Okay, here's one time when I got put in a leadership position and it went wrong because . . ." and the end coming out looking at here's the much bigger issue that I was ignoring, or maybe not even ignoring, that I wasn't aware of. I guess maybe coming to some awareness of an issue that may have impacted the way I looked at leadership. That was a, a big thing for me.

Following the presentation of the case, the consultants work with the presenter to identify the adaptive challenges in the case and to develop organizational hypotheses. Adaptive challenges, according to Heifetz (1994) are problems that are found in the gap between an organization's actual and aspired values and thus require a change in values and beliefs to be addressed. Following Wells' (1985) model, the consultants build organizational hypotheses from multiple levels of analysis beginning with intra-personal and interpersonal (usually the level of analysis offered by the presenter) and moving towards inter-group, group-as-a-whole, and inter-organizational. The generation of multiple and often exclusive hypotheses (Powell, 2002) explicitly encourages the consultants to avoid a kind of pathological certainty (Shapiro & Carr, 1993) about their understanding of the case. It also reminds the consultants of the limits of their perspectives and knowledge and encourages them to ascribe knowledge to the other voices in the group and the often-silenced voices in the case represented in the diversity of the consultation group.

The experiential dimension of case-in-point also engages the consultants with the recognition of their own self-ignorance. The consultants are encouraged to take up their roles using what Shapiro and Carr (1993) call the interpretive stance, which is to use one's experience as a participant-observer to inform development of organizational hypotheses. Using Smith, Simmons, and Thames's (1989) notion of the parallel process, the chairperson of the group and the consultants are using themselves as instruments to attend to the ways in which the consultation process may also mirror the very organizational dynamics of the case. Using the self as an instrument acknowledges the subjective nature of data and the blind spots each brings to his or her interpretations. Many of these blind spots students discover are a result of the social and historical relations in which they are embedded. One example of this occurred during a large group consultation early in the week of one Institute. One of the instructors offered the interpretation that the situation presented in the case might be symptomatic of the adaptive challenges faced by the school in managing the multi-racial demographics of its students. This interpretation led some students to uncover organizational dynamics around race at play in their own cases, which were as one student said "right in front of me but that I didn't see."

One interesting outcome of the Institute is that despite the very general description of the assignment for the case studies, the students' cases show an unexpected common characteristic. All the leadership failure cases that the students brought to the institute involved a failure experienced *during a change of organizational roles.* The students may not attribute their failure to such a change (e.g., several of the students think the root of their failure is an interpersonal conflict with a colleague), yet the context of all the failures involves taking a new organizational role and having to manage shifts in authority relations. Most students were able to engage this dimension in their analyses, although the depth of analysis varied. The implications of this finding are explored elsewhere (Guilleux, 2010), but for the purpose of this chapter about learning from our failures, one observation is that the training of these teacher leaders (pre-service and in-service) did not equip them to explore the processes of authorization—the formal and informal ways one is authorized in relationship to a particular task—and these were the processes often at play in their experiences of leadership failures in schools. Adaptive leadership and case-in-point teaching gave students concepts to reframe their perspectives on their leadership and authority. For some this broadening of perspectives included recognizing the limitations of their perspectives as a result of their social and organizational location. The dynamics of ascribing knowledge to others in relational humility requires a valuing of others' perspectives. For many of the Institute participants, the importance of others' perspectives was a significant part of their shifts in perspectives. As they are confronted by the narrowness of their perspectives (as one of the students called it), the students engage at different levels with the new perspectives offered by their peers. The consultation to Tammy's case reframed for Sally her understanding of her own case that involved being a young white teacher in her first-year teaching in a racially diverse school. Sally's initial sense of failure came from the lack of academic results among her students. She commented that,

> . . . it wasn't until that particular case [Tammy's] that I thought about my school and the kind of problems the students were having with one another. And it came, you know, it came to fruition that race probably was an issue in my school and I didn't even see it.

For some the recognition of the limits of their perspectives is primarily learning to be open to differing opinions. Reflecting on their own evolution, students describe a narrow perspective as a self-centered point of view, limited by a certainty about their interpretation of the leadership situation and the system involved. The broadening of perspective taking described by these students reflects a shift towards a releasing of the certainty with which they hold to their interpretations and an openness to considering others' point of view. This contextualizing of their own interpretations with the views of others can be for some a radical realization. For many, the value of others' points of view becomes an important lesson that they consider as they imagine themselves as principals within complex and changing contexts.

For a couple of students, this loosening of the certainty with which they hold to their points of view reveals a shift away from making meaning in a very concrete and absolute way. Tess, an Institute participant, stated that "as a learner my perspective shifted from thinking that there is always a clear-cut right or wrong answer, but now I learned to think with different perspectives." Seeing the world with certainty in the concrete dualism Tess describes echoes the character of meaning-making systems or epistemological frames identified by a number of developmental theorists (e.g., Perry, Kegan, Belencky, Baxter Magolda). The shift described by Tess could be evidence of an evolving personal epistemology. Since most developmental theories speculate that epistemological changes take place slowly over longer periods of time than a week-long institute, Tess may be describing a micro developmental shift in self-complexity (Garvey Berger, forthcoming) that in time can contribute to whole-meaning making system change.

For many, discovering the value of others perspectives is tied to the function of leadership. Similar to Dalmya's (2007) model of leadership by epistemic contagion, adaptive leadership (Heifetz, 1994; Heifetz, Grashow, & Linsky, 2009) offers a much more relational model of leadership than the dominant superman models or the authoritarian models of leadership that students held prior to the Institute. As one student named Sally said after the Institute, "I learned in class, exercising leadership is a process of diagnosis, experimentation, and reflection. I will need assistance from those around me in the diagnosis step of the leadership process."

For Dalmiya (2007) the social epistemology that stems from the ascription of knowledge to other has strong historical and political dimensions. The other who has knowledge is the other at the margins—the radical other—and the shared meaning-making is across power differentials. For a few students, the importance of the voices at the margins is the way they come to understand valuing others opinions. As their understanding of social systems grows, the participants come to see the way individuals are placed in informal roles to meet the needs of groups and systems—needs that are often the social defenses schools use to manage the social and increasing global complexities of their task (Powell & Barber, 2004). Halfway through the institute, Tammy, an older African American woman with lots of experience in schools, considered whether she might be silencing one of her classmates, Tara, by her choice of seat in the classroom. Tara, a younger white woman with only a few years of teaching experience, had once been Tammy's student. Tammy, who had been sitting next to Tara for the first few days of the Institute, in an experiment in leadership, created some distance between herself and Tara by changing seats in the large group sessions. She was the only student in a group of twelve to change seats in the large group sessions during the whole week of the Institute. As the week continued, Tara did speak more in the large group. While increasing participation is not unusual for students as they become more comfortable, Tara in her end of the course reflections recognized that she had played a role of "the quiet one," a role that was quite unusual for her in learning environments. Tammy's attentiveness to the voices being silenced, in this case by her experience and history, reflected a valuing of others' opinions but also a recognition of the knowledge lost to the cohort in Tara's silence.

One of Dalmiya's (2007) recommendations for leaders is to develop structures that sustain the conversations between the center and the margins. While regional history and past recruiting practices bring some challenges in building the kind of diversity in the cohorts that can facilitate these types of conversations, it is also an area where opportunities for new partnerships exist or need to be renewed. The Institute design and case-in-point teaching encourages people to bring their whole identities to the work. This means an attempt is made to create a space for participants to choose or to authorize the multiple voices they represent to join the class conversations. As a result each person can explore the way his or her various identities can lead to experiences of dominance and oppression and lead to valence to play particular roles in systems. A number of exercises, personality assessments, and the introduction of adult development as a hidden diversity in organizations supports the exploration of identity and roles development.

In addition, case-in-point teaching with its emphasis on the system dynamics and adaptive challenges of schools also introduces the voice of the other. As mentioned earlier, adaptive challenges are the gaps between the espoused values and the actual lived values of a system (Heifetz, 1994). Many of the adaptive challenges faced by schools have to do with issues of poverty and justice (Powell & Barber, 2004). To help reframe the challenges at the heart of the leadership cases in terms of systemic adaptive problems often encourages attention to the minority voices in schools and communities.

Group-as-a-whole analysis (Wells, 1985) offers opportunity to develop "consciousness of oppositional location of gendered and raced bodies" (Dalmiya, 2007, p. 317) in schools by the definitions of roles and organizational dynamics. The inter-group and inter-organizational lenses acknowledge the often conflicted and covert nature of organizational life (Powell, 2002). In learning to identify parallel processes in the consultation groups

(Smith et al., 1989), students begin to identify the relationships between the social defenses of an organization and the informal roles developed to manage organizational anxiety around its adaptive challenges.

Through role analysis, students discover the dynamics of their own investment in the roles they play on behalf of a system. In discovering the propensity they have to play certain roles, students discover the construction of roles to serve various levels of social systems. Tammy's consultation on her leadership failure as the chair of a committee charged with a report for state accreditation led her to recognize the adaptive challenge facing the school around tackling issues of racism in a successful urban school. Reflecting on her case, Tammy and several students came to articulate the difficulties encountered while trying to address issues of racism in schools where a post-racial discourse has become a dominant discourse. Tammy further described how the dynamics of the LIFTS cohort paralleled the post-racial culture of schools and the dilemma this places her in as teacher of color. The dilemma involves the cost to teachers (of color, especially) to take up the roles that are made available to them in schools where post-racial discourse has become dominant.

Dalmiya (2007) suggests that leadership training needs to engage the structures of agency more than management techniques. This chapter suggests that a developmental perspective and case-in-point teaching offer opportunities to address and practice agency through individual and group reflections on personal leadership failures. Through such critical reflections, including reflecting on the historical situatedness that contributes to the blind spots and valence to take up particular organizational roles, and through encounters with new perspectives on their own failures, aspiring principals are challenged towards more complex analysis and meaning-making.[3] These practices encourage the development of relational humility in future educational leaders and give hope for more just and transformative organizations in changing global realities.

CONCLUSIONS AND IMPLICATIONS

In light of the adaptive problems faced by educators in the 21st century (Heifetz & Linksy, 2004; Helsing, Kegan, Howell, 2008) and the implications of globalization on education (Hershock, Mason & Hawkins, 2007), relational humility—as a disposition that encourages a relational, self-reflective praxis on the dynamics of power, privilege and oppression by recognizing the limits of one's knowledge and the importance of knowledge by those at the margins—embodies the ethical and leadership practices often found in the leadership literature for complex and changing organizations and schools (Parks, 2005; Senge, Scharmer, Jaworski, & Flowers, 2004; Wagner & Kegan, 2006).

In this chapter I described the design of the leadership Institute of LIFTS, a new principal preparation program. Reviewing Dalmiya's (2007) call for "unraveling" leadership using her concept of relational humility, I have suggested its alignment with principal preparation standards and offered ways that a developmental framing for case-in-point teaching with its application work rooted in personal leadership failure can support the development of relational humility in educational leaders.

Offering an experience such as the Institute at the beginning of a cohort-based program serves many purposes for LIFTS and better prepares leaders for transformative change in a global context. First, the Institute embodies in challenging ways the themes of the program (ethics, inquiry, and integrity) for developing leaders to transform schools into places of learning for all—adults and children alike. Second, it sets the tone for the culture of the cohort as a community of practice engaged in the deeply personal and hard work of leadership development for schools under significant pressures. Third, it offers several frameworks for participants to make sense of their own learning throughout the year-long program. And fourth, it reframes participants' view of the principalship by challenging their notions of leadership and organizational behavior.

The Institute also invites participants to challenge traditional notions of leadership. Many students came to the Institute with the Superman model of leadership, a view of leadership closely associated with the myth of the hero so prevalent in American culture. Teaching about leadership without addressing issues of authority risks reinforcing dominant and illusory models of leadership. These dominant models are individualistic, supporting the notion that a leader is in control and has all the answers and dismissing the idea that groups and organizations have historically-situated identities of their own that reproduce, often covertly, dynamics of privilege and oppression and influence the thoughts and behaviors of their members. Such views of leadership overlook the complex ways these dynamics might contribute to the perpetuations of relations of injustice in schools and society.

As students learned in the Institute, an openness to examine the social and organizational dynamics in one's experience of failure can point to the limits of one's perspectives. To do so as part of principal preparation within a community of practice is one way to search for ignorance and pursue growth toward relational humility. It is also a way to equip aspiring principals to analyze the complex issues facing schools with an attention to the value of the often missing or minority voices. These practices can help future principals grow in dispositions—such as relational humility—that support more collaborative and distributed leadership for schools and the global contexts in which they practice.

NOTES

1. This chapter is an adaptation of a paper presented at the 2010 University Council of Educational Administration and draws on the findings of a larger study by Guilleux (2010).
2. Joharri's window is a self and group awareness building tool that differentiates information about the individual and group into four types or panes. Two of those panes represent information unknown to the self but which might be known to the group (blind spots) and information unknown to the self and unknown to the group (opportunities for self-discovery and transformative change).
3. Kegan (1982, 1994), building on Winnicott's (1965) notion of holding environment, writes about the culture of embeddedness that facilitates the transitions to more complex epistemological frames by both supporting current meaning making and challenging to consider new ways of making sense of the self and the world. He uses the developmental bridge metaphor emphasizing that the holding environment has to remain in place long enough for the new meaning making system to emerge and become dominant. Heifetz (1994) also draws on this notion to describe the character of the context necessary to sustain adaptive change.

REFERENCES

Cook-Greuter, S. R. (2004). Making the case for a developmental perspective. *Industrial and Commerce Training, 36*(7), 275–281.

Dalmiya, V. (2007). Unraveling leadership: 'Relational humility' and the search for ignorance. In P. Hershock, M. Mason, & J. Hawkins (Eds.), *Changing education: Leadership, innovation and development in a globalizing Asia Pacific* (pp. 297–322). Hong Kong: Comparative Education Research Center.

Darling-Hammond, L., LaPointe, M., Meyerson, D., Orr, M., & Cohen, C. (2007). *Preparing school leaders for a changing world: Lessons from exemplary leadership development programs—Final report.* Stanford, CA: Stanford University, Stanford Educational Leadership Institute.

Davis, S., Darling-Hammond, L., LaPointe, M., & Meyerson, D. (2005). *School leadership study: Developing successful principals (review of research).* Stanford, CA: Stanford University.

Garvey Berger, J. (forthcoming). *Thriving in a complex world: Twenty-first century professional development.* New York: Elsevier: Butterworth-Heinemann Business Books.

Guilleux, F. (2010). *A developmental perspective on leadership education of aspiring principals.* Unpublished doctoral dissertation, University of Pittsburgh, Pittsburgh, PA.

Heifetz, R. (1994). *Leadership without easy answers.* Cambridge, MA: Belknap Press of Harvard University Press.

Heifetz, R., Grashow, A., & Linsky, M. (2009). *The practice of adaptive leadership: tools and tactics for changing your organization and the world.* Boston, MA: Harvard Business Press.

Heifetz, R. A., & Linsky, M. (2004). When leadership spells danger. *Educational Leadership, 61*(7), 33–37.

Heifetz, R., Sinder, R., Jones, A., Hodge, L., & Rowley, K. (1989). Teaching and assessing leadership courses at the John F. Kennedy School of Government. *Journal of Policy Analysis and Management, 8*(3), 536–562.

Helsing, D., Howell, A., Kegan, R., & Lahey, L. (2008). Putting the "development" in professional development: Understanding and overturning educational leaders immunities to change. *Harvard Educational Review, 78*(3), 437–465.

Hershock, P. (2007). Leadership in the context of complex global interdependence: Emerging realities for educational innovation. In P. Hershock, M. Mason, & J. Hawkins (Eds.), *Changing education: Leadership, innovation and development in a globalizing Asia Pacific* (pp. 227–248). Hong Kong: Comparative Education Research Center.

Hershock, P., Mason, M., & Hawkins, J. (2007). *Changing education: Leadership, innovation and development in a globalizing Asia Pacific.* Hong Kong, China: Comparative Education Research Center.

Jackson, B. L. & Kelley, C. (2002). Exceptional and Innovative Programs in Educational Leadership. *Educational Administration Quarterly, 38*(2), 192–212.

Johnstone, M. & Fern, M. (2004). *Case-in-point: An experiential methodology for leadership education.* Columbus, OH: Vantage Point Consulting.

Kegan, R. (1982). *The evolving self: Problem and process in human development.* Cambridge, MA: Harvard University Press.

Kegan, R. (1994). *In over our heads: The mental demands of modern life.* Cambridge, MA: Harvard University Press.

Kegan, R. & Lahey, L. (2009). *Immunity to change.* Cambridge, MA: Harvard Business School Press.

Levine, A. (2005). *Educating school leaders.* Washington, DC: The Education Schools Project.

Luft, J. & Ingham, H. (1955). The Johari window: A graphic model of interpersonal awareness. *The proceedings of the Western Training Laboratory in Group Development.* Los Angeles: UCLA, Extension Office.

Martynowych, P. J. (2006). *Revisiting self-analytic groups.* Unpublished doctoral dissertation, Harvard University, Cambridge, MA.

Miller, S. (2007). *I-skills zone communication and collaborative team skills.* Littleton, CO: Interpersonal Communication Programs.

Mohanty, C. T. (2003). *Feminism without borders: Decolonizing theory, practicing solidarity.* Durham, NC: Duke University Press.

Noddings, N. (2002). *Starting at home: Caring and social policy.* Berkeley: University of California Press.

Ordonez, V. (2007). The changing role of leadership (or a changing leadership for a changing world). In P. Hershock, M. Mason, & J. Hawkins (Eds.), *Changing education: Leadership, Innovation and development in a globalizing Asia Pacific* (pp. 249–272). Hong Kong: Comparative Education Research Center.

Parks, S. D. (2005). *Leadership can be taught: A bold approach for a complex world.* Boston, MA: Harvard Business School Press.

Powell, L. C. (2002). Labouring in the counter story factory: Experiential teaching about authority. *International Journal of Critical Psychology, 4*(1), 141–157.

Powell, L. C. & Barber, M. E. (2004). Savage inequalities indeed: Irrationality and urban school reform. In S. Cytrynbaum & D. Noumair (Eds.), *Group relations reader 3* (pp. 303–320). Jupiter, FL: The A.K. Rice Institute for the Study of Social Systems.

Senge, P., Scharmer, O. C., Jaworski, J., & Flowers, B. (2004). Awakening faith in an alternative future. *Reflections: The Society of Organizational Learning Journal on Knowledge, Learning, and Change, 5*(7), 1–11.

Shapiro, E. R. & Carr, A. W. (1993). *Lost in familiar places.* New Haven, CT: Yale University Press.

Smith, K., Simmons, V., & Thames, T. (1989). "Fix the women": An intervention into an organizational conflict based on parallel process thinking. *Journal of Applied Behavioral Science, 25,* 11–29.

U.S. Department of Education. (2004). *Innovative pathways to school leadership. Innovations in education.* Washington, DC: Author.

van Buitenen, J. A. B. (1973). *The Mah*abh*arata.* Chicago: University of Chicago Press.

Wagner, T., & Kegan, R. (2006). *Change leadership: A practical guide to transforming our schools* (1st ed.). San Francisco: Jossey-Bass.

Wells, L. (1985). The group-as-a-whole perspective and its theoretical roots. In A. G. Colman & M. H. Geller (Eds.), *Group relations reader 2* (pp. 109–126). Ranier, WA: A. K. Rice Institute.

Winnicott, D. W. (1965). *The maturational processes and the facilitating environment: Studies in the theory of emotional development.* New York, NY: International Universities Press.

CHAPTER 13

TRANSFORMATIVE SCHOOL LEADERSHIP

Deconstructing Self and Agency in a Global World

Lyndsay J. Agans and Susan Korach

INTRODUCTION

In the globalized world in which we now live, school leaders must be prepared to think innovatively about how best to prepare students in differing social, political, and cultural contexts. To do so, principals require a model of leadership that transcends epistemological and national boundaries to nurture learning organizations that produce students who are equipped to engage in the global knowledge economy and to participate as citizens of the world. Thus, we offer a model of leadership development that calls for transformational leadership through reflection and deconstruction of self that allows one to unlearn/reconceive and transform self and organizations. During the deconstruction process, individuals are able to confront privilege and learn from the perspectives and values of others. This inquiry-based approach reinforces the growth of the learning organization

Social Justice Leadership for a Global World, pages 227–239
Copyright © 2012 by Information Age Publishing
All rights of reproduction in any form reserved.

while considering the need for proficiency of intercultural communication to empower action toward social justice. This chapter presents an inquiry-based model of reflective practice grounded in critical multiculturalism and field tested with practitioners.

CONCEPTUAL FRAMEWORK

An inquiry-based approach to educational supervision requires learning at the individual, group, and organizational level. We offer an approach to educational leadership preparation programs that utilizes narrative self-reflection for transformation. Empirical evidence reveals a spiraling up process of growth resulting from this approach toward leadership learning. The larger epistemological impact suggests that such a shift in notions of self allows for disruption of the hegemonic discourse, which in turn allows for the interruption of leadership that creates cultures of replication of the dominant power structures within and through schools. We posit that this spiral progression can be made explicit for social justice reform through a process in which the individual reflects, reconsiders, relates, and reframes personal values and organizational culture (see Figure 13.1).

To achieve an authentic-inquiry based approach, we frame the process within layers of a global, national and local (glonacal) agency heuristic (Marginson & Rhoades, 2002) consisting of individual narrative transformational reflection (Rossiter, 1999a), a reconsideration of privilege and culture of power (Delpit, 1988, 2002), a relating and renaming of issues

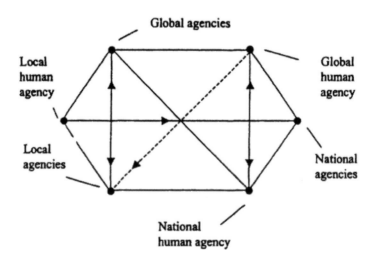

Figure 13.1 Glonacal agency heuristic.

through praxis, and development of intercultural communication (Mohanty, 1990; Freire, 1970) for reframing and leadership action. This inquiry-based model requires that the individual reconsider self at intersections of identity, glonacal level and organizational and sociocultural contexts.

REFRAMING: A GLONACAL AGENCY

Schools hold a unique position in society, and in that position, form and influence the ideologies, beliefs, values, and identities of their students. As nested social systems, schools are influenced by internal and external forces that coerce and shape their work, including expectations for student outcomes. Within this complex landscape, school leaders must navigate social, political, and economic forces to ensure a school culture that allows for safety, learning, and growth for teachers, staff, and students. Increasingly, school leaders find themselves dealing with forces occurring at not only the local and national, but also the international level. Marginson and Rhoades's (2002) work on the "glonacal" realities of academic contexts were first offered in relation to higher education, but we apply them here to better understand the current contexts of school for leaders at the K–12 level.

With the increased attention to international student assessment such as the Program on International Student Assessment (PISA), the context and comparison base for schools and for student outcomes has changed. Not only are 15-year-olds in New York being compared against 15-year-olds in Denver for postsecondary preparedness, but 15-year-olds in the United States are being compared with-15 year-olds in Singapore or Finland. The result of this agenda-setting paradigm of the neoliberal economy has had trickle-down effects on the realities of what it means to be a school leader today, supporting teachers to prepare students for the "new knowledge economy" and for global competition. Concomitantly, as the role and demands placed upon schooling expand, the "flattening" of the world means that students are being prepared to engage as citizens of the world where work occurs beyond borders and across cultural contexts. The corollary imperative in such a context is to develop school cultures that allow for a transformative space for pedagogy that involves a "critical multiculturalism"—a space that disrupts the normative hegemonic discourse and allows for freedom of thought, creativity, and learning.

McLaren (2000) discusses the importance of critical multiculturalism, emphasizing: "Global or structural relations of power must not be ignored . . . Differences are always differences in relation, they are never simply free-floating. Differences are not seen as absolute, irreducible or intractable, but rather as undecidable and socially and culturally relational" (p. 48). Thus, we introduce the importance of a "glonacal agency heuristic" to reframe our model of school leader development to provide for a critical multiculturalist lens occurring through an authentic, inquiry-based approach.

Although there appears to be widespread acknowledgement about the increased need for schools to prepare students for a globalized world, as citizens and knowledge-producers, the power structures and knowledge hierarchies in which this shift is expected to occur have not yet changed. In describing their heuristic of "glonacal agency" Marginson and Rhoades (2002) explain that they mean to:

> . . . emphasize the intersections, interactions, mutual determinations of these levels (global, national, and local) and domains (organizational agencies and the agency of collectivities). We do not see a linear flow from the global to the local; rather, we see simultaneity of flows . . . National and local entities and collective efforts can undermine, challenge and define alternatives to global patterns, they can also shape the configuration of global flows. At every level—global, national, and local—elements and influences of other levels are present. A glonacal agency approach leads us to trace these elements and domains. (p. 289)

When applying the glonacal agency heuristic, one must also consider organizational connectivity and activities, which Marginson and Rhoades (2002) describe as "strength, layers and conditions, and spheres" (p. 291) as well as the concept of reciprocity. Figure 13.1 offers a visual representation of the glonacal agency heuristic.

The glonacal agency heuristic holds implications for college of education as units of higher education, but also for schools and school leaders responsible for creating environments of learning within new market and knowledge realities. If we operationalize the context of schools within the glonacal agency heuristic, we are able to see the complexity of the system and the importance of the human agency work within the global context for school leaders. School leaders are confronted by situations and cultures that they have never encountered nor experienced during their preparation as educators. In *The Reflective Practitioner: How Professionals Think in Action*, Schön (1983) describes the privileges that professionals used to possess due to their "extraordinary knowledge in matters of great social importance" (p. 4). The rapid changes in our technological and global society have altered the professional landscape: "The situations of practice are not problems to be solved but problematic situations characterized by uncertainty, disorder, and indeterminacy" (pp. 15–16). In applying such a heuristic to the development of school leaders, we must layer in space for the development of leaders who can appreciate and make use of glonacal agency to create more equitable organizations within ever changing contexts. To do so, we offer a layered, multi-dimensional approach to preparing principals to be leaders of social justice in a global context. This transformative approach occurs iteratively, through a spiraling process of reflection and leadership development.

DECONSTRUCTION BY DESIGN

The development of school leaders who are able to inquire and deconstruct notions of power and self requires first a deconstruction of their own perceptions and values. In supporting future school leaders to do this work, we engage them in reflective narratives of self, place them in positions that require the confrontation of their place within the culture of power, and evaluate them through expectations of praxis and their exemplified understanding of it in field settings. Narratives in Adult Development

For future school leaders to empower the development of others (specifically, their teachers and staff), they must first be prepared in a way that allows for a reflective understanding of self. Narrative can be a powerful tool in facilitating adult development. In describing the use of narrative for adult development Rossiter (1999b) posits:

> Such an orientation is experience-based, holistic, and in accord with the methods of human science. The storied nature of adult development is understood in terms of the contextual, interpretive, retrospective, and temporal dimensions of narrative. It is through the ongoing construction of the self-narrative that developmental change is experienced and understood. (p. 84)

For future school leaders, transformational development requires introspection, retrospection, and reflection of self, deconstructed within social and cultural meanings. Narrative serves as an essential tool in the process of development, but is an invaluable resource to reposition educational leaders to understand their glonacal agency. As the confrontation of self occurs, a disruption of the hegemonic discourse requires an explication of constructs of power, and agency within that construct must also include considerations of cultural meanings, including the culture of power.

Culture of Power

Social justice leadership is that which confronts aspects of the lived reality of schooling and the influences of power within and across identity groups. Often, this means engaging in a dialogue or difficult conversation that is at odds with the normative social expectations of the organization. Giving voice to the "silenced dialogue" of oppression requires school leaders to be explicit in their instructional leadership and supervision as they deconstruct practices of power and pedagogy with teachers. Delpit's (1988) work introduces how the hegemonic discourse is enacted within classrooms by identifying what she calls the "culture of power." According to Delpit (1988), the concept of the culture of power encompasses the five following aspects of power:

1. Issues of power are enacted in classrooms.
2. There are codes or rules for participating in power; that is, there is a "culture of power."
3. The rules of the culture of power are a reflection of the rules of the culture of those who have power.
4. If you are not already a participant in the culture of power, being told explicitly the rules of that culture makes acquiring power easier.
5. Those with power are frequently least aware of—or least willing to acknowledge—its existence. Those with less power are often most aware of its existence (p. 282).

As educational leaders create space to allow for the silenced dialogue to become "voiced" by students, they must first perpetuate a culture that allows for learning. Put differently, to facilitate this important dialogue, the school itself must become adaptable to disrupt the culture of power and to narrow the gap between espoused values and enacted values, and it must become a learning organization (Argryis & Schön, 1978; Senge, 1990).

Enacting Values: Individual and Organizational Praxis

Individuals deconstructing their own enactment of the culture of power, praxis, or "reflection and action upon the world in order to transform it" (Freire, 1978, p. 36) become an important tool for educational leaders. By applying praxis to the interconnected systems Senge (1990) describes in the learning organization, the oppression so often replicated within schools, as social institutions reifying the hegemonic discourse, true social justice can begin to take root within the educational system and in turn alter the external context. For an educational leader to alter the school environment to such an extent, the organization must be conducive to double-loop learning. Argyris and Schön (1978) describe double-loop learning as " . . . those sort of organizational inquiry which resolve incompatible organizational norms by setting new priorities and weightings of norms, or by restructuring the norms themselves together with associated strategies and assumptions" (p. 18). The inquiry process allows one to critically examine self, practice and consequence, thereby promoting double-loop learning and engaging praxis. Praxis, as a cyclical, ongoing process must be applied at both the individual and organizational level to create true transformative change. In preparing leaders in educational supervision, critical aspects of learning should occur through an inquiry-based approach to ensure preparation as reflective, adaptive, and transformative leaders.

Theory to Practice: An Inquiry-Based Approach through Reflective Narrative

At the individual level, inquiry-based action learning represents a type of professional learning of a school practitioner from direct practices or a type of learning of a student from project-based pedagogical practice (Argyris, 1982; Argyris et al., 1985; Stevenson, 2002). This self-managing process is also a form of organizational learning, involving a cyclic action of inquiry process including environmental analysis, planning, structuring, implementing, monitoring, and evaluations (Cheng, 1996; Cheng & Cheung, 2003, 2004; Senge, 1990). The narrative process in which the individual reflects, reconsiders, relates, and reframes the organizational culture (see Figure 13.2) within a glonacal agency context is necessary for preparing school leaders for a globalized world.

The preparation of school leaders typically focuses on what we know about the knowledge and skills needed to become effective at leading successful schools. Empirical research claims that certain leadership moves increase the potential of impact on improving student learning (Cotton, 2003; Leithwood & Jantzi, 2008; Marzano, Waters, & McNulty, 2005). This leadership research informs a knowledge base for leadership preparation; however, professional education requires an integration of knowledge, skills and values. Shulman (2005) describes professional education as a synthesis of three apprenticeships—cognitive, practical and moral. The glonacal agency context requires the interaction of these three apprenticeships to promote critical inquiry of knowledge and best practice that will challenge the culture of power. This critical inquiry exists primarily through the enactment of the moral apprenticeship where "one learns to think and act in a responsible and ethical manner that integrates across all three domains" (Shulman, 2005, p. 3).

Tapping into the moral apprenticeship requires one to uncover and confront values and assumptions. Only by confronting personal values can one become open to learning and appreciating new perspectives that allow equitable actions and social justice. John Smyth (1989) describes a process of critical reflection composed of sequential stages linked to a series of questions that take individuals through a deconstruction and reconstruction process to unlearn privilege and transform self and organizations. These questions are the foundation of our narrative reflective process that move beyond a record of events to a catalyst for analysis and action. These reflec-

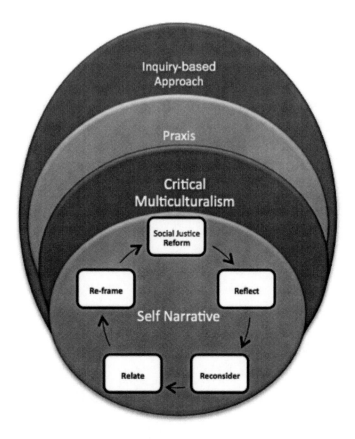

Figure 13.2 Spiral process of learning for social justice reform.

tions are structured to promote the spiral process of learning for social justice reform (see Figure 13.2) through the following questions:

- What do/did I do? (Describe)
- What does this mean? (Inform)
- How did I come to be like this? (Confront)
- How might I do things differently? (Reconstruct) (Smyth,1989)

The first two stages of description and information allow individuals to name and analyze their actions within a context. These two stages are common for reflective processes, and they allow one to remain within one's own value system. Most people are able to describe injustices and analyze actions at an intellectual level through these initial stages. The third stage of confrontation forces the individual to look into the mirror and examine judgments and values. This stage disrupts intellectual understandings, forces the exposure of assumptions and illuminates the "blind spot of leadership"—the inner place from which we operate (Scharmer, 2008). This personalization of learning is often uncomfortable and forces individuals to unlearn their assumptions and reconstruct self through "new eyes" as they become agents of change to challenge the culture of power and build more equitable organizations.

Critical Multiculturalism: Transformational Reflections in Action

We have named Smyth's (1989) reflective framework "transformational reflections" and embedded it as a reflective process within several courses in our principal preparation and Masters and PhD programs in Educational Leadership. The four levels of questions take students through a process where they reflect, reconsider, relate, and reframe their actions and challenge their existing beliefs. Although these courses have been taught by different faculty, the impact on students is strikingly similar. The following is a case example that describes the reflective process a student experienced, along with quotes from the student's journal.

> One white student used the reflective process to describe an incident in her neighborhood where her dog was being chased by a black boy. She reflected that her initial reactions were anger, fear and concern about safety in the neighborhood. Her analysis (What does this mean?) led her to the conclusion that personal stereotypes and assumptions emerged when she was faced with a situation near her home. She works in a school where the majority of families are Latino and African American, and she never felt concerned for her safety at her school. Why did she quickly rush to judgment to an incident near her home? This analysis led to a confrontation of self and a realization that her work within a school with students of color allowed her to claim that she was not racist; 'I am realizing more and more that I have considered myself accepting of all people because I've always had friends of color growing up and have biracial cousins. I think I'm actually accepting of anyone who shares my middle class values and shun those who don't.' The awareness of her bias provided the beginning of the reconceptual process that led to a personal commitment to continually examine and question her assumptions and challenge her biases.

From preparation to practice, educators are asked to reflect and journal about their work and experiences. The word "reflect" has become part of the professional vernacular. The following verbatim excerpt demonstrates how a student perceives the difference in the transformational reflection process from her other reflection experiences.

> I have always felt I was a reflective person. From my first formal journaling experiences during undergrad and student teaching, I was proud of the way I recorded my journey. The transformational reflections asked me much more. It was difficult to look deep within myself and ask the question 'How did I come to be this way?' It felt uncomfortable. As the year progressed, I continued to use this technique and have come to value it. In becoming a leader, you quickly discover that the only person you are really in charge of is yourself. If I expect others to grow and change, I must lead by modeling and sharing my personal journey. (Personal communication, 2008)

Through the transformational reflection process, evidence of personal transformation emerges. Students' reflection on the origination of their values forces them to consider the connections between the personal, group and organizational cultures. The following student reflection represents the depth of personal learning and development of "new eyes" that the transformational reflection process promotes:

> I have also been confronted with evidence that individuals I believed to be culturally proficient do not necessarily reflect behaviors aligned with their talk (but that does not make them bad people). It is difficult to recognize that I may have also been party to some of the acceptance of these behaviors. What I also see in myself is the tendency to be rigid in what I consider correct and incorrect behavior with regards to others, especially students who come from families that are less privileged and students of color. I suspect some of this is based upon the fact that I grew up in a family without a father and with very little economic opportunity. I remember what it was like to be treated as less than because your clothes were hand me downs and your haircuts were never quite right because your mother could not afford to take everyone to the hairdressers. My behavior is not always in the best interest of those I believe I am protecting. After all, it is not my protection they need as much as my willingness to uncover those areas that continue to allow oppression to exist. Being a champion is actually a selfish not selfless behavior.

> I also understand that some of my actions are just as incapacitating when I do not hold a standard for achievement for every student myself. What is most important is that I stop and have dialogue with individuals to better understand their thinking. As I learned from reading about Paulo Freire, dialogue is about building mutual understanding and that praxis in action is based on that dialogue. That is where I believe I need to focus my energies. For if I better understand the individuals I work with, my friends, and family, I can be more interactive in discussions while suspending my own judgments that may be based on inaccurate assumptions about their behaviors as well. It is best to walk the talk. (Personal communication, 2006)

The students in each of these examples demonstrate the power of the third question, "How did I come to be like this?" in confronting personal values and behavior before identifying the cultural and organizational factors. This reflective process provides a catalyst for metatonia, "a shift of mind—from seeing ourselves as separate from the world to connected to the world, from seeing problems as caused by someone or something 'out there' to seeing how our own actions create the problems we experience" (Senge, 1990, p. 13). Metatonia forces them to assume a deeper level of accountability and examine how they personally contribute to issues of social justice and equity that extend beyond self through the glonacal agency heuristic.

CONCLUSION

Overlaying a transformative reflection framework coupled with the glonacal agency heuristic allows for the deconstruction of self for future school leaders to reconsider justice from a global context. Schools are powerful local agencies to disrupt unjust power structures and reshape the critical multiculturalism of schools. Engaging students in reflections of self allows them to deconstruct their personal identities and *reconceive* notions of pedagogy, culture, and power. This process is one of continuous improvement and reframing of leadership that incorporates reflection, reconsideration, relating, and reframing (See Figure 13.2). The successful outcome of the preparation of effective school administrators who can work critically within layered contexts to understand and build a positive school culture requires that school leader preparation programs cultivate the narrative of self and adult identity development. Adult identity development of this kind requires perspectives of critical multiculturalism and the tools of praxis as a way of augmenting the personal reflection of experience and transforming it to a multi-layered, contextualized exploration of power and social structures; the glonacal agency heuristic can serve as an essential device to frame and ground this work.

The spiral process of social justice reform is rooted in the inquiry-based pedagogical approach of the development of school leaders. This field-based, action-oriented, problem-based learning method allows for a mirroring of the role of being an educational administrator while providing the space for support and voice in reflections on power, privilege, and positionality of self. The transformational reflection framework offered by Smyth (1989) of describing, informing, confronting, and reconstructing allows for the praxis of critical multiculturalism to occur. The students themselves recognize their own shift in their understanding of self and others in reflecting on their experiences through the coursework state, "This work was life-altering, I have been changed and now see the world in a new way. Thank you" (Personal communication, 2010). As educational leaders it also means that they develop a habit that supports their work of developing people and building capacity by engaging in the continuation of this process throughout their own organizations. As future school leaders students see the importance of the work, with one commenting, "I've realized so much—not just about what I think about in terms of multiculturalism and diversity—but in my thinking about my thinking. I don't see my role as expert or enforcer but as someone who creates a culture of questioning power, reconsidering norms, and engaging in dialogues about all of these things. It is exciting..." (Personal communication, 2010).

Thus, one of the most powerful implications of incorporating these frameworks and practices into school leadership preparation is the potential for shifts in metacognition about social justice. If principals and educational supervisors are to be transformational leaders and disrupt the normative cycles of oppression, they must first deconstruct themselves and be encouraged to grow continuously as they have been empowered to do through the spiral process of learning. Moreover, the use of narrative in adult learning to allow for students to identify with the work personally allows for a fundamental shift in their thinking of their work as school leaders. To build capacity in schools for social justice means nurturing the individual sense of self, the exchange of power and ability to act on it, and an understanding informed by a reflective and engaged continuously improving approach.

REFERENCES

Argyris, C. (1982). *Reasoning, learning, and action: Individual and organizational.* San Francisco, CA: Jossey-Bass.

Argyris, C., Putnam, R., & McLain-Smith, D. (1985). *Action science: Concepts, methods, and skills for research and intervention.* San Francisco, CA: Jossey-Bass.

Argyris, C., & Schön, D. (1978). *Organizational learning: A theory of action perspective.* Reading, MA: Addison Wesley.

Cheng, Y. C. (1996). A school-based management mechanism for school effectiveness and development. *School Effectiveness and School Improvement: An International Journal of Research, Policy and Practice, 7*(1), 35–61.

Cheng, Y. C., & Cheung, W. M. (2004). Four types of school environment: Multilevel self-management and educational quality. *Educational Research & Evaluation, 10*(1), 71–100.

Cheung, W. M., & Cheng, Y. C. (2003). Developing the multilevel self-management capacity of school through intervention. *Journal of Basic Education, 1,* 69–99.

Cotton, K. (2003). *Principal and student achievement: What the research says.* Alexandria, VA: Association for Supervision and Curriculum Development.

Delpit, L. D. (1988). The silenced dialogue: Power and pedagogy in educating other people's children. *Harvard Educational Review, 58,* 280–298.

Delpit, L. D. (2002). *The skin that we speak: Thoughts on language and culture in the classroom.* New York, NY: New Press.

Freire, P. (1970). *Pedagogy of the oppressed*. New York, NY: Continuum.

Leithwood, K., & Jantzi, D. (2008). Linking leadership to student learning: The contributions of leader efficacy. *Educational Administration Quarterly, 44*(4), 496–528.

Marginson, S., & Rhoades, G. (2002). Beyond national states, markets, and systems of higher education: a global agency heuristic. *Higher Education, 43*(3), 281–309.

Marzano, R., Waters, T., & McNulty, B. (2005). *School leadership that works: From research to results*. Alexandria, VA: Association for Supervision and Curriculum Development.

McLaren, P. (2000). *White terror and oppositional agency: Towards a critical multiculturalism*. Boston, MA: Allyn & Beacon.

Mohanty, C. (1990, Winter). On race and voice: Challenges for liberal education in the 1990s. *Cultural Critique, 14*, 5–26.

Rossiter, M. (1999a). A narrative approach to development: Implications for adult education. *Adult Education Quarterly, 50*(1), 56–71.

Rossiter, M. (1999b). Understanding adult development as narrative. *New directions for adult and continuing education, 1999*, 77–85. doi: 10.1002/ace.8409.

Scharmer, C. (2008). Uncovering the blind spot of leadership. *Leader to Leader, 47*, 52–59.

Schön, D. (1983) *The reflective practitioner: How professionals think in action*. New York, NY: Basic Books.

Senge, P. M. (1990). *The fifth discipline: The art and practice of the learning organization*. New York, NY: Doubleday.

Shulman, L. S. (2005, February). *The signature pedagogies of the professions of law, medicine, engineering, and the clergy: Potential lessons for the education of teachers*. Paper delivered at the Math Science Partnerships (MSP) Workshop: Teacher Education for Effective Teaching and Learning, National Research Council's Center for Education, Irvine, CA. Retrieved March 10, 2011 from http://www.taylorprograms.com/images/Shulman_Signature_Pedagogies.pdf .

Smyth, J. (1989). Developing and sustaining critical reflection in teacher education. *Journal of Teacher Education, 40*(2), 2–9.

Stevenson, T. (2002). Anticipatory action learning: Conversations about the future. *Journal of Forecasting, Planning, and Policy, 34*(5).

CHAPTER 14

PREPARING CULTURALLY COMPETENT INSTRUCTIONAL LEADERS

Maysaa Barakat, Ellen Reames and Lisa Kensler

INTRODUCTION

The demographic composition of the United States is changing rapidly (Shrestha, 2006). Minority and diverse ethnic groups will soon comprise a larger percentage of the student body than the traditional white majority. Large numbers of this minority population will be living in impoverished environments (Southern Education Foundation [SEF], 2007). There are a myriad of studies demonstrating a close relationship between low socio-economic status and a lack of success in schools (Coleman, 1988; Reynolds & Walberg, 1992; Sirin, 2005; Watkins, 1997). The problem is particularly acute in the southern part of the country, where students from low-income minority families comprise approximately 54% of the student population (SEF, 2007). Research findings suggest the achievement gap for low-income students, in several southern states, is often wider than that on the national scale. In addition, low-income students have higher dropout rates from high school and lower college attendance and graduation rates (SEF, 2007). "How the southern states recognize and address this new majority is

Social Justice Leadership for a Global World, pages 241–260
Copyright © 2012 by Information Age Publishing
All rights of reproduction in any form reserved.

the most important challenge that the region and perhaps the nation will face in the early 21st century" (SEF, 2007 p. 13).

Assuring that all students have the opportunity to succeed in school and in life is a vital element in a democracy. Add to this the impact of globalization and how it is changing the social, technological, and economic aspects of our lives, and pressure on teachers and leaders to ensure that our students can succeed in a globalized world is increasing. Thus, it is critical that teachers and school leaders not only believe that all children can succeed, but that they are also prepared to bring about the policies and processes that will expand the school's capacity to meet the needs of all students. These educators must be prepared to effectively facilitate student academic achievement and success in preparation for a changing world. Ingram and Walters (2007) stated, "Today's student population creates a demographic imperative for teachers and administrators to acquire the knowledge, skills, and dispositions that are necessary to respond to diversity and social justice" (p. 24). Our educational institutions are not isolated from the changing economic or demographic cultures of American society. This is especially true in the South because of the increasing minority population projections in this region (SEF, 2007; Southern Regional Educational Board [SREB], 2009). Thus, it is essential that principal preparation programs adequately prepare future school leaders for the cultural competency challenges they will face in these diverse environments. Leaders must understand that today's students will inherit a society that has become progressively more interdependent globally. This chapter presents findings from a study designed to examine one program's efforts in preparing future principals to be culturally competent leaders within a changing global context.

PURPOSE AND SIGNIFICANCE OF THE STUDY

The purpose of the study was to examine the social justice and diversity strands of an educational leadership preparation program we call the Educational Leadership Program (ELP). Researchers wanted to know if the ELP was positively influencing the development of culturally competent leaders. This research is important because of the ongoing call for substantial transformation in educational leadership preparation programs that suggest school leaders are being charged with fostering productive, equitable, and socially just learning environments for all students (Brown, 2004; McKenzie et al., 2008; Murphy, 1999; Theoharis, 2007). While we know that diversity and social justice should be a leadership preparation program tenet, there is little consistent evidence tracking future leaders as they develop cultural competence or showing how well these future leaders practice cultural competence in K–12 settings.

The ELP is located at a major university in the Southeastern portion of the United States. According to the Carnegie Foundation for the Advancement of Teaching (2011), the university is a four-year undergraduate and graduate institution supporting 25,000 students and is classified as a research university with high research activity (RU/H) category. [Southern State] is primarily rural and is ranked as one of the top five Level IV poverty (extreme poverty) states. The state is 10th in total poverty and 9th in child poverty (U.S. Census, 2010). In 2000 [Southern State] was 71% white, 26% black, 3% Hispanic and 1% other (U.S. Census, 2010), but recent estimates report a 100% increase in Hispanics since the 2000 census. The university is located in a small town of 40,000 residents. The surrounding 11 counties are some of the poorest in the state (U.S. Census, 2010). Within these demographics, the Educational Leadership Program has built a strong partnership with the Local Educational Agencies (LEA's).

The University and College of Education have a clear conceptual framework, which promotes diversity and social justice. These institutional conceptual frameworks, along with other guiding standards such as those proposed by the National Council for Accreditation of Teacher Education (NCATE) and the Interstate School Leaders Licensure Consortium (ISLLC), were used to help create a curriculum map of the ideal program.[1] Diversity and social justice were two of seven guiding themes that arose from the ELP curriculum map (Reames, 2010). These two were joined by reflective practice, leadership dispositions, data driven decision making, collaboration and communication and democratic community.

While developing the ELP, leadership faculty were conscious of diversity and social justice and were deliberate in promoting program efforts in this area (Reames, 2010). Each ELP course was mapped using the seven guiding curriculum themes. In other words, diversity and social justice were intentionally addressed in the law and ethics class, supervision, school finance, principal leadership, curriculum and all other courses because these areas were considered overarching programmatic themes.

BACKGROUND OF THE EDUCATIONAL LEADERSHIP PROGRAM

Added responsibilities and accountability measures placed on the school administrators' shoulders as a result of No Child Left Behind (No Child Left Behind [NCLB], 2002) and the high expectations for student and teacher performance have increased the pressure for school leaders to reach performance benchmarks. "Now leaders are increasingly being held accountable for actual performance of those under their charge" (Firestone & Riehl 2005, p. 2). These changes consequently have placed educational leadership programs under the magnifying glass (Bottoms & O'Neil, 2001). As Cunningham and Sherman (2008) stated, "Two major themes of contemporary criticisms are that educational leadership programs lack contextual relevancy and that leadership preparation content lacks focus on instructional leadership and, in turn, student achievement" (p. 309).

Substantial transformation in educational leadership preparation programs are necessary to ensure that school leaders are competent in fostering productive and equitable learning environments for all students. This need to address diversity and social justice issues is especially true in light of the changing student demographics within the public school systems. Additionally, although educational leadership programs have emerged from local contexts, the trend toward understanding cultural competence within a wider, more global sphere is beginning to impact leadership preparation as well (Lumby, 2008). New understandings of the educational leader's role as an instructional leader and advocate for his or her community and beyond has influenced the redesign of the knowledge base, course content, and foundational goal of educational administration preparation programs (Cunningham & Sherman, 2008; Murphy, 2002; Reames, 2010). As stated by Lumby (2008), "Education is indeed a global enterprise... There are resulting implications for how leaders model a stance as citizens of the world and not just of their local community or state" (p. 1).

The literature concerning diversity and social justice in educational leadership preparation programs is growing and becoming more robust (Cambron-McCabe & McCarthy, 2005; Reames, 2010; Theoharis, 2007). One of the leading professional associations, The American Association of School Administrators (AASA), issued a belief and position statement in 2007 stating that "school leaders have a responsibility to create school cultures that recognize and value diversity" (n.p.). The most current education research and best practice literature suggests that our college and university leadership programs should advocate for diversity, and resist any and all forms of discrimination and exclusion (Oplatka, 2009). Currently, state departments of education are addressing the issue of diversity by laying out new standards for licensing educators that incorporate cultural competence (Sanders & Kearney, 2008). Examples of such standards are drawn from leading professional and policy associations such as the core propositions for accomplished educational leaders set by the National Board for Professional Teaching Standards (NBPTS, 2011), NCATE (2008), and ISLLC standards (CSSO, 2008). These accrediting agencies, university educational leadership programs, and state departments of education, who actually grant leadership licensure, are charged to make sure that all leadership preparation programs are operating with diversity and social justice in mind. Thus, it is clear at the national, regional and state levels that diversity and social justice are recognized as important to the preparation of school leaders.

However, subsequent research suggests that we have not yet reached our goal of implementation and evaluation in our programs or in leadership practice (Marshall & Gerstl-Pepin, 2005).

Educational leadership programs carry the great responsibility for preparing school leaders to become agents of social justice in their schools and communities (American Association of Colleges for Teacher Education, 1988; Styron & LeMire, 2009). Currently there are between 450 and 500 university leadership preparation programs across the United States. These programs cover a wide range of expertise between programs offering Master's (M.Ed.), Specialists (Ed.S) and Doctoral (Ph.D, Ed.D) degrees. Approximately 472 higher education institutions offer Master's and Doctoral degrees, while 162 offer the Education Specialist's degree (Young & Brewer, 2008). With college and university educational leadership programs being the primary preparation route and given the pressure these programs are under to provide relevant and rigorous curriculum, it seems important that leadership faculty would pay particular attention to the implementation and evaluation of leadership preparation programs in regards to national standards related to such critical areas as diversity and social justice.

Efforts by educational leadership programs to evaluate their programs, as well as efforts by professional educational associations such as NCATE and the University Council for Educational Administration (UCEA), who serve as strong advocates and positive instigators of "preparation program evaluation and empirical study of leadership preparation in general during the past decade" (Kottkamp, 2011, p.12), have increased. Educational leadership programs across the country have also made efforts to assess their success, specifically in preparing their candidates for leading in diverse contexts (Chan, 2006), as well as in evaluating faculty members' level of commitment to educate towards social justice (Sensoy & DiAngelo, 2009). Even though numerous preparation programs strive to integrate diversity and cultural competency issues into their program designs, the question remains as to whether or not these efforts have yielded the intended results (Chan, 2006). It is toward this effort that this chapter is focused.

CONCEPTUAL FRAMEWORK

"Social justice is a term that is not easily defined, but is associated in education with the idea that all individuals and groups must be treated with fairness and respect and that all are entitled to the resources and benefits that the school has to offer" (Shriberg & Fenning, 2009, p.3). Theoharis (2007) argued that social justice "centers on addressing and eliminating marginalization in schools" (p. 223). For the purpose of this study, social justice encompasses setting high achievement expectations for all students, advocating for diversity, eliminating marginalization, and taking action to promote fairness and equity.

Educational leaders must serve as advocates for social justice and strive to develop a common 21st century understanding of social justice leadership (McKenzie et al., 2008). Historically, the approach for dealing with diversity in the American culture began with a desire to create a homogeneous environment within a heterogeneous culture (melting pot), where a need to blend student differences away was the ultimate goal (Grant & Chapman, 2008). Today, the approach to diversity is one which "strives for an equitable pluralism that works to breakdown social barriers ... while at the same time providing nurturing environments for students who have historically been marginalized" (Reyes & Wagstaff, 2005, p. 102). This line of research is primarily grounded in a newer social justice conceptual framework that "links social justice with academic achievement, critical consciousness and inclusive practices" (McKenzie et al., 2008, p. 116). A number of writers have promoted their concepts of social justice:

- Social justice requires school leaders to work towards raising all students' academic achievements (Bruner, 2008). Bruner suggests that "effective leaders realize that their efforts include both increasing student achievement and becoming an activist for broader social justice issues and change of institutional structures" (p. 484).
- "Social Justice requires the educational leaders to prepare their students to live as critical citizens in society" (McKenzie et al., 2008, p. 116). This means that educational leaders should act as advocates of diversity and social justice as well as encourage their students to become agents of change in their communities (2008). "Educational Leaders not only need to understand research but they also need to understand social justice issues and be trained in how to advocate for their schools, students, teachers, staff, parents and communities" (Gerstl-Pepin, n.d, p. 3). Parker and Shapiro (1993) argued that schools exist within societies and that preparation programs must acknowledge this fact and prepare school leaders to focus on the social context.
- Educational leaders should be able to create an inclusive learning environment for all students (McKenzie et al., 2008). A school principal's set of values together with his/her leadership capabilities and skills strongly affect students' success. Successful school leaders are responsible for and expected to create a learning environment where each individual feels respected and valuable (Reyes &Wagstaff, 2005). "Principals championing the needs of students who have been historically marginalized is a central premise of the

growing call for social justice leadership" (Theoharis & O'Toole, 2011, p. 2).

To summarize, the conceptual framework of the research project proposes socially just educational leaders need to integrate student achievement, advocate for diversity and create an inclusive environment, and that educational leadership preparation programs have both a responsibility and opportunity to influence educational leaders' capacity to do so.

METHODOLOGY

The study sought to investigate the diversity and social justice strand of the educational leadership Master's program. This case study investigation was part of our educational leadership program's ongoing internal evaluation. The researchers wanted to answer the following questions:

1. How did student reported responses on the Cultural Intelligence Scale (CQ) differ between two ELP cohorts of educational leadership students—one just beginning and one just completing the educational leadership preparation program? And, to what extent may any differences between the ELP cohorts relate to students' experiences in the educational leadership preparation program?

2. What knowledge, skills, attitudes and behaviors may be the bridges and/or barriers to increasing cultural competence of school leaders? And how does the ELP curriculum support acquisition of this knowledge and skills?

To answer the first research question, researchers began with the Cultural Intelligence (CQ) Scale (Ang & Van Dyne; 2008). The CQ measures an individual's ability to reason and behave in culturally diverse settings. There are four dimensions comprising the cultural intelligence scale: CQ Strategy, CQ Knowledge, CQ Motivation, and CQ Behavior. The researchers compared the two leadership groups using a developmental rather than a scientific measurement approach. A self-report instrument is used where the participant adds their scores on the four dimensions and reports those as Excellent, Moderate or Red Alert. Excellent means little or no improvement is needed to operate in diverse settings and the respondent scored in the top 25% range. Moderate means improvement is needed and the respondent scored in the middle 50% range. Red Alert is a score falling in the lowest 25% and means a significant amount of work in the CQ dimension is needed in order to enhance individual cultural competence.

The instrument has been used in national and international business and university settings with documented success (Balogh, Gaal, & Szabo, 2011). The CQ is appropriate for use with those who are participating in diversity training or leadership development to facilitate appropriate behavior with cultures other than their own (Balogh, Gaal, & Szabo, 2011). Each of the four dimensions is described briefly:

1. *CQ Strategy: I adjust my cultural knowledge as I interact with people from a culture that is unfamiliar to me.* Individuals with high CQ Strategy scores will reflect and intentionally question their cultural assumptions and knowledge. High CQ individuals are aware that societies and sub-cultures operate with different value and belief systems.
2. *CQ Knowledge: I know the cultural values and religious beliefs of other cultures.* Those with high CQ Knowledge would possess familiarity with norms and beliefs of other cultures as well as their own and would have gained this from education and life experiences.
3. *CQ Motivation: I enjoy interacting with people from different cultures.* Interacting with other cultures requires energy and concentration within unfamiliar settings. An individual with high CQ Motivation will demonstrate confidence to interact in different cultural settings. These individuals will be engaged in the experience and have a sense of confidence in interacting with other cultures.
4. *CQ Behavior: I change my verbal and non-verbal behavior when a cross-cultural interaction requires it.* High CQ Behavior scores suggest that a person is able to practice appropriate verbal and nonverbal actions with persons from different cultures. High CQ Behavior recognizes the need to change behaviors to fit other cultures.

The CQ has a four-factor structure and is a reliable and valid measure of cultural intelligence. The CQ has been tested in numerous settings and times. Cronbach's alpha exceeded .70 (CQ Strategy = .71; CQ Knowledge = .85; CQ Motivation = .85 and CQ Behavior = .83) and discriminant, incremental and predictive validity of the instrument have also been established (Ang, Van Dyne, Koh, Ng, Templer, Tay, & Chandrasekar, 2007; Ang & Van Dyne, 2008; Van Dyne, Ang, & Koh, 2009).

All 14 respondents in our study were students in the Master's level ELP and responded to an online version of the CQ. The 2010 ELP cohort included seven students. These seven were entering their first semester of graduate studies at the university. At the time the researchers administered the survey, the seven members of the 2009 ELP cohort had just completed four semesters of intense leadership studies and were graduating. The 2009 ELP cohort served as our comparison group. Both groups were similar in gender, race, age, educational background and profession. All 14 participants were from LEA's within the 11 partnership counties surrounding the university. Results were given to each and were reported using the Excellent (E), Moderate (M) and Red Alert (X) scores.

The researchers conducted a focus group with the seven 2009 ELP graduates (comparison group) to address the second question, which was to explore the knowledge, skills, attitudes and behaviors that might be considered as bridges and/or barriers of the ELP program. Simply examining differences in the two cohorts' CQ scores would tell us very little, if anything, about our program. However, the focus group interviews would allow us to learn more about student perceptions of the program, their own cultural competence, and the learning they may have experienced during the program. All participants of the focus group were also graduates who had answered the CQ. Thematic analysis of the qualitative data identified themes and patterns using the constant comparative method (Merriam, 2009). The chief limitation of this study is the small sample size.

RESULTS

Research Question 1: *How did student reported responses on the CQ differ between two ELP cohorts of educational leadership students, one just beginning and one just completing the educational leadership preparation program? And, to what extent may any differences between the ELP cohorts relate to students' experiences in the educational leadership preparation program?*

The new 2010 ELP cohort primarily scored Red Alert in all four dimensions (See Table 14.1). One student (Student 7, 2010 cohort) who scored excellent across all four domains had spent a great deal of time living and traveling in the Middle East, Asia and Europe as the child of an engineer and had served

TABLE 14.1   2010 ELP Cohort: Excellent (E); Moderate (M) and Red Alert Status (X) by dimension

Beginning Semester 2010 ELP Cohort	CQ Strategy	CQ Knowledge	CQ Motivation (Drive)	CQ Behavior (Action)
1	X	X	X	X
2	X	X	X	M
3	X	X	X	X
4	X	X	X	X
5	X	M	X	X
6	M	M	M	X
7	E	E	E	E

Source: Ang et al., 2007.

as an educator and state department of education administrator who worked with high poverty and minority populations. This is the only student who scored excellent as a beginning ELP student. All other students in this cohort were primarily Red Alert. This means that beginning Master's ELP students' CQ scores indicated low cultural strategic thinking, low cultural knowledge, low cultural motivation and low cultural behavior based on responses on the CQ Instrument. These results suggest that the educational leadership preparation program has both an opportunity and a responsibility to facilitate improvements in most of these students' cultural competence.

In analysis of the results from the 2009 ELP cohort, these graduates of our program scored moderate to excellent in the areas of Cultural Strategy and Knowledge, but generally scored in Red Alert status in both CQ Motivation and CQ Behavior (See Table 14.2). If we assume that individuals in the 2009 cohort began the program similar to individuals in the 2010 cohort, with most to all scores in the Red Alert range, then these scores suggest that individuals may improve in CQ Strategy and Knowledge during the educational leadership preparation program. The focus group interviews intended to explore this possibility. Combining CQ Strategy and CQ Knowledge suggests that graduates of the ELP may increase in their willingness to think about and approach cultural and diversity issues with mindful and intentional reflection and that knowledge and awareness are at satisfactory levels. It also suggests that these ELP students have yet to develop motivation (drive) and behaviors (action) that express high levels of cultural competence.

Focus Group Interviews

In order to garner a deeper understanding of the students' perceptions of their relationship between the ELP and developing cultural competence,

TABLE 14.2 2009 ELP Cohort Excellent E; Moderate M and Red Alert Status (X) by dimension

2009 Cohort ELP Graduates	CQ Strategy	CQ Knowledge	CQ Motivation (Drive)	CQ Behavior (Action)
1	M	M	X	X
2	E	E	X	X
3	E	E	X	X
4	E	E	X	X
5	E	E	X	X
6	E	E	X	X
7	M	M	X	M

Source: Ang et al., 2007.

researchers conducted a focus group with the seven members of the 2009 graduating ELP cohort. A series of questions designed to extend our understanding of the CQ were asked about the ELP program. Researchers began by asking questions to probe how participating in the ELP had changed their social justice and cultural diversity knowledge, skills and attitudes.

During the focus group, all seven graduates of the 2009 cohort suggested that they developed increased awareness and knowledge regarding diversity and social justice issues through participation in the program. One student spoke to the [Southern State] educational leadership diversity standard and the importance of varied instructional strategies needed to teach specialized populations. Additionally, all seven graduates spoke of their increased responsiveness to cultural diversity and felt compelled to be more compassionate with students and families. One graduate stated,

> Doing one of my internships in a 100% poverty school made me appreciate students and teachers so much more. I never realized how lucky I was to teach in the school district I am in. I didn't realize the challenges so many teachers, administrators and children face every single day. I am so grateful for the experiences related to social justice. It's made me a better teacher and one day I will be a better administrator because of this internship experience.

Another graduate said, "I have begun to focus on looking at each child as unique and special." A third graduate expressed understanding of the contextual necessity and urgency for addressing diversity and social justice and wanted to expand his definitions to include a more global diversity paradigm.

> Before the ELP, I always had the tendency to look at diversity as a black and white issue or a high income versus low income issue. It's not that at all. Diversity is not just what we are used to seeing or knowing. It's much larger than that. We have to think about the way we do things and the way we act every single day.

Research Question #2: *What knowledge, skills, attitudes and behaviors may be the bridges and/or barriers to increasing cultural competence of school leaders? And how does the ELP curriculum support acquisition of this knowledge and skills?*

In probing further, researchers wanted to know if the ELP curriculum had translated into changed behaviors and actions in the workplace because the CQ results were not indicative of this. Two of the graduates mentioned having a better understanding of the need to disaggregate student data so that sub-groups are recognized and studied to improve the learning of all students. As one student stated, "You have to break down the data to look at diverse groups." A second graduate said, "I agree with this and we have to look at different minority groups of students and how they are performing." In regards to behaviors and actions in their schools, one student mentioned using varied instructional strategies for diverse learner needs. "I learned quite a bit in the ELP about instructional strategies but I want to know more. I need to do more."

Towards understanding which ELP activities had the most dramatic effect on knowledge, skills and attitudes in regards to diversity, four out seven students expressed the internship component was most beneficial and three out of seven felt the cohort model had been an important part in their leadership development. Comments such as, "Internships gave us the chance to practice what we learned. We saw social justice up front and personal" and "Spending 10 consecutive days each semester really gave us a taste of what instructional leaders do and how they think about multiculturalism" supported these findings. Being a member of the cohort was important to the students. One ELP graduate said, "We bounced ideas and questions off each other. We studied together . . . like for example looking at school data with the interest of all children, no matter who they were." Another graduate followed with, "I am so satisfied with the entire experience. We have followed a cycle of topics, thinking, reflecting and solving problems together. I have life-long colleagues because of this program." When queried about social justice, course work, guest speakers, and leadership conferences were all mentioned as important components of the program, but they still ranked less valuable than the internships and the cohort model.

In closing, results from the focus group did give researchers reason to ponder why CQ motivation and behavior did not translate into proficient ratings. All seven of the 2009 graduates of the ELP expressed that the program prepared them to be competent leaders who could effectively contend with multiple diversity issues. At the same time several were quite frustrated because they had not been given the opportunity to share what they had learned in regards to social justice, diversity and cultural competence in their schools. As one graduate stated, "We know more than the shopkeepers we are working with." Another said, "Yes it gets very frustrating to know new knowledge and new skills and others have no idea and don't seem to want to know." Because these students were not yet practicing administrators, they perceived their opportunities to apply what they had learned as stifled. One student captured the essence of this finding by saying, "Leaders in our schools are less prepared. We need more hands on in our permanent place of work not just the internship."

DISCUSSION

The focus group interviews led researchers to believe that graduates expressed satisfaction with their present level of knowledge and beliefs concerning diversity and social justice including raising diversity awareness, understanding relevant state and national diversity standards and being more compassionate. The program also seems to relate to graduates' knowledge and views on diversity issues because they expressed understanding how cultural intelligence could positively influence: 1) teaching and learning through data engaged decision making and 2) their repertoire of instructional strategies to target learning styles of diverse student populations. However, in spite of the perceived positive influence in changing student CQ knowledge and strategy from the beginning (enrolled 2010 cohort) to the end (graduating 2009 cohort), there did not seem to be motivation to change behavior and actions in the school environments in which they work. Thus, cultural competence is left unfinished. These findings raise two important questions. *First, why is knowledge and strategic cultural thinking not being supported by motivation and behavior and thus extended to practice?* To answer the first question it may be as simple as one ELP graduate said, "We aren't running the shop." According to Bruner (2008) "school leaders are expected to serve broader social justice goals that urge a focus on diversity" (p. 484). School leaders need to receive sufficient preparation that is based on recent research and best practices so that their awareness, knowledge and skills are developed deeply enough to affect change in school communities and improve student performance.

In a study looking at institutionalizing school diversity plans, Young, Madsen and Young (2010) argue that establishing the plan is not enough; it does not automatically guarantee improvement in principals' action, school environment or students learning experience if school leaders are poorly prepared for the process. Furthermore, "training for leaders cannot focus solely on 'awareness,' we should prepare leaders to feel comfortable in responding to diversity-related conflicts" (Young, Madsen, & Young, 2010, p. 20). Principal preparation programs should aim at increasing diversity self-efficacy of leaders and not just their awareness of diversity issues (Young, Madsen & Young, 2010). As educational leadership faculty, we must dare our students to challenge long standing superficial actions. Perhaps the literature on change process is a good starting point.

Research on change seems to support the need for continuous, long-term development of social justice, diversity and cultural competence. If you want to change professional behaviors and actions, it takes time, resource support and personal and professional development, which includes mentoring (Blake-Beard, 2009; Blake-Beard, Murrell, & Thomas, 2007; Browne-Ferrigno & Muth, 2006; Williams, Matthews, & Baugh, 2004). In addition, it requires leaders who understand the change process and who are willing to be involved. Internships may "wet the whistle," but sustained practice may be what it takes to make deep rooted, second order change that social justice, diversity and cultural competence require (Brown, 2004; Browne-Ferrigno & Muth, 2006; Hernandez & McKenzie, 2010; Marzano, Waters, & McNulty, 2005; McKenzie et al, 2008; Waters, Marzano & McNulty, 2003). In order to better understand *why knowledge and strategic cultural thinking is not being supported by motivation and behavior and thus extended to practice,* ELP faculty and partner LEA's need to be aware of the results of this study and continuously find ways to make programmatic changes to support social justice, diversity and cultural competence of present and future school leaders. This will require ongoing program evaluation with special attention to social justice and diversity.

The second question raised by the finding is the following: *What alterations need to be made in the ELP in order to change the outcomes more positively and ensure graduates are motivated and are willing to take action?* The results of this study point to the idea that the ELP needs to increase efforts to prepare our students and to support the sitting administrators and teachers in the partner LEA's. Murphy (2002) once suggested that social justice should be nested within school improvement. Murphy obviously understood the difficulty diversity and cultural competence issues might be for some school administrators. According to Murphy, if social justice is nested within school improvement, it becomes less caustic because teachers and administrators are compelled to do their job and support student learning. The conversation becomes depersonalized, more objective and focuses on school improvement. There is some evidence to suggest this is true (Reames, 2010; Rivera, 2005; Shields, & Mohan, 2008). In a recent study, when objectively looking at student, teacher and school data and trying to find ways to improve the school and student achievement, leadership was compelled to sideline personal assumptions about a myriad of diverse learner needs (Kensler, Reames, Murray, & Patrick, 2011) and focus solely on success. This led researchers to conclude that supporting the development of the present "shop keepers," will in turn hopefully provide space for new leaders to practice what they have learned in leadership programs.

The ELP, like other school leadership programs, is one of the pillars needed to support social justice and student learning (Nettles & Herrington, 2007; Pounder, 2011; Styron & LeMire, 2009). However, no matter how well designed and executed the ELP is, it cannot achieve social justice and cultural competence in isolation. It must have support from partner LEA's (Sharp, 2003) along with the public policy makers who certainly play a role (Marshall & Gerstl-Pepin, 2005; Murphy, 2003).

Policies like "No Child Left Behind (NCLB) might appear progressive and supportive of multicultural education with its promising title; however… the law presents challenges to the advancement of multicultural education" (Gardiner, Canfield-Davis & Anderson, 2009, p. 143). One such challenge is equity. "Until you can show that every child has equal opportunity to all the things that help students do well in schools, it is unreasonable to hold children, teachers, schools and districts accountable for standardized tests" (Marshall & Gerstl-Pepin, 2005, p. 98). In the [Southern State] districts where the present study took place, equal opportunity remains a huge issue. Current state tax structures do not provide for equal funding in school districts. Local property taxes are used to support much of public education, and poor districts have low property taxes. Poverty stricken communities do not have the depth of support more affluent districts have, and their options for good schools, teachers and leaders are even more limited (Sirin, 2005; Young, Reimer, & Young, 2010).

The McKenzie et al. (2008) conceptual framework is a good ending point for the discussion of this research project. Socially just educational leaders need to integrate student achievement, advocate for their school community and be able to create inclusive learning environments. Cultural competence as measured by the CQ is a portion of being a socially just leader. It gives us a snapshot of the prototype leader. Excellent cultural competence requires leaders to set aside personal assumptions, embrace cultural differences and similarities, and support these with drive and action. It requires leaders to intersect academic achievement of all students, with advocacy and inclusive practices.

Additionally, the culturally competent leader must come to terms with what it means to be a school leader in present times because globalization has changed the face of education forever (Bottery, 1999; Scholte, 2000). As Cambron-McCabe and McCarthy (2005) suggest, school leaders must take a moral stance and operate in local as well as global contexts.

MOVING FORWARD

It would be valuable for the researchers to expand this study to identify the specific reasons that graduates have not implemented meaningful change and to implement curricular and other changes to try to enable future graduates to be more proactive. Forming partnerships with schools systems and with the community to discuss this issue may be one method for creating lasting change.

To determine how the results of this study can be used, ELP program faculty recently began such conversations with partner LEA's. One promising practice will be to bring professional development in diversity and social justice to entire faculties in the schools where our ELP interns are situated. Additionally, we have made conclusions from this study part of our program's continuous improvement plan. One of the program goals this year is to make globalization the theme for our fall Leadership Institute. Each semester ELP students and program faculty, deans and university administrators, and members of our LEA's come together to study leadership best practices. International leadership and globalization is the theme for the upcoming Institute.

One of our far-reaching implementations will be for masters and doctoral level students to participate and lead an international/intercultural experience. Some of our students will travel and participate in the ELP "Australia Leadership Experience;" others will choose to develop an experience with Native Americans or travel to Canada or Costa Rica to spend time engaged in school activities with school leaders.

New cohorts of students shall be challenged by participating in personal CQ analysis as a beginning student of leadership and then again as a graduating student. While in the program students should be expected to confront their diversity and multicultural assumptions and challenged to find ways to become more culturally competent. It would be meaningful if a cadre of preparation programs would conduct similar studies to determine the extent to which these findings are generalizable. If there are programs that are able to implement change more powerfully, factors that allowed them to create this change should be shared.

NOTES

1. The Interstate School Leaders Licensure Consortium (ISLLC) Standards have been developed by the Council of Chief State School Officers (CSSO) in collaboration with the National Policy Board on Educational Administration (NPBEA) to help strengthen preparation programs in school leadership (see Van Meter & Murphy, 1997). The National Council for the Accreditation of Teacher Education (NCATE) serves as the primary professional accrediting body for educator preparation programs in the U.S. What emerged are six major leadership standards that are considered primary national policy agency for educational leadership preparation programs.

REFERENCES

American Association of Colleges for Teacher Education. (1988). *Education reform: Are we on the right track?* Washington, DC: Author.

American Association of school Administrators. (2007). AASA Belief statement. Retrieved from http://archives.aasa.org/about/content.cfm?ItemNumber=9567

Ang, S., & Van Dyne, L. (Eds.). (2008). *Handbook on cultural intelligence: Theory, measurement and applications.* Armonk, NY: M.E. Sharpe.

Ang, S., Van Dyne, L., Koh, C. K. S., Ng, K. Y., Templer, K. J., Tay, C., & Chandrasekar, N. A. (2007). Cultural intelligence: Its measurement and effects on cultural judgment and decision making, cultural adaptation, and task performance. *Management and Organization Review, 3*, 335–371.

Balogh, A., Gaal, Z., & Szabo, L. (2011). Relationship between organizational culture and cultural intelligence. *Management & Marketing, 6*(1), 95–110.

Blake-Beard, S. (2009). Mentoring as a bridge to understanding cultural difference. *Adult Learning, 20*(1–2), 14–18.

Blake-Beard, S. D., Murrell, A. J., & Thomas, D. A. (2007). Unfinished business: The impact of race on understanding mentoring relationships. In B. R. Ragins & K. E. Kram (Eds.), *The handbook of mentoring* (pp. 223–247). Thousand Oaks, CA: Sage.

Bottery, M. (1999). Global forces, national mediations and the management of educational institutions. *Educational Management and Administration, 27*(3), 299–312.

Bottoms, G., & O'Neill, K. (2001). Preparing a new breed of school principals: It's time for action. Atlanta, GA: Southern Regional Education Board. Retrieved from http://www.sreb.org/main/Leadership/pubs/01V17_Time_for_Action.pdf

Brown, K. M. (2004). Leadership for social justice and equity: Weaving a transformative framework and pedagogy. *Educational Administration Quarterly, 40*(1), 77–108.

Browne-Ferrigno, T., & Muth, R. (2006). Leadership mentoring and situated learning: Catalysts for principalship readiness and lifelong mentoring. *Mentoring & Tutoring: Partnership in Learning, 14*(3), 275–295.

Bruner, D. (2008). Aspiring and practicing leaders addressing issues of diversity and social justice. *Race, Ethnicity & Education, 11*(4), 483–500. doi:10.1080/13613320802479059.

Cambron-McCabe, N., & McCarthy, M. M. (2005). Educating school leaders for social justice. *Educational Policy, 19*(1), 201–222.

Carnegie Foundation for the Advancement of Teaching. (2011). Institution profile. Retrieved from http://classifications.carnegiefoundation.org/lookup_listings/index.php

Chan, T. C. (2006). Are educational leaders candidates prepared to address diversity issues in schools? *AASA Journal of Scholarship and Practice, 3*(3), 4–12.

Coleman, J. S. (1988). Social capital in the creation of human capital. *American Journal of Sociology, 94*, 95–120.

Council of Chief State School Officers (CCSSO). (2008). *Educational Leadership Policy Standards: ISLLC.* Washington, DC: Author.

Cunningham, W., & Sherman, W. (2008). Effective internships: Building bridges between theory and practice. *Educational Forum, 72*(4), 308–318. doi:10.1080/00131720802361936.

Firestone, A. W., & Riehl, C. (2005). *A new agenda for research in educational leadership.* New York, NY: Teachers College Press.

Gardiner, M. E., Canfield-Davis, K., & Anderson, K. (2009). Urban School Principals and the "No Child Left Behind" Act. *Urban Review: Issues and Ideas in Public Education, 41*(2), 141–160.

Gerstl-Pepin, C. (n.d). *Accountability, administrative preparation and social justice in Georgia.* Proceedings of the AERA. Retrieved from http://www.aera.net//up-loadedFiles/SIGs/Leadership_for_Social_Justice_%28165%29/R esearch/Gerstl-Pepin_Accountability_Administrative_Preparation_SJ.pdf

Grant, C. A., & Chapman, T. K. (2008). *History of multicultural education, Volume 2: Foundations and stratifications.* New York, NY: Routledge.

Hernandez, F., & McKenzie, K. B. (2010). Resisting social justice in leadership preparation programs: Mechanisms that subvert. *Journal of Research on Leadership Education, 5*(3.2), 48–72.

Ingram, I. L., & Walters, T. S. (2007). A critical reflection model to teach diversity and social justice. *Journal of Praxis in Multicultural Education 2007, 2*(1), 23–41.

Kensler, L. A., Reames, E. H., Murray, J., & Patrick, R. L. (2011, April). Systems thinking tools for improving evidence-based conversations: A cross-case analysis of two high school leadership teams. Paper presented at American Educational Research Association, New Orleans, LA.

Kottkamp, R. B.(2011). Introduction: Leadership preparation in education. *Educational Administration Quarterly, 47*(1), 3–17.

Lumby, J. (2008, September). International perspectives on developing educational leaders. A paper presented at the annual meeting of the Commonwealth Council for Educational Administration and Management, Durban, South Africa.

Marshall, C., & Grestl-Pepin, C. (2005). Reframing educational policies for social justice. Boston, MA: Pearson Education, Inc.

Marzano, R. J., Waters, T., & McNulty, B. A. (2005). *School leadership that works: From research to results.* Alexandria, VA: Association for Supervision and Curriculum Development.

Merriam, S. B. (2009). *Qualitative research: A guide to design and implementation.* San Francisco, CA: Jossey-Bass.

McKenzie, K., Christman, D. E., Hernandez, F., Fierro, E., Capper, C. A., Dantley, M., & Scheurich, J. J. (2008). From the field: A proposal for educating leaders for social justice. *Educational Administration Quarterly, 44*(1), 111–138.

Murphy, J. (2003). Reculturing Educational Leadership: The ISLLC standards ten years out. Paper prepared for the National Policy Board for Educational Administration.

Murphy, J. (2002). Reculturing the profession of educational leadership: New blueprints. *Educational Administration Quarterly, 38*(2) 176–191. doi: 10.1177/0013161X02382004

Murphy, J. (1999). The interstate school leaders licensure consortium: A standards-based approach to strengthening educational leadership. *Journal of Personnel Evaluation in Education, 13*(3), 205–224.

National Board for Professional Teaching Standards (NBPTS). (2011). *Certification for principals: A new way to develop, recognize & retain top school leaders.* Retrieved from http://www.sreb.org/uploads/documents/2010/06/2010060209423162/Topic_5_9.30_am_ Joan_Auctor_NBPTS_4_10.pdf

National Council for Accreditation of Teacher Education (NCATE). (2008). *NCATE unit standards.* Washington, D.C: Author.

Nettles, S. M., & Herrington, C. (2007). Revisiting the importance of the direct effects of school leadership on student achievement: The implications for school improvement policy. *Peabody Journal of Education (0161956X), 82*(4), 724–736. doi:10.1080/01619560701603239

No Child Left Behind Act (NCLB) of 2001, 20 U.S.C. Sec. 6301 (2002).

Oplatka, I. (2009). Shall our leadership preparation programs be focused on proactive leadership for social justice? A rejoinder to Jean-Marie, Normore, and Brooks. *Journal of Research on Leadership Education, 4*(1). Retrieved from http://www.eric.ed.gov/PDFS/EJ875403.pdf

Parker, L., & Shapiro, J. P. (1993). The context of educational administration and social class. In C. A. Capper (Ed.), *Educational administration in pluralistic society* (pp. 36–65). Albany, NY: State University of New York Press.

Pounder, D. G. (2011). Leader preparation special issue: Implications for policy, practice and research. *Educational Administration Quarterly, 47*(1), 258–267.

Reames, E. (2010). Shifting paradigms: Redesigning a principal preparation program's curriculum. *Journal of research on leadership education, 5*(12.5), 436–459.

Reyes, P., & Wagstaff, L. (2005). How does leadership promote successful teaching and learning for diverse students? In A.W. Firestone & C. Riehl (Eds.), *A new agenda for research in educational leadership* (pp. 101–118). New York, NY: Teachers College Press.

Reynolds, A. J., & Walberg, H. J. (1992). A process model of mathematics achievement and attitude. *Journal for Research in Mathematics Education, 23*(4), 306–328.

Rivera, J. (2005). Finding Aristotle's golden mean: Social justice and academic excellence. *Journal of Education, 186*(1), 79–85.

Sanders, N. M., & Kearney, K. M. (2008). Performance expectations and indicators for education leaders. Washington, DC: Council of Chief State School Officers State Consortium on Education Leadership.

Scholte, J. A. (2000). *Globalization: a critical introduction.* Basingstoke, UK: Palgrave.

Sensoy, Ö., & DiAngelo, R. (2009). Developing social justice literacy. *Phi Delta Kappan, 90*(5), 345–352.

Sharp, C. (2003). How can LEAs help schools to use research for school improvement? *Education Journal, 71*, 28–30.

Shields, C. M., & Mohan, E. J. (2008). High-quality education for all students: Putting social justice at its heart. *Teacher Development, 12*(4), 289–300.

Shrestha, L. B., & Heisler, E. J. (2011). *The changing demographic profile of the United States.* CRS Report for Congress. Washington, DC: Congressional Research Service.

Shriberg, D., & Fenning, P. A. (2009). School consultants as agents of social justice: Implications for practice: Introduction to the special issue. *Journal of Educational & Psychological Consultation, 19*(1), 1–7.

Sirin, S. R. (2005). Socioeconomic status and student achievement: A meta-analytic review of research. *Review of Educational Research, 75*(3), 417–453.

Southern Education Foundation. (2007). A new majority: Low income students in the South's public schools. *SEF research report.* Atlanta, GA: Southern Education Foundation, Inc. Southern Regional Education board (SREB). (2009). Criteria and definitions. Retrieved from http://www.sreb.org/page/1135/criteria_and_definitions.html

Styron, R., Jr., & LeMire, S. (2009). Principal preparation programs: Perceptions of high school principals. *Journal of College Teaching & Learning, 6*(6), 51–62.

Theoharis, G. (2007). Social justice educational leaders and resistance: Toward a theory of social justice leadership. *Educational Administration Quarterly, 43*(2), 221–258.

Theoharis, G., & O'Toole, J. (2011). Leading inclusive ELL: Social justice leadership for English language learners. *Educational Administration Quarterly, XX*(X), 1–43. doi: 10.1177/0013161X11401616

United States Census. (2010). Small area income and poverty estimates. Retrieved from http://www.census.gov/did/www/saipe/data/index.html

Van Dyne, L., Ang, S., & Koh, C. K. S. (2009). Cultural intelligence: Measurement and scale development. In M. A. Moodian (Ed.), *Contemporary leadership and intercultural competence: Exploring the cross-cultural dynamics within organizations* (pp. 233–254). Thousand Oaks, CA: Sage.

Waters,T., Marzano, J., & McNulty, B. (2003). Balanced leadership: What 30 years of research tells us about the effect of leadership on student achievement (Working paper). Aurora, CO: Mid-continent regional educational lab.

Watkins, T. J. (1997). Teacher communications, child achievement, and parent traits in parent involvement models. *Journal of Educational Research, 91*(1), 3–14.

Williams, E. J., Matthews, J., & Baugh, S. (2004). Developing a mentoring internship model for school leadership: Using legitimate peripheral participation. *Mentoring & Tutoring: Partnership in Learning, 12*(1), 53–70.

Young, B. L., Madsen, J., & Young, M. A. (2010). Implementing diversity plans: Principals' perception of their ability to address diversity in their schools. *NASSP Bulletin, XX*(X), 1–23. doi: 10.1177/0192636510379901.

Young, M., & Brewer, C. (2008). Fear and the preparation of school leaders: The role of ambiguity, anxiety, and power in meaning making. *Educational policy, 22*(1), 106–129.

Young, P., Reimer, D. P., & Young, K. H. (2010). Staffing at the middle school level: Are the least qualified principals assigned to the neediest school buildings? *Educational Research Quarterly 34*(1), 18–34.

SECTION IV

STRATEGIES FOR K–12 SOCIAL JUSTICE LEADERSHIP

CHAPTER 15

CHANGING COMPLEX EDUCATIONAL SYSTEMS

A Framework for Collaborative Social Justice Leadership

Elizabeth Kozleski, David Gibson and Anne Hynds

INTRODUCTION

Imagine yourself seated at a large table with people from all over the community: parents, teachers, students, business leaders, central administration, workers, and the school board. The school has recently come under fire and faces intense public scrutiny because certain populations of students are not getting a fair shake; students from these groups have higher absenteeism and dropout rates, more failed courses, and they rarely make it to college. Some people are angry, others afraid, some seem resigned and sullen, a few are expectant and want to be optimistic. You are expected to lead the conversation today. What will you say?

People have been meeting like this, particularly since the landmark case of *Brown vs. Board of Education* in 1954, to negotiate, argue their positions, and appeal to each other to resolve one of the perennial questions of educa-

Social Justice Leadership for a Global World, pages 263–286
Copyright © 2012 by Information Age Publishing
All rights of reproduction in any form reserved.

tion: Will the system change to accommodate specific individual and group needs, or will it require people to assimilate to its culture? Many times, a simple solution is offered to bring closure, if not to the issues on the table, at least to the day's meeting. But the complexities of school, home and community guarantee that the simple solution will not fix the underlying problems. People will be back at the table again, to re-negotiate and re-argue their positions. Leadership for engaging the project of social justice must offer ways to influence the conversations and actions to explore and engage more complex and longer-lasting solutions.

A COLLABORATIVE SOCIAL JUSTICE FRAMEWORK FOR COMPLEX SYSTEMS

In this chapter, we develop a framework for addressing issues at that contentious table. The framework synthesizes and integrates knowledge of culture, activity systems, and complex systems, with the aim of engaging people in educational systems change aimed toward the goals of social justice. We remind ourselves, and you, of the medium called culture that percolates all human activity, the imperative of equity in education, of its interrogatory partner, social justice, and the complexity of shifting interlinking systems. In the liminal, or in-between spaces that bound systems, individuals, and practices, we find room to negotiate, purpose, and leverage our collective capital to transform the imbalances and inequities in our conceptions of learning and what it means to be educated. This stance means that when the table is filled with problems such as "under-prepared teachers in science and math classes" and "reading test scores of our 8th graders," leaders need to ask the group to look deeply at the historical and contemporary contexts that have conspired to create the particular issues. In particular, a critical examination of the cultural practices that frame the problem is fundamental to transforming the organization's ability to design and act on changes that rely on shifts in understanding and behavior on the part of the whole community. To embark upon and stay situated in a social justice agenda requires leaders to help people select features of healthy solutions that will improve equity in terms of outcomes, the distribution of resources, and access to opportunities as well as the tools for learning. To measure success in terms of social justice requires complex analyses that shift, amplify, and transform the way people understand and respond to the questions of whose education, for what purpose, and for what world?

Our synthesis introduces concepts from other fields to build a scholarship of interdisciplinary educational leadership, policy, and practice: the conceptual framework of *cultural-historical activity theory*, the tools and processes of *systems thinking* and the *structure and dynamics of complex systems*.

Rather than conceptualize leadership from functionalist or psychological perspectives that embed dispositions, knowledge and skills within actors, we propose scaffolding the collective agency of distributed responsibilities to advance equity and excellence for all participants in learning organizations (e.g., students, parents, teachers, administrators, community members). First, *activity theory* (Artiles, Trent, Hoffman-Kipp, & López-Torres, 2000; Engeström, 1999; Leontyev, 1977) is utilized to foreground human activity as cultural work that grounds the context, genesis, and praxis of innovation and systems transformation. Second, *systems thinking* (Checkland, 1993; Ferguson, Kozleski, & Smith, 2003; Kozleski & Huber, 2010; Meadows, 2008) is discussed to advance notions of how innovation, practice, and policy travel between micro, meso, and macro levels in terms of time, space, and influence. Third, *complexity theory* (Bar-Yam, 1997; Gibson, 2000; Holland, 1995; Holland, Holyoak, Nisbett, & Thagard, 1986; Kozleski & Huber, 2010; Lemke & Sabelli, 2008) is advanced to support modeling and explaining the structures and processes of change in complex systems. We expand upon these existing frameworks, models and toolkits of researchers and educational leaders in order to highlight the complexity of the difficult but highly rewarding challenges of influencing systemic change efforts for social justice.

Our work blends our own experiences from years of interactions with leaders, teachers and community members, in real schools and school systems, with the work of cutting edge theorists and researchers. We have participated at the decision-making table with others and observed as they and we have undertaken difficult systemic change efforts in order to improve outcomes for all students. The plan of the chapter is to present our views about the centrality of culture, the inherent complexity of systems, the need for new ways to frame systems change, and innovative methods for representing and understanding those complexities, as well as the need for social justice leaders to become familiar and comfortable with this way of thinking and influencing change in education. We share two case stories that provide illustrations and take-off points for revisiting our integrated framework.

Terms for Engaging Complex Educational Systems

New terms of engagement are needed for the challenging work of social justice leadership. We draw from three sources we have found to be powerful allies in engaging multi-faceted educational change: activity theory, systems thinking, and complexity theory. By *activity theory* we are referring to a set of sociocultural theories that describe human activities as complex socially situated phenomena that mediate (and are themselves shaped by) tools and other artifacts (Cole, 1992). The opinions expressed by some teachers that separate their students into winners and losers, and likewise, the hidden curriculum of school policy and practice that advantages some students and disadvantages others, are two examples of cultural artifacts that are frozen patterns of thinking embedded into cultural practice. Such practices then limit and mediate current and future possibilities for social justice. Activity theory offers a toolset to interrogate the cultural nature of artifacts and activities within systems in the context of the community in which they have arisen.

By *systems thinking*, we mean holistic and thoroughgoing (i.e., simultaneously *wide* and *deep*) observations, analyses and representations of the networks of relationships that make up educational systems and produce their dynamic behaviors. Those networks of relationships have both *structure* (e.g., what place and history mean to a particular context, how people are connected to each other, which people and offices communicate with each other and the public, and what learning opportunities are present) and *dynamics* (e.g., how people behave with each other, which people and offices send, receive or relay information, how students flow into and out of the learning opportunities).

By *complexity*, we mean an evolutionary perspective on the extent and variety of patterns of behaviors exhibited by educational systems, the higher level processes that emerge from those behaviors, and the interaction of the systems with their surrounding environments as they change over time. Since flux and transformation are occurring all the time in those patterns of behaviors, communities must continuously examine the principles of equity. Thus, achieving equity is not an end game but a *constantly shifting perspective* that changes as the margins of the group are drawn and redrawn to determine who counts and whose needs should be addressed.

Centrality of Culture

Culture is not something that we have. Culture, like air is to our biological systems, permeates our sensibilities, dispositions, analytic tools and conversational moves, and exists not merely inside individuals but in the interactive spaces that we inhabit (Rogoff, 2003). Our cultural imaginations and practices mediate how we see and judge activities around us. But these notions are constantly in play, being shaped and reshaped by the worlds that we inhabit—our personal, professional, and community spaces. Culture is something that inhabits our institutional spaces as well. Our individual and institutional histories inform, calcify, constrain, and afford the way we conceptualize what people are supposed to do, and we pattern our own behavior in response to the ways we understand institutional codes (McDermott & Tylbor, 1996). In this interaction between individuals and the institutional spaces in which they participate, culture is constantly being negotiated and reconstructed in an endless interplay among people and the historical timescales they occupy. In the U.S. in the early part of the 21st century, descriptors of white, black, Hispanic, American Indian, Pacific Islander, and Asian cultures abound. Yet these descriptors often assume within-group homogeneity, glossing over the notion that individual history, local context, access to popular culture, literature, music, and other forms of cultural expression *mediate* cultural practices. This notion of mediation is crucial to the notion of culture and explains why the forms of school in Wellington, New Zealand and Tempe, Arizona might share many features but the specific expression of organization and individual cultures are unique to those contexts and critical geographic spaces (Soja, 1996).

Inherent Complexity of Social Systems

Educational systems are complex human activity arenas in which multiple units of analysis gel activities toward specific outcomes. For instance, classrooms have as their outcome the production of knowledge embodied within the students. The classroom has spaces both mental (figured) and real in which activity is produced and material and intellectual property is exchanged, largely mediated by the teacher. The classroom arena is encompassed by the school, which has other rhythms and sets of transactions that produce other outcomes—for example, for students who progress through levels of proficiency, as well as transactions and outcomes for teachers, administrators, and families. The diversity of outcomes of schools is embedded within a local educational unit, and that unit within the state, which is in turn heavily influenced by the federal government (Kozleski & Smith, 2009). The complex systems perspective recognizes the interlocking nature of small systems that have not only internal agency but are also buffeted by complex social, regulatory, and political manifestations of the ways in which power and privilege have been constructed and accumulated to benefit some.

Systemic improvement is predicated on deep understanding of sociocultural, historical, as well as psychological perspectives (Kozleski & Smith, 2009). For example, organizations and institutions function with specific practices organized into rituals, routines, and cycles of activity. Social reproduction is certainly a part of the cultural work of systems, but systems also engage in their own hydraulics that constantly calibrate disturbance and stasis. Activity cycles at the most molar levels influence larger, more comprehensive cycles. The reverse is also true. Systems are responsive to their constituent parts whether they are people, practices, or policies or some combination of the three (Klingner et al., 2005).

Educational systems are in flux in much the same way. Interactions between students and their teachers are shaped by the design of curriculum materials, classroom rules and regulations. In turn, what teachers and students do together impact how curriculum and classroom policies are delivered, ignored, or modified. Think of schools as bubbles that in turn suspended in larger bubbles called districts, inside states, within federal mandates. Each bubble interacts with and responds to disturbances within and without. And, rather than a bubble only responding to its next larger container, each bubble is buffeted by changes in any of the other levels. Partitions between bubbles are transcended through encounters with what Cobb & McClain (2006) term boundary objects such as rubrics for evaluating teachers, or standardized test scores. Boundary objects like transition plans or grades are assumed to retain their meaning across bubbles. Instead, boundary objects are understood and responded to in specific ways because of the cultural histories and assumptions embedded in any particular bubble, making policy implementation an uncertain affair. Thus, policy and practice are imported not in complete packages but in processes that distort their meanings and their outcomes. This process can be thought of as non-linear which makes the work of innovation diffusion highly idiosyncratic and difficult to predict (Kozleski, 2004).

The *Systemic Change Framework* (Ferguson, Kozleski & Smith, 2003) provides a roadmap for understanding the complex relationships among levels of an education system (Kozleski & Smith, 2009). It provides a way of thinking about educational systems, cautioning us that the interplay between parts of the system occur concurrently and permeably resulting in interaction between any two or more levels of the system. Thus, school psychologists both implement and critique federal policy as federal policy also impacts their practice. Both parts of the system also impact and are influenced by the central district office politics. Thus, human systems like biological or ecological systems influence and accommodate in response to multiple incitements. To think in systemic ways means that planning, assessing, and acting are all accomplished while acknowledging that nuanced and multi-level exchanges are occurring consistently. Systems seek to maintain stability. Change will become the norm when disturbances to the current system are made simultaneously at multiple layers of a system.

Social Justice Leadership and Activity Theory

Social justice leadership embraces and builds new levels of knowledge that intersects with, unifies, and helps leverage enduring philosophies of education toward more equitable systems. In a country such as the U.S., filled with local contextual complexity, the institution of public schooling is resistant to changing its role as a pillar of institutionalizing power and privilege for some groups while excluding and repressing opportunities for other groups. The question that culturally responsive leaders must grapple with is leadership for what and for whom. Engaging this question must be undertaken within the complex political climate of school funding and governance, understanding that school leaders are employees of elected school boards whose values and agendas may differ from that of the professional educator.

Cultural historical activity theory (CHAT) (Kozleski, 2004) provides a theoretical framework for understanding the focus of leadership as well as its functions. The theory helps us to integrate anthropological and sociological views of social organizations with psychological and cognitive models. Using the CHAT theory, social justice leaders can help school communities ask questions and devise strategies for change and renewal in ways that recognize the whole community, understand the division of labor, identify the organizational outcomes for work, make rules for engagement explicit, engage the participants, and use tools and participant structures to mediate the work. The theory helps participants understand the current structure of interaction and activity as well as the gaps between what currently exists and desired outcomes. Engaging classroom communities, school communities, and districts in examining their work requires that the participants engage with information and data about the current status of their arenas and then analyzing what emerges so that the myths and conventional wisdom are taken apart and reassembled so that the participants can better understand the hidden and obvious forces at work.

APPLYING A COLLABORATIVE SOCIAL JUSTICE FRAMEWORK FOR COMPLEX SYSTEMS

Seated at the metaphoric negotiating table engaged in troubling and heated conversations about who is benefiting and not from the educational system "as it stands," social justice leadership will be counted by both its subtlety and capacity to bring about innovative solutions. How can we avoid off-target quick fixes? How can we engage people in a creative process that shares responsibility as well as the rewards of right action? We need to be able to extend the group's collective exploration and engagement over time and at greater depths, in order to create more complex, longer-lasting, real solutions. To do this we need to apply ideas and tools of change to address the *structures* as well as the *dynamics* of the complex system.

Social Justice Leadership and Systemic Thinking

A number of researchers have used systems metaphors to discuss and analyze a wide range of educational situations such as a student's learning, family dynamics, and district and state organizational levels of education (Costa & Kallick, 1995; Ferguson et al., 2003; Fleener, 1995; McLaughlin, 1987; Ramsey, 2002). These theorists are following a general trend seen across all the sciences in the late 20th and early 21st centuries toward understanding complex dynamical systems as networks of relationships (Abraham, 1991; Bongard & Lipson, 2007; Holland, 1995, 1998; Kauffman, 2000; Sporns, 2011; Wolfram, 2002). The relationships are broadly of two kinds: *endogenous* relationships among the members of the system and *exogenous* between the members individually and collectively in relation to larger encompassing contexts. In social networks in particular, exogenous relationships are necessary with both the physical and larger cultural environment. Indigenous scholars in particular have emphasized the importance of understanding specific ecological networks and relationships inherently connected to place, which influence individual and community identity (Penetito, 2009). Social justice leadership can use systems thinking to engage people in seeing their systems from several endogenous and exogenous perspectives.

As an example of an *exogenous* relationship, a variety of critical theorists have suggested that the use of the achievement gap as a centerpiece in educational reform separates groups of students by examining deficits in academic performance (e.g., between whites and their peers by racial/ethnic, language, and ability categories) (Cox, 1997). This "deficits" view privileges some kinds of knowledge and ways of knowing over others (i.e., makes the criteria of achievement *exogenous* to the student) and ignores the rich tapestry of indigenous and migrant knowledge of many students from minority backgrounds (Lemke & Sabelli, 2008). Perhaps more troubling, an educational policy focused on reducing between-group achievement gaps sanctions a monolithic view that reduces our understanding of culture to a static variable. The achievement gap conversation masks the ways in which hidden codes for behaving, using language, and valuing some kinds of knowing are mediated daily by institutional and individual cultural practices that help some while hurting others.

Contrast this with an *endogenous* perspective on cultural uniqueness. While the path to college is based on banking particular kinds of knowledge and using it to demonstrate competence, practical and indigenous ways of knowing also offer great insight and have ecological and social significance. In 2000, Professor Geneva Gay wrote that culturally responsive teaching connects students' cultural knowledge, prior experiences, and performance styles to academic knowledge and intellectual tools in ways that *legitimize what students already know* (Artiles, Kozleski, Trent, Osher, & Ortiz, 2010). By embracing the sociocultural realities and histories of students through what is taught and how, culturally responsive teachers negotiate intellectual and social cultures in ways that reflect the communities *where both teachers and students develop and grow* (Brayboy, 2005). To do this requires that teachers transcend their own cultural biases and preferences to establish and develop patterns for learning and communicating that engage and sustain student participation and achievement.

At the same time, teachers must also negotiate and mediate the *exogenous* social, political, and intellectual traditions that are embedded in the institution of school. Thus, cultural responsivity means simultaneously negotiating and mediating: a) the cultures and embedded assumptions that teachers as well as students bring to school, b) the way that meaning and value is constructed in the classroom, and c) the institutional boundaries, constraints, and affordances (Gay, 2000; Lee, 2007).

The term *systems thinking* means a *discipline of collective thinking and action* that focuses on understanding, representing and interacting with a co-constructed and continuously renewed model of how the system works. In a classroom, for example, it would mean that students and teachers are co-creators of the way the classroom works and how it could be improved for their learning. In a school setting, it would mean that parents, community members, and school personnel co-construct how the school works. Each level of the educational system can be a learning organization that uses systems thinking principles. The discipline builds the capacity of an organization's members to: a) participate in designing and adapting the organization's roles, responsibilities and practices to match valued and intended outcomes; b) recognize when current conditions are different from what is desired; and c) take necessary actions to correct any mismatch while moving toward the desired future.

The discipline requires surfacing the often hidden and unstated mental models and assumptions of how things work and *transforming those ideas into operational terms and relationships*, in order to examine and test new ideas. The collective work is aided considerably by the co-creation of a community constructed representation (e.g., a timeline, a map, a school mission) that is specific to the context and relevant for all the participants so that each person is made more capable of interacting with, suggesting changes, and owning solutions that emerge. In this way, the educational systems change we have in mind is a transformational pedagogy—a new set of methods—that changes the way we think about learning at every level. The pedagogy encompasses the student, the classroom, the school and other surrounding and interpenetrating contexts of learning. A complex activity theory of the system helps conceptualize the leadership needed to *establish systems thinking as a new organizational pattern of thinking and action.*

Our own journey into this way of thinking has led us to new understandings of systemic change that utilize the frameworks and tools of complex systems analysis of culture, which can be described as the *structural relationships* (e.g., the elements, agencies, people, offices) and *interactional dynamics* (e.g., the patterns of energy and communication exchanges and influences). We begin the discussion of structure with a case story of mapping and displaying data to highlight structural challenges in assisting people to understand that equity matters.

CASE STORY 1: MAPPING STRUCTURAL ISSUES

In the fieldwork of the Equity Alliance at ASU (Arizona State University), data maps (topographic representations that display and overlay educational, health and social variables) and individual and group assessments have been created for urban school systems and used to stimulate dialog and group inquiry by leadership teams (Gallego, Cole, & Laboratory of Comparative Human Cognition, 2001; Kozleski & Huber, 2010; Rogoff, 2003). These tools are a part of an involved, highly participatory engagement process of mediating conversations about culture, place, policy and practice that use tools and methods we have assembled for technical assistance.

When a local school system enters into a partnership with the Equity Alliance at ASU, the first step in our work together is to develop a set of maps that overlay the familiar geography of the district with the geographies of equity that are present in the district. So, the district leaders are presented with online maps specifically programmed for their context, using district data to examine the differences and similarities in resources, human capital, and outcomes of the system. In the accompanying map (see Figure 15.1 Mapping Hot Spots), notice that some schools have stronger "halos" around them than others, indicating a degree of safety and lowered risk for certain students. Additional data layers appear over the halos to examine hypotheses that are part of the current conventional wisdom about why some schools are experiencing lower assessment scores than others. For instance, poverty is often hypothesized to be the single most important contributor to student performance. Data maps can show how schools with students with similar economic backgrounds can produce different kinds of data. Disturbing the conventional wisdom creates a space in which new interpretations and hypotheses can be generated. Once this happens, innovation (and more hypothesis testing) can occur.

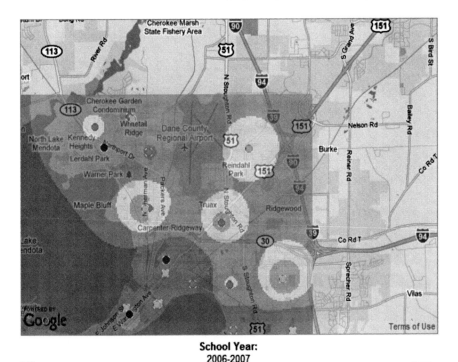

School Year:
2006-2007

Figure 15.1   Mapping hot spots.

Once we begin to disturb thinking, we also spend time in the district interviewing families, students, educators, and administrators. We observe classrooms, tour schools, and collect information about the context. Quantitative data added to these focused collections of qualitative information provide the backdrop for developing an ongoing dialogue with leaders about where privilege is accrued, how the system is structured to distribute informal and formal networks of power, and what constraints and affordances maintain the status quo.

The mapping case story illustrates how we use the multilayered *Systemic Change Framework* (SCF) to represent a variety of intersecting and overlaid action arenas (Figure 15.2). When aligned, efforts in these action arenas can effectively combine to impact student achievement and learning (Kozleski, Mantle, Anderson, Foster, & Wilson, 1999). The framework has richly interconnected layers: 1) student learning and effort, 2) professional effort, 3) school organizational effort, 4) district efforts, and 5) state effort. This way of dividing the system is easy to grasp, which makes it applicable in field-based technical assistance with schools and their communities. We also recog-

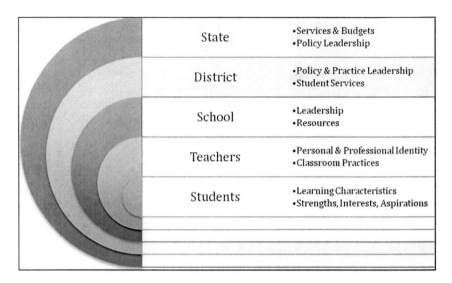

State	•Services & Budgets •Policy Leadership
District	•Policy & Practice Leadership •Student Services
School	•Leadership •Resources
Teachers	•Personal & Professional Identity •Classroom Practices
Students	•Learning Characteristics •Strengths, Interests, Aspirations

Figure 15.2 A systemic change framework with example elements.

nize, however, that alternative ways of talking about structural relationships (e.g., class, gender, ethnicity) are equally valid. Our complexity approach is not limited to any particular or singular structural representation. Here, we are focusing on how students, parents, caregivers, teachers and administrators see themselves in the system and how they can be empowered to make changes that transform their system so that everyone is well served.

There are additional rationales for the nested view of an educational system. Student learning and effort is central to all other people's efforts, because without the student's active engagement and effort influencing their own learning, little learning can occur (Costa & Kallick, 2004; Kozleski, Sands, French, Moore, & Roggow, 1995; Schallert, 2003; Stefanou, 2003; Zito, Adkins, Gavins, Harris, & Graham, 2007). Professional efforts, especially teacher practices that include parents and caregivers, most directly influence the student level (Oppenheimer, 2001) and should ideally be focused on helping the students connect their effort with learning achievement (Biddulph, Biddulph, & Biddulph, 2003; DuFour & Eaker, 1998; McCombs, 2001; TEQ, 2003). Efforts at the school level enhance or constrain the professional efforts and are in turn, constrained or enhanced by district efforts and supports (Darling-Hammond, 2000a, 2000b). Efforts that include the community are critical to the full engagement of the many cultures (e.g,. family and group placed-based histories) that are a vital source of creative and adaptive innovation needed for transformative change (Freire, 1970). When the efforts of practitioners, parents and caregivers, schools, and districts are congruent, the result can be a healthy self-renewing system that better supports student learning (Kozleski, et al, 1999).

It is important to point out that a multilayered structure is not a rigid construction that limits processes of change or confines influences and communications to neighboring layers. Even though many influences do become habituated and solidified into the culture, and these must be unseated in order to effect transformational change, the complex activity system view of culture understands and leverages the idea that powerful influences can skip layers at any time. A student might speak at a school board meeting and have a direct influence on district policy. Or a parent might inspire teachers to visit the families of their students in their homes and create a new way of thinking about the school in the community. Unlike traditional images of relatively inflexible bureaucratic hierarchies, the complex systems viewpoint sees influences at any level potentially impacting change at all other levels.

With an image of the multilayered system in mind, there are also cross-cutting dimensions (Figure 15.3) that serve as *analytic categories* as well as *scaffolds* for action—the technical, contextual and critical dimensions of activity (Van Manen, 1990). These dimensions help us observe stable as well as changing relationships within and among the dimensions, as well as discern underlying clusters of sociocultural activity, such as power relationships between a teacher and a child, or a principal and a teacher, or professionals and a parent.

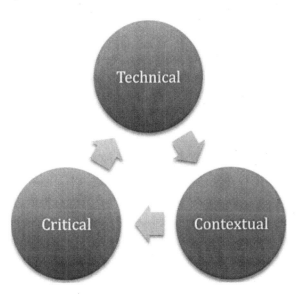

Figure 15.3   Cross cutting dimensions.

As *analytic categories*, we use the technical-contextual-critical dimensions to aggregate observations and bring alternative lenses to our reflections. We unpack the observed relationships by using tools of visualization, social network analysis, participatory analysis, and complex systems concepts while maintaining theoretical and methodological connections with past systemic analysis frameworks that employ mixed methods comprised of both qualitative and quantitative approaches.

As *scaffolds* for action, we introduce these perspectives to social justice leaders and mentor them as they attempt to influence, perturb and transform their educational environments to become more culturally responsive. The *technical* dimension comes into play as educators get to know themselves and their students and change their practices and policies; the *contextual* scaffolds support an understanding of actions as situation-dependent and requiring a deep understanding of the historical and cultural legacies present in the system; and the *critical* dimension scaffolds help leaders to deeply reflect, critique, and act to move their systems forward to benefit all members (Kozleski et al., 1999).

The *technical dimension* takes stock of the mediating tools and artifacts we use; the dimension is generally concerned with how we get things done—what rites, symbols and practices are evident in the system. Tools and artifacts are terms for a broad category of activity patterns, scaffolds, physical and mental tools and frameworks, and models created in previous stages of organizational development. The technical dimension mediates our activity and contributes to the "frozen accidents" (the historical record of an evolutionary path of development, see Van Manen, 1990) of our thought and action—what we know and how we have come to know it, grounded in our activity in particular contexts. The technical dimension is the cultural codification of what we know as well as our know-how.

The *contextual dimension* is the historically situated topology of relationships in complex social networks. We use the term topology because it includes space, time and place but is not limited to specific places and times nor geometries and is instead an expression of a pure *relational totality* that is described with network theory concepts. For example, one can be close to one's mother even though she has died. Topologically, one is still near, even though it is difficult to put a specific place, space and time into relationship with that context. Identity is composed of topologically connected self-concepts. Penetito (2009), for example, in discussing place-based education, emphasizes the specific non-metaphoric "spatial realities" of indigenous cultures between identity and place, and he states "the basic idea behind the person as a relational totality is that there is no sense of the person without the sense of the presence of community" (p. 225). We extend the contextual dimension of identity to "anyplace, anytime, any-connections" including virtual and imagined connections beyond the community, with both topological and realist conceptions of categories such as race, gender, culture, power, capabilities, perceptual acumen and other elements.

The *critical dimension* is the cultural equivalent of metacognition and self-regulation; it is the activity that considers, compares, judges and decides. It is the social-computational "difference engine" that is critical to guidance of complex social systems. The critical dimension continuously provides feedback and improves the system's ability to self-regulate—for example by asking who is being served (and not) by some action or activity in a particular context. Postman and Weingartner (as cited in Ohno, 1973) note, "In order to get people to change something, you have to get them to think about it. In order to get them to think about it, you have to make it visible to them" (p. 6). Just as biodiversity strengthens the flexibility and responsiveness of an ecosystem, ensuring cultural diversity in decision-making increases the chance that different levels of awareness and new insights will be bought to the group. If the organization doesn't continuously seek those differences and bring them into its awareness, it loses flexibility, creativity and responsiveness.

Together these dimensions help categorize, describe and support activity that takes place within and between the structures of the system: what is taking place (Technical), under what conditions (Contextual), and toward what end and for whose benefit (Critical). We next address the dynamics that take place within the structures just outlined.

Dynamics of Change Processes and Social Justice Leadership

From a research and evaluation perspective, remember that *dynamic change processes in social transformation need to be experienced to be understood.* For example, suppose you see an elephant enter a tent, wander around, eat some hay, and run out of the tent. Such an experience can be labeled in a variety of ways, and a label can be shared with someone else, but the label cannot summarize the experience, for two reasons. First, the holistic nature of the experience is richly textured (i.e., many words can describe it and there is essentially no limit to the number of ways it can be described), but a label is just a small word, phrase or storyline (e.g., "the elephant I saw today," which catches only a part of the storyline). Second, the dynamical nature of the experience changes moment to moment and could have been experienced from a variety of perspectives, but a label stays constant and cannot convey the passages of time in the stages of the event.

Labeling, while an important part of knowledge discovery and memory, is naming, not explaining. We might, for example, look at the proverbial elephant's trunk and label that part as a snake, or a leg and identify that part as a tree stump. Traditional ways of evaluating systemic change create labels. Qualitative research searches for patterns in narratives and summarizes those with themes, observations and propositions (i.e., labels and label phrases, including phrases that hypothesize). Quantitative research searches for patterns in numbers, especially correlations among variables, and summarizes these with more numbers and tables of numbers (i.e., labels and label phrases, including tests of the statistical properties of propositions and hypotheses). In addition, labels (e.g., signs, symbols) are the exchange medium of social networks, and as boundary objects (O'Sullivan, 1999) can support trust and understanding or, when contested, abused or via boundary crossing, are misunderstood, then they can be harmful.

To see a system's holistic and dynamic nature, we have to be aware of but also wary of labels. We need a process of stepping back, taking in, and unifying many other aspects in a vibrant picture in our awareness including our responsiveness to the experience. This is where a systemic framework is helpful, and when made dynamic, more closely approaches capturing a complete picture. A systemic framework gives a holistic viewpoint and draws our attention to relevant details, which helps us stay focused on the "big picture" when change is in the air (Penetito, 2009). If the framework also captures a system's *dynamic* aspects (e.g., if the elephant is walking in circles, running out of the tent, or sitting), it helps us to observe its stages of passage (e.g., appearing, enduring, disappearing), or assists us in walking alongside it (e.g., become entrained with it), where we can more fully appreciate not only the wholeness of the event, by simultaneously seeing its unity while it is yet changing over time.

In general there are three observable behavior archetypes that result from the underlying dynamics in such a system: *cycles*, in which the behavior approximately repeats; *events*, in which the behavior either explodes or dies out; and *chaos*, in which the behavior appears random, even when there are rule-like causes underlying the behavior. We begin the discussion of dynamics with a second case story.

CASE STORY 2: TIMELINES OF INNOVATION

In a series of studies of ten years of innovation in five professional development schools in Vermont (Friedrichs & Gibson, 2003), researchers interviewed students, teachers, administrators and parents about "any new innovation" that had made a significant positive impact, that was five or more years old and was still present in the school at the time of the interviews. The innovation sometimes had impacted only one or two departments in the schools (e.g., transforming the teaching of integrated social studies with science and society), and at other places the innovation had impacted the entire school system (e.g., introducing performance assessment as a critical gateway to promotion and graduation). Were there any commonalities among these five very different stories that would inform us about systems change? The researchers used dynamical systems analyses and complexity methodologies to seek an answer.

Each person's story was quantized (Gibson & Clarke, 2000), and the transformed storylines showed the time course (beginning, middle duration and end), the direction of influences, the system levels and the boundary crossing of influences as told by the participants. Then a cross-site research team created a visual representation, which upon inspection led to a series of propositions (Clarke et al., 2000). The data representations, storylines and initial propositions were checked and adjusted with the participants.

A set of dynamical systems models were then created from those generalized propositions with quantitative data support from the quantized and visualized narratives. The dynamical models were then found, through rigorous testing of the limits of each model, to accurately replicate the dynamics (e.g., the evolution of the innovation) of each individual school when the model was seeded with data from that school's known starting conditions. With just a handful of models, the various storylines of the schools were reproducible from different sets of initial data, providing evidence that the complexity approach had found trustworthy generalized computational representations of the structure and dynamics of change from qualitative narratives. The models were then taken into the schools for experimenting with alternative scenario simulations, which stimulated recall and new ideas about the innovations and their history and impacts, leading to appreciative inquiry about enhancement and strengthening of the innovations.

The phases recounted in this case story are an example of what we mean by applying complexity frameworks in collaborative inquiry toward educational systems change:

- Gathering qualitative narratives,
- Transforming story information into time-based visual representations,
- Member-checking visualizations and quantifications with participants,
- Employing transformed data in creating dynamical systems models,
- Testing the models for quantitative validity and qualitative trustworthiness,
- Utilizing the models for collaborative inquiry, reflection and advancement of thinking.

Broadly speaking, this case illustrates a methodology that traverses from qualitative to quantitative approaches through the middle territory of system modeling. It does so not only by *triangulating partial evidence from disparate sources* but also *unifying* all sources into an integrated simulation with both structural as well as dynamical features that mirror the real world. In the next section, we discuss what social justice leadership needs to know and be able to do by summarizing the implications of the complex activity systems framework.

SUMMARIZING A COLLABORATIVE SOCIAL JUSTICE FRAMEWORK FOR COMPLEX SYSTEMS

In the complex activity systems approach to social justice leadership, the goal is to appropriate the tools of both qualitative and quantitative methods, and unify them through new approaches into a dynamical, time-based, *experience* for the participants. The assistance seeks to create an interactive learning environment where people can first appreciate the moving images of change, power and influence in their system, identify with those forces, and then ultimately have control over the variables so they can see and feel the impacts—the transformations, symmetries and asymmetries (the mutually agreeable or antagonistic results that unintentionally or intentionally arise) and the causal relationships—of their actions and experiments.

There are connections here between what Penetito (2009) calls "ecological consciousness" (p. 17) and what social justice leadership needs to know and be able to do—develop the community's capacity through *systemic awareness*. In traditional place-based education, ecological awareness focuses on the local geography and how humans have settled, impacted and changed that physical place. *Systemic awareness* focuses on the cultural historical activity taking place within and surrounding the organization, shaping and mediating its ongoing development. The role of mapping and modeling, using visualizations, and holding reflective dialogs about the changing representations, is to facilitate transformation of the systems participants *from voyeurs to co-creators* of the system. The methods we are advocating go beyond the current toolkits for research, analysis, representation and action planning by emphasizing the dynamic nature of a time-based experience of change from within the system.

Using qualitative and quantitative approaches alone, as we have indicated, falls short in capturing a detailed dynamic model of an experience, and that moment-by-moment connection and understanding is needed for the small, timely, local adjustments that need to be made during a complex change process. No rich description can say enough about an experience to exhaust the possibilities of expression, and no display of numbers, even if collected and analyzed as statistically valid evidence, can do the experience justice either. Both methods approximate and summarize change *over* time, but miss the changing details *during* time.

In traditional mixed methods research, we begin to *appreciate* an experience, but the actors in a change process must also *value* and *interact with living data* during the experience, which introduces the need for a *continuous participatory and creative relationship* to the change process. This is one of the foundations of our approach to stimulating reflective practices in organizations through *continuous improvement* (e.g., constant attention and reflection) and *entrainment* (e.g., acquiring and attaining ownership and commitment) processes that are also necessary for sustaining change. The approach leads to value-forming, aligning, and self-identifying processes that fuel continuous reflection and action, the energy sources for social transformation.

Applying complexity concepts in social justice leadership asserts that detailed information of the evolution of a system is better represented in a dynamical model, where the processes are displayed metaphorically like movies *in time*. Such models can also be structurally accurate, allowing them to generate valid data via simulation, which allows people to generate valid inferences about intersectionalities that hinder equity as well as produce creative responses and innovations in the structures and processes of their system. People can try out new ideas about how they think the system should behave, and then run a simulation to test their theories, then adjust the model, their thinking, or both. This kind of modeling is commonplace in designing a new aircraft, but it is a relative newcomer in educational systems modeling, research and practice. From modeling, people can then move into action, using the models as parts of a continuous feedback system that ingests new data and represents it for collective monitoring, and further innovation.

Multiple Detailed Frameworks and Social Justice Leadership

In social justice leadership, it is important to possess a suite of powerful alternative descriptions of systems that help describe and explain things, and to have these alternatives simultaneously available when reflecting on the current and future states of the system as well as when planning potential actions. Having multiple detailed frameworks is crucial because no one way represents the complete description of a complex system. Having a powerful suite of alternative representations adds to the richly layered perspectives that make up real social systems, and when those representations create new common ground while acknowledging all the layers of meaning, they allow people to re-own their understandings as important contributors to a common system.

The complex activity systems approach to leadership, technical assistance, and evaluation has effective means for dealing with conflicting opinions, breakdowns in communication, and general incoherence in the system. It expects them. Since there are multiple ways of knowing and representing the system, it is expected that both coherent and conflicting ideas will need to be aired and worked through "on the ground," in the local setting, in order for social transformation to begin and be sustained. Recognition of the limits of description and representation reminds leadership to openly seek a diversity of local interpretations and to continuously reflect and integrate alternative ways of thinking and action. At the same time, participants and leaders alike do not have to fear that chaos and incoherence will reign. Resistance and dissonance are signs that something needs to be placed on the table as either a "creative tension" or a "destructive and immobilizing force." Which one will it be is a matter of what Harvey (2000) calls a "relational dialectic" (quoted in Penetito, 2009, p. 22), which the skilled leader influences and shapes, such as through conversational moves (Lambert et al., 1995). Leadership for engaging the project of social justice must offer ways to represent and give credence to both prevailing and counter-narratives to explore and engage more complex and longer-lasting solutions.

As can hopefully be seen, complex activity systems theory applied in educational settings is sensitive to contexts, values, and multiple truths, representations, and expressions, while at the same time, provides a new unifying descriptive language that can integrate qualitative and quantitative approaches. Its unifying modeling method helps bring order to the chaos of overlapping partial representations, by representing the system as a network of actors/agencies and their relationships. In order for social justice leaders to use complexity concepts, activity theory and systems theory in their daily practice, three essential requirements must be met. Leaders need the conceptual tools, the vocabulary of the new domains, and ample practice in using the concepts and tools to resolve leadership dilemmas. With these in hand, leaders can develop over time the ability to reflect on emerging patterns of activity situated in practice settings. Ideally, the skills to conceptualize and use meta-analytic tools are gained best in experienced-based apprenticeships with people who are skilled in negotiating systems change for social justice with complexity tools and frameworks.

Our natural instinct is to seek invariant patterns, to store those as memories, label them, and use them to compare with future experiences of a similar kind. This drive is why we are so inclined to summarize our experiences, and probably why, before the age of computers, we settled on statistical methods and simple linear equations to model and represent things. But now we have a wider array of options for data collection, representation and expression, and we should use them all, we believe, because we can't change what we can't appreciate, value and creatively respond to. Educational research does not yet have a term adequate for the tripartite position of sensing and reporting on wholeness, movements, and detailed, participatory visualization and dynamic modeling. We refer to it as "complex assessment of systems in education"—the CASE process (Kozleski, Gibson & George, in preparation), and will continue to work to outline its main features evident in specific technical assistance fieldwork with schools that are working to transform into more socially just organizations.

Leadership for social justice leadership embraces collective effort that intersects with, deconstructs, and leverages new models of cultural activity with the enduring legacies of a color and class-based education system. In a country such as the U.S., filled with local contextual complexity, public schooling has had great cultural cohesion. Its resistance to change has been sustainable because it has been one of the pillars of institutionalizing power and privilege for some groups while it has simultaneously served as an agent of exclusion and repression for other groups. The question that leaders for social justice must grapple with is leadership *for what* and *for whom*.

NOTES

1. The first author acknowledges the support of the National Institute for Urban School Improvement LeadScape project (H325P060012) awarded by the U.S. Department of Education's Office of Special Education Programs. Both the first and second authors acknowledge the support of the Equity Alliance at ASU under OESE's Grant # S004D080027. Funding agency endorsement of the ideas presented in this article should not be inferred. They do not necessarily support the views expressed in this paper. All errors are attributable to the authors. Address correspondence to elizabeth.kozleski@asu.edu.
2. The Equity Alliance at ASU is an intellectual hub for a variety of funded research and outreach projects that address civil rights issues such as disproportionality, bullying, and opportunities to learn through a social justice, equity-minded lens.

REFERENCES

Abraham, F. (1991). *A visual introduction to dynamical systems theory for psychology.* Santa Cruz, CA: Ariel Press.

Artiles, A., Kozleski, E., Trent, S., Osher, D., & Ortiz, A. (2010). Justifying and explaining disproportionality, 1968-2008: A critique of underlying views of culture. *Exceptional Children, 76,* 279–299.

Artiles, A. J., Trent, S. C., Hoffman-Kipp, P., & López-Torres, L. (2000). From individual acquisition to cultural-historical practices in multicultural teacher education. *Remedial and Special Education, 21,* 79–89.

Bar-Yam, Y. (1997). *Dynamics of complex systems.* Reading, MA: Addison-Wesley.

Biddulph, F., Biddulph, J., & Biddulph, C. (2003). *The complexity of community and family influences on children's achievement in New Zealand: Best evidence synthesis.* Wellington, New Zealand: Ministry of Education.

Bongard, J., & Lipson, H. (2007). Automated reverse engineering of nonlinear dynamical systems. *National Academy of Science, 104,* 9943–9948.

Brayboy, B. (2005). Toward a tribal critical race theory in education. *The Urban Review, 37,* 425–446.

Checkland, P. (1993). *Systems thinking, systems practice.* New York, NY: Wiley.

Clarke, J., Bossange, B., Erb, C., Gibson, D., Nelligan, B., Spencer, C., & Sullivan, M. (2000). *Dynamics of change in high school teaching: A study of innovation in five Vermont professional development schools.* Providence, RI: Brown University.

Cobb, P., & McClain, K. (2006). The collective mediation of a high-stakes accountability program: Communities and networks of practice. *Mind, Culture, and Activity, 13,* 80–100.

Cole, M. (1992). Culture and cognitive development: From cross-cultural comparisons to model systems of cultural mediation. In A. F. Healy, S. M. Kosslyn, & R. M. Shiffrin (Eds.), *From learning theory to cognitive processes: Essays in honor of William K. Estes* (pp. 279–305). Hillsdale: Erlbaum.

Costa, A., & Kallick, B. (1995). Systems thinking: Interactive assessment in holonomous organizations. In A. Costa & B. Kallick (Eds.), *Assessment in the learning organization: Shifting the paradigm.* Alexandria, VA: Association for Supervision and Curriculum Development.

Costa, A., & Kallick, B. (2004). *Assessment strategies for self-directed learning.* Thousand Oaks, CA: Corwin Press.

Cox, M. J. (1997). Families as systems. *Annual Review of Psychology, 48,* 243–267.

Darling-Hammond, L. (2000a). How teacher education matters. *Journal of Teacher Education, 51*(3), 166–173.

Darling-Hammond, L. (2000b). Teacher quality and student achievement: Analysis archives. *Educational Leadership, 8,* 6–11.

DuFour, R., & Eaker, R. (1998). *Professional learning communities at work: Best practices for enhancing student achievement.* Alexandria, VA: Association for Supervision and Curriculum Development.

Engeström, Y. (1999). Activity theory and individual and social transformation. In Y. Engeström, R. Miettinen, & R. L. Punamaki (Eds.), *Perspectives on Activity Theory* (pp. 19–38). Cambridge: Cambridge University Press.

Ferguson, D., Kozleski, E., & Smith, A. (2003). Transformed, inclusive schools: A framework to guide fundamental change in urban schools. *Effective Education for Learners with Exceptionalities, 15,* 43–74.

Fleener, M. J. (1995, April). *Dissipative structures and educational contexts: Transforming schooling for the 21st century.* Paper presented at the Annual Meeting of the American Educational Research Association, San Francisco, CA.

Freire, P. (1970). *Pedagogy of the oppressed.* New York, NY: Continuum.

Friedrichs, A., & Gibson, D. (2003). Personalization and secondary school renewal. In J. DiMartino, J. Clarke, & D. Wolf (Eds.), *Personalized learning: Preparing high school students to create their futures* (pp. 41–68.). Lanham, MD: Scarecrow Education.

Gallego, M., Cole, M., & Laboratory of Comparative Human Cognition (2001). Classroom cultures and cultures in the classroom. In V. Richardson (Ed.), *Handbook of research on teaching* (pp. 951–997). Washington, DC: American Educational Research Association.

Gay, G. (2000). *Culturally responsive teaching: Theory, research, and practice.* New York, NY: Teachers College Press.

Gibson, D. (2000). *Complexity theory as a leadership framework.* Montpelier, VT: VISMT Retrieved from http://wwwvismtorg/pub/ComplexityandLeadershippdf

Gibson, D., & Clarke, J. (2000). Reflections on visual representation. In J. Clarke, J. Bossange, C. Erb, D. Gibson, B. Nelligan, C. Spencer, & M. Sullivan (Eds), *Dynamics of change in high school teaching: A study of innovation in five Vermont professional development schools* (pp. 173–189). Providence, RI: Brown University.

Harvey, D. (2000). *Spaces of hope.* Los Angeles, CA: University of California Press.

Holland, J. (1995). *Hidden order: How adaptation builds complexity.* Cambridge, MA: Perseus Books.

Holland, J. (1998). *Emergence: From chaos to order.* New York, NY: Perseus Books Group.

Holland, J., Holyoak, K., Nisbett, R., & Thagard, P. (1986). *Induction: Processes of inference, learning, and discovery.* Cambridge, MA: MIT Press.

Kauffman, S. (2000). *Investigations.* New York, NY: Oxford University Press.

Klingner, J., Artiles, A., Kozleski, E., Utley, C., Zion, S., Tate, W., et al. (2005). Conceptual framework for addressing the disproportionate representation of culturally and linguistically diverse students in special education. *Educational Policy Analysis Archives, 13,* 38.

Kozleski, E. (2004). Technology transfer and the field of education: The research to practice conundrum. *Technology Transfer and Society, 2,* 176–194.

Kozleski, E., Gibson, D., & George, A. (in preparation). The CASE process: A complex assessment system for education.

Kozleski, E., & Huber, J. (2010). Systemic change for RTI: Embedding change within a critical framework. *Theory into Practice, 49,* 258–264.

Kozleski, E., Mantle, C., Anderson, B., Foster, A., & Wilson, C. (1999, April). *The educational renewal agenda: A synthesis of our findings.* Paper presented at the American Educational Research Association Annual Meeting, Montreal, Canada.

Kozleski, E., Sands, D., French, N., Moore, E., & Roggow, R. (1995). *A systematic approach to supporting inclusive learning communities.* Denver, CO: TRL Associates.

Kozleski, E., & Smith, A. (2009). The role of policy and systems change in creating equity for students with disabilities in urban schools. *Urban Education, 44,* 427–451.

Lambert, L., Walker, D., Zimmerman, D., Cooper, J., Lambert, M., Gardner, M., & Slack, P. (1995). *The constructivist leader.* New York, NY: Teachers College Press.

Lee, C. (2007). *Culture, literacy, and learning: Taking bloom in the midst of the whirlwind.* New York, NY: Teachers College Press.

Lemke, J., & Sabelli, N. (2008). Complex systems and educational change: Towards a new research agenda. *Educational Philosophy and Theory, 40*(1), 118–129.

Leontyev, A. (1977). *Activity and consciousness: Philosophy in the USSR, problems of dialectical materialism.* Retrieved from http://www.marxists.org/archive/leontev/works/1977/leon1977.htm

McCombs, B. L. (2001). What do we know about learners and learning? The learner-centered framework: Bringing the educational system into balance. *Educational Horizons, 79*(4), 182–193.

McDermott, R., & Tylbor, H. (1996). The acquisition of a child by a learning disability. In S. C. J. Lave (Ed.), *Understanding practice: Perspectives on activity and context* (pp. 269–305). Cambridge, UK: Cambridge University Press.

McLaughlin, M. W. (1987). Learning from experience: Lessons from policy implementation. *Educational Evaluation and Policy Analysis, 9*(2), 171–178.

Meadows, D. (2008). *Thinking in systems: A primer.* White River Junction, VT: Chelsea Green.

Ohno, S. (1973). Ancient linkage groups and frozen accidents. *Nature, 244,* 259–262.

Oppenheimer, R. J. (2001). Increasing student motivation and facilitating learning. *College Teaching, 49*(3), 96–98.

O'Sullivan, E. (1999). *Transformative learning: Educational vision for the 21st century.* London: Zed Books.

Penetito, W. (2009). Place-based education: Catering for curriculum, culture and community. *New Zealand Annual Review of Education, 18,* 5–29.

Ramsey, D. C. (2002). Reframing the perfectionist's catch-22 dilemma: A systems thinking approach. *Journal for the Education of the Gifted, 26*(2), 99–111.

Rogoff, B. (2003). *The cultural nature of human development.* New York, NY: Oxford University Press.

Schallert, D. L. (2003). Intellectual, motivational, textual, and cultural considerations in teaching and learning with computer-mediated discussion. *Journal of Research on Technology in Education, 36*(2), 103–118.

Soja, E. (1996). *Thirdspace: Journeys to Los Angeles and other real and imagined places.* Oxford: Blackwell Publishers.

Sporns, O. (2011). *Networks of the brain.* Cambridge, MA: MIT Press.

Stefanou, C. (2003). Effects of classroom assessment on student motivation in fifth-grade science. *The Journal of Educational Research,* 152–162.

TEC. (2003). Pedagogy and community: Understanding situated contexts in learning to teach. Special section. *Teacher Education Quarterly, 30*(4), 7–125.

Van Manen, M. (1990). *Research Lived Experience: Human science for an action sensitive pedagogy.* Albany, NY: State University of New York Press.

Wolfram, S. (2002). *A new kind of science.* Champaign, IL: Wolfram Media.

Zito, J. R., Adkins, M., Gavins, M., Harris, K. R., & Graham, S. (2007). Self-regulated strategy development: Relationship to the social-cognitive perspective and the development of self-regulation. *Reading & Writing Quarterly, 23*(1), 77–95.

CHAPTER 16

CROSS-BOUNDARY LEADERSHIP

A Reform Model in Title I Elementary Schools

Gaetane Jean-Marie and Katherine A. Curry

Leadership in urban schools, particularly in high poverty communities, demands stronger connections between schools and communities to meet the needs of underserved children and families (Bryk, Sebring, Allensworth, Luppescu & Easton, 2010; Jazzar & Algozzine, 2007; Jean-Marie, Ruffin, & Burr, 2010). Often, the communities served by these schools are affected by elements of deprivation and high levels of drug, alcohol and crime rates. Whole school reform, such as the community school approach, is garnering popularity nationally as the antidote to endemic problems facing communities (Adams, 2010).

According to the National Coalition for Community Schools (NCCS), a community school is both a set of partnerships and a place where services, supports, and opportunities are utilized to lead to improved student learning, stronger families, and healthier communities (Coalition for Commu-

Social Justice Leadership for a Global World, pages 287–304
Copyright © 2012 by Information Age Publishing
All rights of reproduction in any form reserved.

nity Schools, 2006, p. 200). While some schools in the NCCS embed health clinics and social services within schools, others address out of school needs of students and families (Adams & Jean-Marie, 2011). The proliferation of community schools across the nation emphasizes an acknowledgement among educational leaders and policy makers of the need for restructuring school governance, policies, and leadership to utilize and mobilize resources to meet the needs of families and children and to, ultimately, support improved achievement (Jean-Marie, Ruffin, & Burr, 2010). The research reported in this chapter is part of an evaluation study on the development and effects of the community school model. Previous evaluations and analyses provided evidence on conditions for learning and stages of development (i.e., inquiring, emerging, mentoring, and sustaining stages) for each of the Tulsa Area Community School Initiative (TACSI) schools. Development stages were determined by cumulative school means across both structural and normative factors, and they indicate the extent to which structural and normative elements are embedded in the school environment. Development stages ranged from: 12–135 sustaining; 108–120 mentoring; 94–108 emerging; and less than 94 inquiring (Adams, 2010). For this study, we focused on ACSI schools at the mentoring and sustaining stages of the community school model. At the mentoring stage, expertise on the structural and normative elements was being developed and refined to change the informal and formal environment. At the sustaining stage, not only were structural and normative elements in place, but also teaching and learning practices were connected to service/support strategies so that stakeholders began to conceptualize services and learning as part of the integrative focus of the school's mission and vision (Adams, 2010).

TACSI AS A COMMUNITY SCHOOL MODEL

In one Midwestern state, the organic emergence of TACSI served as a type of whole school reform in 18 Title I elementary schools (Adams, 2009; Benson, Harkavy, & Puckett, 2007). Program features in this reform model reflect a redesign of traditional school structure to align with each feature of the community school framework (Harkavy & Blank, 2002). As a model for school reform, TACSI was developed and implemented in two school districts—a large urban school district (District 1) and a neighboring suburban fringe district (District 2) of Title I elementary schools. Twelve schools represent District 1, in which the majority of students are black or Hispanic and are from low socioeconomic communities, and six schools represent District 2, in which demographic changes are creating new challenges for meeting the needs of low socioeconomic students.

The mission of TACSI is to enhance student learning by creating and developing community schools that ameliorate social conditions in high poverty communities to strengthen children, families, and the community (Blank, Berg, & Melaville, 2003). Leaders in TACSI schools utilize their leadership skills and influence to engage all members of the school community, both inside and outside of the school, to enhance educational outcomes for all students. The theory of action for TACSI includes the core components of cross-boundary leadership: holistic programs, services and opportunities, family and community engagement, and community based learning. The core components are the mechanisms that promote effective teaching and satisfy the learning needs of students, and they work together to shape the six conditions for learning (i.e, early childhood development, a core instructional program, motivated and engaged students, holistic needs, family school-partnership, and safe school environment). In this study, the focus is on the elements of cross-boundary leadership and how these elements build capacity for improved student learning.

CONCEPTUAL FRAMEWORK

Research on schools emphasizes the principal's role to lead effectively and strengthen school and community partnerships for improved student learning (Hallinger & Murphy, 1985; Jazzar & Algozzine, 2007; Leithwood & Duke, 1999). Leadership as the driver for change is premised on the idea that principals build agency for change within and outside the school, and they nurture the leadership of others through shared vision resulting in systemic school improvement (Bryk et al., 2010). As transformational leader, the principal increases the commitment and capacity of school and community members, creates a culture of high expectations, and provides support for student and teacher growth (Leithwood & Duke, 1999). Further, transformational leadership is displayed "when leaders broaden and elevate the interests of their employees, when they generate awareness and acceptance of the purposes and mission of the group, and when they stir their employees to look beyond their own self-interests for the good of the group" (Bass, 1990, p. 21).

Reform literature suggests that a combination of factors, in addition to principal leadership, leads to school success. Bryk et al. (2010) suggest that the success of a school hinges not only on effective leadership but also a "mix of human and social factors that shape the actual activities that occur and the meaning that individuals attribute to these events" (p. 45). The reform literature on a new agenda for school effectiveness (Firestone & Riehl, 2005; Gronn, 2003; Seashore Louis, Leithwood, Wahlstrom & Anderson, 2010) argues for a more nuanced approach to leadership. This approach to school leadership captures leadership enacted by many people in schools and the implications that shared leadership has for school improvement. One such conceptualization is collective leadership. Collective leadership refers to the influence that role groups and other stakeholders who do not hold formal leadership positions exert on decisions in schools (Jazzar & Algozzine, 2007; Seashore Louis et al., 2010).

Often used interchangeably with "shared leadership," "distributed leadership," and "democratic leadership," collective leadership resides in a communal relationship where participants are both "shapers of" and "shaped by" one another (Donaldson, 2006; Moller & Pankake, 2006). Together, these leaders work to develop and share new ideas and to sustain practices that work to foster a climate of shared purpose, teamwork, and mutual respect (Boris-Schacter & Langer, 2006). Establishing social ties both within and outside of the school community is essential for effective collective leadership. The role of leaders is to build capacity for reform by leveraging the social ties of school members who interact at the boundaries of role groups (Adams & Jean-Marie, 2011; Greenhalgh, Robert, MacFarlane, Bate, & Kyriakidou, 2004; Jean-Marie, Ruffin, & Burr, 2010). The principals, together with all members of the school community, serve as change agents who can slow down, speed-up, or stop reform by tapping into informal authority generated through social networks (Adams & Jean-Marie, 2011).

LEADERSHIP REFORM: CROSS-BOUNDARY LEADERSHIP

Similar to collective leadership, cross-boundary leadership (see Figure 16.1) is based on the idea that educational and social problems require collaborative approaches to leadership that cross structural boundaries and create a network of shared responsibility among the different spheres of influence in children's lives (Adams, 2010; Adams & Jean-Marie, 2011). Cross-boundary leadership brings together community leaders, leaders on the ground, and

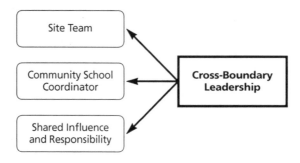

Figure 16.1 Cross-boundary leadership.

leaders in the middle to work collaboratively within the educational process. These leaders represent the civic and business community, the local neighborhood, and different school role groups (i.e., teachers, support staff, parents, students, administrators). Past research emphasizes the principal's role of adopting collaborative leadership approaches to school operations (Reyes & Wagstaff, 2005); however, in cross-boundary leadership, the structural features of the model create processes to invite and allow teachers, parents, community members and other constituents to support and advance the school. An active and diverse community site team and a full-time community school coordinator are structural features of cross-boundary leadership, whereas, a democratic culture (i.e., shared influence and responsibility) is a normative condition that facilitates effective cross-boundary leadership; see Figure 16.1 (Blank, Berg, & Melaville, 2006). Each element is discussed next.

COMMUNITY SITE TEAM AND SCHOOL COORDINATOR

Structural elements of cross-boundary leadership include a community site team and community school coordinator. Both elements are needed to fully implement the model. An effective *community site team* (CST) has representation from every sector of the school community—school administration, teachers, families, community partners, business partners, and community residents. Its purpose is to facilitate the development and maintenance of a shared educational vision for the school. In previous literature on site-based management, the role and function of site leaders lacked clarity, and internal and external role groups had limited to no influence on school and classroom practices (Beck & Murphy, 1998; Leithwood & Menzies, 1998). Unlike site-based management models, cross-boundary leadership does not obfuscate the principal's authority by transferring power to a representative council (Malen & Cochran, 2008). Instead, cross-boundary leadership emphasizes breaking down the walls of separation and isolation between and among groups—teachers, staff, students, parents, and community—as the place for principals to start transforming their schools into productive learning communities (Reyes & Wafstaff, 2005).

An effective *community school coordinator* (CSC) is another essential structural component for the implementation of cross-boundary leadership. The CSC facilitates the development, implementation, and management of community school efforts as they evolve from the school site team. A full-time CSC is the intermediary agent (Fusarelli, 2008), who operates like a connecter and weaver within the school's social network (Jordan, 2006). Networks are important because resources embedded in social networks are made accessible to network members through relational ties (Scott, 1987, 2000). Therefore, individuals within a network, such as the school community, have the potential to benefit from opportunities to exchange information and foster relationships that enhance resource attainment (Curry, 2011). Another commonly accepted effect of social networks is that relationships and structures within a network become stable over time and can either strengthen or inhibit imposed change or reform (Hanneman & Freeman, 1984; Hannan, Polos & Carroll, 2004). As structural components, the CSC and CST work cooperatively with the principal to establish normative conditions of shared influence and shared responsibility among role groups through ties developed in social networks.

SHARED INFLUENCE AND RESPONSIBILITY

The normative conditions of cross-boundary leadership are shared influence and responsibility. Shared influence has its roots in leadership as joint decision-making or participatory leadership (Wagner & Gooding, 1987). However, rather than leadership focused on behaviors and actions of an individual leader (Pearce & Conger, 2003), shared influence refers to a much more distributed or collaborative approach to reform that includes an individual's capacity to inspire, motivate and guide leadership in others to reach desired goals through collaboration and teamwork. Shared influence refers to an individual's interaction with others based on common beliefs about collective actions to pursue. Shared responsibility refers to an individual's willingness to control factors that lead to desired results (Adams, 2009). The control of factors by individuals within all represented role groups in addition to those in key leadership positions further suggests a shift in the distribution of power among constituents into a horizontal network, which is critical to the success of student learning (Reyes & Wagstaff, 2005). This shift is essential in high stakes accountability environments where principals face increasing demands on their time and energy for enhanced instructional leadership. When leadership is practiced from a broad array of role groups and other stakeholders, it strengthens human capacity to improve and change practices within schools to maximize school performance (Seashore Louise et al., 2010). As such, effective leaders encourage others to join in and to work collaboratively within the educational process (Seashore Louis et al., 2010).

In TACSI schools, the norms of shared influence and responsibility are needed as social supports for cooperative interactions between school and community actors. Norms reflect a consistent pattern of social action, and they are often more potent in regulating responsible behavior of school members than formal policies (Adams & Jean-Marie, 2011; Blau, 1955). Normative conditions that support cross-boundary leadership achieve social control through shared influence, cooperative interactions, and collective responsibility. While the structural elements of a community school site team and a community school coordinator are formal mechanisms that unite school members and community leaders within the educational process, the normative conditions of shared influence and responsibility are the lubricant that facilitates effective social interactions within and among school groups. All three elements are necessary to support a fully developed cross-boundary leadership design. Adams and Jean-Marie (2011) assert that cross-boundary leadership is not simply defined by new leadership structures; instead, it is defined by a culture of shared influence and responsibility for student and school performance that takes time and intentional action to develop.

METHODS

This research was part of an ongoing evaluation study on the implementation and effectiveness of the community school model as developed across TACSI schools. For this specific study, a case study design (Yin, 2009) was used to investigate the development of cross-boundary leadership at the mentoring/sustaining stage of community schools. Specifically, the study was designed to gain an understanding of the development of cross-boundary leadership to build capacity to meet social needs and, ultimately, enhance the education of children.

Data Collection

While TACSI network began during the school year of 2006–2007, the evaluation study did not begin until 2008. Qualitative data were collected during the 2009–2010 and 2010–2011 school years. Out of 18 schools, six of the community schools had reached an advanced stage of diffusion of cross-boundary leadership (Adams & Jean-Marie, 2011); therefore, these schools were purposefully selected for the qualitative exploration. Data collection included documents on cross-boundary leadership, in-depth interviews of principals from these six schools, field notes, and observations of implementation meetings in which these six principals participated. Implementation meetings included each of the 18 principals, network and district leaders, and community leaders. In 2009–2010, each principal participated in a one and a half hour semi-structured interview. In 2010–2011, only four of the principals participated in follow-up interviews and observations (i.e., leadership team meetings, staff professional development, school walk thru including global gardens, classrooms and school market). One of the two principals who did not participate the second year of data collection accepted a central office position in her district, and the other principal did not respond to the invitation to further participate in the study. Of those who continued in year two, principals provided documentary (e.g., school newsletter, school wise plan, meeting agendas, and minutes) evidence on the development of cross-boundary leadership during the interview. The interview protocol included an exploration of leadership characteristics and beliefs (i.e., socialization), and the development of normative and structural features of cross-boundary leadership. All the principals were white females with six to15 years at their respective schools.

Data Analysis

Using a grounded theory approach (Glaser & Strauss, 1967), data derived from interviews, field notes, observations, and documents were collected and then thematically coded (Strauss & Corbin, 1998). Open code procedures were used to create information categories on the leadership characteristics and beliefs of principals and on the development of structural and normative features of cross-boundary leadership. Axial coding techniques followed open coding to develop coherent categories of major and minor themes that emerged (Strauss & Corbin, 1998). Member checking of the transcripts was completed to assess for reporting consistency. Principals were provided transcripts to make corrections and provide clarification. In May 2010, researchers presented preliminary findings at a TACSI implementation meeting.

FINDINGS

Using the conceptual framework of cross-boundary leadership (Adams, 2010; Adams & Jean-Marie, 2011; Jean-Marie, Curry, & Bass, 2010; Leithwood & Mascall, 2008), we present findings on how these schools have developed the model by transforming school/community interactions to build capacity to meet social needs and, ultimately, enhance the education of children. The guiding research questions for the qualitative exploration of cross-boundary leadership are: What leadership practices facilitate the development of cross-boundary leadership? How are elements of cross-boundary leadership enabling schools to meet the academic needs of students and social needs of children and families?

The first finding is that *principals articulated how they continue to embrace change despite challenging circumstances in leading in a high-poverty school.* A common challenge noted by principals was working with parents whose roles have diminished over time in their children's lives. One principal stated, "I think the biggest challenge is that the needs of our families are great and very big and more intense. They have more needs that are different than many families had ten, twelve, or fifteen years ago." Another added, "Parents don't have enough time to spend with their children or to spend in schools organizing their students; but time is number one." Another principal discussed instances of neglect, trauma, and abuse experienced by many of her students that impeded the learning process.

Although the principals faced similar challenges, they embraced the challenge of turning around their schools and creating environments conducive to learning. The recurrent theme of "whatever it takes" permeated the kind of learning environment the principals sought to create for their students, parents, and teachers. As indicated by one principal, "My role is to facilitate and to empower my staff, my students, and my community … provide either the time, materials, whatever is needed to help my community. My job also is to make sure that I work for the community partners."

Additionally, principals were not intimidated by change. In fact, they embraced the change process and were even willing to embrace it on a personal level by indicating that they, themselves, had changed as a result of serving in their current positions. They believed it was their responsibility to be and create the change they wanted to see. One stated, "I have changed as much as the school has changed." Another said, "No two years have been the same." Leaders expressed their commitment to continual learning, both for themselves and members of their staff. One leader stated, "I learn something new every day." Another said, "I have that constant belief that we should always continue to learn." Findings suggest that these leaders do not allow obstacles to deter them from focusing on established goals and missions of the school. In fact, several principals viewed challenges as an opportunity for reform and referred to "turning obstacles into successes." These principals suggested that change was something to be embraced as long as change is utilized to fulfill the vision/mission of the school.

One principal had to contend with both structural and behavioral issues before the dream of the community school could be fulfilled in her building. She elaborated:

> When I came to [School X], it was primarily because the school had fallen into a pattern of low achievement. The demographics of the school were beginning to change. Things got a little bit better, then significantly worse … I stayed. I stuck with it because I don't just give up … started working aggressively to make changes and address the economic development of the neighborhood … The community development was huge. Transportation was a problem. So our idea was to bring a therapist here … assume responsibility for them being our clients while they are here. We began to see some of the churches and businesses come to us.

Another spoke of the process she undertook to facilitate change in her school:

> We have paid a lot of attention to the changing needs of our population and have grown that way. We have had to watch over the years that we've monitored carefully what practices needed to continue…We met with faculty, parents, and the community to see what was needed to support the children so they could learn academically…We knew we needed to get them before kindergarten…to help teachers to develop professionally. We needed to provide social services.

And finally, a third discussed the transformation in staff/faculty morale that needed to occur in her building. She asserted:

> I came to a school that was disenfranchised…negative atmosphere, teachers lashing out at communities and families; families lashing into the school over everything…complete chaos…out of control. The transformation has been dramatic. We have broken a lot of myths about poverty and Title I because we look at education from a parent's point of view. Basically it was taking those steps that were broad. They were steep steps, but it had to happen in this particular case because the negativity for so long had escalated to a battle every day.

Capturing the general sentiment of the principals, one principal succinctly stated, "I respond well to a challenge." Principals were acutely aware of the increasing challenges families and communities faced and their effects on their schools. However, they faced these challenges head-on by capitalizing on both human and social resources to address school and community issues.

The second finding is that *principals of TACSI schools shared several common beliefs, leadership and value orientations that influenced their leadership practices.* These principals entered administration to influence decision-making and were motivated by a desire to lead and serve to make a difference for students. The beliefs/values most strongly emphasized were a student-centered focus and a desire to help others find success. Without exception, these principals considered a child-centered focus as the primary influence on their practices and promotion of school culture. One principal indicated her child-centered focus by stating, "My job and my calling in life are to make life better for children." Another said, "I think that my number one belief is that everything I do has to be on behalf of children."

The aspect of valuing all people within the community (parents, students, teachers, and community members) was common across all leaders and was evident in comments such as, "I believe in the value of the people I work with. I believe they all have worth no matter what situations they are coming from in life." Principals saw their position as one of advocacy where those that are often left out of educational discussions were valued as members of the community. Several principals expressed a desire to empower others by "giving a voice to those who have no voice." One principal shared, "It's where the least become the most important, and they drive the educational system in that it is no longer the status quo."

Another common belief among principals was a willingness to do "whatever it takes" to encourage success for everyone within the school community. Leaders recognized the necessity of working harder and longer hours than in their previous positions, and they expected others within the school to do the same. One principal stated, "It's important for me to live by a philosophy of 'I will do whatever it takes.' If it means that I go to three events in one evening to be supportive of teachers and families, then that's what I need to do. If it means that I need to have the building open on weekends, then that's just what we do."

Principals eagerly embraced the role and responsibility of leading reform. One leader stated that her primary responsibility was to serve as "keeper of the dream." Another said, "As the principal, I have to be the keeper of the vision and mission." They did not lose sight of the larger vision and mission, success for all students through empowerment and collaboration across role groups, even when they were involved in day-to-day activities and operations of the school.

Although they emphasized the importance of shared decision-making, they also did not hesitate to make difficult decisions when necessary to protect the vision and mission of the school. Principals emphasized the importance of cultivating an effective human resource plan that communicated high expectations in a supportive environment. This characteristic is evident in statements such as, "If you can't be a part of this team, you need to leave." Another said,

> About one in five people you select to come on the team doesn't really know what they're getting into ... even through the conversation of describing what it is like and what the expectations will be ... every school year, I have to help someone off the train ... if the work isn't productive and it isn't for the children, then I can't let it go on and on.

In the third finding, *principals identified core elements of cross-boundary leadership that are essential to developing the community school model and philosophy.* Similar to the leadership beliefs/philosophy, characteristics, and practices that undergird the collective experiences of the principals, they espoused similar elements that are necessary in facilitating cross-boundary leadership. A normative element of cross-boundary leadership identified by the principals is a culture of inclusion (i.e., shared influence) or that "everyone has a stake in the community." The underlying belief is that schools are nested in communities, and communities are closely tied to schools. Elaborating further, one principal asserted that:

> The ownership belongs to the least as much as the most. It is working side by side with every single person that comes through the door. It's making them a partner even if it's in the enrollment process and the way we greet people. It is engaging everyone in a process of feeling a part of something much bigger than just the school...You are respected, given dignity, and we want you to be a part of us...Every staff member, every child, every parent belongs to the same family...That is shared leadership.

Similarly, another principal viewed shared responsibility as a component of cross-boundary leadership:

> Not just one or two people share the role of leader at the school, but even the leaders of different groups in the school, including partners, discuss the issues, ask questions, and answer questions about the direction of the school...I have to share the responsibility of making the decisions that impact the school with them. It has to be a collective effort from the leaders of multiple aspects of this school. I have to share the leadership with the cafeteria manager and the head custodian. All of those people have to feel they have a piece of that role, and, if they can be empowered to make a decision, then all the other leaders will stand behind it and not just me.

Another principal also emphasized that leadership is an act that must be balanced because it resides within and outside the school (i.e., community):

> It's working together with different entities. It's a give and take...working together internally and externally. It's to meet the needs of your community. It's trusting people and going through those changes. Senior leadership in these agencies changes, and their focus changes. You have to be alert to that and see how they can interface with your school.

Lastly, one principal reiterated the focus on children as the basis for connecting with the community to share leadership within cross-boundary leadership: "It's finding relationships with people in our community who want to help and serve...It's really working together."

In addition to shared responsibility and influence, the structural foundation of CST and CSC to support cross boundary leadership was important to the development of the model. In some cases, the structural features were in place before the leadership model was adopted. One principal talked about having a community site team before becoming part of the TACSI network: "It started off as my Title I committee and then evolved into my team leaders. I've included parents in that." Another principal stated, "My community site team started out with the YMCA, the health department.

As I added each component then that person came to the team. So it really started back in '04 with [X] and Family Children's Services."

The community site team functioned as a social hub that connected teachers, parents, administrators, and community partners in contrast to a governing body that held formal authority and power. As one principal noted, "The [CST] composition is what I call the stakeholders—the parents, teachers, community partners, service providers, myself, community school's coordinator. It's anyone who has an interest in being a part of the leadership of the school." Another principal asserted:

> We need feedback about how to decide what our priorities are and then what our work will be toward those priorities, [which include] how we will leverage our resources toward that. They are connected to the stakeholders who give input to the process of developing calendar, events, budget and concerns/reflection on school improvement and school vision.

The community school coordinator (CSC) was also an essential structural feature of cross-boundary leadership. The CSC was perceived as an important mechanism to build strong connections among school members and to form social bonds between the school and community. Principals emphasized the following responsibilities and characteristics that would be suitable for the person in that role: "ambassador to isolated families and kids having difficulty," "keeper of community school's priorities alongside the principal," "getting to know the community inside and out," "seeking partners we need," "doing grunt work," "liaison between the school and service providers as first point of contact," and "participates in nighttime activities and goes to community meetings." Expressing gratitude for having a CSC, this principal stated the following: "I'm very fortunate to have someone who has been involved in this whole community process since 1985 here and knows the community. He works with the different community members to bring resources to school, to bring more partners into the schools." In essence, the CSC plays an important role in complementing the principal. One principal captured this well: "It's really hard for me to do the academic, the kids, and my meetings as well."

Finally, *principals articulated that the development of the community school coordinator (CSC) was instrumental in enabling them to focus on the operating task of teaching and learning.* The CSC enabled principals to work more closely with teachers to support their professional growth. For one principal, "Once we were able to get a community school coordinator, I was able do more of my job as a principal in the traditional role . . . looking more at the academic success of the student and curriculum and instruction." Another principal reported:

> My time and day are not really interrupted at all by meetings with partners or resource procurement and conversations. That's [the CSC]. My day is spent

in the classroom. I had four formal evaluation conferences yesterday uninterrupted. Three years ago that wouldn't have happened. It would have been like answer the phone, get a message, do this.

One principal who is closer to retirement articulated confidence that the instructional environment that has been established would continue after she leaves her position:

I've created a community of leaders within my building. If I left tomorrow, they would continue this work. They've bought into the instructional practices . . . the environment that needs to be here. I couldn't do it if it were just me. I've created opportunities for teachers to become teacher leaders. You don't do this work by yourself—in isolation.

Similarly, another principal had this to say:

What I probably do best is that I have created a community of leaders within my building. If I left tomorrow, you would still see the same kind of focus because either I've brainwashed them, or they have bought into the instructional practices and the environment that needs to be here to make sure our kids are successful. And I have the most phenomenal leaders in this building . . . I couldn't do it if it was just me, I couldn't do it. And creating that, providing opportunities for people to become teacher leaders, is as I say, priceless.

Additionally, the normative conditions of shared responsibility and influence help to foster positive and improved interactions among role groups in the school. While the principals have high expectations of teachers, they expressed a desire to support and equip teachers to encourage success with students. Informal observations of principals' interactions with teachers also supported this finding. Two principals stated, "Teachers work harder, and it is already a hard job regardless, but we support each other." And, "I can ask people to do a lot of things. But if I don't give them the training or materials to do it, then it's not going to happen." Support came in different forms (i.e., resources, caring relationships, professional development, celebrations of success, modeling, etc.). For this principal, she stated: "I don't ask my staff to do anything that I am not willing to do myself." An outgrowth of the normative conditions is student interactions with teachers. For example, all the principals believed as one principal noted, "Kids here feel safe. They feel like they have someone that they can connect with."

Principals also highlighted the positive interactions between parents and teachers, a change from previous years. Several principals' quotes capture best the overall perceptions of teacher-parent interactions:

I see families engaged...I see great relationships everyday with families with my staff...They [parents] are not angry; they are working together. Children are happy. We see more smiles than frowns.

When they [teachers] willingly do their family nights, they come and participate in the community. Lights on. They do those things as a matter of the way we do business.

We are a team here. It's not the school against the parent or the parent against the school.

Parents feel like they're part of the conversation. It's together, what do you want for your child...we are a team. The kid sees (that) my mom and teacher—they are a team. It's a perfect opportunity to talk about the possibilities of the child.

Relatedly, school and community ties continue to strengthen and are evidenced in decreased mobility rates and parents' interest to capitalize on community resources that are provided through the school (e.g., global garden, medical clinic, adult programs/clubs). One principal stated: "Families don't leave [our school]." Another principal revealed that parents are very engaged at multiple levels: "Parents come now...kind of ask you about things that they want to have. Can we do this? Or they ask questions about afterschool programming or clubs." Lastly, another principal mentioned: "We are giving opportunities in all areas. Churches are coming in. Community retired people are coming in."

DISCUSSION AND CONCLUSIONS

In sum, the principals identified several challenges that hindered their efforts in turning around their schools, but each achieved success over time. They also articulated that by embracing challenges, they became efficacious in addressing them. Principals in TACSI schools shared common leadership characteristics (i.e., keeper of the dream, distributed leadership, children and parent advocates, etc.). Several leadership practices were consistent across these leaders. They described their leadership styles as "collaborative," and all articulated practices of transformational leadership (Bass, 1990; Jean-Marie, Curry & Bass, 2010; Leithwood, & Mascall, 2008). Findings from the study suggest that principals embraced collective leadership along with their formal authority to reach educational goals for students (Seashore Louis et al., 2010). As one principal stated, "I will make decisions and stand behind decisions when I think they need to be made by a leader."

Within cross-boundary leadership, the roles of community school coordinator and community site team continue to develop as the needs of children and families also evolved. The principals recognized that they need the assistance of others, both within and outside the school, to engage in collaborative efforts to develop healthy and engaged learners (Fusarelli, 2008; Jordan, 2006). Hence, the CST and CSC play an important role in developing and sustaining the community school model. Most importantly, clarifying the role and responsibilities of each structural component has the potential to allow the principal to focus on the operating task of teaching and learning. Additionally, the principals indicated that having the right CST and CSC were important to the model. For example, community school coordinators were perceived as important mechanisms to build strong connections among school members and to form social bonds between the school and community. In many ways, the site team functioned as a social hub that connected teachers, parents, administrators, and community partners in contrast to a governing body that held formal authority and power. These conversations reinforced the responsibilities of each role group and created a culture where every voice counted.

In cross-boundary leadership, the benefits of education increase when individuals in the internal and external school environment share some degree of oversight for all children. This study specifies more closely the informal and formal mechanisms that promote a culture where a broad range of individuals embrace a shared responsibility and influence to maximize educational opportunities for students and families.

REFERENCES

Adams, C. M. (2009). *Collective parent responsibility: A normative framework to understand parent involvement.* Unpublished manuscript, Department of Educational Leadership and Policy Studies, University of Oklahoma, Tulsa, OK.

Adams, C. M. (2010). *The community school effect: Evidence from an evaluation of the Tulsa Area Community School Initiative.* Unpublished report, The Oklahoma Center for Educational Policy, University of Oklahoma, Tulsa, OK.

Adams, C. M., & Jean-Marie, G. (2011). A diffusion approach to the study of leadership reform. *Journal of Educational Administration, 49*(4), 354–377.

Bass, B. M. (1990). From transactional to transformational leadership: Learning to share the vision. *Organizational Dynamics, 18*(3), 19–32.

Beck, L., & Murphy, J. (1998). Site-based management and school success. *School Effectiveness and School Improvement, 9*(4), 355–385.

Benson, L., Harkavy, I., & Puckett, J. (2007). *Dewey's dream: Universities and democracies in an age of education reform.* Philadelphia, PA: Temple University Press.

Blank, M., Berg, A., & Melaville, A. (2006). *Growing community schools: The role of cross-boundary leadership.* Washington, DC: Coalition for Community Schools.

Blank, M. J., Berg, A. C., & Melaville, A. (2003). *Making the difference: Research and practice in community schools.* Washington, DC: Coalition for Community Schools.

Blau, P. M. (1955). *The dynamics of bureaucracy.* Chicago, IL: University of Chicago Press.

Boris-Schacter, S., & Langer, S. (2006). *Balanced leadership: How effective principals manage their work.* New York, NY: Teachers College Press.

Bryk, A. S., Sebring, P. B., Allensworth, E., Luppescu, S., & Easton, J. Q. (2010). *Organizing for schools improvement: Lessons from Chicago.* Chicago, IL: University of Chicago Press.

Coalition for Community Schools. (2006). *A handbook for state policy leaders—Community schools: improving student learning/strenthening schools, families, and communities.* Washington, DC: Coalition for Community Schools-Institute for Educational Leadership.

Curry, K. A. (2011). *Parent social networks and parent responsibility.* Unpublished doctoral dissertation, University of Oklahoma, Norman, OK.

Donaldson, G. A. (2006). *Cultivating leadership in schools: Connecting people, purpose, and practice.* New York, NY: Teachers College Press.

Firestone, W. A., & Riehl, C. (2005). *A new agenda for research in educational leadership.* New York, NY: Teachers College Press.

Fusarelli, B. C. (2008). The politics of coordinated services for children: Interinstitutional relations and social justice. In B. S. Cooper, J. G. Cibulka, & L. D. Fusarelli (Eds.), *Handbook of education politics and policy* (pp. 350–373). New York, NY: Routledge.

Glaser, B. G., & Strauss, A. L. (1967). *The discovery of grounded theory.* Chicago, IL: Aldine.

Greenhalgh, T., Robert, G., MacFarlane, F., Bate, P., & Kyriakidou, O. (2004). Diffusion of innovations in service organizations: Systematic review and recommendations. *The Milbank Quarterly, 82*(4), 581–629

Gronn, P. (2003). Distributing and intensifying school leadership. In N. Bennett & L. Anderson (Eds.), *Rethinking educational leadership* (pp. 60–73). London: Sage.

Hallinger, P., & Murphy, J. (1985). Assessing the instructional management behavior of principals. *Elementary School Journal, 86*(2), 217–247.

Hannan, M. T., Polos, L., & Carroll, G. R. (2004, April). *Toward a theory of forms: Similarity & Categorization.* Paper presented at the annual Organizational Ecology Conference, St. Louis, MO.

Hanneman, R. A., & Freeman, M. (1984). *Introduction to social networks.* Riverside, CA: University of California.

Harkavy, I., & Blank, M. J. (2002, April). Community schools: A vision of learning that goes beyond testing. *Education Week, 21*(31), 38–43.

Jazzar, M., & Algozzine, R. (2007). *Keys to successful 21st century educational leadership.* Boston, MA: Allyn & Bacon.

Jean-Marie, G., Curry, K., & Bass, L. (2010). *Examining cross-boundary leadership at the mentoring/sustaining stage of community schools.* Unpublished report prepared for Tulsa Area Community School Initiative.

Jean-Marie, G., Ruffin, V., & Burr, K. (2010). Leading across boundaries: The role of community schools and cross-boundary leadership in school reform. In S. Horsford (Ed.), *New perspectives in educational leadership: Exploring social, political, and community contexts and meaning* (pp. 217–238). New York, NY: Peter Lang.

Jordan, A. (2006). *Tapping the power of social networks: Understanding the role of social networks in strengthening families and transforming communities.* Baltimore, MD: Annie E. Casey Foundation.

Leithwood, K., & Duke, D. L. (1999). A century's quest to understand school Leadership. In J. Murphy & K. S. Lewis (Eds.), *Handbook of Research on Educational Administration, 2nd ed.* (pp. 45–72). San Francisco: Jossey-Bass.

Leithwood, K., & Mascall, B. (2008). Collective leadership effects on student achievement. *Educational Administration Quarterly, 44,* 529–561.

Leithwood, K., & Menzies, T. (1998). Forms and effects of school-based management: A review. *Educational Policy, 12*(3), 325–346.

Malen, B., & Cochran, M. V. (2008). Beyond pluralistic patterns of power: Research on the micro politics of schools. In B. S. Cooper, J. G. Cibulka, & L. D. Fusarelli (Eds.), *Handbook of education politics and policy* (pp. 148–178). New York, NY: Routledge.

Moller, G., & Pankake, A. (2006). *Lead with me: A principal's guide to teacher leadership.* Larchmont, NY: Eye on Education.

Pearce, C. L., & Conger, J. A. (2003). *Shared leadership: Reframing the hows and whys of leadership.* Thousand Oaks, CA: Sage.

Reyes, P., & Wagstaff, L. (2005). How does leadership promote successful teaching and learning for diverse students? In W. A. Firestone & C. Riehl (Eds.), *A new agenda for research in educational leadership* (pp. 101–118). New York, NY: Teachers College Press.

Scott, J. (1987). *Social network analysis: A handbook.* London, UK: Sage.

Scott, J. (2000). *Social network analysis: A handbook (Vol. 2).* Greenwich, CT: Sage.

Seashore Louis, K., Leithwood, K., Wahlstrom, K., & Anderson, S. (2010). *Investigating the links to improved student learning.* Minneapolis, MN: University of Minnesota Center for Applied Research.

Strauss, A. L., & Corbin, J. (1998). *Basics of qualitative research: Techniques and procedures for developing grounded theory* (2nd ed.). Thousand Oaks, CA: Sage.

Wagner, J. A. III & Gooding, R. Z. (1987). Shared influence and organizational behavior: A meta-analysis of situational variables expected to moderate participation-outcome relationships. *Academy of Management Journal, 30*(3), 524–541.

Yin, R. K. (2009). *Case study research: design and methods* (4th ed.). Los Angeles, CA: Sage Publications.

CHAPTER 17

TOWARD A MORE PERFECT UNION

Culturally Responsive Leadership through Social Justice

Rhonda Blackwell-Flanagan

INTRODUCTION

An existing parallel can be drawn between the proposal of the new Constitution at the Constitutional Convention of 1787 and the ideal of social
justice as a platform to lead for educational leaders today. The Articles of
Confederation did not take into account the interest of all colonies to be
served; likewise, in the early days of public schools, school leaders were not
always given to advocating for all learners. The mission of early headmasters
centered on managing the building, resources, and people. Uncovering
the disparity within the Articles of Confederation not being representative gave way to a change in government. In light of school administration,
transitions in the economic, social, political, and demographic landscape
in many of the states caused a shift on the axis upon which school leaders administrated schools. While both ideals represent two controversial

Social Justice Leadership for a Global World, pages 305–323
Copyright © 2012 by Information Age Publishing
All rights of reproduction in any form reserved.

pillars that caused debate as well as resistance, the Articles of Confederation evolved into the establishment of a stronger and more resilient government, and school leaders have had to become change agents, servant leaders, and educational activists to absorb the various national epidemics and local problems of schooling in America. Arguably, the new Constitution has not provided a panacea for governmental relations, nor has the ideal of social justice leadership been a hybrid medium for administrating more equitable conventions of schooling for all students. However, what is admirable is that both endeavors have moved society closer to our shared goals—toward a more perfect union representative of all constituents, and toward the ideal of administrating schools where social justice meets and complements the call to school leadership that is culturally proficient, and responsive to issues related to equity.

As a former middle school teacher, school leader, faculty member and a parent of public school children, I am cognizant of the shift in the purpose of schooling as well as the administrative change that has taken place over the last two decades. In the 1980s, the purpose of schooling was thought to be holistic, comprised of the development of character, sense of self and the ability to think creatively and critically (Graham, 1984). However, the move into the 21st century has masked this purpose of schooling and critics now argue that standards-based reform has hindered the "creation of vibrant and intellectually challenging programs at all levels" (Cambron-McCabe & McCarthy, 2005, p. 205). While some would contend that the emphasis on accountability has improved curriculum for the underserved, others argue that the accountability pressures have forced a narrowing of the curriculum as teachers are ensuring coverage of material that is reflected on standardized tests (Darling-Hammond, 2007). Additionally the accountability movement has been weakened by the seemingly negative effects that it has had on the students who should have benefited most from such reform. Amrein and Berliner (2002) highlighted how scholarship awards for 80% of high performing students in an affluent suburb of Detroit far exceeded the 6% of test takers in Detroit schools that received scholarships. This outcome further establishes lines of inequity that undergird reform initiatives regarding schooling in America—that attaching scholarships to high performance on state tests, in effect, punishes those who do not make the grade.

The current emphasis on accountability and achievement as mandated by federal policy, state interpretation of policy, or district implementation of policy, has made the nation's thrust to leave *no child behind* more crystallized and clear. Cambron-McCabe and McCarthy (2005) synthesized the scope of this level of reform to include an artificial commitment to fairness and educational opportunity. This continued pandemic of schooling has not been a platform to close the achievement gap, but has evolved into a "race to the top"[1] and competition for securing federal funds that will aid in preparing students for college and the workplace (U.S. Department of Education, 2009). While the intent of such reform is positive, it remains another mechanism to marginalize those who do not have access to the information, resources, and experiences to enter the game, let alone to stay in the race. Herein is established the importance of having school leaders ensure that the schooling experiences for all children are more equitable and that all students have access to a rich and full educational experience.

In this chapter, I offer an overview on the entry of social justice into mainstream America, contextualize the ideal of social justice leadership, and explore the implications of social justice leadership in today's school. Finally, to ensure that the school leadership that is currently in place is proficient and prepared for the journey, I provide extant strategies to be considered by leadership preparations programs at the university, district level, and state licensure entities in the United States. Through this discussion, the confluence between school leadership and social justice will at best redefine and create a shift in rethinking how school leaders make an impact on the purpose, process, and outcome of schooling in the 21st century as they sharpen their leadership lens toward the end of social justice and cultural responsiveness in Pre-K–12 settings.

BIRTHING AN IDEAL: SOCIAL JUSTICE IN THE PUBLIC SCHOOLS

The evolution of social justice ideals entering the mainstream of education in the United States has focused on equality and justice for all stemming from the community to the classroom. This evolution was evident in the 1920s and 1930s when early immigrants were welcomed into America's borders. Horace Kallen (1971), one of the founding fathers on the ideals of cultural pluralism, synthesized the events during that time period and asserted that immigrant and ethnic groups had a right to maintain their cultures and traditions in American society and that Americans would benefit from their diversity. In the 1940s and 1950s, the impact of World War II on the social, political, and economic landscape began to take its toll, and tensions among mainstream culture and various ethnic groups began to escalate. The *Intergroup Movement* was developed in response to America's ills, in particular the inability to accept the influx of diverse ethnic groups and shifting demographics from the south to the north that created overpopulated schools and competition for jobs and housing—all of which was undergirded by waves of racism (Banks, 1993). This ideal, which entered into the educational arena, proposed to reduce racial tension, ethnic prejudice and cultural misunderstandings, and help students develop positive attitudes toward diverse groups and more democratic attitudes, beliefs and actions (Banks, 1994).

Spanning forward to the Civil Rights era of the 1960s and into the upheaval and fight for equal educational opportunities, the landmark decision by the Supreme Court in the *Brown vs. Board of Education* case in 1952 now required the desegregation of schools across America (Baird, 1996). After the implementation of integration, two major levels of legislation that would impact federal funding were enacted. In 1964 Title VI of the Civil Rights Act specifically prohibited discrimination in public schools and programs that were funded with federal dollars; and in 1965 the Elementary and Secondary Education Act provided a platform for funding programs for the economically disadvantaged. In 1972, Title IX of the Education Amendments provided protection on the basis of gender, and Section 504 of the Rehabilitation Act of 1973 established provisions for individuals with disabilities.

Additional large scale efforts connected to the synergy of leveling the playing field arose during this historical era as well. The Equal Educational Opportunities Act of 1974 amassed protection for individuals who were discriminated against and denied access based on their race, color, sex, or national origin. Shortly thereafter, the Individuals with Disabilities Education Act of 1975 established the rights and benefits of children with disabilities. Based on this history of legislation centered on educational issues, a movement for multicultural education emerged in the late 1960s and 1970s with a primary purpose of reforming the curriculum to address information relative to ethnicity, women, and other cultural groups (Banks, 1993). Simultaneously as the United States was settling into the equal opportunity era that heavily influenced practice in the workplace and schools, a third wave of immigrants began entering the United States, and educational institutions found it necessary once again to make additional accommodations in the learning environment (Blackwell-Flanagan, 1996). Aside from an emphasis on curriculum, in the 1980s the focus on instructional practices that would facilitate learning for all students evolved as part of the multicultural education movement as well. Villegas' (1991) work and research in the area of culturally responsive pedagogy revealed the need for establishing cultural links between the home and school for Hawaiian and Hispanic children as well as establishing the importance of cultural congruence between teaching activities and students' experiences. From her research in the early 1990s, and in support with the adoption of multicultural education standards by one of the leading professional accrediting bodies in the nation, the National Council for the Accreditation of Teacher Education (NCATE), her work impacted many teacher preparation courses in institutions of higher education. The momentum of Villegas' (1991) research gave rise to a platform for assessing beginning teachers, and as a result, she recommended a set of criteria to the Educational Testing Service to consider when developing its new performance assessments for beginning teachers that reflected the tenets of multicultural teaching. Areas to be assessed included five practices: 1) teachers having an attitude of respect for cultural differences; 2) teachers knowing the cultural resources their students bring to the class; 3) teachers implementing an enriched curriculum for all students; 4) teachers building bridges between the instructional content, materials and methods and the cultural backgrounds of the students in their classes; and 5) teachers being aware of cultural differences when evaluating students. Her work later expanded into a vision for culturally-responsive teaching that guides the examination and revision of curriculum, making issues of diversity central rather than peripheral to the learning that takes place in the classroom. Villegas and Lucas (2002) went on to define the attributes of a culturally responsive teacher as one who is socio-culturally conscious, holds affirming views of students from diverse backgrounds, sees himself or herself as responsible for and capable of bringing about change to make schools more equitable, understands how learners construct knowledge, knows about the lives of his or her students, and who designs instruction that builds on what the students already know.

As the infrastructure of the educational process began changing in response to society's needs, the tenor of the Civil Rights era influenced school leaders to add another dimension onto the face of school leadership, which centered on advocacy for those disenfranchised by policies and practices within public education. It was not until the new millennium was ushered in that the need for school leaders to respond to the call toward reform in creating equitable structures to educate all children became clear. Olivia, Anderson and Byng (as cited in Marshall and Oliva, 2010) cautioned educational leaders "to be mindful of the actions, policies, and processes that they champion in their work" (p. 287). They recognized that the school leader's advocacy for educational outcomes as well as social justice had a direct correlation to the educational advantage and achievement outcomes of all students. Considering the historical frame of reference presented and the plight for equity in schools that remains, the time for mobilizing actions on how school leaders can become better advocates and activists is at hand.

CONCEPTIONS OF LEADERSHIP FOR SOCIAL JUSTICE

Social justice leadership in the context of schooling is about justice, respect, care and equity, with a consciousness of how historical factors of marginalization upon subgroups impacts the learning that takes place within the schools (Cambron-McCabe &McCarthy, 2005; Marshall & Oliva, 2010; Theoharis, 2007). To further narrow the context for discussion applicable to the schoolhouse, Dantley and Tillman (as cited in Marshall & Oliva, 2010) captured a core of issues that revolve around the topic of social justice to include race, diversity, marginalization, gender, spirituality, age, ability, and sexual orientation. However, additional constructs should include religion and social class to broaden the scope of social justice. All of these issues are salient, and when they arise within the context of public schooling, they become the responsibility of the school leader to address and influence the process of decision making toward more equitable outcomes. Jean-Marie (2008) and Theoharis (2007) conducted research examining how school leaders enacted social justice and equity in their schools. Jean-Marie (2008) concluded that the principals in her study engaged in transformative leadership that supports social justice and works to create democratic and equitable schools. In his study of school leaders, Theoharis (2007) found that the practice of social justice leadership is about "leaders creating equitable schools and changing marginalization, and leaders who advocate, lead and keep at the center of their practice, vision, issues of race, class, gender, disability, sexual orientation, and other historically and currently marginalizing conditions in the United States" (p. 223). These studies provide insights on how school leaders are enacting leadership for social justice by disrupting structural barriers and normative conditions that threaten educational equity for all learners.

Karpinski and Lugg (2006) conceptualize social justice for school leaders as "pursuing policies, practices, and politics that enhance the lifetime opportunities for all children, particularly those who have been historically marginalized" (p. 279). In real time, leaders for social justice create integrated learning environments as opposed to segregating students into resource rooms, pullout classes, or continuing systemic tracking practices. They facilitate continuous professional development across landscapes of reform to build stronger professional learning communities and relationships, and they create opportunities for continuous parental engagement to maximize stakeholder involvement (Marshall & Oliva, 2010).

Specific to the conceptions that are highlighted here, the practice of marginalization is subtle and divisive, and in order to counter the outcomes of some groups of students being marginalized, it will require school leaders to engage in levels of activism to erase traditionally held lines and spaces of inequity. In an effort to move the theme of school leadership for social justice forward, it is practical to surmise that there are gradients of frameworks, paradigms, and actions that reside at some point along the social justice continuum—one in which I define as a scale upon which segments of the ideal of social justice can be captured within the range of a moderate awareness to an activists approach. Due to the complexity of defining, embracing, and acting from a social justice conscious, researchers in the field are not promoting "the perfect social justice leader or the perfect social justice school" as a model (McKenzie et al., 2008), but rather urging that leaders recognize their deficiencies in understanding student differences and work to increase their knowledge to make more equitable decisions in the process of administrating schools. As society moves forward, school leadership must be responsive to the changing landscape in schools that mirrors society, thereby advancing forward along the social justice continuum as they administrate schools.

McKenzie et al. (2008) outlined specific leadership tasks that include raising the academic achievement for all students, preparing them to live as critical citizens in society, and structuring schools for learning to take place in heterogeneous and inclusive learning environments. In an era of No Child Left Behind (NCLB) and other accountability mandates, these tasks as suggested by McKenzie are applicable toward the facilitation of equitable leadership that has the welfare of all children at the heart of the decision making process.

SOCIAL JUSTICE LEADERSHIP IN SCHOOLS: FROM THEORY TO PRACTICE

Educational equity, which can be framed as the ideal of ensuring that the principle of equality in the schooling process is practiced, continues to be a misnomer in schools in the United States and internationally. Similar to America, in Australia, achievement in school is closely linked to socioeconomic background and a command of the English language (Christie, 2005). Interestingly, although the participation rate for Australians has increased, the gaps between ndigenous and non-indigenous school retention and attainment remain unsatisfactory. Malin and Maidment (2003) indicated that indigenous youth reach age 15 without being sufficiently literate or able to gain quality employment and as a result have limited options in the future. And while the landscape of Australia is highlighted and compared to schooling in America, the notion of inequities in schooling is a common conversation globally.

Regardless of the fact that the United States has made generations of progress since the days of school desegregation promulgated by Jim Crow laws of the late 1800s, real inequities still exist. As Marshall and Oliva (2010) argue, the disparities may not be as intentional and overt today, but "covert, subconscious, and unintentional acts can be more insidious and damaging" (p. 2). Given the disparities that exist, there is an ongoing need for conversations, research, and theoretical pause that enlightens and engages school leaders toward a higher social conscience for administrating schools; hence, substantive reasons abound for the need for social justice leaders to be at the helm in schools today in the United States and abroad, and merits some consideration.

First, students in culturally diverse settings as well as affluent populated schools continue to be marginalized through tracking and scheduling mechanisms. The infrastructure in which scheduling practices are upheld promotes a sense of privilege among recipients, creates a caste-like system in the social fabric of the school, and disempowers teachers who only teach children in the lower quartiles. Despite the ill effects of marginalization, research consistently posits that academic achievement gains are higher in settings where students are heterogeneously grouped (Peterson & Hittie, 2003; Rea, McLaughlin, & Walther-Thomas, 2002).

Second, despite the interventions in school improvement plans ushered in via the No Child Left Behind reform, the achievement gap between English Language Learners or ELL students and English speaking students is still apparent. For example, the National Assessment of Educational Progress (NAEP) reported that 71 percent of eighth grade students who are English-language learners (ELL) test considerably below grade level in reading, compared with 25 percent of non-ELL students (U.S. Department of Education, 2007). In more recent findings, the National Center for Educational Statistics reported NAEP data that compared 2009 to 1998 reading achievement for 8th grade students in 22 states, and found that the achievement gap between Hispanic and white students did not change significantly in any state (Hemphill & Vanneman, 2010). Disparities that parallel achievement gaps between middle class whites and students of color continue to be reflected in the U.S., Canada, the UK, and Australia (Grothaus, Crum & James, 2010).

Third, the cultural competence of educators, particularly in urban settings, remains and continues to pose challenges to educational leaders (Grothaus et al., 2010). The lack of teachers' cultural knowledge of self as well as diverse groups hinders achievement, creates a divide in the classroom between students and teachers, and affects student engagement. A vital correlation to teachers being culturally responsive is leaders who are also culturally proficient and can provide the instructional leadership and facilitate professional development for teachers as they move the school further along the social justice continuum.

Fourth, Title I schools many times (despite additional federal funding) lack the resources and expertise that, in turn, can adversely impact student achievement (Grothaus et al., 2010). While it may be considered iconic for non-Title I schools to have multimedia and interactive resources to support instructional methods, Title I schools are forced to use more of their operational dollars on securing additional support staff to reduce class size and student-teacher ratios, or on implementing before and afterschool programs in an effort to remediate larger populations of low-performing students. Adding to this disparity that exists across schools, school leaders in Title I schools have a harder time attracting and maintaining larger pools of highly qualified teachers that have the capacity to positively impact student achievement.

Fifth, considering the massive demographic shifts that have occurred over the last several decades, instructional methods, policies and practices have not changed to the point of addressing the needs of a diverse student population (Lim & A'Ole-Bounce, as cited in Grothaus et al., 2010). Students are still rewarded for the cultural capital and experiences that they bring to school and interchanges that they participate in, which aligns with the dominant class (Dumais, 2002). As a result, the cultural capital of those outside the upper class is disregarded. Conversely, Zambrana and Zoppi (2002) offer that in regards to Latinas, the social capital that students bring to school must be valued as assets for building academic success.

Finally, students of different religions, sexual orientation, and economic status on school campuses and universities continue to remain targets of harassment, bullying, and isolation. In 2007, approximately 32 percent of 12- to 18-year-old students reported having been bullied at school during the school year and four percent reported having been cyber-bullied (U.S. Department of Education, 2010). If the White House attention to the matter as seen in the first summit hosted by the Department of Education in August 2010 (Hall, 2011) is any indication of its importance to school communities across the country, then the need for school leaders to ensure a safe and equitable environment for learning is paramount.

Considering the arguments outlined above and the continually changing demographics that color the culture and landscape of schools in America, an advocacy-based leadership at the helm that forges the promise of an equitable education for all students is necessary. Based on these ideas, there is a critical need for school leaders who develop a lens, vision and mission to eradicate the disparities that are evident in schools stateside and internationally (Jean-Marie, Normore & Brooks, 2009). This leads to a discussion of how to prepare leaders for such environments.

LEADERSHIP PREPARATION: A GLOBAL PRESCRIPTION

While leadership preparation programs in the United States are focused on ensuring that aspiring leaders successfully move through the state certification and licensure process, there are specific practices in the leadership making process that are germane to other countries, regions, governmental entities, cities, and schools that are pressed for developing school leaders with a conscience for social justice. In support of this, Jean-Marie and her colleagues (2009) identified three strategies that connect the local practice in the United States and study of educational leadership to activities at a global level and their reciprocal nature of these relationships. These strategies include: a) broadening our conception of the knowledge base that undergirds educational leadership for social justice in order to deepen it, b) reconsidering research designs and outcomes, and c) realizing that local and global are parts of one interrelated whole. In an effort to think globally about what can be learned and shared across international lines and spaces in the leadership preparation process, there are promising practices complementary of programs in the United States that can be extended and tailored to respond to the specific needs of international audiences as well.

The landscape for leadership preparation has experienced a boom in advancing the occupation of a school leader over the last 25 years (Hallinger, 2003; Lumby, Crow & Pashiardis, 2008; Young, 2009). From very little emphasis on requirements for becoming a school leader and retaining the position, leadership preparation has moved to a more focused emphasis on the skills, knowledge, and dispositions needed to be a leader or an agent of change that positively impacts student achievement and school improvement. In fact Hallinger (2003) considered the escalation and emergence toward leadership preparation to be a global enterprise. Not only is the United States continuing to make headway into the industry of leadership, but so are other countries. Thus a global interest in school leadership preparation and development has resulted. Similar to American schools grappling with equity issues of access and resources, other countries share similar challenges related to political, social, and cultural pressures. Demographic and cultural transitions impact schoolhouses in the same way that they do society, as schools tend to be microcosms of the larger culture. Therefore, information on best practices in preparing school leaders to be advocates for social justice should be readily available and shared across school houses and leadership preparation institutions globally.

OPERATIONAL CONSTRUCTS
IN LEADERSHIP PREPARATION

Regardless of the culture, norms, and values that guide education systems, leaders make a difference in schools and leadership development makes a difference in what leaders do in schools (Lumby et al., 2008). The need to understand why a social justice lens is recommended for school leaders to embrace can help to operationalize the concept. One foundational construct for using a social justice approach is targeted at building theoretical underpinnings or "schooling future educational leaders in theories of social justice" (Karpinski & Lugg, 2006, p. 280) so that leaders are more cognizant of the disparities that exist and can work to eliminate them. Another construct to consider is the influence that the school culture has on how leadership is exercised as well as how an individual's cultural experiences impact their actions as a school leader. At this juncture several process and content practices in leadership preparation are explored that align with a social justice platform. It is otherwise assumed that the leadership preparation institution or organization that embraces an interest has a defined curriculum for social justice, or is working to transition aspects of the program toward a social justice approach.

Selection

The process of recruiting and selecting aspiring leaders with the capacity to lead from a social justice platform, is the ingress to maximizing the experience and outcome for aspiring school leaders of social justice. Clearly disaggregating candidates, whose leadership dispositions align with ideals of activism and have a heightened social conscience, will lead to the development of leadership behaviors that promote and advance justice and equity in the process of schooling. Cambron-McCabe and McCarthy (2005) propose that the selection process remains as one of the critical challenges for influencing leadership preparation toward a framework for social justice. However, there exists a creative alliance between the role of school leaders and the nature of social justice leadership. By honing in on and refining the selection process, universities and leadership preparation organizations would improve the quality in the pool of aspiring school leaders who are prepared to take on the charge of administrating schools through a lens for social justice. McKenzie et al. (2008) puts forth three recommendations for the selection process: select individuals who already have a propensity toward critical consciousness; select students who are strong teachers, as instructional leadership is concerned with improving the academic achievement for all students; and select students who can enter the program with solid leadership experience. Amassing the criteria for candidates, or what can be termed as frontloading at the entry point, will allow faculty the opportunity to maximize instruction with students who have a larger capacity to benefit from the experiences that lead to the acquisition of critical inquiry skills, and shape the development of their social conscience.

Instructional Leadership That Impacts Achievement

Leadership preparation programs must place heavy emphasis on training school leaders to lead, model, and assess instruction that takes place in and outside of the classroom. This ultimately means that school leaders will need to demonstrate mastery in pedagogical areas related to skills, knowledge, and assessment (Capper, Theoharis, & Sebastian, 2006). No longer will school leaders be able to delegate critical responsibilities relative to student achievement to academic coaches or assistant principals. Instead, they will need to know what curriculum is being taught, the methods used to yield the highest academic gains, resources that support the teaching and learning process, and the expected outcomes. Additionally, school leaders will need to lead the process of data collection and disaggregation in the school so that teachers can accurately monitor student progress in between reporting periods and administrators can use this data to systematically evaluate teachers. Emphasis on instructional leadership skills undergirded with skills of critical inquiry will shape leadership dispositions toward a social justice approach. One model of critical inquiry found to be applicable to all decision making in the context of "doing what's best for all learners" is synthesized from McKenzie and Scheurich's (2004) discourse in preparation experiences:

> What are we doing? Why are we doing it? What do we value? Why do we value what we do? How are our values evident or not evident in our practice? How is what we're doing affecting all students? Is what we're doing privileging one group over another? Is what we're doing working for all students, why or why not? Are our practices transparent? Is our leadership transparent? (p. 3)

Engaging in this level of inquiry will cause students in leadership preparation programs to challenge historically held norms, values, beliefs, and practices that limit access and pose barriers to certain subgroups of students in relation to their academic success.

A classic example can be seen in the literature that documents the disproportionate numbers of minority students that are placed in special education programs. While Echevarria, Powers, and Elliott (2004) offer that identification can negatively impact self-concept, graduation, and employment, modifications to the Individuals With Disabilities Act have attempted to correct the over identification of minorities by providing services that support the pre-identification phase in addition to Response to Intervention models of service. School leaders with a social justice lens and an expertise in instructional leadership possess a fundamental understanding of patterns and practices that marginalize students of color and can thereby become advocates and change agents to improve schooling disparities.

Culturally Proficient Leadership: A Derivative of Cultural Responsiveness

The research on leadership preparation offers various mechanisms to increase cultural sensitivity, cultural knowledge and advocacy toward promising practices that make educational environments equitable for all students. While the research is rife in promoting programs that increase multicultural proficiency, cultural acculturation, and cultural responsiveness, it could be assumed that all approaches have a relatively high yield in shaping dispositions toward a socially moral and ethically just conscience. With regards to a prescription, the concept of cultural proficiency sharpens the lens toward cultural responsiveness and is endorsed for this discourse due to the nature of activism required to attain a level of proficiency, in addition to how the ideal extends toward a platform for reform that in many instances is the seat of a school leader's charge in an era of school improvement. Lindsey, Robins, and Terrell (2009) promote that "cultural proficiency is a model for shifting the culture of the school or district; is a model for individual transformation and organizational change" (p. 4). The conventions within the model are applicable to various aspects of diversity in the school environment that include culture, language, race, social class, gender, sexual orientation, in addition to the diversity within each of the subgroups as well. Grothaus et al. (2010) asserts that a necessary prerequisite in building cultural proficiency in school leaders begins with understanding one's own cultural identity in order to recognize cultural practices and characteristics in others.

From the work of Lindsey et al. (2009), four tools are promoted that enable leaders to be proactive, facilitate engagement and discourse to embrace difference, and provide a moral framework for decision making and taking action.

Tool 1—Barriers

Within any organizational setting, a privilege to one may impose a barrier on another. In an effort to move school leaders toward cultural proficiency, one needs to be cognizant of the barriers that exist to impede the process of education. Having a good understanding of the context in which decisions are made and the cultural landscape of the school is pivotal to identifying barriers for some populations or subgroups. The tool serves to increase knowledge about the three caveats that comprise the barriers to cultural proficiency, which are outlined as systems of oppression and privilege, the presumption of entitlement, and unawareness for the need to adapt (Lindsey et al., 2009).

Tool 2—Guiding Principles

In most instances when a school leader has a vision to move the school community toward a higher conscience for social justice, great efforts must be made to shape the environment so that all cultures are respected, cultural interactions are positive, and the organization as whole is moving toward cultural competence. Lindsey et al. (2009) provide guiding principles to build an organization that responds to the need for cultural equity within the school community, and outline a framework upon which policies, expectations, communication, and interactions are established.

Tool 3—The Cultural Proficiency Continuum

The cultural proficiency continuum offers a reference point for identifying where an individual or organization's actions, language, and policies are on a scale between healthy and unhealthy, and establishes ideas for responding to differences. Once an individual or organization can identify where they are on the cultural proficiency continuum, they can better target goals for improving their position and develop healthy dispositions for leading and administrating from a social justice platform.

Tool 4—The Essential Elements

The final tool provides elements that are essential for setting standards that guide values, behavior, organizational policies and practices. The essential skills include: assessing culture, valuing diversity, managing the dynamics of difference, adapting to diversity, and institutionalizing cultural knowledge.

Integrating content in the coursework and experiences that lead toward the acquisition of knowledge and application of the tools for cultural proficiency helps to build resilient leaders that have a conscience for activism and the skills for leading change. Instruction in preparation programs geared specifically toward the acquisition of these tools can be integrated into curriculum that explores systemic change and sustainability through reform. For example, a case study methods approach or action research project can be designed to gain an understanding of the barriers that exist within the school and where an organization is on the cultural proficiency continuum. Students can conduct a needs assessment on the organization and analyze the data. The results can be used as a focal point to align with the guiding principles and essential elements, which can then be integrated into school improvement initiatives. While these methods offer a targeted approach to understanding the tools, application of these conventions can be experienced at all levels, and the result is a capstone experience that moves students and school leaders further along on the social justice continuum.

Field Induction and Authentic Mentoring Experiences

Similar to the importance of redefining the selection process for school leadership that builds skills toward a social justice framework is the induction process into the field and the cogent mentoring structures that are necessary to support and maintain skill development and the application of knowledge once new principals are in position. Research suggests that the clinical experiences, if well designed, extend the skills developed and allow students the opportunity to apply knowledge gained to authentic settings (Fry, Bottoms, & O'Neill, 2005). Young (2009) highlight three arrangements of internship experiences, which include job-embedded (ideal as an immersion model of on-the-job training); detached internships, which are more prevalent and require documentation and reflection of experience; and course-embedded field experiences in which students apply information attained in a course in a supporting field experience, which makes the connection between content and application seamless. McKenzie et al. (2008) assert that students who have benefited from a social justice leadership preparation background are likely to meet resistance from districts and schools that are not supportive or actively negative toward the concept of social justice. For this reason, authentic collaboration between leadership preparation organizations and local schools and districts is vital to the entry, induction, and sustainability of effective school leaders that improve student achievement across all populations.

A catalyst for a successful internship program as well as induction into the role of a school leader is a mentoring alliance between the aspiring school leader and an expert in the field. For the large numbers of students who successfully complete the school leader certification and degree programs at Florida State University, a capstone experience has been the Mentoring Initiative in which students self-select a school leader in the field, who mentors them as they matriculate through the program. In particular, this can be useful to those who are in a program that embraces a framework for social justice, as students search to identify a mentor with a vision for equity and values that prompt activism against historically held practices that marginalize and limit access for subgroup populations. The Mentoring Initiative provides an authentic platform for problem-based learning undergirded by the theory acquired through the content and provides space for practice and reflection.

Interestingly, promising practices of leadership preparation highlighted in the research conducted by the Wallace Foundation match the discourse Florida State University's Department of Educational Leadership prescribes for social justice leadership preparation from a global perspective. They contend that a focus on recruitment and selection, instructional leadership to the end of school improvement, fieldwork integrated into coursework, and robust internships are what exemplary leadership preparation programs focus on (Darling-Hammond, LaPointe, Meyerson, Orr, & Cohen, 2007). In the end, and particularly for leadership preparation institutions with a focus on social justice, it is a matter of how to develop school leaders that can successfully transform schools and positively impact achievement for all students.

CONCLUSION

The ever-changing world and society remain in a state of evolution. Politically, economically, socially, and demographically, nothing remains the same. Therefore social justice leaders are to be responsive in finding a balance upon which the ideals of justice, respect, care and equity can be leveraged against the educational norms of mainstream America. As conceptualized by Jean-Marie et al. (2009), leadership preparation programs are embarking upon a new social order of preparing school leaders to lead from a global perspective and courageously promote the ethics of social justice. Embracing a new social order for school leadership will prove to be a delicately orchestrated masterpiece. It will necessitate robust research contributions and voices from scholars in the field, the academy revisiting the content and process of leadership preparation and its role in advancing an agenda of leadership for social justice forward, and collaborative work among coalitions such as Leadership for Social Justice (LSJ), Interstate School Leaders Licensure Consortium (ISLLC), National School Board Associations (NSBA), University Council on Educational Leadership (UCEA), and other professional organizations, all to the end of making the process, preparation, and outcome of education beneficial to those being served. The goal therein as we embrace a new social order in response to our changing society is to move leadership preparation programs as well as current and future school leaders further along the social justice continuum and toward a more perfect union of leadership facilitated through the ideal of social justice. The capstone result would be leaders who are resilient change agents who champion the call toward equity and whose actions create space and access for all students in the school community.

NOTES

1. Race to the Top, abbreviated R2T, RTTT or RTT, is a $4.35 billion United States Department of Education competition designed to spur reforms in state and local district K-12 education. It is funded by the ED Recovery Act as part of the American Recovery and Reinvestment Act of 2009 and was announced by President Barack Obama and Secretary of Education Arne Duncan on July 24, 2009. (http://www.ed.gov/category/program/race-top-fund)

REFERENCES

Amrein, A. L., & Berliner, D. C. (2002). High-stakes testing, uncertainty, and student learning. *Education Policy Analysis Archives, 10*(18). Retrieved August 20, 2011 from http://epaa.asu.edu/epaa/v10n18/

Baird, A. (1996). *Equal educational opportunity project series, Volume I.* Report by the Commission on Civil Rights, Washington, DC. Retrieved October, 2011, from http://www.eric.ed.gov:80/PDFS/ED406472.pdf

Banks, J. A. (1993). Multicultural education: Historical development, dimensions, and practice. *Review of Research in Education, 19*, 3–49.

Banks, J. A. (1994). *An introduction to multicultural education.* Boston: Allyn and Bacon.

Blackwell-Flanagan, R. M. (1996). *Fostering cultural pluralism: An in-depth case study examining how the principal of a culturally diverse middle school facilitates the process.* (Unpublished doctoral dissertation). Florida State University, Tallahassee, FL

Cambron-McCabe, N., & McCarthy, M. M. (2005). Educating school leaders for social justice. *Educational Policy, 19*(1), 201–222.

Capper, C. A., Theoharis, G., & Sebastian, J. (2006). Toward a framework for preparing leaders for social justice. *Journal of Educational Administration, 44*(3), 209–224.

Christie, P. (2005). Towards an ethics of engagement in education in global times. *Australian Journal of Education, 49*(3). Retrieved from http://www.freepatentsonline.com/article/Australian-Journal-Education/139433517.html

Darling-Hammond, L. (2007). Race inequality and educational accountability: the irony of 'No Child Left Behind.' *Race Ethnicity and Education, 10*(3), 245–260.

Darling-Hammond, L., LaPointe, M., Meyerson, D., Orr, M. T., & Cohen, C. (2007). Preparing school leaders for a changing world: Lessons from exemplary leadership development programs. Stanford, CA: Stanford University, Stanford Educational Leadership. Retrieved from http://seli.stanford.edu or http://srnleads.org

Dumais, S. A. (2002). Cultural capital, gender, and school success: The role of habitus. *Sociology of Education, 75*(1), 44–68.

Echevarria, J., Powers, K., & Elliott, J. (2004). Promising practices for curbing disproportionate representation of minority students in special education. *Issues in Teacher Education, 13*(1), 19–33.

Fry, B., Bottoms, G., & O'Neill, K. (2005). The principal internship: How can we get it right? Atlanta, GA: Southern Regional Education Board.

Graham, P. A. (1984). Schools: Cacophony about practice, silence about purpose. *Daedalus, 113*(4), 29–57.

Grothaus, T., Crum, K. S., & James, A. B. (2010). Effective leadership in a culturally diverse learning environment. *Urban Leadership Abstracts, 4*(1), 111.

Hall, M. (2011, March 9). *White house conference tackles bullying.* USA Today. Retrieved from http://www.usatoday.com/news/washington/2011-03-10-bullying10_ST_N.htm

Hallinger, P. (2003). Leading educational change: Reflections on the practice of instructional and transformational leadership. *Cambridge Journal of Education, 33*(3), 329–351.

Hemphill, F. C., & Vanneman, A. (2010). *Achievement gaps: How Hispanic and white students in public schools perform in mathematics and reading on the National Assessment of Educational Progress* (NCES 2011-459). National Center for Education Statistics, Institute of Education Sciences, U.S. Department of Education. Washington, DC.

Jean-Marie, G. (2008). Leadership for social justice: An agenda for 21st century schools. *The Educational Forum, 72*(4), 340–354.

Jean-Marie, G., Normore, A., & Brooks, J. (2009). Leadership for Social Justice: Preparing 21st Century School Leaders for a New Social Order. *Journal of Research on Leadership Education, 4*(1). Retrieved from http://ucealee.square-space.com/storage/jrle/pdf/vol4_issue1_2009/Jean_Marie_Normore%20_Brooks.pdf

Kallen, H. M. (1971). *What I believe and why—maybe: essays for the modern world.* New York: Horizon Press.

Karpinski, C. F., & Lugg, C. A. (2006). Social justice and educational administration: Mutually exclusive? *Journal of Educational Administration, 44*(3), 278–292.

Lindsey, R. B., Robins, K. N., & Terrell, R. D. (2009). *Cultural proficiency: A manual for school leaders* (3rd ed.). Thousand Oaks, CA: Corwin Press.

Lumby, J., Crow, G., & Pashiardis, P. (2008). *International handbook on the preparation and development of school leaders.* New York: Routledge.

Malin, M., & Maidment, D. (2003). Education, indigenous survival and well-being: Emerging ideas and programs. *Australian Journal of Indigenous Education, 32,* 85–100.

Marshall, C., & Oliva, M. (2010). *Leadership for social justice: Making revolutions in education* (2nd ed.). Boston: Allyn & Bacon.

McKenzie, K., & Scheurich, J. (2004, July). Position paper. Presentation conducted at the Miami University Education Summit, Oxford, OH.

McKenzie, K. B., Christman, D. E., Hernandez, F., Fierro, E., Capper, C. A., Dantley, M.,... Scheurich, J. J. (2008). From the field: A proposal for educating leaders for social justice. *Educational Administration Quarterly, 44*(1), 111–138.

Peterson, M. J., & Hittie, M. M. (2003). *Inclusive teaching: Creating effective schools for all learners.* Boston, MA: Allyn and Bacon.

Rea, P., McLaughlin, V., & Walther-Thomas, C. (2002). Outcomes for students with learning disabilities in inclusive and pullout Programs.. *Exceptional Children, 68*(2), 203–222.

Theoharis, G. (2007). Social justice educational leaders and resistance: Toward a theory of social justice leadership. *Educational Administration Quarterly, 43*(2), 221–258.

U.S. Department of Education. (2009). President Obama, U.S. Secretary of Education Duncan Announce National Competition to Advance School Reform. Washington, DC: Author. Retrieved from http://www2.ed.gov/news/pressreleases/2009/07/07242009.html

U.S. Department of Education. (2010). *Indicators of school crime and safety: 2010.* Washington, DC: Author. Retrieved from http://nces.ed.gov/programs/crimeindicators/crimeindicators2010/ind_11.asp

U.S. Department of Education. (2007). *The nation's report card: Reading 2007* (NCES 2007—496). Washington, DC: Author. Retrieved from http://webmail2.fsu.edu/attach/Latino_FactSheet.pdf?sid=&mbox=INBOX&uid=32953&number=2&filename=Latino_FactSheet.pdf.

Villegas, A. M. (1991). *Culturally responsive pedagogy for the 1990s and beyond: Trends and issues paper no. 6.* Washington, DC: ERIC Clearinghouse on Teacher Education. Retrieved from http://search.proquest.com/docview/62936223?accountid=4840

Villegas, A. M., & Lucas, T. (2002). Preparing culturally responsive teachers: Re-thinking the curriculum. *Journal of Teacher Education, 53,* 20.

Young, M. D. (2009). *Handbook of research on the education of school leaders.* New York, NY: Routledge.

Zambrana, R. E., & Zoppi, I. M. (2002). Latina students: Translating cultural wealth into social capital to improve academic success. In D. de Anda (Ed.), *Social work with multicultural youth* (pp. 33–54). New York, NY: Hathworth Press.

CHAPTER 18

NARRATIVE INQUIRY AS A CULTURALLY RELEVANT LEADERSHIP STRATEGY FOR SOCIAL JUSTICE

Alexandre Ilungu Muzaliwa and Mary E. Gardiner

INTRODUCTION

As one of the constellation of approaches to leadership for social justice—global, in other words—inclusive leadership is concerned first and foremost with inclusion in its processes as well as the ends to which it strives. It provides another lens to help those concerned with social justice leadership recognize social injustice in communities and schools and do something about it. We explore what it means to be inclusive school leaders through the lens of social justice discourse that focuses on instructional and supervisory approaches in preparing future school leaders. We want to push the envelope of inclusive leadership practice. The purpose of this chapter is to reveal how, through the development of personal narratives and inquiry, educators were assisted in becoming not only competent in multicultural diversity, but committed to social justice leadership. We report findings from a recent study (Muzaliwa, 2011) illustrating how narratives can be

Social Justice Leadership for a Global World, pages 325–343
Copyright © 2012 by Information Age Publishing

employed to strengthen social justice leadership for teachers and their coaches, mentors, and supervisors.

Educational changes of the 21st century include globalization, changing demographics in schools, and an increased need for social justice in educational leadership (Bogotch 2002, 2005; Bogotch, Beachum, Blount, Brooks & English, 2008; Cochran-Smith, 2004; Marshall & Oliva, 2010; Shoho, 2006). Research indicates that social justice is an essential and continuously relevant topic that should be infused into every aspect of leadership preparation (Bogotch, 2005). Given the demand for schools to prepare children and communities for participation in a multicultural, multiethnic, multi-religious, and a multinational society (Bennett, 2001; Marshall & Oliva, 2010), the role of social justice leadership has become increasingly important.

Today, in the U.S. it is estimated that one out of every three students enrolled in elementary and secondary schools is from a racial or ethnic minority background, one in seven children between the age of five and 17 speaks a language other than English, and one in five children younger than 18 lives in poverty (Bell, 2010; Marshall & Oliva, 2010; Noguera, 2010; U.S. Census Bureau, 2010). Within these changing demographics are disparities in educational outcomes for students who do not have certain advantages related to race, socioeconomic status, language, religion, and culture (Cochran-Smith, 2004; Gay, 1997; Spring, 2001). Diversity among educators within American schools has not kept pace with the rapid growth of minority student populations. White educators remain in the majority within the educational setting (Anderson, 2006; Banks, 2008, 2010; Noguera, 2010) despite calls for recruiting, mentoring and retaining culturally diverse administrators (Gardiner, Enomoto & Grogan, 2000). A growing concern is whether school leaders are prepared to create schools that advocate for education that advances all children (Brooks, 2008; Spring, 2001). Furthermore, studies suggest that leadership preparation programs need to better prepare school leaders to promote a deeper understanding of social justice, democracy, diversity, and equity (Lugg, 2003; Marshall & Oliva, 2010; Young & Mountford, 2006).

In this chapter we examine various considerations as suggested in the literature regarding whether leadership preparation programs are capable of preparing school leaders to think globally and act courageously for social justice. We advocate for a meaningful integration of local and global issues, imperatives, and a concepts approach to leadership preparation, asserting that stories are essential to human experience. Educational supervisors can benefit from using narratives as an instructional and supervisory approach for social justice.

DEFINING LEADERSHIP FOR SOCIAL JUSTICE

In considering the emergence of social justice in the educational field, two strands categorize the paradigmatic shift from indifference or ignorance toward issues of social justice by practitioners and scholars to an embracement of issues. Karpinski and Lugg (2006) drew from the historical work of other researchers to examine the shift of traditional leadership preparation to the emergence of social justice in the field. Similarly, Kumashiro (2004) examined scholarship such as Murphy and Vriesenga (2004), who have debated what makes up the knowledge base of educational administration. They examined other scholarship such as Dantley and Tillman (2006), Gerwitz (1998), Grogan (1999), Larson & Murtadha (2002), and Marshall (2004) to provide an analysis of the scholarship for social justice. We conducted further review of the literature, which included Brooks and Miles' (2008) retrospective on intellectual zeitgeist in educational leadership, English's (2005) handbook of educational leadership, Murphy's (2006) and Murphy and Vriesenga's (2006) examinations of education of school leaders through historical context, Marshall and Oliva's (2010) work on leadership for social justice, and Normore's (2008) analysis of leadership, social justice, equity and excellence. But first, we discuss the changing face of teacher supervision in educational leadership preparation.

Educational Supervision and its Changing Face

Inquiry into whether or not a well-supervised educator was a satisfied teacher was the focus of Danielson's (2000) study that examined the elements of teacher supervision and components of teacher satisfaction that could be affected by administrators. Danielson (2001) suggested that educators have discovered that a well-designed evaluation system improves practices and ensures quality of teaching. Sustaining a school culture in which effective evaluation is encouraged focuses teachers on their own professional growth (Beall, 1999). The push for educator quality grew out of the school reform movements that emphasized increasing student achievement (Danielson, 2001). Publication of *A Nation at Risk* (The National Commission on Teaching, 1993) and *Securing America's Future* (NAFSA, 2003), propelled the concepts of teacher quality and student achievement—particularly for low income and first generation college students—to the forefront of many school districts' and universities' educational policy agendas.

According to Holland and Adams (2010), supervision has traditionally been an activity that placed educators in a relatively passive role. Even though supervisions emphasized educators' abilities to individualize instruction, promote engaged learning, and effectively link standards to instruction, many educator supervision systems continued to rely on anachronistic annual observations. Administrators conducted an observation, wrote a review of the observation, and conducted pre- and post-observation conferences to provide feedback based on their own perception of the observation, with educators documenting non-observable aspects of their practice. Marshall (2004) suggested that observations were conducted too seldom to provide suggestions that could be tried and then reevaluated by both teacher and supervisor.

Iwanicki (2001) found as teaching and learning evolved and became more complex, new models of educator supervision placed the educators in a more active, participative role. New approaches to educator supervision integrated classroom observation and teacher professional development. Educator evaluation methods also encouraged teachers to engage in self-directed professional activities by submitting portfolios and documents that illustrated collaborative events or inquiry-based approaches directly impacting student achievement. Brandt (1996) posed that the principal served as partner, guiding the teacher toward continuous development and improvement. Administrators began to realize that they could not expect educators to develop alternative strategies for teaching and assessing students and then continue to evaluate teachers as they were fifty years ago. Darling-Hammond's research (1990) emphasized that traditional supervision in the rigid, bureaucratically administrated school had not succeeded in implanting necessary school reform. Schools using collective and collaborative problem-solving strategies, valuing the input from people affected by decisions made in the school were successful in improving educator competence and commitment (Danielson, 2000).

Current trends in educator supervision suggest a shift in the primary purpose of teacher supervision from addressing only school district needs to include more collaborative processes focused on professional development (Danielson, 2007; Glatthorn, 1997). It is imperative that educator supervision be conducted fairly to determine the areas where further development and improvement of skills are needed. Teacher supervision could provide a vital step toward providing quality instruction for all students (Beall, 1999) that is culturally relevant (Ladson-Billings & Tate, 1995). The area in which both teachers and administrators lack knowledge and background in the U.S. is diversity and social justice awareness, hence, the need for social justice leadership.

In today's global village (diverse society), leadership preparation programs are now challenged to provide curricula that shed light on and interrogate notions of social justice, democracy, equity and diversity (Evans, 2007; Hafner, 2005; Young & Mountford, 2006). Among the challenges identified in the leadership preparation literature for meeting new demands are: a need for district financial commitment for social justice leadership development programs that will likely draw more candidates to fill the diminishing pipeline for school leadership positions (Jackson & Kelley, 2002); a need to select texts and articles in educational leadership curricula that adequately address issues of how race, ethnicity, gender, socioeconomic status, and other characteristics create a climate that places some students at an educational disadvantage (Beyer & Apple, 1988; Furman & Gruenewald, 2004); a need to adequately prepare educational leaders who will have experiences that will affect their ability and desire to promote and practice social justice leadership (Furman & Shields, 2005; Jean-Marie, 2008; Scheurich & Skrla, 2003; Shields, 2003); a misconception that pre-service training or out-of-district in-service programs will provide aspiring school leaders with all they need to know about effective leadership in a school district; and a need for districts and universities to forge leadership development partnerships to ensure that similar goals and objectives are met with a non-redundant curriculum (Berry, 2001). Narrative inquiry as a strategy holds promise to teach administrators and other school leaders how to support social justice and practice culturally relevant supervision and leadership.

UTILIZING NARRATIVE INQUIRY FOR SOCIAL JUSTICE

Narrative inquiry is a tool for educators to report experiences (Ball, 2002; Cai, 2005; Chavez-Chavez, 1999; Conle, 2003; Gay, 2002, 2004; Phillion, 2002; Phillips, 1997, 1999). Narrative inquiry relies on experience and story to establish research rigor (Bullough & Pinnegar, 2001; Clandinin & Connelly, 2000; Genereux & McKeough, 2007; Reisman, 1993). In the study reported here (Muzaliwa, 2011), the constructs of diversity, democracy, and equity were utilized to examine how personal narratives were developed using narrative instructional methods. Stories transcend borders, languages, race, religions, socio-economic backgrounds and other diversities, and help to eradicate fear of others. Before knowing his/her students, an educator should know him/herself first. Narratives have an integral role for equity in society (Ah Nee-Benham & Cooper, 1998; Banks, 2010; Freire, 1998; Nieto, 2009, 2010; Phillion, 2002; Terrell & Lindsey, 2009; Zeichner & Liston, 1996).

Study Methodology

The study utilized narrative inquiry to develop mindful leaders through research with practicing educators in a school setting. Narrative inquiry is a form of research or a way of conducting and producing research, particularly on school practice, because what happens in a school classroom is a social and cultural construction and can be transformative. Administrators, teachers and students become co-authors of stories about their own educational and life experience and their voices are heard and given legitimate recognition.

In particular, we selected a school district in Idaho that was characterized by educators who were predominantly classified as ethnically "white," thus bringing to the classroom environment their personal cultural backgrounds. The goal of this study was to provide secondary school educators and their principals with valuable information concerning cultural customs, sensitivities, and beliefs of diverse ethnic groups prevalent in this particular school district. The intent was that educators would become aware of cultural contexts that shape not only their culture, but also their students' way of learning (Banks, 2010; Nieto & Bode, 2008; Noguera, 2010). Specifically, in this chapter, we completed an in-depth analysis of one narrative to show how narrative can support social justice leadership development.

The study was designed so that educators can take the lead in providing environments that accept multicultural dialogue and advocate for social justice for all in a classroom, school, or school district. An educator's knowledge must be enhanced by understandings of race, ethnicity, language, social class, and other diversities so that they might be able to see the correlation between these issues and how they influence a student's behavior and success. Administrators who rise from the ranks of teachers have to understand how children develop ideas and attitudes toward people different from themselves. They, too, must research other cultures and lifestyles. Then, and only then, can they help create environments in which children of all cultures and lifestyles feel welcomed, appreciated, valued and respected.

The setting for this study was an urban area of Treasure Valley, Idaho. Two high schools and one middle school were chosen for the project. The schools were chosen because of their access to the researcher, their fit with selection criteria for participants, and their acceptance to participate in the study. Three public school educators were studied in depth through narrative inquiry utilizing interviews, observations, journals, and others artifacts over the course of a school year. Educators were chosen because their graduate studies included at least one course in diversity, and they were viewed by their principals as advocates for social justice. For collection and analysis of data, a combination of narrative inquiry and case study guided the research methods. Issues of race, class, sexual orientation, disability, and other historically marginalizing factors central to social justice and diversity advocacy, teaching and leading practice, and vision were revealed. Educators discussed a critical, transformational incident that led to their commitment and ongoing work in social justice leadership in public secondary schools. What follows below is one story as shared by a teacher, Amanda.

In addition, we conducted a content analysis (Koerin, 2003) on identifiers such as narrative inquiry, leadership preparation, democracy, diversity, equity, social justice, race, gender, culture, ethics, global education, oppression, curricula, social change, social development, social context, and constructivism. The abstracts from the scholarship were reviewed to narrow the focus on issues that dealt specifically with narrative inquiry, leadership preparation, social justice, supervision, culturally relevant curriculum, and strategies for connecting social justice leadership in local, national and global contexts.

FINDINGS

Understanding School Leadership in Multiple Contexts

The findings revealed that narrative inquiry supported a deepening of the participants' understanding of social justice and influenced their ideas about teaching and leading. Narrative inquiry was revealed as both an instructional method for teaching and learning, a supervisory tool for culturally relevant supervision, and an exemplary research method for school leaders seeking to lead for social justice. Narrative inquiry enabled educators to realize their potential as educators and to connect with their diverse students and families. Several themes emerged through the analysis of the narratives:

1. *Teaching Effectiveness.* Through narrative inquiry teachers became aware of ways to assist immigrant and refugee students;
2. *Self Knowledge.* Educators in the study gained self-confidence by exposing themselves to different cultural backgrounds than theirs through interaction with the investigators and the narrative inquiry methodology;
3. *Social Justice Agency.* Educators gained a critical understanding of how they themselves are important agents of change and how their cultural work helps the world.

Drawing upon Muzaliwa's (2011) larger study, we demonstrate the power of narratives by illustrating these three concepts through an abbreviated version of the transformational journey of one educator, whom we will call Amanda.

Amanda's Story. "I can remember the first day Tido walked into my classroom nine years ago as if it were yesterday. I can still feel the fast beating of my heart and the sudden sense of fear as the slender, brown-eyed, dark-haired, handsome young man, a native of San Salvador, walked into my English Language Learner (ESL then) class. I was not surprised by my reaction to him as he made his way to the back of the room and sat down. I had been dreading his arrival all day and when he finally showed up, I immediately felt intimidated and inadequate. Tido, you see, had made it into my high school's ever-so-handy *warning list*. Most educators have encountered this unwritten list at one time or another in their educational careers; it often dominates conversation in the staff lounge. Any child who has the misfortune of being listed, because of his race or ethnicity, is eternally damned in the eyes of school administrators and teachers. Tido was not only unfortunate enough to be on the list; he was at the top. He had been in some fights, he'd been disrespectful to some teachers, harassed some students, and had been painfully honest with an administrator. So his reputation as a troublemaker had preceded him into my classroom.

Although I tried in those first few weeks to maintain my power, as a teacher, over him and let him know who was in charge, something about him left me completely dumbfounded. I couldn't put my finger on it at the time, but Tido was definitely his own person. Maybe, it was the way he sat at his desk: slouched, rolling his eyes, talking to other students and yawning occasionally during the hour. I resented the fact that I couldn't be as effective in drilling and killing my students with insignificant facts and figures because Tido disrupted my concentration, my focus. '*How dare he!*' I thought to myself. It was hard for me to look him in the eye, so I hovered over him, trying my best to intimidate him, just as he was intimidating me. I wanted desperately for him to drop or to be removed from my class, or to do something completely outside the norm so that I could force him to leave.

I didn't realize it at the same time, but my attitude toward Tido reflected our negative feelings some administrators, teachers and students had toward the Latinos/Hispanics and African-Americans who attended our schools in Southeast Idaho. Any person with a bit of common sense could feel the racial hostility that wafted through the hallways and classrooms of our [predominantly white] high schools. It was obvious to everyone, students and staff alike, what areas of the school were reserved for the white students, who constituted 70 percent of the student body, and what areas had been conquered by the students of color, mostly Latinos/Hispanics, mostly the sons and daughters of hardworking migrant farm-workers who moved to this small town to labor in the fields with hope of gaining a better life. Hardly ever, if at all, did these groups mix socially. Crossing into other group's territory was risked only by those students who were brave and strong enough to survive stares, comments and, occasionally, physical abuse, all endured in an attempt to take a shortcut to a destination.

Sadly, little, if anything at all, was ever done to end the school's problem of segregation. Maybe it was because it was easier for us adults to look the other way than to confront head on the issue of this magnitude. Maybe it was unwillingness of the members of the dominant culture to share decision making that could have affected their power. I think, however, that it was the lack of knowledge, respect and appreciation for a different culture that allowed segregation to continue. Some administrators and teachers would complain that the immigrant kids had no respect for the school because they wouldn't stand up when the school song was sung during assemblies. They would complain about having to teach students who didn't speak English. One teacher went so far as to give-after school detentions to students who spoke Spanish as a way of "accelerating" the pace at which they were learning English and keeping them in their place. There were complaints about Latino students' style of clothing, their mannerisms, their low-slung cars, and much more.

Never, however, were there any suggestions about what could be done to make the Latino students feel more welcomed in our school community. Never was there any action taken to reduce the disproportionate numbers of Latino/Hispanic students who were disciplined in comparison to white students. Looking back, I can see why the Latino/Hispanic students refused to stand up during the singing of the school song; they had no ownership of it. In fact, the song was offensive to them because it represented a place that made them feel inferior and unwanted. Consequently, many of our Latino students either did the minimum to get by and graduate, or they dropped out. In a weird way, I think the kids who dropped out were the luckier ones, because the ones who stayed in school traded their own souls for a piece of paper.

As a new teacher trying to fit in and make an impression, it never occurred to me to question the situation. Tido was not afraid to rock the boat. He did not want to be seen as less than what he was: a unique individual who wanted to learn, participate and have a voice in his own education, just like many of the white kids. Finally, one day, Tido gave me the excuse to ask for his removal from my classroom for which I had been praying. He confronted me directly during a dull verb conjugation lesson.

'*What is the point of this? Is this going to teach me how to speak English better?*' He asked with perfect sarcasm in his voice.

'*Tido,*' I said in my most dictatorial tone, '*When you get your degree, you can teach your classes however you like. Until then, I recommend that you pay attention and learn something.*'

Needless to say, Tido did not settle for my ludicrous response, and an ugly confrontation ensued. The bell finally saved me. Although my entire body was trembling as though freezing snow had just enveloped me, I managed to fill out a disciplinary slip and walk it to the assistant principal's office, tears welling up in my eyes. This was my first and last confrontation with Tido.

The Assistant Principal ordered Tido back to my class and made him serve some after-school detentions with me. During those hours we spent together, Tido and I began to talk. The more we talked, the more comfortable we became with each other. Tido shared with me his struggles both in and out of the school; he told me about his girlfriend back in El Salvador, helped me around my classroom and asked me for help when his schoolwork got too difficult. I discovered that Tido was a gifted artist when he volunteered to paint a landscape that I needed for a project in one of my master's degree classes. I ultimately had the pleasure of getting to know his family. It was then

I found the story inside this incredibly intelligent, talented and passionate young man.

Tido was a third oldest son in a family of ten children, five boys and five girls. After leaving El Salvador, his family made their way to Colorado to work in the fields as migrants. One day his father suffered a terrible car accident that left him paralyzed and unable to work. The responsibility of financially supporting the family of twelve had been handed over to the three oldest Garcia boys. At the age of fifteen, Tido inherited the role most teenagers never have to experience.

When the family moved to a small town in southeast Idaho, Tido decided that he wanted better opportunities in life and enrolled in high school. Although he spoke very little English, he was determined to get an education and graduate from high school. To this day, I don't know how he ever made it through. Not only did Tido attend school full-time, but he also worked full-time in a potato factory. His determination to get an education stemmed from his having to live in the depths of miserable poverty that those who have been blessed with privilege will never truly understand. The Garcia family lived in a single-wide, two-bedroom trailer that sometimes didn't have running water or heat. Often they could barely afford to put food on the table.

During the three years that Tido was a student at my high school, I learned some of life's most valuable lessons from my interactions with him. He taught me about compassion, empathy, courage, humility, dignity, sacrifice, perseverance, hope, and love. I taught Tido how to survive in a school with its own soldiers of oppression, administrators, teachers and students who were always ready to smash his self-esteem and undercut his determination to fight for what was rightfully his: an equitable education and a chance to succeed. With my help, Tido was able to stay away from fights that provoked others to make racial slurs, he was able to maintain his composure with teachers who obviously did not welcome him into their classrooms, and he was able to turn the anger living inside him into a positive reflection on his personal journey that helped him become more secure with his own roots and dignity.

Looking back, I now understand more clearly why I was originally intimidated by Tido. He was a constant reminder that I myself was not comfortable in my own skin, that I had not yet earned the honored title of teacher. I still feel guilty when I recall the main reason I entered the master's program in bilingual education. The possibility I might learn something that would help my students was not an expectation. Having a piece of paper that said I had a master's degree would guarantee me a significant pay raise. I even fantasized about ways to spend the extra money. Sadly, I know I was not alone in letting the thought of monetary reward drive my pursuit of higher education. I had become yet another educational foot soldier who obediently kept students in their allotted places, both academically and socially. I kept silent about the injustices I witnessed in order to keep the peace and hold onto my job. I will never forgive myself for not being more vocal about the time a teacher physically threatened a Latino boy and was merely slapped on the hand in response, or the many times another teacher spoke derogatorily about the Latino families in the community, or the times the students leveled the guns of racism at one another. Like a robot, I was automatically following a leader who presented himself as a proponent of multicultural education, not because he truly cared about the students, but because it looked good on his resume. An annual multicultural summit was his claim of fame; the rest of the year, his inappropriate comments at faculty meetings about certain children, his selective open-door policy and his inability to acknowledge the accomplishments of students told the real story about his beliefs.

Unfortunately, we lost many beautiful children during my years at this high school. I wonder how many budding authors I helped to kill and bury alongside their stories. How many students like Tido wanted school to be a place of compassion, caring, love and acceptance, where everyone worked and played together as a true community? How many wanted school to be a place where everyone's feelings and experiences were valued rather than discounted? How many wanted school to be a truly democratic society that balanced out opportunities for everyone, regardless of skin color, language, religion and gender? I am able to raise these questions today partly because of my friendship with Tido . . . a life-changing experience that left me with a deeper understanding of what education should be . . . I am thankful that I found the story of Tido. My last encounter with him, like my first, brought tears to my eyes. It was the day he showed me his high school diploma. Today, Tido works to help support his family and has dreams of going to college. I am proud to honor his voice and our story.

In reading their story, it becomes clear how Amanda became transformed and was able to realize her potential as an advocate for social justice. Through a deeply personal and reflective search of her own values and attitudes, as well as a reframing of her beliefs about teaching, she learned to become a more effective teacher. Time spent with Tido and his family enabled her to engage with those who share a different cultural background, thus supporting a new level of cultural understanding of others as well as her own cultural self-knowledge. Her advocacy and support for Tido during his remaining years at the school surfaced as opportunities to see herself as an agent of change, an advocate for social justice for Tido and all students in her high school. The study's findings revealed that through the process of telling their stories and bringing new meaning to their own beliefs and behaviors, narrative inquiry supported a deepening of the participants' understanding of social justice and influenced their ideas about teaching and leading. Amanda's story of Tido is illustrative of the power of narratives, and readers are referred to the completed study for the transformative stories of other educators (Muzaliwa, 2011).

Through stories, each participant educator in the study became a "transformative intellectual" (Giroux, 1985) describing the journey and struggle in life that led him/her to become involved in activism and advocacy for social justice in his/her classroom, school and community. They understood the power and impact of narratives in leading and on teaching their students. For this reason, as educational leaders, supervisors and teachers, they could no longer remain silent about issues of discrimination, segregation, and injustice, and they became effective with their students.

Implications for Educational Leadership Preparation

Increased attention given to social justice brings to the fore a focus on the moral purposes of leadership in schools and how to achieve these purposes (Furman, 2002). Scholars of globalism and inclusive education have expanded the notion of exclusion and inclusion beyond differently-abled to encompass other axes of dis/advantage such as age, race, class, gender, and sexual identity (Boscardin & Jacobson, 1997; Dei et al., 2000; Riley & Rustique-Forester, 2002). The school principal has a key role in leading for inclusion and asserting multicultural and social justice leadership (Bailey & duPleiss, 1997; Gardiner, Canfield-Davis & Anderson, 2009; Gardiner & Enomoto, 2006; Keyes, Hanley-Maxwell, & Capper, 1999). Inequality persists and students are being excluded from learning processes and activities (Hondo, Gardiner & Sapien, 2008; Ogbu, 1994; Paquette, 1991). These studies, and Amanda's transformative journey as a teacher recounted here, are important because they draw attention to exclusion and inclusion in education. Stories help us understand the ways in which students are excluded, the patterns that this process follows, and the benefits that accompany globalism/inclusion. Social justice cannot be achieved when students and/or their parents are excluded from key educational processes, as Tido was, labeled as an outcast or "troublemaker" in his school. Leadership and a new culturally relevant supervision that emphasizes teaching and leading for diversity and social justice through narrative inquiry can provide us with a way to work toward globalism/inclusion.

Educational leaders themselves should first be aware of and understand differences among cultures, especially those aspects that would impact students and the learning environment. They themselves should be willing and prepared to work with students from backgrounds different from their own. "For, indeed, if all students don't succeed, we fail to meet the democratic ideals, that of providing opportunities to all students to be educated to their fullest potential and thus the very purpose of schooling itself" (Delpit, 1995, p. 2).

Our study, a narrative inquiry, provides a powerful example to support Bredeson (2004) and Young and Mountford's (2006) assertions that there needs to be preparation programs seeking to infuse these issues in their programs of study within the next decade. Cutting edge leadership preparation programs will "emphasize issues of diversity, ethics, and equity, and utilize transformational learning to train leaders who will be better able to advance social justice leadership in their schools and districts as well as in their communities and society at large" (Young & Mountford, 2006, p. 265). In considering culturally relevant curricular and supervision revisions to orient aspiring leaders, consideration must also be given to student resistance to transformational learning around issues of diversity and social justice (Young & Mountford, 2006; Hoff, Yoder, & Hoff, 2006). Preparation programs must consider that when promoting diversity it can be more daunting when the population of potential leaders and their own experiences are themselves homogeneous (Hoff et al., 2006). Many leaders have few opportunities to cross school boundaries and form close linkages with surrounding communities in porous relationships (Furman & Shields, 2005). The need exists to infuse curricula with multiple perspectives to broaden aspiring leaders' experiences beyond their familiarity or limited to their current school setting (Hafner, 2005). Narrative inquiry with educators can be instrumental for teachers seeking professional growth and for school administrators charged with developing and supervising educators.

Given multiculturalism and globalization, there is a need for a better understanding of school leadership in multiple contexts (Dimmock & Walker, 2005). Infusing culture and diversity into educational leadership seeks to inform how practitioner-leaders come to understand their immediate contexts better, while appreciating the contextual differences with their counterparts elsewhere (Dimmock & Walker, 2005). This is a challenge to university educators in educational leadership with which narrative inquiry can assist. As Amanda's story has shown, professors need to reexamine how aspiring leaders are prepared to address the complexity of culture and schooling (Allen, 2006). Theoretically, this will result in developing mindful leaders (Langer, 1989), a critical task for leadership preparation programs (Allen, 2006; Hoff et al., 2006).

In order to prepare leaders to meet social justice leadership responsibilities, university programs must recognize they are in a key position to impact the practices and behaviors of future school leaders (Black & Murtadha, 2007; Hoff et al., 2006). Educators who prepare school leaders must question how well they are cultivating revolutionary educational leaders (Kezar & Carducci, 2007) to embrace social responsibility for creating better schools and better educated students, serving the public and global good. Our study informs the prior studies by illustrating the power of narrative inquiry for culturally relevant supervision for social justice.

CONCLUSION

Students like Amanda who are practicing educators can be guided to reframe the issues surrounding education and develop skills in exploring how they think about schools, as well as cultivating in themselves a more insightful understanding of social justice, diversity, democracy and equity. Culturally relevant supervision begins and ends with personal relationships and connectivity through personal stories. By getting to know diverse others, nurturing and listening deeply to their stories, we learn a great deal about ourselves and our common humanity which is essential for leadership. To respond to the needs of students, both teachers and administrators have the obligation to reflect on themselves to better understand who they are. By so doing, educators put down their traditional lens and put on the new ones through which they see students in a different way. The new way allows for empathizing, understanding, and caring for students. We can no longer afford to lose students, faculty and staff. The achievement of all students, particularly the underrepresented, lies at the heart of understanding social justice leadership. This was the key for Amanda and is the key for bringing about a more humane and inclusive educational leadership and supervision. Culturally relevant supervision is directed towards the ultimate vision of serving an ethic of life, for all.

REFERENCES

Ah Nee-Benham, M., & Cooper, K. (1998). *Let my spirit soar: Narratives of diverse women in school leadership.* Thousand Oaks, CA: Corwin Press.

Allen, A. (2006). The moral life of schools revisited: Preparing educational leaders to build a new social order for social justice and democratic community. *International Journal of Urban Educational Leadership, 1,* 1–13.

Anderson, K. (2006). *Teacher communication with students from different backgrounds: An ethnographic study.* (Unpublished doctoral dissertation). Moscow, ID: University of Idaho.

Bailey, J., & du Plessis, D. (1997). Understanding principals' attitude toward inclusive schooling. *Journal of Educational Administration, 35*(5), 428–438.

Ball, H. (2002). Subversive materials: Quilts as social text. *The Alberta Journal of Educational Research, 3,* 10–39.

Banks, J. (2008). *An introduction to multicultural education.* New York, NY: Pearson.

Banks, J. (2010). *The Routledge international companion to multicultural education.* Boston, MA: Pearson.

Beall, J. (1999). On evaluation and professional development. *Independent school 59*(1), 72–79.

Bell, A. L. (2010). *Storytelling for social justice: Connecting narrative and the arts in anti-racist teaching.* London, UK: Routledge.

Bennett, C. (2001). Genres of research in multicultural education. *Review of Educational Research, 71*(2), 171–217.

Berry, B. (2001). No shortcuts to preparing good teachers. *Education Leadership, 58*(8), 32–36.

Beyer, L., & Apple, M. (1988). *The curriculum: Problems, politics and possibilities.* Albany: SUNY Press.

Black, W., & Murtadha, K. (2007). Toward a signature pedagogy in educational leadership preparation and program assessment. *Journal of Research on Leadership Education.* Retrieved April 12, 2011, from http://www.ucea.org/JRLE/pdfv012/BlackMurtadha%20PDF.pdf

Bogotch, I. (2002). Leadership for social just schooling: More substance and less style in high-risk, low-trust times. *Journal of school leadership, 12,* 198–222.

Bogotch, I. (2005, November). Social justice as an educational construct: Problems and possibilities. Paper presented at the annual meeting of the University Council of Educational Administration, Nashville, TN.

Bogotch, I., Beachum, F., Blount, J., Brooks, J., & English, F. (2008). *Radicalizing educational leadership: toward a theory of social justice.* Netherlands: Sense.

Boscardin, M., & Jacobson, S. (1997). The inclusive school: Integrating diversity and solidarity through community-based management. *Journal of Educational Administration, 35*(5), 466–476.

Brandt, R. (1996). On a new direction of teacher evaluation: A conversation with Tom McGreal. *Educational Leadership, 53*(6), 30–33.

Bredeson, P. (2004). Creating spaces for the development of democratic school leaders: A case of program redesign in the United States. *Journal of educational Administration, 42*(6), 708–723.

Brooks, J. (2008). Freedom and justice: Conceptual and empirical possibilities for the study and practice of educational leadership. In I. Bogotch, F. Beachum, J. Blount, J. Brooks, & F. English (Eds.), *Radicalizing educational leadership: Toward a theory of social justice* (pp. 61–78). Netherlands: Sense.

Brooks, J., & Miles, M. (2008). From scientific management to social justice and back again? Pedagogical shifts in educational leadership. In A. H. Normore (Ed.), *Leadership for social justice: Promoting equity and excellence through inquiry and reflective practice* (pp. 99–114). Charlotte, NC: Information Age.

Bullough, R., & Pinnegar, S. (2001).Guidelines for quality in autobiographical forms of self study research. *Educational Research, 30*(3), 13–21.

Cai, B. (2005). Mythic narratives as rhetorical vehicle for transforming gender inequality and racial justice. *Texas Speech Communication Journal, 29*(2), 79–90.

Chavez-Chavez, R. (1999). W9R)i(t/d)ing on the border: Reading our borderscape of social justice. *Theory and Research in Social Education Journal, 27*(2), 248–272.

Clandinin, J., & Connelly, F. (2000). *Narrative inquiry: Experience and story in qualitative research.* San Francisco, CA: Jossey-Bass Publishers.

Cochran-Smith, M. (2004). *Walking the road: Race, diversity, and social justice in teaching education.* New York: Teacher College, Columbia University.

Conle, C. (2003). An anatomy of narrative curricula. *Educational Researcher, 32*(3), 3–15.

Danielson, C. (2000). *Teacher evaluation: To enhance professional practice.* New York, NY: Association for Supervision and Curriculum Development.

Danielson, C. (2001). New trends in teacher evaluation. *Educational Leadership, 58*(5), 12–15.

Danielson, C. (2007). *Enhancing professional practice: A framework for teaching* (2nd ed.). Alexandria, VA: Association for Supervision and Curriculum Development.

Dantley, M., & Tillman, L. (2006). Social justice and moral transformative leadership. In C. Marshall & M. Oliva (Eds.), *Leadership for social justice: Making revolutions in education,* (pp. 16–30). New York, NY: Pearson.

Darling-Hammond, L. (1990). Teacher evaluation in transition: Emerging roles and evolving methods. In J. Millman, & L. Darling-Hammond (Eds.), *The new handbook of teacher evaluation assessing elementary and secondary schools teachers* (pp. 17–32). Newbury Park, CA: Corwin Press, Inc.

Dei, G., James, I. M., Karumanchery, L. L., James-Wilson, S., & Zine, J. (2000). *Removing the margins: The challenges and possibilities of inclusive schooling.* Toronto: Canadian Scholar's Press.

Delpit, L. (1995). *Others people children: Cultural conflict in the classroom.* Boston, MA: New Press.

Dimmock, C., & Walker, A. (2005). *Educational leadership: Culture and diversity.* Thousand Oaks, CA: Sage.

English, F. (2005). *The Sage handbook of educational leadership: Advances in theory, research and practice.* Thousand Oaks , CA: Sage.

Evans, A. (2007). Horton, Highlander, and leadership: Lessons for preparing educational leaders for social justice. *Journal of School Leadership, 17,* 250–275.

Freire, P. (1998). *Teachers as cultural workers: Letters to those who dare to teach.* Boulder, CO: Westview Press.

Furman, G. (2002). *School as community: From promise to practice.* Albany: State University of New York.

Furman, G. (2012). Social justice leadership as praxis: Developing capacities through preparation programs. *Educational Administration Quarterly, 48*(2), 191–229.

Furman, G., & Gruenewald, D. (2004). Expanding the landscape of social justice: A critical ecological analysis. *Educational Administration Quarterly, 40*(1), 47–76.

Furman, G., & Shields, C. (2005). How can educational leaders promote and support social justice and democratic community in schools? In W. A. Firestone & C. Riehl (Eds.), *A new agenda for educational leadership* (pp. 119–137). New York, NY: Teachers College.

Gardiner, M., Canfield-Davis, K., & Anderson, K. (2009). Urban school principals and the 'No Child Left Behind' Act. *Urban Review, 41,* 141–160.

Gardiner, M., & Enomoto, E. (2006). Urban school principals and their role as multicultural leaders. *Urban Education, 41*(6), 1–25.

Gardiner, M., Enomoto, E., & Grogan, M. (2000). *Coloring outside the lines: Mentoring women into school leadership.* Albany, NY: SUNY Press.

Gay, G. (1997). Multicultural infusion in teacher education: Foundations and applications, *Peabody Journal of Education, 72*(1), 150–177.

Gay, G. (2002). Preparing for culturally responsive teaching. *Journal of Teacher Education, 53*(2), 106–116.

Gay, G. (2004). Beyond Brown: Promoting equality through multicultural education. *Journal of Curriculum and Supervision, 9*(4), 193–216.

Genereux, R., & McKeough, A. (2007). Developing narrative interpretation: structural and content analyses. *British Journal of Educational Psychology. 77,* 849–872.

Gerwitz, S. (1998). Conceptualizing social justice in education: Mapping the territory. *Journal of Education Policy, 13*(4), 469–484.

Giroux, H. (1985). Teachers as transformative intellectuals. *Social Education, 49,* 376–379.

Glatthorn, A. (1997). *Differentiated supervision.* Arlington, VA: Association for Supervision and Curriculum Development.

Grogan, W. (1999). Equity, equality issues of gender, race and class. *Educational Administration Quarterly, 38*(2), 233–256.

Hafner, M. (2005). Teaching strategies for developing leaders for social justice. In C. Marshall & M. Oliva (Eds.), *Leadership for social justice: Making revolutions in Education,* (pp. 167–193). Boston, MA: Pearson.

Hoff, D., Yoder, N., & Hoff, P. (2006). Preparing educational leaders to embrace the public in schools. *Journal of Educational Administration, 44930,* 239–249.

Holland, L., & Adams, M. (2010). *L. N. Holland's and M. P. Adams's core concept in pharmacology.* New York, NY: Prentice Hall.

Hondo, C., Gardiner, M., & Sapien, Y. (2008). *Latino dropouts in rural America: Realities and possibilities.* Albany, NY: SUNY Press.

Iwanicki, E. (2001). Focusing teacher evaluation on student learning. *Educational Leadership, 58*(5), 57–59.

Jackson, B., & Kelley, C. (2002). Exceptional and innovative programs in educational leadership. *Educational Administration Quarterly, 38*(2), 192–212.

Jean-Marie, G. (2008). Leadership for social justice: An agenda for 21st century schools. *The Educational Forum, 72,* 340–354.

Karpinski, C. & Lugg, C. (2006). Social justice and educational administration: Mutually exclusive? *Journal of Educational Administration, 44*(3), 278–292.

Keyes, M., Hanley-Maxwell, C., & Capper, C. (1999). "Spirituality? It is the core of my leadership": Empowering leadership in an inclusive elementary school. *Educational Administration Quarterly, 35*(2), 203–237.

Kezar, A., & Carducci, R. (2007). Cultivating revolutionary leaders. Translating emerging theories into action. *Journal of Research on Leadership Education.* Retrieved from http//www.ucea.org/IRLE/pdf/v012/kezarpdf

Koerin, B. (2003). The settlement house tradition: Current trends and future concerns. *Journal of Sociology and Social Welfare, 30*(2), 53–62.

Kumashiro, K. (2004). *Against common sense: Teaching and learning toward social justice.* New York, NY: Routledge.

Ladson-Billings, G., & Tate, W. (1995). Toward a critical theory of education. *Teachers College Record, 97*(1), 47–68.

Langer, E. (1989). *Mindfulness.* Cambridge, MA: Da Capo Press.

Larson, C., & Murtadha, K. (2002). Leadership for social justice. In Murphy (Ed.), *The educational challenge: Redefining leadership for the 21st century,* (pp. 134–161). Chicago, IL: University of Chicago.

Lugg, C. (2003). Sissies, faggots, lezzies and dykes: Gender, sexual orientation, and a new politics of education. *Educational Administration Quarterly, 39*(1), 95–134.

Marshall, C. (2004). Social justice challenges to educational administration: Introduction to a special issue. *Educational Administration Quarterly, 40*(1) 3–13.

Marshall, C., & Oliva, M. (2010). *Leadership for social justice: Making revolutions in education.* Boston, MA: Pearson Education.

Murphy, J. (2006). *Preparing school leaders: Defining a research and action agenda.* Lanham, MD: Rowman & Littlefield Education.

Murphy, J., & Vriesenga, M. (2004). *Research on preparation programs in educational adminis-tration: An analysis.* Columbia, MO: University Council for Educational Administration.

Murphy, J., & Vriesenga, M. (2006). Research on school leadership preparation in the United States: An analysis. *School Leadership and Management, 26*(2), 183–195.

Muzaliwa, I. (2011). Teaching and leading for diversity and social justice through narrative inquiry in secondary schools. (Unpublished doctoral dissertation). University of Idaho, Moscow, ID.

NAFSA: Association of International Educators. (2003). Securing America's future: Global education for a global age. Strategic task force on education abroad. Washington, DC: Author.

The National Commission on Teaching. (1983). *A nation at risk: The imperative for educational reform.* Washington, DC: U.S. Department of Education.

Nieto, S. (2009). *The light in their eyes: Creating multicultural learning communities.* New York, NY: Teachers College Press.

Nieto, S. (2010). *Language, culture, and teaching: Critical perspectives.* New York, NY: Routledge.

Nieto, S., & Bode, P. (2008). *Affirming diversity: The sociopolitical context of multicultural education.* Boston, MA: Pearson.

Noguera, P. (2010). *Leadership for family and community involvement: The soul of educational leadership series.* New York, NY: Teachers College Press.

Normore, A. (2008). *Leadership for social justice: Promoting equity and excellence through inquiry and reflective practice.* Charlotte, NC: Information age.

Ogbu, J. (1994). Racial stratification in the United States: Why inequality persists. *Teachers College Record, 96,* 264–271.

Paquette, J. (1991). Minority participation in secondary education: A fine grain descriptive methodology. *Educational Evaluation and policy analysis, 13*(2), 139–157.

Phillion, J. (2002). Becoming a narrative inquirer in a multicultural landscape. *Curriculum Studies, 34*(5), 535–556.

Riesman, C. (1993). *Narrative analysis.* Newbury Park, UK: Sage Publications.

Riley, E., & Rustique-Forester, E. (2002). *Working with disaffected students.* London: Paul Chapman.

Scheurich, J., & Skrla, L. (2003). *Leadership for equity and excellence: Creating high-achievement classrooms, schools and districts.* Thousand Oaks, CA: Corwin Press.

Shields, C. (2003). *Good intentions are not enough: Transformative leadership for communities of difference.* Lanham, MD: Scarecrow Press.

Shoho, A. (2006). Dare professors of educational administration build a new social order: Social justice with American perspective. *Journal of Educational Admin-*

istration, 43(3). Retrieved from http://www.emeraldinsight.com/journals. htm?articleid=1556602&show=html

Spring, J. (2001). *Globalization and educational rights: An intercivilizational analysis.* Mahwah, NJ: Lawrence Erlbaum.

Terrell, R. D., & Lindsey, R. B. (2009). *Culturally proficient leadership: The personal journey begins within.* Thousand Oaks, CA: Corwin Press.

United States Census Bureau. (2010). 2010 Census Data [Data set]. Retrieved March 19, 2011 from http://2010.census.gov/2010census/data/

Young, M., & Mountford, M. (2006). Infusing gender and diversity issues into educational leadership programs: Transformational learning and resistance. *Journal of Educational Administration, 44*(3), 264–277.

Zeichner, K. M., & Liston, D. P. (1996). *Culture and teaching.* Hillsdale, NJ: Lawrence Erlbaum Associates, Inc.

CHAPTER 19

CULTURALLY RESPONSIVE LEADERSHIP STRATEGIES TO PROMOTE MULTICULTURAL TEACHING

Jasmine Peña

INTRODUCTION

More than 50 years have passed since the court ruling in *Brown v. Board of Education* (1954) called for making education equal. Although *Brown v. Board of Education* made education possible for all children, schools are more separate now than ever (Jost, Jost, & Whitfield, 2005). There is a void in the present American educational scene, a lack of multicultural education in American schools, and more than ever, a need for multicultural sensitivity in both the content and structure of the learning environment. According to Ukpokodu (2007), "in a multicultural democracy, schooling without educational equality constitutes injustice" (p. 8).

There has been a lack of reference to multicultural education in American schools, especially at-risk schools where the focus is on foundational contextualization (Butin, 2005). Educators will prepare students for lead-

Social Justice Leadership for a Global World, pages 345–360
Copyright © 2012 by Information Age Publishing
All rights of reproduction in any form reserved.

ership and professional roles at the university and in our society with an awareness of social responsibility to the community. Succeeding in school is a challenge for multicultural children, and obtaining a high school diploma with advanced training is imperative in order to get ahead in society and succeed in the future labor market. Add to this the dramatic demographic shift in the United States that is noticeable in American schools, and new challenges arise as to how educators will respond to these changes. These changes are concerning since educational experts predict that there will be a significant increase in enrollment of children of color in American public schools, in particular those whose primary language is not English (Parameswaran, 2007).

Research documents that a lack of multicultural education can affect how well children do in school. A number of issues surface. Students are being educated by teachers who lack training in multicultural education. "Studies indicate that prospective and in-service teachers who are predominantly white, middle-class, and monolingual lack the knowledge, skills, and dispositions needed to successfully work with urban students" (Ukpokodu, 2007, p. 8). Therefore, as Ukpokodu (2007) noted, "Unless teachers are prepared to develop a sense of consciousness and social responsibility as educators, the problems of academic failure and achievement gap will persist" (p. 8). Coupled with a lack of these skills, research shows that the integration of multicultural education in the schools is tied to a closer fit between students' home cultures and the culture of their school. Yet too often there exists a divide between the school and the student's family and cultural upbringing. Brown (2007), for example, stated,

> Researchers have asserted that the academic achievement of students from culturally and linguistically diverse backgrounds would improve if educators were to make the effort to ensure that classroom instruction was conducted in a manner that was responsive to the students' home cultures. (p. 57)

Given these inequities and challenges, educators must learn how to integrate concepts of social justice in their lessons, and unless teachers are prepared to develop a sense of consciousness and social responsibility as educators, the problems of academic failure and the achievement gap will persist (Ukpokodu, 2007). School leaders play an important role in supporting teachers and multicultural education. What follows is a discussion of some of the research related to the importance of multicultural education and improved student achievement for all students, in particular the role of the teacher. The discussion then focuses on ways leaders can help teachers cross cultural barriers in the classroom. The final section describes the role and importance of the multicultural leader, drawing from current research.

MULTICULTURAL EDUCATION AND THE TEACHER

By infusing multicultural education in at-risk schools, outstanding educators can guide students in achieving the highest standard of academic excellence. The implementation of multicultural education in an educator's curriculum is of the utmost importance in order to prepare students to be socially responsible within their communities. Multicultural sensitivity is needed in both the content and structure of the learning environment. Our student population is changing, and demographers predict that by 2035, more than half the school-age population will be non-white Anglo students, although our teacher demographic is not (Timmons Flores, 2007). Timmons Flores (2007) reported that the majority of public educators in this country are monolingual white women with limited experience in other cultures. Timmons Flores also noted that up to 50% of all new teachers in urban schools leave within the first five years. Often their leaving is related to challenges of working with diverse student populations, and "members of mainstream society often want to run away from the harsh realities of race, racism, and poverty, and when confronted with them, quickly retreat to their own safety and comfort zones" (Gay, 2007, p. 57). Clearly, establishing better diversity awareness training for teachers is necessary in a teacher-preparation curriculum.

According to Trent, Kea, and Oh (2008), the *No Child Left Behind Act* (NCLB, 2002) was implemented at a time when schools are "becoming more racially, ethnically, linguistically, and socioeconomically diverse and calls for substantive changes in teacher education programs" (p. 328). Among the recommendations of this report is to increase the diversity among teacher education program faculty and prepare white pre-service and in-service teachers to provide culturally responsive instruction for all learners (Trent et al. 2008).

Cho and DeCastro-Ambrosetti (2006) explained the importance of learning how to teach culturally and linguistically diverse students. Based on their research in the U.S. Census of 2000, the number of culturally and linguistically diverse students is increasing. By the year 2020, culturally and linguistically diverse students will compose approximately half of the public school population in the United States. In their research, they also found that, although there is an increasingly diverse student population, the majority of the teachers are predominantly Caucasian and middle class. Thus, Cho and DeCastro-Ambrosetti (2006) related that "those entering the field of teaching have a lack of knowledge of the experiences, needs, and resources of culturally and linguistically diverse student populations" (p. 24). They suggested that teachers take a multicultural education class to "influence their attitude towards diversity positively" (Cho & DeCastro-Ambrosetti, 2006, p. 24).

Taylor (2004) found that the ideas of Vygotsky (1986), whose theory was related to how social and cultural factors influence the thought processes in children, had a significant impact in the field of multicultural education. Vygotsky believed that the languages people acquire structure their thinking. Students will accommodate information by using a code switch, combining their native language with English. Given that immigrant children are generally at a higher risk for failure than non-immigrant students, the teacher's ability to work with culturally and linguistically diverse students has never been more critical (Taylor, 2004).

In the U.S., there are certain groups of students who do not do well in school. Foster, Lewis, and Onafowora (2003) pointed out that underachieving students are often from racial and ethnic communities that are culturally different from mainstream communities. Foster et al. suggested that the theoretical reason why so many students from these communities fail in school is that psychological approaches to studying education have been problematic in their views of students of color. Hence, Foster et al. (2003) suggested that "researchers need to ascertain how the cultural dynamics of a particular group interact with those of the broader community and to investigate the consequences of those dynamics, both for the education of those in the group as well as for those with a stake in their education" (p. 262). As they stated, "Culture includes knowledge, belief, art, morals, law, custom, and any other capabilities and habits acquired by man" (Foster et al., 2003, p. 262). The approaches used in their study of culture were functional, psychological, cognitive, and linguistic. Thus, for educational researchers, merely asking questions about the meaning and consequences of certain cultural practices is insufficient. Educators must decide which practices might be useful in facilitating change and consider the "cultural and communicative norms" (Foster et al., 2003, p. 261) that affect learning in classroom settings.

What research is suggesting is that as our school student populations are defined by more diversity, the curricular and instructional teaching practices will need to change, and educators will need to attend to all aspects of diversity and its impact on teaching and learning (Ford & Milner, 2005). As stated by Ford and Milner (2005),

> If one defines the curriculum as what students have the opportunity to learn, and if one believes that students learn from a combination of experiences (from what is formally taught, what is indirectly taught, one's personal experiences, as well as what is shared from each other's experiences) then we must consider the significant role of race in opportunities to learn. (p. 31)

There is no doubt that the classroom teacher has much authority in deciding the nature of what gets taught in the classroom. Thus, the ability of educators to see beyond their own worldview to consider teaching and learning through the eyes of their students, so many of whom are racially and culturally diverse can only support improved student achievement for all students. As Ford and Milner (2005) pointed out, "It is these students who we are failing disproportionately in our schools, therefore, we offer the proposition that the achievement gap may be largely determined by a cultural and racial gap between teachers (the majority of whom are white) and their diverse students" (p. 33). Sleeter (2009) gave support to these ideas in recognizing that teachers "are significant curriculum decision makers in their classrooms" (p. 3). As teacher educators, she recommended that teacher preparation curriculum needs to change, suggesting two major approaches:

> (1) disrupt common novice assumptions that there is a "right" way to design and teach multicultural curriculum and that there is a body of "correct" knowledge and attitudes to teach, and (2) help teachers develop more sophisticated epistemological perspectives about the nature of knowledge and their work as teachers. (Sleeter, 2009, p. 3)

According to Sleeter (2009), ideally student success is tied to the degree to which teachers are provided "opportunities to learn from perspectives across racial, ethnic, and cultural boundaries to stretch their beliefs" (p. 4).

Much more can be done to implement multicultural education in the classroom. Research conducted by Ford (2010) indicated the following:

> Cultural clashes in classroom settings are inevitable when teachers and students are culturally different. However, the good news is that teachers can decrease cultural misunderstandings and miscommunication with culturally different students when they become more self-reflective, recognize cultural differences between themselves and students, work to become more culturally competent professionals, and create classrooms that are culturally responsive rather than assaultive. (p. 52)

Ford (2010) provided an interesting discussion of cultural responsiveness. He found that the meaning associated with cultural responsiveness has numerous interpretations. Ford (2010) suggested that "when teachers are culturally responsive, they are student-centered; they eliminate barriers to learning and achievement and, thereby, open doors for culturally different students to reach their potential" (p. 50). For Ford (2010), an important role of the classroom teacher is to "meet the needs of students who come from cultural backgrounds different from their own" (p. 50). He was clear about the importance of multicultural curriculum and that teachers had a responsibility to ask several important questions:

1. Have we tried to ensure that all students are engaged, and motivated by the curriculum?

2. Have we presented a balanced, comprehensive, and multidimensional view of the topic, issue, and event?
3. Have we ensured that multiple viewpoints are shared and discussed?
4. Have we addressed stereotypes, distortions, and omissions in the curriculum? (Ford, 2010)

Based on the ideas of Ford (2010), Sleeter (2009), and others, by using differentiation in their teaching styles teachers can develop curriculum that is intellectually rich, culturally responsive and could help implement multicultural education in a classroom in which the climate is cooperative and family like. The next section will explore how leaders can help teachers cross cultural barriers in their classrooms.

HELPING TEACHERS CROSS CULTURAL BORDERS

Multicultural leaders should aim to help classroom teachers cross cultural borders. Most, if not all, educators and students come to an educational system influenced by their culture, gender, class, age, race, ethnicity, religion, and origins. One of the major goals of multicultural education is for teachers to value these differences through their instruction and to allow students to acquire knowledge, attitudes, and the skills they need to succeed in an ethnically and racially diverse nation and global society (Parameswaran, 2007). This learning begins in the classroom. In other words, teachers must often transcend some of the cultural borders within their own classroom spaces to support student achievement. In these classrooms, "culturally responsive teaching celebrates individual and collective accomplishments, provides academic and personal mentoring in survival skills and self-advocacy, promotes critical thinking, and uses cooperative learning groups or peer tutoring situations" (Parameswaran, 2007, p. 13).

Interestingly, support for cross-cultural teaching can be found in international documents as well. For example, in a statement by Zukang (2009), Under-Secretary-General for Economic and Social Affairs to the Civil Society Forum for the United Nations, he discussed the commitment world leaders made at the World Social Summit in 1995 and how years later social integration is not high on the development agenda. One city Zukang (2009) focused on was Copenhagen and its commitments to building inclusive societies. He pointed out that,

Copenhagen recognized the importance of such broad-based participation in advancing a society for all. It explicitly recommended giving community organizations greater involvement in the design and implementation of local projects, particularly in the areas of education, health care, resource management and social protection. (p. 2)

Zukang also discussed the need for civil society organizations to raise awareness about the importance of promoting social inclusion through multicultural education. Zukang (2009) addressed his audience and said,

> You can mobilize groups and individuals for collective action. You can help to reveal the real impact of government policies and what should be done to improve them. You can support government efforts and help to keep governments accountable for implementing policies that effectively promote social integration. (p. 2)

Teachers Fostering Inclusive Learning Spaces

There are numerous ways that multicultural leaders could help classroom teachers. Crossing borders within classrooms suggests the use of various strategies to encourage discussion on sensitive matters of race and culture in the classroom. Prather and Lovett-Scott (2002) pointed out that "if students are to succeed in a multicultural world, they will need critical and creative thinking skills, competency in communication, the ability to work in groups and teams, and the capacity for self insight" (p. 5). Furthermore, they suggested that "teachers can facilitate learning on sensitive topics like race and gender by drawing boundaries, modeling authenticity, maintaining objectivity, and creating a climate of trust" (p. 5). Educators should be trained in how to hold discussions about race, gender, and ethnicity in non-threatening ways and establish rules of conduct by providing safe and dialogic spaces (Shields, 2004), which provide clarity for students in their learning environment. By incorporating such learning experiences into the school's regular professional development agenda, teachers will improve their own cross-cultural competencies. What is important from the Prather and Lovett-Scott (2002) study is the idea that teachers must maintain objectivity and encourage students to express their ideas. The teacher can do this by listening to the different voices and reframing ideas so that they can be heard with meaning and clarity. Multicultural leaders should train teachers in how to create a climate of trust; it is important to bridge the communication gap.

Another way that teachers can cross cultural borders in the classroom can be enhanced, for example, by having teachers invite multiethnic students to collaborate in small groups and share their diversity through story telling. Athanases (2006) suggested that "such activities serve to allow students to move toward common ground as they engage in compare-and-contrast conversations about cross-cultural themes of diversity and equity" (Athanases, 2006, p. 17). Multicultural leaders could also promote a higher level of cultural awareness within their school communities by asking teachers to have students conduct research and share stories about their own families' ethnic backgrounds. All students have a culture and should be aware of their own ethnic roots as well as respect the cultural values of other ethnic groups. By engaging students in such activities, the teacher will create a fertile learning environment that will help all students develop a multicultural perspective about their world view.

Multicultural leaders also need to train teachers in how to create a classroom environment that fosters intellectual safety, is positive, and helps bridge the gap of diversity. In a classroom, there should not be distinctions between the dominant culture students and minority students. As stated by Rathyen (2004), "Learning is the entitlement of all and I really believe that intellectual safety and existential discussion hold the key to democratizing education for all students" (p. 55). Furthermore, with the efforts of educators and by providing intellectual safety in a classroom, one can create a community of learners and help students overcome the gaps in cultures and class, as well as achieve high levels of literacy for culturally diverse student populations. One way this environment can be achieved is by implementing multicultural professional development for teachers. In a research study by Foster et al. (2003), they looked at a project where master teachers were paired up with less skilled practitioners whereby the less experienced teachers analyzed master teachers, including their role in the motivation of learning and how they created conditions in the classroom that connected with students' backgrounds, identities, interests, and cultural knowledge. The experience gained by new teachers analyzing master teachers was valuable in professional development. According to Foster and his colleagues (2003), the project provided a "theoretically better understanding of the social, affective, and behavioral processes that are prerequisites for cognitive learning in classrooms of teachers who teach for understanding" (p. 262). They found that inexperienced teachers benefited from pairing up with master teachers in their analysis of a multicultural approach to pedagogy.

Additionally, and in support of helping teachers cross borders, multicultural leaders can assist teachers in connecting with culturally different families to begin building global communities to promote multicultural education. If teachers serve as ambassadors of multicultural education, they need to model the value of fostering strong school-community partnerships where diverse cultural backgrounds of students and families can help bridge cultural divides in both the classroom and the community. Teachers should have a global approach to education and increased, respectful communication with people of different nationalities and cultures. Thus, it is incumbent upon the leaders to create school structures and values that support teacher outreach to and inclusion of diverse members in the community.

Another strategy involves technology and multi-media education. As technology rapidly advances, more students are gaining access to computers and other social media in the United States and beyond. Teachers need training in how to use technology effectively in the classroom. Developing and delivering instruction that taps into students' individual learning styles requires more responsive and flexible instructional strategies, environments, and materials (Blackboard, 2008). To begin the integration of technology in the classroom, teachers should know how to provide access to available technological resources. These resources will lead to technological competence in diverse classrooms. The use of technology in the diverse classroom is effective in various ways. According to Sianjina (2000), it can provide opportunities for cooperative learning; meet varying learning-style preferences; increase self-expression and active learning; help students develop greater multicultural understanding; enhance communication skills; and make learning exciting, enjoyable, and relevant. Sianjina (2000) also pointed out that instructional computing seems to benefit both low- and high-achieving children; improve specific content-area skills and knowledge; and promote positive attitudes toward computer use, academic learning, and self. In addition, many colleges and universities are now revamping their education schools to include an increased use of educational technologies, and success of all students who attend college will become more contingent upon the skills and technological knowledge they have leaving high school. Thus, leaders need to work with teachers to address the technology needs and opportunities in support of multicultural education and student success.

Multicultural leaders must help teachers lead diverse classrooms by changing how they deliver the curriculum. With a focus on concepts and principles, Bresnahan and Conderman (2008) indicated that "teachers can lead students in diverse classrooms in the efficient and broad acquisition of knowledge" (p. 176) and stated,

> Imagine a classroom co-taught by a general educator and special educator that includes 11 students with individualized education programs (IEPs), two students with autism, five students from low socioeconomic levels, two students whose parents do not speak English, and five high achievers from enriched backgrounds. (p. 176)

According to Bresnahan and Conderman (2008), "An educator must be prepared to respond to such diverse needs, to ensure the success of each student in this classroom, regardless of ethnicity, background, gender, ability, or income" (p. 176). The duty for all teachers is to successfully meet the challenge of teaching in diverse classrooms. Bresnahan and Conderman (2008) stated that "with the increase of diversity in classrooms and conflicting or confusing advice from experts, teachers may feel pulled in many directions as they race to cover the curriculum" (p. 176). They argued that "to successfully meet the challenge of teaching in diverse classrooms depends, in part, on using research-based instructional methods that boost academic skills and foster independent learning" (p. 176).

Bresnahan and Conderman discovered and used several effective methods that produced significant student academic gains for all students in their classroom. This method they described as "teaching big ideas" (p. 176). According to Bresnahan and Conderman (2008), "American education has been characterized as overstuffed and undernourished" (p. 177). They asserted, "though students are being exposed to a considerable amount of information, they are educationally undernourished because little of this information is explored in-depth" (p. 177). Based on their research, Bresnahan and Conderman reported that with the increase in national and state standards, teachers are more challenged than ever to cover all their content or grade-level state or district learning objectives, which often leads to students learning a little about many topics. However, some students do not benefit from this approach; Bresnahan and Conderman (2008) suggest that "students in diverse classrooms may not be able to distinguish important from trivial facts, memorize facts for exams, or meaningfully associate isolated facts with corresponding main ideas and concepts" (p. 177). In response, creating more "conextualized instruction" may actually better serve students from different cultural backgrounds. Bresnahan and Conderman (2008) stated,

> Perhaps now, more than ever, teachers need to critically examine their instructional practices. As classrooms become more diverse, information and knowledge expands, and schools become even more accountable, educators can focus on teaching big ideas, which are the concepts and principles that lead to the most efficient and broadest acquisition of knowledge. (p. 179)

Because of the importance of attending to diverse classrooms, the multicultural leader should provide teacher training in how to present content texts to students from diverse backgrounds. Smith (2004) suggested teachers should be able to create a rich learning environment by modifying their own talk and appropriate questioning strategies. For example, Smith noted that teachers should use vocabulary role play, which is an effective strategy to encourage learners to make connections with their past experiences. One suggestion was to have groups of students write and perform skits to show the use of vocabulary words. Smith found educators should be trained in how to assist students to understand and connect with content material by tapping, focusing on, and building on students' background knowledge. The author explained that, "in general research has shown that successful background-building activities involve one or multiples of the five senses; they integrate listening, speaking, and reading and are motivating" (Smith, 2004, pp. 48–49).

There is no doubt that the multicultural leader plays a significant role in supporting teachers toward the development of successful multicultural classrooms and helping them navigate the cultural borders within their classrooms. The final section discusses the role of the multicultural leader in bringing about changes in the practices of the classroom teacher from pre-service to in-service development.

MULTICULTURAL LEADERSHIP FROM PRE-SERVICE TO IN-SERVICE

The role of the multicultural leader in bringing about instructional and classroom cultural changes is to implement training and development so that teachers can become better facilitators in a diverse class. Teachers should create opportunities for students to develop positive attitudes towards a diverse class. Garderen and Whittaker (2006) stated, "we must develop classroom communities in which differences can be discussed openly and sensitively and teach conflict resolution skills that provide students with strategies for coping with prejudice" (p. 15). Garderen and Whittaker (2006) reinforced that "culturally responsive teaching celebrates individual and collective accomplishments, provides academic and personal mentoring in survival skills and self-advocacy, promotes critical thinking, and uses cooperative learning groups or peer tutoring situations" (p. 15).

One of the mandates of the NCLB (2002) is to ensure that there is a quality teacher in every U.S. classroom. Subsequently, the need is great for teachers to teach students on both sides of the achievement gap, mainstream English-speaking students and cultural, language, and racial minorities. Sobel and Taylor (2005) noted, "preservice and in-service teachers are being asked to teach in ways they were not taught in their teacher education programs, to learners who often are unfamiliar to them, in classroom contexts that are outside their experiential realm" (p. 84). Furthermore, they pointed out, "many preservice teachers face the probability of teaching in schools where their experiential, cultural, and linguistic backgrounds may differ from those of their students" (Sobel & Taylor, 2005, p. 84). In their study, Sobel and Taylor (2005) reported that "80 percent of teachers polled reported feeling ill-equipped to teach diverse populations" (p. 84). It is the role of the multicultural leader to educate teachers and help them move away from this isolated thinking. By employing the numerous strategies presented in this chapter, a multicultural leader can be successful in making a teacher a change agent.

Multicultural leaders should promote communication among teachers. According to Ukpokodu (2007), "many times, kindergarten through Grade 12 teachers are strangers to each other within their own building and subsequently function in isolation" (p. 12). Furthermore, Ukpokodu (2007) reported, "they lack the empowerment and desire to work together cooperatively and collaboratively to dialogue and solve critical, social, and academic issues" (p. 12). This is why teacher training should be implemented in schools for professional development. Strategies such as team teaching will foster a collaborative community of practice. Ukpokodu (2007) said, "practitioners should learn to become critical colleagues who debate, critique, and challenge one another to go beyond their current ideas and practices" (p. 12).

A multicultural leader must be able to guide teachers to be ethically and legally responsible. Ukpokodu (2007) noted, "traditionally, teacher education has been, and in most cases still is, guided by the thinking of behaviorism" (p. 9). Ukpokodu (2007) further stated, "according to critics of behaviorism, the teacher is merely a rule follower, a guidebook reader of mandated curriculum with standardized materials that determine class activities who is discouraged from interpretative acts" (p. 9). The traditional goal of behaviorism is to prepare teachers to develop technical competence and conform to the existing school structure. Ukpokodu (2007) pointed out that "behaviorist thinking and tradition must become obsolete" (p. 10). Furthermore, Ukpokodu (2007) asserted, "teacher educators are an integral part of a society's ethical, social, and cultural enterprise, and consequently, teachers must be ethically and legally responsible to help students engage in a struggle for a more just and humane world" (p. 10).

A multicultural leader must ensure that teachers engage in teacher education programs that have a social justice perspective. According to Ukpokodu (2007), "if all students are to have equitable opportunities for academic and personal success, teacher education programs must weave a social justice perspective throughout the program to promote teaching as a lifelong journey of transformation" (p. 10). Therefore, Ukpokodu (2007) suggested, "training should offer specific courses on teaching for equity and social justice" (p. 10). Teachers must be given the opportunity to develop their skills further for use in content areas. Ukpokodu (2007) also added, "educators should learn how to integrate concepts of social justice in their lessons" (p. 10).

Furthermore, it is imperative for multicultural leaders to foster a community of practice for teachers and assist them in their struggle for educational change. Educators need to become involved in training and development and engage in thoughtful discussions about how they are meeting the needs of public schools. Ukpokodu (2007) noted, "professional development days should provide an opportunity for teacher dialogues on critical issues, sociocultural and political contexts of education and schooling, color or gender blindness, urban education, and team teaching" (p. 11). Moreover, Ukpokodu (2007) added, "training and development will allow faculty to gain critical perspectives about each other and their work and in the process learn to build connection and interdependency" (p. 11).

Multicultural leaders must assist teachers to use an interactive management process with a central purpose of engagement to enhance teachers' skills in managing all classroom interactions so that they result in substantial change in student behavior and attitude to learning. MacKay (2006) emphasized that "the interactive management process is like a working canvas, whereby teachers follow a specific methodology for managing behavior in order to oversee the ever-changing picture" (p. 5). MacKay pointed out that the interactive management process "enables teachers actively to plan for behavior and develop strategies for student management that focus on building sound working relationships within the classroom" (p. 5).

The role of the multicultural leader is to help teachers to be aware of the impact of their responses on student behavior, need for skilled responses, importance of managing themselves, and importance of understanding their students and their needs. Students learn practical social, emotional, and cognitive responses to any challenging or confronting behavior. Engagement, containment, and consequences replace discipline. The underlying ethos is that students should be allowed to develop within boundaries that enhance their individualization (MacKay, 2006).

It is important for a multicultural leader to provide professional development for teachers. It is critical for new and experienced teachers to have ongoing and regular opportunities to learn from each other. Ongoing professional development keeps teachers up-to-date on new research on how children learn, emerging technology tools for the classroom, new curriculum resources, and more. Teachers are looked upon to contribute meaningfully and substantively to the leadership of the school; thus, the training and development of teachers as leaders should be a substantial investment for school districts (MacKay, 2006). Multicultural leadership is about mobilizing the still largely untapped attributes of teachers.

The role of the multicultural leader should be to promote social equity among teachers. Social equity is more important than ever, as the number of diverse and underserved students increase each year. According to Bradford Smith (2009), "effective teachers in a diverse world need an education that enables them to attain new knowledge, paradigms, and perspectives on the United States and the world, and to deal effectively with both the challenges and opportunities of diversity" (p. 47). Moreover, Bradford Smith (2009) indicated that "teachers must recognize our increasing diversity as well as diversity in nation-states throughout the world" (p. 47). Studies by Bradford Smith showed that racial, cultural, ethnic, language, and religious diversity are increasing in schools in the United States as well as in other nations. Bradford Smith (2009) noted, given this diversity, "it is an excellent context for students to acquire the multicultural understandings and skills needed to function effectively in their local communities, the nation, and the world" (p. 47).

Multicultural leaders must help teachers become change agents in their classrooms. Bradford Smith (2009) pointed out, "the increasing diversity within the nation's schools and classrooms makes it possible to teach students from many different cultures and groups how to live together cooperatively and productively" (p. 49). This diversity, according to Bradford Smith (2009), "provides both opportunities and challenges, since racial prejudice and discrimination may arise when people from diverse groups come together" (p. 49). To help teachers become change agents in education, Gollnick and Chinn (2006) stated that:

> The goal of a multicultural teacher education program is to help prospective teachers become change agents who can impact and alter power relationships through curriculum, instructional practices, and individual and collective action toward more personal and structural relationships in schools, districts, and communities. (p. 49)

Furthermore, Bradford Smith (2009) reported, "in an increasingly diverse society, a multicultural approach to training educators and practitioners is essential" (p. 49). Bradford Smith (2009) noted, "professionals, from all fields, should be able to respond effectively to people from diverse backgrounds" (p. 49). Bradford Smith (2009) ascertained, "if we are to successfully educate all of our children, we must work to remove the blinders built of stereotypes, monocultural instructional methodologies, ignorance, social distance, biased research, and racism" (p. 50). Only then will the intent of *Brown v. Board of Education* (1954) that called for making education equal for all students become a reality.

REFERENCES

Athanases, S. Z. (2006). Deepening teacher knowledge of multicultural literature through a university–schools partnership. *Multicultural Education, 13*(4), 17–23.

Blackboard. (2008). *Expanding learning opportunities: Ensuring student success in the 21st century.* Retrieved from http://www.blackboard.com/resources/k12/K12_ExpandingOpps.pdf

Bradford Smith, E. (2009). Approaches to multicultural education in preservice teacher education: Philosophical frameworks and models for teaching. *Multicultural Education, 16*(3), 45–50.

Bresnahan, V., & Conderman, G. (2008). Teaching big ideas in diverse middle school classrooms. *Kappa Delta Pi Record, 44,* 176–180.

Brown, M. R. (2007). Educating all students: Creating culturally responsive teachers, classrooms, and schools. *Intervention in School and Clinic, 43*(1), 57–62.

Brown v. Board of Education, 347 U.S. 483 (1954).

Butin, D. W. (2005). Is anyone listening? *Educational Studies, 38*, 286–297.

Cho, G., & DeCastro-Ambrosetti, D. (2006). Is ignorance bliss? Pre-service teachers' attitudes toward multicultural education. *High School Journal, 89*(2), 24–28.

Ford, D. Y., & Milner, H. R. (2005). Racial experiences influence us as teachers: Implications for gifted education curriculum development and implementation. *Roeper Review, 28*(1), 30–36.

Ford, D. Y. (2010). Culturally responsive classrooms: Affirming culturally different gifted students. *Gifted Child Today, 33*, 50–53.

Foster, M., Lewis, J., & Onafowora, L. (2003). Anthropology, culture, and research on teaching and learning: Applying what we have learned to improve practice. *Teachers College Record, 105*, 261–277.

Garderen, D. V., & Whittaker, C. (2006). Planning differentiated, multicultural instruction for secondary inclusive classrooms. *Teaching Exceptional Children, 38*(3), 12–20.

Gay, G. (2007). Teaching children of catastrophe. *Multicultural Education, 15*(2), 55–61.

Gollnick, D. M., & Chinn, P. C. (2006). *Multicultural education in a pluralistic society* (7th ed.). Upper Saddle River, NJ: Merrill Prentice Hall.

Jost, M., Jost, M., & Whitfield, E. (2005). When the rules are fair, but the game isn't. *Multicultural Education, 13*(1), 14–21.

MacKay, J. (2006). *Managing classroom interactions: Coat of many pockets.* Camberwell, Victoria, Australia: Acer Press.

No Child Left Behind Act (NCLB) of 2001, 20 U.S.C. Sec. 6301 (2002).

Parameswaran, G. (2007). Enhancing diversity education. *Multicultural Education, 14*(3), 51–55.

Prather, F., & Lovett-Scott, M. (2002). How demographic destinies affect teaching and learning: Innovative strategies for the 21st century educator. *Delta Kappa Gamma Bulletin, 68*(4), 5–14.

Rathyen, C. (2004). Providing safety in a multi-cultural, multi-ability classroom. *Delta Kappa Gamma Bulletin, 71*(1), 52–55.

Shields, C. (2004). Dialogic leadership for social justice: Overcoming pathologies of silence. *Educational Administration Quarterly, 40*(1), 109–132.

Sianjina, R. R. (2000). Educational technology and the diverse classroom. *Kappa Delta Pi Record, 37*(1), 26–29.

Sleeter, C. (2009). Developing teacher epistemological sophistication about multicultural curriculum: A case study. *Action in Teacher Education, 31*(1), 3–13.

Smith, K. M. (2004). Language as we know it, literacy as we know it, and content area instructions: Conscious strategies for teachers. *Multicultural Education, 11*(4), 46–50.

Sobel, D. M., & Taylor, S. V. (2005). Diversity preparedness in teacher education. *Kappa Delta Pi Record, 41*(2), 83–86.

Taylor, J. A. (2004). Teaching children who have immigrated: The new legislation, research, and trends in immigration which affect teachers of diverse student populations. *Multicultural Education, 11*(3), 43–44.

Timmons Flores, M. (2007). Navigating contradictory communities of practice in learning to teach for social justice. *Anthropology and Education Quarterly, 38*, 380–404.

Trent, S. C., Kea, C. D., & Oh, K. (2008). Preparing pre-service educators for cultural diversity: How far have we come? *Exceptional Children, 74*, 328–350.

Ukpokodu, O. N. (2007). Preparing socially conscious teachers: A social justice oriented teacher education. *Multicultural Education, 15*(1), 8–15.

Vygotsky, L. (1986). *Thought and language.* Cambridge, MA: MIT Press.

Zukang, S. (2009). *Social integration: Building a society for all.* New York, NY: United Nations. Retrieved from http://www.un.org/esa/desa/ousg/statements/2009/20090203_civil_society_forum.html

SECTION V

STRATEGIES FOR HIGHER EDUCATION
SOCIAL JUSTICE LEADERSHIP

CHAPTER 20

THINK JUSTICE

Pushing The Boundaries of Black College Presidential Leadership

Marybeth Gasman, Jameel Scott, and Nelson Bowman III

Most historically black colleges and universities (HBCUs) in the U.S. were established shortly after the Civil War in an effort to educate the former slaves. They were created separately from the already existing colleges and universities due to the immense discrimination haunting the country at the time. These institutions are responsible for educating the U.S. African American middle class as we know it today. Although they currently enroll only 16% of African American students, HBCUs graduate nearly 24%—a disproportionate number (Gasman & Tudico, 2008). Despite the important role that HBCUs have played, they are under constant attack and scrutiny from critics and face many resource challenges. The shifting global environment in which HBCUs exist calls for strong leadership and a commitment to social justice.

At several national conferences in 2010, leaders in the HBCU community proclaimed, "We have a leadership crisis." HBCUs have a long legacy of leaders who fought for social justice. Under the confines of Jim Crow and in

Social Justice Leadership for a Global World, pages 363–375
Copyright © 2012 by Information Age Publishing
All rights of reproduction in any form reserved.

efforts to fight for African American civil rights, many black college leaders served as shining examples of thoughtful leadership. Of course there were some leaders who caved under the weight of oppression, but this was not the norm. But, what of today's black college leaders? How do they speak out against injustice? Are they forthright about their opinions on national policy issues given the continually shrinking resources available for higher education? Could a lack of willingness to speak out be part of the leadership crisis currently taking place at HBCUs? This chapter addresses these questions and profiles several HBCU leaders who support social justice in varying ways.

Throughout history there have been HBCU presidents who were highly vocal. These leaders include individuals such as Benjamin E. Mays of Morehouse College. Mays was born to former slaves in 1894. Inspired by some of the black community's great intellectuals and orators, including Frederick Douglas, Booker T. Washington, and Paul Laurence Dunbar, Mays became a Baptist minister and eventually earned a Ph.D. from the University of Chicago (Mays, 2003). The stalwart "spiritual mentor" of Martin Luther King, Jr. was vocal in both the Atlanta community and across the nation. He wrote articles and op-eds, gave speeches in national venues, and was quite controversial in his approach (Mays, 2003; Carter, 1998).

Likewise, Johnnetta B. Cole, the president of both Spelman College and Bennett College for Women, was also an outspoken leader. Cole is an anthropologist who earned her Ph.D. at Northwestern University. She did her undergraduate work at Fisk University and Oberlin College—two institutions known for instilling a sense of responsibility and justice in their students. These two institutions, along with the influence of her parents, shaped her brave and outspoken commitment to advancing the lives of African Americans and issues of social justice (Cole, 1994). Like Mays she wrote op-eds for national venues and authored a book on sexism among African Americans, entitled *Gender Talk* (Cole, 2003), while president and in the midst of the institution's most successful fundraising campaign. She took a chance as some donors might have recoiled after reading her perspectives, which pushed back at gender relations in America. Cole's forthright, confident nature and her ability to capture national attention assisted with Spelman's fundraising success (Barrett, 2006; Gasman, 2001). Prior to Cole's presidency, Spelman had a good reputation but nowhere near the reputation that developed under her leadership and continues to this day.

Johnnetta Cole and Benjamin Mays are considered by most in the HBCU community as well as by researchers as premier HBCU presidents. Some have even labeled them aberrations, showing immense courage and strength often in the midst of an environment that did not support the education of blacks (Riley, 2010; Vedder, 2010). Although speaking out in support of social justice, in our opinion, should be in the lexicon of skills held by all college and university presidents, it is not. Regardless, within the HBCU context there are myriad examples of presidents who demonstrate bravery and speak out against injustice.

CHANGING PERCEPTIONS AND IMAGES

Walter Kimbrough, the president of Philander Smith College in Little Rock, Arkansas, regularly writes op-eds and has blogged about HBCUs for the *New York Times*. Kimbrough is the twelfth president of Philander Smith College and is one of the youngest presidents in the country at 38 years old. He pursued his undergraduate degree at the University of Georgia and a Ph.D. at Georgia State University. Before becoming president of Philander Smith College, Kimbrough served as the Vice President of Student Affairs. Upon becoming president, Kimbrough was tagged the "Hip Hop" president by news outlets. Prior to becoming a college president, Kimbrough (2003) authored a best selling and somewhat controversial book entitled *Black Greek 101: The Culture, Customs and Challenges of Black Fraternities and Sororities*. Of note, Kimbrough has not stayed clear of controversy in his op-eds or his comments to the press. He has taken on *US News and World Report's* ranking of college and universities, especially HBCUs. For example, in 2007, Kimbrough spoke out in a *Diverse Issues in Education* article about the rankings, stating "If there are people looking at the rankings as a measurement of the quality of an institution, they think [HBCUs] do not have any type of qualities. The rankings do not tell you who the best schools are, just the most privileged" (quoted in Kamara, 2007, p. 3). In addition to speaking out in the paper, Kimbrough participated in a letter writing campaign sponsored by Education Conservancy to convince HBCU presidents to boycott the *US News* rankings. At the time that Kimbrough pushed for the boycott, he was a new HBCU president and did not have the political clout among HBCU leaders to gain widespread approval.

In an op-ed in *Inside Higher Education*, Kimbrough (2007) has questioned whether giving to rich, Ivy League institutions that perpetuate privilege is really philanthropy. Specifically, Kimbrough stated:

> On April 11, the president of Columbia University announced that it had received a $400 million pledge from alumnus John W. Kluge, who in 2006 was 52nd on the *Forbes* list of the wealthiest people, earning his fortune through the buying and selling of television and radio stations. This gift, payable upon the 92-year-old's death, will be the fourth largest ever given to a single institution of higher education. With such a massive transfer of wealth, the accolades poured in, justifying such a gift to an Ivy League university. Columbia's president, Lee Bollinger, said: 'The essence of America's greatness lies, in no small measure, in our collective commitment to giving all people the op-

portunity to improve their lives... [Kluge] has chosen to direct his amazing generosity to ensuring that young people will have the chance to benefit from a Columbia education regardless of their wealth or family income.' Mayor Michael Bloomberg indicated that investing in education produces returns that can't be matched. Rep. Charles Rangel said the gift would ensure greater numbers of students can afford a first-class education. Oh please! (p. 2)

Kimbrough (2007) took a hard swing at the nation's wealthy philanthropists who give to elite institutions. He elaborated on the above with,

I am becoming less and less tolerant of people who pass wealth on to the privileged and masquerade it as philanthropy. Philanthropy is the voluntary act of donating money, goods or services to a charitable cause, intended to promote good or improve human well being. When a billionaire gives money that will benefit people who are more than likely already well off or who already have access to huge sums of money, attending the ninth richest university by endowment, this is not philanthropy. This simply extends the gross inequities that exist in our country—inequities that one day will come home to roost. (p. 2)

In speaking out so vehemently, Kimbrough took a calculated risk—one that could have resulted in foundations and philanthropist shunning him and his institution or could have brought him respect from many different constituents including funders.

Kimbrough is also quite forthright when answering the media's inquiries about his leadership and HBCUs overall. He does not try to hide from the media and is upfront about Philander Smith's performance indicators, sharing data even when the data need improvement. In turn the media respects him and have given him and his institution a good amount of positive press (Masterson, 2010; Redden, 2009).

Kimbrough's presence in the media has caught the attention of funders. They see a president who is brave, progressive, and not satisfied with the status quo. They also notice that he makes decisions based on evidence and have made significant grants to Philander Smith based on Kimbrough's actions and vision. One funder in particular, the Kresge Foundation, recently awarded Philanders Smith College a $1.5 million grant to support a center for social justice. When Kimbrough took on the leadership of the small college in Arkansas, he noticed that it did not have an institutional niche or anything truly unique about it. There were no distinctive majors or strengths for students and faculty to rally around. In an effort to increase enthusiasm on campus, elevate the reputation of Philander Smith College, and reach out to the local community, Kimbrough changed the school's motto to "Think Justice." He focused the campus energy on social justice and wove the notion throughout the curriculum and co-curriculum. Most recently, a group of foundations known as the MSI Funders group chose to visit Kimbrough's college in order to learn more about HBCUs and leadership. In their opinion, Kimbrough exemplifies the kind of bravery and leadership skills needed to be president of an HBCU in the 21st century.

Charlie Nelms, the chancellor of North Carolina Central University, has also demonstrated bravery. He recently held a public discussion about the future of HBCUs, encouraging an open and honest conversation about the challenges that HBCUs face. He brought together prominent researchers, including experts on retention, leadership, and fundraising, to push HBCUs forward. Nelms held this conversation publicly in front of funders and the media and as a result of his willingness to discuss tough issues and identify possible results, he has secured additional funding as well as some positive press (Kelderman, 2010). Eric Kelderman of the *Chronicle of Higher Education* highlighted the challenges that HBCUs face but also applauded the HBCU leaders for their frank discussion. Charlie Nelms was lauded for his courage to have the discussion as well as his institution's efforts to create a "university college" to cater to the needs of first year students. Nelms's boldness and openness were the highlight of the *Chronicle* article with Kelderman, quoting him at the conclusion of the article: "If we're [HBCUs] going to be around as a group of institutions 25 years from now, we have to change our narrative and our approach and be strategic" (Kelderman, 2010, n.p.). Most recently, Nelms issued a call to action for HBCUs, asking their leaders to change their ways and move gracefully into the 21st century. This call to action is based on Nelms's recent conference.

Another president who has been using his role to make positive change is Michael Sorrell, the president of Paul Quinn College. Sorrell holds a J.D. from Duke and up until recently, he was a corporate attorney. He decided to take on the leadership role at Paul Quinn despite being advised not to by all of his friends and mentors. In order to save his struggling college, Sorrell has resorted to some innovative and slightly unorthodox strategies. For example, he turned an unused football field into an organic farm. He also secured a donation to demolish 13 abandoned buildings on the Paul Quinn campus. Sorrell could have done this work in isolation. However, he chose not to and instead made the media aware of his efforts, writing op-eds for various Dallas, Texas papers (Sorrell, 2010). By doing this, Sorrell has been able to drum up interest from those in Dallas who had given up on the institution. He has been transparent about the problems on his campus and contextualizes them by describing the state and national climate for higher education in his discussions of Paul Quinn.

Most recently, Sorrell (2010) wrote an op-ed for the *Dallas News* that focused on his institution's rocky past and where he is taking it in the future. Specifically, he proclaimed:

No longer are we prisoners to negative experiences and missteps that occurred 10 to 15 years ago. We have closed that chapter of our history. Today, we celebrate a new truth, a new perception and a new reality. The work being done by the Paul Quinn family is critically important not only to Dallas, but also to under-resourced communities across the country. We are developing a model for others to embrace and replicate. Each member of the Paul Quinn family acknowledges that we still have work to do to become one of America's great small colleges. Somewhere in the Paul Quinn experience is the following advice and an offer for those who cling desperately and rigidly to outdated perceptions and allow those perceptions to define their realities: Stop living in the past. If you will start seeing us for who we are today, we promise to do the same for you. (Sorrell, 2010, para. 7)

Rather than let the locals in Dallas, who could be potential donors, harbor feelings about the college based on past information, Sorrell took responsibility for the institution's missteps and pushed forward a new agenda for the college and its students. He made the education of low-income, first generation students a priority rather than his own ego. This approach has paid off in terms of support from citizens of Dallas, funders, and alumni.

Each of these presidents spoke out in support of HBCUs in order to bolster the education of African Americans. In doing so, the presidents also elevated the reputations of their institutions. These efforts contributed to ensuring social justice for young students of color.

RESPONDING TO CONTROVERSY

On September 28, 2010, Jason L. Riley, an op-ed writer for the *Wall Street Journal*, penned an article entitled "Black Colleges Need a New Mission." In the article, Riley relied on the dated perspective of scholars writing in the 1960s and 1970s and those that compare HBCUs to Ivy League institutions (Jencks & Riesman, 1967; Sowell, 1972). In making this comparison, Riley failed to realize that there are few public or private institutions in the United States that stand up to those comparisons in terms of endowment size and other factors. Riley's judgments are patently unfair and undermine any serious discussions of the true value of HBCUs. A fair assessment of the work of HBCUs places them side by side with historically white institutions (HWIs) with similar student populations. Specifically, HBCUs should be compared to institutions in Southern states with like percentages of Pell Grant eligible students and like SAT scores. Such an evaluation would show that in many cases HBCUs are doing a better job of educating African-American students. Moreover, they have done so with far fewer resources than their HWI counterparts (Gasman, 2010). One of the stinging problems with Riley's op-ed is its placement in the *Wall Street Journal*, a well-known paper with a healthy circulation. Within hours of being published, the op-ed went viral, making its way around HBCU and higher education circles. In looking at the online commentary responding to the article, it was evident that Riley touched a nerve. Riley, an African American editorial board member at the *Wall Street Journal*, gave the anti-HBCU crowd plenty of ammunition to use against these historic institutions and lit a fire under HBCU leaders across the country.

One of the first HBCU presidents to respond to Riley was William R. Harvey, the president of Hampton University in Virginia. Harvey received his undergraduate degree at Talladega College and his doctoral degree at Harvard University. Along with his leadership of Hampton, Harvey is the chair of the board of directors of the White House Initiative on Historically Black Colleges and Universities. He has been a hugely successful president, having served in this role since 1978. He has not only ensured the institutions financial security, but has pushed for more research and academic excellence across the student body. Harvey is admittedly a Republican but puts his role as president of Hampton ahead of his politics. His main emphasis is the education of African American students at all costs.

In Harvey's (2010) op-ed he pointed out the inconsistencies and inaccuracies in Riley's arguments. Harvey pointed toward the economic impact of HBCUs on the nation as a whole and also highlighted their role in providing jobs. For example, HBCUs have a national economic impact of $10 billion annually and provide 180,000 jobs. Harvey also pushed back hard at Riley's assertion that HBCUs should bring in for profit institutions such as the University of Phoenix to manage them. Specifically, he stated "Does he really want HBCUs to model themselves after an institution whose latest graduation rates as reported by the Integrated Postsecondary Education Data System (IPEDS), was 1% at 4 years, 4% at 6 years, and 6% at 8 years?" (para. 6). Because of Harvey's stature within the HBCU world and among the nation's political leaders and policy makers, his voice was a vital part of the rebuttal to Riley.

Another voice of defense for HBCUs was David Wilson, the newly-minted president of Morgan State University in Maryland, who was appointed in 2010. Wilson is the twelfth president of Morgan State, and prior to holding the position he served as the chancellor of the University of Wisconsin Colleges and University of Wisconsin-Extension. He attended Tuskegee University for his undergraduate degree and Harvard for his doctoral degree. Although Wilson had only been in the Morgan presidency for a few months, he spoke out vehemently against Riley's perspective. The *Washington Afro* published his opinion. Wilson (2010) pointed to the inaccuracies in Riley's arguments much like Harvey did, but he also drew on his experience at historically white institutions. According to Wilson (2010), "I have attended and worked at a number of traditionally white institutions and can testify to the fact that little stands between them and HBCUs, save that which a large endowment will buy" (n.p.). He urged Riley to "compare HBCUs with other schools of their size and nature, and not just to the most elite of colleges and universities in the country" (n.p.). In addition, he noted "If he is going to compare HBCUs to the Harvards and MITS of the world, then he also must compare those schools with the smaller, less well-endowed, traditionally white institutions" (Wilson, 2010, n.p.).

In addition to this op-ed article, David Wilson has been vocal at HBCU-focused conferences. In April 2011, for example, he served on a panel at the National Press Club that featured Richard Vedder, a critique of HBCUs, and members of the black and HBCU communities. The panel was sponsored by the National Association for Equal Opportunity and was meant to be a direct response to the HBCU critics who had surfaced over the past year. At the event, Wilson was quite vocal, giving a response that he claimed was not a response to Vedder but merely an overview of the strength of HBCUs. He told the audience that there is no reason to defend HBCUs. In his talk, Wilson discussed the many strengths of Morgan State. For example, Morgan is ranked second in Maryland in the percentage of its students who graduate and go on to graduate school—a percentage that is higher than the state's flagship institution.

The last president to write an op-ed in response to Jason Riley (although she did not name him) was Beverly Daniel Tatum. Tatum is the president of Spelman College in Atlanta and has held the position since 2002. She holds a bachelor's degree from Wesleyan University and a Ph.D. from the University of Michigan. Prior to taking the lead at Spelman, Tatum served as the dean and acting president of Mount Holyoke College. Tatum (1997) is probably best known for her book *Why Are All the Black Kids Sitting Together in the Cafeteria? And Other Conversations About Race.* She is a consistent and vocal supporter of HBCUs and also a national commentator on racial issues.

Tatum (2010) opened her op-ed with examples of the many accolades that her students have received—Luce Fellowships to study child prostitution in Northern Thailand, Fulbright Scholarships to explore women and democracy in India, and the grand prize in the AT&T Big Mobile on Campus Challenge. She used these examples to point to the disconnect between Jason Riley's assessment of HBCUs as inferior and her own daily experiences leading Spelman. Writing for the *Huffington Post,* Tatum also took issue with Riley's commentary on HBCU SAT scores. Riley claimed that HBCU student SAT scores were an indication of the poor quality of the students and HBCUs overall. In her words,

> It has been suggested by some commentators that the fact that average SAT scores are lower at Spelman than at equally selective institutions is an indicator of lower academic quality. I would suggest perhaps it is an indicator of

lower average family income. SAT scores are more highly correlated with family income than almost any other variable—the higher the income, the higher the score is likely to be. According to a 2007 article in *Postsecondary Education Opportunity*, Spelman College is now educating more Pell-Grant eligible students than any other selective liberal arts college in the nation, except Berea College. Of approximately 2,200 students at Spelman that year, 885 of them were Pell-Grant recipients, 40% of our total population. Ivy League institutions with thousands more undergraduates are educating far fewer Pell-Grant recipients. In 2008, Harvard had 543 among an undergraduate population of 6,700, Yale had 469 among 5,350, Princeton only 264 among 4,719. Despite a much smaller endowment than these giants, it is Spelman College that is doing the important work of providing social mobility to talented students like these every year. (Tatum, 2010, para. 4)

Unlike some of her presidential peers, Tatum is armed with an arsenal of data that she can use to defend the reputation of HBCUs. Of course, Tatum was upfront about the fact that Spelman College is the most highly ranked HBCU and has the strongest endowment. She said,

I know that not every HBCU shares the same profile of Spelman College, nor does every majority institution look like Harvard. Yet it is important to understand each institution in its own context—its history, the region it serves, and the service it still provides to a nation in need of every source of talent. (Tatum, 2010, para. 5)

Although these responses are admirable, what HBCU presidents need to do is to take a proactive approach in promoting the reputations of their institutions instead of reacting to criticism. They should be out in front promoting social justice and linking this promotion to the long history of HBCUs. In addition, like Beverly Tatum, HBCU presidents need to stay abreast of the current empirical literature that supports the contributions that HBCU make in order to promote the success of HBCUs with more than mere anecdotal stories.

INFLUENCING POLICY

Another method of speaking out on issues is through policy papers that are disseminated to policymakers, funders, the media, and those in higher education. Mary Sias, president of Kentucky State University; George Wright, president of Prairie View A&M University; and Ron Mason, president of the Southern University of Louisiana System recently co-authored a policy paper on HBCUs and graduation rates. The paper challenged conventional methods for calculating graduation rates as these methods privilege colleges and universities that accept highly prepared, affluent students. When controlling for income and academic preparation, the presidents argued that HBCUs graduation rates are comparable and often surpass those of many similar historically white institutions.[1] The policy paper received considerable media attention. And, the sponsoring organization, the Thurgood Marshall College Fund, shared it with those at the Department of Education and the White House Initiative on HBCUs in an attempt to change the way the federal government assesses college attainment levels (Ashley, Gasman, Sias, Wright, & Mason 2009). When HBCU presidents author policy papers on important issues related to HBCUs, it shows a commitment to improving and a willingness to confront difficult questions.

Perhaps the most vocal president of an HBCU is Julianne Malveaux. Prior to becoming president of Bennett College for Women, Malveaux was a journalist, writing regular columns for *USA Today, Ms. Magazine,* and *Essence.* Coming to the presidency, she had extensive writing experience and was not afraid to speak out—she had been doing it for decades and in a very provocative and public way. Malveaux also has a Ph.D. from MIT in economics, and this gives her considerable credibility with the media as she rarely makes an argument with out a treasure trove of statistics to back up her assertions.

Unlike most of the HBCU presidents mentioned in this chapter, Malveaux speaks out publically on many issues that are not directly related to HBCUs or higher education, including health care, gender and racial inequity, and unemployment. She doesn't bit her tongue often. When Malveaux was appointed president of Bennett College, some in the HBCU community were surprised. As mentioned, she had been an opinionated journalist. Although the institution's previous president Johnnetta B. Cole was also outspoken, she was much more of a traditional academic in her approach. Malveaux is an in-your-face president and is not afraid to speak her mind. According to a story in *Diverse Issues in Higher Education,* "some academics familiar with her often-polarizing punditry wonder if her hard-charging style will mesh well with the demands put upon a college president" (Pluvoise, 2007, p. 7). When she first arrived at Bennett, the board tried to limit her public persona and her op-ed writing. That did not last long and within a year, Malveaux was back writing provocative op-eds.

In 2009, for example, Malveaux wrote an op-ed in the *Chicago Defender* in which she poked and prodded at Republicans and their dislike of Barack Obama's health care plan. Although she nicely laid out the reasons why some Americans oppose health care reform, Malveaux also took several pot shots at Republicans—both the leaders and the masses. Malveaux asked important social justice oriented questions such as "We know there are 50 million uninsured adults and children. What kind of productivity drain exists because people don't have the health insurance they need?" Perhaps her most controversial claim was that the real reason for Republicans' dislike of health care reform is that they dislike Barack Obama. Many college and university presidents stay clear of aligning themselves publically with political parties, but Malveaux makes her stance clear. Although to be fair, she has been very critical of Obama's actions as president as well.

In another op-ed, written for the *Seattle Medium*, Malveaux (2011) took on the issue of gender inequity. Speaking as the president of Bennett College Malveaux argued that the African American community as well as the nation as a whole must come together and support the success and aspirations of women. In her words:

> We must claim this month [women's history month], not simply as a statement of history, but also as an opportunity to remind the nation and the world that gender equity is a human imperative. In other words, we don't just want pay equity for women, but we want pay equity for families and for a nation. When women aren't well paid, families aren't well cared for. When women are kicked to the curb economically, children suffer and we experience generational reverberations. Fair treatment of women is an investment in the growth, development, and success of our nation. (Malveaux, 2011, p. 4)

Because she is president of a women's college, Malveaux's voice on issues related to gender equity appear to be directly linked to her position and expertise.

CONCLUSIONS AND RECOMMENDATIONS

The U.S. HBCU presidents highlighted in this paper are those who speak out on local and national issues and push the boundaries on race and social justice issues. However, these presidents are not the norm for colleges and universities and they are not the norm for HBCUs. Black college presidents operate in a volatile global environment in which their institutions are considered suspect and questioned on a regular basis and global competition is rising. As they are tuition-driven and highly dependent on consistent enrollment, they cannot take chances in terms of funding. Losing a funder as a result of speaking out on controversial issues is not an option for many HBCU presidents. Despite the potential risks involved, our chapter shows that those HBCU presidents who are more vocal and strategically speak out publically on social justice issues are often the most successful. They attract the attention of policy makers and funders. They are seen as brave and commanding respect. In addition, funders see them as innovative and willing to confront challenges related to the mission of HBCUs. Lastly, presidents who speak out against injustice are seen as having a sense of integrity that is worth supporting.

NOTES

1. The policy paper was co-authored by Marybeth Gasman.

REFERENCES

Ashley, D., Gasman, M., Sias, M. Wright, G., & Mason, R. (2009). *HBCU graduation rates.* New York, NY: Thurgood Marshall College Fund.

Barrett, T. G. (2006, October–December). How strategic presidential leadership and institutional culture influenced fund-raising effectiveness at Spelman College. *Planning for Higher Education,* 5–18.

Carter, L. (1998). *Walking integrity: Benjamin E. Mays mentor to Martin Luther King Jr.* Mercer, GA: Mercer University Press.

Cole, J. B. (1994). *Conversations: Straight talk with America's sister president.* New York, NY: Anchor Press.

Cole, J. B. (2003). *Gender talk: The struggle for women's equality in African American communities.* New York, NY: Random House Press.

Gasman, M. (2001). Charles S. Johnson and Johnnetta Cole: Successful role models for fundraising at historically black colleges and universities. *The CASE International Journal of Educational Advancement, 1*(3), 237–252.

Gasman, M. (2010). False comparisons: The plight of historically black colleges and universities. *The Chronicle of Higher Education.* Retrieved from http://chronicle.com/blogs/innovations/false-comparisons-the-plight-of-historically-black-colleges/27406

Gasman, M., & Tudico, C. (2008). *Historically Black colleges and universities: Triumphs, troubles, and taboos.* New York, NY: Palgrave Press.

Harvey, W. R. (2010). Op-ed response to *Wall Street Journal* article. Washington, DC: National Association for Equal Opportunity. Retrieved from http://www.hampton.edu/news/hm/2010_1104_op_ed.cfm

Jencks, C., & Reisman, D. (1967). The American Negro college. *Harvard Educational Review, 37*(2), 3–60.

Kamara, M., & Kimbrough, W. (2007, June 28). Are USNEWS' rankings inherently biased against African Americans? *Diverse Issues in Higher Education.* Retrieved from http://diverseeducation.com/article/7831/

Kelderman, E. (2010, June 27). Black colleges see a need to improve image. *The Chronicle of Higher Education.* Retrieved from http://www.chronicle.com/article/Historically-Black-Colleges/66045/

Kimbrough, W. (2003). *Black Greek 101: The culture, customs and challenges of Black fraternities and sororities.* Madison, NJ: Fairleigh Dickenson University Press.

Kimbrough, W. (2007). The perpetuation of privilege. *Inside Higher Education.* Retrieved from http://www.insidehighered.com/views/2007/06/12/kimbrough

Malveaux, J. (2009, August 26). They don't dislike health care, they dislike Barack Obama. *Chicago Defender.* Retrieved from http://www.chicagodefender.com/article-6203-they-dont-dislike-health-care-they-dislike-barack-obama.html

Malveaux, J. (2011, March 23). Gender equity is everybody's business. *The Seattle Medium.* Retrieved from http://www.seattlemedium.com/News/search/ArchiveContent.asp?NewsID=108071&sID=

Masterson, K. (2010, May 10). Hip hop prez rejuvenates a college using personal touch. *The Chronicle of Higher Education.* Retrieved from http://www.chronicle .com/article/Hip-Hop-Prez-Rejuvenates-a/65350/

Mays, B. E. (2003). *Born to rebel: An autobiography.* Athens, GA: University of Georgia Press.

Pluvoise, D. (2007, March 26). Julianne Malveaux named Bennett College President. *Diverse Issues in Higher Education.* Retrieved from http://diverseeducation.com/article/7158/

Redden, E. (2009, July 14). Reaching Black men. *Inside Higher Education.* Retrieved from http://www.insidehighered.com/news/2009/07/14/blackmale

Riley, J. L. (2010). Black colleges need a new mission. *Wall Street Journal.* Retrieved from http://www.wsj.com/article/SB10001424052748704654004575517822124077834.html

Vedder, R. (2010, October 15). Why do we have HBCUs? *The Chronicle of Higher Education.* Retrieved from http://chronicle.com/blogs/innovations/why-do-we-have-hbcus/27506

Sorrell, M. (2010, December 28). Reality redefines perception at Paul Quinn College. *Dallas News.* Retrieved from http://www.dallasnews.com/opinion/north-south-dallas-project/viewpoints/20101228-michael-sorrell-reality-redefines-perception-at-paul-quinn.ece

Sowell, T. (1972). *Black education: Myths and tragedies.* New York, NY: Longman.

Tatum, B. D. (2010, October 7). And still we rise: One HBCU president's perspective. *Huffington Post.* Retrieved from http://www.huffingtonpost.com/beverly-daniel-tatum/hbcu-president-perspective_b_755144.html

Tatum, B. D. (1997). *Why are all the Black kids sitting together in the cafeteria? And other conversations about race.* New York, NY: Basic Books.

Wilson, D. (2010, October 14). Painting a more accurate picture of HBCUs. *Washington Afro American.* Retrieved from http://www.afro.com/sections/opinion/commentary/story.htm?storyid=69215

CHAPTER 21

USING THE EQUITY SCORECARD TO IDENTIFY AND CLOSE GAPS IN EDUCATIONAL OUTCOMES

Abbie Robinson-Armstrong

INTRODUCTION

While speaking to a Joint Session of Congress, President Obama announced that his budget focused on energy, the cost of health care, and education because these areas were critical to rebuilding the nation's flagging economy (Obama, 2009). The President's concern regarding education derives from the fact that in 2005, over 60 percent of the United States' citizens had not earned a college degree. This reality is especially alarming considering the fact that improvements in the economy and the overall human condition are linked to the nation's college graduation rate (Lumina Foundation, 2009). According to President Obama (2009), a college education is the most valuable commodity in a global economy. Elevated to the national level, the goal is to expand access to higher education, particularly among adults, first-generation college going students, low-income students, and students of color in order "to increase the percentage of Americans with

Social Justice Leadership for a Global World, pages 377–391
Copyright © 2012 by Information Age Publishing

high-quality degrees and credentials from the longstanding rate of 39 percent to 60 percent by the year 2025" (Lumina Foundation, 2009, p. 1).

To make America the leader in educational attainment in the world (Lee & Rawls, 2010), higher education must meet President Obama's (2009) goal to "produce 8 million more college graduates by 2020." In order to achieve President Obama's goal, colleges need not only to increase access to higher education, but also close gaps in educational outcomes between underrepresented and other students. A number of national reports (U. S. Department of Education, National Center for Education Statistics [NCES], 2011) revealed that between 1997 and 2007 undergraduate enrollment of full-time and part-time 18 to 24 year olds (including underrepresented undergraduates) increased 16 percent in degree-granting institutions. Nevertheless, the United States' degree attainment rate remained unchanged during this period due to pervasive graduation gaps for underrepresented students (Harris, 2009). This chapter presents the Equity Scorecard as a critical learning and accountability tool "designed to foster institutional change through the identification and elimination of ethnic disparities among college students" (Harris & Bensimon, 2007, p. 77). The Scorecard differs from other assessment instruments because it "focuses on developing practitioners' contextualized awareness of inequities in educational outcomes" (Harris, Bensimon, & Bishop, 2010, p. 279). This chapter also addresses the role of institutional culture in creating and sustaining an ethos that not only focuses on graduating a diverse constituency, but also on making systemic changes necessary to eliminate graduation gaps.

INSTITUTIONAL CULTURE

Researchers assert that, among other factors, institutional culture plays a critical role in contributing to underrepresented students' academic failure (Bauman, Bustillos, Bensimon, Brown, & Bartee, 2005; Bensimon, Polkinghorne, Bauman, & Vallejo, 2004; Bensimon, 2005). An institutional culture that subscribes to the deficit model views underrepresented students as marginalized individuals coming from dysfunctional backgrounds and lacking motivation (Bauman et al., 2005; Bensimon et al., 2004; Bensimon, 2005). This type of institutional culture does not support the cultural and attitudinal changes necessary to close gaps in educational outcomes.

According to Cameron (2004), culture is "a socially constructed attribute of organizations, which serves as the 'social glue' bonding an organization together" (p. 3). Cameron (2004) also said culture represents "how things are around here or the prevailing ideology that people carry inside their heads" (p. 3). In an effort to distinguish institutional culture from the concept that higher education refers to as campus climate, Cameron (2004) goes on to say that "climate refers to more temporary attitudes, feelings, and perceptions of individuals. Culture is an enduring, slow to change core characteristic of organizations" (p. 3). There are three levels of culture: artifacts, values, and underlying assumptions (Schein, 1988). According to Schein (1988), artifacts comprise "what one feels, observes, and notes with all of one's senses as one enters a new culture. But as clear and palpable as those cues are, they are difficult to decipher unless one asks insiders what they mean" (p. 9). Artifacts in college environments include mission statements, strategic plans, policies, insider language, myths, stories, rituals, ceremonies, dress codes, manners in which various constituencies are addressed (students may address faculty as Dr. Jones, Professor Jones or James), and design of the physical structure (Schein, 1988). Institutional artifacts influence what a college deems to be important, and, as a result, impact priorities, practices, thoughts, and behaviors while stratifying members of the community, services and activities. This makes life in the community predictable. Constituencies who align themselves with the dominant institutional culture develop a sense of identity. In contrast, it can make life unbearable and create a chilly climate for those who find it difficult to adjust to the dominant institutional culture (Cameron, 2004; Schein, 1988).

Values include what Schein (1988) described as organizational "strategies, goals, philosophies, norms, standards, moral principles, and other untestable premises" (p. 9). Organizational values communicate what is good, what works, and what is right (Eckel, Hill & Greene, 1998). They provide for self-perpetuation and ready-made solutions. In college environments, values determine whether administrators and faculty willingly engage in data-driven decision-making for the purposes of identifying and closing gaps in educational outcomes. They also determine who in the campus community is responsible for student retention and success. In colleges where equity and a culture of evidence drive behavior, responsibility for student retention is shared by administrators and faculty; in others that responsibility is shifted to student affairs staff even though they are often unable to impact curriculum, pedagogy, and classroom climate. Schein (1988) said when we "dig beneath the surface of values by observing behavior carefully, noting anomalies, inconsistencies, or phenomena that remain unexplained, we elicit from insiders their underlying assumptions" (p. 9). Underlying assumptions are taken for granted beliefs that are rarely examined or questioned because they are deeply ingrained in people's minds (Cameron, 2004; Schein, 1988). They are often materialized as institutional values, but the longer they "stand the test of time" (Schein, 1988, p. 9), the more it is possible for them to morph into taken for granted assumptions. Within college communities, underlying assumptions can determine how various constituencies define student success. Deans and faculty may use traditional indicators such as grade point average (GPA), learning outcomes, and persistence rates to define student success. In contrast, student affairs staff value academic indicators, but they also know that one needs to focus on a broader set of metrics, such as campus engagement, living accommodations, financial aid package, debt load, employment status, mentoring, academic advising, and climate in order to develop a holistic picture of a student. If academic indicators are the only metrics that drive behaviors within the campus community, it is unlikely that a college will make substantive changes that positively impact underrepresented students' educational outcomes. Therefore, change must be planned or intentional, continuous, and designed to create major shifts in institutional culture (Eckel et al., 1998).

Planned or intentional change involves "charting a deliberate course" (Eckel et al., 1998, p. 3) and implementing strategies that differ from those utilized during when responding to unplanned change. Eckel et al. (1998) asserted that planned change alters institutional culture by changing certain underlying assumptions, individual behaviors, processes, and activities. Planned change positively impacts institutions of higher education because "it is deep and pervasive, affects the whole institution, and occurs over time" (Eckel et al., 1998, p. 3). However, it must be noted that changing institutional culture is not a single, easily performed event that happens overnight. It is a difficult and time consuming process that does not go unchallenged by some in the community who believe that any form of change will be detrimental or ineffective for the college. Other factors, including time, institutional attention span, leadership turnover, uneven progress, and the ever-changing higher education environment, can also deter efforts to alter institutional culture. Eckel and Kezar (2003) identified indicators that provide evidence that institutional culture has been altered. Structural evidence of change or concrete markers can be counted, measured and compared to baseline information. The indicators include changes in polices, budgets, learning and assessment practices, new departments, decision-making models or institutional structures. Attitudinal and cultural indicators reveal changes in the ways groups or individuals interact with one another, language a campus uses to talk about itself, types of conversations that occur, new relationships with stakeholders, and abandonment of old arguments (Eckel & Kezar, 2003).

Realizing that culture impacts institutional behavior, Bensimon (2005) anchored the Equity Scorecard in organizational learning theory because "organizational learning, in both theory and practice, is particularly effective in making the invisible visible and the undiscussable discussable, two conditions that aptly describe the status of race-and ethnic-based unequal outcomes on most campuses" (p. 99).

The following key principles emerge from organizational learning theory: 1) organizational culture and structure can negatively impact individual learning (Kezar, Glenn, Lester & Nakamoto, 2008), 2) every member of the organization must be involved in the learning process (Kezar et al., 2008), and 3) when individuals attack a problem collectively, the solution is often better matched to the needs of a broader group of constituencies (Huber, 1991). These principles can be interpreted to mean that identifying and closing gaps in educational outcomes, such as persistence and graduation, is not the sole responsibility of student affairs staff. Deans, associate deans, department chairs, and faculty are also responsible for graduating diverse groups of highly qualified students who can positively impact the country's global economic growth.

THE EQUITY SCORECARD

This section discusses the Equity Scorecard and includes cases that exemplify changes in institutional culture that a state university system and two-year and four-year colleges made in order to close gaps in educational outcomes. Because new knowledge generated through the Scorecard was sufficient enough to impact institutional culture or educational outcomes, describing the institutions in depth would take unwarranted space. Therefore, brief case examples are embedded in the Scorecard Framework described below.

The Equity Scorecard emerged when it became evident that while educators valued equity in principle, they rarely used it to measure student outcomes (Bensimon, 2004). Equity is the point at which a particular ethnic group's representation across all academic indicators such as majors, programs, transfers to four-year colleges, English and Math placement, persistence rates, and degrees conferred is equal to the group's representation in the student population (Bensimon, 2004). For example, if Latinos make up 25 percent of the student population, a similar percentage of those students should be on the Dean's List.

I use the term "Scorecard Team" to refer to a cross-disciplinary group of faculty and staff that collaborates for the purpose of identifying and closing gaps in educational outcomes (Robinson-Armstrong, King, Killoran, & Fissinger, 2009). According to the University of Southern California (USC) Center for Urban Education, cross-disciplinary Scorecard Teams engage in several interrelated tasks:

- Review disaggregated institutional data and identify gaps
- Define intervention zones—a starting point for inquiry
- Assess campus policies and practices to identify strengths and gaps
- Set equity goals
- Design integrated intervention plans
- Implement action plan
- Assess the results

Since the inception of the Scorecard, Teams have produced outcomes that ranged from the development of a strategic focus on equity and a culture of evidence to changes in policies, practices, programs, budgets, and the language that colleges use to discuss underrepresented students (Robinson-Armstrong, King, Killoran, Ward, Fissinger, & Harrison, 2007; Robinson-Armstrong et al., 2009; Robinson-Armstrong, Clemons, Fissinger, & Sauceda, 2012).

When aligned with institutional mission and goals, the Scorecard process helps teams make clear and compelling cases to key stakeholders about why things must be done differently. The Scorecard stimulates debate about important issues, such as admissions processes and practices, and ways that critical mass, campus climate, faculty diversity, and inclusive curriculum and pedagogy affect underrepresented student success. Conversations of this nature help Scorecard Teams work within the culture of the institution while challenging its comfort zone and provide opportunities for them to plan for change over the long term (Bensimon, 2005).

The Scorecard process begins with analysis of macro and micro measures that emanate from questions posed through the three perspectives: 1) access, 2) retention, and 3) excellence. Macro measures present a large-scale photo of the institution. Analyses of macro measures reveal equity of educational outcomes on the basis of share or rate. Share means the percentage of each underrepresented or gender group present in a given indicator. For example, African Americans' share on the Dean's List means out of all students with a certain academic feature (e.g., Dean's List), what percentage is made up by African Americans? (Bensimon, 2004). Rate means the percentage that students with a certain academic feature (e.g., Dean's List) have out of all students of a certain ethnicity (African American). For indicators in which the data are analyzed by rate, such as graduation and retention, Scorecard Teams often use the highest performing group as the benchmark (Harris et al., 2010).

In contrast, micro measures allow Scorecard Teams to conduct in-depth analysis of trends that impact an institution's educational outcomes. These measures identify specific trends and educational outcomes at a more fine-grained level. Bensimon (2004) asserted that reliance on fine-grained indicators using disaggregated data is based on the assumption that it results in more precise measures. Micro-measures include both institutional and student descriptors. Institutional descriptors identify colleges and programs by discipline, department, and course sequence. When disaggregated by ethnicity and gender, student descriptors, such as sophomore Latino men who declared biology as a major, first-year African American females who earned a minimum of 16 credit hours and a composite Grade Point Average of 3.00 or American Indian women on the Dean's list, produce invaluable new knowledge for Scorecard Teams.

Regardless of whether a Scorecard Team analyzes macro or micro measures, the way in which the data are presented can affect the conclusions. According to Harris et al. (2010), aggregated data hides ethnic patterns of inequity, inhibits dialogue about ethnicity and gender, and allows inequities to persist. On the other hand, disaggregated data reveals patterns of inequity, supports dialogue about ethnicity and gender, promotes awareness, and generates solutions. The Scorecard process helps teams review macro and micro measures, disaggregated by ethnicity and gender, through the perspectives of access, retention and excellence (Bensimon, 2005).

Access

The access perspective in the Scorecard framework helps teams understand the extent to which underrepresented students have access to the institution in terms of courses, majors, minors, programs, and resources such as financial aid, grants, and scholarships (Harris et al., 2010). The following four cases highlight changes in institutional culture that Scorecard teams at three colleges and one state university system made to increase the access of underrepresented students, and thereby close graduation gaps.

Loyola Marymount University Case

Loyola Marymount University (LMU) is a private Catholic Masters institution that enrolls 8,845 undergraduate and graduate students in six colleges and schools, including Loyola Law School. LMU began implementing the Scorecard in 2004. The team included the Vice President for Intercultural Affairs; an Associate Dean from each college and school; and directors of admissions, financial aid, institutional research, university honors, national and international fellowships and scholarships, and the library. Representatives from the division of student affairs and athletics were also team members. While analyzing data through the access perspective, the team discovered that the percentages of African American and Latino students had decreased in five years despite a 21 percent increase in the total undergraduate enrollment in the same time period. Between 1997 and 2001, the African American population decreased from 7.8 to 6.4 percent, and the Latino population decreased from 20.6 to 18.5 percent. White students represented 67 percent of the increase in undergraduates (Robinson-Armstrong et al., 2011). The newly acquired knowledge about the decline in underrepresented student enrollment prompted the team to further explore the data. For example, one team member asked, "Has the proportion of male versus female changed over time?" This led the team to further disaggregate data by gender. The analysis of enrollment by ethnicity and gender revealed that more than 60 percent of African American and

Latino students were female, while other groups had a more balanced gender distribution. Because the Director of Admissions was on the team, it was easy to convince him to create a goal to increase the percentages of African American and Latino males over the next two years (Robinson-Armstrong et al., 2007; Robinson-Armstrong, et al., 2009).

University of Wisconsin System Case

University of Wisconsin System (UW System) is one of the largest systems of public higher education institutions in the United States. It is made up of 13 four-year universities, 13 two-year institutions referred to as University of Wisconsin Colleges (UWC), and a statewide UW-Extension. The System enrolls approximately 182,000 students and employs more than 32,000 faculty and staff statewide. According to V. Washington (personal communication, April 14, 2011), Associate Vice President for Equity, Diversity and Inclusion, the UW System began implementing the Equity Scorecard at all four-year and two-year colleges in the system in 2009. During the process, teams at all of the colleges discovered that the UW System application process presented challenges that negatively affected underrepresented student enrollment. Washington (personal communication, April 14, 2011) reported that Scorecard Teams identified two factors that affected the enrollment of underrepresented students across the UW System: 1) students were submitting incomplete applications because they were unaware of the existence of an application fee waiver, and 2) when students took the ACT late, they did not know what to do to successfully complete the application process. Relying on this new knowledge, admissions staff across the UW System began to be more intentional about initiating personal contact with underrepresented students who submitted incomplete applications, advising them about how to obtain fee waivers or what to do about late test scores (V. Washington, personal communication, April 15, 2011).

University of Wisconsin Colleges Case

University of Wisconsin Colleges (UWC), one of the 13 colleges in the UW System, is a conglomerate of 13 two-year institutions where students can earn an Associate of Arts and Science Degree and take general education courses that are the foundation of a bachelor's degree. After earning a degree, students can transfer to a University of Wisconsin baccalaureate campus or another college to complete a bachelor's degree or complete a collaborative bachelor's degree at one of the UWC sites.

G. Lampe, Provost and Vice Chancellor for Academic Affairs, reported that UWC's Scorecard process created changes in the Academic Department Program Review cycle and the criteria used to evaluate institutional units. UWC has three divisions: Natural Sciences and Mathematics, Humanities, and Social Sciences. Prior to April 2011, all departments across the college were reviewed on the same timeline. It was UWC's goal to take all departments in each division through the review as a group. However, this inhibited the Provost from being able to spend an appropriate amount of time working with departments on each review and discussing goals. The new policy calls for academic departments to be reviewed every three years by division. The new cycle enabled a more rigorous, robust review of curriculum and department goals because fewer departments were involved in the review process in a given year. Also, it enabled more conversation and discussion with the Provost's Office on the facilitation of department goals for the future. In addition, scheduling department reviews by division provided opportunities for a group of Chairs within a division to discuss divisional goals (G. Lampe, personal communication, April 14, 2011).

The UWC Academic Department Program Review consists of three distinct sections: Department Profile, Academic Program Review that includes subsections on curricular overview and curricular analysis, and Department Goals. G. Lampe said "we embedded equity indicators in the Academic Department Program Review so we could maintain a focus on diversity and inclusion" (personal communication, April 14, 2001). As a result, the *Department Profile* section of the revised policy requires that reports include the demographics of the faculty in each unit under review. The section entitled *Academic Program Reviews: Curricular Overview* contains the following questions that demonstrate how UWC embedded equity and inclusion into the Academic Department Program Review process:

- How do the department's current academic goals and focus align with the institutional goals and priorities as detailed in the UW Colleges Strategic Plan? (e.g., Equity Scorecard, ASI, ESFY, Assessment, Service-Learning).
- How do the department's curricular goals address the academic needs of the student population enrolled at the UW Colleges? Do these goals take any initiatives in the area of addressing diversity issues and values in the curriculum?
- How is department or discipline-specific assessment used to improve course content and inform department decision-making? What changes has the department made in course content or teaching approaches to improve student learning based on such assessment outcomes?

This case exemplifies the way in which UWC used the Equity Scorecard to demonstrate the need to embed diversity issues and values in the curriculum and implement inclusive pedagogy in order to improve student learning. It also demonstrates what happens when cross-disciplinary teams obtained consistent streams of information in the same time period and applied new knowledge to the analysis of student outcome data.

Los Medanos Colleges Case

Los Medanos Colleges (LMC), a multi campus two-year institution, began the Scorecard process in 2009. According to R. L. Armendariz, who serves as Project Director of the Hispanic Serving Institution Grant, analysis of the initial data revealed that underrepresented students often experienced difficulty transitioning from assessment tests administered during orientation into recommended Basic Skills courses during their first semester. In order to get a broader understanding of the problem, the LMC Scorecard Team took placement exams, interviewed orientation staff, and surveyed students to determine their perceptions of the experience. The team found that:

- Students did not understand the importance of taking assessment tests
- Test preparation materials were online but were difficult to find
- There was no private space where students could get the results of assessment tests
- During Orientation, students did not make a clear link between assessment tests and enrollment in Basic Skills courses.

To eliminate the problem and enroll students in the correct basic skills courses, LMC began the process of developing a transfer academy by creating partnerships with instructors from the departments of math, English, general education, and counseling. The Scorecard Team also decided to speed up student movement through developmental and transfer courses. Therefore, they invited the Counseling Department to implement their own scorecard to identify gaps in service and establish equity goals (R. L. Armendariz, personal communication, April 14, 2011).

Retention

The retention perspective in the Scorecard framework refers to persistence, course-taking patterns, transfer patterns, and degree completion. This perspective addresses questions about term-to-term or year-to-year persistence; four-year and six-year graduation rates; degree conferred in each college or major; drops, withdrawals or incompletes; rate of completion of gateway/gatekeeper courses; academic probation; credit accumulation; delays in taking math, English, and science courses; and the percentage of mid-semester warnings (Harris et al., 2007).

Long Beach City College Case

Long Beach City College (LBCC) is a point of entry into higher education for underrepresented students. Like all community colleges in California, LBCC was charged with preparing students for transfer to four-year institutions. Thus, the transfer rate is a measure the state uses to judge LBCC. While implementing the Scorecard, the LBCC team learned that only 520 (1.9 percent) students out of a population of 27,422 completed requirements to transfer to University of California (UC) or California State University (CSU) within three years for the 1999–2002 cohorts studied. Among the students, 22 percent had not transferred as of spring 2006. This figure represented a transfer rate-gap (Bensimon, Dowd, Alford, & Trapp, 2007). The LBCC team further examined the transfer rate-gap by disaggregating the data by ethnicity. They found the rate of non-transfers by UC and CSU-eligible Asian/Pacific Islander and Latino students clustered around a mean of 22 percent. The transfer rate-gap for African Americans was 8 percent. In response, LBCC changed its website by adding information on transfer requirements, and established a new transfer academy to better assist students with migrating from two-year to four-year institutions. LBCC also changed its learning and assessment practices by creating new instruments to monitor the transfer rates of African American and Latino students (LBCC and USC Center for Urban Education, 2007). This case exemplifies the steps an institution can take to close transfer gaps between two-year and four-year colleges, and thereby increase student persistence through the Bachelor's degree.

University of Wisconsin Colleges Case

According to G. Lampe (personal communication, April 14, 2011), every University of Wisconsin Colleges (UWC) campus has a Retention Committee charged with analyzing and interpreting student outcome data. Before implementing the Scorecard, the committees analyzed aggregated data because of the size of the underrepresented student population. UWC enrolled 14,300 students across its 13 campuses, but only 9 percent were members of underrepresented groups. However, the UWC Scorecard Team quickly learned that they could not identify gaps in educational outcomes by interpreting aggregated data. Consequently, the institution integrated student success and retention by disseminating disaggregated, rather than aggregated, data for decision-making purposes. For example, UWC Retention Committees reviewed drops and withdraws by ethnicity when 10 or more underrepresented students were enrolled in a course, as evident in a report entitled *UW-Colleges New Freshman Retention Summary* (2010). The report contains the following data sets:

- New freshman retention by course load

- New freshman retention by age range by course load
- New freshman retention by high school rank by course load
- New freshman retention by race by course load
- New freshman retention by 1st Term GPA by course load

G. Lampe summarized the effect that analysis of disaggregated data had on the UWC Scorecard Team: "It created a fundamental change in the way the Office of Institutional Research presents data to the campus community, and that changed the way we talk about students" (personal communication, April 14, 2011).

Excellence

The excellence perspective in the Scorecard Framework comprises both access and achievement. The access component of excellence raises questions about courses becoming gatekeepers into certain majors and the under enrollment of some groups in certain majors such as Science, Technology, Engineering, and Math. The achievement component of excellence raises questions about completion rates. Measures examined through this perspective may include GPA, enrollment in graduate and professional programs, degree attainment, representation in strategic programs, (e.g., University Honors and the percentage of students who graduate in the top 10 percent of the class) (Harris et al., 2010).

Loyola Marymount University Case
In 2003, whites comprised 71 percent of the University Honors population at Loyola Marymount University (LMU); enrollment shares for underrepresented students included: 3% African Americans, 9% Asian/Pacific Islanders, 7% Latinos, and 11% who declined to state ethnicity. In response to the data, the Director gained approval from the Advisory Board to reconfigure the recruitment process, which called for students who were awarded Honors at entrance to receive a letter from the Director within two weeks of receiving a letter of acceptance to LMU. The Director's letter invited them to visit the website and apply to Honors. This change put LMU into a more competitive calendar year with other universities, thereby enabling the program to recruit from a larger diverse pool of eligible students. In 2007, the population of University Honors included 58% whites, 4.8% African Americans, 12% Asian/Pacific Americans, 19% Latinos, and 3.2% American Indians/Alaska Natives (Robinson-Armstrong et al., 2009). The increase in the underrepresented students in LMU's University Honors Program represents a change in institutional policy and makes a compelling case for using

the Scorecard to identify educational gaps that fall within the excellence Framework of the Scorecard.

BEST PRACTICES FOR IMPLEMENTING THE EQUITY SCORECARD

While higher education has been challenged to increase the percentage of college graduates to affect the nation's flagging economy, institutions using the Equity Scorecard process have used it to identify gaps in educational outcomes specific to their culture and students. Colleges interested in using student outcome data to affect change in educational outcomes should consider the following best practices:

- Obtain support for the Equity Scorecard from the President, Chancellor and other administrators at the top of the institution
- Create a cross-disciplinary team, including faculty and staff representatives from all colleges, schools, and strategic programs and divisions
- Build time in the process to train the team, using external consultants who have experienced success implementing the Equity Scorecard in institutions of higher education
- Begin the process with an understanding about the nature and value of change in organizations such as colleges and universities
- Disseminate findings, benchmark goals, improvement strategies, and success stories widely to help others understand the role of equity in higher education

The cases in this chapter demonstrate that the Equity Scorecard is an effective tool for identifying and closing gaps in educational outcomes for underrepresented students. For higher education leaders who ascribe to the values that emanate from social justice, the Scorecard generates indisputable empirical evidence that focuses attention on related issues. Not only does the Scorecard have the potential to impact institutional culture, it can challenge underlying assumptions about underrepresented students. A change from negative to positive perceptions of underrepresented students shifts the focus from implementing programs, to altering their ways of being so they can fit into a particular college environment, to understanding the need to change institutional culture to better serve the students. While it will take time for higher education to increase the United States degree attainment rate in order to compete in a global economy, institutions that utilize the Equity Scorecard will be in a position to play a major role in creating a knowledge based society, strengthening the economy and improving the human condition in this country.

REFERENCES

Bauman, G. L., Bustillos, L. T., Bensimon, E. M., Brown, M. C., & Bartee, R. D. (2005). *Achieving equitable educational outcomes with all students: The institution's roles and responsibilities.* College Park, MD: Association of American Colleges and Universities.

Bensimon, E. M. (2004, January/February). The diversity scorecard: A learning approach to institutional change. *Change,* 44–53.

Bensimon, E. M. (2005). Closing the achievement gap in higher education: An organizational learning perspective. *New Directions for Higher Education, 131,* 99–111.

Bensimon, E. M. (2007). The underestimated significance of practitioner knowledge in the scholarship of student success. *The Review of Higher Education, 30*(4), 441–469.

Bensimon, E. M., Dowd, A. C., Alford, H., & Trapp, F. (2007). *Missing 87: A study of the transfer gap and choice gap.* Long Beach and Los Angeles: Long Beach City College and Center for Urban Education, University of Southern California.

Bensimon, E. M., Polkinghorne, D. E., Bauman, G. L., & Vallejo, E. (2004). Doing research that makes a difference. *Journal of Higher Education, 75*(1), 104–126.

Cameron, K. (2004). A process for changing organizational culture. In T. G. Cummings (Ed.), *The handbook of organizational development* (pp. 429–447). Thousand Oaks, CA: Sage Publications.

Eckel, P., Hill, B., & Green, M. (1998). *On change: En route to transformation.* Washington, DC: American Council on Education.

Eckel, P. D., & Kezar, A. (2003). *Taking the reins: Institutional transformation in higher education.* Westport, CT: Greenwood Publishing.

Harris, L. (2009). *Higher education success among historically marginalized males.* Retrieved April 5, 2011, from http://www.socsci.uci.edu/ssarc/rscholars/webdocs/success-among-historically-marginalized-males.pdf

Harris, F., III & Bensimon, E. M. (2007). The equity scorecard: A collaborative approach to assess and respond to racial/ethnic disparities in student outcomes. *New Directions for Student Services, 120,* 77–84.

Huber, G. P. (1991). Organizational learning: The contributing process and the literatures. *Organization Science, 2*(1), 88–115.

Kezar, A., Glenn, W. J., Lester, J., & Nakamoto, J. (2008). Examining organizational contextual features that affect implementation of equity initiatives. *The Journal of Higher Education, 79*(2), 125–159.

Lee, J. M., & Rawls, A. (2010). The college completion agenda: 2010 progress report. New York, NY: The College Board Advocacy & Policy Center. Retrieved March 15, 2011, from http://completionagenda.collegeboard.org/sites/default/files/reports_pdf/Progress_Report_2010.pdf

Lumina Foundation. (2009). *Lumina Foundation's strategic plan: Goal 2025.* Indianapolis, IN: Author. Retrieved April 5, 2011, from http://www.luminafoundation.org/newsroom/newsletter/Archives/2009-11.html

Obama, B. (2009, February 24). *Address to Joint Session of Congress.* Remarks presented at the Briefing Room, Washington, DC. Retrieved April 5, 2011, from http://www.whitehouse.gov/the_press_office/Remarks-of-President-Barack-Obama-Address-to-Joint-Session-of-Congress/

Robinson-Armstrong, A., Clemons, A. Fissinger, M. X., & Sauceda, M. (2012). *The diversity scorecard at Loyola Marymount University: An exemplary model of dissemination.* Manuscript submitted for publication.

Robinson-Armstrong, A., King, D., Killoran, D., Ward, H., Fissinger, M. X., & Harrison, L. (2007). Creating institutional transformation using the equity scorecard. *Diversity Digest, 10*(2), 7–8.

Robinson-Armstrong, A., King, D., Killoran, D., Ward, H., Fissinger, M. X. (2009). The equity scorecard: An effective tool for assessing diversity initiatives. *The International Journal of Diversity in Organisations, Communities & Nations, 8*(6), 31–39.

Schein, E. H. (1988). *Organizational culture.* WP# 2088-88. Sloan Management School. Retrieved April 11, 2011, from http://dspace.mit.edu/bitstream/handle/1721.1/2224/SWP-2088-24854366.pdf?sequence=1

USC Center for Urban Education. (n.d.). USC Center for Urban Education's equity scorecard model applied at Los Medanos College (LMC). PowerPoint presentation presented at Los Medanos College, Pittsburgh, CA.

U.S. Department of Education. (2011). Fast facts. Alexandria, VA: National Center for Education Statistics (NCES). Retrieved April 11, 2011, from http://nces.ed.gov/fastfacts/display.asp?id=98

CHAPTER 22

MAKING A CASE FOR EDUCATION EVALUATION WITH A DIVERSITY LENS

Diane R. Fuselier-Thompson

INTRODUCTION

The economic and technological growth of the U.S. in response to the rapidly changing global economy presents significant challenges for industry to seek out skilled and diverse workers for the 21st century competitive workforce. The increasing knowledge based economy requires a diversified workforce with highly technical educational skills, specifically in the fields of Science, Technology, Engineering and Mathematics (STEM) in order to adequately meet the needs of industry and remain competitive in the global economy. More specifically, the education and training that engineers receive at selective institutions in the U.S. satisfies a critical source of the skilled and technical labor force needs. According to the most recent 2010 National Academy of Science Report that explores strategies for expanding our labor force in science and engineering fields, a primary source of our science and engineering workforce originates from those who complete at least a Bachelor's degree (National Academy of Sciences, 2010). Yet ethnic minorities and women remain disproportionately underrepresented

Social Justice Leadership for a Global World, pages 393–409
Copyright © 2012 by Information Age Publishing
All rights of reproduction in any form reserved.

among engineering and science degree recipients (National Science Foundation, 2011).

K–12 educators, administrators, and policy makers have long wrestled with ways to develop effective strategies and programs that increase postsecondary access and degree attainment among minority students in the STEM fields of study. A critical approach to evaluation practice that includes a focus on the role of race and racial perceptions provides educators and administrators with vital information that can be tailored to meet their minority program development needs and diversity initiatives. This chapter suggests that an Evaluation with a Diversity Lens (EDL) strategy used in conjunction with a Critical Race Theory (CRT) framework is particularly useful in postsecondary education, where racial disparities persist in the engineering and science fields of study. An evaluator using the tenets of EDL captures and interprets the cultural meaning of program experiences through the "voices" of the program recipients. Yet equally important to the evaluative analysis is the role of race and racism in the institution and/or program under study. In the next sections I will outline CRT, the EDL strategy, and its utility for STEM fields, particularly engineering.

HISTORICAL SIGNIFICANCE OF CRT IN HIGHER EDUCATION

Racial disparities in K–12 education, postsecondary educational access and degree attainment have a unique history that spans many decades in the U.S. Critical Race Theorists provide a perspective that combines legal precedence and race as a central theme in an effort to provide understanding to the persistence of social and educational inequities (Bell, 1992). CRT scholars provide a theoretical framework for understanding historical educational inequities in a way that sheds light on societal differences by race and its impact on educational access and achievement (Lynn & Parker, 2006). The articulated goal of the pivotal *Brown v. Board of Education* historical case was to make education the great equalizer among the races, to provide equal access to education, and to improve the social and economic conditions in the black community (*Brown v. Board of Education*, 1954). The *Brown* decision was intended to desegregate K–12 education and improve the social and educational inequities between whites and blacks. The strategy of this case was that through greater educational access it was believed that blacks could achieve greater opportunity for social and economic advancement.

However, more than fifty years later, the goals of the *Brown* decision remain unfulfilled (Bell, 2004), with the majority of students of color remaining in low performing schools, in contrast to their white counterparts. Bell describes the *Brown* decision as an unfulfilled promise of racial parity in education for minorities and argues that the court ruling and subsequent policies sought to merely replicate the unequal educational structures that existed prior to *Brown* (Bell, 2004). Examples of the failure of *Brown* are numerous, more pronounced in some urban districts like the public school systems in the cities of New York and Chicago that enroll almost 10% of all African American high school males nationwide, yet collectively fail to graduate more than 70% of these students within four years (Holtzman, 2004).

The promise of *Brown* was extended to colleges and universities in 1964 when the federal government passed Title VI of the Civil Rights Act prohibiting institutions of higher learning from receiving federal funds if discriminatory policy or practices were present. Yet, fifty years after *Brown*, predominantly white institutions (PWI) remain predominantly white. Pontius and Harper (2006), in their analysis of U.S. Department of Education data, illustrates that African American males made up only 4.3% of all students enrolled in U.S. higher education in 2002, the same as in 1976. Minority student access to higher education is of historical significance in the evaluation of programs that seek to recruit and assess minority student progress and/or programs. As Guinier (2004) notes,

> The fact is that fifty years later many of the social political and economic problems that the legally trained social engineers thought the Court had addressed through *Brown* are still deeply embedded in our society. Not only in K–12, but also in postsecondary education, Blacks lag behind Whites in multiple measures of educational achievement and within the black [sic] community… (p. 92)

When funding is made available in higher education for an evaluation, the requester of that evaluation is typically situated at the top of the educational hierarchy. However it is important that evaluators not narrowly tailor the formulation of their research questions to the funders and administrators of these programs (Weiss, 1997). The unique history of the underrepresentation of minorities in higher education is of particular importance when evaluating affirmative action and race conscious programs, along with the ensuing political, social and cultural campus climates (Hurtado, 2001). The historical and cultural context provides a meaningful perspective, specifically in the field of engineering where minority students have been historically underrepresented. For this reason, students of color who are the intended program recipients should always be included in the evaluation of a program meant to enhance their academic experience. Minority student perceptions of racial injustices, real or imagined, become critical to the evaluator's understanding of the campus culture. Additionally, the historical underpinnings, unique to each campus, are critical to the understanding of the program and minority academic achievement. Lani Guinier

(2003), in defending the use of race in admissions, spoke of the importance of admissions decisions as it relates to access to the upper echelons of political power in the U.S., indicating that "... at selective institutions of higher education, admissions decisions have a special political impact: rationing access to societal influence and power and training leaders for public office and public life" (para. 4).

Similarly, understanding the historical context of the underrepresentation of other marginalized populations in selective fields of study includes thoughtful discovery of the intricacies of the power structure and the history of the groups' access to and participation in the postsecondary institution. When examining programs and initiatives in the technical fields of study, where minority students are disproportionately underrepresented, the evaluation could become a tool for gate keeping and/or perpetuate existing stereotypes without careful and thoughtful integration of strategies and methodologies. The historical use of race in determining access and equity in education is a historical component legitimating realities that may otherwise be dismissed in traditional evaluations but would be an inclusive element of the EDL. The complexity of the power structure in higher education and the ensuing political climate surrounding issues of affirmative action and race conscious programs necessitate the use of diverse and non-traditional strategies that provide a depth of understanding of the social and educational inequities within the unique historical context of the institution and field of study.

THE NEED FOR EDL

Given historical inequities in achievement of minorities, culturally responsive evaluation strategies (Hood, Hopson, & Frierson, 2005) provide the evaluator with a deeper understanding of the unique perspectives and circumstances of the diverse ethnic group(s) under study. Culturally responsive strategies in evaluation offer a flexible framework for a range of methodological approaches, some non-traditional, in an effort to capture the cultural meanings aimed primarily at communities of color while assessing program outcomes and equity (Hood, 1998). In the absence of a multi-faceted and critical approach to evaluation practice that includes the minority recipient, evaluation outcomes can lead to the misrepresentation of the experiences of marginalized populations we seek to evaluate. Still further, the evaluation results could become a stereotypical tool of student gate keeping in the highly selective and coveted technical fields of study without an accurate interpretation of the cultural meaning of the student experience. Stakeholders should identify early in the evaluation process the relevance and intended use of the evaluation by the organization, which is of critical concern when the evaluation strategy is being designed. Most evaluations are typically initiated by those who occupy a position of power within the ranks of the organization (Weiss, 1997) or the evaluation strategy may serve a social, political or economic function in postsecondary education (Patton & Patrizi, 2010). It is important that educational leaders identify at the onset the audience and purpose an evaluation will serve, along with a myriad of stakeholders. Within the higher education hierarchy, it is important that program managers understand whether programs with minorities as the target recipients achieve intended goals and examine ways to make programmatic changes for improvement. Given the national and global need to diversify the field of engineering and other STEM fields of study, improving minority student access and degree attainment is a commonly stated programmatic goal among postsecondary institutions, usually consistent with institutional goals of diversity. Yet the education evaluation may serve another social or political function. In order to satisfy these sometimes conflicting goals and objectives, an evaluator using an EDL strategic framework would strive to balance the multiple needs of stakeholders along with program recipients.

An EDL is designed to assist the evaluator in gaining an in-depth understanding of the interplay of the social and educational inequities involving race and historical disparities when minority students are the program recipients. In an effort to garner a deeper understanding of the complex socially constructed realities in diverse higher education settings, a non-traditional mixed methodological approach provides the evaluator with a plethora of tools for social inquiry consistent with the EDL framework. The inclusive framework of EDL examines programs with specific attention to the cultural context for racial and/or ethnic minority student populations and includes methods tailored to identify and assess the subtle nuances of race and racism inherent in the power structure of higher education. The complexity of the power structure in higher education and the ensuing political climate surrounding issues of affirmative action and race conscious programs necessitate the use of diverse and non-traditional strategies. These strategies can provide a depth of understanding of the social and educational inequities within the unique historical context of the institution and field of study.

When we apply heuristics to culturally diverse evaluation practice, EDL serves a fundamental purpose by focusing on contextual clarity, close examination of the evaluator's reflexivity and cultural competence, as well as the critical issues of the social, political and cultural context in which the program operates. When examining programs and initiatives in the technical fields of study, where minority students are disproportionately underrepresented, the evaluation could easily become a tool for perpetuating existing stereotypes without careful and thoughtful integration of evaluation strategies and methodologies. The historical use of race in determining access and equity in education is a component of EDL legitimating realities that may otherwise be dismissed in traditional evaluations but would be an integrated element of the EDL.

Inclusive Evaluation

It is the program participants who provide the breadth and depth to the evaluation and allow a deeper understanding of the strengths and challenges of program participation. Additionally, the cultural underpinnings of the programmatic interactions and meanings are lost without the input and interpretations of those who actually experience the program. These cultural interpretations, in conjunction with the meaningful perspective of program managers and others, provides a more holistic view of the program under study.

EDL is an approach that seeks to engage multiple perspectives into the evaluation process, tailored to be inclusive of a range of stakeholders including the voices of intended users (Millett, 2010). While some perspectives may conflict, it is the multiple realities that provide a detailed understanding of a program's origins, intent, outcomes and unintended consequences. EDL, as an inclusive framework of Culturally Responsive Evaluation, has a focus on diverse stakeholders and a deeper understanding of contextually diverse settings and as a strategic approach encourages exploration of culturally specific methods that achieve programmatic goals (Hood, 1998). The broad yet culturally detailed contextualization of EDL brings program meaning and effectiveness through the eyes of the intended user and others by bringing voice to the understanding of the terms and social norms, germane to the culturally responsive evaluation genre. The unique climate of the university setting with its diverse students, faculty and staff, along with the competitiveness and selectivity of the engineering field of study, provides the interplay of key dynamics of institutional power, culture and technical sophistication.

The theoretical framework of EDL provides the latitude and support for mixed methodological approaches in the evaluation of educational programs that serve minority students and other marginalized populations, with an important focus on the understanding and translation of the contextual environment. This deep understanding and interpretation can only be achieved with an evaluation team that possesses the understanding and expertise of the "lived experience." The contributions of the "lived experience" to the evaluation provide both legitimacy and explanation (Schwandt & Burgon, 2006) while providing clarity to the practitioner, who needs to make judgments about program goals and practices (Schwandt,

2003). These judgments are made in conjunction with the social and political influences of the institution. The tenets of EDL, with an emphasis on cultural competency and contextual clarity, provide a holistic approach to understanding programs and are specifically applicable within a racialized and global context. Since the evaluation may serve a social, political or some other kind of function in postsecondary education, it is important that educational leaders understand at the onset the audience and purpose an evaluation will serve. Within the higher education hierarchy, program managers may want to understand whether the program is intended to achieve goals of improving minority student academic achievement, access to postsecondary education or some other institutional goal. It is not uncommon for upper level administrators to have alternate uses for the evaluation, sometimes as a tool for balancing the budget or eliminating programs. In order to satisfy these sometimes conflicting goals and objectives, evaluators will need to balance the multiple needs of stakeholders and the multiple realities of the program.

The Responsive Evaluation

The Client-Centered or Responsive Evaluation supports local autonomy and utility in the program evaluation as a tool for program improvement (Stake, 1972) and social democratization (Greene, 2005) as a way to move towards a more just and equitable society. This approach reflects the philosophy of cultural pluralism and multiple realities (Stufflebeam, 2001), while also providing the institution with information to engage public discourse about inequities in higher education and society. EDL as a responsive type of evaluation approach is expected to be an important tool in shaping future institutional policy and budgetary decisions involving institutional diversity program initiatives. This type of evaluation approach could provide information about intended and unintended results. But in order to achieve the multiplicity of evaluative needs, the evaluator will need to develop strategies and methods that provide context or background for the program with input from multiple stakeholders including, but not limited to, the intended beneficiaries, program managers and administrators responsible for funding the initiative. In other words, how do multi stakeholders view the program, its benefits and challenges? How has the context of the program changed given the social, political and historical context and what are the multi meanings of that reality? How does the program represent the institution's mission of diversity, particularly with respect to the program funding and where it is situated within the institutional hierarchy? In addition to program managers, how do others give meaning to the program? Can conflicting realities among stakeholders be understood within the context of the institutional history by race and/or fields of study?

The purpose of the Responsive Evaluation is to remain open and flexible to what is valued within the cultural context of the phenomena being studied while interpreting multiple realities. This approach allows the evaluator to embrace multiple stakeholder values and interests with regard to the program under study. The history of unequal access to higher education among minority program recipients suggests that a Responsive Evaluation strategy would best meet the assessment needs of an engineering program evaluation, where minority students are the target recipients. The responsive evaluation gives voice to the counter-narrative among the minority and marginalized populations (Solorzano & Yosso, 2002). The counter-narrative is often the untold story within marginalized communities or a story clouded by misinterpretations when being revealed by those unfamiliar with the cultural norms of the community. The historical context of racial disparities in education and more specifically in the engineering fields of study becomes a critical factor in interpreting meanings and context, along with the social and political factors that influence postsecondary access and degree attainment.

EDL/Culturally Responsive Evaluation

Culture is an elusive and amorphous phenomenon and presents both a challenge and opportunity for the evaluator within the context of higher education. Among underrepresented racial and ethnic groups in the U.S. and globally, there exist multiple meanings and interests within and among cultural groups. Culturally Responsive Evaluation is intended to provide an in-depth knowledge and understanding of groups historically underrepresented in American society and parties to an evaluation (Hood, Hopson, & Frierson, 2005). Culturally Responsive Evaluation is strongly influenced by the "lived" experiences of stakeholders, who are the target beneficiaries of the program.

Context is a critical and unique dimension in a Responsive Evaluation, and this includes the strong influence of the programmatic meanings that the recipients themselves attach. For groups that have been historically underrepresented and marginalized in American society, the inclusion of this unique historical dimension is critical to any evaluation that includes underserved program recipients. As Bob Stake (1972) points out when describing responsive evaluation, "an evaluation probably will not be useful if an evaluator does not know the interest and language of his audience" (p. 7). The strength of EDL in examining programs where racial minorities are the primary beneficiaries is the inclusive framework that examines programs, with specific attention to cultural context for a racially and ethnically diverse minority student population with methods tailored to meet the needs of that specific cultural and social context.

In the absence of contextual knowledge, the evaluation could lead to misrepresentation of the marginalized populations we seek to assess, and the evaluation could become a tool of "student gate-keeping," while perpetuating stereotypes in the highly selective and coveted technical fields of study. It is not enough to be sympathetic to the program (Cronbach, 1982), but the evaluator should seek to advance a social agenda that fosters change when examining social and educational programs. The responsive evaluation approach would provide culturally specific information, unique to each cultural community.

CRITICAL COMPONENTS OF EDL

An evaluator operating in the responsive domain of evaluation has the latitude and flexibility to defer the *design* of the study to a range of stakeholders that include authority or funders as well as the underserved population. The *method* of study is best achieved through qualitative methods (case study, observation etc.) or a combination of nontraditional methodological approaches that best interpret the "contextual reality." The relativist orientation of this approach may actually identify multiple realities. The *practice* of Responsive Evaluation employs a defensible assessment of the program while encouraging democratic participation for the common good (Greene, 2005).

The inclusive framework of EDL, with a focus on diverse stakeholders, supports a detailed understanding of cultural context in diverse settings (Hood, Hopson & Frierson, 2005) with historical grounding and exploration of culturally specific methods that achieve these goals. A mixed method study that integrates the needs of the funders for quantitative survey data and the need for contextual clarity using qualitative case study methodology (Campbell, 1975; Guba & Lincoln, 1989; Stake, 2004) can provide the detailed and integrated contextual information needed for a multi perspective and multi level analysis for higher education engineering programs where minority students are recipients. According to Kushner, the methods of the evaluation study should seek to unite the needs of the funders and the evaluator's social values of the program under study (Kushner, 2009). The mixed methodological approach consistent with EDL incorporates the detailed culturally specific program meaning through the eyes of the intended user and others by bringing voice to the understanding of terms and norms, germane to the culturally responsive evaluation (Hood et al., 2005).

This cultural interpretation is critical to the understanding of the program and other contextual influences at the educational institution.

The unique history of minority students in higher education and the university setting with its diverse student body, faculty and staff, along with the disproportionate underrepresentation of minority students in engineering fields, provides the interplay of several key dynamics that are important to this evaluation approach in promoting democratic principles and equity. A multi perspective interpretation of key factors associated with the program is central to the EDL strategy and not easily interpreted or understood by limited stakeholders who are not themselves the intended users of the program.

The mixed methodological approach in the EDL design provides a unique contribution to the body of educational research examining race and student engagement and a unique opportunity for the researcher to inquire at multiple levels with both depth and breadth. A qualitative method of inquiry can provide the detailed counter-narrative that is difficult to achieve using a quantitative framework. The qualitative inquiry can provide the researcher with an understanding of the details of the cultural context in which the phenomenon exists, while a quantitative study can provide historical trends in racial climate and minority student access at institutions with similar characteristics. The combined methodological approaches provide the researcher with the latitude of increased sources and dimensions to examine the subtle nuances of race as it relates to the participation of so few minority engineering students enrolled in postsecondary institutions.

It is important that education administrators and leaders encourage internal stakeholders to embrace the benefits of culturally responsive evaluation, advocating for the cost (which are more costly to perform due to the depth of inquiry) and benefit of completing a culturally responsive evaluation. It is important to work with faculty and other administrators across disciplines to develop action plans for programmatic changes in understanding how intervention programs are evaluated and the methods employed to do so. In light of the in-depth understanding of the cultural context associated with culturally responsive evaluation, the EDL approach provides a unique framework for conducting evaluations when minority students are the target program recipients, and it is necessary to understand the complex social and political influences that operate within the context of the educational institution under study. As unique as language and cultural norms are to each community, the evaluation should be tailored to communicate that unique character to stakeholders and others, and the culturally responsive evaluation appears tailored to meet that need.

A second area of importance in the EDL is the recognition of the ethical and political implications of an evaluation study and its potential impact on educational policy, the power distribution among stakeholders as it relates to their hierarchical position within higher education and within the program specifically, along with ethical considerations and the subtleties of race and racism. It is important that the evaluation include some discussion of the intricacies of the power structure in an educational institution. The ensuing political, social and campus climate surrounding issues of affirmative action and race conscious programs provide meaningful context to an evaluation of programs that include minority students. The role of political influence in evaluation must also be considered (Weiss, 1997), with attention given to the political messages garnered by the results of an evaluation within the highly charged political environment surrounding issues of affirmative action. The EDL strategy of evaluation necessitates the use of diverse methodologies to accommodate divergent stakeholders, while providing a depth of understanding of the social, historical and educational inequities involving race, gender and socioeconomic status. In an effort to garner a deeper understanding of the complex socially constructed realities in diverse higher education settings, a non-traditional mixed methodological approach provides the evaluator with a plethora of tools for social inquiry consistent with the EDL framework.

When educational leaders examine programs and initiatives in the technical fields of study, where minority students are disproportionately underrepresented, the evaluation can easily become a tool for gate keeping and/or perpetuate existing stereotypes without careful and thoughtful integration of strategies and methodologies. The historical use of race in determining access and equity in education is a historical component legitimating realities that may otherwise be dismissed in traditional evaluations using mono methods but would be an inclusive element of the EDL to further contextualize an understanding of the program.

Cultural Competency

Finally, in a diverse setting, it is important that cultural issues be explicitly addressed in the evaluation by competent evaluators who provide "interpersonal validity" (Kirkhart, 2005) through active listening and demonstrative cultural competency (Hood et al., 2005). This competency and sensitivity to cultural issues can best be achieved through the reflexivity of the evaluation team members and competency standards consistent with the American Evaluation Association's (AEA) recommendations for working with culturally different or diverse groups. AEA (2010) recommendations include the following:

> To ensure recognition, accurate interpretation and respect for diversity, evaluators should ensure that the members of the evaluation team collectively demonstrate cultural competence. Cultural competence would be reflected

in evaluators seeking awareness of their own culturally-based assumptions, their understanding of the worldviews of culturally-different participants and stakeholders in the evaluation, and the use of appropriate evaluation strategies and skills in working with culturally different groups. Diversity may be in terms of race, ethnicity, gender, religion, socio-economics, or other factors pertinent to the evaluation context. (n.p.)

The way in which culture affects how people look at the world has been well researched (Hofstede, 2001; House, 1990). The culture of the evaluator also plays a key role in the outcome of the evaluation. Key elements that are important in the evaluation of the program or service include the relevant experience and cultural competency of the evaluator or team. Equally important to the evaluation is recognition of the power distribution among stakeholders as it relates to their hierarchical position within the postsecondary institution, (Weiss, 1997) along with ethical considerations for minority student program participants and the campus racial climate.

Standards/Evaluator Competency

Important to the assessment of any program is the relevant experience and demographic characteristics of the evaluator or team. The evaluator should possess the cultural competencies to interpret the intricacies of the social, historical and cultural phenomena, while balancing democratic participation of each respective stakeholder. Equally important to the strength of the EDL is the relevant experience and demographic characteristics of the evaluator or team. The evaluator's recognition of the position of power among stakeholders as it relates to their hierarchical position within higher education, along with ethical considerations and an understanding of the subtleties of race and racism are critical aspects of the educational evaluation. The experience of the EDL team provides professional prerequisites, similar to the Joint Committee on Standards for Evaluation. In addition, the reflexivity accords historical and contextual knowledge and expertise that is vital to the interpretation and analysis of the multiple perspectives and meanings of the program experience. In fact, the recently passed Guiding Principles for Cultural Competency of the American Evaluation Association (AEA, 2010) provides some additional guidelines on competency in evaluation. The AEA, the foremost organization of professional evaluators, suggest that the evaluation include an accurate reflection of diverse views, recognition of the evaluator's own cultural bias, an understanding of culturally different stakeholders, skills in working with culturally different groups, and understanding appropriate evaluation strategies and methods (AEA, 2010).

Within the area of competency, the AEA Guiding Principles identify some strategies for evaluation approach, given the globally diverse populations, topics and content areas that evaluators must interpret. While AEA does not explicitly identify cultural competency, it does provide guidelines for self-assessment in conducting evaluations and competency in the methodological approach for the target population. Additionally in a diverse setting, it is important that cultural issues be explicitly addressed in the evaluation by competent evaluators who provide interpersonal validity (Elks & Kirkhart, 1993) through active listening and demonstrative cultural competency (Hood et al., 2005). This can best be achieved by reflexive evaluation team members and competency standards consistent with the American Evaluation Association's recommendations for working with culturally diverse populations and should include the following:

> To ensure recognition, accurate interpretation and respect for diversity, evaluators should ensure that the members of the evaluation team collectively demonstrate cultural competence. Cultural competence would be reflected in evaluators seeking awareness of their own culturally-based assumptions, their understanding of the worldviews of culturally-different participants and stakeholders in the evaluation, and the use of appropriate evaluation strategies and skills in working with culturally different groups. Diversity may be in terms of race, ethnicity, gender, religion, socio-economics, or other factors pertinent to the evaluation context. (AEA, 2010, n.p.)

The rationale for the program within a historical context of the institution becomes critically important to understanding the need for such a program, as it relates to racial disparities in education. For example some rationale and evaluation background information may include the racial disparities in K–12 academic preparation, the history of Affirmative Action or higher education access for minority students, the persistent under-representation of African Americans in higher education and engineering, or specific institutional practices in higher education. This contextual information from multiple sources provides meaning to the subtle nuances associated with race and ethnic groups that have been historically marginalized in American society and higher education and provides justification for continued dialogue and institutional introspection.

SUMMARY

In the end, it is imperative that all evaluators recognize their own cultural bias and be aware of the importance of cultural expertise in performing evaluations with diverse populations, and in particular work performed with marginalized communities. While it remains meaningful to include multiple perspectives and stakeholders in EDL, the evaluator must balance the meaningfulness of the stakeholder with his or her own neutrality and usefulness in providing a credible evaluation. Some organizational questions and key principles that educational leaders may want to address before initiating the evaluation include the following: 1) How do evaluators satisfy the interests and goals of funders/administrators who are typically at the top of the educational hierarchy with a multiplicity of perspectives? 2) Has the evaluator achieved balance in the identification of the historical and cultural patterns of disparities among minority students into the evaluation strategy, while satisfying the interests and goals of funders/administrators, taking into consideration the power differential of each respective stakeholder? And 3) What are the competencies of the evaluation team and their "lived experiences" with minority students in providing a valid and accurate interpretation of the cultural and technical experiences? So in summary, the key components of using an EDL strategy within the educational system should include the following:

- It should include deep understanding of the social, political and economic influences within the educational hierarchy as they relate to the program development and participation for minority students.
- An EDL seeks to understand and interpret the cultural context of an educational program including a multiplicity of perspectives inclusive of sometimes conflicting stakeholders and the perceptions acquired from the "lived experience" of program participants.
- An EDL examines the cultural competency of the evaluation team, either by their "lived experience" or other cultural expertise gained.
- When minority groups are the target recipients of the program under study, a critical social theory construct, where race is the focus, provides the framework for understanding the historical disparities of the underserved group within the context of the program and/or institution.

Finally, EDL can only be achieved using methods unique to the environmental context or in most cases a mixed methodological inquiry. It requires mastery of the knowledge of or awareness of culture that can only be acquired through "lived experience" by the evaluators interpreting the experience.

The rationale for the use of an EDL strategy and approach in evaluating STEM programs within a historical and culturally specific context becomes critically important in understanding the need for or funding for such a program, within the context of the institutional diversity mission. This contextual information gives meaning to the subtle nuances associated with race and racial differences that have been historically marginalized in higher education and in American society. However, the evaluator has the need to balance his or her interpretation of the recipients' meaning with the need to remain politically neutral in providing a credible evaluation with diverse meaning that does not seek to advance a specific social agenda. This evaluation goal within the fields of education can be accomplished with EDL.

REFERENCES

American Evaluation Association. (2010). American Evaluation Association guiding principles for evaluators. Retrieved from http://www.eval.org/Publications/GuidingPrinciples.asp

Bell, D. (2004, April 2). The Real Lessons of a 'Magnificent Mirage.' *Chronicle of Higher Education, 50*(30), B10.

Bell, D. (1992). *Faces at the bottom of the well: The permanence of racism.* New York, NY: Basic Books.

Brown v. Board of Education, 347 U.S. 483 (1954).

Campbell, D. T. (1975). Degrees of freedom and the case study. *Comparative Political Studies, 8,* 178–193.

Cronbach, L. J. (1982). *Designing evaluations of educational and social programs.* San Francisco, CA: Jossey-Bass.

Elks, M. A., & Kirkhart, K. (1993). Evaluating effectiveness from the practitioner perspective. *Social Work, 38,* 554–563.

Greene, J. C. (2005). Evaluators as stewards of the public good. In S. Hood, R. Hopson, & H.

Frierson (Eds.), *The role of culture and cultural context* (pp. 7–20). Greenwich, CT: Information Age Publishing.

Guba, E. G., & Lincoln, Y. S. (1989). *Fourth generation evaluation.* Newbury Park, CA: Sage.

Guinier, L. (2003). Admissions rituals as political acts: Guardians at the gates of our democratic ideals. *Harvard Law Review, 117,* 113.

Guinier, L. (2004). From racial liberalism to racial literacy: *Brown v. Board of Education* and the interest- divergence dilemma. *Journal of American History, 91*(1), 92–118.

Harper, S., Patton, L. D., & Wooden, O. S. (2009). Access and equity for African American students in higher education: A critical race historical analysis of policy efforts. *The Journal of Higher Education, 80*(4), 389–414.

Hofstede, G. H. (2001). *Culture's consequences: Comparing values, behaviors, institutions and organizations across nations* (2nd ed.). Thousand Oaks, CA: Sage.

Holtzman, L. (2004). Mining the invisible: Teaching and learning media and diversity. *The American Behavioral Scientist, 48*(1), 108–118.

Hood, S. (1998). Responsive evaluation Amistad style: Perspectives of one African American evaluator. In R. Davis (Ed.), *Proceedings of the Stake symposium on educational evaluation* (pp. 101–112). Urbana-Champaign, IL: University of Illinois at Urbana-Champaign.

Hood, S., Hopson, R., & Frierson, H. (2005). Introduction: This is where we stand. In S. Hood, R. Hopson, & H. Frierson (Eds.), *The role of culture and cultural context: A mandate for inclusion, the discovery of truth, and understanding in evaluative theory and practice* (pp. 1–5). Greenwich CT: Information Age Publishing.

House, E. (1990). Methodology and justice. In K. Sirotnik (Ed.), *Evaluation and social justice: Issues in education* (pp. 23–36). San Francisco, CA: Jossey-Bass.

Hurtado, S. (2001). Linking diversity and educational purpose: How diversity affects the classroom environment and student development. In G. Orfield & M. Kurlaender (Eds.), *Diversity challenged: Evidence on the impact of affirmative action* (pp. 187–203). Cambridge, MA: Harvard Education Publishing Group.

Kirkhart, K. E. (2005). Through a cultural lens: Reflections on validity and theory in evaluation. In S. Hood, R. Hobson, & H. Frierson (Eds.), *The role of cultural and cultural context: A mandate for inclusion, the discovery of truth, and understanding in evaluation theory and practice* (pp. 21–39). Greenwich, CT: Information Age Publishing.

Kushner, S. (2009). Own goals: Democracy, evaluation, and rights in millennium projects. In K. E. Ryan & J. B. Cousins (Eds.), *The Sage international handbook of educational evaluation* (pp. 413–428). Thousand Oaks, CA: SAGE.

Lynn, M., & Parker, L. (2006). Critical race studies in education. Examining a decade of research in U.S. Schools. *The Urban Review, 38*, 257–290.

Millett, R. (2010, June 29). *EDL, an emerging method of evaluation used to assess the merit and worth of programs with culturally diverse populations* [White paper]. Gaithersberg, MD: Ricardo Millett.

National Academy of the Sciences. (2010). *Expanding underrepresented minority participation: America's science and technology talent at the crossroads.* Washington, DC: National Academies Press.

National Science Foundation. (2011). Women, minorities and persons with disabilities in science and engineering. Retrieved from http://www.nsf.gov/statistics/wmpd/race.cfm#degrees

Patton, M. Q., & Patrizi, P. A. (2010). Strategy as the focus for evaluation. In P. A. Patrizi & M. Q. Patton (Eds.), *Evaluating strategy: New directions for evaluation* (pp. 5–28). San Francisco, CA: Jossey-Bass.

Pontius, J. L., & Harper, S. R. (2006, Fall). Principles for good practice in graduate and professional student engagement. *New Directions for Student Services, 115*, 47–58.

Schwandt, T. A. (2003). Back to the rough ground! Beyond theory to practice in evaluation. *Evaluation, 9*(3), 353–364.

Schwandt, T. A., & Burgon, H. (2006). Evaluation and the study of lived experience. In I. F. Shaw, J. C. Greene, & M. M. Mark (Eds.), *The Sage handbook of evaluation* (pp. 98–117). London: Sage.

Solorzano, D., & Yosso, T. (2002). A critical race counter-story of race, racism, and affirmative action. *Equity and Excellence in Education, 35*(2), 155–168.

Stake, R. E. (1972). Responsive Evaluation. ERIC Document ED 075-187.

Stake, R. E. (2004). *Standards-based and responsive evaluation.* Thousand Oaks, CA: Sage.

Stufflebeam, D. L. (2001). *Evaluation models.* San Francisco, CA: Jossey-Bass.

Weiss, C. (1997). *Evaluation* (2nd ed.). Upper Saddle River, NJ. Prentice Hall.

CHAPTER 23

PROVIDING A CULTURALLY RESPONSIVE EXPERIENCE FOR FOREIGN STUDENTS IN U.S. HIGHER EDUCATION

Clementine Msengi, Israel G. Msengi, and Sandra Harris

INTRODUCTION

Due to globalization and an increased need for a high quality education, the number of individuals attending higher education in foreign countries continues to grow (McLachlan & Justice, 2009). International students have indicated their preference to study in the U.S. because of scholarship availability, quality of education and technological advancement, availability of appropriate educational and advanced research facilities, congenial political, socioeconomic environment, and opportunity for general international life experience (Altbach, 1985). Thus, the United States has been the leading host country of international students from all over the world since 1940 (Institute of International Education [IIE], 2010). In fact, the number of foreign students who attended colleges and universities in the U.S. during the 2008–2009 academic year reached an all-time high of

Social Justice Leadership for a Global World, pages 411–431
Copyright © 2012 by Information Age Publishing
All rights of reproduction in any form reserved.

671,616, an increase of 8% from the previous year and the largest increase since 1980 (Open Doors, 2009).

The economic and social benefits of international students attending colleges and universities in the U.S. have been widely documented (Baumgartner, 2009; Chellaraj, Maskus, & Mattoo, 2008; IIE, 2011; McLachlan & Justice, 2009). The National Association of Foreign Student Advisers (NAFSA) estimated international students' contributions to the U.S. economy to be $14.5 billion in the 2006–2008 academic years and $17.8 billion in 2008–2009 (IIE, 2011). This is due to tuition, accommodations, and support for dependants. Socially, international students bring a rich element of diversity to the student body in terms of language, viewpoint, and global understanding (McLachlan & Justice, 2009). In addition, international students can serve as cultural ambassadors between the U.S. and their home countries (Nikias, 2008; Sandhu & Asrabadi, 1994).

Given the increased number of international students and their contributions to their host institutions, however, it is important to understand international students' needs in order to provide appropriate services for them (Brown & Holloway, 2008). This should also contribute to a more positive culturally responsive experience for the students and for those who work with them (Tidwell & Hanassab, 2007). Therefore, the purpose of this chapter is threefold: 1) identify challenges that foreign students face while attending U.S. institutions of higher education, 2) identify coping strategies used to effectively navigate these challenges, and 3) identify suggestions to improve the international student experience.

CHALLENGES INTERNATIONAL STUDENTS FACE

Cross-cultural contacts are inherently stressful (Fasheh, 1984; Neuliep, 2006; Wan, Chapman, & Biggs, 1992). Consequently, in the process of adjustment, the majority of international students in the U.S. experience overwhelming levels of stress (Dillard & Chisolm 1983; Heikinhemo & Shute, 1986; McLachlan & Justice, 2009; Sandhu & Asrabadi, 1994). For international students, cross-cultural contacts require self-adjustment to many issues because this process involves transition from one culture to another and from one type of an environment to the other. Tseng & Newton, (2002) reported that this transition implies adjustment on general life-style (food, housing, transportation, health care) and academics. Other stressors include personal depression (Tseng & Newton, 2002), homesickness (Dillard & Chisolm, 1983; Tseng & Newton, 2002; Msengi, 2007), loneliness (Misra & Castillo, 2004; Msengi, 2007), family concerns (Chun & Poole, 2009), threat to cultural identity, inferiority, anger/disappointments, mistrust, perceived hatred/rejection (Sandhu & Asrabadi, 1994), and perceived alienation or discrimination (Sandhu & Asrabadi, 1994; Tseng & Newton, 2002). Rice (1999) grouped stressors for international students into the following categories: personal and social, adjustment and acculturation, and academics.

According to Rice (1999), personal and social stressors include perceived discrimination, perceived hate and rejection, and homesickness. Perceived discrimination, a widely reported challenge to most international students, reflects the degree to which international students are unable to initiate interactions with host nationals, and to develop or maintain interpersonal relationships with them (Leong & Ward, 2000). Over 40 years ago, Essien (1975) reported that the majority of male Nigerian students participating in the study did not interact adequately with white U.S. citizens in various social situations. Other researchers also have indicated that being a foreign student increases racial and social isolation because they are more likely to favor building friendships with individuals from their home countries (Boyer & Sedlacek, 1986; Chavajay & Skowronek, 2008; Karuppan & Barari, 2011; Mortimer & Bryce-Laporte, 1981). This social isolation, resulting in an inability to reach out to host nationals, influences their perception of being discriminated against (Chavajay & Skowronek, 2008; Charles-Toussaint & Crowson, 2010; Cross, 1995; Karuppan & Barari, 2011).

International students are sensitive and perceive hate and rejection in the verbal and nonverbal communication and behaviors of some U.S. peers according to Sandhu and Asrabadi (1994). This feeling has been attributed to their loss of status, low self-esteem due to deprivation of a family support system, and cultural shock that they experienced after migration. Furthermore, perceived hate and rejection is also a result of U.S. citizen students under-utilizing foreign students' knowledge and skills, having negative attitudes about international students, and lacking competence/sensitivity to the different values of other cultures (Mtika, 2009; Sandhu & Asrabadi, 1994).

Adjustment challenges and associated stress stem from a form of homesickness. Most international students lose their emotional and social support systems when separated from their families and resultant limited social interactions with U.S. students (Lacina, 2002; Olivas & Li, 2006; Poyrazli & Lopez, 2007; Sandhu & Asrabadi, 1994). In addition to struggling to achieve their educational and personal goals, foreign students feel obligated to hold on to their cultural roots, a phenomenon that exacerbates feelings of homesickness (Poyrazli & Lopez, 2007).

Adjustment and acculturation stressors include issues of culture shock and cultural adjustment, as well as fear for safety. Over 30 years ago Stiegelbauer (1979) noted that the process of adopting a new culture involves a number of behavioral changes. These include: a) assimilation, where a foreigner becomes part of a larger culture; b) emulation, where a foreigner manifests behaviors or attitudes common to the dominant culture; c) integration, maintaining, and individualization, an internalization or modification of new information in the group as well as at the individual level; and d) rejection, which may lead to total withdrawal from the environment. Culture shock is widely recognized as a major adjustment challenge for international students, especially when dealing with external matters such as differences in food (Adler, 1975), climate (Adler, 1975; Furnham & Bochner, 1982), language (Kamanakao, 2002; Rice, 1999), mannerisms (Adler, 1975; Furnham & Bochner, 1982), and communication (Chavajay & Skowronek, 2008; Rice, 1999). Students encounter culture shock when trying to adjust to new life-styles such as driving (Furnham, 1988), forming relationships (Knowles, 1977), finances (Sherry, Thomas, & Chui, 2010), managing time (Kagan & Cohen, 1990), adjusting to different education patterns (Andrade, 2006), and conflicting world views (Adler, 1975).

Ryan and Twibell (2000) reported that stress levels experienced by international students were often related to a fear and safety concern. Unfamiliarity of surroundings posed a significant challenge because students feared encountering bad people, criminals, and burglary, or getting lost. Fear of expulsion from school and/or fear related to religious, racial, or cultural differences have also been documented (Mtika, 2009; Tseng & Newton, 2002).

Students also experience stress from academic pressures (Yan & Berliner, 2009). Although both American and international students share common academic stressors over a wide spectrum of issues, the perceptions of academic stress, coping strategies, social and academic conditions in U.S. universities might differ across cultures, consequently international students experience more adjustment complications compared to their American peers (Misra & Castillo, 2004). Such academic stressors include grades, academic standing, major term papers, registration red tape, financial concerns, course workload, and time pressures (Kwon, 2009; Misra et al., 2002; Olivas & Li, 2006).

The major academic stressors are test anxiety and time management (Rice, 1999; Wan et al., 1992). Given that international students often have poor language skills, there is the fear of performing poorly (Eghbali, 1985; Gang, Wei, & Duanmu, 2010; Yan & Berliner, 2009). Academic time management is another critical area, and stress becomes evident when international students are unable to balance the tasks of accomplishing class assignments, finding time for social pursuits, family, recreation, and exercise (Kwon, 2009; Olivas & Li, 2006; Sandhu & Asrabadi, 1994). Consequently, most international students eliminate time for social pursuits to concentrate on academic goals since good performance assures scholarship, as well as retains their student status (Reinicke, 1986).

Communication is another academic stressor (Misra & Castillo, 2004; Sandhu & Asrabadi, 1994). Communication problems are related to the foreign students' self-perceived inability to speak, read, listen to, and understand the language of the host culture (Gang, Wei, & Daunmu, 2010). Students less fluent in English face a particularly difficult task adjusting in the U.S. (Barratt & Huba, 1992; Meloni, 1986; Yan & Berliner, 2009). Furthermore, inadequate language communication skills contribute to social barriers for international students (Karuppan & Barari, 2011; Ryan & Twibell, 2000).

Coping Strategies and Adjustments

In a seminal work, Lazarus and Folkman (1984) identified widely recognized stress adjustment approaches as problem-focused coping (changing the stressful situation through problem solving) and emotion-focused coping (alleviating negative emotional responses through relaxing and meditating). Rice (1999) categorized coping strategies into two main categories called combative coping and preventive coping. Combative coping strategies attempt to suppress stressors by monitoring stress. Preventive coping strategies involve making life adjustments.

Specific coping strategies for international students use several actions. These include: a) utilizing available student services (Sherry, Thomas, Chui, 2010); b) getting into social and/or dating relationships with Americans (Msengi, 2007; Vaz, 1984); c) attending a variety of clubs and organizations to increase the extent of social relations with non-international students (Lee, 1981); d) developing social relations with other student groups in order to satisfy social needs such as friendship (Kamanakao, 2002; Lee, 1981; Msengi, 2007); e) seeking social support (Leavell, 2002); and f) visiting academic advisors (Kamanakao, 2002).

RECOMMENDATIONS TO SUPPORT
INTERNATIONAL STUDENTS

Several adjustment techniques that can be helpful to international students have been recommended. For example, Sherry, Thomas and Chui (2010) emphasized the need for initiatives to raise the profile of international students, improve financial assistance and scholarships, and create opportunities to improve international students' spoken English skills. Other recommendations have included the following: a) encouraging international students to discuss and explore the cultural differences they experience; b) requiring students to undergo a needs assessment evaluation focusing on the identification of needs and the various alternatives employed in meeting those needs; and c) talking to others, keeping journals, seeking information, and developing relationships with natives (McLachlan & Justice, 2009; Olivas & Li, 2006; Tseng & Newton, 2002). Rose-Redwood (2010) recommended several actions for universities to consider, such as developing policies that encourage student volunteer conversation partners or mentors, forming nationality clubs and encouraging members to attend university events, encouraging group work with U.S. students, encouraging departments to create small scale social activities, such as sports events between international and American students, and encouraging trips in the community.

OUR STUDY

We used a qualitative phenomenological narrative design to interview 11 international students about their challenges, coping strategies, and recommendations for improving their student experiences at a regional state university in Texas. This university is diverse, with 14,000 students, 530 of whom were international students, according to the Texas Higher Education Coordinating Board (THECB) (2010). The majority of the international students at this university were graduate students from India ($n = 358$), China ($n = 26$), Nepal ($n = 25$), and Bangladesh ($n = 15$).

Participants

The 11 international students who participated in this study were enrolled in various academic programs, such as engineering, physical education, health education, and occupational therapy. We utilized a snowball approach and began by asking instructors to identify international student from their classes. These students were then invited to participate in an interview about their international student experiences. Initial student participants recommended names of other international students who might be interviewed. Participants were from the following countries: the United Kingdom ($n = 1$), Cameroon ($n = 1$), Barbados ($n = 1$), China ($n = 1$), Venezuela ($n = 1$), Kenya ($n = 2$), and India ($n = 4$). Six students were female and five were male. Four were undergraduates and seven were graduate students. All participants ranged in age from 18 to 30 years old and had been in the U.S. for at least six months.

Data Collection and Analysis

After Internal Review Board (IRB) approval, an informed consent form was obtained from each participant assuring them of confidentiality. Each interview was conducted informally and lasted approximately one hour. Open-ended questions focused on international student experiences regarding challenges, coping strategies, and recommendations to improve their experience. Interviewers took notes and recorded participant responses using a digital audio recorder. Data analysis began with transcribing all of the recorded interviews and reading the transcripts thoroughly to identify and code emerging themes into meaningful units (Hycner, 1985; Lester, 1999).

WHAT WE FOUND

This study confirmed that challenges faced by international students still persist. The specific study findings are discussed by the research questions, which emphasized challenge, coping strategies, and recommendations to improve the international student experience.

Challenges Students Encountered

The discussion of challenges was organized using Rice's (1999) categories. These categories included academic, personal and social, and adjustment and acculturation.

Several academic challenges were noted that caused stress. These stressors included general academic stress conditions, communication, and financial issues. General academic stress resulting from academic pressure was viewed as the most important challenge. Students acknowledged academic demands were "huge." Life in general was fast paced including the instructor-student interaction time and lectures, yet students indicated they were often unaware of any available academic services or support on campus. Students reported the stress level posed by academic demands depended on the type of courses they were taking. A student from India expressed that he "was not used to the American education system and testing approach, but now I am adjusting and understanding and am more comfortable with multiple choice exams." A student from China said, "First year was the toughest, understanding course, lectures, test taking, and writing papers; however some professors were nice; they understood what a student like me was going through." Although in general, students had a positive view of the university faculty and staff as sociable or caring, they noted there were faculty members who were "rigid," and these individuals caused a tremendous amount of stress to students.

Technology and course delivery also created stressful academic concerns. For example a student from India related:

> I struggle to keep pace with academic demands... Back in India we were not
> used to online instruction, never had an online course. Here my first course
> was offered online and had no orientation about this whatsoever. I missed
> deadlines, had problems doing assignments. There were no other interna-
> tional students in my class that I could ask for help, it was hard to meet class-
> mates to seek for help. I did not understand the format and language terms.
> It took time for me to understand. The first semester I was not close to any-
> body, and never was I used to online search in the library database. I wish I got
> orientation to guide me how to search the database.

A Kenyan student expressed similar challenges relating to time management, understanding assignments, and finding study groups. He said,
"Once the class is over, classmates disappear until the next class. People are
busy working; it is just hard to approach people for help."

Further, all 11 of the students stated they encountered some type of
communication challenge. Lack of language proficiency limited their writing skills and sometimes communication skills. As one student emphasized,
"Because English is not my first language it was and still is hard to understand certain phrases and humor." Two students from India suggested, "It
would be very nice to interact with more American students so they can
help us with communication skills; we can help them too somehow." Other
difficulties emanated from different accents and word pronunciation. One
student from India complained, "Americans, including students and professors, sometimes cannot understand my accent." A student from Africa
thought some Americans were impatient in that "they can't spend time to
try to understand what one is trying to say."

Seven participants reported having a hard time being understood when
communicating with others or when they wrote their papers. A student from
China noted, "When I write my papers, to me they look really good... but
one of my professors once commented that I write like a second grader and
was quite aggravated with my writing."

Students from India, Venezuela, Cameroon and Kenya expressed challenges relating to understanding slang and differences in enunciation. Such
difficulties manifested themselves in the classroom, social settings, during
shopping, and when having telephone communications. For example, a
student from Kenya reported not understanding the Texas slang "y'all,"
which he later discovered meant "all of you." Other examples related to
misunderstanding of phrases, such as "taking a nap" instead of "resting," or
"hitting the sack" instead of "going to bed." A student from China reported
misinterpreting a statement from an American student who suggested, "I
would ask him..." to mean that this friend offered and was going to ask the
professor a question for him. But he discovered this phrase really meant
that "I should ask the professor."

A student from the UK noted that some English words were used and written differently and commented, "Some professors thought I was spelling words like 'centre,' 'neighbour,' 'colour,' or 'programme' wrongly; even the computer did not recognize them, so I am learning to spell and use some words the American way."

Another aspect of academic challenge focused on finances. Despite that some international students had scholarships, many still had to find work in order to cover all their living expenses. International students also had difficulty finding a job on campus. For example, one Indian student said:

> I feel that people here are irritated with Indian students and do not want to hire them, sometimes they give them a cold shoulder as soon as they enter the door. I do not understand why they would not hire because most jobs such as those in the dining center do not require much talking just physical work.

Some students received extra financial support from home. However, as one student from India said, "I don't like to depend on my parents all the time." In addition to having extra cash to cover expenses, students indicated that working and having their own money was very rewarding and brought a sense of independence. A student from India shared her excitement:

> Back home parents care for all our expenses; they pay our tuition, during vacations we go home and stay home doing nothing. We are not individualistic as it is here, even if you are 25 or older or even if you make money you would still live with parents. I am very happy that now I am learning to be more responsible for myself. I wish I was able to work earlier and manage certain things like finances, and living expense; I like freedom.

Personal and Social Challenges

Students commented on personal and social challenges that resulted in stress. These included transportation, housing, and safety issues.

All eleven international students reported that transportation was a challenge. A student from India commented, "When we arrived first time at the airport in Houston, we had difficulties finding a way to get to the city." Another student from Venezuela said:

> At first I did not have a car, so I would be begging people to take me to Wal-Mart and sometimes I pay them as much as $40 for a ride to Wal-Mart. After a while I realized that I can take a bus and realized that people have been taking advantage of my ignorance and that $40 per ride was a little too much, but people did not say anything. At first I did not want to take the bus because

people told me it was for the poor people, but when I [did] it was a pleasant experience.

Although public transportation was accessible, a student from England commented, "Public transportation here is not as good and efficient as in my country." Students complained it would take hours to even get to the nearest place in town. Consequently, most of them relied on friends and public transportation for going to a grocery store, the mall, or places of worship.

All eleven students reported a similar view that "a car is very important in this country. You can hardly get anything done if you can't move around fast." One student from Kenya emphasized, "Cycling is good for your health but in [this city] you can't get anywhere with a bicycle. There are no sidewalks that can get you to the main shopping centers; plus it will take you the whole day if you chose to take on this task." Another student from Cameroon complained, "There are many cars here but people ride alone in a roomy car most of the time. They can't give a ride just like that."

International students reported housing to be another stressful challenge. Ten of the participants rented inexpensive housing near campus. A student from India complained:

> Walking to get here early in the morning to attend classes and later work and in addition to my evening classes is challenging to keep up. In a day, I only have a two hour gap to go home, eat, and return. I can handle when the weather [not sunny or raining] is appropriate, but it is quite a hassle when you forget something and have to go back.

When asked why students preferred to live off campus, several pointed out that "housing off-campus is much cheaper compared to the university apartments." A student from Kenya emphasized:

> Housing is tough. I stay off campus. Because I am an athlete I get a stipend but it is not sufficient at all. Instead, I live off campus and I like it there because I can come home anytime, no annoyance, I cook my own food, it is quiet, and I can be alone in a more quiet place and can concentrate on my studies with no yelling around.

In addition, several of the students commented they could co-habit because this made the rent cheaper.

Some students expressed worries about their safety, especially those who lived off-campus. A student from India commented, "Safety is a very big problem. Recently some students got robbed and their wallets were stolen; they called the police and the police just made a note of it...did not do anything about it." Another student from India shared similar concerns regarding safety, "We had our house vandalized and our (shared) laptop and other items were stolen. When we called the police they did not make any follow-up. I think the police should do more on these crimes."

Demonstrating how critical safety issues were, a Venezuelan student complained "even getting grocery is hard because safety in [this city], around campus, and in the nearby off campus housing in addition to transportation issues are bad." A student from Kenya reported they heard gun shots quite often in their neighborhood. Yet another Kenyan student remembered, "During Hurricane Ike [2008] things were worse. Some unknown people broke into our apartment and stole our things, it is really scary."

Adjustment and Acculturation Challenges

Adjustment and acculturation challenges focused on two major themes that caused stress. These themes were cultural issues and lack of social support.

Ten students reported acculturation problems due to culture differences. The cultural issues identified by the students as major stressors were primarily about the difficulty of socializing, the level of individualism and other areas such as dress and food differences. For example, a student from India commented:

> I was surprised to see students here are pretty much couples, that is boy and girls. In India, unless married we can't live together, walk together all the time. In addition, covering is a very important custom. If I would want to get married we would be matched.

Another Indian student stated, "Even that I am here now I am not dating anyone because I respect my parents, they still have control of me. But American students are much freer." A student from Africa commented, "It is hard to integrate here because things that students do here for socializing such as clubbing, partying, drinking, thereafter are quite shocking."

Students noted that U.S. students display strong levels of independence. One student from India expressed this by saying, "I like the level of independence students have here. Our parents still control us even if we are here. We have to consult them for most decisions. But we like our culture." However, a student from India wondered why his professor would not let him help carry some of her book bags as she seemed to struggle to carry them across the hallway to the car. He said, "Every time I see her with heavy bags and I offer to help but she says 'I got it, thanks.' I don't know what it means." A student from Cameroon also emphasized this cultural individualism:

> I think because people here are very individualistic, friendship is not permanent, sort of superficial or is just a short term friendship, it is kind of hard

to form a trusted friendship. When I arrived here the first time most people showed interest in me, everybody was like, 'hi, where are you from?' But after a while it faded out.

Misinterpreting or misunderstanding actions creates a challenge. A student from Kenya pointed out, "I feel that relationships here are built depending on what you have to offer. For example, if you lose what you are capable of doing [offer] they just throw you out." A student from Venezuela added:

Culture has been also a bit different but I am learning to behave like the way they behave here. For example in my county they greet with a kiss and if they see someone they greet them loud even if there are at a long distance, here they will think I m loud and crazy, so I do not do that. I also noticed that people say 'excuse me' for passing close to you. That is not a big deal in my country because there people just pass each other very close pushing you to get out of the way. The issue of space here is important and it is not a big deal over there in Venezuela.

Students commented on other cultural concerns, that female students over-exposed themselves and male students wore their pants below their waist. Food also presented a challenge. The food tasted different, their diet was different, and they saved money by cooking the food of their own choice. A student from India commented, "We eat more of veggies and spices and can hardly eat American food. I can cook a lot of the food I like and save it for the whole week . . . that saves me money."

Furthermore, lack of social support included the sense of feeling lonely, being homesick, and feeling rejected. International students reported they lacked social support at the critical time they needed it, particularly, in their first six months of arrival to the United States. A student from China stated, "In my first and second semester here I struggled to get friend or support to help me in understanding course, lectures, and knowing my way around." Another student from India reported:

It was hard to find true American friends who could help me to understand how things work in this culture, for instance the dos and don'ts. I work at the front desk and whenever someone entered the office I would stand to listen and to greet them. We do that as a gesture of discipline [respect] to someone older or in authority, however I once heard behind my back that this is awkward. I have been here for seven and a half months now and have not had a serious American friend. But this semester I managed to find a friend and we do assignments together.

A student from Venezuela commented:

People are less friendly here, but I think it is not a bad thing because I'm very busy, have to balance my responsibilities, find time to rest, do laundry and relax. I don't have time to socialize anyway, but at my place this will be regarded as abnormal. If I want to be successful here, I have to be selfish and not social.

Coping Strategies for International Students

Coping strategies utilized by international students to overcome challenges focused on several strategies. These included finding time for entertainment and leisure, relying on spirituality, building relationships and socializing in general, and implementing other coping strategies, such as calling home, keeping a positive attitude and car pooling.

All 11 of the international students noted that a primary coping strategy was finding time for entertainment and/or leisure. Common leisure activities identified were watching movies, surfing on the Internet, watching TV, going to the recreation center, and playing games, although these activities usually occurred with other international students. A student from Kenya commented, "My Ugandan roommate and I sometimes we go to movies at the movie theatre, or just rent a movie and watch at home. Also, we occasionally go to dance." Indian students noted they preferred to watch Indian movies.

Religious practices such as praying and reading the scriptures were also reported as an essential coping strategy. A student from Cameroon stated:

I find it very pleasurable getting into church activities. I am so much involved in church activities because that is how I was raised—surrounded by Christianity. The church brings me close to home, reminds me of my family, part of my culture and values. I see that true friends are found in the church.

Similarly, a student from India reiterated, "I find comfort in worshiping; my religion is Hindu. We prepare some place in our house for worshiping. There is no worshiping place here [in this city], but when we have time, sometimes we go to [a large city nearby] for worshiping." A student from China acknowledged, "I pray and read my Bible a lot. My spirituality has helped me a lot. It has uplifted me during hard times." A student from Venezuela said, "I do not pray, but I know those who pray they find comfort in that."

Forming relationships and socializing with others was a coping strategy. Students indicated they attended campus social activities and joined organizations such as the Asian/Indian student association. They also organized social activities and invited friends from similar cultures. One student emphasized:

On weekends or holidays sometimes my roommate and I cook and invite fellow Kenyans or East Africans and get together. In these gatherings there is plenty to laugh and learn. It is so relaxing because we share the culture, have things in common, understand our jokes, and have a similar comprehension of what we talk about.

Nearly all participants found coping easier when they associated or "hung out" with other international students. For example, students from India most of the time clustered together, lived together, worked on assignments together, went shopping together, and partied together. A student from China agreed that because of culture and language similarities it was easier to be together. A student from England said, "I live with friends from home because I feel comfortable with them, although for me making friends with Americans or other students from Europe is not as challenging." A student from Venezuela commented,

I spend most of my time with other international students who are from Spanish speaking countries. Because of that, I am speaking Spanish with them. We speak Spanish mostly because it is more comfortable to them; they do not feel like they have to think of new words and formulate a sentence as it is with English. We also formulate a study group and meet in the library often to study together.

One student emphasized "Americans can't understand exactly what we go through being foreign students; they can't offer me reliable information about how I need to conduct my life here in order to succeed both academically and socially as a student." Therefore, students who have been in the U.S. longer provided the best orientation on how to cope with life in America. For example, an Indian student shared advice from other international students that he was given when he arrived in America:

My Indian colleagues told me welcome to America, and told me I needed to be punctual, on time, work hard and manage finances well, turn in work on time, and always communicate not just sit quiet and assume things, and now I look back all they said is very true.

A student from Barbados emphasized the importance of being able to communicate with the local people and forming friendships in order to find support in times of need. He said:

My church helps with transportation and sometimes with money. I did not shut myself out of the general population, I made efforts to reach out and create friendship with all. It is important to surround yourself with the right people if you want to succeed.

A student from India added, "I find professors and staff who are best and trust them. Those are the ones who help me get through some of the challenges because they are on our side. Focus on those good professors and staff, do not worry so much about the bad ones."

Students mentioned other ways of coping that included carpooling, having a positive attitude, and calling home. Students who had been in the U.S. longer and had the finances to purchase a car helped their colleagues with transportation. Often friends paid for gas and helped with repair costs. A Kenyan student said, "I am a good friend maker and they give me rides, they tell me anytime you need a ride feel free to let us know." By carpooling, students "saved money or avoided buying a car."

A majority of international students reported that a positive attitude towards life was a key toward succeeding in academic pursuits and general social life in America. A student from Cameroon noted, "I think having a good attitude towards other cultures makes you become curious to learn and mingle easily. I find developing a good attitude about things is the best acculturation approach." A student from Venezuela gave this advice, "Be strong and do not listen to discouraging people; remember where you came from and appreciate what you have here; enjoy life, but do it wisely."

International students called home as often as three to four times per week. As a Kenyan student said, "When I am stressed out I call home to talk to my parents, they give me encouragement, I get relief." International students also called families or friends that reside in the States. A student from India said, "I have a cousin sister here [U.S.] and I visit or call her often when I am down or need some advice, she gives me some ideas, and gives some strategies on how to handle things."

RECOMMENDATIONS

Participating international students recommended that universities should consider several actions to improve foreign student experiences. They wished orientations provided when they arrived reflected more accurately the realities of life in the U.S. A student from Venezuela complained, "During the orientation, they give us rules about the campus and also hand you maps of the campus, but no one is there to show us around campus, no one to show where our classes are, where to go take a picture, explain about their I-20 rule."

Students recommended developing a variety of work options that allowed students to work more hours or acquire better paying jobs would be helpful. Students also suggested that the university designate housing for foreign students at a low cost "that are affordable and are safe." Another suggestion was that the university should provide an efficient bus system serving not only foreign students but all students.

Because as a student from India said, "There is a lot we can share with American students, and they can help us too." Students recommended that activities that reflected multicultural views such as cultural dance troops from various countries, student activities, or cultural festivals would improve the campus experience for all students. A Kenyan student suggested having an international student representative on the student government so that there would be a "voice representing international students' issues."

One student suggested mentoring because "international students need mentors or someone who is familiar with our challenges and who can help us and speak for us when we need help." Another student pointed out:

> When we are here away from our parents, if you are not mature enough you can get deviated from your goals. Some of my friends have adopted laziness, drinking, partying and not taking care of themselves. The lack of a role model and a counselor can lead them to a bad path.

CONCLUSION

Despite the extensive documentation of international students' socioeconomic and academic experiences in the U.S., officials at institutions of higher education have been traditionally indifferent to the adjustment problems of international students (Charles-Toussaint & Crowson, 2010; Lacina, 2002; Misra & Castillo, 2004; McLachlan & Justice, 2009; Olivas & Li, 2006; Poyrazli & Lopez, 2007; Yan & Berliner, 2009). Results from this study affirmed that international students who study in the U.S. still experience the challenges associated with adjusting to U.S. culture. Some of the main challenges include academic stressors such as academics, finances, and language; personal and social issues such as transportation, housing, and safety needs; and adjustment and acculturation stressors emphasizing cultural issues and lack of support. On the other hand, students in this study found numerous ways of coping with these stressors. They found time for entertainment, drew strength from their spirituality, built relationships with students from similar and other cultures, carpooled, emphasized positive outlooks on life, and called home. To improve international students' experiences several recommendations were made, which included expanding orientation programs, providing more intercultural social events on campus, offering mentoring services, designating apartments just for foreign students at low cost, and making transportation readily available.

Findings in this study may be useful in assisting university administrators, faculty and staff in understanding challenges international students experience. By understanding their adjustment stressors, educators can devise strategies helpful to international students' acculturation process. For example, culturally sensitive counselors should be hired with multicultural experiences to assist international students. University officials should increase the number of multicultural events where all university students can experience other cultures. Supervision and follow-up of campus life of international students could be done in an annual meeting with international students to exchange ideas and learn more from them. It is evident from this study that when seeking help during challenging times, international students seem to prefer approaching family and friends from similar cultures. Hiring a diverse faculty body could provide a supportive mechanism in a multicultural campus (Olivas & Li, 2006).

Most international students are in the U.S. for a short period of time. Therefore, providing immediate and effective support would assist them in successfully completing their educational endeavors. A university goal should be for international students educated in the U.S. to have a positive experience and return to their own countries as good-will ambassadors (Wang, 2008), which "benefits both US political interests and business interests globally" (Skinner, 2009, p.8). This also provides an opportunity to shape future leaders who may guide the political, economic and social development of their nations and support cross-national relationships.

Although this study has identified challenges international students face, their coping strategies, and recommendations of how to assist them, it is important to note that all the international students who participated in this study expressed their gratitude for the educational opportunities they are receiving in the U.S. They acknowledged that studying in the U.S. will have an important impact on their lives. They stressed their appreciation for the financial and other supports they received and complimented the people both on their campus and in the community who supported them. International students bring with them rich, diverse cultural traditions. Educators at universities participating in international student programs must create a welcoming campus where the experience enriches the lives of the international students, as well as all students and faculty on the campus.

REFERENCES

Adler, P. (1975). The transitional experience: An alternative view of culture-shock. *Journal of Humanistic Psychology, 15*, 13–23.

Altbach, P. G. (1985). *The foreign student dilemma.* Geneva, Switzerland: International Bureau of Education. Retrieved from: http://www.eric.ed.gov/PDFS/ED277284.pdf

Andrade, M. S. (2006). International students in English-speaking universities: adjustment factors. *Journal of Research in International Education, 5*(2), 131–154.

Baumgartner. J. (2009). *Inside the numbers: how foreign students contribute 18.8 billion to U.S. economy.* New York, NY: NAFSA. retrieved from http://blog.nafsa. org/2010/12/21/1963/

Barratt, M. F., & Huba, M. E. (1992). Factors related to international undergraduate student adjustment in an American University. *College Student Journal, 24,* 422–435.

Boyer, S. P., & Sedlacek, W. E. (1986). *Attitudes and perceptions of incoming international students. Research Report* (4–86). College Park, MD: Counseling Center.

Brown, L., & Holloway, I. (2008). The initial stage of the international sojourn: Excitement or culture shock? *British Journal of Guidance & Counseling, 36*(1), 33–49.

Charles-Toussaint, G., & Crowson, H. M. (2010). Prejudice against international students: The role of threat perceptions and authoritarian dispositions in U.S. students. *The Journal of Psychology, 144*(5), 413–428.

Chavajay, P., & Skowronek, J. (2008). Aspects of acculturation stress among international students attending a university in the USA. *Psychological Reports, 103*(3), 827–835.

Chellaraj, G., Maskus, K. E., & Mattoo, A. (2008). The contribution of international graduate students to US innovation. *Review of International Economics, 16*(3), 444–462.

Chun, J., & Poole, D. L. (2009). Conceptualizing stress and coping strategies of Korean social work students in the United States: A concept mapping application. *Journal of Teaching in Social Work, 29*(1), 1–17.

Cross, S. E. (1995). Self-construals, coping, and stress in cross-cultural adaptation. *Journal of Cross-Cultural Psychology, 26*(6), 673–697.

Dillard, J. M., & Chisolm, G. B. (1983). Counseling the international student in a multicultural context. *Journal of College Student Personnel, 24,* 101–105.

Eghbali, I. (1985). *Stress and academic performance of international students: University of Missouri-Columbia* (Unpublished doctoral dissertation). University of Missouri-Columbia, Columbia, MO.

Essien, I. M. (1975). *An investigation of the interaction, perception and attitude of male Nigerian students toward the United States.* Manhattan, KS: Kansas State University.

Fasheh, M. (1984). Foreign students in the United States: An enriching experience or wasteful one? *Contemporary Educational Psychology, 9,* 313–320.

Furnham, A. (1988). The adjustment of sojourners. In Y.Y. Kim & W.B. Gudykunst (Eds.), *Crosscultural adaptation: Current approaches. Intercultural Communication Annual 11* (pp. 42–62). Newberry, CA: Sage.

Furnham, A., & Bochner, S. (1982). Social difficulty in a foreign culture: An empirical analysis of culture shock. In S. Bochner (Ed.), *Cultures in contact: Studies in cross-cultural interaction* (pp. 34–62). Oxford: Pergamon.

Gang, L., Wei, C., & Duanmu, J. (2010). Determinants of international students' academic performance. *Journal of Studies in International Education, 14*(4), 389–405.

Heikinheimo, P. S., & Shute J. C. M. (1986). The adaptation of foreign students: Student views and institutional implications. *Journal of College Student Personnel, 27,* 399–406.

Hycner, R. H. (1985). Some guidelines for the phenomenological analysis of interview data. *Human Studies, 8*(3), 279–303.

Institute of International Education. (2010). Atlas of student mobility. Retrieved from http://www.atlas.iienetwork.org/?p=48048

Institution of International Education. (2011). Special reports: Economic impact of international students. Retrieved from: http://www.iie.org/en/Research-and-Publications/Open-Doors/Data/Special-Reports/Economic-Impact-of-International-Students

Kagan, H., & Cohen, J. (1990). Cultural adjustment of international students. *Psychological Science, 1*, 133–137.

Kamanakao, M. G. (2002). *Acculturative stress experienced by international students at the University of Northern Iowa and their coping options* (Unpublished masters thesis). University of Northern Iowa, Cedar Falls, IA.

Karuppan, C. M., & Barari, M. (2011). Perceived discrimination and international students' learning: An empirical investigation. *Journal of Higher Education Policy and Management, 33*(1), 67–83.

Knowles, A. S. (1977). *The international encyclopedia of higher education.* Washington, DC: Jossey Bass.

Kwon, Y. (2009). Factors affecting international students' transition to higher education institutions in the United States. From the perspective of office of international students. *College Student Journal, 43*(4), 1020–1036.

Lacina, J. (2002). Preparing international students for a successful social experience in higher education. *New Directions for Higher Education, 117*, 21–27.

Lazarus, R. S., & Folkman, S. (1984). *Stress appraisal and coping.* New York, NY: Springer Publishing Company.

Leavell, J. P. (2002). *Coping skills pattern of international college students* (Unpublished doctoral dissertation). Southern University, Baton Rouge, LA.

Lee, M. Y. (1981). *Needs of foreign students from developing nations at U.S. colleges and universities.* Washington, DC: National Association for Foreign Student Affairs.

Leong, C., & Ward, C. (2000). Identity conflict in sojourners. *International Journal of Intercultural Relations, 24*, 763–776.

Lester, S. (1999). *An introduction to phenomenological research.* Taunton, UK: Stan Lester Developments. Retrieved from: http://www.sld.demon.co.uk/resmethy.pdf

McLachlan, D. A., & Justice, J. (2009). A grounded theory of international student well-being. *The Journal of Theory Construction & Testing, 13*(1), 27–32.

Meloni, C. F. (1986). *Adjustment problems of foreign students in U.S. colleges and universities.* Washington DC: Office of Educational Research and Improvement. (ERIC Document Reproduction Service No. ED 276 296).

Misra, R., & Castillo, L. G. (2004). Academic stress among college students: comparison of American and international students. *International Journal of Stress Management, 11*(2), 132–148.

Mortimer, D. M., & Bryce-Laporte, R. (1981). *Female immigrants to the United States: Caribbean, Latin American, and African experiences.* Washington, DC: Research Institute on Immigration and Ethics Studies.

Msengi, I. (2007) Sources of stress and its impact on health behaviors and academic performance of international students at a comprehensive Midwestern University. *International Journal of Global Health and Health Disparities, 5*(1), 55–69.

Mtika, J. (2009). *Common themes, challenges, issues, and aspirations of international students pursuing doctoral degrees in education at a Midwestern University* (Doctoral dissertation). University of South Dakota, Vermillion, SD.

Nikias, M. (2008). Attracting foreign students to America offers more advantages. *The Chronicles of Higher Education.* Retrieved from http://www.usc.edu/academe/faculty/private/8009/Nikias_Attracting_Foreign_Students_to_America_Offers_More_Advantages_2.pdf

Neuliep, J. W. (2006). *Intercultural communication: A contextual approach* (3rd ed.). Thousand Oaks, CA: Sage Publications.

Olivas, M., & Li, C. (2006). Understanding stressors of international students in higher education: What college counselors and personnel need to know. *Journal of Instructional Psychology, 33*(3), 217–222.

Open Doors Report. (2009). *Open Doors 2009: International students in the United States.* New York, NY: Institute of International Education. Retrieved from http://www.iie.org/en/Who-We-Are/News-and-Events/Press-Center/Press-Releases/2009/2009-11-16-Open-Doors-2009-International-Students-in-the-US

Poyrazli, S., & Lopez, M. (2007). An exploratory study of perceived discrimination and homesickness: A comparison of international students and American Students. *Journal of Psychology, 141*(3), 263–280.

Reinicke, M. J. (1986). *Cultural adjustment of international students in the US: A reevaluation using reformulated learned helplessness* (Doctoral research paper). Rosemead School of Psychology, Biola University, La Mirada, CA.

Rice, P. L. (1999). *Stress and health.* Florence, KY: Wadsworth Publishing.

Rose-Redwood, C. R. (2010). The challenge of fostering cross-cultural interactions: A case study of international graduate students' perceptions of diversity initiatives. *College Student Journal, 44*(2), 389–399.

Ryan, M. E., & Twibell, R. S. (2000). Concerns, values, stress, coping, health and educational outcomes of college students who studied abroad. *International Journal of Intercultural Relations, 24*, 409–435.

Sandhu D. S., & Asrabadi, B. R. (1994). Development of an acculturative stress scale for international students: Preliminary findings. *Psychological Reports, 75*, 437–448.

Sherry, M., Thomas, P., & Chui, W. H. (2010). International students: A vulnerable student population. *Higher Education, 60*(1), 33–46.

Skinner, K. (2009). International Students: U.S. colleges and universities, the Global Commerce of Higher Education. Retrieved from: http://education.stateuniversity.com/pages/2129/International-Students.html

Stiegelbauer, S. (1979). *Eskimo printmaking: Acculturation, ethnicity, and art* (Unpublished masters thesis). University of Texas, Austin, TX.

Texas Higher Education Coordinating Board. (2010). Texas higher education data. Austin, TX: Author. Retrieved from: http://www.txhighereddata.org

Tidwell, R., & Hanassab, S. (2007). New challenges for professional counselors: The higher education international student population. *Counselling Psychology Quarterly, 20*(4), 313–324.

Tseng, W., & Newton, F. B. (2002). International students' strategies for well-being. *College Student Journal, 36*(4), 591–598.

Vaz, P. (1984). *Stress adjustment and social relations of foreign students* (Unpublished doctoral dissertation). University of Nebraska, Lincoln, NE.

Wan, T., Chapman, D. W., & Biggs, D. A. (1992). Academic stress of international students attending US universities. *Research in Higher Education, 33*(5), 607–623.

Wang, Y. (2008). *International students' satisfaction with international student services and their college experience* (Unpublished doctoral dissertation). Dowling College, Oakdale, NY.

Yan, K., & Berliner, D. C. (2009). Chinese international students' academic stressors in the United States. *College Student Journal, 43*(4), 939–960.

CHAPTER 24

"DO YOU HEAR WHAT I HEAR?"

Culture and Communication in Teacher Education

Michelle L. Page

INTRODUCTION

As a teacher, and later a teacher educator, I have experienced over and over again what most people already know—relationships are hard. They are complicated. Communication is not always clear or easy. Friends sometimes fight. Spouses do not always understand one another. Bosses and employees occasionally confuse each other. The relationships I am able to develop with my pre-service teachers are wonderful and fulfilling, particularly when I supervise student teachers and am able to have more personal contact with them. But they, too, are complicated. This chapter will explore some aspects of this professional supervisory relationship, in particular in terms of cultural differences and cross-cultural communication approaches.

In my practice, I define supervision as the process of observing pre-service or in-service teachers in the classroom and providing feedback with

Social Justice Leadership for a Global World, pages 433–449
Copyright © 2012 by Information Age Publishing
433

the purposes of supporting and evaluating the teachers. Supervision is the umbrella activity under which specific models can be discussed (such as clinical supervision, developmental supervision, and others). Supervision is set apart from mentorship and induction by its evaluative nature. Mentorship tends to more heavily emphasize support of the teacher, and induction focuses more on support through acculturation. Supervision is distinctive in terms of its dual role of support and evaluation. As teacher educators, supervisors carry the responsibility of implementing these roles, which may sometimes be in conflict with each other: those of advocate and gatekeeper (Page, Rudney, & Marxen, 2004). The evaluative role is evident, as in-service teachers may be evaluated for competency, merit pay, and other purposes, while pre-service teachers are evaluated for their fitness to continue in teacher education programs or to be licensed. Supervisors are often defined as university personnel who visit the field for the purpose of evaluation, support, and feedback. However, it must be noted that cooperating teachers are the primary supervisors of pre-service teachers, and principals and superintendents are supervisors of in-service teachers. Other potential supervisors include department heads, curriculum coaches, and others. This chapter will primarily focus on the supervision of pre-service teachers in teacher education programs by university supervisors and cooperating teachers in relationship to cross-cultural communication patterns.

BACKGROUND OF THE STUDY

Supervision appears to have low status in general. This is evidenced by several factors such as who is hired to engage in supervision, the availability of training and education in supervision, and the research literature in supervision. In teacher education, field supervision often seems to be conducted by graduate students and adjunct faculty who, no matter how excellent their performance may be, typically are considered as lower status employees than tenure-line faculty. There may be uneven training or guidance in terms of preparing or training university supervisors. For example, when I recently examined several large universities' program curricula (via institution web sites), there were no formal courses or trainings mentioned that were geared toward students in Ph.D. programs in Curriculum and Instruction or toward cooperating teachers.[1] Training or education in supervision does not seem to be universally required for university supervisors; formal guidance and education offered to cooperating teachers may also be uneven. While some institutions offer or require workshops or online modules to be completed by cooperating teachers, other teacher education programs do not have the resources to offer or require these experiences or may take for granted cooperating teachers' abilities to supervise. When courses or training related to supervision (either those geared toward university supervisors or cooperating teachers) are listed, it is exceedingly rare for culture and race, primary emphases of this chapter, to be key areas of focus in these learning experiences. This lack of visibility may mean that such training is not common or, if in existence, is not spotlighted in public materials. Both possibilities lead one to conclude that supervision does not have a very high profile.

Moreover, the literature related to supervision is thin as compared to other areas of curriculum and instruction[2] (Page, 2003). While the 1980s and 1990s saw growth in the amount of literature on supervision in general, this appears to have dropped off after 2000. Within the subset of supervision, literature with an emphasis on race and culture and how these affect relationships and other supervisory processes often is not discussed (Vander Kolk, 1974; Fong, 1994; Page, 2003). While occasionally researchers will discuss how supervision can enhance teachers' understandings of classroom culture; help teachers to become more multiculturally aware and effective educators; and guide teachers in becoming more reflective in their practice as it relates to race, culture, gender, and other identity factors, the actual supervisory relationship and the communication between supervisor and supervisee is largely neglected. Commonly used texts on clinical supervision might discuss the need for supervisors to be good communicators, but rarely is the role of race or culture in the communication interchange mentioned. These topics also are neglected in the literature of other fields (i.e., counseling, social work) that have outpaced education in this area (D'Andrea & Heckman, 2008). I argue that the supervisory process can be vitally enhanced by supervisors' understanding of cultural values as well as principles and knowledge related to cross-cultural interpersonal (intercultural) communication.

As most educators realize, the teaching field is primarily composed of white teachers and teacher educators, while the student body is much more diverse. As stated by Gay (2005), "the increase in ethnic, racial, cultural, and linguistic diversity in U.S. society and schools is indisputable" (p. 111). It is critical that the teaching field be diversified. This includes training all pre-service teachers to be culturally competent and, in particular, to support and retain teachers of color through supervision and other means. This has particular ramifications for pre-service teachers of color who often find themselves as numeric minorities in teacher education programs, working with a large number of white classmates, instructors, and supervisors. As can be seen in the cases presented later in this chapter, the supervisory process can be instrumental in retaining pre-service teachers of color or disenfranchising them. Literature on supervision from fields such as social work and psychology points out that supervisees of color can be vulnerable to uneven power relationships, can perceive a lower level of empathy or respect from their supervisors, and can anticipate the supervisory process differently with different goals and expectations. Sometimes there is perceived or actual racism in the supervision process (Miller, 2009). Supervisors of color can be perceived by supervisees who do not share their racial identity as less competent than their white counterparts (McRoy, Freeman, Logan & Blackmon, 1986).

Teacher educators must not assume that university supervisors and cooperating teachers have met the standards for working cross-culturally with student teachers. One cannot assume that success as a classroom teacher will automatically lead to success as a supervisor or that supervisors will automatically be able to apply their knowledge and expertise to a different situation and different interpersonal dynamic. Supervision requires a different role for the supervisor than does classroom teaching, and it has different dynamics than a teacher-student relationship in a K–12 classroom. Supervisors must consciously and consistently apply knowledge of culture and intercultural communication to their practice.

THE CASES

Some of the complications that may arise during cross-racial and cross-cultural supervision, as well as the benefits of understanding intercultural communication, can be seen in two cases.[3] Both cases relate the experiences of supervisors and student teachers who participated in a teacher education program located in a rural area. According to census data, the region is 99% white and has a high level of socioeconomic need. Within the university and teacher education programs, the demographics vary slightly. The university's students have a very high level of financial need; the student body is comprised of 80% white students and 20% students of color. Nearly 12% of the student body is Native American. Approximately 15% of the pre-service teachers in the teacher education program each year identify themselves as students of color, most of them Native American. All of the instructors and supervisors in the program self-identified as white, European American. Not all cooperating teachers were surveyed as to their identities, but of those asked, all cooperating teachers also identified as white, European American. In the region and in the university, pre-service teachers of color find themselves in the minority.

Eric

The first case is that of Eric, a Native American pre-service teacher from the Dakota nation. Eric was a nontraditional student who had previously served in the military. Upon admission to the program he seemed academically prepared and very committed to being a teacher. Halfway through the first semester of the program, while Eric was enrolled in an intensive field experience,[4] the university supervisor began receiving calls from the cooperating teacher. The cooperating teacher voiced concerns about Eric's readiness to take over the full time portion of the field experience, concerns over a lack of communication between the two of them, and concerns about a lack of initiative and attention on Eric's part. Soon after the supervisor began receiving calls, she also began to hear rumors from the teacher education students that Eric was going to quit and drop out of the program. The university supervisor, also one of Eric's course instructors, decided to speak to Eric to find out what was happening.

When the supervisor and Eric met, the supervisor integrated a large amount of "wait time" and silences into the discussion. Eric gradually revealed that he was thinking about dropping out of the education program because he didn't feel like he could successfully complete the field experience or student teaching. He seemed to doubt his own ability and thought that the cooperating teacher disliked him, suggesting that she "glared" at him, and that he had let her down somehow. By the end of the conversation, it became clear that not only was Eric having difficulty communicating with the cooperating teacher, but he also was uncomfortable with the unit he was to teach, a research paper unit. He felt that he hadn't yet had much exposure to teaching skills like writing and he didn't think he was up to the task. When asked if he had discussed this with the cooperating teacher, Eric indicated that he had tried to let the teacher know through comments he had made, but that he had found it difficult to have this type of discussion with the teacher, who was very direct in her communication style. He also was afraid that she would think him incompetent or that she wouldn't respect him. He thought that perhaps his lack of readiness to teach the research paper unit meant that he shouldn't be a teacher and he should drop out of the program.

Insights from Intercultural Communication

The supervisor met with the cooperating teacher to discuss working with Eric as well as conversing many times by phone. Though the supervisor did not consider herself an expert on communication, she had learned several things about intercultural communication, cultural values, and learning styles that she thought might help in this situation. In particular, the elements were visual learning, field dependent learning, learning by observation, and communication style.[5]

The supervisor pointed out that, while every individual is unique, research into cultural values and learning styles indicated that it was more common for Native Americans to embrace visual learning (Pewewardy,

2002; More, 1989). The use of models and demonstrations is often valued by Native American learners, as is learning from observation and private practice before public demonstration (More, 1989; Pewewardy, 2002; Rhodes, 1988; Swisher, 1991; Swisher & Dehyle, 1998). In addition, Native Americans can often be global, field dependent learners who benefit from seeing the "big picture" (Irvine & York, 1995; Gardner, 1980; Morgan, 2009; Pewewardy, 2002). In other words, they often benefit from understanding the "forest" first and then how all the "trees" fit in rather than looking at individual trees first (Lustig & Koester, 2003; Schultz & Kroeger, 1996). The supervisor also shared with the cooperating teacher that many Native American groups hesitate to engage in self-disclosure until there is a trusting relationship between individuals—this may be one reason that Eric had not directly approached the cooperating teacher with his difficulties. Finally, the supervisor wondered if Eric's concern over performance was somewhat related to his cultural values as "making mistakes in public [is] not...accepted as a way to learn" (Swisher, 1991, p.2).

In another conversation, the teacher and supervisor discussed communication style. It is not uncommon for Native American students to display less frequent eye contact than their European American counterparts. In addition, the tone of voice used is often softer than that of European Americans or African Americans and the turn-taking rules are a bit different. (Lustig & Koester, 2003; Diller & Moule, 2005). The supervisor shared that many Native Americans value wait time and silence in conversation, for this is a respectful silence. Often Native Americans make sure to wait until the speaker has completely finished and use long pauses to gather their thoughts and communicate that they value what the speaker has just said. European Americans can sometimes experience this as a very "slow-paced" type of communication and may unwittingly prevent Native Americans from speaking by rushing to fill the silence (Diller & Moule, 2005; Swisher, 1991; Heit, 1987; Pewewardy, 2002).

All of these discussions had an effect on the relationship between Eric and his cooperating teacher as well as the supervisory visit when the university supervisor went to the field to observe. As a result of these many discussions, the cooperating teacher changed her approach with Eric. She had a long conversation with Eric wherein she provided the "gestalt" of the research paper unit—she discussed the "big picture" ideas such as what the major goals of the unit were, what a final research paper should look like and why, and common problems that students would encounter. She then taught a couple of sample lessons that laid the groundwork for Eric's unit—she modeled for him how a skills lesson might unfold—and then they discussed the lessons and how he could build on them. She showed him her own lesson planning techniques and old lessons that she had created on the same topic.

Previously, the teacher had wondered if Eric was truly listening to her and understanding her, since he did not look her in the eyes as often as she expected. Now, she no longer interpreted Eric's avoidance of her gaze or his relatively slower rate of speech as a lack of initiative or engagement and her positive affirmation of Eric and his abilities increased. No doubt many of these strategies (such as modeling) would have benefited a large variety of pre-service teachers. However, these were particularly vital to Eric in that they tapped into communication and learning styles that were more comfortable and culturally appropriate for him. In turn, Eric learned to be more direct in asking for assistance and he learned how to articulate his learning style. This benefited him in his student teaching placement in New Zealand where he was able to relate strongly to his native Maori students, who share some of the same historical anti-colonial struggles as Native Americans, and also to navigate the discourses of the New Zealand-European teachers and administrators. Eric finished his field experience and teacher education program successfully. If the university supervisor had not had some rudimentary understanding of intercultural communication and if the cooperating teacher had not been willing to increase her knowledge in this area, it is likely that Eric would have followed his instinct to drop out of the program.[6]

Susan

Susan, another Native American pre-service teacher (Nez Perce/Apache), was a very talented student who was able to navigate the dominant discourses of higher education well. She was extremely dedicated to helping others understand Native Americans' customs, values, and heritage and tirelessly took on the role of educating her classmates, her students, and her instructors. Susan received good evaluations for her fall field experience and it appeared that her student teaching experience would go just as smoothly. All appeared well at the beginning—the cooperating teacher had no concerns about Susan's performance and thought she was doing a good job. Susan's journals mentioned some discomfort and some incidents that were upsetting to her, but the journals did not seem to the supervisor to be overly emotional and did not contain many details; therefore the supervisor did not react. Student teaching is full of challenges, and the supervisor thought that these journal entries were simply a new teacher experiencing growing pains.

For several weeks, Susan did not directly discuss with her supervisor what was happening in the field. She made brief mention in her journal of an incident where a student made a "war cry" type sound in the hallway, but it appeared that Susan had resolved the situation. However, as time went on, Susan began to withdraw and seemed depressed. Her work was no longer submitted with the same punctuality that had been evident previously. The supervisor, becoming concerned, began to actively email and phone Susan more frequently. The supervisor began to understand that something was not right, but still was unsure what exactly had happened or how serious it was. Susan discussed her experiences with family and with an American Indian staff member who worked in the diversity office on the campus. After these individuals counseled her that she might receive assistance from the education program, she approached her university supervisor directly. Both the university supervisor and the program director met with Susan at her home one evening to hear the entire story.

That night, the supervisor and director learned that, as the student teaching experience continued, the incidents once thought to be small annoyances or discomforts actually were more serious. Susan was being racially harassed at school on a regular basis. More than once, students passed by in the hallway and, covering their mouths, made "war cry" type sounds (the first of these incidents was discussed in Susan's journal). In class, some students were disrespectful, asking her to do a rain dance. When Susan asked the cooperating teacher for guidance, the teacher merely said, "I think you handled it fine." Sometimes students waited until the cooperating teacher was out of the room to make sounds or comments about Susan's Native American identity. When a student in class wrote about how he had learned that "white people could kill people of color with impunity," a comment made in response to a Civil Rights unit, Susan was disturbed and went to the principal, who seemed to believe that Susan just needed to adjust and "be the adult," for these were "good kids" and even good kids did stupid and insensitive things sometimes. Neither the cooperating teacher nor principal appeared to Susan to take the incidents seriously. Both seemed to view the incidents not as harassment but as challenges of classroom management. They seemed to think that Susan was overreacting.

The university supervisor conferred with the cooperating teacher, who seemed to believe that none of these issues was "a big deal." Susan continued in the placement for another week. When yet another incident of harassment occurred and was dismissed as a misunderstanding, Susan was ready to quit student teaching and not be licensed. Complicating the issue was the fact that the school had an American Indian mascot that Susan found offensive.[7] When students cheered for their team, it often seemed to Susan to be demeaning rather than an expression of respect of pride. Though the school did not actively support such cheers, they still occurred on a regular basis. Even worse were the comments and jeers of opposing teams who occasionally utilized epithets and slurs or demeaning comments about Native Americans ("Scalp those Indians!" for example) as an expression of their own team loyalty.

When the program coordinator conferred with the principal and the cooperating teacher about how to help support Susan, the school personnel seemed unwilling to make changes and did not acknowledge that the problem even existed. They approached the issue from a classroom management point of view, believing that Susan was the teacher and the adult and that she should handle this in the same way as one would handle a student shouting out in class or some other inappropriate behavior. They were unwilling to assist Susan in working with the students or to consider this an opportunity to work with students on prejudice reduction even though Susan had been willing to use the incidents as teachable moments and do a unit or some lessons on prejudice or American Indian history or other topics. They appeared not to understand the history of Native American genocide in America which, in part, caused these incidents to be so troubling to Susan and the university staff. Subsequently, since the school personnel seemed unresponsive, Susan was placed at a different school where she completed student teaching very successfully and no longer experienced the stress of being harassed.

Insights from Intercultural Communication

Though the situation had a positive resolution for Susan, the university supervisor felt that if she had better understood Susan's cultural communication style, had taken steps at the beginning of supervision to establish the expectations of supervision and to open up cultural lines of discussion, and had better understood Susan's hesitance to ask for assistance that perhaps the supervisor could have determined more quickly and effectively what was happening in the placement and thus made the placement more appropriate or at least considered an alternative placement sooner.

Some Native American peoples are more emotionally restrained[8] (Diller & Moule, 2005; Manning & Baruth, 2004; Heit 1987) and expect to have a relationship of trust established before they are willing to self-disclose (Heit, 1987). Susan and the supervisor had a previous positive relationship, which enabled Susan to open up to the supervisor, but the supervisor did not immediately understand that though Susan was not overly emotional in her communications and assignments that this did not mean everything was going well. The university supervisor had worked hard and cared deeply and benefited from a previous relationship with Susan, but, in spite of this, it had been difficult for the supervisor to listen with cultural ears. The school-based supervisors most certainly were unwilling to hear what Susan had to say; their attitude was that it was her responsibility to adapt to the culture of their school, even if that meant suffering harassment on a regular basis. Had the school supervisors understood intercultural communication, American Indian history regarding extermination and oppression, and issues surrounding mascots, they might have been more ready to understand why the situation was so disturbing to Susan and to others at the university.

Though initially resistant, Susan's cooperating teacher later was persuaded to enhance his knowledge of diversity, prejudice, social justice, and other ideas through taking courses offered by the Anti-Defamation League. He found that he learned about many topics such as internalized racism and white privilege that might have helped him to better understand Susan's perspective. He became determined to continue to work with student teachers but to learn more about their cultural values, personalities, and personal and cultural histories. In addition, the cases of Susan and Eric have prompted the university to begin to explore a collaborative training program for university supervisors and cooperating teachers where race, culture, communication styles, and other topics are addressed within the context of supervision.

Insights from Critical Whiteness Studies

The supervisor, program coordinator, cooperating teacher, principal, and students in Susan's classes, with the exception of one student of color, were all white. It is vital that whiteness be a category of examination since it so clearly permeated the situation. Critical Whiteness Studies examines whiteness through a critical theory lens.[9] In other words, relationships of power and structural relationship are examined and analysis is not limited solely to interpersonal relationships. It examines and challenges white racism and white privilege. Frankenberg (1993) writes,

> Whiteness... has a set of linked dimensions. First, whiteness is a location of structural advantage, of race privilege. Second, it is a 'standpoint, a place from which white people look at ourselves, at others, and at society. Third, 'whiteness' refers to a set of cultural practices that are usually unmarked and unnamed. (p. 1)

When we understand whiteness as a frame of reference and as a set of invisible and often unacknowledged cultural practices, this can help to shed light on what happened to Susan. The school personnel in this case had a "sink or swim" mentality. This attitude toward challenge is characteristic of individualistic cultures like European American culture. The expectation in the school appeared to be that Susan should handle the situation on her own and that this would be a sign of success if she did so. Again, this is a point of view that conflicts with the values of collectivist cultures such as Native American and Asian American, where collaboration and cooperation are valued (Bennett, 2009; Pewewardy, 2002).

Racial privilege allows white people to claim colorblindness ("I don't see color—people are people."). Embracing such a colorblind view essentially allows white people to ignore the experiences of people of color and to say that race is not relevant (Fine, Weis, Powell, & Wong, 1997). Of Franken-berg's (1993) three dimensions of whiteness, the dimension of structural advantage or privilege can powerfully inform our understandings of Su-san's story. Structural advantage is more than the sum of individual actions; however, individual actions do serve to perpetuate and instantiate privilege. In Susan's case, she was already in a situation where she lacked privilege simply by being in such a severe minority—both in her teacher education program and in the school where she student taught. In addition, she was the inheritor of a history of oppression that was symbolized to her every day through the image of the school mascot. Susan's situation exemplified white privilege in that everyone who was in power over her (supervisors) was white; they did not have to try to understand where Susan was coming from—if they did make this effort it would likely be perceived as a choice, a "going above and beyond," or a favor to Susan. Susan was the one obliged to get along, to navigate, and to figure things out. This is the price of having less power, and Susan had less power not only due to her position as a stu-dent but also due to her race and its construction in our schools and society.

Supervisors (including cooperating teachers) must understand how race, and whiteness in particular, function in our society. Pre-service teach-ers of color, like Eric and Susan, face barriers that often remain unseen and unexamined. These barriers are hallmarks of a racially striated society built on differentiation of privilege. If supervisors can understand the challenges faced by pre-service teachers of color, then perhaps they can help these new professionals to navigate the system, and perhaps they can help to change the system itself to be more equitable and just. "Good intentions," states Gay (2005) about dealing with diversity in education are insufficient; "they must also be accompanied by appropriate knowledge, skills, and actions" (p. 113). Therefore, it is important that both supervisors and cooperating teachers understand the different ethnic groups with whom they work in order to become better cross-cultural facilitators.

RECOMMENDATIONS

Literature and research, as well as experiences like in the cases of Susan and Eric, can yield recommendations for practice for university supervisors and cooperating teachers. University supervisors should apply their knowl-edge of principles of multicultural education to the practice of supervision and not assume that this knowledge automatically carries over. Within the changing demographics that define our educational institutions, we must attempt to destabilize the often unexamined practices of supervisors and cooperating teachers who may too often react to the "other" with uncon-scious assumptions about cultural differences. For example, supervisors should learn about their students (pre-service teachers) and their cultures, engage in sociocultural analysis of pedagogy and curriculum, and acknowledge and value difference. University supervisors can benefit from increasing their knowledge of intercultural communication, cultural values, and histories of marginalized groups. A challenge inherent in this is to apply general findings from research without essentializing or stereotyping individual pre-service teachers. One should refrain from assuming that individuals all fit the group patterns—instead, one should use the information to question what one is seeing. "Is it possible that x is happening because of the cultural value of y?" Verify the interpretations with pre-service teachers in a non-threatening manner. Supervisors should also know themselves and be aware of how their own cultural values and biases affect their own lives. Difference should be acknowledged and valued.

Additional goals for university supervisors should include regular communication with cooperating teachers, being open to teachers' knowledge and expertise about race and culture—particularly the culture of the classroom—and being ready to provide teachers information they lack if necessary. Supervisors should provide cooperating teachers guidance about multiple ways to communicate with the pre-service teachers, and be ready to model culturally sensitive communication. The university supervisor must work hard to establish an environment of trust and safety. This may be a challenge if the pre-service teacher does not have a previous relationship with a supervisor, but it is not impossible. The time invested in establishing this trust not only leads to enhanced communication and self-disclosure but also allows the supervisor to assist the pre-service teacher in self-evaluation, reflection, and goal-setting.

Cooperating teachers share many of the same goals and recommendations as university supervisors, particularly the need to understand themselves as cultural beings, understand cultures that are different from their own, and build empathy with the student teacher. Specifically, increasing knowledge of intercultural communication and cultural values is important. Teachers cannot assume that the student teacher interprets a situation the same way the teacher does or that the pre-service teacher receives the teacher's communication in the way that the teacher intends.

Additionally, cooperating teachers should refrain from making assumptions about the pre-service teacher (for example, that the student teacher is not engaged or not listening as in the cases above). Cooperating teachers should be open to learning new skills—the benefit of which Susan's cooperating teacher later discovered—and should understand that being recognized as an excellent classroom teacher does not automatically translate into being an excellent mentor to adult learners. Teachers should discuss the goals and procedures for supervision as well as get to know the pre-service teacher as a person. Cooperating teachers are encouraged to take advantage of any training or learning opportunities offered by the institution. Teachers may learn new skills or at the least they will learn more about the philosophies and expectations of the program. Teachers should consider multiple ways that they can guide the student teacher—for example, telling, modeling, questioning. Finally, cooperating teachers need to be willing to share their expertise and knowledge with both the student teacher and university supervisor (university supervisors are not all culturally aware any more than are all classroom teachers).

CONCLUSION

Supervision is an under-researched and often under-valued area of teacher education. Supervisors (both university supervisors and classroom cooperating teachers) can radically affect the experience and learning of pre-service teachers in field placements. The cases discussed above demonstrate how complex supervision can be. These cases highlight how knowledge of cultural values and intercultural communication in supervision was beneficial in retaining and supporting pre-service teachers of color and where lack of knowledge and understanding served to undermine and discourage these novice educators.

The field of teacher education is facing challenges when it comes to supervision. In the tight budget climates of higher education, it can be tempting to cut back training and services available to university supervisors and cooperating teachers, justified by the view that supervision is a sort of "common sense" activity geared toward honing the technical skills of teaching. A lack of status associated with supervision may also contribute to supervision not being placed center stage in teacher education.

In several states, not only are high stakes standardized tests gatekeepers of licensure, but standardized performance assessments also are becoming means of evaluating teacher education programs and pre-service teachers.[10] While performance assessments can be a welcome counterbalance to standardized exams, teacher educators should be mindful of how these are implemented. For example, in an effort to create reliability, these performance assessments in many cases are scored by individuals who are not part of the teacher education program. While providing a benefit (reliability), a potential drawback to this is that it is unknown how these scorers view race and culture, and they do not know the pre-service teachers being assessed or their cultural values or communication styles. Another potential drawback of these high stakes performance assessments may be that institutions may see less need for in-person supervision if the program or students will be evaluated by the performance assessment structure, which in many cases requires video of a lesson, not in-person observation As with any tool, such standardized performance assessments may be a great benefit to teacher preparation; however, teacher educators must be cognizant of the potential pitfalls as well so that pre-service teachers and their future students will fully benefit from these reforms and not lose other valuable support.

The cases of Eric and Susan demonstrate the complexities of cross-cultural communication in supervision and the need for "hands on" supervisors who value diversity and who are committed, knowledgeable, and present. Now, more than ever, we need to prepare educational supervisors and leaders who can lead across borders. These cases also show us the need to focus on areas of teaching that are not simply about skills such as planning and assessment but which relate to the cultures, characteristics, values, and priorities of the pre-service teachers. One size does not fit all. Supervisors should understand and value their pre-service teachers the same way we want classroom teachers to understand and value their K–12 students. How to apply understanding about cross-cultural relationships into a set of standards that can help supervisors better accomplish higher levels of cross-cultural knowledge and skills is an important outcome of this study.

FUTURE RESEARCH

Future research should address areas such as the following: What type of training would help supervisors be more effective in cross-cultural situations? How do race and culture affect the supervisory relationship and the effectiveness of supervision? What are the implications for supervision within the changing global context? How can teacher education programs overcome the barriers to investing in supervision and create systems that support all pre-service teachers? Assuring that university and classroom-based supervisors have adequate working knowledge of cultural values, history of racism and oppression, and intercultural communication styles and techniques is one place we can begin. Though Eric and Susan were ultimately successful in their teacher education programs, they experienced barriers and a lack of support that other (white) teacher education students did not encounter. Supervisors' knowledge (and lack thereof) radically impacted their field experiences in positive and negative ways. Establishing effective supervisory relationships that include attention to race and culture should be a priority of teacher educators as we seek to make teacher education more equitable and just.

NOTES

1. In contrast, about one half of the program curricula examined (via institutional web sites) in the area of Educational Leadership or Educational Ad-

ministration did have such courses or trainings. Attention to supervision of in-service teachers seems more common than attention to supervision of pre-service teachers. It is unclear, however, what materials are used in these courses and whether the texts and materials are specific to education, are drawn from business and management, or are a blend.

2. Just by way of example, I searched two keyword terms that are of interest to me: multicultural education and teacher supervision. While over 11,000 sources appeared for multicultural education, only 1,100 or so appeared for teacher supervision.

3. Case study methodology was used (Stake, 1995a and 1995b) to analyze these cases. Qualitative methods of analysis such as coding were used as well.

4. The field experience required pre-service teachers to be in the field 10 hours per week for eight weeks and then culminated in a two-week-long full time field experience where the pre-service teachers taught a full unit and took over classes for at least two to three hours per day. The total number of hours exceeded 150.

5. Whenever one discusses the cultural impact on values, communication, and learning style, one runs the risk of stereotyping. It is helpful to distinguish between generalizations and stereotypes in this discussion. Generalizations are descriptors that apply to whole groups and arise from research—for example, it is more likely or more common for Asian American students to perceive the teacher as a strong authority figure that should not be questioned. Stereotypes apply generalizations to individuals across the board—for example, my student John is Asian American, so I automatically assume that he will see me as a strong authority figure. Generalizations can help us to understand and explain behaviors, but they cannot automatically be applied to all individuals.

6. It might be tempting for some readers to take the small bits of information about communication of Native Americans and apply them inappropriately to all Native learners or to discount the information completely out of a fear of stereotyping. The goal is to find the middle ground and to allow research to inform us but to continually recognize that each person is an individual who is shaped by his or her culture and experiences in different ways. The goal for the supervisor is not necessarily to memorize information about all cultural groups but to remain open to reframing a situation and finding multiple interpretations of it. Information from research on communication and learning styles can help supervisors do this.

7. For a discussion of Native American mascots, see Pewewardy (2004).

8. Though there is research to support this, one must beware of the deeply engrained stereotype of the "stoic Indian." Though in my own experiences with Eric and Susan, both seemed to fit this description, none of the other Native Americans I am close to could be described as "emotionally restrained."

9. Due to the scope of the chapter and space constraints, this is a highly simplified explanation. For a fuller discussion of critical race theory, see Delgado and Stefancic (2000). For a summary of the literature on whiteness, see Page (2009).

10. Examples include the Performance Assessment for California Teachers (PACT) in California and the Teacher Performance Assessment (TPA) in

Minnesota, modeled after PACT. Several other states, along with Minnesota, are early adopters of this performance assessment. The assessment includes writing a context paper about the educational setting, videotaping a chunk of instruction of about 20 minutes, analyzing the videotape, analyzing lesson planning for the instruction, and collecting and analyzing assessment data related to the instructional segment.

REFERENCES

Bennett, J. (2009) *Building intercultural competence for educators.* Presentation to the University of Minnesota-Morris, Alexandria, MN, August 2009.

D'Andrea, M. & Heckman, E. F. (2008). A 40-year review of multicultural counseling outcome research: Outlining a future research agenda for the multicultural counseling movement. *Journal of Counseling and Development 86* (3), 356–363.

Delgado, R. & Stefancic, J. (Eds.). (2000). *Critical race theory: The cutting edge.* Philadelphia, PA: Temple University Press.

Diller, J. V. & Moule, J. (2005). *Cultural competence: A primer for educators.* Toronto, Ontario: Wadsworth.

Fine, M., Weis, L., Powell, L., & Wong, L. M. (Eds.). (1997). *Off white: Readings on race, power, and society.* New York, NY: Routledge.

Fong, M. L. (1994). Multicultural issues in supervising. (Greensboro, ND: ERIC Clearinghouse on Counseling and Student Services, ERIC Document Reproduction Services No. ED 372 346).

Frankenberg, R. (1993). *The social construction of whiteness: White women, race matters.* Minneapolis, MN: University of Minnesota Press.

Gardner, R. C. (1980). *Learning styles: What every teacher should consider.* Retrieved from ERIC database (ED 198058).

Gay, G. (2005). Standards of diversity. In S. P. Gordon (Ed.), *Standards for instructional supervision: Enhancing teaching and learning* (pp. 107–119). Larchmont, NY: Eye on Education.

Heit, M. (1987, March). Research Summary: Communication Styles of Indian Peoples. *AWASIS Journal.* Retrieved July 10, 2010 from http://www.lpi.usra.edu/education/lpsc_wksp_2007/resources/heit_report.pdf

Irvine, J. J., & York, P. (1995). *Learning styles and culturally diverse students: A literature review.* Retrieved from ERIC database. (ED 382722).

Lustig, M. W. & Koester, J. (2003). *Intercultural competence: Interpersonal communication across cultures* (4th ed). Boston, MA: Allyn & Bacon.

Manning, M. L. & Baruth, L. G. (2004). *Multicultural education of children and adolescents* (4th ed.). Boston, MA: Pearson Education, Inc.

McRoy, R. G., Freeman, E. M., Logan, S. L., & Blackmon, B. (1986). Cross-cultural field supervision, *Journal of Social Work Education 22*, 50–56

Miller, T. (2009). *Investigating elementary teachers' perceptions about and experiences with Ontario's teacher performance appraisal system, 2002* (Unpublished doctoral dissertation). Ontario Institute of Studies in Education, University of Toronto, Toronto, Ontario, Canada.

More, A. J. (1989). Native Indian learning styles: A review for researchers and teachers. *Journal of American Indian Education, Special Edition,* 15–28.

Morgan, H. (2009). What every teacher needs to know to teach Native American students. *Multicultural Education, 16*(4), 10–12.

Page, M. L. (2003). Race, culture, and the supervisory relationship: A review of literature and call to action, *Journal of Curriculum and Supervision, 18*(2), 161–174.

Page, M. L. (2009). Pedagogy of privilege: White preservice teachers learn about whiteness. *Teaching and Learning: The Journal of Natural Inquiry and Reflective Practice, 24*(1), 3–21.

Page, M. L., Rudney, G. L., & Marxen, C. E. (2004). Leading preservice teachers to water . . . and helping them drink: How candidate teachability affects the gatekeeping and advocacy roles of teacher educators. *Teacher Education Quarterly, 31*(2), 25–41.

Pewewardy, C. D. (2002). Learning styles of American Indian/Alaska Native students: A review of the literature and implications for practice. *Journal of American Indian Education, 41*(3), 22–56.

Pewewardy, C. D. (2004). Playing Indian at halftime: The controversy over American Indian mascots, logos, and nicknames in school-related events. *Clearing House, 77*(5), 180–187.

Rhodes, R. W. (1988). Holistic teaching/learning for Native American students. *Journal of American Indian Education, 27*(2) 21–29.

Schultz, M. & Kroeger, M. (1996). *Teaching and learning with Native Americans: A handbook for Non-Native American adult educators.* Retrieved July 12, 2010 from http://literacynet.org/lp/namericans/values.html

Stake, R. E. (1995a). Case studies. In N. Denzin & Y. Lincoln (Eds.), *The Handbook of Qualitative Research* (pp. 236–247). Thousand Oaks, CA: Sage.

Stake, R. E. (1995b). *The art of case study research.* Thousand Oaks, CA: Sage.

Swisher, K. G. & Dehyle, D. (1989). The styles of learning are different, but the teaching is just the same: Suggestions for teachers of American Indian youth [Special issue]. *Journal of American Indian Education,* 1–14.

Swisher, K. (1991). American Indian/Alaskan Native learning styles: Research and practice. Charleston, WV: ERIC Clearinghouse on Rural Education and Small Schools. (ERIC Document Reproduction Service No. ED 335 175)

Vander Kolk, C. J. (1974). The relationship of personality, values, and race to the anticipation of the supervisory relationship. *Rehabilitation Counseling Bulletin 18,* 41–46.

ABOUT THE EDITORS

Cynthia Gerstl-Pepin is a Professor and Associate Dean for the College of Education and Social Services at the University of Vermont. Dr. Gerstl-Pepin is an interdisciplinary scholar who explores the social justice implications concerning how poverty and other forms of discrimination may have an impact on education inequity. As a policy scholar and qualitative methodologist, she is specifically interested in the frequent disconnect between public policies and their portrayals in the media and the lived realities of the children, teachers, staff, and administrators who inhabit schools and the communities they serve. Dr. Gerstl-Pepin served as a Fulbright Scholar in 2010 at Beijing Normal University in the People's Republic of China. Her teaching interests center on the politics of education, qualitative methodology, and diversity issues. She is the co-author of *Reframing Educational Politics for Social Justice* (with Catherine Marshall) and is currently working on two additional edited books. The first book (with Li Qi) compares the challenges facing the U.S. and Chinese university systems, entitled *Survival of the Fittest: The Shifting Contours of Higher Education in China and the U.S.* The second book (with Cynthia Reyes) examines the lack of connection between rigorous educational research and media coverage of educational reform issues and is titled *Reclaiming the Public Dialog on Education.* She has been published in such journals as the *Journal of School Leadership, Educational Policy, Teachers College Record,* the *International Journal of Qualitative Studies in Education, Qualitative Research,* and the *Review of Higher Education.*

Judith Aiken is an Associate Professor of Educational Leadership in the Department of Integrated Professional Studies at the University of Vermont. Her research interests center on the preparation and development of edu-

Social Justice Leadership for a Global World, pages 451–452
Copyright © 2012 by Information Age Publishing

cational leaders and an understanding of how research informs ways leaders can engage in democratic and ethical practices that support highly successful and collaborative learning cultures. Dr. Aiken provides professional development and technical assistance to many school districts in Vermont in the areas of teacher supervision and evaluation and the ongoing professional development of school leaders. She has served on the Vermont Standards Board for Professional Educators, the New England School Development Council, and she currently sits on the Board of Examiners for NCATE. She coordinates the Administrator Licensure Program for school administrators at UVM and directs the field-based internship/mentoring program for students pursuing endorsements as school principals. Professor Aiken's research interests also focus on women and leadership, school governance, educational supervision, and positive aspects of leadership preparation and practice. Her research has been published in the *Journal of School Leadership, Planning and Changing: An Educational Leadership and Policy Journal,* the *Journal of Leadership Studies, NASSP Bulletin, Educational Leadership Review* and other scholarly journals. Professor Aiken is a member of the editorial board of the *Journal of Women in Educational Leadership.* She has contributed numerous book chapters, including a chapter in the *Handbook of Research on Supervision* and has published in the yearbook for the *National Council of Professors of Educational Administration (NCPEA).*

ABOUT THE CONTRIBUTORS

Lyndsay J. Agans is an Assistant Professor of Educational Leadership & Policy Studies at the University of Denver in the Morgridge College of Education. Her scholarship focus is on technology, teaching, and learning with an emphasis on inclusive excellence. She teaches in the areas of higher education, educational leadership, and curriculum and instruction. Current research by Dr. Agans includes motivation for college-going and STEM motivation, the development of technology resources for school leadership, and capacity-building throughout the educational pipeline for improved outcomes. In addition, Dr. Agans works on postsecondary readiness, instructional technology, and data systems for P-20 innovation toward 21st century educational transformation. She approaches her work from a social justice perspective, viewing educational equality as an issue of intergenerational equity and social sustainability.

Maysaa Barakat has served as a school administrator in private schools in Cairo, Egypt for twelve years. She is currently a Ph.D. candidate at Auburn University. Her research interests include: Diversity, Social Justice, and educational leadership preparation programs. She is the Senior Graduate Student representative for the AERA Social Justice Special Interest Group (SIG).

Lisa Bass is an Assistant Professor of Educational Leadership and Policy at North Carolina State University. She completed a post-doc at the University of Vermont, and a dual major Ph.D. at The Pennsylvania State University in Educational Leadership and Policy Studies, and Comparative and International Education. Her primary research interests are ethics and urban

Social Justice Leadership for a Global World, pages 453–461
Copyright © 2012 by Information Age Publishing
All rights of reproduction in any form reserved.

school reform through alternative approaches to schooling. Her goal is to positively impact urban education and the perceptions of urban youth.

Risha R. Berry completed her doctoral coursework at Virginia Commonwealth University in the School of Education, and is a graduate research assistant with the Department of Educational Leadership. Risha's research interests focus on educational equity, school exclusion, technology use, and systems change. Her dissertation focuses on the systematic construction of pushout.

Rhonda Blackwell-Flanagan is an Associate In Professor of Educational Administration in the Department of Educational Leadership and Policy Studies, College of Education, Florida State University. Dr. Blackwell-Flanagan's background experiences of over 20 years include middle school teaching, elementary school administration, working collaboratively with school districts in professionally developing aspiring school leaders, and consultant work with the Florida Department of Education. Presently she coordinates the educational leadership programs that lead to state level certificate and teaches graduate courses in leadership preparation. Her research interests include leadership for equity and social justice and innovative methods in the leadership preparation process.

Nelson Bowman, III is the Director of Development at Prairie View A&M University where he joined the team in 2005 following a career in corporate management. He received his B.A. from Morehouse College and is currently pursuing a M.A. Mr. Bowman is also the co-author of a two books entitled, *Unearthing Promise and Potential: Our Nation's Historically Black Colleges and Universities* and *Fundraising at Historically Black Colleges and Universities: An All Campus Approach.*

Yu-min Chien received her Ph.D. from the University of Wisconsin-:Madison. She is an Assistant Professor of the Graduate School ofEducation and the Center for Teacher Education at Chung-Yuan Christian University, Taiwan. Her research interests focus on leadership of multicultural education, organizational theories, and school principalship. She teaches multicultural education, educational administration, organizational theories and behaviors, and qualitative research. She served as a member of the Student Council Committee and as a consultant of the Center for Teacher Professional Development. She was the Director of the Center for Teaching and Learning Excellence for two years at Chung-Yuan Christian University.

Hsiang-I Chiu earned her M.S. degree at the Graduate School of Education, Chung-Yuan Christian University. She is currently a teacher at Beisin

Elementary School, New Taipei City, Taiwan. Her research interests are in multicultural leadership and new immigrant education.

Kelly Clark/Keefe is Associate Professor in the Reich College of Education at Appalachian State University, Boone, NC. Kelly teaches research methodologies, educational leadership, social foundations and writing. Her research involves utilizing poststructural, materialist and complexity theories to examine the role of bodies, subjectivity, and creativity in learning, leadership, and social inquiry. Kelly is author of the book *Invoking Mnemosyne: Art, Memory, and the Uncertain Emergence of a Feminist Embodied Methodology* (2010).

Deborah J. Conrad (Associate Professor) holds a Ph.D. in Curriculum and Instruction (Literacy Education) from Virginia Tech. Deborah is also a graduate of Sheffield University (UK), the University of the West Indies (Trinidad), and Corinth Teachers' College (Trinidad). She has taught extensively in elementary and special education. Deborah is currently the Co-Chair of the Department of Curriculum and Instruction. Prior to this Deborah was the coordinator for Early Childhood/Childhood Education for eight years.

Dennis Conrad (Associate Professor) holds a Ph.D. from Virginia Tech. Dennis is also a graduate of Sheffield and London universities, and Mausica Teachers College. He has taught in regular and special schools, been an alternate school principal, and a pioneer in addressing special education teacher preparation in Trinidad and Tobago. His awards include the President's Award for Research and Scholarship related to Cultural Pluralism and the 1995 Trinidad and Tobago National Award for Excellence in Teaching.

Katherine Curry, Ed.D. is an Assistant Professor of Educational Leadership at Oklahoma State University in Stillwater, Oklahoma. Her research interests include social network analysis, parent responsibility in education, leadership development and preparation, leadership ethics, and moral literacy. She is a former Headmaster, Middle School Principal, Director of Curriculum and Instruction, and Research Associate for the Oklahoma Center for Educational Policy at the University of Oklahoma. She is co-founder of a research and development center that promotes parent/school partnerships for student educational success through school-university-community collaboration.

Diane Fuselier-Thompson is a graduate student at the University of Illinois, Urbana-Champaign in the Department of Educational Policy Studies. Her research interests include issues of access and equity, culturally responsive evaluation practices that examine P-20 educational initiatives in the fields of Science, Technology, Engineering and Mathematics (STEM) and the educational efficacy of diversity initiatives in higher education.

Mary Gardiner is an immigrant to the U.S. from Australia. She has served as a teacher, administrator and university professor in Educational Administration & Supervision at Washington State University (1990–2001) and Educational Leadership at the University of Idaho, Boise (2001–present). Given these global experiences as Americans of diverse origin, the study reveals the importance of collaboration, culturally relevant and social justice leadership through the implementation of narrative inquiry.

Marybeth Gasman is a Professor of Higher Education in the Graduate School of Education at the University of Pennsylvania. Her expertise pertains to the history of higher education, African American leadership and philanthropy, and historically Black colleges and universities.

David Gibson is an educational researcher, professor, learning scientist and technology innovator. His research focuses on complex systems, web applications and the future of learning, and the use of technology to personalize education via cognitive modeling, design and implementation. He is creator of *simSchool*, a classroom flight simulator for preparing educators, and eFolio an online performance-based assessment system.

Taucia Gonzalez is a doctoral student at Arizona State University pursing a Ph.D. in curriculum and instruction with an emphasis in special education. Her work focuses on the intersections of culture, language, and disability within an urban context. She specializes in spatial ideologies of difference with particular interest in how ideologies create and control spaces.

Francois Guilleux holds an Ed.M. from Harvard University and a Ph.D. from the University of Pittsburgh, where he was involved in the development of a new principal preparation program and continues to teach part-time in the Administrative and Policy Studies department. Francois' research focuses on adult development and leadership education.

Sandra Harris, Ph.D. is Professor and Director of the Center for Doctoral Studies in Educational Leadership at Lamar University in Beaumont, Texas, where she teaches courses in Qualitative Research and Social Justice. She has authored or co-authored 14 books and over 100 journal articles or book chapters. Her research interests are leadership and building relationships that value others.

Jennifer J. Huber, Ph.D. has been teaching for over 22 years, in general education, special education, and inclusive settings. She received her Ph.D. at Clemson University in South Carolina in curriculum and instruction with an emphasis in special education. Her research interests center around the topics of inclusive teaching and learning, collaboration, and teacher learning.

Anne Hynds is a Pākeha Researcher/Senior Lecturer in the School of Educational Psychology and Pedagogy, Faculty of Education at Victoria University of Wellington, New Zealand. She is also a Research Associate for the Jessie Herrington Research Centre at the Faculty of Education. As a teacher, Anne taught in primary, intermediate and secondary school settings, and in mainstream and Deaf education. Anne has a real interest in collaborative research/action research methodologies and has worked in a number of bi-cultural evaluation projects including the National Evaluation of Te Kotahitanga; the coordination of the Quality Teaching Research and Development in Practice Project (QTR&D) and the National Evaluation of Te Kauhua: Maori in the mainstream pilot project.

Lisa Kensler is an assistant professor in educational leadership at Auburn University. Her research interests include the ecology of democratic learning communities, schools as living systems, and school leaders' role in developing green, more sustainable schools—schools that aim to meet human needs now and in the future in a healthy and socially just manner, while also reducing negative impacts on natural ecosystems.

Susan Korach is an Assistant Professor of Educational Leadership & Policy Studies at the University of Denver in the Morgridge College of Education. She co-designed and serves as the director of a district/university partnership principal preparation program that received a United States Department of Education School Leadership Program grant in 2008. She is an active participant with the UCEA/LTEL Taskforce on Evaluating Leadership Preparation Programs and a Research Associate with The National Center for the Evaluation of Educational Leadership Preparation and Practice. She also serves on an Advisory Committee for the Utah Education Policy Center. Her research focus is on leadership preparation, learning transfer, university/district partnerships and institutional change.

Elizabeth B. Kozleski, a Professor of Culture, Society, and Education in Arizona State University's School of Social Transformation, is recognized internationally for her work theorizing systems change for equity, inclusive education, and professional learning. She was awarded the UNESCO Chair in Inclusive International Research in 2005 and received the TED-Merrill award for her leadership in special education teacher education in 2011.

Lisa Marie Lacy, I currently live in Arizona and attend Arizona State University (ASU), pursuing a doctoral degree in Curriculum and Instruction in Special Education. I am interested in the examination of social justice and equity issues as they relate to inclusive education settings for all students regardless of racial, linguistic, and dis/ability diversity.

Vachel Miller is an Assistant Professor in the Reich College of Education at Appalachian State University in Boone, North Carolina. In the doctoral program in educational leadership at ASU, Dr. Miller teaches courses in research methodologies, leadership, globalization and diversity. Prior to joining the faculty at Appalachian State in 2008, Dr. Miller worked as a regional monitoring and evaluation, policy and research specialist on a project focused on child labor and education in East Africa. He holds an Ed.D. in educational policy and leadership from the University of Massachusetts Amherst (UMASS).

Anjali Misra holds a Ph.D. in Special Education from Pennsylvania State University, and also a graduate of Delhi University, India. Anjali has several years experience teaching children with disabilities; and has earned several awards including the Nehru Memorial Award, the Council for Exceptional Children-Mental Retardation Division Herbert J. Prehm Presentation Award, and the President's Award for Excellence in Research and Scholarship. She has nine years leadership experience in higher education as Department Chair.

Clementine Msengi is a doctoral student in Educational Leadership, a graduate research assistant at the Center for Doctoral Studies in Educational Leadership and an adjunct instructor in Health and Kinesiology Department at Lamar University. Her research interests focus on health education especialy among international students, refugees, immigrants, minorities and other underserved populations.

Israel Msengi is an Assistant Professor, a coordinator of health program in the Health and Kinesiology Department, and a chair of the multicultural enhancement committee in the college of education at Lamar University. His research interests are in environmental health, health behaviors, and disparities.

In his country of origin, **Alexandre Ilungu Muzaliwa** was a high school teacher, and a principal. He taught French and various subjects for many years. In the late eighties, he fled his country to Kenya where he spent seven years. In Kenya, he taught French at Menengai high school in Nakuru in the Rift Valley province, at Ole Tipis high in Narok in the Masailand, and at the French Alliance in the capital city Nairobi. He recently completed his doctoral dissertation, University of Idaho, Boise, and currently is a Scholar in Residence.

Michelle Page is Associate Professor in the Division of Education at the University of Minnesota, Morris. Her teaching includes general education courses as well as courses in diversity and content reading. Her research has focused on issues of race and culture in teaching and teacher education. Her current work is centered on gender and sexual orientation in the teaching of language arts and literature.

Amy Papacek is pursuing a Ph.D. in Curriculum and Instruction with an emphasis in special education. She is dedicated to understanding how intersectionality helps to explain the ways in which ability, culture, language, race, and other dimensions of human variation intersect in particular ways to complicate the structural and hegemonic forces that produce and maintain deficit views of children and adults.

Michele Pinard is a doctoral candidate at McGill University and an instructional support specialist/clinical faculty member in the Department of Curriculum and Instruction. She also a graduate of SUNY – Potsdam and the School for International Training, Vermont. Her leadership experience over a decade includes the areas of International Education Group Leader in South Korea and Intermediate multi-age Team Leader. Her research interests include Comparative/International Education, Culture & Values, the Teaching English as a Second Language.

Joseph A. Polizzi, Ph.D. is a former New York City Public high school English teacher, and is currently an Assistant Professor of Educational Leadership at Marywood University. His research revolves around the many aspects, approaches and applications of transformational learning.

Ellen H. Reames spent thirty years as a public school teacher and administrator before joining the College of Education faculty at Auburn University. Her research interests include learning communities, educational leadership program design and evaluation, leadership and K–12 issues of school safety such as bullying and alternative schools. She is currently the editor of the *Southern Regional Council for Educational Administration Yearbook*.

R. Martin Reardon is an Assistant Professor in the Educational Leadership Department of the School of Education at Virginia Commonwealth University. His research interests include learning-centered leadership, educational quality and equality, and technology-infused learning. He is currently the Chair of the School-University Collaborative Research SIG of the American Educational Research Association (AERA).

Abbie Robinson-Armstrong is Professor and Vice President for Intercultural Affairs at Loyola Marymount University. She earned a Bachelor of Science degree at University of Indianapolis, a Master of Science at Indiana University Bloomington, and a Ph.D. in Higher Education at University of Toledo. She held faculty positions at institutions of higher education in the United States and Canadaincluding Seneca College, Centennial College and Durham College. Her research interests include organizational development and change,and underrepresented students and faculty in predominantly whiteinstitutions of higher education.

Erin San Clementi holds a B.A from Sarah Lawrence College in Liberal Arts She is currently working towards her Master's Degree in Special Education at Marywood University. Her research interests include visual culture, media theory and their application to the classroom context.

Jameel Alexander Scott earned his BA in African-American studies with an emphasis in religious studies at Morehouse College in Atlanta, GA. While earning his M.Th. degree at Drew University in Madison, NJ he analyzed the intersection of religion and education. He later earned a M.S. degree in Higher Education Policy, primarily focused on Historically Black Colleges and Universities from the University of Pennsylvania. Jameel also completed an Advanced Graduate Certificate at the University of Maryland, College Park where his research interest centered on higher education philanthropy, economics and finance.

Saeeda Shah is currently working at the School of Education, University of Leicester, teaching on Masters and doctoral programmes. She is also visiting Professor of Education at the University of Derby. Previously, she has worked in higher education in Pakistan, holding senior leadership positions with both academic and administrative responsibilities. Her research interests include educational leadership with a focus on Muslim education, faith, culture, gender and power issues. She has published widely in the areas of education, leadership, Islam and society, gender, diversity, inclusion, and identity/ethnicity. She has presented her work at international conferences in many parts of the world and is recognised as an international authority in her field of expertise. Saeeda has also been actively involved in the voluntary sector in Britain since 1995, and has participated in the United Nation's Human Rights Commission's sessions in relation to her work for human rights, particularly for the rights of women and youth.

Seena M. Skelton is Assistant Director of professional learning at the Great Lakes Equity Center, Indiana University, Purdue University Indianapolis. She has more than 15 years of experience in the areas of systems change and educational equity. Dr. Skelton received her Ph.D. in School Psychology from the University of Cincinnati and has provided leadership in implementing various school improvement initiatives.

Nancy J. Smith has over 40 years experience as a teacher, administrator and social justice advocate. She taught high school and middle school English before earning a Ph.D. while teaching at the University of Georgia. She taught at Kansas State University and served as a dean and professor at Millersville University of Pennsylvania where she is Professor Emeritus of Educational Foundations.

Anna Q. Sun earned her Ph.D. in Educational Administration in the Department of Educational Leadership and Policy at the State University of New York at Buffalo. Her research interests include the effectiveness of school leadership, with a focus on the assistant principalship and the principalship, school reforms, educational policies at state, national and international levels, and the development of international school partnership. Dr. Sun has presented at 13 national and international conferences, including at University Council for Educational Administration (UCEA) and American Educational Research Association (AERA). Her career includes 17 years of teaching in public, charter, and private schools, with 4 years of an administrator. Currently Dr. Sun serves as a coordinator of The Learning Center at Buffalo Academy of Sacred Heart, with the responsibility to develop international student programs with China. Dr. Sun has received her MEd. in Comparative and Global Studies in Education from State University of New York at Buffalo and a B.A. in Foreign Language and Literature from Tianjin Teacher College in China.

Charles A. Williams, Ph.D. is a member of the faculty the School of Education and director of the Center for the Prevention of School-Aged Violence at the Goodwin College of Drexel University. His work focuses on mentoring, bullying, the achievement of minority and special needs youth, and child welfare. He's been featured on Fox News, CNN, MSNBC, in *USA Today*, the Associated Press and the Christian Science Monitor.

Tiffany Wright has served in various settings over 15 years, i.e., juvenile facilities, a comprehensive high school, and a career/technical high school. She taught English and served as a school administrator while earning her Ed.D. from Johns Hopkins (JHU). She taught part-time at JHU and Millersville University and recently was hired full-time in the Educational Foundations department at Millersville.

INDEX

V

visual critical literacy, 179

W

Wall Street Journal, 368
Washington, Booker T., 364
Waiting for Superman (film), 176–177
Which Way Home (film), 182–184

Z

zanana (female) colleges (Pakistan),
       60, 71